## JEWELS OF A LADY OF THE COURT IN THE GREAT DAYS OF UR

Most distinctive item of the attire of a Sumerian lady of court rank, as proved by the remains found in the great death-pit shown in page 21, was her headdress of gold ribbons and bands of beads, with leaves and flowers entwined and pendant among them, and on the crown an erect floral spray wrought in gold and lapis lazuli. Gold rings were threaded among her tresses, heavy gold rings hung from her ears, a collar of gold and lapis lazuli encircled her throat, and round her neck she wore many chains of gold and lapis lazuli and carnelian.

# WONDERS OF THE PAST

A World-Wide Survey of the Marvellous
Works of Man in Ancient Times Written by
the Leading Modern Authorities and Edited by

### Sir J. A. HAMMERTON

With upwards of 1450 photographic illustrations
many maps and 45 plates in color

### New Edition in Two Volumes

★

Pages 1-628

## New York
## WISE & CO.
1952

# CONTENTS OF THIS VOLUME

## The Study of the Past
PAGE

I. THE WALLS OF JERICHO: *C. B. Mortlock* .. 3
II. THE MODERNITY OF THE ANCIENT WORLD. *The Editor* .. .. .. .. 7
III. A STONE-AGE "POMPEII" IN THE ORKNEYS *Lewis Spence* .. .. 48
IV. TRAGEDY OF THE MAMMOTH. *C. E. Benson* 109
V. THE DOOM OF CITIES. *Hamilton Fyfe* .. 135
VI. THE REAL ACADEMY OF PLATO. *F. N. Pryce* .. .. .. 215
VII. THE ROSETTA STONE. *H. R. Hall* .. .. 250
VIII. CAVE OF THE CUMAEAN SIBYL. *F. N. Pryce* 375
IX. THE LOST TREASURES OF MEXICO AND PERU. *Lewis Spence* .. .. 410
X. WHEN AND WHERE DID CIVILIZATION BEGIN ? *M. C. Burkitt* .. .. 429
XI. WHAT THE DAWN-MAN WAS LIKE. *Sir Arthur Smith Woodward* .. .. 490
XII. WONDER SHIPS OF LAKE NEMI. *The Editor* 600
XIII. AERIAL DISCOVERY OF THE HIDDEN PAST. *E. Cecil Curwen* .. .. .. 612

## The Wonder Cities

I. UR: CITY OF 'THE FLOOD.' *C. L. Woolley* 18
II. TIMGAD: GRANDEST RUIN OF COLONIAL ROME. *The Editor* .. .. 61
III. PETRA, THE ROSE-RED CITY OF MYSTERY. *The Editor* .. .. .. 83
IV. THEBES IN ITS SPLENDOUR. *A. Weigall* 190
V. LONDON'S ROMAN REMAINS. *R.E.M.Wheeler* 290
VI. PAGAN: CITY OF TEN THOUSAND TEMPLES. *Richard Curle* .. .. 312
VII. TROY: THE CITY SUNG BY HOMER. *A. H. Smith* .. .. .. 323
VIII. POMPEII. *George Sampson* .. .. 353
IX. ATHENS IN THE DAYS OF HER GLORY. *J. L. Myres* .. .. .. 381
X. KISH, THE WORLD'S OLDEST CITY. *S. G. Blaxland Stubbs* .. .. 413
XI. THE SPLENDOURS OF ANCIENT PERGAMUM. *F. N. Pryce* .. .. 419
XII. THE SPLENDOURS OF IMPERIAL ROME. *Edward Hutton* .. .. 494
XIII. PALMYRA, QUEEN CITY OF THE DESERT. *Edward Wright* .. .. 531
XIV. JERUSALEM UNDER HEROD THE GREAT. *J. Garstang* .. .. .. 567

## Records of the Tombs

I. THE AMAZING RICHES OF TUTANKHAMEN. *T. Eric Peet* .. .. .. 41
II. WEIRD HORSE SACRIFICES OF ANCIENT SIBERIA. *E. Royston Pike* .. 70
III. ALGERIA'S AMAZING TOMBS. *A. MacCallum Scott* .. .. 169
IV. WONDER MODELS OF THE DAILY LIFE OF EGYPT 4,000 YEARS AGO. *Donald A. Mackenzie* .. .. 261
V. CAVE TOMBS AND CHAIR BURIALS OF THE MYSTERIOUS ETRUSCANS. *The Editor* 445
VI. WONDER OF THE MUMMY. *G. Elliot Smith* 549

## The Royal Palaces

I. MARVELS OF PERSEPOLIS. *Lewis Spence* .. 51
II. A WONDER PALACE ON A ROCK. *G. E. Mitton* .. .. 114
III. DIOCLETIAN'S PALACE AT SPALATO. *F. N. Pryce* .. .. .. 130
IV. THE CITADEL PALACE OF TIBERIUS AT CAPRI. *F. N. Pryce* .. .. 181
V. THE SUPERB SCULPTURES OF THE GREAT PALACES AT PERSEPOLIS. *Lewis Spence* 252
VI. CHOSROES' PALACE AT CTESIPHON. *W. Ewing* .. .. .. 609

## The Great Monuments
PAGE

I. THE MYSTERY OF THE EASTER ISLAND IMAGES. *T. A. Joyce* .. .. 29
II. THE COLOSSI OF "MEMNON." *W. F. Aitken* 68
III. THE SPHINX. *Margaret A. Murray* .. 154
IV. WONDER OF THE OBELISK. *R. Engelbach* 403
V. THE PYRAMIDS OF EGYPT. *T. Eric Peet* 453

## Temples of the Gods

I. THE MYSTERIOUS GIANT SCULPTURES OF TELL HALAF. *E. Royston Pike* .. 14
II. GREAT SHRINES OF SICILY. *F. N. Pryce* 35
III. ANGKOR: A MARVEL HIDDEN IN THE JUNGLE. *Edmund Candler* .. 73
IV. THE PARTHENON: CROWN OF ATHENS. *F. H. Marshall* .. .. .. 96
V. THE SHRINES OF ISIS AT PHILAE. *Margaret A. Murray* .. .. 122
VI. BORO BUDUR: THE SOUL OF JAVA. *T. Athol Joyce* .. .. 162
VII. THE ROCK TEMPLES AT ABU SIMBEL. *Margaret A. Murray* .. 176
VIII. A TEMPLE OF THE GREAT GOD BAAL. *E. Royston Pike* .. .. 187
IX. MYSTERY GODS OF EARLY CYPRUS. *E. Royston Pike* .. .. 232
X. OLYMPIA AND ITS SACRED GAMES. *The Editor* .. .. 277
XI. THE ROCK-HEWN TEMPLES OF ELLORA. *F. Deaville Walker* .. 283
XII. DELPHI OF THE ORACLE. *Edward Wright* 317
XIII. SAKKARA. *Margaret Murray* .. .. 347
XIV. BAALBEK: SPLENDID IN ITS RUIN. *R. Curle* 435
XV. THE GREAT DAGOBAS OF CEYLON. *G. E. Mitton* .. .. 560
XVI. THE GODS OF ANCIENT GREECE. *W. R. Halliday* .. .. .. 619

## The Master Builders

I. THE STRANGE FORTS OF ARAN. *E. W. Lynam* .. .. .. 91
II. THE MARVEL OF THE ROMAN AQUEDUCTS. *F. A. Wright* .. .. 205
III. THE MAYA MARVELS OF CENTRAL AMERICA. *L. E. Elliott* .. .. 217
IV. THE GREAT WALL OF CHINA. *F. H. Davis* 303
V. HADRIAN'S WALL: RELIC OF ROMAN BRITAIN. *Jessie Mothersole* .. 474
VI. SOUTH AMERICA'S MARVELS IN MASONRY. *T. Athol Joyce* .. .. 584

## Ancient Arts and Crafts

I. MASTER ARTISTS OF THE STONE AGE. *E. G. Harmer* .. .. 143
II. PEERLESS GEMS OF GREEK SCULPTURE. *Frank Rutter* .. .. 239
III. THE EXQUISITE ARTISTRY OF ANCIENT EGYPT. *Donald A. Mackenzie* .. 332
IV. MASTERPIECES OF ROMAN SCULPTURE. *Frank Rutter* .. .. 463
V. ARTS AND CRAFTS OF ANCIENT BRITAIN. *Sir Bertram Windle* .. .. 525

## The Seven Wonders

I. THE COLOSSUS OF RHODES. *J. A. Brendon* 27
II. THE STATUE OF ZEUS AT OLYMPIA. *A. H. Smith* .. .. 237
III. THE MAUSOLEUM AT HALICARNASSUS. *F. Norman Pryce* .. .. 271
IV. THE GREAT PYRAMID. *Margaret A. Murray* 543
V. THE HANGING GARDENS OF BABYLON. *J. A. Brendon* .. .. 605

# SPECIAL COLOR PLATES
# IN THIS VOLUME

FACING
PAGE

Jewels of a Lady of the Court in the Great Days of Ur .. .. *Frontispiece*

Giant Figures of the Divine Triad at Tell Halaf .. .. .. .. 16

Colossus Commemorating the Deliverance of Rhodes .. .. .. .. 28

Silent Custodians of the Secrets of an Old Polynesian Culture .. .. 33

Doric Columns of the Temple of Castor and Pollux, Girgenti .. .. 40

Propylaea of Xerxes at Persepolis .. .. .. .. .. .. 52

Temple Front at Petra, Chiselled from the Living Rock .. .. .. 88

The Parthenon, Shining Diadem of Athens .. .. .. .. .. 104

Boro Budur, Java's Mammoth Buddhist Shrine .. .. .. .. 164

Beautiful Propylon of the Third Ptolemy at Karnak .. .. .. .. 197

The Zeus of Pheidias, Loftiest Embodiment of Divinity in Art .. .. 236

Hand-Maidens for Mehenkwetre in the Otherworld .. .. .. .. 261

"The Wall of Ten Thousand Miles": China's Mighty Triumph in Stone .. 312

Ancient Egypt's Artist-Craftsmanship in Carving and Ceramics .. .. 330

Beauty Destined for the Darkness of the Tomb .. .. .. .. 340

The Acropolis, Rocky Heart of the "City of the Violet Crown" .. .. 385

Centre of Athenian Life, the Tradition-haunted Agora below the Acropolis .. 393

Reconstruction of the Three Pyramids at Abusir .. .. .. .. 453

Pyramids at Gizeh seen through the Feathery Palms that Fringe the Nile .. 461

Tepidarium of the Baths of Caracalla in its Pristine Beauty .. .. 500

Arab Splendour and Classic Grace of the Haram el Sherif .. .. .. 580

Reconstruction of the Hanging Gardens of Babylon .. .. .. .. 604

# WONDERS OF THE PAST

## The Endless Romance of Antiquity

### How the Dead Past is Made to Live Again

#### Some Introductory Remarks by the Editor

IT is unfortunate that one of the most fascinating pursuits to which the human mind can devote itself should have so forbidding a name as Archaeology. To that much-mentioned personage, "the Man in the Street," the word probably suggests chilly museums with dusty shelves and potsherds with little tickets in glass cases. And he has good warranty for this, as only within recent years has the science of recovering the past been brought to something like perfection in its methods, attaining results that enthral the intelligent and stir the sense of wonder in all persons of average imagination.

#### Digging through the Dust of Ages to Recapture the Hidden Past

Thanks in some measure to the superabundance of wealth with which the United States found herself—shall we say encumbered ?—in the years immediately following the war, numerous expeditions from the great American universities, either independently or in conjunction with the British Museum and our own universities, were organized to search for the buried remains of past ages in many different parts of the world, so that at present important expeditions are exploring many sites identified with the strange civilizations of the Mayas, the Incas, the Aztecs, and other once powerful races of the American Continent ; such age-old city-sites as Ur and Kish and Babylon, and various others in Mesopotamia are being deeper and more deeply dug into with the most fruitful results, as the ensuing pages vividly illustrate ; expeditions are even at work in different regions of China and the great deserts of Asia, searching for anything that throws light upon that vast stretch of the world's existence which, for convenience, we describe as Prehistory.

NEARER home there is great activity on the classic sites of western Europe. Anyone who first visited Pompeii thirty years ago and again today would be astounded at the change that has come over that little town of Ancient Rome, the tragedy of whose destruction has given it a place in the imagination of mankind beyond its intrinsic interest.

It is instructive to recall that the first unearthing of Pompeii seems to confirm the idea that the common domestic architecture of Imperial Rome was somewhat similar to that of the Spanish country residence of today : a rectangular series of rooms enclosing an inner courtyard, the *atrium* of the Romans, the *patio* of the Spaniards, whence doors gave immediate access to the surrounding apartments, which were all on the ground level, excepting certain upstairs quarters for the domestic slaves.

#### Wherein The New Archaeologist Rivals " Sherlock Holmes "

The meticulous examination of every spadeful of earth dug by the modern archaeologist—whose methods are precisely those of " Sherlock Holmes " —and the laborious assembling of fragments as in a jig-saw puzzle—have revealed a remarkable variety of domestic architecture as to style, mass, and principle of construction. Pompeiian houses that thirty years ago were mere outlines of foundations have actually been made to arise from their ashes by the ingenious refitting and building-up of their tiniest fragments until they are now seen to have had two and sometimes more floors with massive balconies.

WE know from the tenement houses of Ostia, the ancient port of Rome, and the large villas of Pompeii, which were divided into self-contained flats and residences among a considerable number of tenants, that the populous Roman cities must have had an appearance of mass by no means inferior to that of our modern cities before steel and concrete enabled our builders to soar to previously undreamt-of heights. But the builders of Ancient Rome had little to learn from those who put up Mayfair's latest block of flats.

When we come much closer to our own doors than even Herculaneum or Pompeii ; when we come to Verulamium (St. Albans), to Caerleon in Wales, or to any one of the scores of historic sites all easily accessible within the narrow compass of the British Isles, we are confronted with the most pleasing manifestation of intelligent energy seeking to recover from his native soil for the Briton of to-day authentic and tangible evidence of the sort of life that was lived in his own country ages ago, and the measure of civilization enjoyed by the remoter and long-extinct races that peopled the British Isles.

To make these dead cities of the distant past live again in the popular mind of our own time is the fascinating work that is known by the forbidding name of Archaeology : a work of endless allure, of continual surprises, and richer than almost any other field of human study, as from the past with its miseries and its splendours, its gallant strivings towards great things and its catastrophic failures, we can derive knowledge to help us in the living of our own lives today.

### The Earth as a Vast Cemetery of the Human Race

The Earth is really a vast cemetery of the human race. From the objects dug up in its ancient graves and tombs we can piece together tolerably accurate pictures of the life lived by the men and women who returned to Mother Earth many thousands of years ago. Hardly a week passes without some news of new and exciting archaeological finds, for there is scarcely any limit to the explorer's range : wherever primitive man had his temporary place of shelter, wherever savage or civilized communities dwelt, wherever temples, palaces, or tombs were built by men of the vanished races, the archaeologist finds objects that thrill with significance when interpreted by experts of today.

In designing WONDERS OF THE PAST my object has been to provide a work of a " popular " kind which yet would be as accurate and considered in its information as attractive in appearance. Those best capable of judging have expressed the opinion that the object in view has been attained in this work. Perhaps I may, with pardonable editorial pride, mention that several years after our first edition had been issued, and an American impression of WONDERS OF THE PAST had been widely sold throughout the United States, I was being shown through the wonderful tomb built five thousand years ago by Hetepheres, mother of Khufu, for her daughter, and then newly discovered by that veteran Egyptologist, Prof. G. A. Reisner, of Boston ; his other guest on the occasion of my visit being the Harvard professor of Archaeology, from whom I learnt that WONDERS OF THE PAST was so esteemed in the United States that at Harvard papers in the Archaeology course were set from its pages. Here, indeed, was proof that it is possible to make a publication " popular " and attractive in its appearance without surrendering anything of accuracy or seriousness.

I DO not suppose than any of my new readers will be less pleased with WONDERS OF THE PAST because it does not follow any sort of historic sequence in the presentation of its contents. The systematic study of any subject can too easily be made over-systematic, and to attempt to build up in strict historical sequence a conception of the many and various cultures of prehistoric and ancient times might result in a work that would be worthy of praise but could scarcely be described as " popular." The attention of the ordinary non-specialised reader, to whom this work makes its chief appeal, would be less likely to be engaged in that way than by the method here adopted.

### Our Varying Interests in the Study of the Past

Not everyone is interested in the same periods of history or in the same aspects of civilization. There are those to whom everything concerning the history and civilization of Ancient Rome is electrical with interest, and others to whom Egypt or Assyria are far more alluring than anything of a later date. Those who find themselves peculiarly attracted to speculation on primitive man and the earlier forms of human society, such as we study in objects of the Old Stone Age, probably would not be stirred by anything so very recent as the collapse of the Western Empire.

And yet I am hopeful that in WONDERS OF THE PAST readers of all tastes will find something to attract them, and to whet their appetite for knowledge of the ancient times. Even the expert will find abundant data in our profusely illustrated chapters, which merely as collections of pictorial documents are unrivalled in any publication known to me, and which, in most cases, require only the mention of their authors' names to give authority to their literary contents.

Our original classification of the contents has been followed again, with the addition of a new section somewhat more general in character than any of the rest : The Study of the Past. No attempt has been made to obtain uniformity of length between these sections, which are long or short according to the number of subjects presenting themselves for inclusion :

| | |
|---|---|
| The Study of the Past | The Great Monuments |
| The Wonder Cities | Temples of the Gods |
| Records of the Tombs | The Master Builders |
| The Royal Palaces | Ancient Arts and Crafts |
| The Seven Wonders | |

Some important new chapters have been added to the work, and the whole has been subjected to careful revision, so that WONDERS OF THE PAST has become a more extensive and more valuable survey of a subject that is as endlessly interesting as it is unlimited in extent and variety.

## The Study of the Past. I.

# The Walls of Jericho: Why they Fell

## By C. B. Mortlock

Special Correspondent of " The Daily Telegraph " in Palestine

OF all the cities of antiquity the name of none is more familiar than that of Jericho. Until Professor Garstang began his excavation of the site it was no more than a low mound lying somewhat to the west of the rather squalid modern village of the same name. The visitor to-day may not be able to discern much of the history of the place without guidance, but he cannot mistake the remains of massive works of fortification and the ruins of the houses that once clustered against the walls.

Unlike many other ancient sites, that of Jericho has raised no doubts concerning its identification. One reason for this is that the place became a favourite winter resort of Herod in the Roman period. Fortunately the buildings of that age left the old mound uninhabited. Even the name survives in the modern Arab form el Riha.

The strategic importance of Jericho is revealed at the first glance. Seven miles west of Jordan it commands the steep ascent to the highlands of the interior. Like so many of the cities of antiquity, Jericho can be better envisaged as a large fort, rather than as a town in the modern understanding of the term. In all, it occupied an area of a little more than six acres. And even that extent—about the size of an ordinary cricket ground — is not abnormally small. Sir Flinders Petrie has pointed out that the ancient city of Troy could have been comfortably accommodated in Hanover-square, one of the smallest London squares.

Jericho was one of the first of the historic sites of Palestine to be scientifically investigated. Two eminent German archaeologists, Drs. Stellin and Watzinger, excavated it in part a few years before the war, and their work attracted widespread interest on account of the correspondence of some of their results with the Biblical narrative. A great deal was written about their discoveries, but nothing conclusive was forthcoming at that time.

For many years Professor Garstang of Liverpool had desired to make an exhaustive investigation of the site. He had the advantage of being deeply read in the history of Joshua's campaigns. From 1920 to 1926 he had been Director of the Department of Antiquities set up by the High Commissioner under the British mandate in Palestine. During that time he followed on foot the precise itinerary of Joshua's army. Thus he visited the site of every battle and succeeded in identifying the sites of some of the cities, the exact location of which had even been forgotten.

In the early months of 1930, thanks to the generosity of Sir Charles Marston, it became possible for Professor Garstang to re-open the investigation of Jericho. One of the difficulties of the German excavators was that there was at the time of their digging no systematic classification of Palestinian pottery and other remains. They had been obliged to go far afield, to Egypt, Cyprus, and elsewhere, to compare the data which their spades turned up.

By the time Dr. Garstang started work on

**EVIDENCE OF JOSHUA'S CAMPAIGN: BURNT WALLS OF JERICHO**

The walls of the citadel of Jericho, destroyed by the Israelites under Joshua, date from the late Bronze Age, 1600–1400 B.C. In this photograph are seen the burnt brick walls which rose to a height of 28 feet, showing the line of fire with the reddened upper parts.

THE BRICK-WALLED CITY OF JERICHO ON ITS MOUND AS IT APPEARED WHEN JOSHUA FIRST SAW IT

This reconstruction drawing made by Miss M. Ratcliffe under Professor Garstang's supervision, shows the city of Jericho in the time of Joshua. On the left is the Great Tower, built some time before 1400 B.C., while round the city runs a double brick wall, the inner wall being 12 feet thick. The excavations have shown continuous signs of destruction and burning along the west side. The outer wall fell down the slope of the mound, so that the Israelites easily entered the city, and, as described in the Old Testament, "burned it with fire." The primary cause of the collapse of the walls seems to have been earthquake shock. There is no question now that the walls of the city did actually fall in Joshua's day, and the Bible narrative is further confirmed by ample evidence throughout the ruins of the city of Joshua's day of destruction by burning, as seen in the photograph in the previous page. These walls remained in ruins for 500 years. On the outer edge of the mound are ruins of the older Canaanite city with its stone rampart. This city was about double the area of the one destroyed by Joshua.

4

THE MOUND OF THE CITIES OF JERICHO AS IT STANDS IN THE PLAIN OF CANAAN TODAY

Lying under the hills of Judea deep in the Jordan rift, 4,000 feet lower than Jerusalem and 800 feet lower than sea level, Jericho was a point of strategic importance. It covered routes from the north and south, as well as the main trade route from Jerusalem to the east. Traces of at least three cities have been found which flourished in various parts of the Bronze Age between 1800–1200 B.C. The excavations here not only dated Joshua's campaigns but have established a new date for the Exodus itself.

Jericho there was a good deal of classified knowledge about pottery—the importance of which lies in the fact that in every age it is easily broken and yet is virtually indestructible, and lies in fragments until it is trampled into the earth and forgotten.

In his first season Dr. Garstang and his assistants examined tens of thousands of potsherds. In the end over a hundred thousand had been washed, examined and charted. The reason for such exhaustive thoroughness was the paramount importance of discovering the latest period at which the ancient city was inhabited, or in other words, when it was destroyed. Dates are not always important within a hundred years or two but in the case of Jericho it is otherwise. For generations scholars have disputed the date of the Exodus and upon that date depends all the subsequent chronology of the history of Israel.

The result of Dr. Garstang's investigation of pottery remains was to point to the middle of the late Bronze Age (c. 1400 B.C.) as the date of the destruction of the city. The generally accepted belief, based on precarious evidence, was that the Exodus had occurred two centuries later. That theory was supported vigorously. The knowledge that there were Israelites in Palestine at that period was answered by alleging that not all had gone into captivity! Professor Garstang's

deductions from the pottery of Jericho were challenged. It was suggested that the classifications were wrong.

Fortunately for the excavators they came on a wealth of evidence the existence of which had never before been suspected. To the west of the city site, in a small valley, was a necropolis entirely concealed by the drifting sand of the plain. It is rare in the East for tombs to escape the plunderers, but here was a complete necropolis untouched since the days, 4,000 years ago, when the bodies were laid to rest with their weapons and trinkets and such-like. Dr. Garstang was confronted with the prospect of some 70,000 tombs. They yielded all manner of archaeological treasure. From one tomb alone were taken 300 unbroken pots. But most precious of all were the scarabs found in some of the richer tombs. Altogether about eighty were recovered. Their importance lay in the fact that they bore the cartouches of the Pharaohs and so could be dated with precision. Nothing was found later than two royal seals of Amenhetep III (1413–1377 B.C.). There were no burials after that date. Thus the evidence of the pottery was confirmed. Everything pointed, as Sir Charles Marston observes in his excellent little book, "The New Knowledge of the Old Testament," to the reign of Amenhetep III as marking the period when Jericho fell.

CANAANITE WALL BUILT ON ROCK

This finely-constructed stone walling at Jericho is part of the
earlier Canaanite city of the middle Bronze Age (1800–1600 B.C.).
It reaches down to the solid rock and on it was built a brick wall,
remains of which are seen in the upper part of the photograph.

But what of the walls of Jericho ? That is the
point about which curiosity is liveliest. Well, in the
first place Dr. Garstang found that the use of the
plural number in speaking of them was justified
by the facts. He found two parallel walls built of
sun-dried brick. The outer was about 6 feet thick and
the inner about 12 feet thick.
Their height was roughly 30
feet and there was room between them for such houses
as that in which Rahab lived
and from whose window the
spies of the Israelites were
let down outside the wall in
a basket.

The statement that the
walls were built of brick must
not be taken to imply a neat
regularity of construction.
The bricks were of all sizes
and their gaps were very
irregularly filled with mud
mortar. There was also an
outer sloping stone wall, probably built about 1800 B.C.
and remaining in use for two
hundred years. The main defences of the city in the late
Bronze Age, the period when

Joshua attacked it, consisted of the two inner
walls. Dr. Garstang hesitated a good deal about
ascribing a cause for the fall of the walls, but
he is inclined to the view that the catastrophe
was caused by an earthquake, though the walls
did not at first show traces of splitting or frac-
ture. On the other hand, faulty foundations
would have made the walls an easy victim of
earth tremors much less disruptive than that
experienced in Palestine in 1927. However
that may be, one part of the outer wall was
certainly tilted bodily forward and resting on a
bed of fine earth. It must thus have provided
a clear path to the invaders.

The Biblical narrative states that the city
was burned with fire, and Dr. Garstang found
abundant evidence of a vast conflagration. He
came, indeed, to the conclusion that Joshua and
his men, after the capture, systematically
collected wood and other combustible material
from all around the district to make a holo-
caust of the city. In addition to reddened
walls, layers of white ash and masses of charcoal, Dr. Garstang found store-rooms filled with
vessels the contents of which were burned ;
others were filled with food stuffs which had
been left untouched by the captors.

The evidences of the deliberate destruction of
the city are deeply impressive. Dr. Garstang
formed the opinion that the conflagration which finally effaced the city was not
only general but must have needed weeks of
preparation. The Israelites sacrificed Jericho
of the Late Bronze Age, the first-fruits of
the Promised Land, as a burnt offering to
Jehovah with method and deliberation.

THE TWO WALLS OF JOSHUA'S TIME

Here are seen portions still standing of the two brick ramparts of the city Joshua captured. On the left is the inner wall, 12 ft. thick, which, in places, still stands 18 ft. high.
The outer wall, right, was only 6 ft. thick. It was this wall that "fell flat." Both walls
are in a ruinous condition.

# The Modernity of the Ancient World

## By The Editor

THOSE who like to visualise the social life of dead ages, while studying the ruins of ancient domestic architecture that still remain in the classic lands of Europe and in the near East, must often have occasion to marvel at the evidences of the high degree of inventiveness in the provision of creature comfort which had been attained by the beginning of the Christian era—indeed, more than three thousand years earlier, as we can see from the wells and bath-rooms of 3500 B.C. found at Mohenjo–Daro in India (see page 434).

I do not mean the barbaric luxury of oriental potentates, of which the ruins that bestrew many desert places of the East are eloquent, and which did not necessarily connote comfort. I mean the style of the houses in which many thousands of Roman citizens were accustomed to reside. For the Romans were the first of the great peoples who, on a national scale, properly appreciated ' home comforts,' and designed their dwellings accordingly. So alert were their architects to all details of house-planning that they would have had very little to learn from the architects of to-day.

The decline of the western power and the coming of the Gothic age, when the passion for religious design absorbed the creative genius of the architects, lost to Europe for some eight centuries the development of certain building features which we moderns are apt to regard as peculiarly of our time. Central heating, drainage, hot baths, service flats, efficiently designed shops: these had all approximated to perfection under Imperial Rome, and not only in Italy but as distant from the capital city as our own Bath (Aquae Sulis) or St. Albans (Verulamium). The ideas of comfort that obtained among the great nobles in the England of the Conqueror were primitive by comparison with those that prevailed a thousand years before in Rome and among the Roman officials who held Britannia for the Caesars.

There are many things made and used by man in his social state that have suffered scarcely any change in thousands of years and are little likely to alter radically in ten thousand more. The modern plough, for instance. It is essentially the same instrument as the first plough, once the idea of adapting a hoe for animal haulage had stirred in the mind of some prehistoric Edison. The stone-built quays of Tyre and Sidon, with their iron cleats and mooring rings, were hardly different in any detail from thousands along the coasts of Europe and America to-day, at which, perhaps, a greater variety of vessels tie up. The anchor of any great modern liner is in principle, and indeed in appearance, the same implement as the Carthaginian mariners used for making their vessels ride at anchor in Cornish bays when they came trading for tin and lead before the rise of Roman sea power had sealed the doom of the Punic cities. One could compile a ponderous list of such instances, but they are less illustrative of modernity in the ancient world than of the survival of ancient crafts in the modern. Such a list would lack the element of surprise, however instructive it might be.

As striking examples of modernity in the ancient world it would be hard to beat the planning and equipment of the public baths, lavatories, markets and libraries at Timgad, that astonishing little city of ruins in North Africa, so cleverly restored by the French authorities. The sanitation of Timgad about nineteen centuries ago would, I think, have passed the scrutiny of any modern Medical Officer of Health : it was incomparably better than the sanitation of Edinburgh at the beginning of last century! The public lavatories are certainly surprising even in their utter ruin. They were splendidly fitted, decorated in sculptured marbles ; a fountain in the centre of the building played continually, its overflow water being carried off through little channels as a constant means of flushing. There

Beck & Macgregor

**A BOOTBLACK OF ANCIENT GREECE**

Among numerous odd little bits of evidence of the modernity of old time conditions, this Greek bronze statuette of a negro slave cleaning a boot is signal It dates from about 460 B.C., and the boot itself is an early model of the Roman outdoor calceus and its modern successor.

Courtesy of Dr. T. Ashby

MANSION FLATS FOR MIDDLE-CLASS PEOPLE IN THE FIRST CENTURY OF THE CHRISTIAN ERA

In Rome the tenement houses occupied by the lower classes were usually built around courtyards and were by no means above criticism. At Ostia they seem to have been built along the line of the street, with courtyards or gardens at the back overlooked by pleasant balconies. This reconstruction drawing by Gismondi of the House of Frescoes at Ostia, based upon facts deducible from existing remains, shows the surprising resemblance of the Roman ' insulae ' to the mansion flats found in good residential quarters of many towns to-day. Sun blinds, window boxes and bright pigments in the exterior decoration gave these blocks of self-contained flats a most attractive appearance.

**LUXURIOUS SANITARY METHODS OF EIGHTEEN CENTURIES AGO IN ROMAN AFRICA**

The finest lavatories of the great cities of to-day show hardly any advance on those of Timgad, where the sanitation was extra-ordinarily " up to date." Here is seen a corner of the great public lavatories hard by the Forum, with 26 carved stone seats, each enclosed by two gracefully chiselled dolphins. In the centre an ornamental fountain served to flush out the drains. Timgad was founded by the Emperor Trajan in A.D. 100 and completed in about twenty years.

was an attendant, for whom a little lodge at the entrance was provided.

One of the markets at Timgad, that erected by a soldier-priest named Sertius as a practical thank-offering for his prosperous career in the Augustan Legion, remains in a good state of preservation to remind us that the Romans were more than modern in their market arrangements : no town of the same size in England to-day can boast a market so ' up-to-date ' in design and decoration as this which flourished at Timgad eighteen hundred years ago. Each of the enclosures of the different traders bore a charming little sculpture symbolising the particular wares dealt in at that counter. For centuries until the Vandals came smashing up the fine work of Rome in North Africa there must have been many happy days spent by busy traders in fruit and flowers and other commodities in this ideal little market of Sertius

WITHOUT leaving this wonder place of Roman Africa (held of so little account in its own day that its name, Thamugadi, is mentioned only three or four times in contemporary chronicles), furthei examples of modernity confront us in the remains of the once lovely little building that was the gift of another grateful townsman. A public library, it was evidently furnished exactly like any modern institution of the kind with tables and chairs for consulting the parchment rolls which served as books and were neatly stored in deep pigeon holes around the walls of the building. Above all, there are the numerous baths whose elaborate and efficient heating systems are disclosed in their ruin, showing how well the ancient builders understood the system of warming by hot air.

I do not remember to have seen at Timgad examples of central heating applied to ordinary dwelling houses. Perhaps the winter season there in Roman times, when the surrounding land that is now barren and treeless was well wooded, may have been mild enough to call but rarely for any special heating devices. At Ostia, at the mouth of the Tiber, however, one can see central heating as cleverly arranged in a block of flats as any heating engineer could do it to-day.

Not many visitors find their way to Ostia, which strikes me as hardly less interesting than Pompeii or Herculaneum. For centuries it was the port of Rome, and a place of great consequence, its harbour bustling with merchants and shippers and its hotels equipped for dealing with the sea-borne travellers to and from the world's capital. You can walk into the ruined shipping offices to-day and see the names and trademarks of the different firms set in mosaic in the floors ; you can visit the wreckage of a hotel in which every room was heated from a furnace

ROMAN DRAIN 2,500 YEARS OLD AND STILL IN USE

One of the greatest achievements of Roman engineering skill was the cloaca maxima, the main sewage system draining the low-lying district of the Forum. The walls are possibly Etruscan, and were vaulted in about 150–100 B.C. It averages fourteen feet in height with a width of eleven feet, and still serves as a drain, discharging into the Tiber through this great triple-coursed archway.

to the ancient Roman villa type. But the archaeologists have shown us that even in Pompeii some of the larger dwellings were apartment houses of several floors, sheltering a considerable number of families. At Ostia, on the other hand, apartment houses were the rule rather than the exception, and buildings of four storeys were common. Even in their ruined state some of those that remain are sufficiently surprising : the famous House of Diana, for instance, shown in page 686. It must have been very similar to a well-built block of flats in modern Rome, except that bright pigments were more freely used in its exterior decoration.

Some of these blocks of flats were also warmed throughout in winter by means of hot-air from underground furnaces. They had fine central stairs with apartment doors on the landings, and the flat roofs were used for drying clothes or the sunning of the dwellers, just as similar roofs serve to-day. The grocers' boys also used to scratch on the walls of the stairs nasty remarks about the grumpy old lady of the third floor back.

in the basement by means of intramural tunnels, and in which you can still see the position of the night porter's office in the entrance hall !

The idea used to be common that Roman buildings were chiefly one-storey structures, like the modern patio houses of Spain, which conform very nearly

Nearly two thousand years ago on a sunny day in Ostia—and most days were sunny there—when the

CENTRAL HEATING AND CONSTANT WATER IN OLD ROMAN VILLAS

As early as the reign of Augustus nearly every Roman private house had its own water supply drawn from the main by lead pipes like these (right) from the House of Livia on the Palatine. The blown joint in one of these has a remarkable look of modern plumbing. Where climatic conditions made it desirable Roman villas also had central heating. A villa at Darenth, Kent (left), is an example. Hot air passed from a furnace below through the tiled supports of the raised floor and through flues in the wall to the upper storey.

Courtesy of Dr. T. Ashby

## STRIKING ANTICIPATION OF NEO-GEORGIAN ARCHITECTURE

Ostia, even more than Pompeii, furnishes proof that there was no lack of variety in Roman domestic architecture. Gismondi's reconstruction here shows a five-storeyed building in a principal street with shops on the ground floor and generous provision of balconies and loggias on the upper storeys.   Buildings almost identical in appearance are being built in many towns in this twentieth century, and, save for the absence of wheeled traffic, the ill-paved roadway and the deficiency in street lighting  this corner of Ostia might be a corner of post-war Mayfair.

blocks of flats had their sun-blinds down and their window and balcony boxes were gay with flowers, save for the absence of all motor-car noises and the difference of costume, the place must have presented an absolutely 'modern' aspect, such as would have in no way appeared strange to the eye of a beholder who had strayed backward from the twentieth century. At Ostia, too, the great quayside warehouses, like those that were once the pride of Carthage would differ hardly at all from those of modern Havana or Valparaiso, though I suspect that the grain elevator would be noticeably absent.

In the British Museum you will find a bronze statuette of a negro house-boy cleaning one of his master's boots. It is a scene from ancient Greece, and if the little slave had only been shown in some sort of trousers it might have passed for a domestic study from Tennessee or Kentucky, the boot (like the later Roman 'calceus' worn out-of-doors only) being extraordinarily like a modern one. Another modern glimpse of the ancient world, and still more striking, is afforded by a Roman tomb sculpture preserved in a museum at Treves, the ancient capital of Gaul. It shows a Roman lady (doubtless the wife of a

**11**

TABLE APPOINTMENTS 1,900 YEARS OLD

Prof. Halbherr

Pompeii's destruction in A.D. 79 was the means of preserving for us much material evidence of the conditions of life in those days, and quantities of kitchen utensils and table appointments virtually identical with those in use to-day have been recovered. This photograph shows a table as found laid ready for a meal, with jugs and platters and a bronze balance used as kitchen scales

thought of. When we notice a particularly tidy and nicely-arranged butcher's shop in the newest London suburb we are seeing a thing that was the commonest sight in ancient Rome, as we have monumental evidence to prove; and when we see, as we may any day in France, the wife of the *patron* seated in a high chair at a desk attending carefully to the financial side of the business, we are also looking at a familiar shopping scene from the ancient world.

The extremely varied collection of dishes arrested in the act of cooking by the catastrophe that overwhelmed Pompeii in the year 79, and now assembled in the Naples Museum, includes so many meats and sweets that figure on the menu of any European restaurant every day of the year

provincial official) seated in a wicker-work chair of extremely modern appearance, with three servant maids attending her, none of whom, so far as costume and toilets are concerned, would attract any particular attention if they were seen walking to-day in any town of France.

The shopping methods of the ancient world were much the same as those of to-day, although the modern idea of the 'multiple shop' had not been

that we are reminded how slight, if any, is the progress that has been made in the culinary art in the last two thousand years. Indeed, the nearer we approach the life of the remote past, by means of the material fragments of those vanished ages that may still be found in situ or scattered among the museums of the world, the more often we must ask ourselves what does all our vaunted progress amount to? Very little indeed, if we could ignore the purely mechanical

'SMALL TRADESMAN' METHODS UNMODIFIED BY TIME

This cast of a relief in the Dresden Museum depicting the interior of a pork butcher's shop in the second and first centuries B.C. proves that nothing essential has been added to the outfit of such a retail business in the intervening 2,000 years. The block on which the man is jointing a side of bacon could be matched in any butcher's shop to-day; so could the steel yard, if not replaced by a modern spring balance: the joints hung on the bar are familiar objects; and still to-day the tradesman's wife sits in the shop making up the books.

FEMININE PREOCCUPATION OF STILL UNDIMINISHED INTEREST

Rich gentlewomen in imperial Rome led rather indolent lives, owing partly to their exclusion from active participation in the intellectual and athletic pursuits engaged in by women to-day, and partly to the large number of slaves employed, relieving them of all domestic occupation. Their toilet thus engrossed a disproportionate amount of their attention, and one of them is actually depicted on her tomb seated in a quite up-to-date basket-chair, submitting to the ministrations of four maids and watching their dressing of her hair in a mirror held by one of them. The simple costumes are such that, as Dr Mortimer Wheeler has pointed out, they might well be found in a modern drapery store

side of life. This, however, we may not do, as it is undeniable that a vast amount of our present-day comforts and fullness of life rests entirely upon the development of mechanical contrivances of the last two centuries.

The ability to move rapidly from place to place, to become familiar in a short space of time with hundreds of towns and changing scenes which, no more than two generations back, would have taken a lifetime is due to the modern perfection of mechanical transit. And herein we have moved immeasurably beyond the wildest dreams of the ancients. The development of the mechanical arts, the success of the industrial revolution, may not

be an unmixed blessing, but it would be foolish to suggest that it has not made happier the lot of the working classes, both as regards their domestic conditions and the facilities offered for the rational enjoyment of life. For we must remember that throughout the whole of the ancient world, from the earliest days of Babylonia to the latest of Greece and Rome, with all its evidences of social comfort and enjoyment which we find recorded in the wrack of it, there was an immense class of the community whose lives were divorced from all forms of enjoyment and who existed as the slave class that performed so much of the work which in the modern world is discharged by machinery.

## The Temples of the Gods. I.

# The Mysterious Giant Sculptures of Tell Halaf

### By E. Royston Pike

#### Author of "The Story of the Crusades," etc.

*AMONG the many remarkable and romantic archaeological discoveries of the present century not the least striking is that presented here in brief and fully described by Baron Max von Oppenheim in his "Tell Halaf: A New Culture in Oldest Mesopotamia." The English translation is published by G. P. Putnam's Sons, by whose permission most of the illustrations in these pages are given.—*EDITOR.

IN 1899 Baron Max von Oppenheim, a member of the Imperial German diplomatic service in Egypt, was prospecting in Syria for the proposed Bagdad railway. From Syria he passed into Mesopotamia, to the region in which the Khabur, the only all-the-year-round tributary of the Euphrates, has its source. It was there one day, sitting in the great tent of the local chieftain before the heaped-up mound of rice and chopped mutton, that he heard a half-whispered tale that at once aroused his interest

**MYTHOLOGICAL MONSTER AND ITS DISCOVERER**

Here we see Baron Max von Oppenheim, the German archaeologist who restored the mysterious sculptures of Tell Halaf to the world, gazing questioningly at one of the gems of his collection—a fantastically-shaped creature of stone, with human head, bird body and scorpion tail. Several of these great figures stood before the entrance of the sacred enclosure.

A year or two before, he gathered, some tribesmen when digging a grave near Ras el Ain had come upon great and mysterious stone statues of animals such as were unknown on earth, animals with human heads. The sudden appearance of these monsters filled them with fear and they hastily flung back the earth and hid them once more from the sight of men. But, it appeared, evil, irreparable evil, had been done, for that very year the rains failed, locusts devoured every green thing, and cholera took a heavy toll of human life. It was only too plain that the statues were the home of noxious spirits whom the brief uncovering had released to work their malign will. Hence men spoke but little of the mysterious find, for fear that others, bolder or more careless than themselves, should again disinter the statues.

A strange story—so strange and so intriguing that the Baron at once made his way to the village Ras el Ain, and after much argument was conducted to the statues' burial-place, on the hill of Tell Halaf, and there began to dig. In three days parts of a temple-palace were laid bare, together with several slabs carved in relief, some animal statues and, most marvellous of all, a great throned goddess. "The uncovering of the veiled goddess was a great event," writes Baron von Oppenheim in the story of his work; "this large, dark-coloured woman's figure with its retreating forehead, thin lips and mysterious cast of countenance—whose effect was further heightened by the large, black oval eyeball with a very narrow white rim—threw a spell over me."

After three days his duties made him leave Tell Halaf — not before, however, he had carefully re-interred the statues. In 1911 he returned fully equipped to excavate, and in quick

CONJOINED IN MYSTERY: TELL HALAF'S ENIGMATIC DOUBLE STATUE

Not far from the temple-palace at Tell Halaf was unearthed another temple building, a cult-room containing statues of deities, household idols, necklaces of stone and other fragments representing offerings made to the local divinities just before temple and town were involved in a common ruin. The most remarkable of these "finds" was this double statue of a man and woman—possibly the Hittite god Teshup and his consort Hepet—sitting on a bench together, with their feet resting on a slab.

succession his workers uncovered colossal statues of animals, monstrous gods and veiled sphinxes. Gradually they cleared the floor on which the great figures stood, and then, amongst the remains of charred and fallen beams, they were halted by the skeleton of a girl, wearing still the ornaments that had been her delight and pride in life, but whose contorted shape spoke all too eloquently of her tragic, sudden end.

At the end of 1913 it seemed that the site had been thoroughly dug over. The statues were removed to the expedition's house, and operations were suspended until the winter of 1914. But the war intervened and it was not until 1926 that Baron von Oppenheim was able to make his way back to Tell Halaf, now included in the Syrian mandate of France. The house he had built in 1911 had been destroyed by gunfire, but the statues had been safely preserved beneath the débris. In 1929 work was definitely restarted.

So much for the history of Tell Halaf's unveiling. Now let us turn to consider the "finds" and their implications. Most striking and important

are the colossal statues which were found lying together outside the north front of the temple-palace. Five once stood in the portico—a trinity of roof-supporting deities erect on animal mounts, and two flanking sphinxes, winged and watchful. Restored and replaced (as may be seen in the colour plate facing page 1), they impress even the beholder of today, used though he be to the wonders of Ur and Egypt ; what must have been the impression made on the worshippers of that far distant age, to whom the figures were not weird shapes of basalt but were filled with a dreadful meaning at which we can only guess !

The three statues, each about 8 feet high, stood on cube-shaped bases placed on the backs of colossal sculptured animals. The centre figure was smashed into fragments when the temple-palace was burnt some thousands of years since, but the other two were protected by the falling beams and were found in a comparatively good state of preservation. The left-hand figure facing the observer stood on a lion and is of a man or god, broad-faced, hook-nosed, with protruding

15

MYSTERIOUS OBJECTS OF WORSHIP 3,500 YEARS OLD

This stone eagle, weird and huge, kept watch before the front of the temple-palace ; reminiscent of the phoenix, it probably represents the sun god. On the right is the female member (believed to be the goddess Hepet) of the divine triad (see colour plate facing page 1) that stood like caryatids in the building's portico.

Hittite trinity — Teshup, the supreme god, Lord of Heaven and Earth, God of Rain and Storm, in the centre ; and to right and left the sun god, mounted on the lion, and the goddess Hepet, corresponding to the Babylonian Ishtar, on the lioness

In front of the façade and the statues just mentioned was an altar, and beside this was dug up a huge sculptured bird of grotesque appearance  Its wings are folded close to the body and its eyes—of polished black stone set in disks of white limestone— project above its tremendous beak  Not quite so remarkable but still sufficiently impressive are the wonderfully-preserved statues of scorpion bird men—recumbent figures with human heads, bird's body and legs and scorpion's tail—that guarded the gate to the sacred enclosure. Then in a "cult room" of another temple not far away, was found a double statue worked from one stone and representing a man and a woman sitting together on a bench  The man is serious, almost woe-begone ; the woman is milder-countenanced, and her inset eyes stare straight before her. What would one not give to know what passed in front of them before they were blinded by destroying flame and smoke and buried for those thousands of years beneath the dust ?

One more figure may be mentioned, perhaps the most impressive of all. This is the great goddess already referred to, which was found beneath a close-packed mass of bricks above a tomb. Without any feminine lines, almost without bodily form, the statue is built

lips and long, neatly arranged beard  On his head is a diadem of seven-leaved rosettes, above which is a pair of thick horns, a frequent symbol of divinity or leadership — Moses, for example, is so represented in certain sculptures at Rome. As for his dress, he is garbed in a short-sleeved coat and a cloak  In his right hand he holds a boomerang, while his left grasps the pommel of a sword. Judging from its remains, the middle statue was very similar. On the right stood the statue of a goddess, fully clothed in indeterminate garments, with rows of beads round the neck and bracelets about wrists and ankles  The lioness on which it stood was found near by. There seems to be little doubt that the three figures constituted a divine triad, the supreme deities of the ancient folk who once lived at Tell Halaf. They have been identified, indeed, with the

ANIMAL MASTERPIECE OF AN ARCHAIC SCULPTOR

In addition to the colossal statues, Tell Halaf has disgorged a number of orthostats—stone slabs carved in relief with details of the life of the prehistoric sculptors. A typical specimen is this splendidly realistic representation of a lion such as in those far distant days roamed the Mesopotamian plain.

## GIANT FIGURES OF THE DIVINE TRIAD AT TELL HALAF

Retrieved from beneath the accumulated debris of three thousand years and restored with well-informed care to something approaching their ancient grandeur, the three colossal statues that once supported the portico of Tell-Halaf's temple-palace now stand in a museum at Berlin. Their discoverer, Baron von Oppenheim, is seen leaning against the lioness mount of the goddess Hepet.

*Specially coloured for " Wonders of the Past," from a photograph*

up of three cubes set one above the other, and resembles nothing so much as the " cubist " art with which we have been made familiar of recent years. But the moon-shaped face, the tremendous beak of a nose, the retreating forehead have no parallel elsewhere.

Still we have not described all, or nearly all, the archaeological spoil won by Baron von Oppenheim from Tell Halaf's soil; in particular we have said nothing of the magnificent collection of orthostats—relief-carved stone slabs nearly two hundred in number, which stood round the base of the temple-palace, and which throw a flood of light on the daily existence of the people of pre-historic Tell Halaf. Yet when we have seen them all, the prevailing sense is still one of mystery. Who were these Tell Halaf folk, who sacrificed before their dreaded trinity, who carved the fantastic bird-man and the cubist goddess, who went hunting in chariots, who rode on horses and camels? What was their race? When did they live? What tale of horror could be told by that girl whose calcined bones were found near the altar of which, perhaps, she was the last ministrant priestess?

Some of the statues bear the name in cuneiform inscription of one Kapara, an Aramaic prince who is believed to have lived about the twelfth century B.C., but Baron von Oppenheim maintains that the statues of the temple-front were made about 2500 B.C. and stood originally in a temple-palace of the Subaraic-Hittite folk that was

ANCIENT ARTIST'S CUBIST CREATION

Cubism is generally regarded as an essentially modern development. Yet here in this statue from Tell Halaf of a huge goddess wanly smiling an archaic smile, we have a well-nigh perfect specimen of cubist art. It is composed of three cubes, mounting like a pyramid to the massive head.

wrecked several hundred years later; and that after they had lain buried for a thousand years or so they were resurrected about 1200 B.C. by Kapara, touched up and replaced in much the same positions they had originally occupied. The orthostats are given a still earlier date, about 2900 B.C. Then at some much later date there was another invading wave and Tell Halaf was burnt and its statues were wrapped in flame and buried in the dust.

Whether or not the Tell Halaf sculptures be as old as their discoverer would have them to be, it would seem clear that they are evidence of an independent culture which was apparently distributed throughout a wide area in southern Asia Minor, western Syria and upper Mesopotamia—in other words, in a district which for a thousand years prior to 1200 B.C. was included within the dominions of that most mysterious of ancient folk, the Hittites. This " Subaraic " culture, it is claimed, dates back to the fourth millennium B.C. If this be so, then Tell Halaf was the source of a large part of what has been hitherto known as Hittite culture.

NATURALISM IN CARVEN STONE

Another example of the realistic carving displayed on the orthostats. This gazelle turns its head as if it detected the presence of the observer who immortalized it in stone.

This mighty Ziggurat, the "Mountain of God" at Ur, was erected by Ur-Engur, a king of the Third Dynasty of Ur, about 2400 B.C., probably on the site of an even earlier temple. The shrine in the centre was of blue glazed brick. The Ziggurat remained in this form until it was restored by Nabonidus in the 6th century B.C. This reconstruction is by Mr. F. G. Newton.

### THE MOUNTAIN OF THE GOD AND THE GREAT TEMPLE OF UR OF THE CHALDEES

Coming down into the plains of Mesopotamia from mountainous country, the Sumerians, originators of the ziggurats, raised artificial mountains of brickwork as substitutes for the holy hills on which their gods formerly had their seats. The great ziggurat at Ur whose surviving ruins, as seen from the air, are shown in the photograph, measured 200 feet long by 150 feet broad and 50 feet high. Outside the temple enclosure lie the excavated remains of numerous domestic and business buildings.

# The Wonder Cities.   I.

# Ur: the City of 'The Flood'

## By C. Leonard Woolley

Director of the British Museum and University of Pennsylvania Joint Expedition to Ur

A TANGLE of low mounds, sandy yellow and grey, littered with broken bricks and potsherds, rising out of a plain which stretches flat and desolate as far as the eye can see ; in the centre of the mounds one higher than the rest whose steep curves are broken by projecting corners of weathered brickwork ; such, before excavation began, was " al Mughair," the Mound of Pitch, as the Arabs named it. Dig into the upper part of these crumbling hillocks and you find the stout girdle wall of mud brick, the temples and the houses which two thousand five hundred years ago Nebuchadrezzar built at Ur. These are almost the latest monuments, for about four hundred years before Christ the last inhabitants moved away from the dying town and left its buildings to solitude and decay ; but during many ages before that men had lived here continuously and city had been piled upon city, each generation building over the wreckage of the last, so that a section cut through one of the mounds will give in successive layers of rubbish and ruin as many chapters in the life history of a people.

The foundations of Nebuchadrezzar's walls are cut down through the walls and floors of buildings put up by Kassite kings five hundred and nine hundred years older than he ; still deeper down comes the Ur which Abraham knew, a city partly built in his time, partly surviving from the great days when Ur-Engur made Ur the capital of an empire and embellished it with temples worthy of his grandeur. We are back now at 2300 B.C., but still below us there are perhaps sixty feet of accumulated rubbish representing no one can say how many more centuries of man's occupation. Sometimes underneath Ur-Engur's temple floors there are found fragmentary walls built with curious

round-topped bricks witnessing to another glorious age in the city's history, when about 3100 B.C. a local ruler, Mes-anni-padda, rebelled against his overlord and set himself up as master of the Valley Land with Ur as his seat of government : he founded the First Dynasty of Ur and it was his son who built at al 'Ubaid near Ur the little temple whose discovery first threw light upon the astonishingly rich architecture of the early Sumerians.

DEEPER yet, thirty and forty feet below the modern surface, older remains reward the digger. At the bottom of shafts cut down through stratum after stratum of rubbish belonging to a still earlier time lie the tombs of the prehistoric kings. In arched and vaulted chambers of rubble masonry there lie concealed such treasures of art as revolutionise our ideas of early civilization ; as far back in time as 3500 B.C., when Egypt was still barbarous, here in the Euphrates valley the Sumerian workers in gold and silver, in copper, stone and shell were turning out veritable masterpieces of design and technique, while their architects were familiar with all the main principles of modern construction There is no written history of that age, but even from the offerings placed in the graves we can see how highly organized civilization had already become.

Take the few objects illustrated here ; the materials of which every one of them is made had to be imported from abroad : by land and by sea, from the Pamir mountains, from Oman at the foot of the Persian gulf, from Persia, from the hills of Lebanon, were brought the lapis lazuli, the copper and alabaster, the silver and the cedar wood which the craftsmen of Ur used in their manufacture,

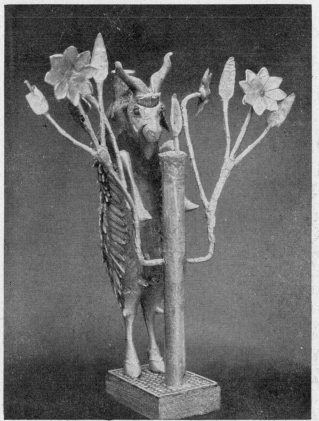

Joint Expedition

**THE RAM CAUGHT IN A THICKET**

Among the most remarkable objects disinterred at Ur were two figures of rams, so well preserved that this restoration has been practicable. The fleece is composed of shell and lapis lazuli encrusted on a wooden core and the plants of wood overlaid with gold.

and since their own country produced nothing but grain and dates it must have been in manufactured goods that they paid for their imports. All this meant an elaborate system of trade and a foreign policy which by treaties or by force of arms secured the far-flung trade routes : the art of writing had been developed to meet the merchants' needs, and, as the "Standard" shows, the Sumerian army with its heavy-armed phalanx and its chariotry had become a formidable weapon for opening up communications or resisting attack. We have evidence of a material prosperity seldom equalled in antiquity ; that there was another side to this civilization we can gather from the discovery of the "death pits" attached to the royal graves. When a king died not only were his treasures buried with him but outside the door of the stone-built house wherein his body lay in state were buried his guards, his servants, his musicians, his women and the officials of his court, even his chariot with its asses and their grooms, all sacrificed that they might accompany their master to another world. Probably the king was deified in his lifetime, and the sacrifice, to a god and not to a mortal, was perhaps gladly made as ensuring a better chance in a future life ; but the grim relics of it seem strangely at variance with such gay sophisticated things as the ram statue and the gold-headed lyre.

It must be clear to anyone that the objects from the tombs are the product of a civilization already old and experienced : it is not surprising then to find that not only are the tombs buried in mounds of rubbish whose accumulation would require many centuries, but that the same rubbish layers continue far down below them. The site of the cemetery is

UR-ENGUR BUILDS THE ZIGGURAT

In this stele set up by Ur-Engur, founder of the Third Dynasty of Ur, the king is seen pouring a libation and receiving instructions from Nannar, the moon god, to build the great Ziggurat and shrine seen in page 18. The god holds measuring rod, cord and adze

VICTIMS OF A BARBAROUS CUSTOM AWAITING THE MOMENT OF THEIR RITUAL SACRIFICE

This reconstruction of the burial scene of a king in Ur between 4,000 and 5,000 years ago is based upon an actual plan of a death pit similar to that in page 21. A retinue of 59 men and women, including nine ladies of the court, was butchered to attend their king in the next world

indeed the waste-heap of the ancient town, and the strata of brick rubble, broken pottery, house ashes and disintegrated mud brick running steeply down hill show plainly how the refuse was first flung over the town wall, and later, as the mound grew in height, carried out and emptied down the slope. By 3500 B.C. the refuse-pile stretching from the outskirts of the city to a water-channel at the mound's foot had reached an average height of more than fifty feet ; to what date the lowest stratum belongs it would be hard to say, but it can scarcely be less than six thousand years old. Yet throughout all the successive layers which represent the passing of so many centuries the remains, pottery and beads, etc., found in the soil show practically no change from what is normal in the tombs ; scanty as these relics are they prove that the civilization illustrated at its prime in the graves of the kings had its roots in a very distant past and had developed slowly and consistently throughout the period

during which the rubbish heaps were formed.

Then comes a sudden break. Under the rubbish there lies banked against the hillside a bed of clean water-laid clay eight feet thick and more, the deposit of a great flood ; and below this again we find, and can trace up into the settlement above, the remains of an older civilization one side of which at least is completely different from that which lies above the clay. Here we find, with implements of flint and volcanic glass, painted and decorated pottery such as has no parallel in the higher strata, the handiwork of a race almost certainly northern and non-Sumerian. Just as Sumerian legend would lead us to suppose ; so archaeological evidence tends to prove that an alien people shared with the Sumerians the ownership of the lower valley of the Euphrates ; suddenly all trace of them disappears, and while local tradition would make the Sumerians at least the paramount race in their own

Courtesy of Joint Expedition

## ROMANCE AND TRAGEDY REVEALED BY THE SPADE

In the death pit shown in this photograph—the outer chamber of a royal tomb—no fewer than 74 skeletons were found, disposed as shown in the plan above ; six of them were the bodies of armed men servants, and 68 were women. The floor of the pit was strewn with gold and jewelled ornaments of the sacrificed victims and with other priceless relics of Sumerian art

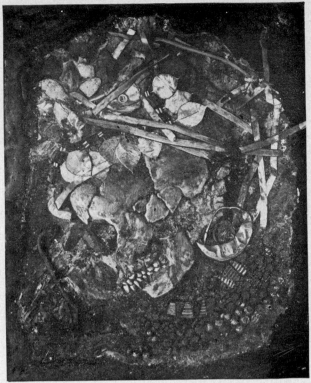

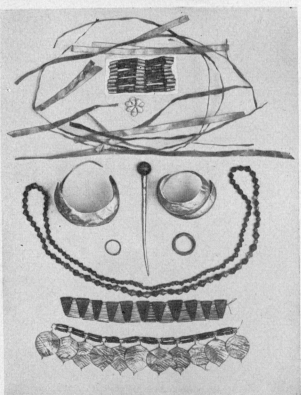

## POMPS AND VANITIES OF LONG AGO

Of the upper photographs, that on the right shows a gold-flowered, gold-ribboned headdress as actually found upon a broken skull ; that on the left Queen Shub-ad's headdress restored and mounted on a head moulded over a female skull of the period. Below is a group of ornaments recovered from the same death pit.

territories, the painted pottery which we may attribute to the other stock ceases to be made in the south country. The clay bank supplies the explanation. The Flood which figures in Sumerian history and legend drowned out the low-lying villages in which the more barbarous element in the mixed population lived, and left the city-dwelling Sumerians to occupy the empty country and to develop their own civilization undisturbed : that this Flood is also the Flood of which we read in Genesis gives additional interest to a discovery whose importance for the archaeology of Mesopotamia is very great.

THE story of the Flood was still remembered when, in the twentieth century before Christ, Abraham walked the streets of Ur, but men had long since forgotten even the names of the old kings whose tombs lay hidden so deeply underground ; if by chance in digging the drains for one of their own houses they came upon a grave with its loot of gold and lapis and carnelian beads and mouldering copper weapons, these things must have seemed to them to belong to a past almost as far away and dead as it is for us. For a citizen of Ur the great days of the Third Dynasty had eclipsed all that had gone before. Those days were gone and Ur was no longer the capital of an empire, but a city long subject to the rulers of old rival states and now threatened, together with all Sumer, by the Semitic lord of Babylon ; but they were commemorated and epitomised by one monument beyond which there was no need to look. Still dominating the town

A fine head of a bull in copper, an admirable example of Sumerian animal sculpture, of about 2800 B.C.

Two of the most ancient sculptures from Ur. These mysterious figurines of bird-headed women with black wigs were found in the earliest graves dating from before 3200 B.C. They probably have religious significance.

**EXAMPLES GROTESQUE AND FINE OF SUMERIAN SCULPTURE OF REMOTE ANTIQUITY**

Left, another of the strange figures of bird-headed women carrying a child. The bodies of these figures are well modelled but the heads and faces are grotesque. Right, two sculptures from wayside shrines at Ur dated about 2000 B.C. The first is a finely carved ram's head in black steatite, and the second is a cult statue of a seated goddess in white limestone. Both were found in little wayside chapels.

rose the vast Ziggurat which Ur-Engur had erected in honour of Nannar, the Moon god, who had established his throne ; its sheer walls supported terrace after terrace green with trees and leading up to the little shrine which was the centre of the city's worship ; up and down its threefold flight of steps the priests still went in procession carrying the image of their god, as they had done for four hundred years.

The Ziggurat, "the Mountain of God," stood for Ur's lost independence, but even the later time had not been so inglorious. The temple of Nannar which Ur-Engur and his son Dungi had built under the shadow of the great Tower had been destroyed, but a king of Larsa, when Larsa was the paramount city, had rebuilt it on a yet more ambitious scale and had adorned its walls in the modern style with half columns and recesses which added an intricate grace to the building's four-square bulk. The temple, too, of Nin-Gal, Nannar's wife, was now more splendid than it had been under the Third Dynasty, for the mud brick walls had been replaced by walls of burnt brick, the sanctuaries were rich with panelling and inlay, and in the side chapels dedicated to the lesser gods and in the temple courts carved and inscribed monuments testified to the piety of a whole list of kings ; nor was the old tradition broken, for still in the heart of Nin-Gal's temple you could pass through a maze of corridors and crossing one end of a narrow chamber see at the other end the round-topped inscribed stela of white stone flanked by the symbols of power, and pay homage to the founder of the building, Bur-Sin, grandson of Ur-Engur, King of Ur, King of Sumer and Akkad, King of the four quarters of the earth, and God.

Other temples besides these were crowded under the high terrace of the Ziggurat and helped to form the Sacred Area of the city ; E-Nun-Makh, where in a little secret shrine were performed the double rites of the Moon god and his consort, Dublal-Makh, " the

This wooden lyre, decorated with mosaic and a superb bull's head in gold, was found with two other lyres crushed in a grave. The mosaic was still in place and thus gave the measurements for exact restoration.

Courtesy of Joint Expedition

**OLDEST KNOWN EXAMPLES OF THE GOLDSMITH'S ART**
Right, a marvellous gold dagger with a solid lapis lazuli hilt studded with gold and enclosed in an intricate filigree sheath in gold, dating from at least 3500 B.C. Its design and workmanship would have been remarkable in any age. Left, a bull's head of gold with a beard of lapis lazuli from a king's grave at Ur. The beard is an attribute of deity.

Great Gate," where from the sanctuary door the judges gave out their sentence to the people assembled in the wide courtyard below, and the row of small shrines dedicated probably to the gods of the Underworld.

These temples were not merely places of worship ; about their courts were store-houses and magazines

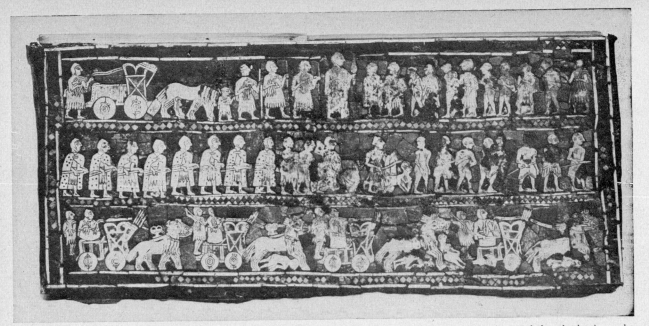

This panel is a war scene. In the bottom row, four-wheeled chariots—perhaps the earliest representation in art of the wheel—drawn by four asses and each carrying a driver and a fighting man are driving over fallen enemies. In the middle row, on the left, are the heavy infantry wearing copper helmets and felt cloaks and armed with short stabbing spears, and, on the right, light-armed skirmishers. In the centre of the top row, the king, dismounted from the chariot behind him, is passing judgement on captives

In this lower panel, in the top row, the royal family are seen at a banquet, with their servants below bringing sheep and oxen for the feast. This elaborate piece of inlay work, discovered in the oldest royal tomb yet excavated at Ur, dates from about 3500 B.C. It consists of two plaques of shell, lapis lazuli and pink limestone mosaic set in bitumen ; the plaques were set back to back at a slight angle, with triangular pieces between the ends, suggesting that the whole may have been carried as a standard. As a work of art this mosaic is unparalleled ; as a historic document giving a contemporary picture of Sumerian customs and costumes both civil and military at this early stage of civilisation when Western Europe was still in the Stone Age, it is priceless.

## EVERYDAY LIFE OF PRINCE AND PEOPLE IN PEACE AND WAR 5,500 YEARS AGO

for the multitudinous offerings in kind brought by faithful worshippers or paid as rent by tenants of the sacred estates ; there were living-quarters for the priests and the temple servants, and there were workshops and factories wherein the men and women attached to the temple were employed, spinning and weaving into cloth the raw wool which the farmers brought, casting and hammering into objects for the god's use the copper and the silver paid as tithes by the merchants of the city, cutting and carving the timber imported from the north ; here too were the schools where

25

the professional scribes were taught and libraries where sacred texts and historical records and court precedents were stored.

Round the Sacred Area lay the town, and from the ruins of it we can see something of how the contemporaries of the patriarch lived. The houses were built of burnt and crude brick, plastered and whitewashed; they stood two storeys high, all the rooms opening on to a little central court round which ran a wooden gallery approached by an internal flight of stairs and giving access to the upper floor. A moderate-sized house might contain thirteen rooms—reception room, kitchen and servants' quarters on the ground floor, the living quarters for the family above. Very different from the life of the Beduin was that to which Abraham was accustomed in his early days, and if later he adopted the pastoral life he took with him into the desert pasturelands the thoughts, customs and traditions of a civilization which had become stereotyped for Sumerian and Semite alike in the great age of the Third Dynasty of Ur, had led the world when Shub-ad and Mes-kalam-dug were buried with their treasures in the rubbish heaps of the prehistoric town, and had its roots in the immemorial past before the Flood.

Courtesy of Joint Expedition

SUMERIAN DOMESTIC ARCHITECTURE IN THE DAYS OF ABRAHAM

Excavation of a great mound outside the wall of the Sacred Area of Ur disclosed a residential quarter of the city built about 2100 B.C. Careful study of the remains of the house shown in the lower photograph warrants the reconstruction drawing above it. All the rooms opened on to a central, brick-paved courtyard. The reception room faced the entry, the kitchen was on one side, and near the entrance a staircase led to a similarly planned upper storey, the rooms of which opened on to a wooden gallery. The roof was nearly flat, but sloped slightly inwards, leaving a square patch open in the centre.

## The Seven Wonders. I.

# The Colossus of Rhodes

### By J. A. Brendon, F.R.Hist.S.

Author of " The Story of the Ancient World," etc.

YOU may seek, but you will seek in vain, at Rhodes for any trace of the famous Colossus. Of this great statue, accounted one of the Seven Wonders of the World, nothing remains; there is nothing even to indicate where it stood. More than two hundred years before our era, it fell. The bronze giant has now been entirely demolished—sold as scrap, it is said.

Wrote the Roman historian, Pliny, who visited the islands in the Aegean in the first century A.D.: " Most worthy of admiration is the colossal statue of the sun which stood formerly at Rhodes, and was the work of Chares the Lindian, no less than seventy cubits in height. The statue, fifty-six years after it was erected, was thrown down by an earthquake, but even as it lies it excites our wonder and imagination. Few men can clasp the thumb in their arms, and the fingers are larger than most statues. Where the limbs are broken asunder, vast caverns are seen yawning in the interior. Within, too, are to be seen large masses of rocks, by the aid of which the artist steadied it while erecting it."

So meagre are the reliable descriptions which have been handed down to us that it is difficult to visualize a reconstruction of this wonder. The Colossus was an immense statue of Helios (Apollo), the sun god and protecting deity of Rhodes. Chares of Lindus designed it, and for twelve years, 292 to 280 B.C., laboured at its construction. It stood at the entrance to Rhodes Harbour, and in the year 224 B.C. was overthrown by an earthquake. These are facts, beyond the range of controversy.

Shakespeare's allusion to the Colossus was inspired by medieval tradition. Cassius, speaking of Julius Caesar, it will be remembered, says:

He doth bestride the narrow world
Like a Colossus; and we petty men
Walk under his huge legs, and peep about
To find ourselves dishonourable graves.
—(" Julius Cæsar," Act I., Scene 2.)

We know that the old harbour of Rhodes had a very narrow entrance. The popular belief, however, that the Colossus stood actually astride it, that all ships approaching or leaving the city had to pass between the statue's legs, is certainly false. Not one of the ancient writers has assigned this position to the statue, and it is highly improbable that a Greek sculptor would have placed the figure of a god in an attitude so inartistic and undignified. The statue, an immense nude form with out-stretched arms, stood really, it would seem, with feet together at the end of the long pier or mole which divided the old harbour into two parts.

Pliny's estimate of its height can be accepted. Other writers have endorsed it. Seventy cubits are the equivalent of, roughly, 105 feet. The Colossus, therefore, was rather more than half as tall as that fluted column, the Monument, which stands in Pudding Lane, London, to remind us where the Great Fire of 1666 first broke out.

The statue was made of bronze, cast in moulds, and was gradually raised upward, section by section, from its foundation in the harbour. The huge legs were strengthened inside with masonry, lest the weight of the body should prove to be greater than they could bear; and within ran a spiral staircase from feet to head. In the eyes, according to some accounts, the Rhodians kept burning a beacon light to serve as a guide to ships.

The story is told that Chares, when he had nearly finished his task, discovered an error in his calculations, and committed suicide. The error, however, could not have been a serious one. Those who saw the Colossus have proclaimed it not merely the largest but the most perfect model of a human form ever fashioned by man. And the Greeks of old were exacting critics in such matters.

Why was the Colossus erected?

The answer to that question is a story of heroism hard to match. In the sixteenth century the blight of Turkish rule fell on Rhodes, and the island to-day is an insignificant place, sparsely populated, unprogressive, poor. But it has not always been like that. There was a time when it played a big part in the affairs of the world. Of its very early history little can be said. The island was civilized, however, long before Homer sang, and, under the influence of that wonderful civilization which radiated from Crete, its people prospered mightily. As workers in metals, they were famed for centuries from the Euphrates to the Nile.

After the power of Crete had declined, Greeks

colonised Rhodes, and built at its north-eastern end a great harbour—now filled with sand—and a city so splendid that it came even to rival Athens. With this as their capital, the Rhodians, seafarers and merchants, were for many years the richest people in the Aegean. At length troublous times befell them. Their wealth kindled jealousy, and they were forced to acknowledge in turn the supremacy of Sparta and Athens. Their ships,

under the command of his son, Demetrius. With three hundred and seventy ships, we are told, Demetrius sailed, and 40,000 men, and a powerful and awe-inspiring siege artillery. The Macedonian host outnumbered the entire population of Rhodes. How could the islanders hope to repel the serried might of this terrible armada?

Undaunted they made their city ready for a siege, and for twelve months offered a desperate resistance. Slaves were armed, and promised freedom if victory should be won. Women worked night and day preparing munitions, and gave their hair as bow strings. Temples were pulled down that the stones might be used to strengthen the walls and repair breaches.

ILLUMINATED LANDSCAPE OVER WHICH THE COLOSSUS GAZED

It must have been somewhere in the neighbourhood of the Fort of S. Nicholas, a relic from the days of the Knights Hospitallers guarding the harbour of Rhodes, that the Colossus once stood, masterpiece of Chares and Wonder of the World. But it never stood, as here, in the unearthly glare of a searchlight

Demetrius, meanwhile, delivered attack after attack. Steadily he approached his goal, and it became clearer to the devoted defenders as each new day dawned that they could not hold out indefinitely, that only help from outside could save them and their city. In 306 B.C. that help came. Ptolemy, mindful of the services which the Rhodians had rendered to him, arrived off the island with a fleet, and forced the Macedonians to withdraw. The Rhodians then gave to Ptolemy the name of "Soter" (the saviour), by which he is still known to history, and to commemorate their deliverance raised the famous Colossus in honour of their protecting deity, the sun-god.

however, continued to dominate Mediterranean trade routes and maintain their prosperity.

Next, Mausolus conquered them—that Carian king whose tomb at Halicarnassus (see page 273) ranks with the Colossus among the Seven Wonders of the World. Then Persians captured the island.

In 340 B.C. Alexander the Great delivered Rhodes from Persian thraldom, and, on the death of the mighty Macedonian, it regained its freedom. Then began the most successful period of its career. Alexandria was at that time the chief centre of Mediterranean trade; but they were Rhodian ships which brought to it the riches of the East, Rhodian ships which distributed over the world its merchandise from Egypt and the South.

In 312 B.C. Ptolemy, the king of Egypt, once a general in the service of Alexander the Great, became involved in a struggle with his former brother-in-arms, Antigonus, the ruler of Macedon. Self-interest induced the people of Rhodes to rally to the side of Ptolemy. And gallantly they fought for him; the valour of their seamen contributed materially to the defeat of the Macedonians.

Antigonus resolved to punish Rhodes, and in 307 B.C. sent a great expedition against the island,

They made it wholly of metal taken from the engines of war left behind by Demetrius, and naturally entrusted its building to Chares. Was not Chares the favourite pupil of the renowned Lysippus, the sculptor on whom, by royal decree, the great Alexander had conferred the exclusive privilege of carving his statue? And had he not fought gallantly in defence of Rhodes?

Alas, the Colossus stood for a short while only. In 224 B.C. an earthquake shook Rhodes, and the huge bronze figure crashed on the rocks in the harbour, where for centuries it lay, as Pliny saw it, prone and pathetic, a giant dismembered.

Numerous attempts were made to restore it to its place. But, though the cleverest engineers of Greece and Egypt were engaged in the task, no means could be found of raising it. In A.D. 672 the Arabs, when they gained possession of Rhodes, sold what remained as waste metal to a Jew. That old Jew, it is said, carried away nine hundred camel loads—three hundred tons—of bronze.

## COLOSSUS COMMEMORATING THE HEROISM AND DELIVERANCE OF RHODES

None of the Seven Wonders have suffered so piteously as the Colossus of Rhodes; there is more than a likelihood that the Hang
Gardens of Babylon have been identified, but the exact site of the Colossus is lost to memory. From ancient writers, however, we kn
that it stood somewhere at the entrance to the harbour; that it was 100 feet high, or a little over; that it was made of bronze, in sectio
strengthened with masonry within; and that the popular idea of it, standing with legs astride, is false.

*Based on a portion of a picture by T. Kiyza, and specially coloured for "Wonders of the Past"*

## The Great Monuments.  I.

# The Mystery of the Easter Island Images

## By T. A. Joyce

Of the Ethnological Department, British Museum

FAR away in the bright blue waters of the South Pacific, two thousand miles away from land to the westward and more than four hundred miles from the nearest island to the east, lies Easter Island, the home of a mysterious phase of human culture.

The inhabitants, of whom about 250 still survive, gathered together in a settlement at Mataveri, at the western end of the island, are members of the Polynesian stock, speaking a dialect akin to that of Tahiti. The fact that the colour of their skins varies from light creamy tint to dark brown, and that clan barriers, jealously maintained, divided the community from the earliest historic times, points to successive waves of immigration—a suggestion borne out by legend ; but, whatever their origin, these antagonistic groups, flung together upon this lonely little outpost of the Pacific Ocean, nevertheless developed in unity a series of arts and crafts differing in certain details not only from those of any other part of Polynesia but from the culture of any other part of the world. The system of writing evolved by the guild of learned men—of whom none survives to-day to tell its secret—is unique ; the curious series of ' emaciated ancestor ' figurines, beautifully carved from a variety of mimosa wood still found upon the island, are entirely distinct ; the same can be said of the ' lizard ' series of carvings and the ceremonial paddles eagerly sought by international collectors ; while strangest and rarest of all the demonstrations of the Easter Islanders' genius are the huge bizarre statues of stone which these people quarried, carved and set up in extraordinary numbers.

The islanders possessed no metal ; their tools were none but crude and weak implements of volcanic glass and rock ; life was not particularly easy, since all food supplies had to be cultivated or snared ; and there could never have been any considerable body of labourers to spare. Yet tremendous concerted energy must have been expended in cutting away blocks of stone sometimes more than thirty feet in length and weighing in some instances as much as 50 tons, in moving these great masses, by means at which we can only guess, considerable distances over broken country, and finally in erecting them at the sides of roads, at the limits of clan territories, or upon the long stone terraces or platforms which were the burial places of the ancient islanders.

THE statues set up on these burial platforms, or ' ahu,' were possibly associated with the honour paid to venerated ancestors, and probably for this reason bore as a badge of rank the fantastic head-dress whose posing is another of the problems of Easter Island ; this was a great hat or crown of red tufa, quarried from the exterior slope of Punapau. Only upon Punapau could this deep crimson rock be found, and the ' hats,' five to eight feet in diameter, were transported all over the island from this one quarry, to be placed, by some ingenious device, upon the heads of figures 20 to 30 feet high. No one knows the precise significance of these singular ornaments ; but when the first European discoverers, chancing upon this out-of-the-way island in a Dutch ship commanded by Admiral Roggeveen on Easter Day in the year 1722, sighted the tawny shores, they were astonished to see the coast ringed by stone statues, surmounted with their red hats, and standing with their backs turned to the sea.

This remarkable series of images was not the sole expression

**HALF-WAY STAGE IN QUARRYING AN IMAGE**

Here we see a stage in the process of undercutting an image partly quarried from the moderately soft rock. After being roughed out as shown in page 30, it was steadily undercut until it rested on a narrow ridge, as seen here. On either side are trenches in which the workmen stood.

**CRIMSON CROWNS FOR STATUES OF HONOUR**
Huge red tufa hats like that seen here were placed on the statues after their erection. These head-dresses were cut out of a special rock and were from five to eight feet in diameter

of the sculptural activity of these artists of the Pacific ; all over the island, except upon the two bald headlands that guard the east and west, figures were erected. Rows of gigantic busts stand looking into the extinct crater of Raraku ; scores of others were set up on the exterior slopes ; three main roads leading from Raraku to the west, north and south were lined with avenues of great figures ; they seem to have marked boundaries, to have presided over ceremonial, and to have been the objects of affection ; their influence was beneficent. When the Routledge expedition made a scientific examination of the island in 1914–15 there was only a single statue left standing on the coastal burial platforms, all having been broken or overthrown during racial feuds or through the action of the sea constantly eroding the sandy shore ; but there were still to be seen, almost perfect, although many are partially buried in sand, one hundred and fifty images on Raraku volcano alone. In addition to their work of carving and erecting statues, the old inhabitants seem to have had a passion for sculpturing every outcropping of rock, numbers of these having been worked in situ. The reason for this great impetus, urging a small group of primitive tribes to this astounding stone-carving effort ; the reason for the beginning, and the ending, of the sculptural era ; and

**COLOSSAL STATUE LEFT UNCOMPLETED IN ITS CRADLE OF ORIGIN**
Nearly all the statues on Easter Island were quarried from the compressed volcanic ash of which the mountain Rano Raraku is composed. The features and the upper outlines of the body were roughed out first and the work was then carried on downwards in grooves or trenches cut on each side of the figure. The figure was then undercut, being propped up on stones while the last keel or ridge was shorn away. It was then ready for erection on the slope of the mountain or for transport e'sewhere.

From Scoresby Routledge, ' The Mystery of Easter Island

## STONE CHISELLED MONOLITHS POLISHED TO THE NAIL

Most of the decoration on the statues appears on the back; the design usually comprises a girdle of from one to three bands, surmounted by one, sometimes two, rings and, frequently, a figure below it shaped like the letter M, all in relief. In front the nipples, navel and hands are carved, these last having very tapering fingers and long thumbs. Exposure of unweathered surface shows that the statues were highly polished, pumice—pieces of which have been found in the quarry—being used for the purpose.

31

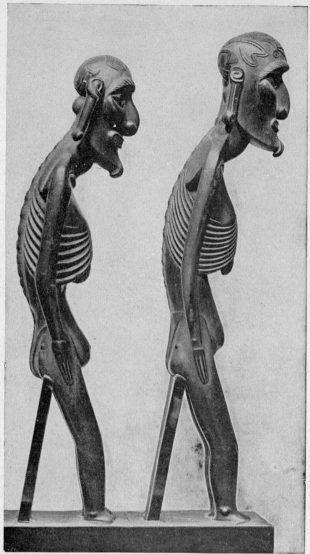

British Museum

SMALL FIGURES OF MYSTERY

In addition to the remarkable stone figures, wooden carvings of nude male and female figures have been found. Probably portraits or memorial statuettes, they are twenty to thirty inches in height and, like the great stone images, have long ears with disk-distended lobes and show a similar design of girdle and ring upon the back. The most remarkable of the wooden figures are those called the moai kava-kava, meaning statues with ribs, which seem to have been intended to represent supernatural beings. Another distinctive feature of the male figures is their small goatee beard.

the data of that era, are amongst the mysteries of humanity; chances of recovering the islanders' historical records were lost when the art of inscribing and reading the hieroglyphs perished.

Of volcanic origin, and of recent creation geologically speaking, Easter Island has a total surface area of less than one hundred square miles; the extreme length is thirteen miles, the width no more than seven. There are no trees, no veins of metal, and few springs or streams, the main source of water supply being the rain-pools that collect in the craters of extinct volcanic heads. The highest of these peaks is about 1,700 feet high, and the country

rock is basaltic. A firm from Chile operates the only commercial enterprise of the island, running sheep on the scant grassy areas of the east; but much of the interior is an undulating plain of black broken lava that can be crossed on foot only with difficulty. and which radiates the sun's heat to a distressing degree. The thin patches of soil produce sweet potatoes, a little sugar-cane, a few roots and bananas. The only native quadrupeds are species of rodents; fishing is poor, owing to the conformity of the island, a shallow and narrow sill about its margin dropping to great depths; and the most important birds seen on the island are the migrants which appear annually in the breeding season.

Here, according to their own traditions, the forebears of the present inhabitants arrived from far over the sea, leaving their native island on account of a contest between the sons of a dead chief; supporting this tale is a legend found in one of the Gambier Islands, 1,200 miles away, that the followers of a defeated chieftain set out in two big canoes, with their women and children and food supplies, a west wind carrying them safely to an island in the middle of the seas. The Easter Islanders retain circumstantial accounts of their migration. including the revelation of the island in a dream, with its 'beautiful road' and a 'big hole'—identified with the crater of Rano Kao—the first planting of yams, and the arrival of the ariki (learned) Tuukoihu, who first made wooden images, and whose sons were the ancestors of the still proud Miru clan.

Legend also tells of the distinction between the 'Long Ears' and the 'Short Ears,' the fighting between them, and the defeat of the 'Long Ears' at their last ditch on the eastern headland; and this tale of the two chief immigrant waves is borne out by the variety of racial types still to be observed, and the conformation of skulls. This evidence points to the existence on the island of two main types, Melanesian—woolly-haired, dark-skinned, long headed, characteristic of the Solomons and other isles adjacent to Australia—and Polynesian, broadheaded, pale-skinned, and straight-haired, and in this connexion Sir Arthur Keith remarks that the people of Easter Island are the 'largest-brained people yet discovered on the islands or shores of the Pacific.'

The immigrants may have brought from Melanesia the idea of distending the ear-lobes, of making weapons from flakes of obsidian, and carving wooden figurines; while the curious bird-cult of Easter Island, connected with the annual coming of the sooty tern, has its analogy in the same area, the Solomon islanders carrying out ceremonies in connexion with the frigate-bird or fish-hawk. But the evolution of a form of writing, and the development of what seems to have been at one time a national passion for making stone statues, cannot be ascribed to any other island or continent.

Two hundred years ago, when Roggeveen found Easter Island during his search for the 'Davis Island' of rumour, the various clans were occupying

From Scoresby Routledge, 'The Mystery of Easter Island'

*SILENT CUSTODIANS OF THE SECRETS OF AN OLD POLYNESIAN CULTURE*

Strange monuments of a forgotten past, scores of these enormous figures stud the bald slopes of Rano Raraku on Easter Island. When set up by the sculptors who shaped the great monoliths in their virgin rock their entire torso was exposed to view; but time in its passage has crumbled the surface of the mountain and soil has gradually accumulated around the base of most of the statues, burying them ever deeper until now only their heads emerge above the sparse herbage, still turning their enigmatic gaze seaward as if challenging the curiosity of rare visitants from the civilized world beyond. As shown in page 33, the peculiar long ears appear also in the wooden carvings of the Easter Islanders.

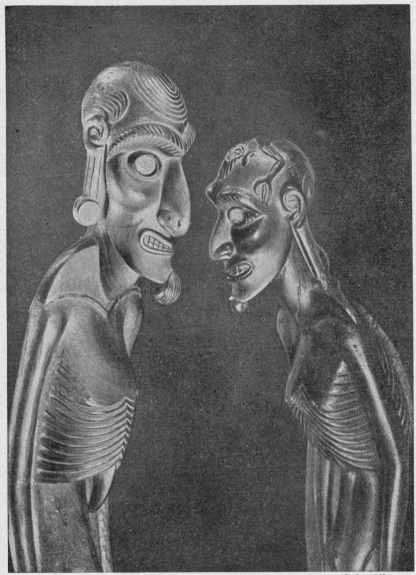

Beck and Macgregor

**ASTONISHING EXAMPLES OF EARLY PACIFIC ART**

Although they have been open to public inspection in the British Museum since the 'eighties of last century, the moai miro, or wooden carvings of the Easter Islanders have attracted singularly little attention considering their high artistic quality. These two reveal a knowledge of anatomy without parallel among primitive people. The custom of carving them is supposed by some to have been Melanesian in origin

with their red hats in place. Apparently, during the interval, the tribal feuds between Long and Short Ears had half ruined the island. In 1774 Cook was here, his officers reporting the natives as about 700 in number, noticing particularly their long ears, and stating that the images, ' so disproportionate to the strength of the nation,' were no longer venerated, their cult belonging to the past. La Pérouse cast anchor off the island in 1780, considered the natives particularly ungrateful thieves, with a special penchant for hats ; did not notice the long ears, and, while observing that the statues were not venerated, thought that there was no reason why the then inhabitants should not carve and erect them. Forty-five years later, when H.M.S. Blossom visited the island, a few Long Ears were still to be seen, even the existence of statues was regarded as ' doubtful,' and the natives still purloined sailors' caps.

By this time the disintegration of the culture of Easter Island, begun from within, had been seriously attacked from without. From the first years of the nineteenth century American sailing-vessels, lacking hands, began to seize the unfortunate natives, and about 1860 raiding expeditions, seeking labour for the Peruvian guano fields, took away something like a thousand islanders ; among these slaves were the last of the learned l e a d e r s, the ' ariki,' readers and writers of the peculiar script of the island. At the instance of French missionaries interested in Pacific islands, the remnants of the guano slaves were eventually returned ; their numbers had been decimated by smallpox, however, and only fifteen reached Easter Island ; these carried the disease with them, and the unhappy islanders suffered from this scourge and at the same time from consumption unwittingly introduced by the missionaries. To these enthusiasts, too, is due the destruction, as pagan symbols, of quantities of the wooden tablets inscribed with Easter Island hieroglyphics.

When H.M.S. Topaze called here in 1868 and took away the typical statue now standing in the portico of the British Museum—Hoa-Haka-Nana-Ia, or There is a Friend Who Watches—there were only about 175 inhabitants surviving, and these had been

the whole of the area, cultivating the ' rich soil,' and appearing well supplied with food ; they were friendly, although thievish as regards head-gear ; varied in the colour of their skins, wore clothes of tapa, and large disks in their long, distended ear-lobes ; they lighted fires in front of the coastal statues and did reverence to them. Fifty years later, in 1770, a Spanish ship arrived, took possession for the King of Spain, made a map, which the natives signed in their own writing, and called the island ' San Carlos ' ; they estimated the inhabitants at 900 to 1,000, and said that the soil was then mostly uncultivated. Many shore statues were still standing, gathered together by French traders at the west end of the island. In 1888 the Chilean Government took formal possession of Easter Island and granted a concession to a company engaged in pastoral development ; besides the visits of the company's vessels, the Chilean Government send a training ship once every year.

The Routledge expedition in 1914–15 arrived just in time to find the last inhabitant with any knowledge of the tablets and their records—chiefly legends, war lists and, apparently, to preserve the account of the bird cult connected with the sooty tern and the competition for the ' First Egg ' ; and to make careful surveys of the remaining ' ahu.' These platforms, sloping gradually from solid shore to the sea's edge and ending in a small artificial cliff, strongly buttressed, were built of worked stone blocks, in which were vaults used as graves.

**BIRD MAN AS A RELIGIOUS MOTIF**

References to the strange bird cult of Easter Island are numerous in the native art. A remarkable example is this representation of the bird man holding an egg in his hand carved upon a block of stone, itself egg-shaped. The wooden club above represents the fish man, but the blade of the weapon is adorned with numerous figures of the bird man in various attitudes.

From Scoresby Routledge, "The Mystery of Easter Island"

**MEMORIALS OF THE ANCIENT "LONG EARS" OF EASTER ISLAND**

The erection of the statues on the seaward slope of Rano Raraku was a comparatively simple matter. Eased down the incline to the destined spot the earth was cut away from their base and they were hauled upright. Scores are still erect, but many more have only their heads and faces exposed. The " long ears " referred to in page 32 are well seen.

Upon these terraces the statues were erected, their big, serene heads with concave noses, pursed lips, and elongated ears, facing inland, while their ornamented backs were turned seawards. No fewer than 260 of these platforms were found by the Routledge expedition, the finest measuring 300 feet in length and rising 15 feet high. Many were suffering from coastal erosion.

To-day the most striking evidence of the mysterious culture of Easter Island is found on the inner and outer slopes of Raraku volcano, where many scores of statues stand in perfect condition, while others lie partly completed, witness to the methods used by the ancient sculptors. All about the slopes of Raraku are countless quantities of stone and obsidian chisels, lying as if they had been flung down by the prehistoric artists and abandoned for ever in answer to a sudden call

# The Great Shrines of Sicily

By F. N. Pryce, M.A.

Assistant keeper, Department of Greek and Roman Antiquities, British Museum

IT was in Sicily, an island ruled for twenty-five centuries by a succession of masters, including almost every race but its own inhabitants, that, in point of material prosperity, Greek civilization probably attained its zenith. The island completely outstripped Greece proper, and its reactive influence on the motherland is clearly traceable. The culmination of Greek art, as we know it in the Parthenon of Athens, would have been impossible and inexplicable without the long evolution and development which is to be traced in the forty odd Doric shrines of Sicily of which the remains are still preserved to us.

It is probable that Sicily had attained a measure of civilization long prior to the arrival of the Greeks. Apart from vague traditions of lotus-eaters and Cyclopes, the earliest inhabitants of whom anything definite is recorded were the Sicani, who, perhaps about 1,500 B.C., were driven into the western half by the Siceli, a race of invaders who seem to have come from Italy, and whose tombs have yielded bronze implements and pottery proving them to have been considerably advanced beyond the stage of barbarism.

The Greeks who came to Naxos, the earliest Greek colony in Sicily, in 735 B.C. were of the Ionian branch of their race, to which the Athenians belonged; several other Ionian colonies followed in the north-east corner of the island, among them being cities on the sites of the modern Messina and Catania. But the most numerous colonists were the Dorians, who settled along the southern and eastern coasts. The Phoenicians, timid traders and far from their base, shrank from competition with the newcomers and, abandoning most of their own stations, confined themselves to a few posts at the far west of the island. It was through these Phoenician colonies,

however, that danger first arose for the Greek communities. Fearing to be excluded altogether from the trade of the island, they sought the protection of their countrymen of Carthage. In the year 480 B.C. a powerful Carthaginian army under Hamilcar advanced along the north coast and besieged Himera, a few miles west of the modern Cefalù. Here it was surprised by the Greeks and utterly routed. It is to the period following the battle of Himera that we owe most of the existing remains, including the later and larger temples. If they lack the perfection of detail and the beauty of material which is sometimes, though not always, to be found in the shrines of Greece proper, they show in a pre-eminent degree a variety of planning and a happiness of position, while in scale and bulk they have never been surpassed. The Parthenon at Athens is 228 feet in length along the platform; but at least two of the Sicilian temples attained a length of over 370 feet.

Throughout the greater part of the fifth century B.C. the island seems to have enjoyed peace. But internal revolutions and change of government were common within the cities, so when in 409 B.C. a second Carthaginian army landed in the west, the Greek cities failed to combine as they had in face of the former invasion and were conquered piecemeal. One after the other the rich and populous communities were sacked and destroyed, and from this point until the Roman conquest the history of Sicily is the history of Syracuse, which was almost the only city able to resist the invaders and preserve its prosperity.

The material remains of this flourishing age are of varied nature, comprising fortifications, aqueducts, tombs, houses, some superb theatres, and, above all, temples of the " Doric " order, the development of which may be traced

IMPORTANT SITES OF ANCIENT SICILY

VIEW ALONG THE MAJOR AXIS OF THE GREEK TEMPLE AT SEGESTA

One of the most impressive monuments which the Hellenic world has left us is neither in Greece nor built by native Greeks. Egesta in Sicily, or Segesta, as it is now better known, was a town of the Elymians, to whom the Greeks assigned a Trojan origin, but who were more probably a branch of the native Sicilians; Eryx was another of their settlements. They became completely Hellenized, however—sufficiently so towards the end of the fifth century B.C. to start the construction of this typically Greek temple.

in Sicily from the rude and clumsy proportion of primitive architecture to the perfection of a finished art. Apart from Syracuse, the most important sites to-day are Girgenti, Selinunte, and Segesta. Girgenti is a flourishing town of 20,000 inhabitants about the centre of the southern coast-line, but the modern town occupies only a corner of the area covered by the ancient city, which in its prime counted over 200,000 inhabitants. Known to the Greeks as Akragas, to the Romans as Agrigentum, it was one of the latest establishments of the Greeks, founded as late as 582 B.C. as an offshoot of another colony farther east. It rapidly grew under a succession of able rulers, one of whom, Phalaris, earned an unenviable reputation in later tradition as a cruel tyrant; he is said to have roasted his victims alive within a hollow bull of brass. Another ruler, Theron, was one of the heroes of the great victory of Himera.

During the early part of the fifth century B.C. Akragas disputed the primacy of the island with Syracuse, and war broke out between the two cities, but Akragas suffered a heavy defeat (446 B.C.). Thirty years later, when Syracuse was fighting for existence against the Athenians, Akragas remained sullenly neutral, but in 406 B.C. the Syracusans were sufficiently magnanimous to send help to

their rivals against the Carthaginians. Despite this assistance, however, after an eight months' siege, Akragas was taken and plundered. In the following century it was recolonised and, in contrast to the fate of most of the destroyed cities, a second time rapidly rose to prosperity. On more than one occasion it again endeavoured to challenge the leadership of Syracuse, and it was the last city of Sicily to pass under the domination of Rome, holding out long after the rest of the island had submitted, and then only won by treachery.

The site of Girgenti is of extraordinary beauty. Two long ridges, bounded on each side by small rivers, rise from the fertile coastal plain. On the northern ridge is the modern town; between the two lies the ancient city, of which few remains are now to be seen; but the southern ridge is crowned by a line of half a dozen great temples, of which one is in almost perfect preservation. This array of colonnaded buildings of bright golden stone must have been extraordinarily impressive; the Greek poet, Pindar, calls Akragas " the most beautiful city of mortals."

The ancient names of the temples have been largely lost, and their modern designations are simply adopted for the sake of distinction. At the eastern end of the ridge is the Temple of Juno,

36

gloriously situated on a high rock. It dates from the fifth century B.C., the period of finest art, and is still extensively preserved ; traces can still be observed of the fire which consumed it on the night that the Carthaginians took Akragas. A little farther west comes the Temple of Concord, of the same date, and, with the exception of the Theseion at Athens, the most perfectly preserved Greek temple in existence. The only part lacking is the roof, which has fallen in ; the staircases leading to the roof, the colonnade, and pediments are undamaged. It owes its preservation to the fact that during the Middle Ages it was converted into a church. Both these temples are a little under 140 feet in length.

Still farther west comes the Temple of Zeus, the largest temple in all Sicily, over 370 feet long. The architecture of this is peculiar, as the columns, instead of standing free, were engaged into the walls. There are thirty-eight of these half-columns, each fifty-five feet high ; the flutings of the shafts are sufficiently deep to contain a man. In the interior the roof was supported by thirty-eight human figures, each twenty-five feet high. One of these has been reassembled from fragments and now lies amid the ruins. This temple was commenced in celebration of the victory of Himera and was still unfinished when Akragas was stormed in 406 B.C. ; at present it is wholly ruinous.

Beyond this are other temples, an angle of one of which—known as the Temple of Castor and Pollux—has been re-erected. It is a graceful piece of architecture, still showing traces of the richly coloured decoration. In all there are no less than ten temples to be traced around Girgenti ; one of the finest is built into the crypt of a medieval church. Of other remains perhaps the most remarkable are the aqueducts for the water supply

MEMORIAL AT SEGESTA TO THE SPREAD OF HELLENIC CULTURE

The temple, as shown by this comprehensive view, was of the type known as "peripteros-hexastylos," with six pillars at either end and fourteen on the sides, a total of thirty-six, and it was built in the purest Doric style, which, with its severe, unornate capitals, is perhaps the most pleasing form of Greek architecture  The dimensions are as follows · length of stylobate 200 feet, breadth 8⁵ feet, height of columns and capitals 2y feet, width at base 6 feet, space between columns 8 feet.

Photo by Alinari

TEMPLE OF CONCORD AT GIRGENTI, STILL STANDING SOLID AND FOURSQUARE

Another illustration of the so-called Temple of Concord, already mentioned as having been used as a church, which gives an admirable idea of its preservation. Not all its details have remained unaltered, as the arched openings in the cella wall were pierced in Christian times ; but, especially if viewed from the northern ridge, it looks almost as it must have looked in the beginning. It is a peripteros-hexastylos, that is, the ceila is completely surrounded by columns, of which there are six at either end.

Photo by The Autotype Co.

of the ancient city, large enough to walk through. It is said that the prisoners taken at Himera were forced to labour at their construction.

Fifty miles west of Girgenti lies an even more important site, Selinunte, the most westerly Greek settlement in Sicily. Selinus, to give it its ancient name, was founded in 628 B.C., being, like Girgenti, the offshoot of an older colony. The settlement was of ill omen to the Greeks of Sicily, for the quarrels between Selinus and its neighbour Segesta were the cause of two great disasters in Sicilian history. It was the appeal of Segesta for help which was directly responsible for the Athenian expedition of 415 B.C. and the Carthaginian invasion of six years later. On the latter occasion Selinus had to endure the first fury of the storm, and was taken and razed to the ground within a week ; of the 60,000 inhabitants, over one-third were massacred outright in the most barbarous fashion, and many others were sold into slavery.

A little later, in the course of the war, Hermocrates, a Syracusan soldier, seized the citadel of Selinus and fortified it as a strong point, but the town never again prospered, and after about 250 B.C. the site appears to have been deserted. This fact accounts for the preservation of the complete town-plan and of all the temples of Selinus. Not a building is standing ; the Carthaginians levelled everything to the ground, but the fragments have not been touched, and in some cases every stone is lying where the Carthaginians hurled it. So complete are the remains that in some cases it would be possible to rebuild the entire temple from the original material.

Selinus originally occupied a pear-shaped plateau washed by the sea on the south. On the north the fortifications of Hermocrates still remain, an astonishing complex of battlemented walls, subterranean passages, flanking towers, and case-mates for catapults, the ancient artillery. On

**WEATHER-WORN COLUMNS OF THE TEMPLE OF JUNO LACINIA AT GIRGENTI**
Another imposing ruin at Girgenti is that called the Temple of Juno Lacinia. Although not in such a perfect state of preservation as the Temple of Concord, it enjoys an even finer situation, standing on the brink of an abrupt cliff over the sea. Of the original thirty-four columns only twenty-two are still intact, but a few more have been partially restored. Akragas, the name by which Girgenti was known to the Greeks, was destroyed in 406 B.C. by the Carthaginians under Himilco. The temple was a peripteros-hexastylos, and the height of the columns was five times their diameter.
Photo by The Autotype Co.

east and west were formerly harbours, now filled up. In its prime the town extended far beyond the limits of the plateau, not only inland but also on either side of these harbours. The temples, styled by one authority "the grandest in Europe," lie in three groups. The first group is at the southern end of the plateau and comprises five temples, including the most ancient of all; the second group, of three, lies beyond the eastern harbour; and a single temple has been found beyond the western harbour. All are built of limestone, with a fine coating of plaster, which largely remains perfect with the original colouring. Remains of sculptured decoration have also been found on three temples. These are now in the Museum of Palermo, and illustrate in a remarkable degree the development of Greek sculpture from the grotesque awkwardness of primitive times to the beauty of the fifth century.

One of the temples of the eastern group deserves special mention, as it is almost exactly the same size as the colossal Temple of Zeus at Girgenti

It has not the peculiar arrangements of the latter, but follows the normal plan, being surrounded by a colonnade. The columns are fifty-three feet in height, one still exists to give some idea of the vast scale of this shrine, which was dedicated to Apollo. This edifice seems to have been begun before 500 B.C., but was still incomplete in 409 B.C., when the Carthaginians destroyed it. So vast and imposing are its ruins that it is almost difficult to believe them other than the work of nature.

Going inland, twenty miles north of Selinunte are the remains of its old enemy, Segesta, or, as the Greeks knew it, Egesta. This is a city of another type; it is no Greek colony, but was a settlement of the Elymians, a people of somewhat doubtful origin; they may have been a section of the aboriginal inhabitants of Sicily; but there is also an unfounded tradition that they were descended from the ancient Trojans, who fled to Sicily after the capture of Troy. The city was perpetually on terms of hostility with the Greek colonists.

# The Amazing Riches of Tutankhamen

## By Prof. T. Eric Peet

Brunner Professor of Egyptology, University of Liverpool

THE tourist who pays a visit to Egypt for the first time, or who has not been there since 1925, will undoubtedly receive a great surprise on his first pilgrimage to the Cairo Museum. However closely he may have followed the newspaper reports of the finds in the tomb of Tutankhamen, however vivid his imagination, he will hardly be prepared for the discovery that the material completely fills the long East Gallery of the upper floor of the museum, and even overflows into the North. Now the East Gallery is 80 yards long and 10 yards broad, and the cases in it are placed no farther apart than is necessary to allow visitors to move freely. Only after seeing this can anyone realize the quantity of material which was packed into the famous tomb in the Valley of the Kings.

Why and for whom were these treasures collected into these insignificant underground chambers? When Amenhotep III, one of the greatest of the kings of Egypt, died in 1375 B.C., he left as heir to the throne his son Amenhotep IV, afterwards re-named Akhnaton, a boy with views of his own on the subject of religion. This youth, within a few years of his accession, had suppressed the national worship of Amen, and substituted that of the Sun's Disk or Aton, at the same time moving his capital from Thebes, the modern Luxor, to Tell el-Amarna, some 350 miles farther down the Nile. There, after a reign of about 17 years, he died, leaving apparently no son, but a number of daughters. One of these was married to a certain Smenkhkara, who for a year or two succeeded his father-in-law and then disappeared. A younger sister had been married to Tutankhamen, of whose birth we know

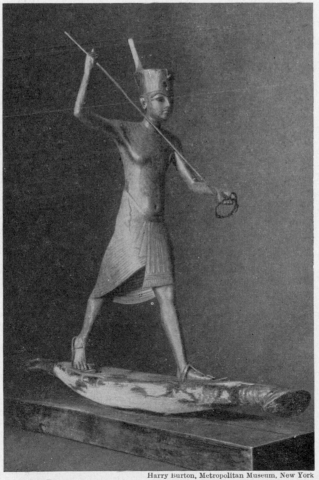

Harry Burton, Metropolitan Museum, New York

### TUTANKHAMEN AS HORUS THE AVENGER

Pretty grace and much animation characterise this gold-plated wooden statuette of Tutankhamen posed as Horus the Avenger, one of more than thirty found in the store chamber of the tomb. It represents the youthful Horus in his canoe about to launch his javelin at the hippopotamus, the river demon lurking to destroy him.

nothing, though some now think he may have been a brother of Akhnaton. On Smenkhkara's death, shortly before 1350 B.C., Tutankhamen, a boy of perhaps only ten years of age, followed him on the throne. The religion of the Disk was already becoming unpopular, and the young king was soon persuaded to return to Thebes and to the religion of his ancestors. There, after a reign of at least nine years, he died.

Now according to Egyptian belief the life beyond differed little from life on earth. It was still a physical life, though of a slightly more ethereal kind, and a dead king, in order to attain happiness, would need not only his body but provision for its wants, first and foremost food and drink, and next tables, chairs, chariots, clothes and jewels; everything, in fact, which would enable him to lead the life of a king there as here. Hence the presence in the tomb of loaves of bread, joints of meat, jars of water, wine and beer, oils and unguents, together with the king's clothes, jewels and personal belongings, and a considerable part of the furniture of the royal palace.

To provide for all these bodily needs was easy. More difficult was the preservation of the body itself. For not only must it be preserved from the natural processes of decay, it must also be protected against destruction by sacrilegious thieves, heedless of Tutankhamen's future life, might actually pull the mummy to pieces in their search for the wealth with which it was known to be covered. The first need was provided for by mummification. The second was more difficult, for it was well known that even the vast pyramids which earlier kings had caused

**THIRTY-THREE CENTURIES ON GUARD**
One of the two life-size figures in bitumenized wood decorated in
beaten gold that stood at the entrance to the actual burial
chamber since it was closed in 1353 B.C. The outermost of the
series of shrines found in it is illustrated in page 45.

to be heaped over their bodies had failed to
protect them from violation. Taught by this lesson
the monarchs of Tutankhamen's dynasty hewed
their tombs out of the solid rock of the lonely Western
Valley at Thebes, and instead of placing in front of
them the chapels where the daily supplies of food
and drink were to be brought, they built these several
miles away on the plain, where they could give no
clue to the whereabouts of the tomb. Even this
precaution, to which we owe the treasure of
Tutankhamen, was of little avail, for his is the only
royal tomb which was not completely plundered in
ancient times.

For us the value of the wealth of material found
in the tomb is not in the main historical, for,
apart from the fact, gathered from a vintage-year
inscribed on a wine-jar, that the king reigned at
least nine years, it has not given us a single
new historical datum. Its value is rather social
and artistic ; social because it teaches us how
an Egyptian king and his family lived, what
means they had at their disposal, what clothes
they wore, what food they ate, what chairs
they sat on ; artistic because it shows us what were
the ideas of the Egyptian artists of that age, and how
they applied them to the decoration of objects of
daily use.

The artistic value of the objects is rather variable ;
there are a few very beautiful things, large numbers
of quite good things, and a few very bad ones.
Egyptian art reached its high-water mark in the
Old Kingdom between 2800 and 2500 B.C. The

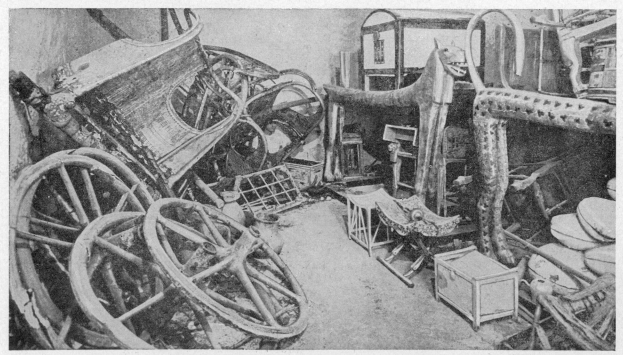

**WEALTH BEYOND THE DREAMS OF AVARICE CONSIGNED TO THE TOMB**
An astonishing welter of objects of superb artistic quality and immense intrinsic value met the eyes of Lord Carnarvon and Dr. Carter
when they opened the antechamber of the tomb at the end of the corridor. Prominent among them was the ceremonial couch
supported by typhonic kine, a clothes chest with the royal cartouches and the jewelled gold and silver throne. But the crowning
discovery was made when they forced their way through the closed portal of the sepulchral chamber.

Middle Kingdom (2000–1800 B.C.) hardly equalled the standard set by the Old, and the New Empire, 1580 B.C. onward, though it occasionally produced a work of the first order, fell on the whole definitely behind its predecessors. The great days of Egyptian art were in reality gone, and we must remember this when we try to judge the contents of the tomb.

It would be a difficult task to pick out among such a wealth of material the most beautiful objects. It is, however, not so difficult for one who has seen it to select those which impressed him most, and in some cases to give the reasons. Undoubtedly the most striking objects are the gold inner coffin, and the mask of beaten gold which lay within it, over the head of the king ; they impress not so much because they are of gold, but because both are magnificent pieces of the sculptor's and metal worker's art. Both are strong and virile portraits of the king, and they are among the very few portraits in metal which have survived from ancient Egypt. Superb objects are the four miniature mummies which were found in the Canopic jars, and which contain the inner parts of the king's body removed during the process of mummification.

Harry Burton. Metropolitan Museum, New York

AN ARTISTIC MASTERPIECE IN GOLD AND ALABASTER

Inside a richly-carved canopic shrine this chest was found. It stood upon a silver-handled sledge-like base, and is of semi-translucent alabaster with lovely figures of the goddesses at the corners standing upon a dado of gold. Within the chest were four receptacles, each stoppered with a portrait bust of the dead king, and each containing an exquisite miniature of the second coffin, within which his viscera were preserved.

They are of gold, with coloured inlays, replicas on a small scale of the second coffin. Lovely, too, is the gold covered Canopic box which contained these jars, with its four guardian goddesses at the corners, which stood in the inner chamber of the tomb itself.

Many visitors to the museum stand in long admiration before the gay throne with its delicate figures of the young king and his bride, inlaid in glass, faïence and precious stones on a background of pure gold. And yet one has only to turn round to see, in the opposite show-case, a chair of plain cedar wood carved with a delicacy of which the more brilliant materials of the throne are incapable, and to wonder whether the simpler thing be not the more beautiful. The famous painted casket, with its scenes of war and hunting, done with a delicacy worthy of the modern miniature painter, is an object from which it is not easy to tear oneself away. Yet it is hard to say whether it is more exquisite than some of the plainer boxes, more especially one of wood inlaid with ivory, which, both in design and proportions, seems unsurpassable.

One may spend hours in the Gold Room admiring, for instance, the king's diadem, a lovely piece of designing, perfectly carried out. It is in this room, however, that Dr. Carter's observation that some of the objects were rapidly and roughly made for the special purpose of the king's burial is most clearly borne out, for side by side with many admirable things there are some which are poorly designed and still worse finished ; indeed a comparison of the contents of the room as a whole with the work of the Middle Kingdom jewellers in the other Gold Room turns very much to the advantage of the latter.

Among the hundreds of smaller decorated objects, sticks, bows, swords, staffs, a word of special praise is due to the walking-sticks with crooks of ebony and ivory respectively in the form of Negro and Semite prisoners. The characterisation of the two races is superb, and these sticks certainly rank among

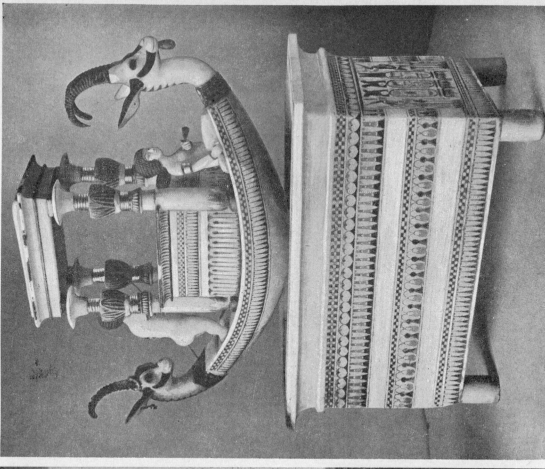

Harry Burton. Metropolitan Museum, New York (World copyright)

**MASTERPIECES OF GOLD AND ALABASTER LAVISHED ON ONE OF EGYPT'S LEAST GLORIOUS KINGS**

Standing within the innermost store chamber or treasure house, surrounded by an amazing collection of funerary paraphernalia, was this magnificently carved and gilded shrine. Four goddesses—Isis, Nephthys, Neith and Selkit—keep watch with protective arms outstretched against its sides ; and above are double tiers of uraei, the serpent emblem of Egyptian divinities and divine kings. On the right is Tutankhamen's "funeral barque" in alabaster—one of the finest examples of ancient Egyptian lapidary work, 27 inches high by 23 inches long. In the prow is the squatting figure of a charming girl, holding a lotus flower to her naked bosom. At the helm, steering the barque, is a Sudanese slave girl, whose short and sturdy form reveals unmistakable traces of dwarfism due to achondroplasia. The boat rests on an island in an ornamental tank, and, it is thought, was designed to serve as the funeral ship for the young Pharaoh's celestial journey ; according to another view, however, as a centrepiece for the royal banqueting table.

44

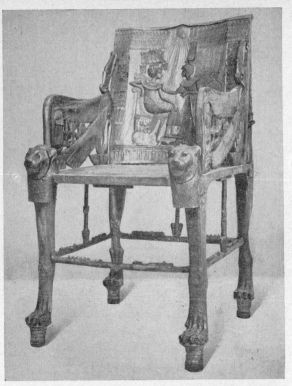

## SUMPTUOUS FURNITURE FROM THE PHARAOH'S COURT

The chambers of Tutankhamen's tomb contained an extraordinarily varied collection of articles, some made specially but most, it is evident, coming from the palace of the boy Pharaoh. Left, an ornate lamp on which is painted the seated figure of the Pharaoh, visible only when a wick floating in oil is lit within the lamp. Next, a white alabaster perfume vase; and right, the royal chair or throne on the back of which Tutankhamen and his queen are depicted in carnelian, red glass, silver, and faience.

Harry Burton, Metropolitan Museum, New York

## THE OUTERMOST OF TUTANKHAMEN'S FOUR GOLDEN SHRINES

When Lord Carnarvon and Dr. Howard Carter pierced the wall that alone stood between them and the sepulchral chamber they saw at last the Pharaoh's actual shrine, gilded from top to bottom with superb and lavish artistry and with sides composed of panels inlaid with blue faience, on which were repeated in long succession the magic symbols deemed potent to protect the royal corpse from the touch of time and sacrilegious men. At the shrine's eastern end are massive folding doors each decorated (as will be seen from our illustration) with a headless yet still guardian demon.

TRIPLE NEST OF GOLDEN CASKETS TO PRESERVE POOR HUMAN CLAY

When the actual sepulchral chamber was opened it was found to be nearly filled by an enormous sarcophagus of yellow quartzite. Within this were three golden coffins fitted closely into one another, each with a sculptured effigy of the king holding the royal emblems, the crook and flail. The innermost coffin of pure gold in which the mummy lay is shown in the accompanying colour plate. Above is the second of the three. This is made of carved wood covered with sheet gold and encrusted with polychrome glass in an intricate design in which the protecting vulture goddess Nekhebet is prominent. The nicety with which the coffins fitted into each other was such that in the process of investigation jacks had to be used to lower the first from the second.

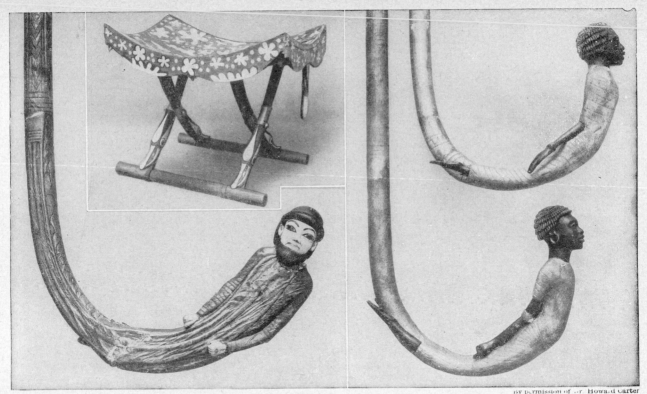

'UNCONSIDERED TRIFLES' OF INESTIMABLE VALUE

In brief compass it is not possible to enumerate the treasures found in Tutankhamen's tomb, since they include every kind of article of furniture and wearing apparel used or usable by the king. The specimens shown here are a gold mounted stool of ebony with legs inlaid with ivory to represent ducks' heads, and several walking-sticks, one (bottom left) a ceremonial stick of gold and ivory with for handle a figure of a turbaned prisoner, whose painted ivory face is of Semitic cast, and two with crook handles representing negroes in ebony and gold.

the finest pieces of decoration, not only in ancient Egypt, but in the world.

From an artistic point of view the most disappointing objects in the tomb are those made of alabaster. The great alabaster vases on stands, with the plants of Upper and Lower Egypt on either side of them, cut in the same material, look unattractive in the photographs, but one hoped that in the originals the beauty of the translucent material would more than make up for clumsy designing. It does not, and these must be reckoned among the few aesthetic failures of the tomb. The same is true of several of the more ambitious objects in this material, though an exception must be made in favour of the four Canopic jars with their delicately cut portrait heads, touched with colour to show the beauty of the stone.

Summing up the impression made by the whole treasure, we may say that the dominant note is one of brightness. The Egyptians were a good-tempered, merry people—' Let us make a happy day ' was one of their favourite maxims—and they loved to be surrounded by beautiful and gaily coloured things in life—and in death.

And the other point which strikes us is its wealth in gold and precious stones—not diamonds, rubies and emeralds, such as modern taste loves, but carnelian, amethyst, turquoise and lapis lazuli, which many of us find even more beautiful. Go

into the jewel room, and look at the inner coffin. It is more than six feet long, it is of solid gold a quarter of an inch thick, and its value in metal alone is said to be about £50,000. You have not in the rest of your life put together seen so much gold as now lies before you. And in what form ? In a coffin meant to remain buried in the valley ' until eternity and everlasting ' as the Egyptians said. What a vivid glimpse it gives us into their astonishing minds! How heavily they must have drawn on the gold mines of Nubia to be able to consign this fabulous amount to the tomb each time a king died ! And what a prestige the old funerary beliefs must have had to countenance this drain on the nation's resources, and for a mere boy who had never led an army !

One last reflection, one that is almost awe-inspiring. Tutankhamen reigned for a few inglorious years at one of the low-water marks of Egyptian history, and was buried in the poorest and smallest of the royal tombs in the valley. Yet his inner coffin was made of solid gold, and his body was covered with jewels whose value in precious metal alone is immense. Suppose that Lord Carnarvon had discovered intact the tomb of Seti I or Rameses the Great, tombs fifty and a hundred times the size of that of Tutankhamen, tombs of kings whose armies struck fear into the Hittites and held the gorgeous East in fee ' ! What would he have found ?

# The Study of the Past. III.

# A Stone-Age "Pompeii" in the Orkneys

## By Lewis Spence, F.R.A.I.

### Author of 'An Introduction to Mythology,' etc.

THAT an entire village of the New Stone Age, complete in every detail, should have been embalmed in the sands of Orkney as Pompeii was in the preserving lava of Vesuvius, seems to savour too much of the miraculous to approach reality. It is, indeed, an archaeologist's dream come true, a thing unique in the history of British prehistoric science, and it is scarcely to be wondered at that nearly 3,000 people visited it during the summer months of 1933, urged by curiosity to see for themselves the manner in which our remote ancestors actually lived and conducted their domestic affairs.

Upon the sandy sheltered Bay of Skail on the western side of the mainland of Orkney, flanked by hills rising to lofty cliffs, stands Skara Brae, the village which has been so strangely preserved like a fly in amber. Hundreds of years ago the terrific gales which rush in from the North Sea smothered it in driving sands, and although its existence has been known of since 1850, it was only in 1927 that serious excavation was undertaken at the site by the Office of Works under the expert guidance of Professor V. Gordon Childe.

At first it had the appearance of a

**STAIRWAY OF AN ORKNEY STRONGHOLD**
Of late years archaeologists have been exploring certain mounds in the Orkneys dating from the New Stone Age. The results of their excavations at Skara Brae are described in this article. Above is the stone stairway leading into the Broch of Aikerness in the parish of Evie, another Orkney prehistoric site which as yet awaits investigation.

grass-grown sand dune showing the protruding ruins of five huts, and surrounded by midden heaps of refuse, but by 1929 eight huts had been cleared. These were entered by narrow doorways leading to a short tunnel through which it was necessary to creep to gain entrance. The walls of the huts were carefully but crudely built of flat slabs laid in horizontal courses without any mortar. The builders had at hand a plentiful supply of material, as the beach is littered with excellent Caithness slabs, ready made, and employed by the folk of Skara, much as a child's box of bricks.

When dug out of their dense covering of sand and midden, the huts were found to be rectangular in design, with rounded corners, the walls averaging from five to eight feet in thickness. Their inmates had evidently housed there during four successive periods ranging over a very considerable time, and a good deal of alteration and remodelling had been effected during consecutive generations. The appearance of the upper part of the walls has led to the surmise that the huts may have been covered by domed roofs, indeed the fact that the jaw bones of a large whale were found lying across the hearth of one of the huts, has led a good authority to believe that the roof was formed of whalebone rafters supporting slates or thatch.

The doorways were secured by slabs of stone, held in place by a bar which fitted into sockets in the wall, and one of these bars has actually been found in place. The furniture of the huts is entirely of stone, and displays extraordinary ingenuity of design. In every house rectangular hearths have been found, in which peat was burned. Stone bed-places, formed by three slabs built out from the wall, were filled with grass or heather, and when they retired to these cubicles for the night, the men of Skara Brae carried their supper with them in the shape of large beef or mutton bones which they gnawed clean before they dropped off to sleep. Some of the bed-places were cluttered with such bones. That they also concealed their personal treasures under their " mattresses " of heather is plain from the beads and paint-pots found in these sleeping enclosures.

The family settle or bench was evidently the

**SMITHY OF A PREHISTORIC CRAFTSMAN**

Opening on to a stone-paved, enclosed space just outside the group of dwellings at Skara Brae is another chamber (seen in this photograph) which, judging from the remains of tools and weapons and pottery fragments that have been recovered from its floor, was the workshop of the communal craftsman—the Stone Age equivalent of the village blacksmith of a later day.

front slab of the bed nearest the hearth, as is evident from the signs of wear in these particular stones, but in some huts between the larger beds and the hearths are tiny sleeping-places which were evidently those of children.

Cupboards for the careful keeping of the family treasures were in places let into the wall above the beds, and dressers made of large flagstones were built against the rear walls of every hut. These usually consist of two shelves, and probably held the domestic utensils. Opening off every hut are small enclosures, let into the thickness of the walls. These are low, oblong chambers, the doors of which were secured by bars, and the presence of drains in some of them suggests that they were used as sanitary conveniences.

The nine huts of which the village was composed were connected with each other and with the outer world by long alleys or passages, flanked on each side by retaining walls, which were either the walls of the huts themselves, or dykes specially constructed for the purpose.

**A ONE-CHAMBER STONE AGE HOME**

Here we see the interior of one of the nine dwellings at Skara Brae—a prehistoric kitchen, parlour and bedroom combined. On the right is the larder or " dresser," in front of which, let into the floor, is a stone tank in which, very probably, limpets were stored in sea-water. The open hearth is in the centre of the chamber, and at the back is a stone box-bed. Above the bed is a cupboard or " safe," where perchance the housewife kept her trinkets.

In every case these walls are backed by the all-pervading substance of the midden refuse, which finally invaded every part of the village excepting the interiors of the dwellings. The passages were roofed over for the greater part of their length by flagstones or slates and the ends of the dim alley-ways were secured by enormous stones.

Dumb witness of the last panic flight of the inhabitants along these passages, when at length the ever-threatening sandstorm compelled them to evacuate their dwellings, was found in a trail of beads discovered in one of them. A terrified woman, in her fear, dashed through a doorway, breaking her necklace against the jamb. The beads continued to fall from her neck as she rushed along the dark alley, and were found just as she had left them, by the excavators.

whale bones and carved stone balls, stone hammers and celts. In the days of its occupation the village had the appearance of a great mound with the roofs of the huts protruding from it, and curling smoke arising from fissures in the soil.

Although the village was hastily abandoned, it was re-occupied on at least three separate occasions, at lengthy intervals. It must, indeed, have taken generations to heap up the 2,400 cubic feet of midden refuse which surrounded and at last covered the site. The habits of the folk, too, changed completely in the course of these long occupations. At first they seem to have been a pastoral people, living exclusively on sheep and cattle, but later deposits reveal that these sources of food disappeared, and that the villagers' diet was reduced to the flesh of the red deer of the hinterland and the limpets found on the shore in large quantities. The village was not originally subterranean and the midden heaps seem to have been allowed to accumulate as an insurance against the ever encroaching sand from the shore. The sand, powerful as the lava of Pompeii and Herculaneum, conquered at last, and transformed a series of free-standing huts into a subterranean labyrinth.

SKARA BRAE'S "HIGH STREET"

The huts at Skara Brae were linked by passage-ways, roofed over with slabs of stone or slate, and so narrow, dark and tortuous as to hinder the approach of any foe who managed to make an entry into the stronghold. This photograph shows what seems to have been the principal "street."

Who were the people of Skara Brae, to what race did they belong? They used no metal, they were not agriculturists or grain-growers. They caught and ate few fish, though dwelling in a maritime region. They employed stone for every industrial purpose. The skull-shapes of these skeletons indicate that they were part of a mixed population very much the same as the present-day inhabitants of Orkney, a mingling of what is known as the Mediterranean race of long-skulled folk with "Alpines" or round-headed people, although then there was no Norse intrusion. That they were not of like culture or race with the later people of the brochs or sea-coast towns of Northern Scotland is clear enough, as the latter were users of iron, and sea-farers. As regards the epoch at which they dwelt at Skara Brae, that must for the present remain uncertain, but the circumstances seem to point to the early Christian centuries—a local stone age still flourishing when the rest of Europe had adopted an iron culture.

Outside one of the large gates stood what has come to be known as "the Market Place." This area was paved and was enclosed by walls pierced by several doorways. It seems to have been the industrial quarter of the village. From the implements found in one of the huts abutting on it, it is plain that it was a communal workshop, scrapers to prepare skins, clay for making pottery, and cores and rejected pieces of broken chert proving that the tanners, potters and flint-knappers of the community laboured therein.

The superincumbent midden which at one period roofed the entire settlement was found to be rich in remains—shells, the bones of sheep and oxen, pottery of crude make but artistic pattern,

## The Royal Palaces. I.

# Marvels of Persepolis and its Palaces

### By Lewis Spence, F.R.A.I.

Author of "Myths of Babylonia and Assyria," etc.

THE plain of Mervdasht, selected by Darius I. of Persia at the beginning of the fifth century B.C. as the site of the great palace-city of Persepolis, is one of the most fertile and pleasantly situated districts in the Persian province of Fars. To-day it is a rural neighbourhood occupied by a cluster of farms and villages, and only the vast level platform on which the King of Kings built his metropolis of pillars remains as a proof of the former existence of one of the most famous cities of antiquity. Not many miles away Lake Miris drains the turgid waters of that almost legendary river the Araxes, a name which appears with such frequency in the pages of classical writers that it seems much more familiar than its modern Arabic title Bend Amir. This green plain is overhung by a dark mountain-chain of fantastic outline which traverses it diagonally from north-west to south-east, and it was on a rocky spur beneath the shadow of those heights that the imperial Darius constructed the great artificial plateau on which some nameless school of visionary architects raised a series of palaces, that for sheer dream-like l o v e l i n e s s must ever seem to the builder of cities as the dome of Kubla Khan to the poet—a glimpse of that ideal paradise which art must ever strive to mirror, but the exquisite reflection of which it eternally fails to capture, save in vague outlines, imperfect and distorted. The few tottering

pillars which men still sadly call Persepolis seem to the traveller to-day like a leafless and lightning-stricken grove on a deserted plateau. Scarcely a vestige remains of the glowing façades of the Hall of a Hundred Columns or the Hypostyle Hall of Xerxes, the restored plans of which show with startling clearness whence the Moorish architects of the Alhambra drew their aesthetic lineage. But if these lofty palaces of the Achaemenian monarchs are now wrecks on the shoal and bank of time, they survive in human imagination as an assembled and dazzling picture, eternal and indestructible. The walls of Carthage may have vanished, but they are as impregnable in human poetry as the glorious ramparts of Verdun. Troy is burnt ! Then Troy is immortal.

Let us then, assisted by the science of the architect and the skill of the archæologist, as well as by any clairvoyance of the imagination we may possess, try to restore in words the shattered glories of the Persepolis of Darius and Xerxes, those magnificent monarchs who took the world for their footstool, and boasted of their conquests in the crooked letters of that strange cuneiform script which Persia borrowed from the Assyrians. The mighty platform which the architect of Darius designed as the foundation of his enchanted city is in itself a work of imperishable marvel. It forms three sides of a parallelogram, the extreme length of which

**THE PROPYLAEA OF XERXES**
These two great piers, standing about 11 yards high and carved in deep relief with two bulls in the Assyrian manner symbolising power, are the principal remains of the monumental entrance built by Xerxes on the Platform of the Palaces at Persepolis.

PERSIAN  KING  AT  THE  "ENTERING  IN  OF  THE  WAY"

On the inner face of this doorway may be seen a Persian monarch seated on his throne, with an
attendant standing behind him ; below there is a procession of his subjects, and above, the
Persian god Auramazda (or Ormuzd) presides over his royal counterpart from within the
conventional winged disk in which he is always portrayed.

inscriptions  vaunt  the glories of Darius.  In one he invokes the great god Auramazda, in another he enumerates  the  many tribes  and  peoples  tributary  to  his  rule.  Two are written in the Persian tongue,  another  is  in Susian, and the last in the abrupt  but  yet  more polished Assyrian.  A road for carts or chariots led from  the  plain  to  the platform,  winding  round its southern face, but the true  and  more  kingly approach  to  the  palace buildings  was  by  the magnificent staircase which still serves as the ascent to this artificial plateau.

This great processional way of the Persian kings consists  of  two  separate flights of steps parallel with  the  wall  of  the platform.  Its first flight was reached by a ramp or gentle slope, admirably adapted to the approach of a large body of people. There are in all a hundred and eleven steps in the staircase, and the gradient is  so  gentle  that  Arab writers assure us a horseman  ascend  and descend it without difficulty.  The  whole  was founded with consummate art on a rocky promontory.

The floor of this platform shows evidence of the former existence of four distinct  planes.  The lowest of these, as regards elevation,  seems  to  have been unbuilt upon.  The second is that which abuts upon the grand staircase, and occupies nearly two-thirds of the whole area.  Here stood the Propylaea and the Hall of a Hundred Columns. Behind this site is the level which supported the Hypostyle Hall of Xerxes, and again to the rear of this is the terrace on which were erected the palaces of Darius and Xerxes, his son.  Here, too,

is 1458 feet, and its greatest breadth 929 feet. The whole was surrounded by a perpendicular wall from 32 to 39 feet in height, according to the state of the ground.  The masonry is solid, but shows signs of repair in places, and is almost destitute of ornament.  The projecting cornice which topped it has almost entirely crumbled away. On  the  southern  face  of  the  platform  four

## PROPYLAEA OF XERXES AT PERSEPOLIS FACING THE GRAND STAIRCASE

There is relatively little of the fanciful in our restorations of Persian buildings, because the rock-cut tombs in the hillside still reproduce in relief the vanished architecture of the plain below. Thus while there is no direct evidence that a frieze of lions in enamelled brick actually ran round the cornice of the Propylaea, we know that it would certainly not be out of place. The lintels, door-posts, and columns were of uncemented stone, the beams of wood, and the remainder of brick.

*After a reconstruction by Ch. Chipiez*

are to be seen the great conduits which supplied the palaces with water drawn from reservoirs on the slopes of the overhanging mountains, and the drains, still covered with a thick layer of mud, designed to carry off the heavy rains which must occasionally have drenched the flat timber roofs of the great buildings and poured off in streams.

Strabo and Diodorus have both given us descriptions of Persepolis, the first a scanty and vague account, the second a more precise picture, but by no means compatible with the archæological evidence. The palace was without fortifications. Its situation alone sufficed for perfect safety—or so it seemed to the sublimely confident Darius who, like all truly great men, was oblivious to the very possibility of failure or defeat.

The Propylaea stood at the head of the grand staircase. Its remains, sentinelled by w i n g e d monsters in the style of Assyrian architecture, are the first to confront the traveller who climbs that gentle gradient. Two vast piers of masonry, 34 feet high and hewn from large blocks of limestone, form a description of passage beyond which rises a pair of slender columns, whose graceful symmetry irresistibly recalls that of the Corinthian model. Beyond these stands another pair of pillars similar in design, and twin gigantic bulls guard the rear entrance. The Propylaea thus composed two great portals or entrances to the platform, a kind of gigantic guard-house or pavilion, massive in front and rear, but graceful at the sides as a Grecian portico. Indeed, it seems clear that the n i m b l e  P e r s i a n  m i n d caught and wedded together the more graceful

Hellenic and the heavier Assyrian architectural styles in this composite structure, which also bears the unmistakable stamp of Egypt—a strange mingling of the three great architectures of the ancient world by the energetic genius of a younger and more eclectic race.

Between this great canopy in stone and the noble Hypostyle Hall, there stretched in the days

IMPOSING RELIC FROM THE HALL OF A HUNDRED COLUMNS

A favourite theme of Persian sculptors was to depict the king, with all the attributes of royal dignity, as though coming out of his palace to meet a procession of his subjects, either loaded with offerings or about to discharge the duties of their office. He is preparing to expose his august head to the light of day so that a fan would be inadequate protection; a second attendant therefore presses forward to cover and shelter him with a large umbrella.

Photo from Sir Percy Sykes' "From Isfahan to Shiraz, 1916"

SOARING PILLARS OF THE HYPOSTYLE HALL OF XERXES, WITH THE PALACE OF DARIUS BEYOND

In the background are the ruins of the dwelling-place or Palace of Darius, seen silhouetted against the sky between the few remaining pillars that once upheld the Hypostyle Hall of Xerxes like a forest of stone. Faintly seen on the supporting platform of the hall are the carvings and reliefs that encrusted it. The "well" on the right is a re-entrant in the main platform containing one of the staircases by which it was negotiated; against the secondary platform of the hall are other staircases. Note the almost Greek proportions of some of the pillars.

Photo from Sir Percy Sykes' "From Istahan to Shiraz, 1916"

of Xerxes a paradise o delightful garden watered from a grea reservoir excavated in th living rock. Here th king had his pleasance i the cool of the evening and from its path which crossed in diamon fashion the radiant par terres, could gaze back ward at a scene no les brilliant, a garden i painted stone, flower beds in living colour the memory of the red greens, and magica yellows of which mus surely have inspired th later story-tellers o Arabia and the Eas with many of their glow ing descriptions of en chanted fairy palaces.

What Persia ha achieved in colour, surel only the Genius of A who records such triump could tell. But whe colour in its most tend and entrancing shades matched with the elf beauty of Oriental desig as in the Hypostyle Ha of Xerxes, we feel th these sagas of the Ea which tell of the creatio of dream-like palaces supernatural beings we in a manner justifie Here stood a marvel stone which the untutor peoples who followed the evacuation of Pers polis could not accou for otherwise than as t work of jinns. From base carven in likeness a processional triump the struggles of lions a the deeds of Auramazd rose a series of rich fluted columns crowned the capitals by doub headed bulls which, Caryatid form, upheld light and wondrous

SKILL OF PERSIAN ARCHITECTS SHOWN IN MAIN PLATFORM-STAIRCASE OF THE HYPOSTYLE HALL

Where buildings are constructed on different terraced levels, and they in turn are built on a platform high above the ground, staircases and approaches are bound to be a problem, and the Persian architects adequately solved it. Here we see the successive ramps of the grand entrance-stairway to the great platform of the Hall of Xerxes whose remaining pillars are shown in the photograph in the opposite page. On the right may be seen the Propylaea of Xerxes

fretted entablature. From between the pillars hung curtains of that embroidery which even to-day demonstrates the peculiar cunning of the Persian hand to capture and make manifest the unearthly hues of dreamland. Behind this rich frontage were gathered group upon group of pillars so magnificently adapted to the general effect that, though the central mass is square, the substructures which surround it at intervals give one the impression of that sublime irregularity seen in a grove of noble trees, that natural harmony which is always so much more enchanting than mere uniformity. This Hypostyle Hall in its heyday was a fairy forest in stone, an architectural Broceliande, labyrinthine, umbrageous, a carven grove painted in the hues of an undying sunset. Ever mighty in art through the centuries, the race who fashioned this marvel of unexampled loveliness conquered and displaced at one essay the squat and plantigrade traditions of Assyrian architecture, and indicated to the future the way to an emancipated beauty in palatial construction.

The Hypostyle Hall was surrounded on three sides by colonnades of pillars, each of which was 65 feet in height. The Arab population of the plain has denuded it almost of its last stone. Only some twelve poor pillars or fragments of pillars remain, the last broken trunks of that amazing forest of masonry. We know it chiefly from the wonderful restoration of Charles Chipiez. That it was by far the most imposing building in Persepolis is witnessed by the wealth of ornament which overlaid the stairs that approached it, by the lofty magnificence of its colonnade, and the extent of the ground it covered. Its purpose was evidently that of a reception hall, and it seems clear that it was divided up into sections to be occupied by the several castes or classes in the court life of Persepolis. There were no enclosures between the central and other colonnades, but a balustrade the height of a man's breast sufficed to keep the less distinguished guests at a proper distance from the throne, but not at such a distance that they were unable to see the monarch, or to obtain a good view of the proceedings.

The gorgeous roof of the Hypostyle Hall merits brief description. It was of cedar with a facing of enamelled brick or faience, bronze, and ivory. The metal plates which capped the ends of the wooden joists protected them from rain and rot, and bronze rosettes set in iron clamps gleamed and glittered among the intervals of the paler ivory and shining

RESTORED HALL OF A HUNDRED COLUMNS AT PERSEPOLIS—

In this imposing structure, sculptor and architect have joined hands in impressing upon the mind an idea of the power and quasi-divine majesty of their lord and master. And whether he was Darius or Xerxes, the proportions and magnificence of the Hall certainly enabled him to show himself to his subjects with a majesty and in a setting befitting a monarch whom so many millions of men obeyed from the banks of the Indus to the borders of the Aegean Sea. In shape the built surface is a parallelogram about

enamel Such wood as was visible was lavishly adorned with paint. The wood-panelled ceiling was arranged in compartments which broke the monotony of the mass and added to the richness of the interior The centre or canopy beneath which the king sat was thickly inlaid with plates of gold and silver When we remember that iron, though well known for weapons and tools, had not as yet been made use of for the purposes of building construction, our wonder at the extraordinary achievements of Persepolis widens into amazement. But as regards site, unity of plan, and variety of detail, the happy contrast of the massive platform and the rich and airy pillars, the rhythm and

mingling of curved and straight lines, and the delicate vigour of the whole conception and creation, the Hypostyle Hall built by King Xerxes must be regarded as the last and crowning triumph of the Age of Bronze.

The Hall of a Hundred Columns occupied the centre of the platform It covered a space of 21,073 square feet, but its plan was more simple than that of the Hypostyle Hall. Only one of all its hundred pillars remains. In shape it was a parallelogram, about 230 feet long from east to west, and 296 feet long from north to south The principal façade abutted on the north side, as is shown by the two great columns flanked by gigantic bulls. Two

56

## —A VISIBLE EXPRESSION OF GRANDEUR, WEALTH AND POWER

77 yards from east to west, and about 99 yards from north to south.    Excepting Karnak in Egypt, it is said that there was no building in the ancient world which enclosed so vast an area as this ; whose roof was upheld by so many pillars ; or the splendour of whose decoration was in better correspondence with the enormous dimensions.    There are evident traces that the royal house which Alexander burnt down at Persepolis, urged thereto by the courtesan Thais, must have been the Hall of a Hundred Columns.

After a reconstruction by Ch. Chipiez

immense portals opened upon the pronaos, which was decorated with paintings of mythological figures.

Within, the floor shows the traces where stood the hundred pillars from which the hall has taken its name. These shafts were distributed in rows of ten. The entrances were without doors, veils or curtains taking the place of these. The space within was so thronged with pillars that they must have seriously interfered with any spectacle or court function held therein. From about the middle of the wall, a panelling of cedar, walnut or cypress was carried up to the architrave. The lower portion was hung with tapestry. With the exception of the great temple at Karnak in Egypt, there is no building of the ancient world so large in area as this, or with so magnificent an interior.

This hall, like the Hypostyle Hall, was also an audience-chamber, a species of throne-room. Indeed, the two bear remarkable resemblances although differences existed. The Hypostyle Hall rested on a platform, whereas the Hall of a Hundred Columns is on the flat, and carven ornaments cover its walls, whereas the ornamentation of the Hypostyle Hall is confined to the basement. The one is an open pavilion, the other a walled edifice. The Hall of a Hundred Columns was probably the older, the less complex, and its pillars are not so lofty—a sign of greater

57

**ASSYRIAN BULLS AS ADOPTED IN PERSIAN ARCHITECTURE**

This illustration shows the opposite (or inner) façade of the Propylaea of Xerxes to that in page 51. The great winged, human-headed bulls were a legacy to Persia from Assyrian art, and as at Nineveh were disposed at the doorways of palaces; note, however, that the "extra leg" (see the chapter on Nineveh) has been discarded. Xerxes I., who built the Propylaea, was the son of Darius I., original founder of the Persepolitan palaces and first of the Achaemenid kings. He continued his father's work on even more ambitious lines

greatest glory. Darius, son of Hystaspes, firmly established himself on the throne on the death of Cambyses, and, acting with extraordinary energy, succeeded in quelling rebellions in Babylon and other tributary states. On the rock-face of Behistun, in Kermanshah, on the road from Babylon to Ecbatana, he has left us sculptural portraits of himself and the rebel leaders he subdued ; these are illustrated in later pages. He caused Greece and Egypt to tremble, but still in his brief leisure contrived to raise his capital of Persepolis to heights of magnificence until then unsurpassed. His son Xerxes, during his short reign, was no less active in the work of embellishment. The dwellings in which these great kings passed that part of their lives which was not occupied with war or conquest stood on the southern side of the platform. They were four or five in number, and differed slightly in dimensions and arrangements. The Palace of Darius is situated on a platform some seven feet higher than the level on which Xerxes later erected his great hall. Approach was gained to it by four ramps or inclines held by retaining walls richly sculptured. A portico supported by eight pillars arranged in two rows led to a hypostyle hall of sixteen columns, and its remains present a very fair idea of what the building was like in the days of the great kings. It would at first sight seem to be a reduced copy of the Hall of a Hundred Columns. But a number of rectangular chambers help to fill its space —guard-rooms, living-rooms, sleeping-chambers, doubtless. All of these face the central hall, so that the heat and

antiquity. Nor were its sculptures so fine as those of the Hypostyle Hall, which was probably used as a summer reception pavilion, while the sheltered aisles of the other seem to have been more suited to levées during the rainy season.

To Darius I. (522-486 B.C.) and his son Xerxes I. (486-465 B.C.) are due, if not the foundation of Persepolis, at least the consummation of its

**LOFTY SHAFTS AND SHADY COLONNADES OF THE HYPOSTYLE HALL OF XERXES**

The Hypostyle Hall of Xerxes, of which this is a reconstruction, served as a throne-room or hall of audience; it was open to the air all the way round, but the spaces between the columns could no doubt be closed with gorgeous hangings on the sunny side. Detached colonnades surrounded it on three sides, the style of the pillars being slightly different from that in the body of the hall; they were all, however, crowned with the double bulls' head capital, and their height was 65 feet.

After a reconstruction by Ch. Chipiez

dust of the plain might not trouble the royal occupants. The entrances to the greater rooms looked down the spaces between the columns, and did not face them, as did the minor apartments. The central hall had few pretensions to magnificence, but made up for the lack of this in elegance and beauty of design. Precious metals, rare woods, ivory and faience, and the wonderful weaves from the Persian looms harmonized to form no unworthy background to a royal existence.

After the two great throne-rooms or pavilions, the Hypostyle Hall and the Hall of a Hundred Columns, the Palace of Xerxes was the largest building on the esplanade, with a ground surface of about 6,900 square feet. It bore a close resemblance to the Palace of Darius, but was on a larger

**ROYAL POMP AS MURAL DECORATION AT PERSEPOLIS**
A relief on a solitary pier of masonry rising from the great platform at Persepolis shows an Achaemenid monarch emerging from the doorway of his palace followed by two attendants, one of whom bears a fly-whisk and the other the state umbrella. It will be noticed how much freer from inscription are the Persian sculptures than those in Assyria, where the bands of hieroglyphic lettering often ran across figures and background alike.

depicted, carrying ewers, napkins, and perfumes, a striking commentary upon the growth of luxury in the reign of Darius. This palace is the only one which faces north, probably because Xerxes had grown dissatisfied with his father's house, which was extremely exposed to the merciless sunshine of Fars. But few of these buildings are in so utterly ruinous a condition as the Palace of Xerxes. The modern restorations of it show its interior as a pillared hall having extensive living-rooms on either side, saloons, sleeping-cubicles, and guard-rooms for the various officers of the army stationed at Persepolis.

At last Persepolis fell —Macedonian, Seleucid, Parthian, and Sassanid swept over it in succession, not well knowing the wealth and wonder of that which they destroyed. The halls burnt at the whim of Thais, the light o' love of Alexander the Great, fell into blackened ruin. Those that she spared, shaken and neglected, soon perished through the falling in of their heavily timbered and over-ornamented roofs; the runlets from the hills gnawed mercilessly at the wooden architraves and slowly crumbled the clay which covered them. In the course of half a century or so from the period in which they had been last inhabited, they had sunk into almost the same degree of ruin in which we now behold them. Then came the Arab, who quarried among their pillars for the building materials out of which his farm or homestead was to be constructed. And lastly fell utter desolation— noiseless, silent, sun-drenched ruin, where once stood on their platform the snow-white colonnades of the throne-rooms of the great kings.

scale; its chambers were more spacious, and in some cases their roofs were supported by pillars. So that there might be space for a broad terrace in front, the building was set back as far as possible, till its central hall hung over the very edge of the southern terrace. It was approached in front by several flights of steps, and its façade, instead of being carven with the usual mythological figures and legendary motifs, displays a more "modern" tendency by the substitution for these outworn themes of scenes from the life of the palaces. Trains of attendants and eunuchs are

# Timgad: Grandest Ruin of Colonial Rome

## By the Editor

### With illustrations from photographs by Crété, Paris

IN all that vast area of the earth which knew the rule of Rome, there exists to-day no memorial of her imperial splendour that surpasses, and few that equal in interest and fascination, the ruins of Timgad. Anciently Thamugadi, this wonder city of the North African highlands cut so small a figure in the history of Rome that contemporary references to its name could be counted on the fingers of one hand. Unlike Palmyra, it had no Zenobia, no Longinus to immortalise it; there was not even a Juba II. to cast a romantic glamour over its broken stones as with the sparse fragments of Cherchel; the name of no great Roman sheds radiance on Timgad. And, withal, Timgad, by some sarcasm of Fate, stands foremost to-day amid all the litter of a vanished empire as the most tangible evidence of its civic grandeur.

Little has been written in English concerning "The African Pompeii," as the French are fond of calling Timgad, but photographs of its multitudinous pillars have often enough been seen in descriptions of North Africa, and, so far as the present writer is concerned, these photographs, more eloquent than any description, awakened in him a full score years ago the desire to tread the ancient pavements of the town and to see its wonders for himself. Not until the closing days of 1922 did the opportunity arrive, when he was able to add another to his list of famous places that have not fallen short of long-sustained expectation.

The first impression, when one approaches it on a winter forenoon along the open road, through the bleak and windy uplands of the Aurés, is the strangeness of its site. It is difficult to suppose that the neighbourhood could have been so barren of trees when the city was built, and there is reason for believing that the surrounding hills were then well timbered. The heights around are not picturesque and individual; there is merely a sense of travelling over rising ground and in a mighty saucer-like region, where natural vegetation is sparse, and the gracious touch of the woodlands is unknown. Suddenly, far eastward, under the remote lip of the saucer, your guide points to a grey patch on the grey-green hillside, and says: "Timgad!"

In all the landscape there are not more than a handful of human habitations in view, and the whiteness of the walls of the little hotel that stands close to the entrance gate of our wonder city draws the eye away from the myriad grey columns which at a distance, would scarce be discerned save for the shadows they cast in the morning sunshine. But how the imagination thrills as one passes the site of the northern gate and treads the broad paving-stones of the Cardo, the main street of the northern part of the ancient city! The distant greyness is now resolved into a most astonishing collection of majestic columns and hewn stones, all so clearly indicating their original uses that scarcely any effort of the imagination is needed to rebuild the

**WHERE ONCE A LITTLE GARDEN BLOOMED**
This striking scene in Timgad's ruins is taken from the house of the flower-boxes, where plants were grown in stone boxes.

missing parts, and to repeople the stately halls and porticoes with the retired military officers and legionaries who formed the chief element of its population some eighteen hundred years ago.

It is a grey ghost of a city, but a ghost that speaks of glorious days and days of terror to all who know anything of Rome's enthralling story.

Photo, Crété

TRAJAN'S ARCH DOMINATES THE RUINS OF TIMGAD

Popularly known as Trajan's Arch, this splendid piece of Roman architecture served as the western gateway to the city, and an inscription at its base reads : " The Emperor Trajan Augustus, the Germanic, son of the divine Nerva, High Pontiff, Consul for the third time, and for the fourth time invested with tribunal power, father of the country, founded the colony of Timgad by the Third Augustan Legion, Lucius Munatius Gallus being legate propraetor."

Timgad came into existence at the behest of the Emperor Trajan, as a colony where time-expired veterans from Lambessa, the great city-camp of the Third Augustan Legion sixteen miles to the south-west, might settle down with their families to an easeful life. And it was the soldiers of Lambessa who built it while they were still carrying on frontier warfare with the Berbers, whose descendants were one day to destroy the city after four centuries of splendid prosperity.

On its sloping hillside, ideal for drainage purposes, Lucius Munatius Gallus, the commander of the Third Legion, a man of great culture and admirable taste, saw to the building of the city in the most regular plan, the original ramparts enclosing a space of 387 yards by 351, the area within being equally divided into blocks by eleven streets that ran east and west, and eleven from north to south. A noble paved road, the Decumanus Maximus, stretching from east to west, bisected the city north and south into two equal parts, the northern part having the equally imposing highway, the Cardo, which at the exact centre of the town led to the splendid colonnaded square of the Forum.

Here was the great basilica in which justice was administered, and here was the Curia or municipal building where the city fathers provided a miniature edition of the pomp and circumstance of the imperial city by the Tiber. Massive and elegant buildings these must have been, to judge from their remains to-day, but a great door in one of them gave trouble to the custodian for years, as we can plainly see the curved rut it scraped in the stone flags of the hall until it was repaired or re-hung !

Immediately south of the Forum was the site chosen for the splendid theatre, which must have been a glory of marble and porphyry, and even in its direst ruin to-day offers features of dignity and impressiveness. The majestic Capitol, modelled upon that of Rome, was built outside the original wall in a rising position at the south-west angle, probably at a later date, when the ramparts had been razed to the ground as the city had grown in population and the conquest of the native tribes seemed complete.

Generally speaking, there was nothing novel in all this work of town building. Small provincial centres and a network of cemented paved roads marked the victorious track of thirty Roman legions. But the Third Legion, formed of men from all parts of the conquered world, possessed admirable artists. With all the renowned, costly Numidian marbles at hand, and artist sappers eager to display their talents after years of rough fortification, Gallus had made Timgad a jewel of architecture. No doubt, in a grand proconsular manner he had carved out a great domain of fine corn land for himself in the newly-conquered territory, and he saw to it that the new town should be a remarkable memorial of his connoisseurship in art. Fine artistic activity was then the best way of winning imperial favour. Nowhere else in the country were precious marbles used with such profusion and variety, while the work of the army sculptors had the restrained classic beauty of good Greek work, instead of the over-ornamentation of Asiatic and later Roman styles.

## THE MAIN ARTERY OF TIMGAD'S LIFE IN THE SECOND CENTURY OF OUR ERA

The above photograph has been taken near the point where the Cardo, the chief street of the north, joins the city highway from east to west, known as Decumanus Maximus. In the days of its prosperity this would be the very centre of the thronging city life, and, as at Pompeii, one can clearly see in the great stone blocks with which the road was paved the ruts worn by the wheels of the chariots. A few feet below the street levels lie the drains of the city, still wonderfully preserved.

## THE ELABORATE UNDERWORLD OF A GREAT ROMAN BATH CLUB

Fifteen public bath establishments have been excavated at Timgad. These magnificent buildings were not merely devoted to bathing, like the so-called Turkish baths of modern times, which are really their lineal descendants. They were centres of social life, more resembling the modern club. Here is seen the ruin of the great northern baths. Numerous stone supports carried the gorgeous mosaic floors of the hot rooms. The blackened traces of the smoke, and the very ashes burnt in the ancient furnaces 1,500 years ago, can still be seen.

**TIMGAD, THE WONDER CITY OF ROME'S NORTH AFRICAN EMPIRE**

In its entirety Timgad, in the modern department of Constantine, Algeria, is the finest relic of the Roman Empire in the world. The twin columns in the distance to the right mark where the stately Capitol once stood ; in the foreground are the remains of the market Sertius ; and on the left, best preserved of all, an Arch of Trajan that formed the western gateway of the city.

Thus the fine shell of the town had been completed. It filled with life immediately. Its situation was doubly attractive. Soldiers who were finishing their years of service and retiring with their wives and children from camp usually had sufficient money to buy or build a house. As their sons were sure to follow a military career, they were the salt of the empire, and likely to be favoured by their old leader in the matter of a land grant. There were also thousands of traders in the wake of the Legion, who saw that Timgad would draw, through the El Kantara gap in the Atlas mountains, the export trade of the best and unexploited part of the southern Atlas and the Sahara, and tap caravan commerce from the far south. Timgad therefore flourished amazingly, and the prospering town-folk soon began to continue the work of the soldier builders. Officer settlers were particularly keen on further beautifying the work of their men, and saved hard to afford the cost of fine statues by army

sculptors who had also retired, and charged about £40 for their best works in fine marble.

Marcus Plotius Faustus, called Sertius, was a Timgad-bred boy, who entered the army and rose to the command of cohorts and wings of the auxiliary forces of the Legion, won a Roman wife and a Roman knighthood, and at the end of his career returned to his native city and accepted the position of a priest. Out of the fortune he had won by fighting he built a beautiful basilica, set in a fountain court and surrounded with porticoes, and dedicated it as a market place. There were refreshment rooms and drinking bars for the retailers and shoppers, who bargained in the shade of the arcades, while the wholesale merchants and brokers conducted their large operations within the walls of the basilica. It was not often, however, that army officers spent their money in favour of the merchants. Their hobby was to put up statues to the gods and the imperial family, as

CORNER OF THE MYRIAD-PILLARED EXPANSE ON THE UPLANDS OF THE AURES

agad, though a stricken shell, is still a wonder city. One may pace its two great avenues, the Cardo and Decumanus, tread the great anse of marble, quarried by slave labour, with which the forum is paved, linger over the richness of the mosaics, and see the niches in the great triumphal arch where the statues of the Caesars stood.

became pious, loyal, hard-working frontier fighters, proud of the strength of the empire and uncorrupted by the loose life of Rome.

Great villas rose beyond the suburbs, and these manor-like villages, with their pleasure pavilions, increased the pomp of festivities in Timgad and enlarged the market for the work of the craftsmen artists. The mosaic workers, who had given Timgad's many public baths remarkable decorative pavements, developed a fine pictorial style, as the splendid collection of mosaics in the Timgad museum bears witness, and the sculptors were not behind them in talent and invention. At the end of the first generation of town-folk the frontier city was a lovely frame for a most picturesque medley of civilization and barbarism. The shy Berbers came down from the mountains and in from the desert to taste the strangeness of city life. There was no mixture of Arab or negro blood then in them, and the tall, grey-eyed northern

Vandals had not yet come to inter-marry with them. For the most part they were small, thick-set men, with fair or red hair and blue eyes or brown; roughly dressed in a belted tunic, but proudly careful of their waved and curly beards and hair.

Above the shores of the Mediterranean were the settled farming tribes, who were fairly peaceful, but on the Atlas heights and round the desert oases were wandering shepherds riding bareback on fine, hardy horses, men who made the best cavalry in the world, that had often shattered the armies of Rome in the days of Hannibal and had lately assisted Trajan to victories. Neither under Hadrian nor any later emperor could Rome conquer them, though the best legions from Europe and Asia were added to the famous Third Augustan Legion in repeated compaigns, each of which was intended to be conclusive. Yet, though the wild Berber could not be won by arms, he could be wooed, and Timgad, rising in majestic beauty within hail of

65

the Sahara, lured him into peaceful civilization. The brave, sun-dried savages, coming in with their caravans to trade, wandered in amazement in the statue-crowded Forum, and found a foretaste of paradise in some of the fourteen great baths, where they could be steamed out of their fatigue, cooled, massaged with oil and scented.

But what pleased them most was the superb open-air theatre.   Timgad was remarkable for its passion for literary drama at the time when the mob of Rome had lost all fineness of mind and delighted only in racing, indecent pantomimes, and gladiator shows.  In this remote African town the gentry of retired army men were sick of human bloodshed, and fond either of literature or hunting. They set the taste for good drama.   The settled

names and Roman ways of life.  Timgad was far from pleased when Rome lost her power and the Greeks of Constantinople acquired it.  After considerable trouble the city and surrounding country accepted the Christian faith, but the folk displayed their unexhausted energy of mind in the invention of strange heresies.  It was partly because of their passionate revolt against the persecuting Christians of the orthodox faith that they welcomed the Vandals from Spain.   At Timgad a Vandal-Berber army was at last, in A.D. 535, broken by the Byzantine general Solomon, the remains of whose great fortress now stand by the ruined city.  The city, however, was an absolute ruin before the Byzantine forces arrived, and their fortress was built out of the wreckage of the lovely work of the old

GENERAL VIEW OF THE MARKET OF SERTIUS, LOOKING TOWARDS TRAJAN'S ARCH
This photograph has been taken from a point of view behind the semi-circular part of the market, and shows, beyond, some of the remaining pillars of the large square basilica within which the merchants conducted their bargaining, much on the same lines as in many a corn or wool exchange in modern countries.

natives, in search of a Roman education, also supported the theatre ; while the wild Berbers, without troubling to learn the language of Greek tragedy and Roman comedy, enjoyed the scenes somewhat in the manner of modern kinema plays.

Likewise the market prices tempted them into Timgad.  One third of the wheat required to feed Rome came from Africa, and light rains often made a general shortage, when prices went desperately high.  The Berbers therefore began to leave their mountain nests and settle round the well-watered city.   Their sons entered the army, and by inherited skill often rose to high position and returned in glory, having almost forgotten in their new Roman culture their native speech.

But the Berber remained a Berber, even in the days of his conversion, when he came to be the main working force of the Third Legion, as well as of the Mauritanian army, and had as officers mostly men of his own stock, disguised under Roman

Third Legion, most of the glorious bits of marble sculpture having been ground into powder for the mortar.  For before the decisive battle the mountaineers resolved that Timgad should not be a prize of victory and house a large hostile garrison that might subdue the mountains and countryside.  So they completely destroyed the town.  They fired the Capitol and the other great buildings, and made so hasty a retreat to the hills that, not many years ago, when the Market of Sertius was dug out of the sand, with which tempests had covered it, there were found in the wineshop bottles of desiccated drinks which the fugitives had not stopped to consume !

The marks bitten by the flames of fourteen hundred years ago can still be seen upon some of Timgad's stones.  During the course of the generations that followed there were people who came and rebuilt some of the fine old Roman houses, and lived amid the wilderness of ruin, but only another Augustan Legion could have restored the splendid life of Timgad  This was quenched for ever that day of A.D 535

France, who has attempted to re-establish in our own day a new Roman Empire in North Africa—and seems in a fair way to success—has dealt most reverently and most ingeniously with these stones of Timgad  Her archæologists have unearthed most of the city that had disappeared beneath the sand and dust of ages, have set up again many of the fallen columns, have even searched among the remains of the fortress, which Solomon, the Byzantine general, built from the debris of the city, for such items as theatre seats, and restored them to their places, so that in the weird ghost of a town we may walk again the very pavements once thronged with joyous life and muse, amid the roofless columns of its once elegant and spacious public library, on that great enigma of life—the meaning of progress

It is difficult to believe that in any of the real essentials of a full and reasonable life we are to-day one step advanced upon the Timgad of seventeen centuries ago  The public buildings of the city were all vastly finer than any existing in any town of like dimension or importance in the world to-day. The public baths, immense as cathedrals some of them, were great centres of social enjoyment, where lectures were given, entertainments held, and the pleasures of friendship and cultivated human intercourse experienced to the full

The public markets were as practical as, and incomparably more artistic than, any in modern Europe or America ; the public lavatories were astoundingly like those of the greatest hotels of New York or London and probably more beautiful in their marble decoration, while the sanitation was far ahead of anything that even cultured France could boast a generation or two back  The houses of the people, too, as we can trace them in the distinct outline of their enduring foundations, were commodious and attractive, and free from the horrid ugliness of undue ostentation

And all this splendid life, so seemingly wisely directed, was suffered to perish and to leave a husk of carven stone behind—perhaps as a warning to all of us who dwell in great stone-built cities that, often when a civilization seems to be attaining to its highest, it may, imperceptibly, but none the less surely, be nearing its extinction

RUINS OF TIMGAD'S TEMPLE TO THE PROTECTING SPIRIT OF THE TOWN

Throughout the whole Roman world the worship of the genius of place was observed, in the humblest provincial city as in the capital of the empire itself.  The inhabitants of Timgad set up a very beautiful votive temple to the protecting genius of their town, and even the remains of it, as will be seen from this photograph, are not without a certain impressive dignity. The custom has its equivalent in modern times in the patron saints of cities.

THE FAMOUS COLOSSI OF "MEMNON": SURVIVALS OF 3,000 YEARS

Erected at Thebes to represent Amenhotep III. and his consort, these colossal figures are about 65 feet in height. That on the right was known to Greeks and Romans as the statue of the mythical god Memnon. To it pilgrims once flocked from far distances to listen to the musical sound it is said to have emitted at sunrise.

## The Great Monuments. II.

# The Colossi of "Memnon"

### By W. Francis Aitken

TOWERING giants of the plain and the most prominent landmarks on the west bank of the Nile at Thebes, the so-called Colossi of "Memnon" stand facing the east, midway between Medinet Habu and the Ramesseum. With the waters of the Nile bathing their feet when the life-giving river is at flood, at other times with a carpet of vivid green, the green of growing crops, spread around them, they are best observed from a distance. Then one can more easily reconstruct what time and earthquake and man's hands have destroyed, especially if the hour chosen is at sunrise, or when the solar disk is sinking in the west ; or, again, in the silence of the night, when moon and stars alone are visible in the firmament. Then, as one thinks of the vast storehouse of history in the temple ruins around and in the silent rock-tombs in the valleys of the distant hills, the Colossi appear sentient, individual, as if gazing across the Nile valley for some new divine manifestation to add to their already age-long experiences.

They were fashioned some three thousand years ago, under the direction of the chief architect and namesake of the Pharaoh Amenhotep III., to stand in front of the pylon of a temple. Carved from a conglomerate quarried in the red mountain, Gebel el-Ahmar, or in the sandstone hills of Edfu, and brought along the Nile in eight specially constructed ships, they mark the introduction of the huge statue in place of the obelisk in monumental and symbolical building. The record of their arrival at Thebes glows with contemporary enthusiasm. "They were wonderful for size and height, and they will last as long as heaven," says Amenhotep the architect.

When the Greeks and Romans came, the wonderful architecture around, including the Colossi, was attributed to the mythical Memnon, son of Eos or Aurora, who fell at Troy. One of the Colossi was a portrait statue of Amenhotep III., the other represented his Libyan consort Tiyi. The northern figure, that on the right of the photographs, was broken in two during the earthquake of about A.D. 27, referred to in the "Thebaid" of Statius (A.D. 61-96). Thereafter this statue is said to have achieved its name of "the vocal Memnon" by emitting at sunrise a musical strain, which fancy likened to a lament. Witness is borne to the world-interest aroused by this sound phenomenon—which modern science attributes to the action of the sun's heat on cold stone—by numerous Greek and Latin inscriptions on the statue. The earliest of these belongs to A.D. 65 ; many were inscribed in the time of Hadrian, who visited the spot in A.D. 130 with his wife Sabina ; some date from the days of Septimius Severus and Caracalla. Hadrian's visit is celebrated in verse, of which two lines run (as translated) :

"Sea-born Thetis, learn that Memnon never suffered pangs of dying.
Still, where Libyan mountains rise, sounds the voice of his loud crying——"

The first author to refer to the "vocal Memnon" is Strabo, who came here with the governor Aelius Gallus, and was sceptical ; but the legend was accepted by Pausanias and Juvenal. Septimius Severus (A.D. 193-211) repaired the statue with large blocks of sandstone placed horizontally in five layers to form body, head, and upper part of the arms. The work was done somewhat crudely, but so effectually that the plaint has never been heard since.

Originally, when each statue was adorned with the tiara of united Egypt, the Colossi stood nearly 70 feet high. Their present dimensions are as follows : Height of figure, 52 feet ; pedestal, 13 feet ; legs from sole to knee, 19½ feet ; each foot, 10½ feet ; shoulder breadth, 20 feet ; arm from elbow to finger-tip, 15½ feet ; middle finger, 4½ feet. The Nile, which has swallowed up so much of that it once created, has deposited over 6 feet of soil around the base of the figures. The ornamentation includes representations of the Nile-god holding papyrus and lily, and figures of the mother and wife of Amenhotep III., whose name is given in hieroglyphs.

The beautiful temple they were made to adorn has gone; so has the shrine that Merenptah built for himself with the white stone he took from the work of his great predecessor. But the Colossi, corollaries of the Sphinx, remain dominant, if scarred beyond recognition, among the wonders of Egypt's inscrutable past.

## Records of the Tombs. II.

# Weird Horse Sacrifices of Ancient Siberia

## By E. Royston Pike

Author of " Slayers of Superstition," " Story of the Crusades," etc.

*AMONG the many forms of burial-sacrifice practised in the ancient world one of the most widely spread was that of sending a man's horses to accompany him to the next world. Firmly adopted by the Scythian nomads of the Black Sea region over 2,600 years ago, it has persisted among the modern nomads of the Altai, even under the Soviet régime, as an aspect of Shamanism. In this same Mongol-Siberian region Bronze Age tombs have recently been excavated which, as here described, present elaborate forms of horse sacrifice. The photographs illustrating the article are given by courtesy of the Pennsylvania University Museum and its Director, Mr Horace H. F. Jayne.*—EDITOR.

OF late years the attention of archaeologists has been directed towards the numerous mounds, resembling the barrows that are so prominent a feature of our downland landscape, that are to be found here and there, singly but more often in groups, on the eastern Siberian plain and its extension into Europe towards the Danube. In the Black Sea area and in the Kuban, north of the Caucasus, they are known as kurgans, and have been identified as the last resting-places of the chieftains of a nomadic people, given greatly to war and only in slight measure agriculturists, who came from central Asia and probably constituted the first Aryan wave

In 1929 the field of investigation was extended to the eastern Altai mountains in what may have been these people's homeland, where the burial mounds are concentrated into cemetery-like areas ; and in one of the barrows, in what has become known as the " Pazirik burial," M P Griaznov, of the Russian State Museum, came upon a rich find—not of buried men, but of the horses which were the staple of the ancient Siberians' economy. Beneath a mound and several layers of logs two burial chambers were unearthed, constructed of logs and thick planks, and adjoining the chambers to the north was an area containing the remains of ten horses The tomb of the chief had been rifled, though his sarcophagus was discovered intact; his mounts, however, were still practically as they had been left by the savage sacrificers, for, thanks to the unending frost of more than two thousand years, the processes of decay had been arrested, with the result that we can see today in an extraordinary state of preservation the yellow mares that carried a Siberian chieftain over the steppe during the Bronze Age, before the commencement of our era, or Rome had become an empire, while Britain was still barbaric.

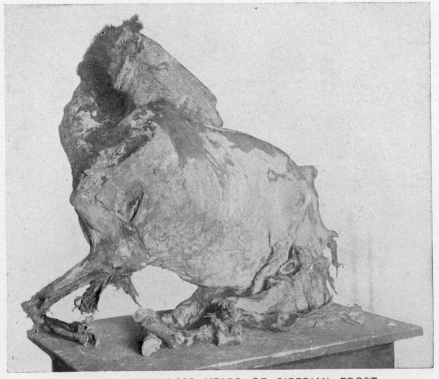

**" MUMMIFIED " BY 2,000 YEARS OF SIBERIAN FROST**

Some time before the commencement of our era a chieftain of the Altai died and was buried ; and after the fashion of his people, his favourite steeds, ten in number, were slaughtered and laid beside him beneath the same funeral mound. In 1929 the mound was opened, and though no human remains were found, the ten horses were there very much as they had been on their day of sacrifice ; the continuous frost of 2,000 years had acted as a mummifier and had successfully arrested the processes of decay. One of the horses—a yellow mare—is shown above.

BARBARIC TRAPPINGS OF A BRONZE AGE WAR-HORSE

Some idea of the horse-furniture found with the buried mares may be gained from this reconstruction drawing showing a set of the harness as it would have appeared in position. Saddle, bridle, saddle-trappings and horse-cover are all richly ornamented.

bloodthirsty as their worshippers, gods who delighted in holocausts of cattle and of horses.

In the light of the Pazirik discovery, however, what is of still greater interest is Herodotus' account of the funerary procedure adopted on the occasion of a great chieftain's demise. Placing the corpse in the grave on a bed of leaves, he says, they fixed spears upright beside it, and then over all laid pieces of wood covered with mats. " In the remaining space of the grave," he continues, " they bury one of the king's concubines, having strangled her, and his cup-bearer, a cook, a groom, a page, a courier, and horses, and firstlings of everything else, and golden goblets.

The harness, too, is in an excellent state of preservation, and from it we may gather some conception of the culture of its fashioners—a culture which obviously had much in common with that of the ancient Scythians. The saddles were richly ornamented and embroidered ; carved wood pendants, gilded or silvered, hung from bridles and saddle trappings ; the saddle covers were embroidered with figures of birds or with animal designs—one shows a beast of prey attacking a reindeer, and in another a carrion bird flutters its wings in triumph above a stricken deer ; and in two cases the horses were provided with masks, the one representing a reindeer and the other a griffin at grips with a bear. Shields of stick and leather, digging tools, sacks of fur, and the remains of a chariot, were among the other " finds " in this one burial.

The Pazirik discovery is intensely interesting and important in itself, but it derives an added interest from the light it throws on the Scythians, that unprepossessing folk who appear so often in Herodotus' lively pages. Those who are well-read in the " Father of History " will remember his vivid and detailed descriptions of the nomads who wandered from place to place with their horses, cattle, and sheep in the eternal search for water and fresh grass. They will recall how relentless they were in their private quarrels, ferocious in the extreme against a foe not of their tribe or race—how their goblets were the skulls of their slaughtered enemies, and how their cloaks and shields were made of human skins, flayed from the corpses of the fallen. Then their gods—how fearsome they were, fearsome and

REINDEER MASK FOR A SIBERIAN MARE

Among the material recovered from the Pazirik kurgan were two horse-masks, of which one—devised evidently to make its wearer look like a reindeer—is illustrated here in reconstruction. The mask is made of felt, leather, fur, and gold leaf ; the horns are life-size.

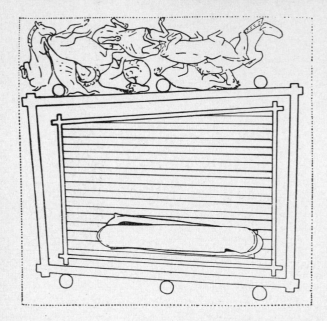

ANIMAL MOTIFS OF SIBERIAN CARVERS

The craftsmen who fashioned the harness found at Pazirik employed in almost every instance animal designs. Here we see one of the bridle ornaments of gilded wood, representing a reindeer in vigorous movement. Similar use of the "animal style" of decoration was made by the Scythians of the 6th century B.C.

the great plains of the nomads' heaven. Very much as Herodotus described the Scythian interments, then, so the archaeologists of today have found matters in the sites they have explored.

Here we are not concerned, however, with Herodotus' reputation, but with horse sacrifice as an institution among the Siberian folk, not only of the long past yesterdays, but of today. Yes, of today, for some trace of the idea that inspired the hecatomb still lingers among the peoples of the steppes.

Among the Altai nomads it is the custom to hold tribal festivals at which in addition to displays of horsemanship, wrestling and the like, horses are sacrificed and their skulls and hides hung on birch trees above a bower, or "yurta" of leafy branches. At least, it was so until recently; but the anti-religious propaganda of the Soviets has probably won yet another victory, and the sacrifice that came down from the Bronze Age is banished from the steppe that now is shaken by the march of locomotives and motor-driven ploughs.

Having done this, they all heap up a large mound, striving and vieing with each other to make it as large as possible." Then, after the lapse of a year fifty male servants and fifty horses were slain, mounted on half-wheels, and set up round the mound as ghastly sentinels So detailed is the old writer's description, that he tells us that the young men were fixed in position on their steeds by long straight pieces of wood passed down their body from the neck into the frame of the horse.

Elsewhere in Siberia and the steppe land other mounds have been opened, and some of these have been proved to contain bones of men surrounded by the skeletons of obviously sacrificed horses, slain to accompany their masters through the gates of death into

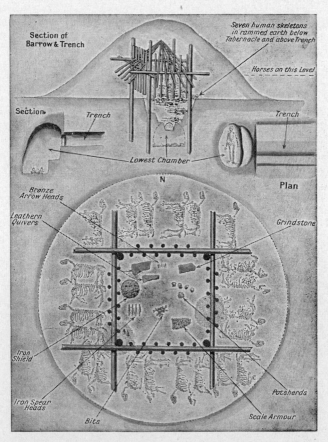

SCENES OF SLAUGHTER ROUND NOMADIC TOMBS

Below, plan of a Scythian burial in the Black Sea Region. Over the chamber containing the dead chief were laid his wives and leading members of his household, and then the whole tomb was ringed with sacrificed horses and covered with a tumulus. Above, is a ground plan of the Pazirik kurgan for comparison. The sarcophagus contained originally the body of the Siberian chieftain, placed within the sepulchral pit and covered over with logs. Closely adjoining, to the north, were packed ten horses.

Lower illustration, after E. H. Minns' "Scythians and Greeks"

# Temples of the Gods. III.

# Angkor: A Marvel Hidden in the Jungle

## By Edmund Candler

Traveller and Descriptive Writer ; author of " The Unveiling of Lhasa," etc.

UNTIL quite recently Angkor was little known to Western travellers. The temple lies, buried away in the jungle, to the north of Cambodia in the Mekong basin, not a day's journey from the inland sea of Tonle Sap. Owing to the beauty and grandeur of its architecture, the mystery of its origin and its isolation, Angkor has exercised a greater spell on those who have visited it than any other Oriental shrine. In spite of its thirteen centuries and the ravages of the encroaching forest, this monument of a lost civilization is almost intact, though there is no trace of the empire builders who conceived it—only the ruins of neighbouring cities and temples, shrouded in the same mystery, strangled in the same vegetation.

Life in Cambodia to-day is centred in the districts bordering on the lake and rivers. Angkor lies to the north, a league or two outside the fringe of the populous cultivated zone. A few yellow-robed priests dream away their life in the ruins. Otherwise the temple is deserted save at the time of the annual festival when the Cambodians carry offerings to their dead. They regard the shrine as some supernatural emanation planted there inscrutably by giants or genii. They approach ignorantly, careless of its inspiration and significance. If you ask them who built it, they will look at you vacantly and say, " The Gods." The founders of Angkor have passed away from the face of the earth, leaving no trace of their influence on the races who absorbed them. The old forgotten Hindu deities they enshrined in the temple are as dead as Pan. There is no tradition in modern Cambodia of the builders.

The riddle of these enigmatic ruins, so far from being solved, is, if anything, obscured by the contradictory conclusions of French archæologists, sent out by the French Government to study early Cambodian architecture and history. It is the most difficult field of research. Khmer architecture is distinctive and unique, and nobody has been able to speak with authority as to the sources from which its salient features are derived.

The Khmers have left no record save in stone. Historic data is confined to legends, oral and written, of Cambodia, China, and Siam, puerile and contradictory fables of which the aim, as in most Oriental chronicles, is the glorification of the dynasties concerned. The earliest inhabitants of the country were the Ciampas, whose cult was serpent-worship, a race which received a large admixture of Malay blood. Later, they were known as the Khomen. Fournereau fixes the date of the Aryan invasion in the fifth century (A.D.), and believes that Prea-Thang, the founder of the Khmer Empire, was the son of the sovereign of Indrapat, the earliest of the strata of capitals on which the modern Delhi is built. He revolted against his father, was defeated and banished ; then, with his army of followers, broke across the southern continent, devastated, destroyed, created, and was only checked in his eastward course by the marshes of the Mekong valley and the Tonle Sap.

This was the beginning of the Khmer Empire. It endured as a great military and civilizing power until the tenth century. Brahmanism succeeded the cult of the serpent. The Hindu invaders built the temple of Angkor Vat. But in the seventh century, when the work was completed, it seems, save for the chiselling of a single pillar, the sacred Buddhist books were introduced into Cambodia from Ceylon and the temple was given over to the new cult. It was a peaceful revolution. In the statuary and friezes of Angkor the images of the Brahmanic and Buddhist ideal exist side by side to-day. Architecturally, Angkor owes little to the Buddhists save that their tolerance has left the shrine intact. Perhaps with the new influence the religious aspirations of the Khmers were idealised, they were filled with the sense of the pervading

SCULPTURE THAT LIVES

The embodiment of lithe movement, this dancing girl, one of sculptured myriads, almost seems to move on the walls of the Angkor temple.

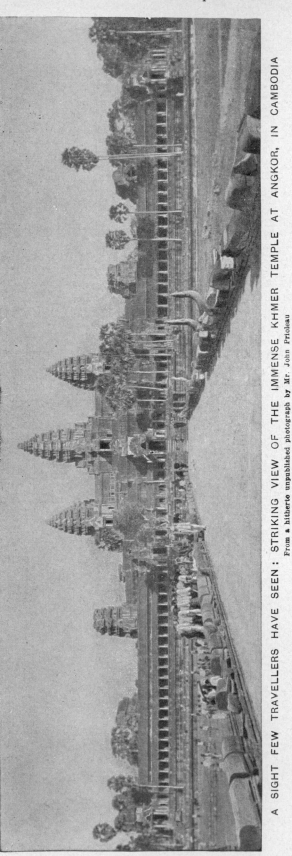

A SIGHT FEW TRAVELLERS HAVE SEEN : STRIKING VIEW OF THE IMMENSE KHMER TEMPLE AT ANGKOR, IN CAMBODIA

From a hitherto unpublished photograph by Mr. John Prioleau

vanity of things, and the motive for this monumental labour vanished. Anyhow, the adaptation of Buddhism as the state religion marks the beginning of the decadence of Khmer architecture. No monuments dating from the eighth century or after approach Angkor in vigour or imaginative expression.

Angkor Vat in any other geographical situation would be the goal of pilgrims from the four continents, but situated as it is in a country where the highest flight of the architect's imagination seldom soars beyond a draughty cowshed on stilts its appearance is doubly imposing. My first distant view of its towers and battlements in the dim light before sunrise suggested an old-world Dutch garden with its fantastically-clipped yews and mounting terraces ; then, as the slanting rays of the sun fell on the ruins and transfigured them, I knew that the rhapsodies of the French travellers which prompted my journey were not vain.

The fascination of Angkor is incommunicable. Its beauty, mystery, and symmetry may be dimly suggested by illustrations as to the massive solidity of its stone-work ; but to convey an idea of the grandeur and dimensions of the building one has to fall back on the uncongenial medium of statistics.

Like other ancient shrines of the Khmers, Angkor stands in a walled enclosure defended by a broad moat traversed by causeways. One crosses a bridge and passes under a gate guarded by huge stone lions to an inner raised causeway which leads to the main entrance of the shrine. The foundations are ten feet in height, and massively built of volcanic rock. The whole building, including the roof, is of stone, but without cement, and so close-fitting that the joints in many places are scarcely discernible.

The temple is built as an oblong, 796 feet in length, 588 feet in breadth. The central pagoda rises some 250 feet above the foundations, and the four others at the angles of the court are each about 150 feet in height. The grouping of them differs from the design in Indian shrines where the height of the towers diminishes progressively towards the centre of the temple, with the result that the greater part of the building is often hidden by the walls of the enceinte. In the Khmer temple the towers increase in height from the circumference inwards to the central shrine. Thus one gains a view of the whole building and much of the subordinate detail from the outside. The origin of these conical-pyramidal towers of the Khmers, and of their ogival vaulted roofs, is one of the mysteries of Angkor. Another distinctive feature is the stairway that leads from terrace to terrace and, unlike the stairs in Indian temples,

E.N A

## A PRIEST-RULED CITY OF CAMBODIA SAVED FROM THE CHOKING JUNGLE LIVES AGAIN

For many centuries the city of Angkor Vat, the second and greater capital of the Khmer Empire, lay hidden within the vast forest and jungle that still encircles it. Even when rediscovered, it was for long so inaccessible that nothing like complete exploration was possible To-day French enterprise has brought the city within a few hours' journey of Saigon by an air service. Above, part of the great complex of buildings with a paved way from the city's outer wall, now cleared of entangling growth ; be'ow, the main temple.

DANCING IN RHYTHMIC MEASURES AT THE TEMPLE OF THE ANCIENT KHMER GODS

Part of the training for the Cambodian Royal Corps de Balet consists of dancing on the threshold of the Temple. Two of the dancers shown here are old women practised in religious dancing and in the arts of costume and make-up, and two are young girls. They dress in special robes, with diadems of gilded bronze and metal masks, in a small courtyard, and the novices enter upon their performance in a spirit of the utmost piety. They imitate closely the sculptured dancers seen on the wall behind.

enclosed within the thickness of the walls, contributes impressively to the general plan.

Angkor Vat was completed in the first half of the seventh century (A.D.) Neither the Siamese nor the Cambodians have concerned themselves with its preservation. It is doubtful if, before the coming of the French, any guardian of the shrine cut away a single destructive root or creeper, or spent an hour in its repair. The outer walls enclose 400 acres, and it would take an army constantly employed to cope with the vegetation. Nevertheless, in spite of the encroachments of the jungle, the temple is wonderfully preserved. Enough is left to reconstruct the whole in the imagination.

The pre-eminence of Angkor Vat over other Hindu temples lies in its simplicity and restraint. There is nothing which may be compared with it in the land from which the Khmers sprang. India contains no supreme monument of Hindu architecture. Beside Angkor the conception of temples like Madura and Trivandrum, with their heavily overcharged ornament and exuberance of design, appear morbid excesses of fancy, the play of a diseased mind. Angkor has its profusion of ornament, but the general impression

is harmonious. Everything is in its right place ; there is little in excess. The architects have achieved a paradox in preserving a sense of moderation in the multiplication of detail, whether in the statuary or in the bas-reliefs.

The interior courts with their colonnades in the form of cloisters are on the Indian model ; only the Khmer corridors have an ogival vaulted roof supported on the inside by pillars. There is not an inch of these galleries which is not richly carved in bas-relief. The temple contains 1,025 yards of sculpture ; hundreds of thousands of figures are represented with surprisingly little repetition. Rame and Hanuman draw bows, slash swords, and thrust savagely with knives in the wildest fury and hate. The ferocity implicit in the features and gestures of the Rakshashas is most realistic.

When I visited Angkor Vat, I had the shrine very much to myself. Perhaps the grand old ruin was the more impressive in that it showed no trace of human meddling for the last thousand years. The chaos of vegetation had penetrated to the inner courts of the temple ; one could see the roots at grips with the masonry. A block was overthrown here and there, a pillar wrested from its portico, but the greenery and shade were welcome associations. Stripped of its verdure, its naked stones exposed to the glare of the sun, Angkor would lose much of its sombre fascination. To-day the French custodians are repairing the ruin. They can arrest or postpone its decay, but they cannot restore its ancient charm. The more one sees of their diagrams of the reconstructed Angkor in its hard and cold perfection—Angkor as it ought to be—the more one appreciates Angkor as it is.

I slept two moonlight nights in the temple, alone save for a small company of yellow-robed Buddhist priests—a solitude probably unpurchasable to-day. The sound of one's footsteps in the deserted colonnades awoke myriads of bats. Every night, as the sun sinks, they sweep along the vaulted roofs with a rushing sound like a great wind. The smell of them is like some fœtid incense to age and decay. Then, when they were still, I could hear the gentle stir of the palms inside the walls. The moonlight patterned on the stones, silhouetting their plume-like fronds, is associated in my mind with an atmosphere of nirvanic calm and rest. Now and then an owl wailed plaintively from a tree by the moat, and I heard other strange noises nearer by, the labouring of the stones, rustlings as of snakes, sounds without reason, voices of the night.

Sometimes the darkness of the corridors took tangible shape and a shadowy priest appeared out of the silence. A quiet old priest glided by me with noiseless feet like a shadow; he lit a taper at the end of the cloister; a little shrine before a Buddha was illumined by the flicker of a joss-stick; then he turned and passed me again, as silently as he had come, without a look or a word, devoutly incurious, walking in a trance. The flag-stones were haunted with pious feet.

Angkor Thom, which lies three miles to the north, the capital of the Aryan invaders who built the temple, is of an earlier date, and has suffered more from the ceaseless sapping of roots and creepers, the secular war which is being waged between the masonry and the sacred fig tree, the

**DANCERS IN THE HEAVEN OF THE GODS**

To show the immense acreage of mural decoration on the Angkor temple is beyond the power of camera. This photograph at least enables one to appreciate what an immense amount of loving labour must have been given to produce effects so superbly delicate. The gracefully posed dancing-girls are inimitably carved, and the pillared window, though sadly damaged, is still a thing of entrancing beauty.

shadow of whose branches, arched and embossed like a cathedral, has caressed the temple for centuries, while its roots have spread their slow and secret ruin. The ruined city lacks the sublimity of the temple owing to this decay, but in wonder and mystery and suggestiveness it transcends it.

The city is spread over miles. The grandeur of the shrine is repeated in fragments. Stumbling through the thick, tropical tangle one comes upon a tower with a human face. One creeps through crumbling galleries, scrambles over fallen pillars, and in the struggle to keep one's feet finds oneself clasping the knee of an elephant or the waist of some grotesque Hindu goddess.

The traveller enters a massive gateway through which elephants have passed to war; sculptured bowmen peep out at you above the lintel, grin, and attitudinise. On either side of them are stone

THE "STAIR OF HONOUR," ALSO OF WONDER

In the centre of the west side of the great temple of Angkor. The impression of height and immensity given, to those who behold it, by this long, unbroken flight of steps can be only faintly conveyed by a photograph. In the preceding page may be seen a near view of one of the many remarkable and graceful pillared windows through which the light of day penetrates into the temple.

chambers, in which slept the guard. It is easy to people these ruins with the figures one has seen in the sculpture galleries of Angkor—the monks, the dancing girls, the courtiers making their obeisance with their foreheads on the ground as the king and his guards ride out to war.

Then one breaks through a thicket and is held up by a wall of bas-relief, on which a troup of demons afflict the damned. One surprises the elephant-headed god Ganesh under his green canopy, or looks up and meets the nirvanic smile of a Buddha. Other faces leer at you enigmatically through the forest, draped with creepers and parasites, like hair. Everywhere lifted above the vegetation you meet the cobra's cowl, the sacred seven-headed Naga, its fan-shaped hood erect, the genius of Angkor. Sometimes it forms an immense horizontal balustrade supported by squat archers, its head the newel; or it rises life-like from the centre of a tank. Rows of them guard the terraces and causeways of Angkor and figure on the friezes.

Right in the heart of this forest is a shrine only less immense than Angkor, half smothered in the exuberant jungle. Arches of foliage interlace its arches of stone. Its thirty-seven towers are grouped round the central pagoda, the sanctuary, and each has four Brahmanic faces, which embrace the four points of the compass in a mystic secular smile. Bapuon and Pimean Acas, some way to the west and north, are other miracles in the efflorescence of stone.

All the Lower Mekong Valley and the borders of the great lake are rich in monuments of a dead civilization. Forgotten temples, fortresses, cities, bridges, and roads are scattered over Indo-China from the Laos country in the north to Thop-moi south of Pnom Penh, from Korat in Siam to Quinhon on the coast of Annam. Altogether, archæologists have numbered a hundred shrines. Some of them are almost as vast as Angkor, and might perhaps have rivalled her in grandeur and beauty and strength of line, if they had survived

FRAGMENT OF A VAST TEMPLE SMOTHERED IN EXUBERANT JUNGLE

This extraordinary edifice lingers a sorry ruin some 80 miles to the north of Angkor. In all thirty-seven towers, each bearing four colossal faces and about 24 feet in height, still stand in various stages of decay, strangled by creepers, eaten by parasites. The one-time immensity and grandeur of the building cannot be imagined, much less portrayed, for—to adapt a popular saying—none can see the ruin for the trees.

ALONG THE APPROACH TO THE EASTERN GATE OF ANGKOR THOM—

Once the capital city of the Khmer Empire, Angkor Thom, in the jungles of northern Cambodia, has an incommunicable fascination for the traveller who ventures thus far into this little-travelled part of French Indo-China. And everywhere, its head raised above the tangled vegetation, he meets the sacred Naga, symbolic of that snake worship dear to ancient mythology. Who fashioned these things? The present natives of the land, when questioned, say, "The Gods," and even savants can only conjecture. Some authorities maintain that the

–GIANT SEVEN-HEADED SERPENT SUPPORTED BY ITS ATTENDANT BEARERS

Khmers came from Indrapat, the ancient Delhi; others believe that the founders of this wonderful civilization were traders who ventured up the rivers Menam and Mekong from the sea. But the riddle of their coming and their going is insoluble; in the 5th century A.D. these people mysteriously rose to greatness, in the 10th century they mysteriously disappeared, leaving as traces of their culture such amazing structures as the temple of Angkor, strong enough to defy even the destruction of the jungle, as puzzles to the modern antiquarian.

the vandalism of the races who succeeded the Khmers. For there is evidence of other agents of destruction than the strangling jungle. Pakhan, an older shrine than Angkor, which stood within its four and a half miles of surrounding wall, has been reduced to a heap of ruins, and the riot of the iconoclasts is witnessed in the stones. Adjacent temples seem to have been destroyed or spared according to caprice.

This is another riddle of Angkor. Who were the iconoclasts? What inspired their fury or stayed their hand?

The disappearance of the Khmers and the manner of their dispossession is as mysterious as the wave of immigration that established them within the basin of the Mekong. There is a great divergence of opinion among French savants as to when and how they came. Fournereau's story of the exodus of Prea-Thang and his host from Indrapat, the ancient Delhi, and the breaking across the Burmese peninsula is not generally accepted as history. M. Foucher has ascribed the Hinduisation of Angkor to Sivaite priests who came from the basin of the Ganges in successive human waves and were absorbed in the indigenous population of the country. General Beylie, on the contrary, believes that the founders of Khmer civilization were adventurers, exiles, or traders who entered the mouths of the Menam and the Mekong by sea, a theory based on the evidence of Chinese annals and the orographical study of the Cambodian hinterland It does not seem probable that if the invaders followed the land route from India they would have left no traces of their communications behind.

Early last century there existed no data for the study of Khmer civilization. Travellers indulged in the wildest surmise, even attributing the ruins to the Egyptians or the lost tribe of Israel. During recent years French archæologists have carried out investigations on scientific lines.

The mystery that veils the origin and disappearance is only one of the riddles of Angkor. Equally inexplicable is the derivation of their architecture. The characteristic features to which we have drawn attention, as well as a number of other distinctive details, are entirely original. The Aryans did not bring these traditions from India. There is, of course, no trace of Mussulman influence, and the inspiration is not of the Far East. There is no suggestion in the Khmer temple of the tent-like pagoda roof of the Chinese or of the Islamic dome. Fournereau has traced fanciful analogies between the Khmer and Egyptian temples and the Khmer and Assyrian sculptures and bas-reliefs. Not that he presupposes any commerce between these ancient civilizations, though he

cannot accept the theory that Khmer civilization is indigenous. The problem would appear insuperable. There is no architecture in Cambodia prior to the Aryan invasion—a fact that would dismiss the supposition that the architects can have derived their model from the primitive Khomen or Malay. Yet if the principles of Khmer architecture were introduced by the Hindus, how comes it that they have transmitted a style that is unknown in their own country? The Indian builders have never evolved or adopted the salient features of the Khmer temple.

M. Groslier, the distinguished archæologist who was charged with a recent mission to Cambodia, believes that he has unravelled the mystery. He deprecates the expression "Hindu architecture" in relation to the relics of the Khmers. The Hindus, he argues, found what we call the Khmer architecture already evolved when they invaded the country—but not in masonry. All they did was to translate the tradition from wood into stone. Thus the Aryan genius has made what was else perishable immortal. It has adopted the practical traditions of the Cambodians; the intellectual, religious, and æsthetic inspiration is its own.

An ingenious solution, but it does not evade the paradox that the master builders derived the symmetry, the proportion, the ordered grouping, which is lacking in their own temples—that is to say, the æsthetic and intellectual impulse—from the subject race. The dweller in the jungle, it might be argued, has only to look around him to adopt from nature the model of the vaulted arch. The best roof to a cloister is suggested by the natural corridor in an overarching bamboo grove. But the Cambodian seems to have neglected the hint. He is not to-day remarkable for his initiative or resource, and it is doubtful if, in the days when he was the subject of a great empire, he was ever more than a complacent drudge.

It is difficult, too, to believe that the Aryans were absorbed in the indigenous stock. They have left behind nothing—there is no trace of Hindu inspiration in modern Cambodia, whether in dress, ornaments, vessels, architecture, manners, customs, or thought—beyond the common supineness of the East. When the native builds a house he drives four piles into the earth, or perhaps six or eight, not more, and stretches across them a bamboo floor. This, with four walls and a slanting roof, also of bamboo, satisfies his architectural aspirations. Villages built in this way stand among the ruins of the ancient Khmers. No wonder the Cambodian believes that Angkor is an exhalation conjured up out of the earth by genii or giants. To the European traveller Angkor compels moralising more than any other shrine in the East.

## The Wonder Cities. III.

# Petra, The Rose-Red City of Mystery

## By the Editor

With a special series of Photographs by Mr. Donald McLeish, including one in Colour

*BY reason of its difficulty of access, the scene of natural grandeur in which it is set, the beauty of its rock-hewn tomb-temples, and the secretive character of the Arab race of Nabataeans who made it the rich and luxurious capital of a prosperous trading empire, Petra has always exercised a spell over the imagination of the student of ancient history since its site was rediscovered in the early years of the nineteenth century. " A rose-red city half as old as Time" it has been called, in allusion to the colour of the mighty walls of rock which enclose on every side the valley wherein it stood, the only approach in Nabataean times and that chiefly used to-day being through a narrow and tortuous defile, now known as Es-Sik.*

COMING in from the desert, the traveller fronted a fantastic maze of rose-red, mauve, scarlet and golden peaks, cliffs, crags and ravines, surging, like a frozen sea of tempestuous colour, against the grey uplands of Northern Arabia. As the caravan from the Orient arrived, laden with scent, pearls, spice, and rare fabrics, there seemed no path by which the weary camels and horsemen could cross the mountain border to Palestine and Egypt. But there was a way, though neither Beduin on the desert side nor Jew on the seaward side dared to take it.

For hundreds of years vague tales had been told, along the Mediterranean, Red Sea, and Indian Ocean, of a strange gorge in the Arabian wilderness, leading to a marvellous City of Rock. All that men definitely knew, however, was that most of the trade between the Western and Eastern worlds passed through the strong hands of a mysterious race that held the mountains between the Dead Sea and the Red Sea. The few adventurers who set out to solve the mystery never returned, and a horrible suggestion ran that they formed part of the sacrifices that were continually offered up in the City of Rock.

Persians, Macedonians, and Romans tried in turn to break the secret desert kingdom. Some of these expeditions reached the City of Rock, and finding the fables true, took wonderful spoil; but the men of the mountains managed to maintain their

dominion for centuries after these raids, and took toll on the growing commerce between the Mediterranean and the Indian Ocean. As the mystery of their seat of power deepened, the marvels of their Rock increased. Around them empires and religions flourished and faded; but as they had refused entrance to the disciples of Zoroaster, so they kept away the followers of Christ, and became so hostile to the Jews that they helped the Romans in the last attack upon Jerusalem.

Night and day a score or two of tall, lean, hawk-faced men watched the great gorge, while outposts peered and listened above all the lesser ravines. Occasionally some foreign craftsman was invited to adorn the City of Rock in the last period of its triumphant pride. After a long, fatiguing, roundabout desert journey with his guides, he would enter a narrow cleft in a wall of rock. This was the gorge of the river Mûsâ, so called because the Arabs believe it was made by the rod of Moses. The stream that now flows through it was then diverted in flood time through a tunnel into a neighbouring ravine. Close to the entrance was a decorative arch across the ravine, at a height of about fifty feet, forming the Grand Portal, with statues and altar niches below. The air, still as pond water on a windless day, would be stifling, the heat hard to bear. Oleanders in flower half curtained the passage,

MAP SHOWING POSITION OF PETRA

GENERAL VIEW, LOOKING NORTHWARD, OF THE TOMB-COVERED HILLSIDE IN PETRA'S ENCHANTED VALLEY

The solemn grandeur of these lofty and now desolate hills, faced with the crumbling mementoes of a long bygone worship, cannot be described in words. Some of the temple tombs of the rose-red city, claimed by the poet to be "half as old as Time," date back to the sixth century B.C., and for something like a thousand years Petra, held first by Edomites, then by Nabataeans, and next by Romans, to fall finally before the onrush of some desert horde, flourished as a great commercial centre of the East. Its decline began in the fourth century A.D., and after the Arab conquest of Western Asia the city disappeared from history to wait through the years for rediscovery in modern times.

SECRET OF THE PETRAEAN SCULPTORS

On this mass of rock known as the Hill of the Acropolis, an unfinished temple tomb (marked with a X and enlarged in the inset) shows how the Petraeans built without the aid of scaffolding, working downwards from the top of the living rock. Crowning this hill are remains of a Crusaders' Castle and of a Place of Sacrifice, sacred to the primitive Semites.

but greenery and blossom grew rarer as the sky narrowed into a distant thread of brightest azure, and the gorgeous colourings of the rock dimmed in a gathering twilight. Down to a depth of twelve hundred feet the tortuous paved way sank and shrank in width, until a man could touch with outstretched arms the two dark red walls. What with the stagnant air and the eye-straining dimness and immensity of the rocky defile, the soul of a strange visitor, even under friendly guidance, was overborne by a feeling of superstitious terror. Never had any fortress possessed so impregnable and sublime an entrance as this great winding gorge of the secret city. It was a natural trap for invaders coming in strength, or for lonely spies.

Suddenly light and beauty touched the traveller with a relieving sense of joy. A great sideways gash in the mountain enlarged the sunken way, making a pool of gleaming sunshine, and in the

radiance shone a temple carven in the rose and golden rock of the eastern precipice. It was the rosy marvel now known as El-Khazneh or " the Treasury," but then a temple of Isis. Some horses and camels might be tethered on the worn grass, and a priest in white linen thanking the riders for their offering ; for here every man of the city stopped and prayed for protection when he set out for the desert, and gave thanks when he safely returned. But the Egyptian-like priest and the Arab-like worshippers would not count—the temple, a lovely thing possibly of Greek art, would enrapture the sight with its richly sculptured capitals and cornices, its graceful Corinthian columns, its sphinxes and its statue of the goddess Isis, to whom it was dedicated, all hewn with incredible labour and loving skill out of the living rock and glowing rosy in the bright sunshine and clear air.

Beyond this travellers' temple the gorge narrowed again, and then widened, revealing the mystery of Arabia. All the mountains had fallen back, leaving an oval space a little more than a mile long and about three-quarters of a mile wide. Here, out of the steep sides of the many-coloured sandstone heights, a great city of roseate glory had been hewn. Where they lived, the hillfolk had been buried. By the hundred, their carven tombs were ranged in close tiers on the iridescent mountain flanks. These rock-hewn tombs are the wonder of Petra to-day, and will remain for ages to come one of the greatest monuments of antiquity.

Some of the majestic burial caves were as large as temples, and probably two were used as Christian churches in a later age. There were other tombs sculptured from the rock in the style of imperial palaces, with two or three storeys of richly-wrought pillars. In them were laid the bodies of the kings and queens, whose successors lived in proud splendour in the gorgeous palaces that once stood among royal gardens on the valley floor, and worshipped, with strange rites, in the grandiose temples of the living city. The hillside region of the dead was a reflection of the valley floor region of the living. Small, plain-faced tomb caves of working folk were modelled on the style of their small square cottages, and the houses of middle-class men and mansions of rich merchants were represented in the style of their family tombs.

There were tombs with exterior heights ranging to about sixty-five feet, with large, finely-carved porches, windows, and outside altars on which offerings were made to the spirits. The inside walls were unadorned, and the family mummies were placed in hollows along the sides and in graves in

UNIQUE OF ITS KIND—THE ROCK-HEWN COLUMBARIUM OF PETRA

Petra (Gr. " rock "), the mysterious mountain stronghold of the Nabataeans, an Arab race who came into written history about 312 B.C., is the rock-hewn wonder city of North Arabia. It became a Roman province, was destroyed about the sixth century A.D., and sank into obscurity until explored in the early part of the nineteenth century. Of its many marvels not the least noteworthy is the tomb shown above and called the Columbarium, a name given by the ancient Romans to their sepulchral vaults, and used in our time in connexion with crematoria. The walls of the Columbarium of Petra are remarkable for their network of quadrangular cavities.

MASSIVE BUT SAND-ERODED PILLARS OF THE TOMB WITH THE URN

Here the camera shows how the sand storms of centuries have eaten into the columns of the rock-cut porticoes of the Tomb with the Urn, so-called on account of the great urn which crowns the monument. Two massive substructions of the tomb contain ten vaults and support a square terrace. In the inner chamber, 56 feet by 59 feet, is an inscription suggesting that at one time it was used for Christian worship. The architrave over the door is decorated in Roman style with circular shields between the triglyphs.

the rock floor. Closer and closer they were set as the generations passed. When filled, a new family tomb would be excavated, and the slow change of architectural styles marked the historic development of the Nabataean empire. In the oldest work were pylons telling of intercourse with Egypt, and sculpture showing Persian influence. Next came finely-moulded columns and graceful figures and ornament from the Greeks, while Syrian arches told of the expansion of Petra's power to Damascus, and late works showed the impress of Rome, whose hand eventually stretched out to Petra. Finally, there was a native blend of foreign influences, the first faint token of a tremendous awakening of a creative spirit in the Arab that was to shake and break apart the Old World, when Petra could no longer hold the desert nomads in check.

Meanwhile, the men of Petra had absorbed the ideas and arts of Greece and Rome, and were spreading them among the wilder Arabs. The Nabataean tongue which they used was a dialect of Syria, but they delighted in the Greco-Roman theatre, and at the foot of their sacred mountain, on which stood the Great Place of Sacrifice, was a fine open-air theatre, with thirty-three tiers of sandstone seats on which an audience of three thousand persons could comfortably rest. As the fighting-men of Petra numbered about ten thousand, and a high proportion of them were always absent, guarding caravans and outpost positions, and garrisoning towns, the theatre was of ample size for the city. There were royal seats for the king and his court, and above the highest tier, and forming part of the theatre, were the tombs of the dead.

Working, playing, fighting, and trading, the Rockmen liked the protecting, inspiring company of the souls of fellow-tribesmen. They hovered by tombs in the entrance gorges, and by military stations and trade depots in the sand wastes and along the Red Sea. From the city, burial caves,

**PETRA'S GREAT OPEN-AIR THEATRE HEWN OUT OF THE PRECIPITOUS CLIFF**

To the north of the Mount of the Obelisks and near to the mouth of Es-Sik, the narrow, sinuous gorge which gives entrance to the valley, are the remains of a fine theatre. Semi-circular in form and of Greek design, this theatre had thirty-three tiers of seats and afforded accommodation for more than 3,000 spectators. In the rock-wall towering in the rear are some of the oldest of the Petraean tombs, disposed in rows one above another. Some of them were cut away when the theatre was constructed.

houses, and temples extended down a triumphal way, and along a westward ravine that climbed the rocky height of Ed-Deir (the Convent). And here, at a distance of an hour's march from the capital, was another wonder of the wilderness. By the mountain top a colossal temple was hewn from the high rock in a large, solemn, classic style. Overpowering in strength and majesty, it seemed a work that would endure as long as the mountain tops about it. Stark in its grandeur, it embodied better than anything else the energy of soul that made the Rockmen lords of the desert.

The origin of the extraordinary cult of the dead in Petra, that led the mountaineers to encircle their city with tiers of tombs until death reigned above life, may possibly be found in ancient Arab superstition. In their view a mortal had several souls, and one remained by a well-preserved corpse, like a kind of guardian spirit. As it could revenge wrongs done to its body, it was presumed to have sufficient tribal feeling left to help in guarding the

store place for tribal plunder. This the shadowy army of the dead was supposed to have done in the first Macedonian and Roman invasions, and, encouraged by such achievements of their ghostly forbears, the Rockmen settled permanently under their protection, and very cheerfully lived with the spirits of their dead.

The Rockmen, known abroad as Nabataeans, began as a robber clan of nomad Arabs. They won and ranged over the grey limestone upland of Edom and the red heights between Sinai and the Dead Sea, and held up the caravan traffic along the desert marches of Arabia and Egypt. While living in shifting camps of black tents, they used the Petra basin as a secret storing-place for plunder. After interrupting the commerce of the Eastern and Western civilizations, they found that a combination of honesty, monopoly, and hard bargaining was far more profitable than brigandage that frightened caravans from the old routes, and piracy that led to the Persian and Persian-Egyptian

## TEMPLE FRONT AS BIG AS A CATHEDRAL, CHISELLED FROM LIVING ROCK

nceive the façade of S. Paul's Cathedral, not as built up stone by stone, but as a hill of red sandstone chiselled into an imposing piece of chitecture! Such is this Temple of Ed-Deir, 147 feet wide by 138 feet high, cut in the rock at a great height above Petra, and reached by airways through a gulley that splits the mountain to the north-west. Its one chamber, less than 40 feet square, still contains the ancient altar.

*From a photograph by Donald McLeish, specially coloured for " Wonders of the Past "*

governments increasing their naval forces in the Red Sea. So as honest brokers they reorganized the caravan routes and started to police the desert. Still they did not settle in Petra, but buried and warehoused there. A strong line of kings, with sustained ability in war and commerce, gave them strength, riches, national organization, and wider dominion. Definitely they housed themselves in Petra in the fourth century before the birth of Christ, and for a century before our era they were, with large numbers of slaves, cultivating the arts of civilization.

The air of romantic mystery which they maintained regarding their Rock City and hidden

**ONE OF THE OBELISKS**

On the terrace of the Sacrificial Mount are two of these columns or mazzeboth, hewn from the living rock. Divine symbols, these stone columns are common to the Holy Places of ancient Semitic peoples.

villages in Arabia was a matter of shrewd, practical business. The less aliens knew regarding the details of their mountain stronghold and the intricate organization of their trade routes, the safer the Rockmen were against invasion and competition. They took the iron, bronze, and purple dye of Mediterranean races, and, at usurious rates, traded these goods for myrrh, gold, silver, pearls, and other fine Orient produce. On the desert side they kept the Beduin in order by subsidies based on transit insurances for their caravans, and when subsidies failed to overcome

**NORTH-WEST FACE OF THE MOUNT OF OBELISKS**

At the summit of the mount, the height of which may be gauged by the figure on the right of the photograph, was Petra's principal Place of Sacrifice. At its base, now remarkable for the strangely-hewn tombs, first nestled the nucleus of the city, whose founders, the Edomites, could not have dreamt of its later wonders.

**THE ONLY APPROACH IN ANCIENT TIMES TO PETRA**

This photograph was taken midway in the magnificent gorge between towering rocks of red sandstone that stand sentinel over the winding way that in former times afforded the only means of access to the mysterious city. The torrent bed of the defile, now rough with stones, was in Roman days a regular paved way.

Photo by American Colony, Jerusalem

garden to their splendid warehouses, where trains of slaves tended them. Their womenfolk, with eyes like pools of passion and finely-moulded features, displayed their pride of body through gowns of gauze-like silk. Pride it was that kept them true to their men, amid all the pleasures of the senses that great wealth had won for them.

The main trouble of the prosperous people of the Rock City was that they could not spread. Their huge profits would diminish by sharing the traffic with colonies or amalgamated countries. As families grew, they could extend their native agencies in foreign lands, but it did not pay to unite Arabia, as the Romans united Italy. The Rock system was based upon a monopoly of the caravan trade, and the soul of the people of mystery, in spite of their bodily grace and cultivated charm of intellect, was as narrow and hard as the rockway to their lovely carven city.

Above their rose-red, lilac, and golden-yellow vale of pleasures and treasures rose a terrible hill, inaccessible except on the south side, where a great stairway had been cut. It was the Great Place of Sacrifice, to which the priests, king, and elders climbed in procession towards the blood basin

the nomads' love of plunder they used methods of extermination. Rumours that have not faded from the Beduin mind, and which were collected by Lord Kitchener in his adventurous, scientific exploration of the Petra region, speak of still larger secret cities lying in limestone hollows by the Red Sea coastland, and witnessing to the might and mysterious ways of the fighting merchant princes of Petra.

As they would stroll in family groups from the great theatre to the stream-fed valley and glowing ring of rose-red heights, they would look what they were—men of a lean, lithe, sun-hardened, desert-hammered stock, which had before been master of milder civilizations, and would again, shattering, spread. In flowing robes of Tyrian colour and headdresses of far-brought silk, with weapons by their hand, they moved with an air of graceful strength by palmgrove and scented

and the altar where the throats of victims were cut and the bodies burnt to the glory of Duchara, the divine lord of the kingdom of Aretas, chief of the Nabataeans, who, in Egyptian fashion, took to wife his own sister.

In the struggle of Mark Antony and Augustus, it was the Nabataeans who completed the overthrow of Cleopatra, by destroying the Egyptian Red Sea fleet. This enormously increased their trade, strength, and influence.

At last the Emperor Trajan, in A.D. 106, could not resist the lure of the Nabataeans' wealth, and reduced Petra to the rank of a Roman province. For many years the Orient trade continued, much to the profit of Rome, but the best Nabataeans vanished, and secretly diverted the desert traffic to Palmyra. The Beduin swept over the weakened frontier, and Petra, when rediscovered in 1807, was a ruin-ringed waste held by Arab robbers.

## The Master Builders. I.

# The Strange Forts of Aran

### By E. W. Lynam

#### Assistant in the British Museum

With Photos from " Notes on Irish Architecture," by the Earl of Dunraven

THE three Aran islands lie in the Atlantic on the western rim of the old known world, six miles from the nearest point on the coast of Galway. In the ancient traditions of the people of the mainland they figure as the home of giants and workers in magic ; in later legend they are identified with the enchanted western isles of Hy Brasil and Tir Nan Oge.

Two of the islands are quite small, with populations of less than 500. The third, Inismor (Great Island), which is nine miles long by one mile and a half broad, rises in high, precipitous cliffs along the Atlantic side, but is low, with many little coves, on the landward, or north-east shore. Sheets of grey limestone, broken by hundreds of crannies, warm hollows, and little fields, cover half the extent of the islands. Not a single tree occurs to break the quiet, lonely slopes of grey and green, or to shut out the wide encircling blue of sky and sea : but many unusual plants, such as maidenhair fern and spring gentian, grow profusely in the rock-crannies and fields. The Gulf Stream, which flows close to these islands, renders the climate exceptionally mild. The inhabitants, some 2,500 souls in all, are a handsome, hardy race, whose fair skin, blue-grey eyes, and dark hair and eyebrows seem to indicate an early mingling of fair and dark stocks in their ancestry. Very conservative and preserving many ancient customs and beliefs, they still wear the " pampootie " shoe, and use the " coracle " boat described by Himilco, the Phoenician traveller, 2,400 years ago.

These ocean-girt rocks, with their dreamy atmosphere and primitive customs, are crowded, even beyond expectation, with ancient stone monuments of the most varied types and dates. Among these a group of great stone forts stands out conspicuously. Four of them are on Inismor. Dun Aengusa (Fort of Aengus), the largest, was evidently the residence and walled citadel of a ruler. It stands on the edge of a beetling cliff, 300 feet above the Atlantic, on the south side of the island, and overlooks much of the island and a wide expanse of sea. Going outwards from the centre, the ruins consist of a strong oval enclosure or citadel, now measuring 150 feet by 130 feet internally, an outer wall defended by an abattis of large stones, and a second outer wall.

Although part of the citadel and of an old outer wall have crumbled with the cliff into the sea, the ruins still cover over sixteen acres. The present outer walls and the abattis never formed complete rings, but ended, as now, on the cliff edge. The walls vary from 7 feet in the outer, to 13 feet thick in the inner, and still rise in places to 18 feet high. The citadel is built on a natural platform artificially scarped, and overlooks the outer courts and walls. Terraces, which are reached by flights of steps from the interior, run along the tops of the walls. The abattis is made of pointed stones, placed on end close together, and projecting 3 feet to 4 feet above ground. It forms an effectual barrier, 30 feet to 80 feet deep.

The wooden houses and huts which once crowded the citadel and courts, as well as the booths, galleries, and light structures which were the flesh

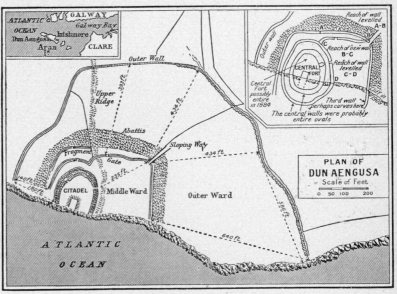

After plans by T. J. Westropp, M.A.

DUN CONOR OR DUN CONCHOBHAIR, "THE NOBLEST FORT OF ALL," ON THE—

Situated in an imposing position on the crest of the island's central hill 250 feet above the sea, it consists of an oval-shaped fort measuring 221 feet by 115 feet, protected for about half its circumference, where the cliff is not steep, by an outer wall. Its walls, still standing nearly 20 feet high in places, are double, sometimes triple, attaining thereby a thickness as great as 18½ feet. A feature unique among

GREY STONES OF DUBH CATHAIR, HEADLAND FORT OF INISMOR

Dubh Cathair, the Black Fort ("cathair" is a later word for fort than "dun"), stands on Inismor, and is the only one of its kind in the group, consisting as it does of a single wall between the precipitous cliffs of a headland projecting into the sea. The wall is 220 feet long, and the space which it encloses measures 354 feet from wall to sea. The masonry is laid in "headers" as at Dun Aengusa, but the stones are smallish and neither so well shaped nor so well laid, which may point to its being the oldest of the series.

—HILL-CREST OF INISMEADHON, MIDMOST OF THE THREE ARAN ISLANDS

the forts of Aran is a kind of outwork projecting on the north-east side, a rough rectangle of 51 feet by 70 feet. Legend states that this fort was built by Conor or Concraid, brother of Aengus and son of the Firbolg chieftain Umor, who fled with his kindred for protection to these islands of the utmost west. More probably the Aran forts were the last piratic strongholds of a pre-Gaelic race.

REMAINS OF THE CIRCULAR HILL-FORTRESS OF DUN ONACHT. INISMOR

Built on a steep knoll which rises from the rocky plain of Inismor, Dun Onacht is roughly circular, measuring 93 feet by 97 feet; the wall, which appears to be single and is in places nearly 15 feet thick, is remarkably well laid and consists of even larger blocks than is the case at Dun Aengusa. A platform runs round the wall within the fort, and was once approached by four flights of steps. At present the wall is nowhere more than 16 feet in height. The doorway, much ruined, is on the eastern side.

of the great stone skeleton that remains, have vanished with the men who built them and the lords who owned them. Some stone foundations, as well as chambers which are said to have existed in the walls, disappeared in the nineteenth century. An oblong raised table-stone within the citadel was probably connected with the inauguration of kings. Like the other forts, Dun Aengusa is built of blocks of local limestone, unworked and unmortared, laid in courses of "headers." The stones are usually large, from 4 feet to as much as 7 feet long.

Dun Oghil (Fort of the Oak Grove) and Dun Onacht (Fort of the Descendants of Owen) stand on commanding ridges in the interior of Inismor, three and two miles respectively from Dun Aengusa. They would seem to have been subsidiary courts and outposts to the great fort, as well as centres of considerable settlements. On the hillside to the north of Dun Oghil, the ruins of four lesser forts and of some forty primitive stone huts are still preserved. Dun Oghil has an oval citadel, measuring 91 feet by 75 feet in the interior, and an outer wall. The inner wall, 19 feet thick and still 15 feet high, is well built of large stones, beautifully laid, and gives, more than any of the forts, an impression of immense strength and immense antiquity. Dun Onacht, though small, rivals Dun Oghil in the excellence of its masonry and the size of the stones used. Its single wall is 14 feet thick and encloses a circular space 90 feet in diameter. Both forts have the same system of wall-terraces and flights of steps as Dun Aengusa, and there are foundations of stone huts in both.

Dun Conor (Conor's or Concraid's Fort), which, though not the largest, has been called "the noblest of all," crowns the central hill of Inismeadhon (Middle Island). It is built on a natural rock-platform 20 feet high, and is visible for miles out at sea. The fort is oval, enclosing a space 221 feet long by 115 feet broad. Its wall is the most massive of all, being 18½ feet thick and rising even now 20 feet high above the platform. It is terraced with steps. From the gate of the fort one descends into a wide, strongly-walled court, and thence through a sort of circular guard-house with narrow doorways, out to the open hillside. While here also all the ancient wooden buildings have disappeared, the foundations of several stone huts and chambers, round and oblong, survive within the citadel.

Dubh Cathair (Black Fort) on Inismor differs from the others in some respects, particularly in being a promontory fort—i.e., it depends on cliffs for protection on three sides, and has only one wall across the landward neck. It is in a perilous and most striking position on a precipitous head-land, 400 feet high, which is separated from the adjacent cliffs by great chasms, through which the sea booms continually. The wall, 220 feet long, is built of smallish stones loosely heaped, and is 16 feet to 18 feet thick and 20 feet high. It is terraced, a loose abattis protects it, and there are remains of hut foundations inside and outside.

Massive though these structures are—and, if they belong to the Bronze Age, truly wonderful for their time and place—they were more in the nature of fortified homesteads than of regular forts. In case of need, however, the Aran forts could shelter 3,000 persons. That they were not intended to stand a siege is evident from the fact that only one of them has a spring of water within or near it. This peculiarity has been noticed in some early forts in Greece. The entrances of all the forts open towards the landing-places on the north-east shores, but this does not necessarily imply that an invader was expected. On the other hand, nearly all the forts were certainly improved and extended by their ancient inhabitants at different times. The alterations at Dun Aengusa, which included the building of the outermost wall and the rebuilding of part of the middle wall, are calculated to have lasted over a period of some two hundred years.

Early forts occur in many parts of Europe, from England, Brittany, and Sweden down to Thessaly ; and they were in use from neolithic right down to medieval times. But it is hardly too much to say of the whole group of Aran forts what has been said of Dun Aengusa, " it has become, with most antiquaries, the type and symbol of countless similar structures, all subordinate to it in interest."

While the lack of conclusive " finds " in the forts has greatly hampered archæologists, the most recent investigators are inclined to assign them to the late Bronze Age. In that period (c. 1800-400 B.C. in Ireland) Ireland held a position of some importance in North Europe, partly owing to her possession of gold and copper. Irish bronze objects show great beauty and some originality of workmanship, and her gold lunulae and sun-disks, which were associated with sun-worship, found their way even to Germany and Denmark, and were probably bartered for Cornish tin.

The earliest literary reference to the forts appears in an eleventh century Irish poem, written from earlier, lost records. It is related that the sons of Umor, of the Firbolg race, were expelled from Ireland by Milesian invaders. After long wanderings in the western isles of Scotland and possibly among the Picts of Scotland, they returned, a few hundred strong, to Ireland about the beginning of our era. They were allowed to settle near Tara, surety for their good conduct having been given by the powerful body called the Red Branch warriors. The king, however, exacted such a heavy tribute from them that they fled westwards to Connacht, where the famous Queen Maev granted them lands round Galway Bay and Clew Bay. "They settled westward at Dun Aenghusa" and "Concraid obtained his just portion at Inismedhoin." But when they fled the king appealed to their guarantors, the four sons of Aengus of Dun Aengusa were compelled to fight four of the greatest champions of the Red Branch, and the four Firbolgs were slain. Soon afterwards, the story goes, their settlements were broken up.

The date, the names, and most of the incidents of this story may be rejected as more than doubtful. Early Irish history was written by Gaels for the glorification of Gaels, but for the confusion of their struggle with the Gael. It is believed that the story of the sons of Umor may preserve a memory of that struggle. The "Firbolg" inhabitants of Connacht appear to have been a warlike people, and some hundreds of forts in west Connacht are attributed to them and to the sons of Umor by tradition and early history. It is considered probable that some of these people, hard pressed on the mainland, emigrated to Aran. There the fugitive chieftains and their descendants organized a polity and a system of fortified manors such as they had known on the mainland, and being little disturbed in their island kingdom, maintained their independence and an increasing prosperity for at least two hundred years.

If they practised piracy on the high seas and along the west Irish coast, the comparative wealth

**WITH WALLS STILL 18 FEET HIGH: THE CENTRAL CITADEL OF DUN AENGUSA**

This photograph is a view of Dun Aengusa from the north; the reader should refer to the plan in page **91** and imagine himself standing not far from the words "Upper Ridge" and looking towards the citadel. Behind him will be the outer wall, and in front a kind of abattis of rough blocks set on end and leaning slightly outwards. Between the abattis and the fort in the background will be seen two lines of wall, somewhat complicated in arrangement owing to alterations in the distant past.

Photo by Dr. G. Fogerty, R.N.

later generations. In plain language, the Firbolgs and Milesians of early Irish literature were respectively, the pre-Gaelic or Bronze Age inhabitants of the country, and their Gaelic conquerors. The Gaels, a branch of the tall, fair Celtic race, reached Ireland about 400 B.C., probably by the north. They were armed with iron weapons, and brought that metal into general use in Ireland. Though comparatively few in numbers, they established a military ascendancy over all the north and over portions of the east and west of Ireland. Their language and to some extent their culture were accepted by the whole country before they became merged, in Christian times, in the earlier and more numerous population.

Whether the Bronze Age inhabitants of Ireland were dark-complexioned Iberians, mysterious Picts, or Celts of an earlier colonization, little is known of these island lords could be easily understood. Their islands were admirably adapted for that, and the west coast of Ireland has hundreds of convenient creeks where raiders might land unobserved. It may well be that the fort entrances opened towards the landing-places of the islands simply to facilitate the transport of booty. In this they would only be imitating the Scandinavian sea-rovers, who, elsewhere, had carried off Irish gold ornaments, and the Gaels themselves, who had raided Ireland, and later on frequently plundered Britain.

The Aran forts form the western end of that long chain of hill forts which has its other end in Thessaly and Mycenae. If the pre-Gaelic theory as to their origin be correct, they are also the last great monuments, in time and place, of the proud Bronze Age civilization in Europe; an adventurous survival on forgotten islands of the Atlantic.

Temples of the Gods. IV.

# The Parthenon: Crown of Athens

## By Prof. F. H. Marshall

Koraes Professor of Modern Greek, London University ; Author of " Discovery in Greek Lands"

*WHENEVER Greek architecture is mentioned it is probable that the first individual achievement of the ancient builders to be visualised in the mind's eye, even by those unskilled in things Greek, is the Parthenon. In its broken and ruined condition this majestic building still preserves a dignity that seems unimpaired ; its very fragments still impress the beholder with a sense of beauty and proportion hardly less pleasing to the mind than the perfected beauty of its original state must have been. To conceive Athens without the Parthenon or the Parthenon without its Acropolis site is hardly possible, but it has been found that a general chapter on Athens dealing adequately with the Parthenon would be of undue length. Accordingly a special study of the Parthenon is here presented, to be followed in later pages by a chapter on the city and its Acropolis by Prof. J. L. Myres —*EDITOR.

THE Parthenon may be said to epitomise all the merits which distinguish Greek art at its best period. It is at once strong, simple, graceful, and harmonious. It was nearly finished just before the disastrous Peloponnesian war dealt a fatal blow to Athenian supremacy. It embodies the peculiar qualities associated with the virgin goddess Athene, the goddess of wisdom and the arts, in whose honour the temple was erected.

The supremacy which is accorded to the Parthenon in the history of Greek architecture is not due to its size ; though a large temple for its time, it sinks into insignificance when compared with such a building as S. Peter's at Rome. The English reader will be better able to grasp its dimensions by a comparison with the famous London church of S. Martin's-in-the-Fields. The Parthenon measures 228 by 101 feet ; S. Martin's, 160 by 80 feet. The palm accorded to the Parthenon is due to the sound instinct which prefers perfection of symmetry and perfection of finish to the merely colossal. It is fitting that this great work of art should be associated with the names of Perikles, the greatest Greek statesman, and Pheidias, the greatest of Greek sculptors.

The site and the building are worthy of one another. Placed upon the great rock of the Acropolis, which rises more than 500 feet above the sea, the building dominated the city which lay below, and could be seen from far and wide. It commanded in the clear atmosphere of Attica a magnificent prospect, whether towards the sea and Salamis, or inland towards the mountain masses of Parnes, Pentelikon, and Hymettos. The site had been previously destined for two temples, neither of which was ever finished. The second was probably destroyed by the Persians in 480 B.C., and its foundations were partly used for the Periklean Parthenon, though enlargement and elaborate additions were necessary.

The history of this last building may be briefly traced. It was begun in 447 B.C., and by 438 it was ready for the reception of the great statue of Athene Parthenos, but the finishing touches do not appear to have been placed to the building when the Peloponnesian war broke out in 431. The temple seems to have remained practically intact until its conversion into a church in Byzantine times ; we have the definite evidence of the traveller Pausanias, in the second century after Christ, that it was then standing unimpaired. The

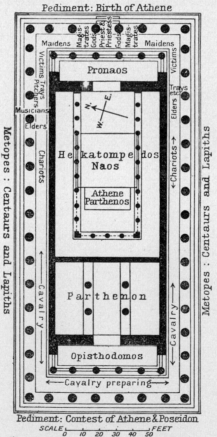

Pediment: Birth of Athene

PLAN OF THE PARTHENON

The inner shrine or Hekatompedos [Naos] was 100 feet long and contained the great statue ; the Parthenon proper housed the temple gear The Pronaos (fore-temple) was an outer portico, while the Opisthodomos (house behind) was a porch at the opposite end used as a treasury.

96

conversion into a church apparently took place in the fifth century, and the alterations necessary for this purpose are instructive as showing the essential difference between the Greek temple and a Christian church. The central object in the ancient temple was the cult-statue of the god or goddess, and a fixed liturgy played no part in the worship. A long and uninterrupted space was not required, and the converters of the Parthenon found it necessary to remove the partition wall which divided the building into two separate portions in Greek and Roman times, and further to build an apse at the east end. In 1458 the Turks captured Athens, and again the temple suffered conversion—this time into a mosque, but little structural damage apparently resulted. The building remained practically undamaged till the fatal year 1687, when the Venetians under Morosini were besieging the Turks in the Acropolis, and a shell landed on the Turkish powder-magazine placed in the Parthenon and blew out the middle of the building. Morosini caused further damage through an attempt to remove the horses of Anthene's chariot from the western pediment; in the

## SECTION THROUGH A PEDIMENT OF THE PARTHENON

The great pediment, or triangular gable, contained groups of symbolic statuary; it was supported by the stone beams of the architrave, along the top of which were placed, at regular intervals, the triglyphs, or triple-fluted slabs. In the interspaces, called metopes, were sculptured episodes of the fabled war of the Centaurs and Lapiths. The frieze ran round the four walls of the cella, or temple proper, within the colonnade.

After a drawing by Niemann

## RELIEFS THAT MAY BE BASED ON THE PARTHENON SCULPTURES

A slab from a "puteal" or well-head, now in Madrid, is used as the basis for most recent reconstructions of the eastern pediment of the Parthenon, as it is thought that its inspiration may have been drawn thence; with the necessary reservation imposed by the rectangular shape of the puteal compared with the triangular pediment. The scene is immediately after the delivery of Athene from the head of Zeus by a blow from the axe of Hephaistos. From left to right: Hephaistos, Zeus, Nike (Victory), Athene, the three Fates. What so commends the puteal as a useful clue is the fact that Athene is shown full-size and in the centre of the field—a much more likely arrangement than that adopted in many previous reconstructions which portray her of diminutive stature and still poised on the head of Zeus, who is the central figure.

SCULPTURE AND PAINTING OF THE EASTERN PORTICO

Acknowledged though the Parthenon was, in ancient times as to-day, to be without peer among Greek temples, its supreme merits seem to have been so taken for granted that little has come down to us of contemporary accounts. Thus the painting on the cella wall in this reconstruction of the eastern end is conjectural, although a conflict of Greeks and Persians would be a very likely subject; while the restoration of the central figures in the pediment is only one of many attempts (see the puteal in page 97).

After a reconstruction by Loviot from "Monuments Antiques"

process they fell to the ground and were irretrievably damaged The next important incident is the removal by Lord Elgin, in 1801 and the following years, of most of the sculptures left in the pediments, together with a large portion of the frieze, several metopes, and other portions of the building. After romantic vicissitudes and acrimonious debates in Parliament these (with some other sculptures) were ultimately purchased for the British Nation in 1816 for the sum of £35,000, and have since been one of the chief glories of the British Museum.

We pass to a description of the building itself with its sculptures. The Greek temple has a long history, and in that history the Parthenon holds, as it were, a central position. The earlier Greek Doric temples are characterised by the heaviness and squatness of the columns, which have a very marked diminution in thickness from the bottom upwards. The architraves are correspondingly heavy, and this stage is well illustrated by the remains of the sixth century temples of Poseidon at Corinth and Paestum in South Italy, or the ruinous remains at Selinunte, referred to in page 38 of this work. Later, the Doric order in Roman hands is marked by the comparative slightness of the columns In the Parthenon, however, the tapering of the columns, a little over 34 feet high, though marked, is free from exaggeration If we look at a plan of the temple, we see that it has an outer colonnade of eight columns at the short ends and seventeen on the long sides; this colonnade rests on a platform (the stylobate) rising in three steps. On the columns rests the architrave, and above this are the square sculptured panels called metopes, separated from each other by the grooved triglyphs. Over these at the short ends are the triangular gables or pediments The roof was originally covered with marble tiles resting on wooden supports. Inside the outer colonnade runs a corridor which separates it from the temple proper. The latter consisted of four parts; at the east end was an antechamber called the "Pronaos," which led into the main chamber of the temple, the "Hekatompedos Naos," a shrine 100 feet long, like the old "Hekatompedon," the ancient temple which the Parthenon replaced, containing the great statue of Athene by Pheidias; this chamber was completely separated by a wall from the rooms on the western side—the " Parthenon," or Maiden's Chamber, which gave its name to the whole temple, and another ante-chamber corresponding to the pronaos, and probably known as the " Opisthodomos." Both ante-chambers have a portico of six Doric columns, and behind these was originally an iron grating which converted them into closed rooms. Over the columns ran the sculptured frieze, which was carried right round the walls of the temple proper, or cella. This frieze, which is one of the noblest monuments of Greek art, will be described later.

To return to the arrangements of the Hekatompedos and Parthenon. The former was divided into a nave and surrounding aisles by means of two long parallel rows and a short cross-row of Doric columns ; a second series of Doric columns superimposed on the first supported the ceiling. A balustrade railed off a space in front of the cult statue, the position of which is still marked by the dark stone flooring. A description of the statue will be given later. On the western side the Parthenon chamber had its ceiling supported by four tall columns, probably of the Ionic order. It served mainly as a repository for precious objects dedicated to the goddess, and these were recorded with meticulous accuracy in lists inscribed on stone, several of which, witnessing to the temple's wealth, have come down to us.

The lighting of the temple was probably (apart from artificial light) supplied through the great doorways at the east and west ends. In estimating the effect we must bear in mind how much greater is the intensity of light in Greece than in England. This intensity explains another feature of the Parthenon—the free employment of bright colours in combination with the dazzling white of the

WALL OF THE HEKATOMPEDOS AND EXTERIOR DORIC COLONNADE ON THE SOUTH SIDE

The wall on the left is that of the cella, or temple proper. Round this wall, on the outside, were friezes sculptured by Pheidias to represent the glory and power of Athens in the service of her goddess. These must indeed have been executed with rare ingenuity, for it is said that when the sun threw the shadows of the columns on the inner wall as here, it seemed to a person walking down the pillared aisle that the whole procession was in movement towards its glorious climax at the eastern end.

CRUDE REPLICA OF A PEERLESS STATUE
The glorious statue of the Virgin Goddess, that was to the
Athenians an ideal symbol of all that their city meant, has
vanished beyond recall ; and the few extant copies are rude and
amateurish efforts.    Nevertheless this cast of the so-called
" Varvakeion " statuette (the original is in Athens) enables us
to realize the pose in which the goddess was portrayed.

marble.   The brilliant success of the effect thus
produced can be judged to-day from several of the
buildings of modern Athens which are built in this
style.   It must be remembered that the Pentelic
marble of which the Parthenon is built was originally a pure white, though in the course of centuries
it has weathered to a rich gold owing to the admixture of iron in the substance of the marble.

The sculptures of the Parthenon were produced
at a time when Greek art was at its acme, and it is
the singular good fortune of Britain that she has
these (as so many other masterpieces of Greek

sculpture) ready at hand for those who care to
study them.   There are three principal groups of
sculptures from the Parthenon—those from the two
gables, the metopes, and, above all, the great
frieze.   In studying these we must bear in mind
that they were intended in their subjects to symbolise the highest aspirations of the Greek and
especially the Athenian mind.   Every aid to their
proper understanding will be found in the Elgin
Room of the British Museum.

The great pedimental groups have suffered most
from the vicissitudes of time, but we have assistance
in reconstructing them, notably in the descriptions
of the traveller Pausanias in the second century
after Christ, and in drawings made by a French
artist (usually supposed to be Jacques Carrey) in
1674.   The east pediment, which surmounted the
principal entrance to the temple, appropriately
represented the birth of the virgin goddess Athene
from the brain of Zeus ; these figures are entirely
lost, but a probable reconstruction can be made
with the aid of a relief-sculpture on an ancient
marble well-head at Madrid and representations
of the myth on vases.   From this central group the
figures on either side were ranged in diminishing
height to suit the triangular frame.   Behind Zeus
probably stood Hephaistos, who had delivered the
goddess from the head of Zeus by a blow with his
axe.   The interpretation of the extant figures,
with the exception of the Sun-god rising in his four-
horse chariot on the left and the Moon-goddess
sinking with her team on the right, is uncertain.
But whether we regard them as deities or as local
personifications, there can be no disagreement as
to the merits of the sculptures.   The group of three
draped women on the right, commonly known as
the three Fates, and the splendid nude figure
usually and with great probability called Theseus
are masterpieces of the sculptor's art.

The western pediment depicted the struggle between Athene and Poseidon, Lord of the Sea, for
the possession of Attica.   Here Carrey's drawing is
of great importance, for it shows the original
composition admirably and enables us to have a
proper understanding of the mere fragments which
remain.   Athene and Poseidon start back from one
another, probably after the creation of their special
attributes, the olive-tree and the salt   spring.
Each had a chariot in attendance, but the fate of
Athene's horses has already been described.   The
figures on either hand have been variously interpreted, but they are probably Attic heroes and hero-
ines interested in the struggle.   There is general
agreement that the recumbent figures in the
corners represent river-gods.   That on the left,
usually called the Ilissos, is famous for its soft
modelling suggestive of a river's flowing water.

MASTERPIECE OF PHEIDIAS: THE STATUE OF ATHENE IN HER CHOSEN SHRINE

The Hekatompedos, as seen in this reconstruction, was divided longitudinally into three aisles by two rows of Doric columns. In a commanding position against the back wall of this temple stood Athene. Her right hand held a representation of Nike (Victory), while her left rested on the shield on whose surface was depicted the battle of the Amazons with the Greeks. Athene's breastplate was the "aegis," a goat-skin plated with scales, having the Gorgon's head in the centre. The cost of the statue was fabulous, for the flesh parts were of ivory and the drapings of pure gold.

Based upon a model reconstruction in the Metropolitan Museum of Art, New York City

**METOPE FROM THE PARTHENON**
Of much less skilled workmanship than the frieze, the metopes were probably executed by disciples in the school of Pheidias. The subjects are contests of the mythical Lapiths and Centaurs, arising from a quarrel at a marriage feast.

Of the ninety-two metopes the British Museum possesses fifteen, all from the south side of the temple ; forty-one still remain in position, but all are badly weathered. The metopes in the British Museum represent the struggle between the Lapiths and the horse-monster Centaurs ; such scenes of combat are frequent in Greek art, and in the case of the Parthenon it is hardly fanciful to read into them a symbol of the triumph of Greek civilization over Persian barbarism. The metopes vary greatly in artistic merit ; some are comparatively poor in composition and execution, others admirable. We must conceive of the background being picked out in colour to understand the full effect of these groups. Different scenes of combat are represented on other metopes, but their bad preservation makes any more exact interpretation difficult.

There can be no doubt that the interest of the Parthenon sculptures culminates in the frieze, which, it is generally admitted, represents the great Panathenaic Procession held every four years in honour of Athene. This vast composition occupied 524 feet in length, and is 3 feet 4 inches in

**COWS LED ALL UNWITTING TO THE SACRIFICE**
In the Panathenaic festival sacrifices and offerings of various descriptions were laid before the goddess Athene. Amongst these sacrifices were cows and bulls, led by the owners, who wished to propitiate their guardian deity. In this fragment of frieze from the south wall can be seen the hindquarters of one cow, its leader being on its right side and holding his cloak with his left hand, and the head and forequarters of another animal whose leader walks on its left.

DEITIES OF ANCIENT GREECE VIVIDLY PORTRAYED IN MARBLE

On the eastern frontage of the frieze we have Poseidon (extreme left), now reconciled with Athene and a guest at the celebrations at her temple. Reclining on the stool next to him is Apollo, seated side by side with Artemis, the divine epitome of the beauty of maidens. The mutilated figure on her right is Aphrodite (Venus of the Romans), who has her boy Eros, or Cupid (not shown in the photograph), by her knee. All save Apollo are watching the procession, and he, from his attitude, seems to talk of it to Poseidon.

height. The British Museum is singularly fortunate in possessing some 247 feet of it.

The position round the wall of the cella was carefully chosen for its effective display; as seen in alternate light and shadow by one walking round the columns of the outer colonnade it must have appeared to be in actual movement. Now, as exhibited in the British Museum, it both gains and loses. It can be studied in minute detail because it is nearer to the eye; but it is arranged internally instead of externally, and the effect of the view from between columns is lost.

The moment in the procession depicted is the presentation of a new robe to Athene, and this takes place on the east side in the presence of the gods and goddesses seated in a semicircle. On the western side the procession is starting, and it proceeds in two long streams up the north and south sides towards the seated deities. These deities are arranged in two admirably-balanced groups. On the left are Zeus and Hera, on the right is Athene; most of the other deities can be identified with reasonable certainty. Between these two groups are five persons standing: a woman, presumably a priestess, receives two girls who appear to be carrying stools on their heads; to the right of them is a bearded priest who takes a

RIVAL DEITIES FOR THE WORSHIP OF ATTICA

A reconstruction by Schwerzek of the statues that once occupied the centre of the west pediment; they were a representation of the legendary struggle of Athene and Poseidon for the control of Athens—a contest won, of course, by Athene.

## COLD MARBLE QUICKENED WITH THE BREATH OF LIFE

The bearded figure in the upper of these two slabs from the Parthenon frieze is a Marshal, who points the way to the youth with the horse. The reins and trappings are gone, for they were of bronze; only the rivet-holes in the marble remain. The restive horse in the lower example is in acute contrast with the meek cows in page 102; the veins of his limbs almost seem to pulsate.

large folded robe—no doubt Athene's—from a boy.

We may now turn to the different elements in the procession. At the west end, where most of the slabs are still in position, a number of knights are about to mount or have just mounted their horses. On the long side these riders are in full procession, and are portrayed with admirable life and variety as they ride in groups nearly abreast. Before the cavalry move four-horse chariots, preceded by a group of elderly men. In front of these again are lyre-players and flute-players and youths with trays and jars of wine. At the head of the procession are sacrificial victims—on the north side cows and sheep (perhaps offerings from

THE PARTHENON, SHINING DIADEM OF ATHENS-

This magnificent pile, raised at the zenith of the finest period of Greek architecture, the essence of whose beauty would appear to lie in its ve
simplicity, is nevertheless built with an amazing skill. Details of its construction which have been minutely scrutinised reveal the fact that
architects must have been scientists and mathematicians as well as artists. This is abundantly evident in such subtle points as these : that apparen

*Based on a model in the Metropolitan Museum of Art, New York City—*

## —AND TREASURE-HOUSE OF PEERLESS STATUARY

rizontal planes are imperceptibly curved ; that perpendicular lines incline slightly towards the centre of the temple ; and that the seemingly flat or is rather higher towards the centre than at the base—everything was studied for the finest effects.  But the great glory of the Parthenon was e decorative sculpture by Pheidias and his disciples ; the Athene statue, the frieze, the metopes—all were masterpieces impossible to excel.

—and specially coloured for " Wonders of the Past "

the colonies), on the south side cows alone. Continuity is preserved by the introduction of marshals at the corners of the frieze. As the procession turns from the two long sides to the east front it is headed by maidens carrying bowls and jugs. The arrival of the procession is awaited by groups of elders who stand on either side of the deities. This short description enables us to realize how nearly every element in Athenian life was introduced into this great composition, and was brought thereby into the closest touch with the protecting deities.

Though occasionally unequal in execution, the frieze as a whole is sculptured with great spirit, the fire introduced into the horses being sometimes wonderful. The composition shows a master mind and may be associated with the name of Pheidias.

LIFE'S UNTRAMMELLED GESTURES WROUGHT IN STONE

The realism of Pheidias' art, vivid but not crudely obtrusive, is well shown in these portions of the frieze. Particularly noteworthy is the vigorous treatment of the noble central figure of the Attic knight and the strong, sweeping curve of the horse's neck in the upper picture. Below are most vigorous animals bearing riders, whose eager attitudes are instinct with dashing energy, while the flying cloak of the rear horseman suggests triumphant speed

To allow for the effect of the lighting from below the upper part of the frieze is in rather higher relief than the lower (about 2 inches against 1¼). Accessories, such as bridles, were introduced separately in bronze and riveted to the marble.

The greatest of all the sculptures of the Parthenon, the cult-statue of Athene Parthenos, the position of which has been already indicated, has perished. We have, however, an elaborate description of this masterpiece of Pheidias by the traveller Pausanias, and several antique copies, none of which worthily represents the splendour of the original. The goddess stood in long tunic with the "aegis" on her breast. Her helmet was adorned with a sphinx in the centre and griffins on the sides. Her outstretched right arm held an image of victory, her left rested on a shield adorned with a representation of a battle between Greeks and Amazons. About this shield we have the story that Pheidias introduced portraits of Perikles and himself into it—Pheidias as a bald old man raising

slight backward tilt of the columns, with the object of counteracting optical illusions. But these refinements had long been employed by the Greek architect. The happy mean struck between excess of heaviness and excess of lightness in the proportions might seem due to the natural evolution of the Greek temple. The peculiar meaning of the Parthenon is best grasped by contrasting its sculptures with those of the slightly earlier temple of Zeus at Olympia.

The temple of Zeus is the expression of pan-Hellenism, the Parthenon of Atticism. The subjects of the sculptures of the Zeus temple—the preparations for the chariot race between Pelops and Oinomaos, the combat between the Centaurs and the Lapiths, and the exploits of Herakles—concern the great precinct at Olympia " where all men meet." The Parthenon sculptures also include the struggle between the Centaurs and the Lapiths ; but greater stress is laid upon the essentially Athenian subjects—the birth of Athene,

GRAND CLIMAX OF THE PARTHENON FRIEZE: PRESENTATION OF HER ROBE TO ATHENE

a stone, and Perikles poising a spear, with his arm raised so as partially to conceal his face. These figures can be identified on the "Strangford" shield in the British Museum. The materials of this colossal statue, which, according to Pliny, was about 40 feet high, were of gold and ivory—gold for the robes, ivory for the flesh—and the gold and ivory could be detached from the statue. The base was decorated with elaborate reliefs. We cannot doubt that the grandeur of the statue was worthy of the people's ideal conception of their patron goddess.

If we look for the real significance of the Parthenon, it is to be found, I think, in its expression of the Attic ideal. This is revealed rather in the sculptures adorning the temple than in the actual architecture. It is true that subtle refinements are introduced into the structure, such as the gentle curving of seemingly straight lines and the

the contest between Athene and Poseidon, and above all upon the Panathenaic Procession. In the execution of the pedimental groups the free flow of the Parthenon sculptures is in striking contrast to the stiff balance of the Olympia groups, and herein it is hardly fanciful to detect the essential difference of the Attic spirit. At Olympia the cult-statue of Zeus was also the work of Pheidias, and it is significant that it was an Attic sculptor who gave a satisfying ideal interpretation both of the pan-Hellenic god and of the Athenian goddess. The visitor at Olympia would be dominated by a sense of the majesty of Zeus ; on the Acropolis at Athens he would be under the spell of the goddess who typified the Attic spirit, which sought to free the human intellect from all that might hamper it in its natural development and to enable it to express its highest aspirations in sublime forms of imperishable beauty.

# The Study of the Past. IV.

# The Tragedy of the Mammoth

## By Claude E. Benson

A MONSTROUS eft of old was lord and master of earth, For him did his high sun flame and his river billowing ran.'
Years passed, and again years upon years, and very gradually, imperceptibly, the crust of the earth became less viscous. Wherefore, gradually also, ' Dragons of the prime That tare each other in the slime,' passed away, slime and dragon, and the increasingly coherent soil was trodden by creatures of higher development. So, at long last, it came about that, in place of the monster dragon, a monster elephant was overlord, if not of earth, at least of the northern hemisphere. Alone of all the creatures of that period we can tell exactly what he was like, because we can see him exactly as he was, with his shaggy, fulvous coat still fresh on him, his eyes glazed, with the life as it were just gone out of them, and in his stomach, and even between his teeth, the food he was chewing and digesting when he was cut off.

That the foregoing sentence contains a fallacy is patent. Man was, as always, the master, but he was a timorous, self-effacing master, holding most precarious dominion over the beasts of the field. By arboreal shelters, by lacustrine dwellings, by fastnesses among the rocks, by fire, he evaded or checked the attacks of creatures against which he, one of the most impotent of animals, defective in sight, hearing, scent, and strength, was defenceless, his stone hatchets and puny missiles about as effective as straws and twigs against the assault of the large mammalia. Yet was man the master and aggressive. By traps and pitfalls he overcame the great brutes of forest and field, fed himself on their flesh, lighted his home with their fat. Master and hunter, he was artist to boot. In the caves of France and elsewhere in southern Europe we can see his handiwork to-day. Curiously accurate he was withal, as can be tested by comparison of his 'counterfeit presentments' with the stone-cold original, preserved in Siberian snows. He even engraved a mammoth on a mammoth's tusk, possibly a record of personal prowess, or triumph over his gigantic quarry.

Such infinitesimal casualties in no way affected the herds of **numberless mammoths roaming unassailable** over the immeasurable forest lands of northern Asia. No living creature could stand up in combat with a mammoth save a mammoth only. Only in the mastodon could he have encountered a fit challenger. The mastodon, however, appears to have affected sunnier climes, albeit there is no doubt that the temperature of northern Asia was at that time far less severe than it is to-day. There is never a tide that washes the northern coast but casts up mammoth ivory. The Aleutian Islands may be said to be built up of their bones.

IT is clear then that the Asiatic continent must have extended at one time much farther towards the Pole than it does to-day. It is clear also that the climate must have been less severe, otherwise neither the mammoth nor its food could have existed, much less thriven. It is clear also that a very considerable portion of northern Asia must have been submerged at some date subsequent to the coming of the mammoth.

The existence of the mammoth, either unpieced and in the bone or complete and in the flesh, is no modern discovery. Kamschatkan natives have realized that mammoth beef from cold storage is excellent provender and have used mammoth fat as fuel for their lamps in their shelters and igloos for who knows how long. Mammoth ivory has been a commercial asset ever since the tenth century, probably from many years earlier. It was then exported east and west, to Russia and China, but by far the greater quantity went to China. Even so, two hundred tusks may be taken as a moderate average annual export westwards. Quite recently, only last century, Western commerce became alive to the fact that mammoth ivory was to be had for the picking up and that there was an inexhaustible supply available for those hardy enough to brave the climate. Consequently, in spite of having been despoiled steadily for a thousand years at the rate indicated, the market furnished sixteen thousand pounds weight of mammoth ivory, which was all bought up in one year. A little later sixteen hundred tusks were imported into London, and there was plenty

**THE MAMMOTH DRAWN BY ONE WHO KNEW HIM**
Both in cave paintings in colour and in drawings and engravings in monochrome the Aurignacian and Magdalenian hunter artists of 10,000 years ago left excellent pictures of the animals that then roamed the earth, including several, such as the woolly rhinoceros and the mammoth, that are now extinct. This finely impressionist study of the mammoth was found in the Font de Gaume cave near Les Eyzies in the Dordogne, southern France.

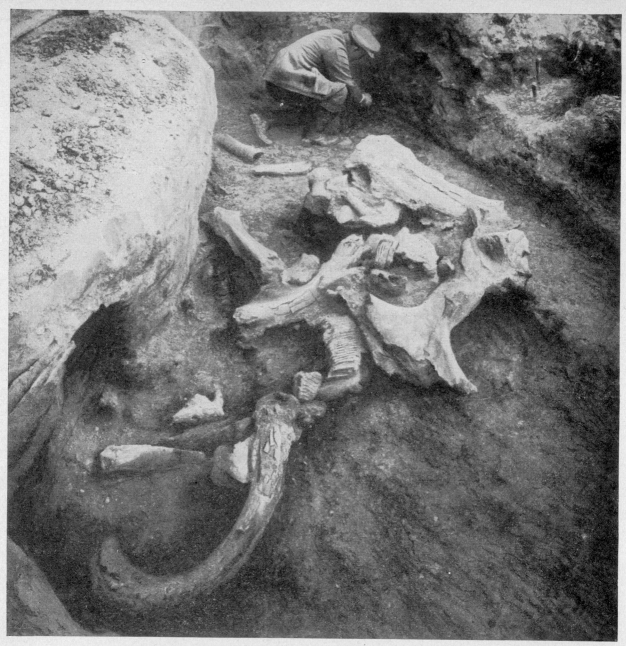

GRAVEYARD OF PREHISTORIC MAMMOTHS IN MORAVIA

Traces of hunter cavemen and their contemporary fauna have been found in numerous places in Moravia.  The most interesting find was made on a hillside near Dolmi Vistonice in the south of the province, where excavation disclosed a quantity of weapons, tools and cups of carved ivory and worked reindeer horns, pointing to a considerable assemblage of these people ; and just beyond this a veritable graveyard of mammoths, a large area being covered with heaps of legs, shoulder blades, skulls, jaws and teeth of mammoths both great and small. The presence of partly calcined bones in a large cinder heap suggested that they had been used as fuel by the hunters when cooking the flesh.

more where that came from.  The ivory, however, was too brittle to find favour in Western markets. It was useless for billiard balls, a very uncertain proposition for knife handles, frames and what-not, and Westerners are not adept at carving miniature pagodas, or half a dozen balls, beautifully pierced and decorated, one inside the other, as the Oriental craftsman can do.

With regard to the 'cold storage' mammoths there is a popular pronouncement, accepted as scientific, to which allusion will be made later, but of such wise men are shy.  Science is modest and tentative.  It knows that the 'progress of science' consists largely in correcting the mistakes of the past and that sundry of these mistakes were popularly proclaimed not so very long ago as established facts.

It seems, then, highly probable that in some remote age a vast subsidence of the land along the north coast of Asia, extending hundreds of miles east and west and of great depth, occurred.  As a counterpoise

A MAMMOTH BROUGHT TO LIGHT BY AN OLD STONE-AGE ROCK PICTURE

Apart from a few fossilised grinders preserved in the Vaal River gravels there was no evidence of the former existence of the mammoth in South Africa until the quite recent discovery at Delarey of some rock sculptures depicting animals of the Glacial Period with such fidelity that the actual species can be identified. Above is a representation of the woolly mammoth, Archidiskodon. The high-domed head with tufts of hair, small ears, short hairy body, tall pillar-like hind limbs and tail with long tassel have many points of resemblance to the Dordogne specimen shown in page 109. In front of the mammoth a woolly rhinoceros was sculptured upon this same stone

to this it would be reasonable to expect a corresponding rise of the earth's surface farther south. These premises conceded, it would also be reasonable to expect that the climate of northern Siberia would be markedly affected. Any considerable elevation to the south would screen off the northern regions from the influences of the heated atmosphere of the tropics. If this elevation touched the snow-line the warm airs stealing northward over plains of not dissimilar temperature would be actually frozen to

death during their transit over the high lands, and all along the northern coast a reign of intense and enduring frost would be established—and that is exactly what it would seem did happen. The climate of that part of the world to-day is intolerably severe. At Yakutsk, for example, the temperature of the soil is many degrees below the average of the Polar Ocean.

Careful examination suggests very strongly that these changes were rapid, of the nature of a cataclysm, that, in fact, the bulk of the mammoth race was

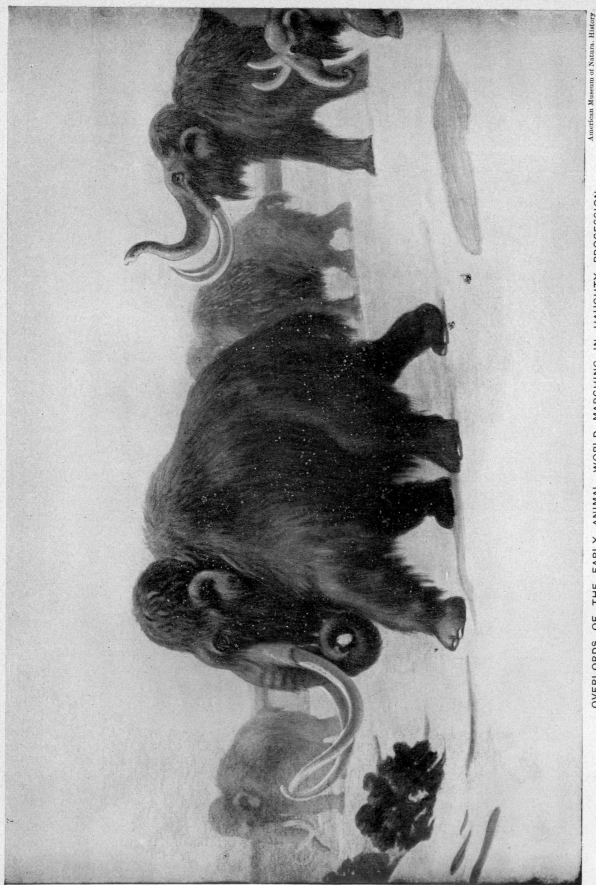

**OVERLORDS OF THE EARLY ANIMAL WORLD MARCHING IN HAUGHTY PROCESSION**

With the advent of the Ice Age mammalian forms of animal life appeared, highly specialised to withstand the extreme cold—notably the woolly rhinoceros. This reconstruction drawing by Osborn and Knight depicts a herd of woolly mammoths—Mammonteus primigenius—such as roamed over Europe in late glacial times in vast numbers. With their immense bulk and spirally coiled tusks they must have presented a formidable appearance to hunters armed only with crude stone weapons. Yet these men slew the monstrous brutes in thousands, greatly thinning the herds long before with the increasing mildness of the climate, these moved slowly after the retreating glaciers into the wastes of northern Asia.

American Museum of Natural History

**AN ACTUAL MAMMOTH THAT ONCE TROD THE SIBERIAN PLAIN**

Actual specimens of the mammoth have been found entombed in ice in the Siberian tundra, and so perfectly preserved that their flesh was edible. The mammoth did not greatly exceed the African elephant in stature. It bore a general resemblance to the Indian elephant, but differed in having long, slender tusks curled upwards and outwards, and in being covered with long, reddish brown hair with a thick woolly **under fur**. The specimen shown here, found in the Beresovka, is now in the Leningrad museum.

swept suddenly out of existence. The destructive agency is not far to seek. Fire it assuredly was not. Fire on such a scale would have calcined its victims. Assuredly, too, these were not overwhelmed by the glacial nightmare. Ice in motion has a rough and brutal way of dealing with such as fall into its grip. There remains then water, and with it the conclusion that the mammoths were simply drowned out by some overwhelming catastrophe. Those far to the north would have been engulfed without so much as a chance of attempted flight. Those farther south would have been between the devil and the deep sea—' death in the front, destruction in the rear,' assuming that the convulsion to the south was of similar scale and violence. In any case the fleeing beasts would have been caught by the pursuing water before such distant safety was attained, if such safety existed. The fountains of the great deep were broken up and the ocean rushed headlong over the continent till checked and repulsed by the barrier rising inland to the south, and in this catastrophe perished the mammoth stock.

As to the nature of this barrier, it has been asserted with some appearance of authority that at this time the giant range of the Hindu Kush rose majestically into the air. It was objected that the earth could never have stood such a shaking, retorted that the old earth was thoroughly used to such shakings, and so forth, all which is something of the scuffling of kites and crows inasmuch as a corresponding depression could be made to scale by pressing the tip of a finger on an india-rubber ball. There was no need to summon up the Hindu Kush to the whole of its majestic elevation. As has been indicated, as soon as the rising land to the south touched the snow-line northern Siberia was condemned to eternal winter. Such occurrences do not happen in five minutes. The inrush of the sea may have been, probably was, impetuous, but the process of reflux and contributory causes only relatively rapid.

The popular explanation of the ' cold-storage ' mammoth, to wit that the great beasts had fallen into slime pits and there got frozen in, does not cover much ground. It is not very important. If the number of such mammoths approaches those estimated by some, this form of sepulture must have been something of a habit. Let it be conceded that in their wanderings some mammoths did get stuck in the mud. That does not account for the vast ocean graveyard of mammoths to the north. It is far more probable that the preserved specimens were first drowned and afterwards smothered in the detritus of the ebbing inundation and there left to be frozen in with the frozen soil.

113

GREAT CISTERN ROCK OF THE FORTRESS-PALACE OF SIGIRI, CEYLON

View taken from about halfway up the rock of Sigiri, showing the wide-spreading jungle from which it springs stretching out towards the sharp cones of Mihintale in the distance. The rounded mass on the left is called the Cistern Rock. In ordinary seasons there was no necessity for the dwellers on the summit to convey water for their needs from the large lake at the south end of the rock-base, the large tank and the smaller cisterns being filled by the monsoon rains.

Photo by F. Burnett

114

## The Royal Palaces. II.

# A Wonder Palace on a Rock

## By G. E. Mitton

### Author of "The Lost Cities of Ceylon," etc.

*THIS fascinating chapter is one of three in our work dealing with the past wonders of Ceylon, the others describing the famous Lost Cities and the hardly less notable Buddhist Dagobas. Sigiri is a great boss of granite rising out of the jungle, upon which in the sixth century King Kasyapa built a fortress-palace whose construction remains a marvel to the modern engineer.*—EDITOR.

THE sunset light caught the western face of the giant boss of rock as it reared itself to a height of four hundred feet above the rolling jungle. It brought out the dark red of the granite, streaked black by the soil washed down by the heavy monsoon rains from the overhanging mushroom cap. Even with the naked eye a ragged fringe of growth could be seen on this cap, and with the glasses this resolved itself into sparse trees and stunted shrubs.

Such was my first view of this strange rock-fortress in the midst of Ceylon, the only specimen in the island of one of those scarped cylindrical masses of rock which, rising abruptly with height vastly greater than their area, always compel attention whatever their surroundings.

The rock of Sigiri can be reached by road from Kurunegala station, distant about thirty miles. As far as Dambulla, some eleven miles south-west, the way lies along the metalled trunk road north. After this it forks, one branch going on to the ancient royal city of Anuradhapura, and the other to Trincomalee. We follow the latter for another four miles, then branch off into the true jungle, halting a couple of miles farther on by the pretty but very small rest-house, where a night or two may be spent under primitive conditions. From the tiny compound of this can be seen the mighty mass of Sigiri, on the summit of which a king built his palace in the sixth century, and from which he ruled Ceylon—or that part of it which was under any sort of rule—for eighteen years.

Kasyapa was the younger of the two sons of King Datu Sena. He rose against his father (A.D. 511), attempted to extort his treasure from him, and finally had him walled up in a rock cell to die of starvation. The elder son, Moggallana, had fled. But Kasyapa knew no peace while his brother lived to take vengeance, and he flew south-west to the commanding rock of Sigiri, distant from the capital city of Anuradhapura some thirty-five miles in a straight line. There he established

himself and his court. What Moggallana did meantime, and why he did not seize the government himself, ignoring his brother, the chronicle does not say. Probably Kasyapa carried with him the Sacred Tooth, which was an emblem and signet of the royal power, and could not be withstood.

The work accomplished by Kasyapa's engineers in dealing with the difficult ascent of the rock is a marvel even at the present day. The cap bellies out around the top, and these clever workmen carried up the stages of the mighty stairway exactly at the one point where it was feasible on the northern face. This was in A.D. 511, when Britain was suffering under the invasions of the West Saxons.

From the north side of the main rock, about half-way up, a boss projects, and the top of this forms a large area comparatively level. The ascent began on the west face of the cliff, and was carried upwards by flights of quartzite steps, some of which still exist, though they have been "restored." From the high point to which this carries us, at the "waist" or smallest diameter of the rock, a gallery was made resting on a wall that rose with it, having its base on the part of the rock which spread below. This gallery, running in a quadrant round about a quarter of the rock face, was thus firmly supported, and the supporting wall rose beyond its floor and became a high retaining wall.

The gallery is supplemented by a modern iron bridge at the north-west corner, where the older work no longer exists, having been at this point subject to the violence of the monsoon rains. Thus we are carried on to the great northern boss or platform, where was planned and executed the most effective and startling of the conceptions of these great artist-workmen, whose qualities seem to have died with them.

For long the name of the rock had been a puzzle to antiquaries. The Sinhalese derive their name from the word "sinha," a lion, and in the national chronicle, the Mahawansa, we are told that

**SPIRAL GALLERY OF THE FORTRESS ROCK OF SIGIRI**

The ascent to the Palace of King Kasyapa at the summit of the giant rock of Sigiri was made easy by a great spiral gallery, having short flights of steps, two of which are seen in the photograph. This gallery was protected by a wall about 9 feet high, built on the outer edge, and giving a sense of perfect security to those who made the ascent.

Photo by Frank Burnett

revealed the key to this quaint conceit—the "Lion-staircase House"!

Four enormous claws, about four feet in height, shaped of brick and partly plaster-covered, after the manner of the Sinhalese when they wanted to make enduring work, were unearthed, and by their means it became possible to reconstruct in imagination the form taken by the rest of the fallen brick-work. This must have been the head and shoulders of a gigantic lion, between whose paws ran up the staircase to the king's palace on the summit above. Visitors now ascend this part by means of iron ladders, supplemented above by footholds cut in the face of the rock.

Once the summit is gained, there stretches out a scene of desolation where once stood the palace and citadel of the king. The whole area is about an acre in extent. Tall grass grows amid the brown-red courses of brick which remain. A high ridge runs along the western side of the summit; otherwise the whole surface slopes considerably from west to east.

It is still easy to trace the backbone of the citadel, as a paved way runs from end to end, though broken with steps here and there to fit it to the different levels. From this passages and stairways give access to each side. Steps appear most unexpectedly, and the foundations of the brickwork are set, wherever possible, on the solid rock. The bricks are well baked, of a dark red-brown, and unusually long. They are set in plaster where it has been found necessary to strengthen them to bear the weight above. Of the super-structure nothing remains; it was probably made in great part of wood that time has destroyed.

Kasyapa "built galleries in it (Sigiri) ornamented with figures of lions, wherefore it took its name of Sihagiri (the Lion Rock)." But for long the question was, where were the lions?

On the northern platform already alluded to, there was a mass of rubble brick, apparently falling down in an avalanche from the face of the rising rock. As excavations progressed, and the encumbering falls were removed, there was

The terracing was a special feature of the work. The 1896 Report of the Archæological Survey says : " That part of the ancient citadel lying south of the pond, and east of the high level strip, was laid out in a series of cross terraces east and west, varying in width and falling away southwards. From the ' pokuna ' (tank) to the foot of the last staircase at the extreme south are seven or eight distinct terraces. The centre is taken up with an open courtyard, and passages leading to the pond, and round it on either side by stairs and intermediate landings, all admirably planned to suit the physical conditions, and displaying great ingenuity in turning to full account the limited space and surface inequalities of the rock's summit. . . . On the left, skirting the east edge of the rock, was a range of minor rooms and passages,

doubtless communicating with an outermost corridor which almost encircled the citadel. This series of side chambers was continued on to near the south end of the rock."

The " pokuna," or tank here referred to, still remains as a marshy lake. It is rock-hewn, and measures thirty yards square. Such a receptacle, filled by the monsoon rains, and supplemented by smaller cisterns, would no doubt form an adequate water supply in ordinary seasons, and do away with any necessity for conveying water from the large lake at the south end of the rock base, up the steep ascent to the summit.

The most remarkable object remaining on the summit, facing the eastern jungle, is the great throne of red gneiss, on which doubtless the king sat to dispense justice or give audience. These

RUINS OF KING KASYAPA'S PALACE ON THE ROCK OF SIGIRI

The work of bygone Sinhalese engineers in providing for the ascent of the rock was equalled by their work in the citadel and palace at the summit, which covered about an acre. Whenever possible, the foundations of the brickwork were set on the solid rock. The superstructure, of which nothing remains, was probably in great part of wood. Tall grass grows luxuriantly amid the brown-red courses of brick, and here and there a few trees, like gaunt spectres of the past, rear their heads above the ruins.

Photo by Frank Burnett

kings, we know, were accessible to any of their subjects who claimed the privilege. The throne stands untouched by time, its severe plainness of line bringing out its excellent and unobscured design.

The palace was a world in itself, a labyrinth of passages and corners and store-rooms. In trying to reconstruct the life of this strange epoch, we must remember that the Sinhalese of those days had attained a splendour of luxury and refinement which were not to be found in the British Isles for centuries later. Silken hangings, woven carpets, chambers decorated with festoons of pearls hanging from pillars, and utensils

SIGIRI, THE "LION ROCK"
Below the summit of the rock is a natural boss, and on its platform, the first stage in the ascent, is the "Lion-staircase House."

of silver and gold, were to be found in their kings' houses. Couches, chairs, and even bell-pulls are mentioned as commonplaces of furniture. The sanitary arrangements were efficiently attended to, baths were frequently taken, and perfumes freely used.

Perhaps the most wonderful feature of this jungle court remaining to us are the paintings of the ladies of Kasyapa's entourage. High above the great western gallery, by which the ascent is made, are hollow caves in the cliff face, and on the "ceilings" of these are painted frescoes in colour of contemporary date, representing some score of these ladies and their attendants going to the nearest "vihara" (temple) with offerings of flowers. They are almost certainly actual portraits. They are so inaccessible that for long it was considered impossible to reach them, even

WHERE KING KASYAPA HELD HIS COURT
The warm red granite of the rock of Sigiri, streaked with black by soil carried down in the monsoon rains, and the lotus-covered pool in which it is reflected, make it one of the most romantic sights in Ceylon, and the impression on the visitor is deepened when he learns its old-world story of intrigue and battle.
Ceylon Government Photos

with modern appliances, and they could only be glimpsed from below. But in 1889 staging was carried up the rock-face, and a flooring fixed, for the " floor " of the cave is as curved as the " roof." Copies in chalk were made of the details of the colouring with infinite labour and difficulty. Nearly a decade later Muhandiram Perera, now in charge of the ruins at Anuradhapura, whose skill as a draughtsman is well known, was swung up by cables in a chair, 150 feet above the ground, and in this uncomfortable and unstable position made careful copies in oils of the series. He has himself told me of the almost insuperable difficulties he had to overcome. He had to lie on his back on an improvised scaffolding to get a proper view of the originals, and it took him nineteen weeks to complete the task, fighting all the time against cramp and fever (which nearly laid him low), as well as the minor ills of flies and the great bambara bees, who in the first instance had honeycombed the walls with their nests.

Yellow, sienna, umber, green, and so on had to be employed in copying the originals, but no blue. These wonderful reproductions can be seen in Colombo Museum. It is another proof of the weird fancy of the sixth century Sinhalese that such portraits should ever have been executed in such a position. A stranger picture-gallery was surely never chosen. However that may be, its inaccessibility has preserved them ; they have survived the bees and mud-nesting birds, and are now covered in with wire netting. The colours are still brilliant.

BASTION-GUARDED STAIRWAY OF THE FORTRESS-PALACE ON SIGIRI

This bastion was constructed by King Kasyapa's engineers for the purpose of guarding the winding stairway, which was conceived and carried out so that the ascents were led up through the body of a gigantic lion. According to the national chronicle, the " Mahawansa," the gallery was ornamented with figures of lions. Sigiri or Sihagiri means the Lion Rock, but the name remained unsupported by evidence until excavations revealed the remains of the " Lion-staircase House " (see page 120).

Photo by G. E. Mitton

Here we have, then, twenty-one female figures, three-quarter length, diaphanously dressed, and, in the case of the mistresses, covered with costly ornaments, such as jewelled pins, rings, hair decorations, and many chains in heavy settings. They are usually alternate, first a lady and then her attendant ; the flesh of the higher class being

**THE LION'S CLAWS OF SIGIRI**
Half-way up the great rock, in a mass of brick débris, were found remains of the famous " Lion-staircase House." These comprised giant claws of brick about four feet high, partly plaster covered, which once held the staircase that rose through the body up the scarped face of the rock. Their discovery revealed the long forgotten origin of the name Sigiri—Lion Rock.
*Photo by G. E. Mitton*

shown of lighter or darker yellow, that of the serving-women of a greenish dusky hue, to indicate an alien race. They carry flowers, and are moving in procession northward. The position for the work has evidently been chosen with some reason, for as they march forward through the centuries they are ever going towards the smaller hill of Piduragala, lying some distance northward of Sigiri, where King Kasyapa had built a " vihara," and called it after his two daughters.

The faces of the women are carefully executed, evidently as actual likenesses. The outlines of the figures are full, the almond eyes dark and lustrous. The style is that of the much better known cave paintings at Ajanta in Hyderabad.

Thus we have it on direct evidence that the

ladies did, at all events, descend the hill occasionally ; whether Kasyapa did, we do not know. But even if he remained in his eyrie on the summit, he had a wide range of interest to overlook. The lake on the south side was evidently, judging by its bund, formerly of much greater extent then than now. There are moated islands in it. It may have been a feature of one of those pleasure parks in which the ancient Sinhalese delighted—a park with well-kept sward, with flower-beds, with pavilions and open-air baths, where the air was fragrant with the scent of jasmine, and the eye pleased by the rainbow hues of peacocks and the gay dresses of the crowd worn on festival days.

Hives of workers dependent on that aerial domain are to be found all round the base of the rock. The remains of huts and shelters in caves are frequent. A great army of artificers, soldiers, messengers, and others was constantly coming and going. Half-way down the rock on the north side is the projecting boss facing the Lion-staircase House. Here, it is surmised, dwelt the nobles and court officials, and others who, while not actually attendants at the court, had yet to be in constant touch with the throne. Their rooms are seen to have been built round the edge ; doubtless they faced inward to some sort of courtyard.

On the east side of this platform was built a great retaining wall, which held up the mass of masonry employed in building the Lion House. This had fallen into ruin, and threatened to collapse altogether, when the archæological authorities took it in hand and painstakingly rebuilt it with concrete blocks.

There are smaller outcrops of rock, rearing themselves above the jungle all around Sigiri Rock. These can best be seen by looking down from the summit. The most noticeable of them are the Audience Hall and the Cistern Rock near the western ascent. In the Audience Hall remains a stone seat for the king or his representative, and behind it a small round stone, possibly for the umbrella bearer. On the summit of the Cistern Rock, reached by foot-holes cut in one of the rounded " angles," is a beautifully hewn bath or cistern. And all around and about swings up the jungle, rolling like a dark green sea to the far horizon. Faintly in the distance rise the twin peaks of the sacred hill of Mihintale, where the apostle of the Buddha alighted when he brought the religion of Buddhism over from India to Ceylon.

Often must Kasyapa have scanned the distance, as he sat in the cool of the day, and heard the challenges of innumerable jungle cocks, the monotonous note of the coppersmith bird, the belling of the deer, and perhaps the hunting scream of a leopard. Often must he have wondered if he were destined to die on his isolated height, far distant from the city of his boyhood's days.

Whether he descended or not during the eighteen years he reigned there we do not know, but we do know that he descended at last, and met his doom in combat with the justly incensed and patient avenger, his brother Moggallana. The "two armies met like two seas that had burst their bounds" ("Mahawansa"). Kasyapa was completely beaten, and died either by his own or his brother's hand, tragic end to a reign that began in tragedy.

After that the Palace on the Rock was left to fall to ruin, and the great ascents began to decay; but so fine and durable had been the work of the sixth century artificers that even in the nineteenth century sufficient was left to afford some foothold and enable them to be faithfully reconstructed.

ON THE EAST SIDE OF THE LION STAIRCASE OF SIGIRI

Here we see modern Sinhalese engaged in the work of rebuilding the retaining wall of the platform to hold up the remains of the Lion-staircase House built by their forbears some fourteen hundred years ago—one of the engineering marvels of the palace-fortress of King Kasyapa, who, having starved his father to death and usurped the throne, lived here for some eighteen years, surrounded by all the pomp and circumstance of the royal state, but in constant fear of his brother's vengeance.

Ceylon Government Photo

"PHARAOH'S BED": A GEM OF PHILAE PARTLY SUBMERGED BY THE NILE

Sometimes called the Temple of Trajan, or referred to simply as the Kiosk, this beautiful structure was never finished. The roof was never put on, nor were the high blocks above the capitals of the columns cut back, as seems to have been intended, into Hathor heads like those shown on page 124. There are five columns on each side and four at each end, and the inter-columnar walls rise to about half the height of the columns. As might be said of the whole island, the temple was dedicated to Isis. Reliefs on the walls represent Trajan presenting wine to Isis and Horus, and as standing before Osiris and Isis. The lovely pale yellow of the stonework has been changed by the Nile into a dreary grey

Photo by Donald McLeish

122

# The Shrines of Isis at Philae

### By Margaret A. Murray, D. Lit., F.S.A. (Scot.)

Assistant Professor of Egyptology at University College, London

PHILAE—known in ancient times as P-aa-lek, "the island of Lek"—has always been considered as one of the most beautiful places in Egypt. In pre-Christian times it was also one of the holiest. The buildings are not so ancient as the temples farther down the Nile, for the earliest dated object found there bears the name of Tirhakah, who is mentioned in the Bible as King of Ethiopia; he reigned about 700 B.C. But there were undoubtedly temples and shrines on the island before that date, probably as early as the eighteenth dynasty. The temples of Philae were considered so sacred that the very rocks shared their sanctity, and the rugged granite appears unexpectedly among the buildings, for no chisel or other tool might cut away a fragment.

The temples now standing are of late date, chiefly of the Ptolemaic period, and many of them are dedicated to Isis, that great mother-goddess whose worship was carried far and wide over the ancient world. Philae was one of her chief shrines, and it was thronged with pilgrims. So strong was the feeling towards these temples that even after the establishment of Christianity in Egypt the worship of Isis still continued at Philae, and pilgrims still came to pray at the shrine of the goddess. It was not until churches dedicated to the Virgin were built on the sites of some of the Isis chapels that the worship was diverted into Christian lines; this was about the fifth century A.D.

When a pilgrim visited the holy shrines, he landed at the south end of the island and ascended a flight of steps from the river; he then came into an open court forming the quay. He turned to the left, and found himself between two small temples, one on each side of the entrance to the colonnade. The little temple on the south was built by Nectanebo II., the last native King of Egypt. Here the pilgrim stopped to pay his devotions, and to be purified with the double purification. In the northern temple the pilgrim made offerings to various gods, and was again purified with water and burning incense. He was now fit to proceed towards the great Temple of Isis. He passed slowly up the long double colonnade, either in the open air, under the blinding glare of the sun, or walking in the shade in the roofed aisle at the side, stopping as he went to pray and make offerings at the chapels which led off the eastern colonnade. At the north end of the colonnade towered the great pylon; this he reached and passed through, and found himself in an open court, with a colonnade and chapels on the east side, and on

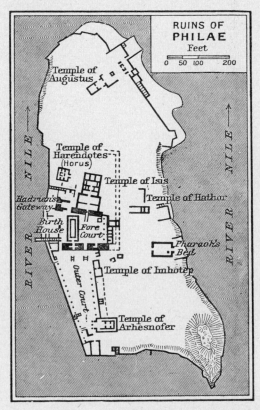

RUINS OF
**PHILAE**
Feet
0   50  100    200

Temple of Augustus

Temple of Harendotes (Horus)

Temple of Isis

Temple of Hathor

Hadrian's Gateway

Birth House

Fore Court

Pharaoh's Bed

Temple of Imhotep

Outer Court

Temple of Arhesnofer

the west the beautiful Birth House. This building was one of the most sacred spots in holy Philae, for it was built to celebrate the birth of Horus, and to honour the divine motherhood of Isis. In this shrine the capitals of the columns are surmounted by the head of Hathor, who at this late period was often regarded as only another form of Isis. Passing through the court, the pilgrim arrived at the second pylon, and there, on ascending a flight of steps, he entered the actual temple of the goddess.

On this temple the Ptolemies had lavished much wealth, each king endeavouring to outdo his predecessor in the splendour of the decoration of the buildings. On every side the walls and pillars glowed with colour, soft and brilliant, for to the artist of the Ptolemaic period it was an honour to give of his best to Isis of Philae.

Passing through the second pylon the pilgrim found himself in a columned hall, of which part was open to the sky and part was roofed in.

Hurrying forward, for his goal was almost reached, the pilgrim entered a little court, which led into the outer and inner vestibules, and at last he bowed before the shrine of the goddess herself. We have no knowledge of what the figure was

**SISTRUM COLUMNS OF THE TEMPLE OF NECTANEBO II. AT PHILAE**

Two sandstone obelisks once stood at the temple gateway; only the base is left of one, the other has lost its apex. The capitals of the sistrum columns represent Hathor (woman's head with heifer's ears) carved in relief on each side of a square block, each head supporting a fluted cornice on which stands a naos flanked by two volutes and crowned by a shallow abacus. The columns are connected by a screen about 6 feet high, surmounted by a concave cornice crowned with rows of uraeus serpents.

Photo from W. M. Flinders Petrie

**SCULPTURED PYLON AND FLOODED FORECOURT OF THE TEMPLE OF ISIS**

The forecourt lies between the two pylons, the second of which is seen in the photograph. On the west side is the colonnaded Birth House dedicated to Hathor, Isis, and Horus. The columns of the Birth House and those in the east side of the forecourt are surmounted with Hathor-headed sistrum capitals. North of the second pylon is a hypostyle hall, and beyond several small chambers lies the secret sanctuary containing a pedestal on which stood the sacred boat with the image of Isis.

Photo by Donald McLeish

like that stood in that holy of holies, but from Greek sources we learn how the goddess appeared in a vision to her votaries. Rising out of the sea, crowned with a wreath of blossoms among which the full moon shone resplendent, she appeared to those who worshipped her. Her robe was the colour of the sunset glow, shot with gold and flame; her cloak was of the velvety blackness of night, scattered over with glittering stars like points of light, and twined about with an endless

PARTIALLY SUBMERGED RUINS OF THE HOLY ISLAND OF PHILAE—

The top photograph shows in the background the island of Biggeh, behind the colonnaded outer court of the Temple of Isis; the first pylon, 150 feet broad and 60 feet high; the forecourt and the second pylon, 105 feet broad and 40 feet high; and, in right foreground, the building familiarly known as Pharaoh's Bed, of which a closer view is given in page 122. Below (left) is a general view of the island before it was flooded. On the right is a photograph (by Francis Frith) of Pharaoh's Bed, as it appeared about the middle of the nineteenth century,

—FAMOUS FOR CENTURIES AS A CENTRE OF THE WORSHIP OF ISIS

when palm trees provided a graceful setting for the beautiful little building. After the Nile dam was completed in 1902, the greater part of the island was submerged during the first half of the year, and only between the months of August and December did the river regain its previous level. With the further raising of the Assuan dam in 1912 and 1932 the buildings are completely submerged during the greater part of the year, and consequent upon water erosion Philae will become in time little more than a treasured memory.

127

garland of fruit and flowers ; and " the ambrosial feet were shod with sandals woven of the leaves of victorious palm."

On each side of both vestibules were small chambers, roofed in and dark ; they were probably chapels in which special rites were celebrated, and would therefore not be often used. If the pilgrim were an initiate into the mysteries of either Isis or Osiris, he would turn back from the shrine after he had paid his devotions to the goddess, and returning through the two vestibules into the little court, he would enter the chamber on the west side. There he would ascend a flight of steps to the flat roof, at each corner of which was a chapel. But it was to only one of these chapels that the initiate would turn—to the one which still bears on its walls the representations of the resurrection of Osiris from the dead.

This was the great Temple of Isis, sculptured and painted in every part, overpowering by its greatness and magnificence the smaller temples which clustered round it on that holy island. Of these smaller temples two are important. One is dedicated to Hathor, goddess of love and beauty, whom the Greeks identified with their own Aphrodite. Here the sculptures are all of a joyous character befitting the ritual of the goddess. The other temple, known as the Kiosk or Pharaoh's Bed, stands on the east side of the island ; it is a rectangle enclosed by pillars with inter-columnar slabs, and is open to the sky above and to all the winds that blow. It also was dedicated to the goddess Isis. Standing as it does high on the rocks above the river, it must have been to the worshippers of Isis, as they approached the island, a visible sign of the beauty and splendour of her temples.

EAST FACADE OF THE BIRTH HOUSE, TEMPLE OF ISIS, PHILAE

The doorway at the head of the steps opens on to the small court leading to the hypostyle hall. The Hathor-headed columns seen in the photograph are on the east side of the Birth House. The small court, in which sacrifices used to be made, is embellished with reliefs of Ptolemy III presenting gifts and pouring water upon a small altar. Near the sanctuary are the Osiris chambers with reliefs referring to the tragic death of the god after whom they are named.

Photo from W. M. Flinders Petrie

**GATEWAY OF PTOLEMY PHILADELPHUS SHOWING PART OF THE COLONNADE**

The granite-covered height in the background is part of the island of Biggeh, the Egyptian Senmet. Each part of the Temple of Isis was appropriated to some special service in the ceremonial worship of the goddess. Courts, chambers, and colonnades are elaborately inscribed, and have afforded much material for the study of Egyptian mythology, the mysteries of the nature and offices of the deities being expressed in more explicit and intelligible terms than was the case before the Ptolemaic and Roman periods.

Photo from W. M. Flinders Petrie

When Isis-worship was finally ousted by Christianity, and Christianity in its turn bowed under the yoke of Islam, Philae's temples fell into decay; but the natural beauty of the island and its surroundings made it one of the most romantic spots in all the Nile valley. The ruins of its marvellous temples, on which the colour still blazed, were seen rising clear and distinct amid feathery palm trees, contrasting in their exquisite beauty with the rugged granite rocks of the island.

The great barrage of Assuan was opened during the early years of this century, and has since been twice increased in height and the last increase in 1932 causes the temples of Philae to be totally submerged during the period of high Nile. The water, heavily laden with red silt, washes through the temples, and every vestige of colour has vanished. The slime of the river stains those walls and pillars which once glowed so brilliantly in the sun. Visitors to those once holy shrines pass by boat through the colonnades and halls where pilgrims knelt in adoration to the mother of all. Though beautiful effects are seen when the pylons and temples are reflected in the placid stream, yet the day must come when the steady lapping of the water will undermine the buildings, and they will fall and become a tumbled heap of ruins. Ichabod, the glory has departed!

GLORIOUS ANTIQUITY OBSCURED IN A POOR MODERN SHROUD

In pages 136 and 137 is a restoration showing the great sea-face of the palace illustrated above ; it will be noticed how the mean erections of modern days have found their support in the ancient masonry of Diocletian's building, and also that the sea has retreated
considerably since ancient times.   Below, the Golden Gate, which is still in fair preservation ; arches once supported by Corinthian
colonnettes and niches for statues are the decoration of its exterior façade of large unmortared blocks.

Upper photo from " La Dalmazia nell' Arte Italiana," by Dudan

## The Royal Palaces. III.

# Diocletian's Palace at Spalato

## By F. N. Pryce

Of the Department of Greek and Roman Antiquities, British Museum

*OF the many architectural legacies that give us an inkling of Rome's great glory in ancient days, probably none is less known to the general reader than the country palace of Diocletian, that Emperor whose inborn astuteness and organizing ability held the Empire together when its state seemed precarious and whose simple ideals led him to renounce the glory of the purple while still in his prime for the pastoral delights of his native province. The great palace is situated on the coast of Dalmatia, that most debatable of all lands, and the fact that this district is off the beaten track of the tourist may account for the cloak of oblivion that overlies the building; yet I should feel that such a work as* WONDERS OF THE PAST *were incomplete if it lacked an account of this great monument.*—EDITOR.

TO a person of average intelligence the Roman Emperors of the first and second centuries of our era are at least vaguely familiar; we can roughly discriminate between the cautious Augustus, the unspeakable Nero, the saintly Marcus Aurelius; we may see their features and physical peculiarities reproduced for us in hard marble in the galleries of the British Museum. But the succeeding third century is an age of wars and rebellions, in the midst of which Emperors rise and fall, leaving little more than a bare name in a dusty chronicle as a record of their existence. Of Diocletian few know more than that he persecuted the Christians, and abdicated to grow cabbages in a garden; indeed, the whole sum of our knowledge is confined to the most meagre outline of his career. Even his personal appearance is unfamiliar: his coins show a bull-necked man with long, straight nose and close-cropped hair and beard; but of the sculptured heads which are sometimes labelled as Diocletian in museums not one can be called a certain identification.

Yet in the long list of Emperors there is no one of whom we so much desire fuller knowledge, for his claim to rank among the greatest of all will not be disputed. If Augustus founded the Empire and ended the civil wars, Diocletian equally founded it anew and gave civilization a respite after fifty terrible years of anarchy. And whereas Augustus possessed all the prestige of nobility as the heir to the dead Julius Caesar, Diocletian started on the lowest rung of the ladder. His parents were slaves in a small provincial town and he entered the army as a private soldier. How he won advancement we do not know, but in A.D. 285, at the age of thirty-nine, he was raised to the Imperial purple by the troops. He was chosen for his fighting abilities, for in those critical times the first duty of a Roman Emperor was to fight; and it does not surprise us that he succeeded in crushing internal rebellions and barbarian invasions, and reestablished the Roman peace. But what is surprising about this uneducated soldier is that, having put down his enemies, he boldly attacked the social and political disorders of the age and strove by a series of reforms as far reaching

**IMPERIAL BUILDER OF SPALATO**

Of obscure Dalmatian parentage, but a born military genius, Diocletian rose to be Emperor in A.D. 285 and became one of the greatest of Rome's later rulers. When the cares of state wearied him, he built as a country retreat the Palace of Spalato.

Capitoline Museum, Rome; photo by Alinari

GRACEFUL ARCADE IN THE SOUTH WALL OF DIOCLETIAN'S PALACE ON THE ADRIATIC

The reader who wishes to gather an adequate conception of the wonderful and lavish style of Diocletian's great house is advised to study this picture in its relation to the most illuminating birds-eye view in the special double page illustration (pp. 136 and 137). This restoration of the southern face shows the fine cloister running along the entire façade between the corner towers, with the decorative arched gates in the middle and at the ends. Before the postern door in the centre of the solid lower wall projects a stone platform used as a landing stage. The present condition of this part of the palace is shown in the photograph in page 130.

After a reconstruction by Hébrard in "Monuments Antiques"

as original to rebuild fundamentally the whole fabric of society in the Roman world.

With one of his reforms we are concerned—his attempt to regulate the succession to the Imperial throne. Historians are agreed that the disasters which befell the Roman world in the third century —disasters from which the western half of the Empire never fully recovered—were largely due to the fact that no fixed principle of legitimacy existed whereby, when an Emperor died or proved incapable, a successor could be peacefully chosen and legally installed. Hence came general insecurity and frequent civil wars in the midst of which the barbarians seized their opportunity. To prevent further confusion and to ensure adequate supervision of the threatened frontiers, Diocletian ordained that there should always be two Emperors reigning contemporaneously, together with two "Caesars," who were to succeed automatically. And having thus done what lay in his power for the future welfare of the State, on May 1, 305, at Ismid near Constantinople, he divested himself of the diadem which he, first of all the Emperors, had dared to wear, and retired into private life. He was not yet sixty years of age and though twenty years of strenuous rule had left their mark on him, there can be little doubt that his object was largely to put his system to the test of a practical experiment. This much can be said, that his abdication was due to no sudden impulse, as some years previously he had commenced the building of a residence to house him in his retirement.

The site he had selected was one of the fairest spots on the beautiful coast of Dalmatia, his native province, a few miles from the city of Salona. Here between the mountains and the sea the modern town of Spalato stands largely within the walls of Diocletian's palace, which include an area of over nine acres. Some idea of the pomp which surrounded a Roman Emperor may be gained when we reflect that at a time when the Empire was long past its zenith in wealth and population an Emperor could build a palace larger than the Escurial of Spain as a country villa in which to spend his declining years. More than six centuries later a Byzantine Emperor, himself born in the purple, declared that in its ruin it surpassed all powers of description. Even to-day, when the mean edifices of the modern town have overgrown it, its vast proportions and solid construction excite astonishment. Fortunately, despite all modern alterations, the principal internal buildings and most of the exterior walls are still standing.

Like many other Roman buildings, the palace had but little of beauty or of the picturesque in its external appearance. It was a quadrangle surrounded by walls of uniform height, broken by low towers. The general proportions were low and squat and the impression must have been that of a walled town rather than of a single residence. It is only on a near approach that the vast scale is perceived. Though low relatively to the length of the sides which vary from 570 to 700 feet, the walls themselves are nowhere less than 50 feet in height, which in some places, owing to the fall of the ground, becomes over 70 feet. The material is a fine limestone little inferior to marble.

The external decoration is limited to the south side, facing the sea, where an open cloister runs along the whole of the upper part of the front, and to the gates, of which one opens in the centre of each side. Otherwise the exterior walls are those of a fortress, plain and unbroken save for a defensive gallery. On the sea front little danger was to be apprehended and here the long range of cloister arches not only provides a fine architectural feature, but reveals an appreciation of natural beauty hardly to be expected of the designer of the grim battlemented walls. The four gates are named respectively the Golden on the north, Silver on the south, Brazen on the east, and Iron on the west. The Golden Gate is richly adorned with Corinthian colonnettes and arcades; the others are similarly but less abundantly decorated; the Brazen Gate no longer exists, having been replaced by a mean modern doorway.

Within the gates the plan is cunningly contrived on a scale of increasing splendour. Two streets crossing one another divide the palace into quarters, save that the main street, running north and south, does not extend through to the south, but stops in front of the Imperial apartments which occupy the whole south front, facing the sea. This arrangement, like the exterior, recalls to us the traditional lay-out of a Roman camp. Entering at the Golden Gate, we should originally have found ourselves in a street about 36 feet wide, running south to the vestibule of the palace proper, and intersected in the centre by a similar street running east and west. Both streets were lined with arcades, as was usual in the Roman cities of the Orient, one of many reasons which have led archæologists to suppose that the architects of the palace came from the eastern half of the Empire.

Much of this has now disappeared, and the two blocks of buildings which occupied the northern quarters are in too ruinous a state for a certain determination of their purpose. One may have been the quarters of the officers of the guard, the other may have contained domestic offices. Around them, inside the walls, ran a row of small chambers which were probably the barracks and stables of the guard. Continuing our advance southward from the crossing, everything up to the palace entrance remains practically complete to this day. The low side arcades of the street are replaced by lofty and graceful rows of columns of " cipollino " marble and red granite, which form open screens through which on either side was seen an enclosed court containing a temple.

On the east is the Temple of Jupiter, now the cathedral. This is an octagon surrounded externally by a colonnade; in front was originally a projecting portico, which has been removed to make way for the superb medieval Campanile, the most conspicuous feature of the modern town. The interior is circular with a domed roof and two tiers of columns, the lower of granite, the upper alternately porphyry and granite. The tradition that this building was a temple of Jupiter is very ancient, but some authorities have suggested that it was originally Diocletian's tomb. It has been a Christian church since A.D. 650. Two Egyptian sphinxes of black granite, probably of the eighteenth dynasty, originally stood one on each side of the entrance. One is still to be seen in the court, the other is in the museum. In the western court is a small oblong shrine, on a lofty base, originally faced with a portico of four columns which has now disappeared. The doorway is richly sculptured; it is $15\frac{3}{4}$ feet in height, $7\frac{3}{4}$ feet in width, and with true Roman magnificence is composed of only three stones. At present it is used as the baptistery; but the same tradition which assigns its neighbour to Jupiter gives it the title of Temple of Aesculapius.

Between these two courts the peristyle ends in a flight of steps and another portico, the entrance to the Imperial apartments; beyond this was the vestibule, a circular room with a dome, now fallen, which leads into the grand hall or throne room, a stately saloon nearly 100 feet in length. The whole of this area is now thickly built over with modern habitations and the actual arrangement of the interior is largely a matter of conjecture based on such scraps of ancient stonework as are still visible. The most recent investigators consider that on each side of the grand hall was a corridor flanked by six small rooms, perhaps sleeping apartments or guest chambers. To the west of these came a second large saloon, perhaps a library, and beyond were the Emperor's private apartments which included another large reception room and a set of baths. To the east came first the state dining-room, and beyond this the private suite of the Empress Prisca. At a lower level, leading from each side of the vestibule, were various apartments some of which no doubt were used as kitchens; the others would be domestic offices.

It is not impossible that another storey may have extended over at least parts of the ground floor, but of this there are no remains. In any case, the main halls were only one storey high and lighted from the top or by clerestories. Internally they were no doubt bright with marble and mosaic and the courts must have been gay with flowers and plants, but there was no view of the outside save from the portico along the southern face, or perhaps from terraces on the roof.

Such was the home Diocletian built himself. As the monument of a remarkable man, and also as the best preserved of all Roman Imperial palaces and the most eloquent witness to a magnificence of which we can form but an imperfect conception, its interest is abiding. To lovers of art it has another value in that it marks an era in architecture—the end of the ancient, the beginning of the medieval styles. Gibbon observes icily that the " awful ruins of Spalato are not less expressive of the decline of the arts than of the greatness of the Empire." But a more recent critic, Freeman, gives to the architect of Spalato the honour of " taking the greatest step ever taken, the beginning of all later forms of consistent arched architecture."

Greek architecture is one of flat lintels, medieval architecture is one of arches. Roman building shows the transition between the two. The Roman inherited the Greek tradition and set to work to improve on it. The old criticism of Roman architecture that it is a degraded copy of the Greek, because Roman buildings do not show the exquisite proportions or the finished detail of Greece, misses the point ; the Roman was pre-occupied with experiments in construction which had never entered the head of a Greek. And seeing that his experiments led him towards the arch and the vault, the Roman architect was in constant revolt against his Greek masters who had refused to accept the arch.

As an example of this clash of styles, we may take the exterior of the great Colosseum at Rome. Here is a Roman building with a Greek covering to satisfy contemporary taste. The rows of pilasters and flat architraves are Greek, but they are entirely unstructural ; they are simply orna-ment added to the vaulted Roman building behind them. Now, the interest of the Palace of Spalato lies in the fact that it is the earliest building known to us in which the two styles are successfully blended, and in it we may even trace the develop-ment in the mind of the architect. At the Golden Gate (see page 130) the whole of the structural

work is performed by the massive discharging arch, but the flat Greek lintel is still retained ; it is a useless encumbrance, but the architect has not been able to shake free from tradition. But in the colonnades of the interior the true solution has been reached after centuries of experiment : the architect has omitted the flat architrave, and made his arches spring directly from the columns. From this innovation dates the birth of the Byzantine, the Romanesque and, eventually, the Gothic styles of building.

Diocletian lived to occupy the palace for about nine years. They were not years of peaceful rest such as he had anticipated and merited. Scarcely had he resigned authority when the civil wars he had so painfully suppressed broke out anew between the men among whom he had divided the Empire. To us such an event seems the inevitable result of the division, but it is curious how Diocletian's scheme haunted the minds of succeed-ing Emperors ; the Roman Empire was quite beyond the control of any single man. Less than two years after his abdication, the contending parties appealed to him to resume office and once again to save the State ; this is a striking proof of the prestige he enjoyed. But he rejected the proposal, observing to the ambassadors that if they could but see the cabbages he had planted with his own hands, they would not urge him to abandon his simple happiness for the pursuit of power. This answer was probably prompted less by a love of nature than by a feeling of anger that his life work had been wrecked ; but it would have been well for Rome and for him had he listened to the appeal. The civil wars continued with increasing intensity and ferocity. His wife and daughter were captured by one of the factions and barbarously murdered ; and it is said that he himself committed suicide to escape insult from men whom he had originally raised to power.

After his death in A.D. 313, the palace was never again used as an Imperial residence but was allowed to fall into decay ; merchants from Salona established rope-walks in the porticoes. In 639 Salona fell into the hands of Slav invaders and was destroyed and the inhabitants sought refuge within the massive walls of Diocletian's home until such time as the barbarians should depart ; but finding that the intruders were like to settle permanently in the land, they obtained permission from the Court of Constantinople to abandon Salona and to make a permanent home within the now desolate palace. This was the beginning of the modern town of Spalato.

# The Study of the Past. V.

# The Doom of Cities

## by Hamilton Fyfe

WRITING about the ruins of Babylon, Sir Austen Layard, the explorer of dead cities, said: ' The traveller visits with no common emotion the scene of so many great and solemn events. Here Nebuchadnezzar boasted of his glories and was punished for his pride. To those deserted halls were brought the captives of Judea. In them Daniel, undazzled by the glories round him, remained steadfast to his faith, rose to be a governor amongst his rulers, and prophesied the downfall of the kingdom. There was held Belshazzar's feast and was seen the writing on the wall. Between those crumbling mounds Cyrus entered the neglected gates. Those massive ruins cover the spot where Alexander died.'

Wherever the feet tread upon ground that once was the site of a famous city, the same feeling is stirred. Not many ruins have for our imaginations such a stimulating charm as those of Babylon. But from all the cities of ancient times, of which there now remain only faint memories and heaps of mouldering stone, we draw something of the same stimulus. Tiryns, Mycenae, Troy, Persepolis — their very names sound grand and melancholy. As we walk over the spots where stood their temples and palaces, where ran their streets and stood their market places, we are forced to reflect upon the insubstantial reality of all the works of man, even those that seem most surely destined to endure.

How can it be that the populations of cities decrease, their edifices perish, their very sites become uncertain? Their being torn down by enemies we can understand. The destruction of Pompeii and Herculaneum by lava and ash from volcanoes we can picture. But how does it happen that cities are covered gradually with soil, buried, hidden? Even though it takes centuries to accomplish, such a doom is hard to comprehend. Yet upon all the famous cities of the past it fell, and in course of time must fall on those of our own age.

Babylon is the one among all the cities of remote antiquity which we can best picture to ourselves. We know that it was of vast size, though how long exactly the circuit of its walls we cannot tell. Herodotus said the city covered 126 square miles. But it must have increased very much by the time the final walls were built, since they were fifteen miles each way, and the area thus enclosed would amount to 225 square miles. The size of Greater London at the present time runs into about seven hundred square miles, which have nearly eight millions of people living on them. In the ancient world there were no such populations as this. Yet Babylon was assuredly a great city, even by our standards.

BABYLONIA (of which it was the capital) and Chaldaea, its next-door neighbour, were countries teeming with inhabitants. To-day they are known as Irak, and Irak is sparsely inhabited. The reason for the change is that the irrigation once so carefully provided and maintained was allowed to cease. The land therefore ceased to be fertile. The need for a great city passed away. Of Babylon's greatness we have ample testimony. In the walls were a hundred gates of brass, upon them were 250 towers. The plan of the city was rectangular. All the streets were straight, and round the squares which they formed the private houses were built, with gardens in the middle. The houses were detached, and most had three or four storeys. They were decorated inside and out with tiles. Pottery and glass used by the Babylonians was of fine quality. Carpets and rugs of silk and wool abounded; rich garments of those materials were worn.

The river Euphrates ran past the city, and its water was distributed by a very efficient canal system. Herodotus thought these canals were for purposes of defence, but it seems clear that they were made to keep the soil well watered. Within the walls, which were of

**RESTORED TO DAYLIGHT AFTER CENTURIES**
Lava 100 feet deep in places buried Herculaneum so that for centuries even its site was forgotten. To-day, with scientific care excavators are bringing to light its public buildings, private houses and shops with all their treasures of art and appointments of its highly cultured life.

## WONDER PALACE OF A ROMAN EMPEROR WHO RESIGNED—

Resembling more a walled and turreted township than the country seat of an emperor, Diocletian's Palace was singularly plain as to exterior decoration, and it is only on the southern façade in which appears the pillared terrace that this plainness is not found. Built in quadrilateral plan, the walls rise in places to 70 feet, varying in length from 570 to 700 feet, and are of limestone. Inside are two main streets that cross in the centre of the complex and run to the wall gates, these being on the north the Golden, on the east the Brazen, on the

*After a reconstruction by—*

## —THE MASTERY OF THE WORLD FOR A COUNTRY LIFE

south the Silver and on the west the Iron. Just behind the south wall are the great halls of the Imperial quarters with a view over the Adriatic from their windows, having in the centre the vestibule, an architectural feature which is remarkable because its interior arches rise directly from supporting Corinthian columns; here for the first time in Roman architecture we find no lintel or architrave. The octagonal building behind it is the Temple of Jupiter, and the oblong shrine to its left is that of Aesculapius. Colonnades flanked both streets.

*—Hébrard in " Monuments Antiques "*

## MARTS AND STREETS WHERE THE LIFE OF POMPEII ONCE PULSED

The baleful lava of Vesuvius proved to be an excellent preservative, and thus the completeness with which it buried Pompeii renders it one of the most instructive places in the world. The Civil Forum (top) is a better revelation than anything in Rome itself of this feature of Roman urban life. Even more eloquent is the lower photograph of a recently excavated street with houses and taverns. It tells us that they were protected by substantial awnings such as that over the quadruple windows of the second house on the left.

immense thickness in places, at any rate sixty feet, was included much agricultural land and pasture, enough to make the city self-supporting and to save it from famine in the event of a siege. But its prosperous commerce, due to its position, filled it with luxuries from afar, and men of all climes were to be seen in its streets, drawn by curiosity or business. On rafts of skins and in boats made of reeds plastered together with bitumen, the merchandise came and went, while caravans started frequently to trade by land. So the 'golden city,' as it was called, became 'the praise of the whole earth' until one of its rulers decided to move his capital to the Tigris and pulled down many of Babylon's buildings to serve as material for the new city (Seleucia). By the beginning of the Christian era there was next to no Babylon left. The doom foretold by the prophets Isaiah and Jeremiah had been fulfilled. It had been 'swept with the besom of destruction'; where it stood so proudly was 'the possession of the bittern and pools of water.' It had 'become heaps, if not 'a dwelling-place for dragons'; it was 'an astonishment' and almost 'without a habitation.'

NINEVEH the splendid was on the Tigris also. In the Bible it is described as 'an exceeding great city.' Its walls, a hundred feet in height, with more than a thousand towers, were broad enough to allow of three chariots being driven on them side by side. The total circuit of this formidable defence was some sixty miles. Here, as in Babylon, orchards, gardens, cultivated fields and grass meadows formed part of the city. There was evidently a desire to live inside rather than outside the walls, not only for purposes of society, but because life there was more secure.

Courtesy of The Daily Telegraph

**STATELY STAIRWAY RUINED BY THE FOOTSTEPS OF TIME**

Jerash in Transjordania is an example of the completeness with which a neglected city may gradually become covered over with earth. The cracked lintel of a gateway above a mass of soil and broken masonry (bottom) was the clue to the excavation of the magnificent stairway to the Church (top), called the Fountain Church from the fountain in its courtyard.

**LOST CITIES AND HISTORIC SITES THAT ECHO ALEXANDER'S NAME**

Many cities have been built upon the Bhir mound of Taxila in the Punjab, where Alexander the Great rested his Macedonians before advancing to his victorious attack upon Porus, King of India. A corner of the uppermost of these cities is shown in ruin in the lower photograph. Alexander founded several cities bearing his name on his way to India. Some of these are known under their modern names—Herat, Khojend, Kandahar : but in the deserts of Afghanistan are ruins of other towns (top), quite probably other Alexandrias.

Not that the inhabitants were altogether free from anxiety. The Tigris overflowed at times and caused great damage. A vast dam was built, however, both to control the turbulence of the stream in spring, and to keep the supply of water to the city steady in the summer heats.

That they were skilled in arts and industries is sure. Even before the rise of Babylon Nineveh had silversmiths and engravers of gems. Before any systematic excavation was started many finds of such work must have been made, and the objects destroyed. For example, a Turk building a house and digging for stone discovered in a hillside tomb a woman's ankle ornament and a child's, both of silver ; a bracelet of gold beads, an engraved agate.

The ornaments were at once melted down and the agate thrown away. So perished much that would have helped us to reconstitute the life and habits of the Assyrians ruled over by kings with names as familiar to us as Tiglath-Pileser and Sennacherib.

Flourishing in Egypt at the time of Nineveh's splendour were Memphis and Thebes, capitals of the northern and the southern Kingdoms into which that land was divided. Of Memphis there is left nothing but the Pyramids and the Sphinx (see page 155) ; they were outside the city and were erected before it grew to its full extent. Two colossal statues of a Rameses probably adorned Memphis, but of the city itself there seemed to be no traces left until in the latter part of the

RAISED FROM A DESERT TOMB: TWO CAPITAL CITIES OF A VANISHED PAST

Capital of the Southern Kingdom of Egypt, Thebes in its long story received the attention of all the builder Pharaohs. Yet the Temple of Karnak (see also pages 190 to 198) is all that remains of that once proud city. All else is laid in ruins as here shown. Even greater ruin has overtaken El Amarna, the city built by the religious reformer Akhnaton. Of that vainglorious attempt only the eastern portion (top) has been recovered from the sands, the houses where lived the men who quarried the stone for its building.

nineteenth century excavators were able to show what its lay-out was and to exhibit many interesting things which have lain under the desert sand for thousands of years.

Of Thebes much more remained though the ruins were buried beneath rubbish and in places actually built over. Great clearances have been made and the plan of the city, with some of its buildings, revealed. Most valuable in adding to our knowledge was the discovery of the royal and other tombs. That there were kings and other persons of importance buried near Thebes was suspected. Objects which had pretty clearly come from such places of burial were offered for sale in the bazaars of Cairo. Yet all efforts to learn where they came from failed.

Then in 1881 a clue was obtained, with the result that a well was sunk in the hope of striking an underground passage. Into this the well-shaft broke at a depth of thirty-eight feet, and when the passage had been followed for about an eighth of a mile the explorers found themselves in a large rock-hewn chamber filled with coffins and mummies which had at some time been collected and stored away here for safety.

Thebes at one time suffered a set-back. Akhnaton, the King of Egypt who turned sun-worshipper and did his best to change the old religion of Amen, resolved to build a new capital. At El Amarna he laid out his city with temples, palaces, gardens, streets of houses. It must have been a

THE EXCEEDING GREAT CITY ON THE TIGRIS

Where stands the little Irak town of Nebi Yunus, conspicuous for little except the mound that holds the tomb of Jonah and a mosque where the Prophet is said to have preached, there was once the great Assyrian city of Nineveh. Its doom was overwhelming. Not a trace remains of its walls, which were 100 feet high, and so broad that three chariots could be driven abreast.

impressive in the Egyptian style. Then Thebes became a world-wonder. The very name of El Amarna would to-day be forgotten but for a chance find by some Arab peasants (in 1888) of cuneiform tablets which were deciphered by scholars and proved to be letters exchanged between certain Pharaohs and the kings and governors of western Asia. These Tell-el-Amarna tablets changed all previous ideas about the history of this period (round about 1400 B.C.) and added greatly to our knowledge of the ancient world.

Coming down to the opening of the Christian era we find that Ephesus claimed at that time to be the 'first city in Asia.' It was important for many reasons, chief among them the wide fame of the goddess Artemis, or Diana, as she is called in the Bible. She was not the slim, graceful huntress of the Greeks, 'Maiden most perfect, lady of light.' She was the goddess of fertility and was represented as enormous in bulk and with many breasts. Yet, strangely enough, the priests of Artemis were all celibate and none but virgins could serve her as priestesses. The temple of 'Diana of the Ephesians' was immensely rich through gifts and legacies. It was noted for its architecture and magnificence. When the Goths fell upon it in 262, they found it an easy prey. After that malaria raged and doom descended upon the city.

place of rare beauty, for this was the best period of Egyptian art and the king was a man of taste, a poet, a lover of the beautiful. In glaze and colour the pottery of that period was very fine ; so was the glass-ware. The court moved to El Amarna. A large number of the inhabitants of Thebes went with it. It seemed as if the great days of the city which had long been the Southern capital were over.

But Akhnaton had under-estimated the power of the priesthood. He fancied it was only necessary to preach a nobler religion and everyone would gladly adopt it. He learned that the old religion, because it was familiar and traditional, had a firm hold on the public mind. The priests waited sullenly for his death, and then all signs of sun-worship disappeared. Akhnaton's successor went back to Thebes, which became more prosperous and magnificent than ever. Then arose the temple of Karnak, with its massive columns, many of which can still be seen, heavily

Dramatic and terrible was the fate of the cities on the Mediterranean shore overwhelmed by the eruption of Vesuvius in A.D. 79. Yet their doom was our advantage, for when the cinders and the lava came to be cleared away after many centuries, Pompeii especially and, to a less degree, Herculaneum were found so well preserved that we can understand, as we never could have understood without them, the way in which Romans of the early Empire lived. To many Pompeii is the most interesting place in the world. Studying its ruins, reconstructing the lives of its inhabitants, we get a grip on the reasons why civilizations break up, why cities decay. For Vesuvius only hastened an end which would have come in any event from internal causes, as the end came to ancient Rome, though in her case as in no other a second great city arose after a long interval to take the doomed one's place.

Ancient Arts and Crafts I.

# Master Artists of the Stone Age

## Pictures that were Painted more than 12,000 Years ago.

### By E. G. Harmer, F.R.A.I.

#### Writer on Anthropology and Archæology

*OF all wonders of the past, there is none that makes a stronger appeal to the imagination than the paintings that still survive from the Stone Age in the caves of Altamira and Font-de-Gaume ; none that so stuns the mind with a sense of awesome antiquity, compared to which the Pyramids themselves seem modern ! It is humiliating to our pride of progress to contemplate the perfection of line and technique attained by artists who painted in dark caverns more than 12,000 years ago. These drawings, copied by the Abbé Henri Breuil, are here reproduced from the two great works " La Caverne de Font-de-Gaume Aux Eyzies (Dordogne)," by Capitan, Breuil and Peyrony, and " La Caverne d'Altamira à Santillane (Espagne)," by Cartailhac and Breuil. Other aspects of the art of the Old Stone Age are considered and illustrated in a later chapter by Dr R. R. Marett.*—EDITOR.

ON a bleak winter day late in 1879 a Spanish nobleman, Don Marcelino de Sautuola, was engaged in exploring a prehistoric cave close by his home at Santillana. It was one of the many long and tortuous galleries which ancient rainstorms carved out of the limestone ridges overlooking the Bay of Biscay behind Santander. Some years before a hound followed a fox into this unknown " earth," and in order to save it the huntsmen enlarged the hole, but had no eyes for what lay within. Even when, as time went on, the explorer turned his thoughts to this fox-hole, his sole hope was to add to the store of flint implements, fossil bones, and other Stone Age remains which he had unearthed within its entrance four years before.

On this fateful November day Don Marcelino was groping about in a gallery so low that he could not stand upright in it. His little girl, who chanced to be with him, was making observations of her own in greater freedom, when she suddenly stood still, and cried out " Toros " (bulls). When her father turned to her he found her pointing to the roof, where, to his amazement, he descried a group of fresco paintings. Even with his dim illuminant there were revealed, drawn with lifelike vigour in gleaming reds, blacks and yellows, a score of bison, some boar, a deer, and other game.

When, a few months afterwards, the existence of a prehistoric academy in a Spanish cave was announced to the world, its discoverer drew upon himself much scornful scepticism. But before very long the walls of other caves, far and near, revealed, one by one, examples of the same vivacious art, and to-day thousands of these paintings and engravings, enshrined in more than fifty caves, are recognized as the authentic achievements of the world's first artists.

Let us select for consideration the three outermost subjects in the great ceiling fresco already mentioned. It lies over an alcove within a cavern now immortalized under the name of a neighbouring meadow, Altamira. The bison which, like many of its companions, is 5 feet long, is the best conserved of them all. The red and black body-colour was lightened by scraping on the loins and other salient parts, while a stone burin gave definiteness to eye, horn and muzzle, the fore hoof, and the whip of the quivering tail.

The deer, $7\frac{1}{2}$ feet long, exhibits equal mastery of form with a somewhat different technique. The subject is firmly and yet delicately outlined in black. After the addition of the red body-colour in a uniform layer the effect of chiaroscuro was secured by scraping, while near the rump a dry chalky mass was impasted, as if by a palette knife. The eye was badly placed, and an ineffective attempt made to efface it. The galloping boar, $5\frac{1}{2}$ feet long, being nearest to the entrance, has suffered most from recent atmospheric condensation. Yet it still retains its pristine vitality, and the skilful way in which it was worked over imparts to the drawing a singular quality of brightness.

Two decades elapsed before a learned French abbé, Henri Breuil, lit upon another great subterranean gallery high up on a cliff side in a romantic Dordogne valley. This cavern of Font-de-Gaume, separated from the Cantabrian art centre by more than three hundred miles, maintained a school of painting animated by the same high purpose, the same vivacity of portraiture. So uniform is the style that it would not be easy at a glance to say

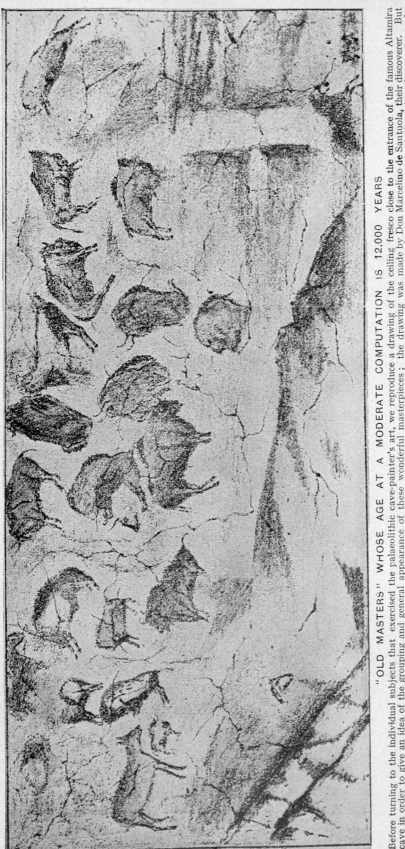

"OLD MASTERS" WHOSE AGE AT A MODERATE COMPUTATION IS 12,000 YEARS

Before turning to the individual subjects that exercised the palaeolithic cave-painter's art, we reproduce a drawing of the ceiling fresco close to the entrance of the famous Altamira cave in order to give an idea of the grouping and general appearance of these wonderful masterpieces; the drawing was made by Don Marcelino de Sautuola, their discoverer. But no less important is it for their true appreciation to get some idea of their immeasurable antiquity. Bald figures at best mean little, and in any case the dating of such remote epochs is so uncertain that some authorities double or halve the results of others. Let it be said then that the Palaeolithic or Old Stone Age, to the latter part of which these paintings belong, covered at the lowest estimate a period of 100,000 years

of an unlabelled bison that it was a "Font-de-Gaume" and not an "Altamira." But this more northerly academy also drew animals of which the Cantabrian painters seem to have known little, if anything at all.

There is, for example, a drawing of the long extinct woolly rhinoceros, sketched in with swift red strokes upon the wall. The economy of effort which suggests not only the woolliness of the pelt but also the rotundity of the body, the careful delineation of the horns and other details of the anatomy, all merit unstinted praise. Another experiment, equally successful, is observable in the mural drawing of a wolf. The animal was drawn in black upon a panel of red paint, and then touched up by skilful scraping. Still more agreeable is a group of two reindeer facing each other, the heads lowered as if browsing. The antlers are shown partly in full face, and the whole composition exhibits the marvellous proficiency of this primeval art at its best.

Of these polychrome frescoes the reproduction has been made possible by the assiduity and skill of the Abbé Breuil himself. Others, done in monochrome, reveal a similar level of artistry. Among them line drawings in black of the mammoth abound. The massive bulk, hairy integument and purposeful tusks are delineated with a sureness of touch that points to their having been drawn from the life by contemporary man. So too with the horse, which in every period covered by the cave art may have been as yet no more than

PAINTING RIVALLING MODERN SCHOOLS OF AN ANIMAL LONG EXTINCT

Unlike the browsing reindeer, this woolly rhinoceros (one-fifth original size) is an outline drawing done in red with bold, free, un-hesitating strokes that admirably indicate his pelt and anticipate the impressionist art of to-day. But even as we realize this there comes the thought that the animal thus portrayed *is now extinct*. How long is it since reindeer roamed a glacial Southern France ? How long since the woolly rhinoceros was a danger to hunters ? About 10,000 years is the least ever proposed, but 15,000 years or more would be considered a moderate reckoning by some experts exact dating is practically impossible.

wild game. Several varieties are clearly distinguished, as in the admirable sketches of heads at Altamira and elsewhere, or the virile profiles of Hornos de la Pena and Niaux, on opposite slopes of the Pyrenees.

As for cave-bear, there is a fine study of one in an erect posture at Font-de-Gaume, and another, in the act of ambling, in the neighbouring grotto of Les Combarelles. Fish are rarer, but on the floor of the great Niaux cave sanctuary are engraved some salmon-trout, while on the wall of the romantic cavern of El Pindal on the Spanish coast, approachable only from the sea, there is a fine engraving of a tunny. Birds are scantier still, both in art and in the kitchen refuse, perhaps because the bow and arrow had not as yet been born.

Of the remote antiquity of this remarkable art there is now no question. Some examples have been preserved behind films of stalactite whose deposition demands prolonged periods of time. Some lay concealed beneath the household litter of later tribal communities whose handiwork is mingled with the bones of animals which became extinct, either in Western Europe or in the whole wide world, before recorded history began. At the great Spanish cave of Castillo, a rival of Altamira, some works were clawed by cave-bears of a type that did not survive the artists themselves.

This whole art movement, indeed, pertains to a civilization whose apogee was reached before ever man smelted a metallic ore, burned a clay pot

wove garments out of wool or flax, or knew aught of the tillage of the ground and the taming of animals. It synchronises with what are called the Aurignacian and Magdalenian epochs of the Upper Palaeolithic or Old Stone Age—the first-named epoch being so called from the cave of Aurignac, in Haute-Garonne, France, where industrial remains of the age and type in question were first reported in 1861, and the other epoch deriving its name from the ruins of La Madeleine in Dordogne. At that time Western Europe was occupied by a long-headed race, whose livelihood depended upon the toilsome quest of game and the cunning of the fisher's art. It was the hunting life at its highest, and yet, for all its remoteness, it was the threshold of the modern world.

The palette of these first artists was resourceful in the extreme. From ferruginous earths they prepared reds, yellows and browns. For black they used manganese oxide as well as lamp-black. For white they had chalk and, later on, china clay. Where ochreous deposits were plentiful, as at Noailles, eastward of Font-de-Gaume, the gamut ranged from pale yellow, orange, rose and vermilion to purple, maroon, brown, sepia, dark blue and black. Sometimes the pigments were stored in tubular bones, and after being rubbed down in stone or horn mortars were spread with animal fat by bone spatulas upon schist palettes, shoulder-blades or bivalve shells. Crayons were fashioned from lumps of pigment, and sometimes

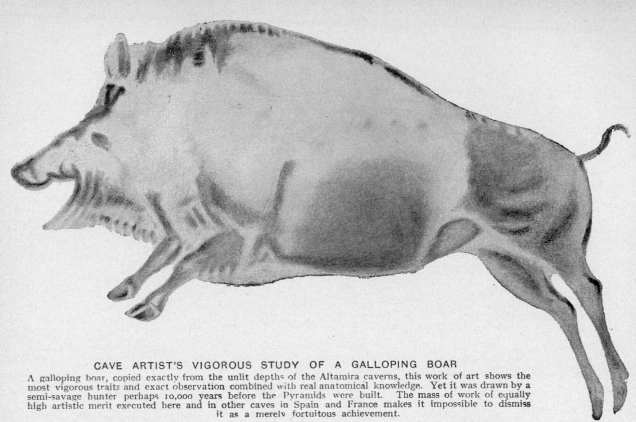

## CAVE ARTIST'S VIGOROUS STUDY OF A GALLOPING BOAR

A galloping boar, copied exactly from the unlit depths of the Altamira caverns, this work of art shows the most vigorous traits and exact observation combined with real anatomical knowledge. Yet it was drawn by a semi-savage hunter perhaps 10,000 years before the Pyramids were built. The mass of work of equally high artistic merit executed here and in other caves in Spain and France makes it impossible to dismiss it as a merely fortuitous achievement.

## SLENDER DEER DEFTLY DRAWN

This delicate drawing of a red deer could hardly be surpassed by any modern painter of animal life although it was " hung " in its palaeolithic gallery something like 15,000 years ago. In the opposite page are examples of the signs that puzzle interpretation; some, as those in the centre, have been called " tectiform " from a supposed resemblance to houses and it has also been suggested that they represent traps.

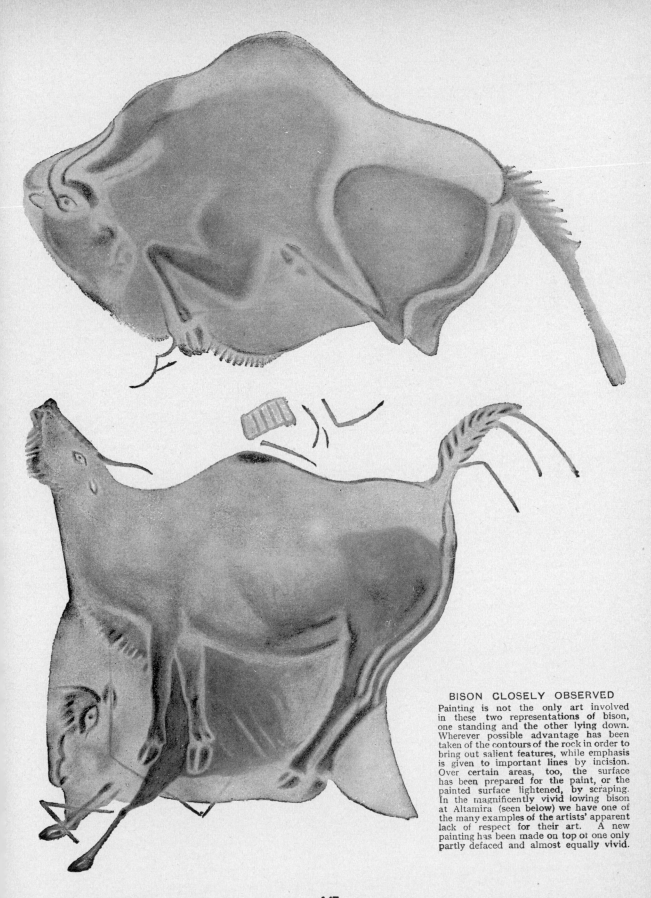

### BISON CLOSELY OBSERVED

Painting is not the only art involved in these two representations of bison, one standing and the other lying down. Wherever possible advantage has been taken of the contours of the rock in order to bring out salient features, while emphasis is given to important lines by incision. Over certain areas, too, the surface has been prepared for the paint, or the painted surface lightened, by scraping. In the magnificently vivid lowing bison at Altamira (seen below) we have one of the many examples of the artists' apparent lack of respect for their art. A new painting has been made on top of one only partly defaced and almost equally vivid.

**UPSTANDING BULL THAT SEEMS ARRESTED IN MID-GALLOP**
Hitherto we have been considering painting in which colours, one or several, were employed. But Font-de-Gaume can also produce works executed in black that stand in relation to our modern charcoal drawings ; the pigment was obtained from lamp-black or manganese oxide. Such is this bull whose proud spirit seems unabated by the lapse of time. Reproduction between one-seventh and one-eighth original size , that of the wolf below about one-fourteenth.

nomad hunters of the pre-metallic age, utilising to the full the resources at their command, were ever reaching out for new conquests of the mind.

At first the contours were made upon soft clays by the bare fingers, or by pronged substitutes for them. When harder surfaces were attacked graving tools were contrived out of flint points and scrapers, until these in their turn gave way before the brush and the chisel-edged pencil. At one stage the natural projections of the rock were utilised for forms of low relief : sometimes the flattening of the rock around the contour achieved similar results. The value of line and stipple was appreciated, and there was thus no lack of variety in the art forms.

While the palaeolithic " old masters " are best known by their mural frescoes, they doubtless used other media as well. The presumption that, in

pierced for suspension round the neck. Of all these artists' materials actual specimens survive, with the exception of the brushes themselves.

This astonishing art did not spring up in a night. Its development has been patiently traced out by the unrivalled genius of Henri Breuil and by a host of other workers. There are to be recognized four main phases in its history, beginning with the early Aurignacian meanders and culminating in the Magdalenian frescoes ; it was a time of progress, of unceasing purpose. These primeval hunters were not degenerate savages, but the flower of mankind, bearing within themselves the promise and potency of ages yet to be. The

**THE SCOURGE OF THE PALAEOLITHIC HUNTSMAN**
Another procedure is illustrated by the head and forequarters of a wolf from the cave at Font-de-Gaume ; it is done in black outline and shading on a prepared surface of red. What is so striking about these paintings is their absolute sureness of touch. Of many animals drawn in later ages we can only say that they are animals ; but who could doubt that this is a wolf ?

Master Artists of the Stone Age

the forest glades and on the river banks, they made preliminary studies upon slices of bark or prepared skins, and employed them as memory aids for the subterranean works, is not unreasonable. That in the useful crafts, as well as for art training, materials were enlisted which have long since perished cannot be doubted. The cave art, unequal though it be, was essentially mature. Art students no more dreamed of misusing the cave walls as a practising school than their living successors would desecrate a chancel with elementary studies. Except on engraved stones and horns the trial pieces have passed away. An inspection of these early works, however casual, inevitably incites an inquiry as to their motive and purpose. Were the drawings the outcome of a desire, on the part of the beholder no less than of the craftsman, for

THE HORSE PORTRAYED IN BLACK AND GREY

Two horses are placed together in this page for comparison, this from Font-de-Gaume, and the one below from Altamira. The example above is done in shaded black, and apart from the unrivalled vigour of the pose shows the complete mastery attained over chiaroscuro effects. It must be remembered that the horse was undomesticated as yet and hunted as game.

the pure pleasures of art? Are we here in the presence of a manifestation of the aesthetic sense, the feeling after ideal beauty, and of that alone?

To answer this question the conditions under which the pictorial art is presented claim attention. The most primitive works were executed, not only in tortuous caves bereft of daylight, but almost always in their remotest recesses, and in these alone. Among the many caverns near Font-de-Gaume there are two called La Mouthe and Les Combarelles. In the one the engravings do not begin until after 100 yards have been traversed; in the other they are 135 yards from the entrance. At Niaux, which is nearly 1,600 yards long, a full half mile must be penetrated before the animal drawings begin, and some of them have been purposely wrought in almost inaccessible corners. The great Altamira fresco is in a side-chamber nearer the entrance, but the height of the roof varies from 3 to 6 feet, so that both artists and beholders

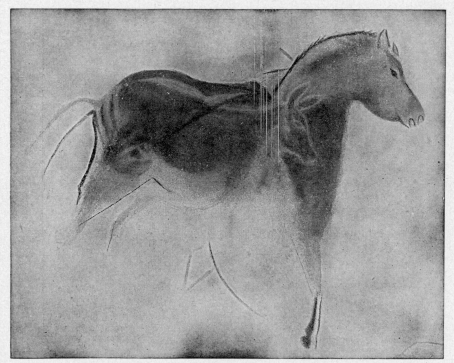

THE HORSE IN SHADES OF RED AND BROWN

This horse from Altamira is of interest as showing the haphazard way in which one picture encroached or was superimposed upon another when, for some reason, the first had become obsolete. Here the horse has been painted in polychrome over an earlier rendering of a doe. Further examples of the polychrome work of Altamira are shown in the colour plate and pp 146-7.

ENTRANCE TO ONE OF THE OLDEST PICTURE-GALLERIES IN THE WORLD

The complete fresco in page 144 comes from Altamira in Spain, but the artistic culture which it revealed extended on both sides of the Pyrenees. These photographs show the setting of a cave on French soil that has yielded a rich store of paintings. Above, the rocky, water-tunnelled bluff of Font-de-Gaume, commanding the valley of the Beune in the Dordogne—the entrance to the cave is marked with a cross; and below, a closer view of the entrance—the tunnel on the right is the principal one.

From "La Caverne de Font-de-Gaume," by Capitan, Breuil, and Peyrony

which this art was slowly climbing to its apex the main purpose of the artist was to depict single animals. Of these the useful big game predominate. At Font-de-Gaume, apart from its untinted outlines, there are paintings of about eighty bison, forty horses, twenty-three mammoths, seventeen reindeer and stags, and a dozen oxen and goats. Cave-lions, wolves, and other beasts of prey are rarely portrayed. The range of themes is conditioned by their economic importance and not by their aptitude for yielding a good picture. That they were not treasured as masterpieces is shown by the fact that again and again an artist used for his " canvas " a surface already painted without troubling to erase it. It was as if the earlier one had become, not old fashioned, but impotent to fulfil some purpose. But besides the " fine art " of these primitive

SORCERER GARBED AS AN ANIMAL

Figures of human beings are not very common until an age slightly later than that represented by the wall-paintings under consideration. But in the cavern of the " Trois Frères," near St. Girons, there is a wonderful representation, part painted part engraved, of what is supposed to be a sorcerer wearing antlers, mask, beard and tail for some magic rite.

had to stoop, if not even to lie upon the back. On the other hand, engravings were sometimes executed in daylight on shallow rock shelters, having been preserved through the ages solely by the accidental fall of débris.

The artificial light needed for these studies was furnished in part by stone lamps, such as the Eskimo use to this day. One of them, carved out of sandstone, with an ibex engraved upon its concavity, still bears a blackened film left by the desiccation of the grease. Hardly ever are paintings found in chambers occupied by the hunters themselves at the time, or such as could be visited by them, as one nowadays resorts to the Royal Academy for a private view. They were never drawing-room pieces. The explorers of Font-de-Gaume were convinced that it was devoted wholly to ritual uses, and that its mural pictures were executed for the community whose habitat lay in neighbouring caves and rock shelters at Les Eyzies. Here numerous decorated implements attest a steadfast regard for magical potency, as well as for artistic excellence, in the commonplace accessories of life. But the walls themselves are bare.

The very nature of the subjects portrayed has its tale to tell. Over the prolonged period during

RELIEF OF A WOMAN HOLDING A HORN

The ancient artists engaged not only in painting, but in modelling and sculpture ; the two, however, are found predominant on separate sites and represent different art phases. This figure of a steatopygous female comes from a rock shelter at Laussel in the Dordogne district—steatopygy, or a fatty development of the thighs, still characterises certain backward races.

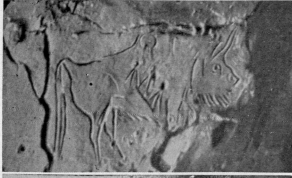

**STUDIES FROM THE LIVING MODELS**

Since these figures of a bison and a trout in the cave of Niaux are executed in sand, it seems reasonable to suppose that they were impressionistic sketches made by the artist while the originals were vivid in his mind—sketches that would refresh his memory when he came to draw on rock.

*After Breuill, " L'Anthropologie "*

draughtsmen other forms of graphic expression were also practised. Some caves contain silhouettes of human hands, stencilled around, or impressed by, the living hand. At Gargas, in the French Pyrenees district, where there are 150 such designs, most of them show amputated fingers. That they are of early date is determined by the crude mud outlines of the same age, and indeed the first pictures ever painted may have been these very hands that we are considering.

Elsewhere a multitude of designs of artificial objects, seldom rendered with realistic care, appear to symbolise traps for securing big game, sledges for transporting prime joints to the homestead, curved throwing-clubs, and other appliances of the chase. In the great Niaux sanctuary there is on the floor a sand drawing of a wounded bison, and even a human footprint, both glazed with stalagmite by the hand of time. So also lances, traps and sledges are often depicted

upon the flanks of bison, clearly for practical ends. Indeed, the drawings compel the inference that they were a kind of sympathetic magic, produced primarily as aids to good hunting.

From the use of animal masks as accessories for stalking big game there arose the practice of masked dances and ritual masking. In a recently explored Pyrenean cave, called the Three Brothers, there occurs a chamber presenting a whole galaxy of animal drawings. They are all dominated by a picture, twelve feet from the ground, of a sorcerer masked in a skin overall, with stag antlers, a horsehair beard and a horse's tail. The portrayal of the human form in that age was apparently tabooed, lest evil should be wrought upon the person. Such examples as remain, whether in sculptured relief or in flat outline, are rude and poor in the extreme.

Thus the general conclusion emerges that the impulse behind this pictorial art was a magical one. It was an expression of the emotions in a magico-religious atmosphere. Recognizing the existence of invisible powers more potent than their own, these early worshippers sought to bring themselves and their daily needs into contact with the unseen by graphic means. The pictures served to rivet the attention of the hunter when making ready for the chase, and by their mystic influence, aided by the ritual acts of the sorcerer, attuned his thoughts to the expectation of success.

It is tempting to speculate upon the social organization developed by these early hunters.

**ANIMAL MASTERPIECES OF PREHISTORIC ENGRAVERS**

This photograph shows the actual appearance today of the engravings on a cave wall at La Loja, Cantabria, with horses and cattle confused and superimposed. As drawings they show an economy and excellence of line equal to the best modern work.

The very existence of graphic art shows that life was no mere drudgery. Division of labour was carried far. There were not only industrial experts but from time to time dominant thinkers and other outstanding men. That the magico-religious leaders were not themselves the producers of the pictorial accessories of their cult is a reasonable inference. There was apparently a caste of trained painters, perhaps in part hereditary, who exploited their skill in the treatment of line and colour as a vocation. This is why their works not only came to be ritually efficient, but also to be aesthetically good. This also is why the craftsman now and then poured out his soul in a riot of artistic feeling. An interesting work of this genre is an engraved reindeer antler found in a French Pyrenean cave at Lortet. It portrays a group of stags and salmon, perhaps to denote the crossing of a stream. It is much weathered, but with the aid of a charming restoration proposed by himself Sir Edwin Ray Lankester claims it as the oldest picture in the world.

STONE HORSE THAT COMES TO US FROM THE DAWN OF TIME

At Cap Blanc is to be found this stone sculpture in deep relief of the head and body of a horse. While apparently later than the cave paintings in date, there is no reason not to assign it to the same race and to the same art impulse; it exhibits identical features of ease and fidelity to nature. It is now preserved as one of the national monuments of France.

This amazing outburst of art, after reaching its zenith, seems to have faded more or less suddenly into oblivion. For an explanation of this episode in the history of painting we may perhaps invoke the relative scantiness of the painters' order, which arose at the bidding of a self-contained community by which the hunting industry was raised to a high level of opulence. The manner of its decline may be hinted at by turning to another school of prehistoric art in Eastern Spain.

Upon the exposed background of rock shelters, such as the famous localities of Alpera and Cogul, there have been traced out strange medleys of ancient designs. Among them prehistoric scholars discern vestiges of an inspiration derived from the Magdalenian school. These peoples, perhaps swarming up from the southward, learned to practise new elements of style, and to present a new outlook upon life. There are scenes of warfare and the chase, besides ritual dances and domestic incidents. Accuracy of drawing was sacrificed to vitality of movement. A strong human interest was introduced. At Alpera, out of 150 figures, half of them are men and women. These are not delineated with the careful eye for portraiture observed in the Altamira animals, but the aesthetic impulse is more marked. From the technical standpoint they represent a decadence of the early art, and pass by stages into careless stylism.

By that time Europe was being peopled by new immigrants from the east. No longer huntsmen, they sought their subsistence in pasture and tillage. Nowhere does neolithic Eurasia offer evidence either of a knowledge of the Magdalenian paintings or a capacity to emulate them. No great pictorial art was to arise in the world again until, after millenniums of years, it emerged once more under the incentive of the new civilization due to the conquest of metals. The Old Masters were by then unknown, and the "art nouveau" of Egypt, Crete and Hellas had to grow by slow and painful stages, until at length there dawned upon the world another age of gold.

Some remarkable cave paintings in other parts of the world demand a passing word. Those produced by the Australian blackfellow and the South African Bushman yield interesting parallels, reminiscent of man's earliest art. They also have delineated, upon cave walls and rocky surfaces, useful animals, as well as mutilated hands, masked dances, ground drawings and the like, under conditions pointing to a ritual intention. That this art is not intuitive is clear from the many lowly hunting peoples, such as the Andamanese, to whom it is unknown. This is not to say that in Australia and South Africa there survive direct descendants of Magdalenian man. But one may with advantage speculate how far their cruder efforts are due to the persistence in racial memory of artistic impulses that first became part of man's mental equipment and inheritance in South-Western Europe, in those far off days when all the world was young.

## A KING'S UNIQUE MEMORIAL: THE SPHINX OF GIZEH

It is generally thought that it was Khafra, King of Egypt from about 2867 to 2811 B.C., who distinguished himself from the other great pyramid builders of the Fourth Dynasty by causing a rock adjoining his pyramid to be carved into the semblance of a sphinx, with a lion's body and a human face presenting his own features. In A.D. 1926 clearance of the sand disclosed once more the sphinx's massive outstretched paws, with a Roman altar to the sun god between them, and behind this a stele or tablet erected by Thothmes IV in the 15th century B.C. After each excavation the sand has always quickly piled up again round the great sculptured rock, as seen in the lower photograph taken as late as 1925.

"The Times"

## The Great Monuments. III.

# The Sphinx

**By Margaret A. Murray,** D.Lit., F.S.A. (Scot.)

Assistant Professor of Egyptology at University College, London

THERE is no relic of antiquity in the world round which so many legends have gathered as the Sphinx. This is not remarkable when the stately figure is seen rising above the desert sands, dominating even the pyramids themselves by its sheer majesty.

Many of the legends are due to a confusion between the Egyptian and the Greek sphinx. The Greek sphinx, though an equally fabulous animal, is derived from an entirely different source. The Egyptian sphinx is always male, and is a lion with a man's head or face; whereas the Greek sphinx is female, a lioness with a woman's head. The Greek form comes probably from the harpy, and seems to be the origin of the modern idea of an angel, that is, a winged human being with a woman's face. The Egyptian sphinx is an emblem of the king in his aspect as the incarnate God, and represents omnipotence. It is impossible to imagine so majestic a being as the Egyptian sphinx propounding silly riddles and committing suicide when the right answer is given.

The date of the Great Sphinx is not known accurately—it is usually ascribed to the reign of King Khafra, who built the Second Pyramid. It is partly sculptured in the solid rock, partly built, and represents a couchant lion with a human head; the headdress is of a form worn only by a Pharaoh, and on the brow was the royal snake; therefore, it clearly represents a king. Though the paws were rebuilt in Roman times, the tiny temple, only five feet wide, which lies between them is probably as early as the Sphinx itself. Standing at the end of this temple against the breast of the Sphinx is the Dream-stele of Thothmes (or Thutmosis) IV., placed there probably in the twenty-first dynasty. It is a poetical account of how the monarch, wearied with hunting, slept at midday under the shadow of the Sphinx and beheld a vision. The Sphinx is there called Harmakhis or Khepra, both of whom were at that time regarded as sun-gods. " Great and exalted is this figure of the god, resting in his chosen place; mighty is his power, for the Shadow of the Sun is upon him. The temples of Memphis and the temples of every town on both sides adore him, they stretch out their hands to him in adoration; sacrifices and libations are made before him."

The approach to the Sphinx in ancient times was by a processional way which led across the desert, then down a flight of thirteen steps, across a stone platform, and again down another flight of steps, thirty in number, to the level of the little temple between the paws. The visitor to this temple, on arriving at the top of the processional way, would be on a level with the breast of the Sphinx; as he descended, the figure would appear to grow more and more gigantic, until, when he reached the temple, the great statue towered above him, gazing into space with the far-seeing eyes and aspect of calm contemplation which, in spite of the mutilation of the face, makes the Great Sphinx the most impressive of all the remains of the ancient civilization of Egypt. By day or by night, at broad noontide or by the mysterious light of the moon, the majestic quality of this monument, its regal air and divine calm, prove it one of the masterpieces of the world.

Excavations were made round the Great Sphinx by Captain Caviglia in 1818, when the processional way and the temple between the paws were discovered. In 1837, Col. Howard Vyse made borings to the depth of more than twenty-seven feet in the back of the Sphinx, finding only solid rock. Maspero dug out the sands in 1886 and uncovered the paws stele and altar. In 1926 the whole was again cleared. a Roman protective wall revealed and the head restored.

The Sphinx is about 75 feet high and over 160 feet long overall, but the gigantic size is perhaps best realized by the measurements of the face, which is 13 feet 8 inches across, the nose is 5 feet 7 inches, and the mouth 7 feet 7 inches long. The face was mutilated by a fanatical sheikh, and afterwards by the Mamelukes; the nose, beard, and headdress have suffered most. Part of the beard is now in the British Museum—it shows the plaited form characteristic of Egyptian royal statues.

The Great Sphinx is not mentioned by classical authors until the time of Pliny (in the first century A.D.), who says that it was traditionally reputed to be the tomb of Amasis II. of the twenty-sixth dynasty. This is probably due to the fact that the remembrance of the romantic and gallant figure of that successful leader and general still

ONE OF THE SPHINX-LINED CEREMONIAL AVENUES OF THE GREAT TEMPLE AT KARNAK

Among the products of the royal workshops at Karnak, whence came official portraits of the Pharaohs, were some remarkable sphinxes, some shaped like kneeling rams (krio-sphinxes), some like human-headed lions (andro-sphinxes). They were fashioned to line the ceremonial pathways of the temples. One such avenue led from the Temple of Khensu to the Temple of Luxor, between the forelegs of the sphinxes being small figures of Amenhotep III. That shown on this page leads from Karnak to the ancient river-quay, and is about 200 feet in length. The view is taken from the first or north pylon of the Great Temple of Ammon. In former times the Nile took a more easterly course, and ran under the house seen in the photograph

*Photo by Gaddis & Seif*

## SUPPOSED TO COMMEMORATE KING KHAFRA

The Great Sphinx of Gizeh in Egypt, most ancient and renowned of all sphinxes in all countries, and known to the
Egyptians as " Hu," gazes due east across the Nile valley,
with its back to the Second Pyramid shown on the right of
the photograph, with which it appears to be associated.

**Photo by Ewing Galloway**

lingered even after the lapse of six centuries.
The modern name of this giant figure is " abu 'l
hol " (father of terror), a name which appears to be
derived through the Coptic " belhèt," from the
Egyptian " hu," and means guardian, watcher.
The Arabs consider it a talisman against the
drifting sand which continually threatens to
overwhelm the cultivated land. Tradition also
says that at one time there were two Great Sphinxes
which guarded the whole country ; like most
traditions, this contains a substratum of fact, for
colossal statues of the king were usually in pairs.

Sphinxes of all sizes are known from the time
of the Great Sphinx onwards. The largest of these
is the alabaster sphinx found by Mackay at
Memphis in 1912 ; from the style of the workmanship it is evidently of the reign of Rameses II.
The quaintest of all are the tiny amulets carved
in amethyst and other stones which occur in the
twelfth dynasty ; they represent a feline animal,
possibly a cat, with a human face ; but it is

## KHAFRA AS CHISELLED 5,000 YEARS AGO

Everything points to the Sphinx being a product of the fourth
dynasty, and it is possible that its head is a portrait of Khafra,
the builder of the Second Pyramid ; although some think that
alterations were carried out under the twelfth dynasty,
especially of the headdress.

**Museum of Egyptian Antiquities, Cairo**

represented sitting, whereas the lion-sphinx is
couchant.

Avenues of sphinxes are often found at the great
temples ; the most celebrated are the crio-sphinxes

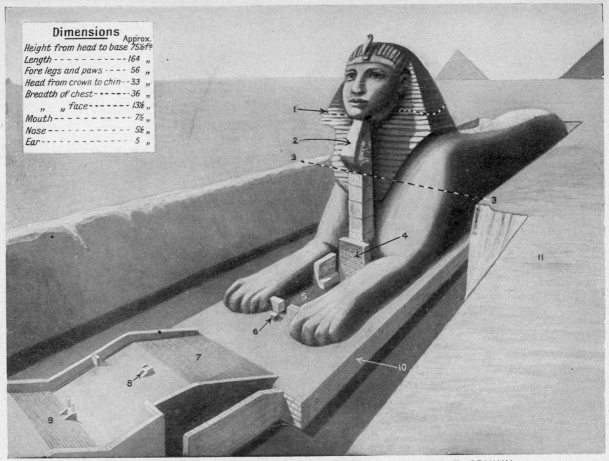

**Dimensions** Approx.
Height from head to base 75½ft
Length - - - - - - - - - - - 164 "
Fore legs and paws - - - - 56 "
Head from crown to chin - - 33 "
Breadth of chest - - - - - - 36 "
  "     "   face - - - - - - - 13½ "
Mouth - - - - - - - - - - - 7½ "
Nose - - - - - - - - - - - 5½ "
Ear - - - - - - - - - - - - 5 "

EXCAVATION TO SHOW THE DIMENSIONS OF THE GREAT SPHINX

1. Present size of headdress; only the upper part is still preserved.   2. The beard has disappeared, only parts of its support remaining intact.   3. Level of surrounding desert.   4. Stele of Thothmes IV.   5. Small roofless temple, once uncovered, excavated by Caviglia. 6. Altar in front of entrance.   7. Thirty steps.   8. Small raised altar set up in Roman times.   9. Thirteen steps.   10. Wall of sun-dried bricks.   11. Sand ; after each excavation the flow of sand has overcome the protective walls.

at Karnak (see illustration page 156), which outline the sacred way from the river to the temple.   These are couchant lions with rams' heads, and are emblematic of the god Ammon of Karnak, who was worshipped in primitive times under the form of a ram.   Even in this strange form the sphinx is impressive, and the avenue of crio-sphinxes is a fitting prelude to the majestic solemnity of the temple of Karnak.

Another form of sphinx is the lion with a hawk's head.   This is the emblem of the king in battle, and it is represented standing and trampling the enemy —negroes and Syrians— under its feet.   It is a favourite motif in the decoration of objects for

SPHINX OF THOTHMES III. FROM KARNAK

Before the entrance to the Museum at Cairo, where so many of the Egyptian antiquities illustrated in this work are preserved, stand two andro-sphinxes, of which this is one, bearing the name of the eighteenth dynasty king, Thothmes III.

Photo by Ewing Galloway

royal use, and is used with great effect in jewelry and in ornamenting caskets.   In jewelry the colouring of the hawk's head and the contrast of the fair Syrian and the dark negro gave the artist-designer great scope ; and the calm dignity of the creature contrasts with the undignified attitudes of the overthrown enemies.

The sphinx does not occur as a hieroglyph until the late period when the language had been considerably changed by foreign influences, chiefly Greek and Persian.   It reads " neb " as lord, and is used in the name of Nectanebo, one of the last native kings of ancient Egypt.

## SIDE VIEW OF THE SPHINX UNCOVERED ONCE AGAIN FROM THE SHIFTING SANDS

For at least sixty years the Sphinx had been undisturbed, but the removal of immense quantities of sand in 1926 permitted this complete side view showing a portion of a protective wall built by the Romans. At the same time certain repair work was carried out including the dilapidated crown of the head. Even in Thothmes' day it was necessary to free the Sphinx from sand, and the Romans also carried out restorations by refacing certain stone blocks set in the sculptured rock.

Photo by "The Times"

## TWO VIEWS OF THE ANDRO-SPHINX DISCOVERED ON THE SITE OF MEMPHIS

From the Fourth Dynasty onwards we meet many sphinxes of many kinds—lions with human heads, like the Great Sphinx; crio-sphinxes with rams' heads; falcon-headed sphinxes or wingless gryphons; and couchant rams which resemble sphinxes only in their attitude. Most notable are the vast avenue of sphinxes at Karnak (see illustration in page 156); the above example was discovered on the site of Memphis, and is an andro-sphinx, probably from the reign of Rameses II of the Nineteenth Dynasty.

ASCENDING FROM THE WORLD TO A REGION OF CELESTIAL PEACE

On each of the four sides of the Boro Budur a long stairway leads from the base to the top of the temple. From the first landing platforms the visitor was conducted by a priest along the galleries and was instructed in the significance of hundreds of reliefs showing episodes in the life of Buddha. Then, mounting higher, he reached the terraces, to find himself in the presence only of the statues of the celestial Buddha, in an atmosphere of silence and contemplative peace that contrasted vividly with the stir of mundane things left behind.

## Temples of the Gods. VI.

# Boro Budur: The Soul of Java

### By T. Athol Joyce, M.A.

Deputy Keeper, Department of Ethnography, British Museum

With a special series of photographs by Mr. Geo. P. Lewis

IN the Kedu residency of Central Java stands one of the finest and most elaborate monuments ever inspired by a great world-religion. A masterpiece of human art and craftsmanship in a setting of superb beauty. The Kedu plateau, rightly named the Garden of Java, is skirted by the peaks of four imposing volcanoes, which stand in virile contrast to the soft luxuriance of the plain. Beneath a vault of blue sky is stretched a plateau brilliant with every shade of green, from the emerald of young rice-crops to the almost-blue of tropical forest. Amid such surroundings the ancient builders selected their site, a low hill, as a foundation for the colossal pyramid-like structure which they reared in honour of some great saint. For the building is less a temple than a gigantic reliquary, since it is clear that the dagoba, or shrine, at the apex once enclosed relics of some personage of great holiness, perhaps even of Gautama Buddha himself.

Boro Budur, then, is Buddhist, and as such is evidence of the widespread appeal made by this Indian religion throughout the Orient, and also of the close

**IN INSCRUTABLE CONTEMPLATION**

Statue of the Buddha, moved from its proper niche—no one knows when—by some thoughtless or vandal hand, still wonderfully preserved amid the ruins of Boro Budur. This great Buddhist shrine in Central Java dates from the ninth century of our era, and is the most remarkable, perhaps, of all the buildings and monuments which remain to testify to the past glories of the now Dutch island.

connexion between religion and art, because the art of Boro Budur comes straight from its native source in Northern India.

Dates are dull, but necessary if a true perspective of old-world monuments is to be obtained. The death of Buddha is supposed to have taken place early in the fifth century before Christ. Indian influence is apparent in Java as early as the first or second century A.D. That influence, however, is Hindu rather than Buddhist. It was not until some two centuries before William the Conqueror invaded England that the Buddhist community in the island attained such numbers and power that they could commence, and carry to its achievement, so colossal a monument of their faith. Meanwhile the Buddhist doctrines had undergone great development, and an important schism had taken place. The so-called Northern School had elaborated the simple rules of life enunciated by the Founder into a metaphysical and mystical doctrine in which, not only a succession of earthly Buddhas, but a series of celestial counterparts (the so-called Dhyani-Buddhas),

TWO MILES OF WALL CARVED CUNNINGLY WITH LEGEND AND STORY

G. P. Lewis

From this section of the outside walls richly decorated with reliefs illustrating the earthly life of the Gautama, one may gain an inkling of the stupendous feat of sculpture accomplished by those ancient Indian and Javanese craftsmen who made and embellished the shrine. There is no less than two linear miles of these reliefs altogether, carved with an exquisite art and characterised by a rhythm that makes of each series a veritable poem in stone. Note the colossal Buddha above—one of more than 400 enshrined in niches

together with their spiritual emanations (the Dhyani-Bodhisattvas), had their place.

This school was destined later to be degraded by the incorporation of elements derived from the worship of Siva, the old Hindu god of destruction. Boro Budur, however, shows no signs of decline, and exhibits the art and doctrines of the Northern School in its highest form. The history of the Northern School affords a crucial instance of the fact that humankind as a whole needs something more than a rule of life. Mankind in bulk cannot live without gods, and so even to Buddhism, which was in a sense a revolt against gods and priest-craft, the gods came back. The smaller Southern School, which maintained the original teachings in simpler and purer form, persists in Ceylon, Burma, and Siam, but has never produced an architectural monument comparable with that of Boro Budur.

Boro Budur was begun about the year 850 A.D., but its construction must have been extended over many years, and indeed a close study of the remains suggests that the builders made more than one modification of their original plan. In broad outline the shrine is a stepped pyramid, built around a low hill as core, with a square base measuring no less than 520 feet each way. But the impression left upon the beholder is not that of, for instance, an Egyptian pyramid, nor even of one of the pyramidal temple-mounds of Central America. In the first place, the base line is not straight, nor are the lines of the succeeding courses ; they are recessed backwards at intervals from the centre, so as to present a succession of cornices. This peculiarity produces that clever combination of horizontal and perpendicular lines which is so characteristic of Indian architecture.

In the second place, the numerous niches and miniature dagobas which adorn the terraces are surmounted with pinnacles which accentuate the perpendicular lines of the shrine and obscure its triangular outline.

Another peculiarity lies in the change in the form of the terraces as the visitor climbs upwards, for the three topmost tiers are circular instead of square. A stairway leads up each face of the

*BORO BUDUR, JAVA'S MAMMOTH BUDDHIST SHRINE—*

Constructed and adorned by unknown hands to hold a long-lost relic of a Buddhist saint, this polygonal pyramid of dark trachyte, known as Boro Budur, rises in terraced splendour some 150 feet from the surrounding plain. Crowned by a great dagoba or cupola, it presents to the eye a series of jutting walls and projecting cornices, a front of " star y-pointing " pinnacles, its terraces elaborately decorated with sculptures of forceful imagery, full of astonishing detail and once adorned with hundreds of life-size figures of the Buddha. It is, as Mr. J. F. Scheltema, in his " Monumental

Specially coloured for "Wonders of the Past"

## —ONE OF THE WORLD'S ARCHITECTURAL MARVELS

Java," well says, " a source of spiritual quickening to whoso tries to understand," for this masterpiece of stone was raised, as were so many master-pieces of the Western world, by the hands of faith. Boro Budur dates from the ninth century of our era. Left for long years, almost as forgotten as its builders, a prey to the fretting tooth of time and the merciless hand of the spoiler, but now the object of careful preservation by the Dutch authorities, it grows in dignity and beauty the more closely it is observed.

structure to the shrine at the summit, passing under arches crowned with the grim face of the Makara monster. Apart from the foundation terrace, which is an open platform, the four lower terraces are bordered by an exterior wall, and so form a series of narrow galleries to which the stairways give access. The view along these galleries is, of course, broken by the recessing of the walls, so that from every point of view the eye is held by the harmonious outline of jutting cornices and rising domes. The interior wall of the gallery, of which the upper portion is the outer wall of the gallery above, is covered with two classes of ornamentation, each fulfilling a definite function.

The upper portion is conceived on a large scale, because it is visible from a distance. Here we have a series of deep niches, each originally

tenanted by a colossal figure of one of the Celestial Buddhas, sitting with interlocked legs (the so-called "adamantine position") wrapped in serene meditation. The simple, yet majestic, aloofness of these figures renders each one a masterpiece of Indian sculpture. Yet there are more than four hundred of them.

Their very perfection has contributed to their destruction. Boro Budur has suffered much from the casual plunderer, who, unable to cope with the entire image, has often succeeded in breaking off and carrying away one of these serene heads. These Buddhas in their niches constitute the most prominent feature of the decoration of the lower terraces as seen from the plain, but between them are sculptured panels, on a smaller scale and in lower relief, for the architects of those days

SUPERB RELIEFS ON BORO BUDUR'S SCULPTURED WALLS

The terrace walls of the great square structure which supports the actual shrine are adorned with a series of superb reliefs, unrivalled anywhere. These reliefs, which, for the most part, illustrate incidents in the life of the Buddha, number, or rather numbered, no fewer than 2,141—for many, alas! have been lost or so badly damaged as to be beyond hope of repair—and they extend along a distance of nearly two English linear miles. We know nothing of the master chisellers who fashioned them.

## THE LORD BUDDHA RECEIVES TREATMENT AT THE HAND OF HIS MASSEUSE

This amazingly realistic relief on the wall of one of the terraces of the Boro Budur belongs to the series which is illustrated also on the opposite page. The series tells, with an almost incredible wealth of detail, the whole story of the Buddha's life, from the hour of his birth to the hour of his death, and is so arranged that the pilgrim approaching the venerable shrine which crowns the edifice may be gradually educated up to a proper appreciation of that supreme excellence which is the Buddhist ideal.

covered every available square foot at their disposal with ornament; and all ornament had a ceremonial significance.

The lower portion of the inner walls is divided into panels adorned with sculpture on a lesser scale, because it was meant for the eyes of intimate observers who trod the galleries. These are carved in bold relief, models of technique and composition, and imbued with all that sensuous and rhythmic beauty of form which made so strong an appeal to the Indian artist. The scenes depicted are of almost infinite variety, and are evidently intended as illustrations to certain works of Indian literature. Here we have incidents from the life of Gautama Buddha, either in his last, or some previous, incarnation. The figure of Maitreya Buddha, the "Buddha of kindness," who has yet to come, is prominent in the reliefs of the third gallery.

In the fourth gallery are scenes which appear to deal with the Dhyani-Buddhas, those mysterious and supra-mundane counterparts of the earthly Messiah, and the paradises which they inhabit, together with their spiritual emanations, the Bodhisattvas. The whole is an amazing wealth of detail, which, when the eye becomes accustomed to the canons of Oriental art, stands out as a masterpiece of harmonious beauty.

The setting of these sculptures is perfect from the point of view of their intimate study. The monotony of a long series of reliefs, however beautiful in themselves, is broken by the recessing of the walls; while the cornices themselves are diversified by large gargoyles, which, in connexion with a cleverly-planned system of gutters, served to drain the terraces.

From the series of lower terraces rise the three upper, which are circular, and which, moreover, are not provided with an outer wall. Here the

**RESCUED TREASURE OF BORO BUDUR**

This broken statue was one of the treasures rescued when, in the
early years of the nineteenth century, the debris of some remote
volcanic disturbance was removed from the glorious terraces of
the wonderful temple of Boro Budur.

There are signs that this dagoba, the innermost
shrine of the whole structure, originally contained
two chambers, an upper and a lower. But what is
there within ? Nothing—now. What was the
object which was so important an element in the
local faith and worship that hundreds of men for
many years toiled to build and cover with lavish
ornament so huge a shrine ? We do not know. It
is an ironical fact that this, one of the most superb
pieces of architecture in the world, should be to us
empty both of content and ultimate meaning.
There is no lack of conjecture, and the probable
alternatives are few.

Most probable is the suggestion that the dagoba
was intended as the last resting-place of the ashes
or some portion of them, of one of the greatest
Buddhist saints, possibly even of Gautama
Buddha himself.

Buddhism waned in Java, and was finally
replaced by Islam, which laid a sterilizing hand
upon the ancient traditions. The old shrines fell
into decay, some have suffered from Moslem
iconoclasm, but more from the unscientific
pilfering of " excavators." Fortunately, of recent
years the Dutch Government have realised that
Boro Budur is something more than an interesting
local ruin. Steps have been taken to safeguard
the structure, pilfered sculptures have been
traced and replaced, and a very considerable
amount of restoration, carried out upon sound
scientific lines, has been performed.

So, if the soul has left it, the body remains, the
dark trachyte blocks of which it is composed
taking upon themselves unimagined shades of
colour from the tropical sun ; the brilliant light
giving a depth to the architectural relief which
makes Indian sculpture so wonderful in its
proper surroundings and so cold in northern
latitudes.

Even the very elaboration of detail, which might
so easily have impaired the grandeur of the conception by a suggestion of the trumpery, adds a
richness to the mass of the building because the
details are appropriate in arrangement and harmonious in spacing.

As seen to-day, in its beautiful geographical
surroundings, Boro Budur does not convey the
impression of something dead. It needs so small
an effort of the imagination to see the stairways
thronged with worshippers and pilgrims, slowly
encircling each gallery in their progress to the
sanctuary above, becoming gradually more and
more attuned to the last rite of reverence by the
sculptured scenes, taken from the tradition of the
scriptures, which border their path. Regarded as
an architectural achievement, or as an expression
of the devotional sense in man, Boro Budur has
few compeers.

scheme is entirely different. The observer no longer
walks in enclosed galleries, elaborately sculptured
with religious scenes, but moves in freer air with,
on the one side, the wonderful tropical panorama
in full view, on the other, the mysterious shrine
which still towers above. From the pavement of
these last tiers rise small pinnacled domes in
orderly series, each containing the figure of a
seated Buddha, who may be dimly descried
through the stone lattice-work of his shrine.

Finally, the summit, crowned with a plain dome,
entirely without ornament, as if by this time the
visitor had been elevated above all human art.
Merely a surmounting pinnacle still pointing
upwards.

# Records of the Tombs. III.

# Algeria's Amazing Tombs

## The Medrassen and the Tombeau de la Chrétienne

### By A. MacCallum Scott

#### Author of "Barbary: the Romance of the Near East"

*A MONG the ancient monuments that make North Africa so rich in archæological interest there is none more impressive than the two immense Algerian structures known as the Tombeau de la Chrétienne and the Medrassen, both standing in peculiarly imposing positions widely distant from each other in Algeria. Little has been written concerning these very remarkable memorials of a distant past; in English works of travel, especially, readers will have difficulty in finding references to them. We are peculiarly fortunate in being able to include the fine photographs of these monuments taken recently by the French Colonial Government authorities at the suggestion of the Editor's friend, Mr. W. H. Miller of Algiers, whose knowledge of the remains in Algeria is very extensive, and under whose guidance the Editor first made acquaintance with these astonishing monuments.*—EDITOR.

ABOUT fifty miles west of Algiers, on the summit of one of a low range of hills overlooking the Barbary coast and the blue Mediterranean, the traveller by sea or land beholds a strange and unexpected edifice. Far from the Nile, it nevertheless, by its shape and by its colossal proportions, recalls the pyramids. In the distance it seems half-pyramid, half-tower, an African Tower of Babel, a hill piled by man upon a hill. It has stood sentinel there for 2,000 years.

This strange Egyptian shape overlooking the Barbary coast is known to the French as the "Tombeau de la Chrétienne," the Tomb of the Christian Woman. The Arabs call it "Kubr-er-Roumia." To the Arab the Christian is still "Roumi," the Roman, whom his ancestors from the desert dispossessed. The French title is therefore simply a translation of the native name in common use. There is evidence, however, that this structure was contemporary with the origin of Christianity itself, and that it is to be associated not with the name of any Christian woman, but with that of Selene Cleopatra, the daughter whom Cleopatra, Queen of Egypt, bore to Antony.

In the first place there is documentary evidence. Pomponius Mela was a Latin author who flourished early in the first century. In his work, "De Situ Orbis," written before the middle of that century, he refers to this tomb as "Monumentum Commune Regiae Gentis," the Public Memorial of the Royal Family, the tomb of the native Kings of Mauretania.

Dr. Judas, an Oriental scholar, has pointed out that the native name, Kubr-er-Roumia, is not of Arab but of Phoenician origin. In the old Phoenician or Punic language, which survived for centuries after Roman times all along this coast, "Roumiah" means "Royal," and from the similarity of the name to the Arab word, and a false derivation,

the legend of the Christian Woman was evolved. Colour was given to the legend by the fact that on the four blind stone doors of the monument the panelling made the Sign of the Cross.

Not far from Constantine, the most ancient capital of the native Berber princes, is to be found another structure known as the Medrassen, so similar to the "Tombeau" as to make it certain that one has suggested the other. This building, on which the Egyptian characteristics are even more plainly marked, was erected about 150 B.C. by Massinissa, the native ally of the Romans against Carthage, to be the sepulchre of his dynasty. What more natural than that his great-great-grandson Juba, when established in a new kingdom on the western frontier, should build near the new capital a sepulchre like that of his fathers?

The story of Juba II. is one of the most romantic episodes in African history and it has one curious link with the Bible narrative, for his daughter Drusilla was the wife of Felix, Governor of Judea, upon whom the Apostle Paul's preaching produced so powerful an effect. His father, Juba I., King of Numidia, had rashly taken the side of Pompey in the Roman Civil War, and had been crushed by Julius Caesar, his kingdom being incorporated in the Empire. The boy, Juba II., was taken a prisoner to Rome, and there, instead of suffering the miserable fate of so many other captive princes, he found an education, a fortune, a wife and a kingdom.

Augustus, the new Caesar, took a fancy to the little captive and marked him out as a pawn in his great schemes. He placed him in charge of his sister Octavia, the widow of Antony, and in her family he became familiar with all that was best in the literature, art and philosophy of Rome and Greece. Octavia had also taken another

THE MEDRASSEN : TOMB OF MASSINISSA, AND PROTOTYPE OF THE TOMBEAU

Massinissa was an ally of Rome in her final victorious campaign against Carthage, and because of this, succeeded in preserving intact his throne and his frontiers. This great mausoleum which contained his remains was built as a solid conical pile of tufa-stone blocks each several feet square, and had a secret entrance, with funerary chamber in the centre. From Egypt, land of the great pyramids of the Pharaohs, must have come the inspiration for the erection of this tomb. Through time the legend arose that it was a repository of fabulous treasure and many were the attempts to rifle it, but all of them unsuccessful. The break in the symmetry of the structure, shown above, marks the point where a forced entrance was essayed by bombardment by French artillery about the middle of last century.

170

NORTH AFRICAN EVOLUTION OF THE PYRAMIDS OF THE PHARAOHS, THE MEDRASSEN

In 204 B.C., with the help of Scipio Africanus, Massinissa razed Cirta, capital of King Syphax, to the ground, and carried off Syphax's wife, Sophonisba. Her father, Hasdrubal of Carthage, had thought to gain a more powerful ally to his cause by giving her in marriage to Syphax, although she had previously been betrothed to Massinissa. After defeating Syphax, Massinissa naturally wished to marry Sophonisba, but Scipio, fearing her power, refused to allow this, and she died through drinking a cup of poison sent to her by Massinissa. In 148 B.C., at the age of ninety, Massinissa died, just after having erected this great monument as the burying-place for himself and his successors—an expectation which was never realized.

little refugee into her home, Selene Cleopatra, the daughter of her own fickle husband and Cleopatra of Egypt. When the children became of age, Augustus, in pursuit of his subtle policy, arranged a marriage between them, and established Juba as king of the dependent native state of Mauretania on the western frontier of his African province.

The experiment was a triumphant success. Juba and his queen had a long and prosperous reign. They established their capital at the little Phoenician town of Jol, about 70 miles west of Algiers, and rechristened it Caesarea in honour of their Imperial patron. It is now known by the Arab name of Cherchel. The city grew rapidly in wealth and splendour. Architects, sculptors, painters, writers, teachers, thronged to the Court of Juba and Selene from the best schools of Athens, Rome and Alexandria. Within the walls a theatre was built, and a hippodrome, and luxurious baths, and palaces and temples resplendent with marble pillars and statues. The colossal ruins of the aqueduct (illustrated in page 212) which brought the water of the distant hills may still be seen striding across a valley seven miles away. Caesarea

became known as the Athens of the west. All has perished. The looted pillars adorn many an Arab mosque, and some relics of statuary and mosaic may be found in the museums of Algiers and Paris. Corn and vines grow upon the site. For miles around the ploughshare turns up in every field fragments of statues, columns, capitals, inscribed stones and exquisitely carved marbles. What treasures still lie underground we can but guess.

Before his death Juba caused to be built on the coast hills, about twenty miles east of his capital, a mausoleum which would be worthy of the new African dynasty he hoped to found. Taking the ancestral Medrassen as a model he built on a larger and more massive scale, challenging comparison with the pyramids of the Nile. He was crowned in the year 26 B.C., and he reigned forty-five years. And here, in the recesses of this mountain of stone, he and his queen would be buried, with a magnificence befitting the glories of their lineage and of their reign, and the traditions of the tombs of Egypt.

For nearly two thousand years the legend of buried treasure attached to the tomb and many were the efforts made to wrest it from its rocky strong-room. But the clue to the entrance had been lost, and generation after generation of would-be plunderers expended their strength in vain in trying to force the secret. Battered and torn, scarred and defaced, its huge bulk still preserved the ancient pyramidal outline, and served as a beacon over sea and land. Soil settled on it, and seeds were dropped by wind and by birds, so that, at a near view, it was shaggy like the hillside with herbs and plants. A French botanist has even published a pamphlet on the flora of the " Tombeau." A rank growth of legend as well as of plants clings to the monument.

The Arabs believed that the " Kubr-er-Roumia" was guarded by spirits in the shape of black, poisonous wasps whose sting was certain death. This myth took various forms. According to one legend a certain Ben-Kassem, having been taken prisoner by the Christians, was sold as a slave in Spain to an old scholar who was an adept in magic. His master gave him his freedom on his promising to return to his home near the " Tombeau de la Chrétienne," and on the fourth day after his arrival to carry out certain instructions. He was to burn a scroll of paper at the tomb and to go away immediately. No sooner had the liberated slave burned the paper than the tomb opened,

and a stream of gold and silver pieces issued forth and flew over sea towards Spain. Overcome by cupidity, Ben-Kassem spread out his burnous and tried to stop some of the flying treasure. The spell was broken, the stream of money stopped, and the tomb closed fast again.

News of this extraordinary adventure was carried to the pasha, who resolved to demolish the tomb and find what remained of the treasure. But no sooner did the workmen lay hands on the stones than the figure of a woman appeared on the top, shouting " Alloula! Alloula! Come to my help!" Alloula was the name of a small lake at the foot of the hill. Immediately a swarm of virulent mosquitoes issued from the lake and drove away the desecrators of the tomb in headlong flight.

In 1855 the Emperor Napoleon commissioned two well-known Algerian antiquaries, M. Berbrugger and M. MacCarthy, to carry out a complete exploration of the monument. Although they had at their command all the resources of science, it took them seven months to force an entrance.

The monument, which is circular in form, stands upon a square platform. Its base is like a huge drum, 36½ feet high and 198 feet in diameter. The circumference is divided into sixty equal spaces by sixty Ionic columns, attached to the wall and

VICTIM OF TOMB ROBBERS AND TREASURE SEEKERS: THE TOMBEAU DE LA CHRETIENNE

Since its erection about 2,000 years ago the tomb of Juba II. has undergone innumerable assaults, first at the hands of tomb robbers, and then from the Arabs, who firmly believed the tradition of its concealed wealth. The very solidity of its structure must have baffled them, but that some unknown band of robbers did penetrate to the sepulchral chamber was definitely discovered in 1885 when MM. Berbrugger and MacCarthy bored their shaft to the inner cavity to find only empty caskets, and the broken bead-strings of Selene Cleopatra, lying on the floor.

THE MASSIVE PILE OF THE TOMBEAU DE LA CHRETIENNE AS IT IS AFTER 2,000 YEARS
From a comparison of its height with that of the large bell-tent in the foreground, or with the figure of the man seen standing among the debris of boulders on the right, a rough idea of the size of this great monument may be gathered. Its drum-like base stands on a square foundation and is about 36 feet high and 200 feet in diameter. The conical upper portion is 75 feet in height, thus making the total height of the tomb about 110 feet.

surmounted by a frieze and cornice. North, south, east, and west are what appear to be four doors of stone, but they are false doors, for the masonry is quite solid behind them. The upper part of the monument is in appearance like a blunt cone, or rounded pyramid. It rises in a series of high steps some 75 feet above the cornice. The total height is about 110 feet, and it may originally have been as much as 130 feet from base to summit.

Armed with an artesian well-sinking outfit, the two explorers set to work to probe the mountain of stone in search of the secret chamber. They put down the first bore from what they believed to be the geometrical centre. Unfortunately they were misled by a land survey mark on the top, and missed what they sought by a few feet. They proceeded to put down a series of bores between that and the eastern false door. All these efforts were unsuccessful. Other bores were put down at various points. For six months they laboured in vain, then the plunger in the thirteenth bore suddenly fell a clear eight feet, precipitating the workmen on to the stone blocks. The long-sought cavity had at last been located.

The successful bore had been sunk opposite the false door on the south. At this point a mine was driven into the mass of the solid masonry.

It took ten days to cut a way through, and then the explorers found themselves in a long gallery about 8 feet high and 6½ feet broad. The walls were formed of large blocks of squared and dressed limestone, finely jointed. There were niches along the walls which seemed as if they had been made to hold lamps. This gallery, which was about 500 feet long, circled almost completely round the monument, and then, turning inwards like a spiral, ended in two vaulted chambers in the centre. They were shut off by doors of stone which slid up and down in grooves like a portcullis.

Alas, the casket was empty! For all these centuries the assailants had been attacking an empty shell. The tomb had been rifled at some early date before the secret of the entrance was lost. Ample evidence was found of the visits of early robbers who knew the secret and who, from the gallery itself, had made excavations into the solid mass in search of other concealed chambers.

In the dust of the floor the modern explorers found two relics to show what had been the nature of the booty, the scattered beads of an Oriental necklace of cornelians and pearls, and a pendant broken from some Egyptian jewel. The latter is significant as a link with Selene Cleopatra. From the harbour of Cherchel there has also been dredged

TOMB OF THE DAUGHTER OF ANTONY AND CLEOPATRA, THE AMAZING TOMBEAU DE LA CHRETIENNE

After Julius Caesar was murdered in 44 B.C., he was succeeded in the imperatorial office by Octavianus Augustus, the people's idol ever since Antony had left Rome and fallen slave to the woman of whom it was said : " Age shall not wither her, nor custom stale her infinite variety "—the romance-encircled Cleopatra. The daughter of their liaison, Selene Cleopatra, was adopted after Antony's death by his wife Octavia, sister of Augustus, and guardian, too, of Juba, son of the King of Numidia. An attachment soon sprang up between these young people, and on their coming of age they were married, after which Augustus established Juba as ruler of Numidia. This great monument was erected to receive the bodies of his queen and himself at death : like all such conspicuous tombs, it has been plundered by treasure seekers

174

EXCAVATIONS IN A TOMB TWENTY CENTURIES OLD

In this photograph may be seen the remains of five Ionic columns and one of the " blind " doors. All told, there were sixty such columns round the immense drum, and at the four cardinal points of the compass were four of these false doors having on their surface a large cross, one of which is plainly visible here. Above the drum were a frieze and a cornice and then the uppermost cone. Notice the deep indentation made by the excavators in the solid mass of the upper part.

a portion of an Egyptian statue in black basalt, bearing the cartouche of King Thothmes III. The Mauretanian queen had not forgotten the land of her birth and of her mother's tragic story.

Now that the clue had been discovered it was comparatively easy to find the original entrance. The gallery, winding round from the central vault, rose seven steps, and came to an abrupt end in another chamber exactly opposite the eastern false door. Here the entrance was found where no one had suspected it, outside the structure altogether, underground, and buried, ironically enough, beneath the debris of previous attempts to demolish the tomb. Very simple, like most secrets when one holds the clue.

Ptolemy, the son of Juba and Selene, died miserably in a dungeon in Rome. He is said to have been a weak and dissolute ruler, but history is apt to be partial to the conqueror. He perished, and with him the dynasty for whose names this monument was designed to secure immortality. In the Louvre may be seen two portrait busts of Ptolemy which were dug up from the ruins in the neighbourhood of Cherchel. One can recognize in that Oriental countenance the mingled strains of Egypt, Phoenicia and Barbary.

The glory has departed but the Berber race endures. It still populates the land and preserves the ancient language. It has persisted throughout the domination of Phoenician, Roman, Arab and French. Under French protection the vine, the orange, the fig and the olive flourish on the rich plains around. But, while the Roman temples of Caesarea and Tipasa have disappeared, this un-European monument still crowns the hill and looks over the Mitidja valley on the one side, the Mediterranean on the other, proclaiming that the soul of the land is of Africa, not of Europe.

175

COLOSSAL PORTRAIT STATUES OF A VAINGLORIOUS PHARAOH

Illimitable pride and personal vanity characterised Rameses II, and were the chief animating motive behind the grandiose schemes of conquest and empire that make his reign notable in the brilliant period of the Nineteenth Dynasty. They are reflected in the four colossal figures representing him enthroned, each 65 feet high and the largest sculptured figures in Egypt, carved on the façade of the vast temple of Ra that he caused to be hewn out of the sandstone cliff beside the Nile at Abu Simbel in Nubia.

## Temples of the Gods. VII.

# The Rock Temples at Abu-Simbel

### By Margaret A. Murray, D. Lit., F.S.A. (Scot.)

**Assistant Professor of Egyptology at University College, London**

THE Great Temple of Abu-Simbel (Ipsambul), on the left bank of the Nile, about forty miles north of Wady Halfa, is hewn out of the solid rock where the river takes a bend and runs eastward. Almost all temples in Egypt are orientated by the river, and the Temple of Abu-Simbel is no exception. The entrance faces due east, so that at sunrise the sunlight strikes along the straight axis of the temple and shines upon the figures in the innermost sanctuary. The temple is dedicated to Ra-Harmakhis, the Rising Sun, and daily at sunrise the Glory of the Lord illumines the darkness of the shrine.

Four gigantic statues are at the entrance, two on each side, sculptured in the rock. They represent the Pharaoh Rameses II. seated on his throne and wearing all the insignia of royalty; on his head is the striped linen headdress which was worn only by kings, and above that is the double diadem of Egypt, while the royal serpent is on his brow. The figures sit with the hands on the knees, gazing out to the sunrise with that calm consciousness of power which is one of the attributes of the divine.

At each side of each colossus is a female figure, representing the queen and some of the princesses; these do not reach to the knees of the seated statues, though elsewhere they would be considered colossal; as it is, they are completely dwarfed by the majestic proportions of the figures by which they stand. Between the legs of each colossus is another small figure, a son or daughter of the king. The colossus immediately to the south of the doorway is partially destroyed owing to the disintegration of the stone itself.

The plan of this great temple has a cruciform effect, which is probably accidental, and is due to the lateral chambers on each side. To enter the temple one must pass between the two middle colossi and through a square-headed doorway. Above this entrance, raised high so that his head is on a level with the heads of the colossi, is a statue of Ra-Harmakhis, the sun-god himself. "At early morning the sun's rays strike full upon it, so that the figure appears to be stepping forward to greet the sunrise."

The doorway leads directly into the Great Hall. Four square pillars support the roof, and in front of each pillar is a gigantic figure of the king in the attitude, and bearing the insignia, of the god Osiris. The sides and backs of the pillars are covered with representations of the Pharaoh in the presence of various gods and goddesses.

The effect of these enormous figures is very impressive; seen as they are in the faint light which filters through the narrow doorway, they tower above the head of the spectator; dimly visible in the darkness, they gaze in silence for ever across the hall in which they stand sentinel.

A door at the west end of the Great Hall gives access into a small pillared hall; then, still going due west, through a small vestibule, the innermost shrine is reached. Four statues sit with their backs to the west wall, facing towards the daybreak, and on them the rays of the rising sun fall when "the majesty of Ra rises in the eastern horizon" and the earth is flooded with light.

The lateral chambers on the north and south of the temple are entered from the Great Hall. All these chambers are sculptured with reliefs which indicate that these inner rooms were for the cult of the divine king. To the ancient Egyptian the Pharaoh was god incarnate, in him dwelt the spirit of the living god, and he was worshipped in all parts of Egypt as a god. But it is not often that the sculptures show this belief so clearly as at Abu-Simbel, for here in these inner chambers the king is represented among the gods and at the same time worshipping his own divinity.

The walls of the whole temple are covered with sculptures, and in the Great Hall is the account of the Battle of Kadesh. It was the one dashing exploit of Rameses II.'s life, and he caused it to be recorded on every temple which he built or restored. The record is always elucidated with illustrations, and the poem of the court-poet Penta-ur invariably accompanies it. Though Rameses undoubtedly acted with conspicuous gallantry, and at great personal risk turned defeat into victory, it is quite evident, even from his own account, that the happy result was due as much to good luck as to good management.

In his campaign in Syria Rameses had reached as far north as the Orontes, and proposed to take the city of Kadesh. Deceived by the reports of Hittite spies, who claimed to be deserters from the Hittite army, Rameses pushed on to Kadesh with only his bodyguard and one out of the four divisions of his army. He marched up the west side of the town, and proceeded to encamp, while the Hittite army slipped round the eastern side of " the deceitful city of Kadesh," fell upon the army of Rameses, which was totally unprepared and at a distance from its supports, and put the second division to flight. The routed division fled in all directions; the greater number in the wake of the king. They burst panic-stricken into the camp and communicated their terror to the first division, who also fled. The Hittite chariotry came up in hot pursuit, and seeing that the king and the royal bodyguard had remained, they wheeled round with a wide circling movement to kill or capture the now dangerously imperilled Pharaoh.

This was Rameses' great moment, and Penta-ur describes it, omitting with poetic licence the fact that the bodyguard also stood their ground : " There was never a chief with me, never a charioteer, not an officer of troops nor a horseman ; the infantry abandoned me, the chariots fled away,

SMALLER NORTHERN TEMPLE AT ABU-SIMBEL DEDICATED TO HATHOR AND NEFERTARI

To the north of the Great Temple of Abu-Simbel is a smaller one, dedicated to Hathor, in which Nefertari, wife of Rameses, plays the same part in relation to the gods as her husband in the larger temple. The façade, here illustrated, is made even more to resemble a pylon, with 33-foot figures representing Rameses and Nefertari standing in niches. As before, there are smaller figures of princes and princesses, while on the buttresses between are dedicatory inscriptions. This façade is 90 feet long and 40 feet high, but the cornice which once surmounted it has fallen. Within there is only one hypostyle hall, instead of the two the other temple, and six Hathor-headed columns.

GREAT HALL OF THE TEMPLE LEADING TO THE INNER HALL AND SANCTUARY

Immediately within the doorway of the Temple of Abu-Simbel is the great hypostyle hall, corresponding to the open forecourt of an ordinary temple, even as the doorway, with its colossi, represents the pylon. The hall is 58 feet long by 54 feet broad, and is supported by eight pillars 30 feet high against the inner faces of which stand Osiris-figures of the king between 17 and 18 feet high. The ceiling of the nave so formed is decorated with flying vultures, and on the walls are painted historical scenes, representing in particular Rameses' great victory over the Hittites at Kadesh.

FACADE OF THE GREAT TEMPLE OF ABU-SIMBEL, HEWN FROM THE LIVING ROCK

The colossal sandstone figures of Rameses II., one with the rock of the cliff, are 65 feet high, and on either side of each, and between their legs, are smaller figures representing various members of the royal household. The statue between the legs of the second colossus from the left represents his son Amenherkhepeshef (not to be confused with the son of Rameses III similarly named), while his wife Nefertari stands on the right. To the left of the door is a falcon, above the lintel a relief of Ra-Harmakhis.

not one of them remained to fight at my side." Then he called upon the god Ammon, who heard and came to the rescue, "striking on the right hand, seizing on the left hand, like Baal in wrath."

Encouraged by this divine help, Rameses charged into the midst of the enemy, finally driving them across the river. "I came up to them quicker than fire. I was carried among them. I was like Mentu, god of war. I gave to them the taste of my hand in the passing of an instant. I was a devouring flame among them, slaying them as they stood." The Hittites in their turn were seized with panic and fled, crying : "This is no mortal man. It is Sutekh, great of might. It is Baal in the flesh." Egyptian reinforcements came

up before the Hittites had time to rally from the sudden onslaught, and the victory was complete. Many of the Hittites fell into the river and were drowned by the overturning of the chariots. The unfortunate Prince of Aleppo, an ally of the Hittites, was dragged half-drowned out of the water by his faithful followers, who rendered first aid by holding him up by the heels in order to get rid of the water he had swallowed.

This incident struck the sense of humour of the ancient Egyptians, and the prince is always represented in that ridiculous position. The sense of humour has altered very little in the course of centuries, and the modern tourist laughs just as heartily at the predicament of the Prince of Aleppo as the ancient Egyptian did.

# The Citadel Palace of Tiberius at Capri

By F. N. Pryce, M.A.

Assistant Keeper, Department of Greek and Roman Antiquities, British Museum

MANY thousands of tourists cross the Bay of Naples every year to the little isle of Capri and, probably most of them, undertake the short excursion to the eastern extremity of the island to visit the ruins of the Palace of Tiberius. The site is not only one of the beauty spots of the world, with a glorious prospect over the rest of the island and over the blue waters of the bay, into which the cliffs fall with a sheer drop of a thousand feet ; but it has also given Capri a place in history for all time. For the crumbling walls that crown the promontory once housed the master of the world, the terrible emperor Tiberius, who more than any other Roman emperor, more even than the unspeakable Nero, remains in our minds as the embodiment of cold cruelty and vice.

Here the eyes of the known world were focussed for eleven long years ; here was played out one of the most thrilling dramas of history. In the palace on the cliff the old emperor lay sick and trembling, awaiting the news that the obsequious Senate had obeyed his order to execute his trusted but traitorous minister Sejanus ; while on the beach below were moored the fast warships that were to convey him to the farthest Orient should Sejanus succeed in winning over the Senate and in gaining for himself the imperial purple. And here later Tiberius died, lonely and worn-out ; poisoned by his heir, so Roman gossip ran.

Excavations have recently been undertaken on the site by a well-known Italian archaeologist, Professor Maiuri, with the object of ascertaining the ground-plan and arrangement of the building. It must be understood that what now remains is little more than the substructures and cellars of brick and concrete ; the staterooms above with all their magnificence have vanished, and what local guides point out as the apartments of Tiberius were probably slaves' quarters.

On the western side of the palace, facing the island and landing-place, a long terrace extends across the entire front. This is a common feature of a large Roman residence ; laid out as a garden or colonnade, it provided space in which the lord might perambulate. Behind this the main body of the palace rose in terraces, arranged around colonnaded courts, or peristyles, going back to the edge of the cliff. The first of these courts would be devoted to reception rooms, the more retired ones

would contain the private apartments. In the centre at the back, a large room with curving walls at the end supported a saloon with a bay-window commanding the view across to the mainland. Other points of vantage along the cliff were occupied by detached pavilions. Thus the ground-plan is fairly certain, displaying the normal elements of a Roman palace adapted to the site.

We may also hazard some conjectures as to the elevation. So massive are the foundation-walls that it is reasonable to suppose that the building rose up in several storeys like a skyscraper. At one point, where they are set against the side of the cliff, the ruins of at least three storeys are still to be traced, nor is it likely that these were all. It is supposed that here were the baths, an

**MEMORIAL OF IMPERIAL CREDULITY**
Like many tyrants Tiberius was extremely superstitious and attached great importance to the intimations of future events to be learned from the heavenly bodies. In this observatory tower, recently rebuilt, he spent long hours in company with the astrologer Thrasylus, in whose prophetic skill he had unshakable faith.

**WHERE ONE OF THE MOST NOTORIOUS ROMAN EMPERORS SPENT THE LAST YEARS OF HIS LIFE—**

Hardly anything remains of the superstructure of Tiberius' villa at Capri, but sufficient of the brick and concrete substructure and cellars has been uncovered by Professor Maiuri and his associate workers to reveal the general plan and arrangement of the building and to warrant this ambitious reconstruction of the palace as it may have appeared at the time of the emperor's residence there. It stood at the eastern point of the island with one face at the extreme edge of the cliffs. Here were the private apartments with windows commanding a view across to the mainland.

—THE PALACE OF TIBERIUS AT CAPRI AS IT MAY HAVE APPEARED DURING HIS RETIREMENT

On the western side the main body of the palace was built on terraces overlooking the island and arranged round colonnaded courts. A notable feature of this lordly pleasure house were the great open spaces laid out as gardens; one like a stadium lay at the foot of the residential buildings. The precincts ended in a long terrace extending across the entire front. With regard to the height of the structure the ruins of at least three storeys can be traced on the eastern face of the cliff, and the massiveness of the foundations justifies the assumption that these were not all but that the building towered up like a sky-scraper

"THE LEAP OF TIBERIUS": TOWERING PEAK AROUND WHOSE SUMMIT GRIM LEGEND HAS GROWN

Rising to a height of 974 feet sheer from the sea this great rock is called Salto di Tiberio, the Leap of Tiberius, from an old story that the emperor was wont to order victims of his displeasure to be hurled to death from its summit. Cruel and tyrannical as Tiberius was, this particular story is almost certainly without foundation in fact. It was given perpetual currency by Suetonius who, like Tacitus, wrote with a strong bias against the emperor and was ready to believe the worst scandals that were spread about him.

His private life had been a tragedy. Step-son of Augustus, he had quickly been promoted to high rank and had justified his promotion when suddenly, for no reason known to us, he was disgraced and condemned to years of exile. His marriage, contracted for dynastic reasons, had been most unhappy. In the end he succeeded Augustus, but rather from lack of other heirs than from any favour of Augustus. Small wonder that the world accounted him morose and reserved.

He had difficulties to face that were unknown to Augustus. By the proud Roman aristocracy the institution of empire was loathed. They looked back to the days when they were free to misgovern and to plunder provinces, and took it ill that one of their own number should have the power to restrain them. This jealousy had led to many years of civil war; and after these all parties had acquiesced from sheer exhaustion in the government of Augustus. But when Tiberius succeeded, and it was patent that the empire was going to continue, the aristocratic opposition raised its head.

The most probable explanation we can give of Tiberius's retirement to Capri is that, acutely sensitive to his own lack of popularity, he supposed the growing opposition to be directed against him personally, not against the imperial system, and argued that the machine would work more smoothly if he eliminated himself and ruled through a deputy. The treachery of the deputy aroused him to the truth. If the tale be true that henceforth he encouraged spies and struck cruelly at potential enemies, he might well plead self-defence; the empire had to continue, despite the Roman nobility.

Let us remember that the popular idea of him is derived from the pages of the historian Tacitus, who also belonged to the aristocratic opposition and wrote with a definite bias against him. How far prejudice could blind Tacitus to the good in an emperor has been amusingly illustrated of late in the case of his contemporary the Emperor Domitian. To him Domitian was simply a savage tyrant; whereas modern historians, working from the results of recent archaeological research, find themselves compelled to rate Domitian's achievements ever higher and higher. Perhaps one day we shall be able similarly to form an independent estimate of Tiberius.

## Temples of the Gods. VIII.

# A Temple of the Great God Baal

### By E. Royston Pike

#### Author of " Temple Bells "

*LITTLE has so far been known of the actual rites of the Semitic god Baal whose worship is prominent in Old Testament accounts, but probably he was an abstraction represented by groups of local gods. Some further light is thrown on the problem by the recent excavations at Ras Shamra in Syria, a short account of which is given here. The photos are copyright by Professor F. A. Claude Schaeffer, Director of the French Archaeological Mission at Ras Shamra, and Curator of the Prehistoric and Gallo-Roman Museum at Strasbourg. Other aspects of Baal worship come up for consideration in later chapters on Carthage and Baalbek.—*EDITOR.

OF the multitudinous divinities of the ancient East, perhaps the best known is the one who in our Scriptures is denominated Baal, the god whom the children of Israel preferred time and again to Jahveh, for whom Ahab reared an altar; the god whose priests, egged on by Elijah's mockings, leaped up and down, slashed themselves with knives and lancets, from morning even until noon; the god for whom the chosen youth of Judah's kingdom passed through the fires of sacrifice.

Despite his repute, however, we know little of the details of Baal's worship, of the ceremonies that were performed beside his altars on the high places, of the mystic ritual of the groves, of the forms in which the god was made apparent to his worshippers. Some have maintained that there were no visible representations of Baal, but only upright stones whose phallic shape suggested the god's fructifying power. Others, however, have argued that the barbaric folk who embraced the Baal cultus were not likely

to be content with symbols of a symbol, and that the deity was represented in sculptured stone after the pattern of the Eastern pantheon.

That the latter view is the correct one would appear to be established by the archaeologists' unearthing in Syria and Palestine of what we are assured are carven portraits of the local Baal—local, for there was not one Baal, but many baals or baalim, each the embodiment, so far as a particular town or district was concerned, of the male principle.

One of the finest of these representations so far discovered is that found in 1932 by the French Archaeological Mission, under the direction of Professor F. A. Claude Schaeffer, at Ras Shamra, near the bay of Minet-el-Beida on the north Syrian coast. As will be seen from our illustration, it depicts the god standing in a warlike, fear-inspiring attitude, brandishing in one hand a club, while in the other he grasps a thunderbolt with a spear-pointed tip. Beside him is a much smaller figure, arrayed in a long Syrian robe and mounted on a

**BAAL. HURLER OF THUNDERBOLTS**

This stele of Baal, found in the mound of Ras Shamra in northern Syria, is one of the few representations of the god so far discovered. Essentially a nature deity, the embodiment of the generative principle, he here represents nature's destructive aspect, for in his hands are a thunderbolt and club. The smaller figure is believed to be that of a king of Ras Shamra.

**WATER FOR THE DEAD IN A ROYAL TOMB**
Many graves and tombs have been located at Ras Shamra and the near-by Minet-el-Beida. This royal tomb is remarkable not only for its coursed masonry and pointed arch but for the window in the far end—placed there to enable the grave's occupant to reach the jar of water which, with vessels for drawing the water and drinking, was placed without.

the finding of the Babylonian tablets at Tell-el-Amarna in 1887, comprises, in addition to the dictionaries, business accounts, lists of various kinds, letters, notes of religious ritual and — most valuable—on a broken tablet nearly 800 lines of a kind of epic poem in which feature more than twenty deities, including Astarte, Dagon (of Bible fame), and a son of Baal. All would appear to date from towards the end of the second millennium B.C.—*i.e.* about the time when the Israelites were invading the land of Canaan to the south.

The stele of Baal, to which reference has been already made, was found close by, and in the neighbourhood several other representations of gods and goddesses have been brought to light. These include a votive tablet dedicated to Baal by " Mami, royal scribe and overseer of the treasury," on which the god and his worshipper are both depicted ; a stele representing a male divinity

pedestal, who is believed to represent a king of Ras Shamra—perhaps the monarch at whose order the stele came into being, and who wished at one and the same time to express his comparative unworthiness and his reliance upon the protective care of mighty Baal.

Three thousand or more years ago, Ras Shamra seems to have been the metropolis, commercial, religious and intellectual, of northern Syria. It was rich and flourishing, for to the adjacent harbour came the galleys laden with copper ore from the Cyprus mines, and through its landward gates passed the goods that Syria and Mesopotamia traded for those of Egypt and the islands of the Aegean. Being wealthy, its merchant princes had the means to patronize the learned, and one of the most remarkable of Professor Schaeffer's discoveries is that of the remains of a great library and school or institute of book-making scribes. The foundations of a large room, surrounded with smaller chambers and with a staircase indicative of an upper storey, have been laid bare ; and among the broken stone and brick were found a number of tablets inscribed with cuneiform lettering—the books which the students of those far-distant days perused with eager zeal or yawning boredom, which perhaps in that same room were made by scribes with pointed stylus on soft clay. Some of these antique tablets contained lists of words, even dictionaries, of the languages used by the scribes—Babylonian, Sumerian, Hittite, Egyptian, Phoenician and a mysterious sixth, known to us only through the Ras Shamra tablets. This literary treasure-trove, constituting the most important discovery of its kind since

**BEAUTY IN PORCELAIN**
Bizarre though their divinities appear to us, this remarkable head fashioned in porcelain satisfies the modern aesthetic sense. It was discovered in one of the tombs, believed to date from the 14th or 13th centuries B.C., at Minet-el-Beida.
Photographs copyright by Professor F. A. Claude Schaeffer

with horns and wearing short breeches and sandals, and statuettes of a divine couple (illustrated in this page). The latter in particular are really remarkable. Only a few inches in height made of silver enriched with gold their style is extremely primitive, even barbaric. Speculation is busy as to whom they represent, but as yet the identity of the strange little pair, so huge-nosed, so monstrous-eyed, remains a secret. This we know, however, that before the glitter of their silver bodies was dimmed and dirtied by contact with millenniums of superimposed dust, they were held in great esteem, for they were found enclosed in an earthen jar buried amid the débris of the temple. Evidently their guardians, priests or scribes, seeing ruin approach in the guise, perchance, of a relentless foe who knew not their cherished divinities, did their best to secure them from sacrilegious hands. They succeeded so well that for thousands of years the figures lay buried; and now today, when they see once again the light, they engender not iconoclastic anger but vexatious puzzlement.

There was a temple at Ras Shamra, a wondrous library, a scriptorium; there were also tombs—layer upon layer of them, suggestive of a holy,

GROTESQUE DIVINITIES OF ANCIENT SYRIA

Among the most remarkable of the finds at Ras Shamra are these statuettes, believed to represent a god and companion goddess, executed in silver but evidently the work of a barbaric or rustic craftsman. They were discovered enclosed in the pottery vase in which they had lain hid for more than 3,000 years.

highly-regarded site. Indeed, inasmuch as the graves are beneath the temple, it would seem that it was from the presence of the dead that the spot first acquired its sanctity. A number of the burials were made as far back as 1700 B.C., and in these some of the corpses were interred in a crouching posture, while others were first stripped of their flesh and then the trunk was placed in a large vase and the limbs and head buried beside it. Of somewhat later date are the chamber-tombs (see illustration in page 188), the burial-places, as likely as not, of the local sovereigns and their entourage. In one were found the fragmented skeletons of twenty-eight men, women and children; and in most lay goblets and drinking-cups and vases of the choicest Cyprian or Mycenaean ware, placed there for the use of the deceased.

As a cemetery, then, Ras Shamra probably had its origin. Traders came and went, priests and priestesses performed Baal's libidinous rites, youthful scribes sat at the feet of the old and incised their tablets of brick. Then disaster struck the town, or may be it merely succumbed to the touch of Time's finger, so today it is a cemetery again—of dead races, dead tongues, dead faiths.

AMEN'S TEMPLE AT KARNAK: THE MOST STUPENDOUS RELIGIOUS MONUMENT IN EXISTENCE

As the chief local deity of Thebes, Amen had a temple at Karnak at a very early period, but after his elevation to the supreme place in the Egyptian pantheon the rulers of the Twelfth Dynasty replanned the early building on a much larger scale, and their successors developed it until the temple of Amen at Karnak became not merely a cathedral but the cathedral city of Egypt. In this air view the obelisk slightly out of the perpendicular in the left foreground is one of the pair set up in front of the Osiris Court by Thothmes I; the obelisk beyond is one of the two erected by Queen Hatshepsut. The tall columns somewhat to the right mark the entrance to the Hypostyle Hall, the maze of whose columns occupies most of the middle distance.

## The Wonder Cities. IV.

# Thebes in its Splendour

## By Arthur Weigall

Author of " The Glory of the Pharaohs," etc.

WHEN Diodorus visited the city of Thebes in 57 B.C. he found it very largely in ruins, but the priests and scribes were able to show him evidence of its past greatness, and he has left a record of what he heard and saw. In former times, he says, its circumference was about twelve miles (100 stadia), and it was adorned with stately public buildings, magnificent temples, and rich memorials, while some of its private houses were four or five storeys high. It was, in fact, he says, the most beautiful and most stately city, not only of Egypt, but of all the world, for there was no metropolis under the sun adorned with such a multiplicity of monuments of gold, silver, and ivory, and so many multitudes of colossi and obelisks.

Strabo, writing in 24 B.C., says that its ruins at that time extended some nine miles (80 stadia) in length, and he recalls the lines of Homer, written many centuries before, in which the poet speaks of the city's hundred gates, of its gleaming gold, and of its soldiers and horses and chariots.

Modern excavations have not laid bare many important remains of the city itself, but the vast temple-ruins on both banks of the Nile, and the thousands of tombs on the western side, are clear evidence of the might of Thebes. The ancient Egyptians built their houses very largely of unbaked bricks, covering the walls and floors with whitewashed and decorated plaster ; and only those buildings which were erected on the dry sand of the neighbouring desert have left any trace behind. All the walls of the houses in the city itself have long since collapsed, and their ruins have become part of the soil which is annually soaked by the flooded Nile. The modern towns of Luxor and Karnak have grown up on top of the compressed and trodden-down remains of the ancient houses and palaces, and excavation generally reveals only a mass of formless earth and potsherds, with here and there a fragment of stonework, or an almost indistinguishable portion of an ancient wall.

Fortunately, however, there is a quantity of material available—paintings, inscriptions, documents, and objects by which we can reconstruct the life of this ancient city ; and, after all, its main features, such as the Avenue of Sphinxes, the great temples, the quays, and so forth, still exist in great part, and the magnificent background of the desert hills, the verdant fields around, and the Nile itself, are all unchanged in general aspect.

Thebes stood mainly on the east bank of the river, some 450 miles above Memphis (near the modern Cairo) and about 140 miles below the First Cataract. Although it was in existence from a very remote period, its real history begins about 2100 B.C. when the Pharaohs of the eleventh

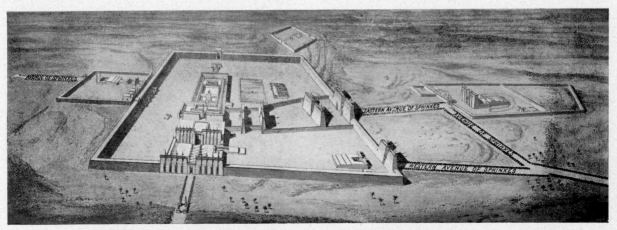

RECONSTRUCTION OF THE GREAT TEMPLES AND SACRED ENCLOSURES AT KARNAK
For details of buildings see plan in page 195

COLOSSAL PILLARS IN THE COURT OF THE TEMPLE OF RAMESES III. AT KARNAK

Despite its relatively small size—it is only 170 feet in length—the Temple of Rameses III. at Karnak is probably the best extant example of a complete temple of a simple kind, having been constructed throughout on a harmonious plan. The photograph shows part of the open court beyond the pylon or gateway of the façade. This court is flanked with passages, the roofs of each of which are supported by eight massive Osiris pillars. The temple, dedicated to Ammon, was excavated in 1896-7 by M. Legrain.

Photo by Donald McLeish

dynasty reigned there in some magnificence, and the city is referred to in one inscription as being "like a splendid sea." The height of its power, however, was attained between the eighteenth and twenty-first dynasties, that is to say between 1550 B.C. and 950 B.C.—six hundred years of wonderful prosperity, during which time its fame and its wealth were the talk of the civilized world.

The name Thebes was given to it by the Greeks, who thus transformed the native Ta-apé ; but the city was often called by the Egyptians Nu-Ammon, "The Town of Ammon," which name is rendered in the Bible as No-Ammon, or simply No. The Greeks identified Ammon with Zeus, and therefore called it "The Town of Zeus," or Diospolis, as well as Thebes. It is known by many other names in Egyptian inscriptions : "The Mysterious City," "The City of the Hidden Name," "The City of the Lord of Eternity," "The Mistress of Might," and so on. It was the centre of the worship of the god Ammon, who had once been a local deity of no great importance, but whose power increased with the rise of the city until he became identified with the ancient sun-god Ra, under the name Ammon-Ra, king of the

gods, and was adored together with Mut, the mother-goddess, and Khensu (sometimes spelt Khons or Khonsu), the god of the moon, these three forming the great Theban Trinity.

After 950 B.C. its power declined, and in 661 B.C. the city was destroyed by the conquering Assyrians, a catastrophe to which the prophet Nahum refers in his warning to Nineveh : "Art thou better than populous No, that was situate among the rivers, that had the waters round about it, whose rampart was the sea (river ?), and her wall was from the sea ? Ethiopia and Egypt were her strength, and it was infinite ; Put and Lubim were thy helpers. Yet was she carried away, she went into captivity : her young children also were dashed in pieces at the top of all the streets : and they cast lots for her honourable men, and all her great men were bound in chains."

The city was rebuilt after this disaster, but in 525 B.C. it was again destroyed, this time by Cambyses ; and though later Egyptian kings of the Ptolemaic dynasty restored its temples and carried out great building works, the place was never again of first-rate importance. Let us here, however, try to picture it as it was in the height

**LOOKING THROUGH THE PILLARED CATHEDRAL HALL OF KARNAK'S GREAT TEMPLE**

For a hundred years three Pharaohs laboured to bring the Hypostyle Hall to perfection. According to Maspero, it was planned by Rameses I., while the building was finished by Seti I., and Rameses II. almost completed the decorations. Pharaohs of later dynasties endeavoured to share the glory of the three founders, but nearly three hundred years elapsed before the final pylon and colonnaded court were attempted. Revolts in Thebes hindered the efforts of the Ptolemies, the earthquake of 27 B.C. overthrew part of the temple, and the pylon was never completed.

of its power, somewhere about 1250 B.C., when Rameses II. sat upon the Egyptian throne.

In imagination let us take our stand upon the roof of some tower in the midst of the city, and turn towards the rising sun in the east. Looking across the housetops, our backs being towards the river, we see the open fields stretched out for many a mile ; and in the distance there are the peaks of the three desert hills which are a landmark to all travellers who approach the metropolis from the north or south.

Turning now to look westward, we see the great

the peasants are scattered. Behind these again is the desert necropolis at the foot of the magnificent hills which are dedicated to the goddess Hathor, who each evening, to use the figurative language of mythology, receives the setting sun into her bosom.

These hills tower up opposite the city like a rugged wall of gold in the sunshine, but to the north and south they pass into the distance in lower undulations, carrying the eye into the eternal mystery of the desert. At about the middle of the main range there is a great wall of cliffs, and at the foot of these the white terraces of the temple

RUINS OF THE GREAT TEMPLE OF AMMON SEEN FROM THE SACRED LAKE

First built on a large scale by kings of the twelfth dynasty, and altered and embellished by later monarchs down to the Ptolemies, the Temple of Ammon at Karnak was Egypt's greatest sanctuary. Its Hypostyle Hall (illustrated in colour facing p. 197), its Temple of Thothmes III., its great court, massive pylons, fine colonnades and sculptures awake our wonder still. On the sacred lake once floated the boats of the gods, and across it at night-time, once a year—according to a tradition favoured by the fellahin —may be seen passing a ghostly golden dahabiyeh.

Photo by Donald McLeish

Temple of Ammon, erected already a hundred and fifty years ago by Amenhotep III., on the edge of the river, the main building being at the south end, the open, sun-bathed courtyard, surrounded by a colonnade of pillars, linking it to the court and pylons lately built by Rameses II. at the north end. Beside this mighty temple are the quays where the river-craft, with their tall masts, lie moored ; and across the wide stretch of the waters of the Nile there are again open fields and palm-groves, among which the white villas of the wealthy and the drab-coloured houses and huts of

built by Queen Hatshepsut nearly three centuries earlier, can plainly be seen rising above the intervening trees and fields ; while beside it is the ancient temple of the Pharaoh Nebhapetra-Mentuhotep, already 800 years old in the time of Rameses II.

Out of sight, on the far side of these cliffs, lies the lonely Valley of the Tombs of the Kings, where the Pharaohs are buried. A little to the south rises a hill which is honeycombed with the rock-cut mortuary chapels and tombs of the nobles of Thebes who have been buried there for the last six hundred years and more; and near its foot is the great temple just built in honour of the reigning Pharaoh, Rameses II. Farther south stands the mortuary-temple of Amenhotep III., 150 years old, its gateway guarded by two great colossi; and to the south of this again are the temples of Amenhotep I. and Thothmes I., erected more than 300 years ago, and the ruined palace of Amenhotep III., where he once lived in splendour with his beautiful queen, Tiyi.

As our eyes sweep in imagination along this desert necropolis, we see various smaller temples built by the different Pharaohs of the past. A little to the north of Hatshepsut's temple, but on the edge of the fields, is the temple of her brother, Thothmes III., the great warrior Pharaoh, whose memory is greatly revered; and to the north of this again is the temple erected by Seti I., the father of Rameses II.

It is a magnificent prospect, this range of great buildings, backed by the splendid hills of the desert; but directing our eyes across the river to the city once more, we gaze with equal wonder, over the noisy streets and flat-roofed houses of Thebes, northwards to the huge temples of Karnak, where the god Ammon has his chief centre of worship. Here white pylons and obelisks of pink granite rise into the blue of the sky, and the huge Hypostyle Hall, recently finished by Rameses II., can be seen towering above the more ancient part of the temple. A little to the south of the main buildings is the temple of Mut, the mother-goddess, with its gardens and beautiful artificial lake; and to the west is a little shrine of Khensu (the moon) which presently will be rebuilt on a larger scale.

Now let us descend from our imaginary tower and look at some of these buildings more closely. The Temple of Amenhotep III. (known to the modern visitor as the Temple of Luxor) first commands our attention by its size and beauty, and we approach it by the broad Avenue of Sphinxes which runs from here all the way to Karnak, like a great boulevard bisecting the city. Beautiful gardens have recently been planted in front of the new pylons of the temple; and the colour of the flowers, the red and white pennants fluttering from the tall flagstaffs which stand on either side of the doorway, the gold-capped obelisks of pink granite, and the vivid paintings on the white walls of the building itself, combine to create a picture of extreme brilliance. The huge doorway of the temple is plated with electrum and studded with gold, and through it we enter the forecourt, surrounded by richly painted pillars, between which stand huge statues of Rameses as though stepping out into the sunshine from the shadow of the magnificent colonnade

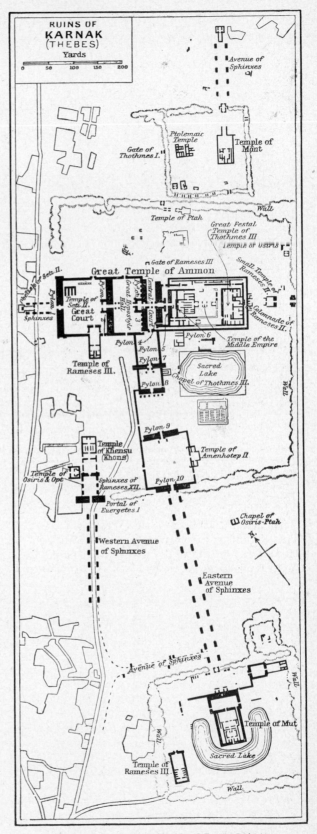

PLAN OF THE RUINS OF KARNAK

PAPYRUS-BUD PILLARS OF THE TEMPLE OF AMENHOTEP III. AT LUXOR

Unlike some other wonders of the past in Egypt, the ruins of the Temple of Amenhotep III., known familiarly as the Temple of Luxor, are devoid of darkness. Its magnificent columns, now full of air and sunlight, front the busy Nile, while behind ebbs and flows the varied life of the modern village. Children play and pigeons fly around them, and Christian and Moslem—hard by the very court of Rameses II. is a mosque—pursue their religious observances where, some fifteen hundred years before Christ, the people of Thebes paid homage to Ammon-Ra and Mut, and their son Khensu.

Photo from W. M. Flinders Petrie

Thence we pass into the great hall built by Tutankhamen a century ago, and finished by Horemheb, on the walls of which are painted and sculptured scenes representing a festival of the god Ammon, and showing the procession which passed on that occasion between this temple and Karnak. So we come to the large forecourt built by Amenhotep III., the pavement of which is partly covered with sheets of silver; and beyond it, approached through a forest of pillars, is the main temple, only open to the priests, where, in a superb shrine, the golden ark of Ammon rests.

We leave the temple and walk out on to the embankment facing the Nile. This is paved with stone, and there are flights of stone steps leading down to the water. Here great river-going vessels are moored, some with richly-decorated cabins built on their decks, and with furled sails of many colours which are reflected in the mirror of the water. Here, on the quays, merchants from distant lands are to be seen moving among the bales and boxes which contain their wares, and groups of

sailors sit about in the sunshine. Richly dressed priests, officials, and dignitaries of the city pass to and fro; and here and there a little chariot is to be seen, drawn by two small horses with coloured plumes tossing upon their heads. Carts with wheels are rare, but heavy sledges drawn by oxen are to be observed, and pack donkeys are used, for as yet the camel is unknown.

We walk around the north end of the temple, and so pass once more through the gardens to the great avenue, and make our way between the two seemingly endless rows of ram-headed sphinxes (see page 156) through the city, out to Karnak. Just before we reach the main temple we turn off to the right, by another short avenue of sphinxes, and so reach the Temple of Mut, half surrounded by the crescent-shaped sacred lake among the trees, the whole area being encompassed by a high wall. Inside the court of the temple there are long rows of grey granite statues of the lioness-headed goddess, Sekhmet (or Sekhet), the divine wife of Ptah, she being at this period identified with Mut, and

RECONSTRUCTION OF THE GREAT HYPOSTYLE HALL IN THE TEMPLE OF AMMON AT KARNAK

One of the wonders of the world, the Great Hypostyle Hall measures 170 feet by 338 feet. Its twelve central roof-supporting clustered papyrus columns, with calyx capitals, are 80 feet in height, 11½ feet in diameter, and 33 feet in circumference. The additional 122 smaller columns, also in a reddish sandstone, have bud capitals, and are 42½ feet in height and 27½ feet in circumference. This great cathedral-like structure, 5,450 square yards in area, is divided into nave and aisles, the nave being subdivided into three aisles. The walls and columns are covered with coloured inscriptions and reliefs (see colour plate facing page 197). From its stone-barred windows was derived the Arab name of Karnak (window).

Courtesy of the Metropolitan Museum of Art. New York City

198

GREAT FORECOURT OF THE TEMPLE OF AMENHOTEP III. AT LUXOR, LOOKING NORTH-EAST

Measuring about 185 feet in length and 167 feet in breadth the Great Court of Rameses II., which lies within the pylon of the Temple of Amenhotep III., was surrounded by a double row of pillars. These pillars, to the total number of 74, are in the form known as papyrus columns, with smooth shafts and bud capitals. Raised above the ground level within the court is a chapel, built by Thothmes III., and restored by Rameses II., and containing three chambers dedicated respectively to Ammon, Mut, and Khensu. The walls of the court are covered with inscriptions and reliefs, and in the southern side are standing statues of Rameses II. averaging 23 feet in height, one in black and the others in red granite.

Photo by Gaddis & Seif

199

in all directions we are confronted with her mysterious, leonine smile.

Yet another avenue of sphinxes, running more or less parallel to the main avenue, brings us to the great Temple of Ammon, the doors of which are made of Asiatic copper, studded with gold. The main feature of this building is the huge Hypostyle Hall, only lately finished, the roof being supported by 134 enormous pillars, the largest of which are 80 feet high and over 30 feet in circumference. It is a vast and dimly-lit hall, the light being admitted through grated windows set high under the roof ; but the columns and walls are richly decorated with coloured reliefs, the strong pigments of which counteract the otherwise forbidding aspect of the building. The tremendous size of the columns, however, is awe-inspiring ; and the shaven-headed priests who pass to and fro seem like little creeping things, intimidated by the fearful majesty of these courts of Ammon.

Beyond this hall we come to the colonnades and forecourts which stand before the sanctuary, where only the feet of the priests may tread, and here we pause to gaze in admiration at the great obelisks erected by Queen Hatshepsut, which pass up into the blue of the sky as though they were pointing the way from earth to heaven. Making a detour around these sacred buildings we enter an open, sunny court, at the far side of which is the great Festival Hall erected by Thothmes III., a spacious building having on its western side a number of chambers wherein the King had caused to be sculptured a pictorial catalogue of the flowers, plants, birds, and animals which he had brought back from his wars in Syria. Near by there is the sacred lake, surrounded by trees and gardens, and here, against the stone quay, the festival barque of Ammon is moored, its sides shining with gold.

The buildings and gardens of this great group of temples cover an area of over a square mile, and are surrounded by a stout rampart of brick,

**SECOND PYLON OF THE MAIN TEMPLE OF RAMESES III. AT MEDINET HABU**

Dedicated to Ammon and planned like the Ramesseum, the main Temple of Rameses III. at Medinet Habu is part of the temple group of the Theban necropolis. The pylon or towered gateway shown in the photograph is remarkable for its inscriptions and sculptures. On the left tower the king is depicted leading before Ammon and Mut three rows of prisoners (Philistines), taken in a campaign of the eighth year of his reign, the successful issue of which is chronicled in the inscriptions on the companion tower

Photo from W. M. Flinders Petrie

VIEW OF THE SPLENDID COLONNADE IN THE LUXOR TEMPLE

It is described as the most beautiful group of columns in Egypt. What must it have been when first completed, its lovely contours glowing with colour under the tropic sky, framed with verdure and waving palms, fresh from the hands of architect and artist? The seven pairs of columns are about 52 feet in height, and at each side are colossal seated figures of Rameses II. After the introduction of Christianity, the temple, about 284 yards in length when completed, was converted into a church.

Photo by Donald McLeish

RESTORATION OF THE "PAVILION" OF THE TEMPLE OF RAMESES III. AT MEDINET HABU

The so-called "Pavilion" in the outer wall of the temple, and forming the entrance thereto, represents an attempt to reproduce a fortress of the kind made familiar to Egyptians in their campaigns in North Syria. Flanked by two small guard chambers, it is built of hewn stone, and its towers, about 26 feet wide, were originally about 72 feet in height. On the façades of the towers Rameses is shown smiting his foes. The reproduction is from a design by Charles Chipiez.

outside which the houses of the city are clustered, the main streets and largest dwellings being situated on the east side of the Avenue of Sphinxes, in the direction of the Temple of Amenhotep III.

The houses of the nobles and richer citizens are surrounded by gardens, and are shut in by high walls, so that, even in the city, considerable seclusion is obtained. There is usually a group of palms and sometimes a little vineyard in front of the house, and often a small ornamental pond, wherein lotus flowers grow in profusion. As we walk along the streets we can only see the tops of the palm-trees and acacias above the white-washed walls, but if we enter through some gateway and walk up the neatly swept garden path to the house itself, we shall see a pillared portico or veranda, beyond which is the main hall where the meals are served, and where comfortable armchairs stand about. In the interior of the house are the bedrooms and kitchens, or, sometimes, these are on the upper floors. There is generally a loggia or veranda on the northern side, where, in summer, the cool north wind may be enjoyed, and another on the southern side, where, in winter, there is protection from the breeze, and the full strength of the sun can be felt.

The dwellings of the middle classes are simple, flat-roofed little buildings, having sometimes an upper room with awnings spread before the doorway. Both these and the houses of the wealthy are designed to meet the extremes of the weather, for in winter Thebes is sunny, but frequently cold, there being often actual frost at nights, and in summer it is intensely hot. Rain falls so seldom that it has hardly to be considered, and therefore the roofs are flat, and little protection against a downpour is necessary. This absence of rain, however, causes the roads to be very dusty, and everywhere we meet with water-carriers sprinkling the water upon the parched earth. The irrigation of the gardens has to be continuous, and near each of the larger houses there is a well whence the water is raised and directed into small channels which bring it to the flower beds.

In summer-time the court moves north to Memphis or to Lower Egypt, where the breeze from the sea cools the air ; but most of the ordinary townspeople have been born and bred here in the south, and do not mind the great heat prevailing from May to August. At the end of the latter month the Nile rises into flood, and the fields around the city are soon inundated, so that Thebes is almost like an island, and the north wind, blowing across the water, brings some degree of coolness into the streets.

The Palace of the Pharaoh is an extensive building just outside the city, standing in beautiful gardens wherein are artificial lakes, and many little kiosks charmingly decorated in bright colours. In the main halls of the palace, the walls, ceiling, and floor are covered with paintings executed with great skill. Flights of duck are shown rising from the papyrus swamps into the air, and seem to be winging their way towards the open casements; butterflies are depicted fluttering amongst the poppies; and beneath our feet fishes swim amongst the lotus flowers. The pillars are often inlaid with coloured glass; and the furniture is rich with gold and inlay.

As we walk through the streets of the city we cannot fail to be surprised at the wide contrast between the elegance and luxury enjoyed by the wealthy, and the primitive conditions in which the poorer citizens dwell. It is not so much the contrast between affluence and actual want that

## "PAVILION" OF THE TEMPLE OF RAMESES III. AS IT IS TO-DAY

The "Pavilion," of which a reconstruction is shown in the opposite page, serves as a memorial of the triumphant campaigns of Rameses III. and of the twenty-one years of peace which followed his victories over the Libyans and invading barbarians, for it was during this peace that the temple at Medinet Habu was constructed. The pictures on the façades of the towers show Rameses smiting his Nubian and Libyan foes before Ammon-Ra, and seven fettered princes representing the conquered peoples.

Photo from W. M. Flinders Petrie

**HEADLESS STATUES IN THE MORTUARY CHAPEL OF RAMESES II. AT THEBES**

Of the Ramesseum, or mortuary chapel of Rameses II., at Thebes, only about one-half remains. On the four sides of the second court were colonnades, partly of papyrus-bud columns, partly of square pillars with statues of the god Osiris. The figures of Osiris, which also represent Rameses II., are mostly headless. On the shafts of the columns and the sides of the pillars are represented the monarch, the most celebrated of the Egyptian kings, and one of the greatest of temple builders, sacrificing to the gods.

Photo by Donald McLeish

strikes us, but rather a difference between the manner of life of the upper and lower ranks of society. The poor people are simple and rudimentary in their requirements. Their houses, or rather huts, are almost unfurnished ; their garments are few, and their food is of the plainest. Yet they are contented and law-abiding ; and since the Egyptians have never been a cruel people like some of their Asiatic neighbours, there is little misery or oppression to be observed. Nevertheless, their condition is almost primeval in its absence of the refinements of civilization, and their ignorance and superstition are astonishing.

On the other hand the life of the upper classes is elegant in the extreme, and we can see at once that thousands of years of culture have passed in its formation. The houses of the wealthy are very luxurious and very clean ; the furniture and ornaments of life all display the highest state of civilization ; and learning and education are to be observed wherever the members of the privileged classes are gathered.

Under such conditions, of course, it is only natural to find that the people are priest-ridden, and everywhere in the city we see signs of the domination of the priesthood of Ammon. The shaven heads of these " servants of the god," as they are called, are to be observed in every street, and the various rites and services in the temples are the events of the day. The air is full of incense and the savour of burnt offerings, and the strange chants of the holy choristers are heard on all sides. Thebes, in fact, is well named " The Mysterious City," for Ammon, who is called "The Hidden One," is master of the lives of all its inhabitants, and, through his learned priests, rules every hovel and every mansion.

Thus, as we leave its busy streets to return to our own times, we carry away with us an impression of a vast area of small dwellings and unimportant streets relieved here and there by a fine house, a lordly highway, or a beautiful garden ; but, rising from this jumble, the great and splendid temples of Ammon, King of the Gods, remain in our memory, dominating the picture and uttering a challenge to Time itself.

## The Master Builders. II.

# The Marvel of the Roman Aqueducts

## By Prof. F. A. Wright

Professor of Classics, London University ; author of " The Girdle of Aphrodite "

EVERY nation, ancient and modern, has some concrete achievement which symbolises the character of the people. Modern America has its skyscrapers rising with gay audacity to heaven. Modern England has its fleets of ships, from the lordly liner to the tiny fishing-smack, questing a livelihood on the water. Ancient Greece, enamoured of beauty, had its temples and its statues to appeal to the imagination and fascinate the eye. Ancient Rome embodied its love of effort, of order, and of practical utility in its leagues of roads and its mighty aqueducts.

" Tantae molis erat "—Virgil's immortal lines come back to one's mind when we consider the work of his countrymen in building, in making laws, and in governing the world. I remember still my first pilgrimage to Rome, many years ago, and of all the pictures that then impressed themselves upon my consciousness the two most vivid were the first view of the Alps shining rosy in the morning sun as the train wound its way up laboriously from Culoz, and, later, the first view of the Campagna in the soft twilight of an Italian evening, the dark clumps of scattered and melancholy trees, the white strip of road with an occasional bullock-cart wending its way slowly home, and by its side the long line of huge broken arches, memorials of the mighty past, stretching towards the dim and distant outlines of the Alban hills. Those arches, serene in their shattered grandeur, are all that remain of the Claudia aqueduct, and modern Rome still draws some of its abundant water supply from the actual conduits of which they once formed part.

In A.D 537 Rome was besieged by the Goths and Burgundians, and the very accessibility of the aqueducts rendered them an obvious mark for attack. The conduits were broken, and at a point where several lines of aqueducts converged from different parts of the plain the barbarians established a walled camp, using the masonry as part of the fortification. One of the towers they then built, the Torre Fiscale, is standing to this day. After A.D. 537 the aqueducts were left neglected for over two hundred years ; the water, instead of bringing life and health to Rome, flowed in stagnant streams over the plain, and thus it was probably that the dreary marshes of the Campagna, with their air of peculiar desolation, came into being. In A.D. 776 the great Pope, Adrian I., put in power by Charlemagne, began their partial restoration, substituting underground conduits for overhead arches, and the work was continued by his successors

The Greeks, before the Romans, had seen the importance of a good water supply for cities, and some traces of the sluices they constructed from Lake Copais, in Boeotia, are still left to bear witness to their engineering skill. But the aqueduct, as we know it, was a Roman discovery, and derived its origin from several causes. First, perhaps, we should put the sheer love of building for itself—the same passion that animates the child with its box of bricks and its sand-castle—which was one of the strongest features of the Roman character. Second, comes one of their great material inventions, the arch, which rendered possible both the huge mass of the Colosseum and the aqueducts with their unbroken line of conduits supported by tiers of arcades beneath. The arch was to the Romans what the steel frame is to an American architect, and although there are traces of its use before them by the Asiatic Greeks, the development of its resources, which they realized, practically made it their own. The third, and in itself sufficient, reason is that guiding rule of architecture, the use of those materials that lie ready to your hand.

It has sometimes, rather foolishly, been supposed that the Romans preferred the raised aqueduct to the hidden conduit or pipe because they were unacquainted with the fact that water always rises to the level of its source. As a matter of fact, they were expert water engineers, and both Vitruvius and Frontinus show themselves well acquainted with most of our modern devices. The reason why they so often chose the aqueduct was that building materials, travertine stone, bricks, concrete, cement, and mortar, were all cheap, plentiful, and readily adapted for use. Pipes, on the other hand, of the size necessary for a main supply of water, were expensive and unreliable. Steel they did not possess ; cast iron they could not work with facility ; bronze was very

FRAGMENTS THAT REMAIN OF HADRIAN'S AQUEDUCT AT CARTHAGE, AND THE AQUA CLAUDIA AT ROME

The illustrations given on this page show two noble aqueducts from widely distant lands.—Rome itself and one of her most important provinces. Top, the aqueduct at Tunis (originally 60 miles long); it was built by the Emperor Hadrian to bring water from the inland mountains to Carthage. After its complete destruction in 146 B.C. Carthage was rebuilt and eventually, in imperial times, regained no small measure of its old importance as a Roman provincial town. Below, the Aqua Claudia crossing the Campagna; it is also illustrated and described in the opposite page. Above it are remains of the concrete-lined brick structure known as the " Anio Novus " or New Anio; the two conduits finally mingled just outside Rome.

206

THE FAR-STRETCHING LINE OF ARCHES OF THE AQUA CLAUDIA AT ROME

Of all the remains in the neighbourhood of Rome few are more impressive than that long line of arches which was once the Aqua Claudia stretching interminably across the Campagna. The Aqua Claudia was built in A.D. 38 to meet the ever-increasing needs of Rome's swelling population, although there were already seven constructed before that date. It drew water from springs in the neighbourhood of Tivoli and entered Rome by what is now the Porta Maggiore; above it was a row of brick arches carrying the supply known as Anio Novus or new River Anio.

costly; and lead, although employed for city use, was unsuitable for a continuous line of large bore pipes. So considerations both of economy and expediency drove the Roman engineer to his arched aqueducts; and we may be thankful that it was so, for they are, perhaps, the most beautiful things that the Romans have left us.

Of the nine aqueducts that served Rome at the period of her greatest prosperity in Hadrian's reign, Frontinus gives us full information in his treatise "De Aquis." Frontinus, after governing Britain with some distinction, was appointed by Hadrian "curator aquarum" (A.D. 97), Chairman of the Metropolitan Water Board in our tongue, and therefore writes from first-hand knowledge. In the early days of Rome, he tells us, people got their water from the Tiber, from wells, from rain-water cisterns, and from the numerous springs, such as the Fountain of the Nymphs and the Fountain of Juturna, which lie at the foot of the Seven Hills, and in the valleys between them. The first aqueduct—"Appia"—was made by the censor, Appius Claudius, in 312 B.C., and drew water from a spring about ten miles south of Rome, still to be seen at the bottom of some stone quarries near the River Anio. Just before it entered the city it was brought across a valley on a series of low arches, but for most of its course it was an underground conduit beneath the road. It discharged its water into a large receiving tank near the present Porta Maggiore, and was thence distributed, as described below, over the town.

While the Appia was constructed like a sewer, the "Anio Vetus" (272 B.C.) is an aqueduct, although a low-level one, in the restricted use of the word. Its intake from one of the mountain valleys through which the Anio flows, some forty-three miles from Rome, was skilfully chosen for the purpose of getting elevation, and the contours of the country were cleverly used to maintain elevation. The line followed that of the modern railway to Tivoli, and for the structure solid blocks of stone were used, laid in cement and plastered on the inside with a special sort of concrete in which pottery pounded up into fine fragments was mixed with the mortar. The "Marcia" came next (146 B.C.), the first high-level aqueduct, carrying spring water at an elevation of 195 feet above sea-level. Built of rough hewn stone it was nearly fifty-eight miles long, and one of the three most famous of the aqueducts. From Tivoli it passed to Gallicano, being carried on arches across the valleys and by tunnels through the hills until it reached the Via Latina. Sinking there into a conduit beneath the road it was taken again, seven miles from Rome, upon an arched aqueduct, remains of which can be seen now near the Porta Furba, and distributed to three sections of the city. The Marcian springs in the country above Tivoli are still used to supply the mains which an English company laid in 1870, and in ancient times the "Marcius liquor" was regarded as the best of all waters for drinking. Nero, with his usual wilfulness, insisted one day on bathing

*BUILT OF MASSIVE BLOCKS UNSTRENGTHENED BY CEMENT—*

Aqueducts, the noblest memorials of Roman architectural genius left to delight and astonish modern eyes, are not due to ignorance of elementary hydraulics on the part of the Romans—namely that water will rise to its own level ; rather are they the result of the difficulty and the cost, with the materials available, of laying the simplest pipe-line system, as compared with these stupendous structures of straight-forward stone, which rely on gravity and a non-hermetic conduit. Not only are they plentiful round Rome itself, but throughout the whole

—*GIANT SPAN OF THE PONT DU GARD, CLOSE TO NIMES*

Roman Empire, Britain excepted ; and of them none is better preserved than the Pont du Gard, three magnificent tiers of arches one above the other, 880 feet long and 160 feet high at the highest. The " bridge " was built to carry the waters of the Eure and Airon in southern France, ultimately destined for the town of Nîmes, across the broad and steep-banked gully of the Gard, and the spot chosen is just above the town of Remoulins. *Photograph by Braun, Paris*

SEGOVIA'S STREETS AND HOUSES CLUSTERING BENEATH THE BULK OF THE PUENTE DEL DIABLO

The universal instinct to say "here is perfection" is baffled when one must choose between the "Puente del Diablo" at Segovia and the Pont du Gard. If the latter (illustrated in pages 208-9) has the more airy grace where it takes the Gard in its stride, the Devil's Bridge is the more solidly massive above the city streets; moreover, it justifies itself by being still in use to-day. Both are inimitable. The "Puente," of course, is not a bridge, but an aqueduct like the rest; it was constructed probably in the reign of Trajan to serve the Roman pleasure resort of Segovia. In the fifteenth century it was restored at the command of Queen Isabella of Spain, and still pours its refreshing burden into the town.

## SO MARVELLOUS THAT THE BARBARIANS CALLED IT THE "DEVIL'S BRIDGE"

The aqueduct brings the Rio Frio to Segovia, and its total length is ten miles; but in our restricted use of the word—that portion which crosses the valley supported on tall arches—it is 847 yards long and its highest point 132 feet above the ground. The arches—there are a hundred and nine of them—are built of a grey granite-like stone in two superimposed tiers, without the aid of cement, mortar, or rivets of any kind, and are still in perfect condition although they have been standing thus for eighteen centuries; the piers scarcely seem strong enough to bear the weight of masonry and water combined. In the centre, where the arches span the roadway, is a broad entablature which bore an inscription, now defaced.

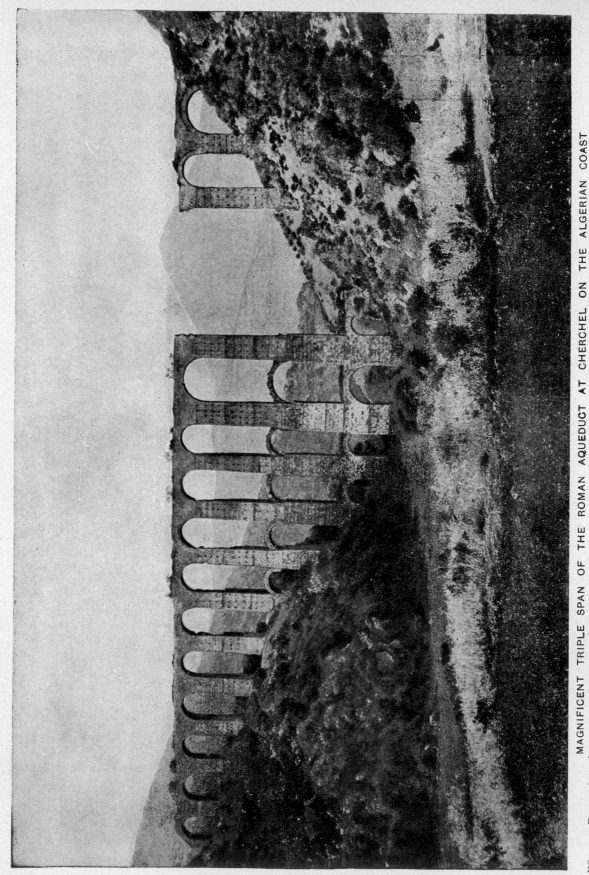

MAGNIFICENT TRIPLE SPAN OF THE ROMAN AQUEDUCT AT CHERCHEL, ON THE ALGERIAN COAST

Wherever Rome colonised we find remains of aqueducts. Serving Caesarea on the Algerian coast, where Juba II. built a lovely capital for the Kingdom of Mauretania given him by the Emperor Augustus. was a splendid aqueduct, still in some parts, as this photograph shows, in a remarkable state of preservation. Built in three superimposed tiers of arches it is the largest Roman work of its kind in Algeria. When the traveller along the main road from Algiers first sees this imposing sight he receives an impression of Roman greatness such as comes to him who first beholds the amphitheatre at El Djem, or the Pont du Gard, all these wonderful monuments being remote from the imperial city of the people whose genius created them

in the fountain-head; the severe chill that resulted was held as a righteous retribution.

The "Tepula," built in 125 B.C. of concrete and mortar, drew from some slightly warm volcanic springs near Frascati; in 33 B.C. Agrippa made a new aqueduct, the "Julia," drawing from some larger cold springs in the same vicinity, and the two supplies after that date were amalgamated. They flowed together for several miles, and finally entered Rome in two channels, both of them built over the Marcia, at the Porta Tiburtina, discharging into a reservoir near the modern Ministry of Finance. When Aurelian, in A.D. 272, built his hasty wall of defence round Rome the arches of Marcia, Tepula, and Julia were all incorporated in the new structure, and there they can still be seen.

Another famous aqueduct, built in the time of Augustus, was the "Virgo" (19 B.C.), which drew from springs near Salone, about eight miles from Rome. It followed the same line as the other aqueducts, until half a mile from the Porta Maggiore, but there turned northward, and, passing under the Via Salaria, entered Rome near the Pincian Hill, just north of the Piazza di Spagna. "Virgo" was a low-level aqueduct, and still supplies the ship fountain in the Piazza di Spagna, passing thence behind the Via Nazzareno, and ending at the well known Fontana di Trevi. To Augustus also is due the "Alsietina" (A.D. 2), made for the express purpose of supplying water to the huge circus he constructed under the Janiculum for mimic sea fights. It drew from a lake twenty miles from Rome, and its water was of inferior quality. Lastly, we have the "Claudia" and the "Anio Novus" (A.D. 38), the Romans' highest achievements, which cost together fifty-five million sesterces, some half a million sterling. Drawing from springs near the sources of "Marcia," the "Claudia" was brought on arches across the Campagna, with "Anio Novus" above it, the "Claudia" being built of stone, the "Anio Novus" of brick lined with concrete. On reaching Rome, by the Porta Maggiore, the two waters were mixed and carried on the Neronian Arches, many of which are still standing, to the Caelian.

These nine aqueducts, supplemented by two others, the "Trajana" and the "Alexandria," built after Frontinus' time, probably brought about forty million gallons of water into Rome every day. The poorer folk fetched their supply from the public fountains, the rich had lead pipes, laid at their own expense and stamped with their names, which conveyed the water into the house. One gang of public slaves, first organized by Agrippa, managed the public service; another gang was available for private owners. Taking the population of Rome as about a million, each person had an allowance of forty gallons a day; a large figure, but not improbable considering the waste which their system of a continuous flow involved, and also the immense amount of time the Romans gave to the bath. Bathing was their favourite recreation, and under the empire no less than six huge establishments were built, one of which alone, the Baths of Diocletian, could accommodate more than two thousand bathers at the same time.

So much then for the aqueducts that brought water to Rome. But Rome was only one city, and wherever the Romans went they took with them their aqueducts, their roads, and their sewers. It has been computed that the ruins of at least two hundred Roman aqueducts are still in existence, and a brief tour round the Mediterranean may here, in imagination, be made.

Starting from Italy eastwards we shall find little to detain us in Greece, for in Roman times the days of Greek prosperity were over, and the dwindling cities needed no enlargement of their old supplies. Athens alone maintained something of its former position, and here the conduit that Hadrian made is even to-day in use. But in Asia Minor there are remains in plenty, the most remarkable being at the greater Antioch, at Mitylene and at Metropolis. Antioch, with its pleasure suburb of Daphne, was renowned for its abundant water supply, and the ruins of one aqueduct, the lower part a solid wall surmounted by a line of pillared arches, 200 feet high at the deepest point, can still be seen. Equally impressive is the bridge of the aqueduct that stands about three miles north-west of Mitylene with its massive pillars of grey marble and three superimposed rows of arches. And besides these three places, Pergamum, Laodicea, Tralles, Smyrna, and Aphrodisias all have their examples to show.

But, striking as are these remains amid the squalor of their present surroundings, the Roman aqueducts in North Africa are even more impressive. Near Carthage, for example, is the marvellous line of arches, the Aqueduct of Zaghouan, built by Hadrian, to bring spring water from the mountains of Tunis to the chief town of the province of Africa. They stretch for miles, useless and abandoned, across the plains of Oued-Milian and Manouba, and in the hills under the bare side of Mount Zaghouan there still remains the stone reservoir, built with all the grace of an ancient temple, in which the water was collected. Intact also are the cisterns at the other end of the aqueduct in Carthage, "Muadjel-esh-Shaitan," Cisterns of the Devil, as the Arabs call them—but, while some of these are still used for storing water, others serve as shelters for Arabs and stables for animals.

Readers of Flaubert's " Salammbô " will recall the exciting episode of the perilous swim of Matho and Spendius through the aqueduct to the reservoirs on the night of their adventure in the Temple of Tanit, a triumph of imaginative description, as the period of the story predated by two centuries or more the construction of the great aqueduct whose remains are still to be seen by the visitor to Tunis.

And Carthage is only one example of many. In Roman times North Africa contained dozens of flourishing towns, and in most cases their water supply had to be brought for distances of twenty miles or more from the hills. The admirable work of French archæologists is gradually revealing the wonders of Timgad, Dougga, Lambessa, and Tebessa, and near all these places the ruins of aqueducts have been found, notably the bridge aqueduct with its two massive, rounded piers at Sbéitla, the graceful three-tiered arcade across the valley at Cherchel, and the one squat little arch that spans a lonely ravine near Khamissa.

In passing from Africa to Southern Spain we are still in a land where water is a prime necessity, and once again we find the Roman aqueduct. Tarragona and Merida, in addition to their Roman names, have each a glorious line of ancient arches, and at Segovia is to be found one of the best preserved of all Roman works. The aqueduct there, commonly called " El Puente del Diablo," the Devil's Bridge, though built by Trajan, is still in perfect order, and brings the water of the Rio Frio from the Sierra Guadarrama mountains ten miles away. It is made of rough hewn granite blocks laid without lime or cement, and is 2,700 feet long and 8 feet wide, and the tallest arch is 95 feet high.

Coming into France we find the nearest rival to Segovia in the Pont du Gard, near Nîmes. This aqueduct was probably built by Agrippa, about 18 B.C., and the reservoir into which its water flowed has been discovered in Nîmes itself near the Tour Magne. The Pont du Gard is 900 feet long, 160 feet high, and 10 feet wide at its top storey. There are six arches in the lowest tier, eleven in the second, and thirty-five in the third. The road bridge over the Gard is a medieval addition. Space forbids more than a mention of the aqueducts at Jouy aux Arches, near Metz, and at Mainz, and we have now been our round of the Roman Empire. On one province only we have not touched, the province of Britain. There, for reasons with which we are familiar, the Romans had no need to construct aqueducts.

LICHENED ARCHES OF THE AQUEDUCT AT SMYRNA

At Smyrna, too, in the Roman province of Asia, the city that vied with Ephesus and Pergamum for pride of place, there still stands an old aqueduct, by no means among the greatest of its class, but perhaps the most pleasing in appearance. For not only is it lichened and covered with creeping things that have rooted in the crannies of its masonry, but where it crosses a river at the bottom of a valley the monotony of its arches is varied in the central span to give a bridge-like effect. And so, wherever we go in the lands that formed the Roman Empire, we find these aqueducts, mute witnesses not only to the power of Rome and to her far-flung rule, not only to the patience and skill of her engineers, but to the cleanliness of a civilization which kept open spacious baths for rich and poor alike; a cleanliness which with other scorned and discarded legacies from Rome we are only gradually regaining to-day.

## The Study of the Past. VI.

# The Real Academy of Plato

## By F. N. Pryce, M.A.

### Assistant Keeper, Department of Greek and Roman Antiquities, British Museum

*THE Dialogues of Plato remain one of the supreme achievements in the literature of mankind, and they have been regarded throughout the ages with the reverence due to the words of a master mind. Yet Plato himself gave his teaching only by word of mouth to his disciples in the Academy at Athens. It is not to be wondered at, therefore, that speculation has long centred upon the actual building whose precise locality has been unknown since the 6th century A.D. In 1933, after numerous guesses, the modern Academy of Athens crowned the labours of three years' excavation by uncovering the walls of the ancient Academy where the golden words of the great philosopher were spoken. This discovery, although it presents to the eye but a few stone blocks, is therefore of such importance and interest as to justify inclusion in these pages.*—EDITOR.

ACADEMUS is one of those half-remembered names which survive to remind us that the ancient Greeks, who seem to us to stand at the dawn of history, had a past of their own stretching back like ours into misty darkness. There was a tradition that long, long ago Castor and Pollux had come from Sparta to Athens in search of their sister, Helen, with whom Theseus had eloped, and that Academus helped them by revealing the lady's hiding-place. Why he did this, who he was, and what the story really means, the Greeks had forgotten; but there was a shrine to his honour outside the city of Athens on a piece of ground called from him Academy; and whenever it befell that Sparta was at war with Athens and Spartan armies invaded Attic territory, they forebore to damage the Academy on account of the legend that Academus had been a friend to Sparta.

This ground lay about three-quarters of a mile outside the city wall in a north-westerly direction. It is low-lying, with springs of water which made it famous for its verdure in the midst of arid, dusty Attica. In the fifth century B.C. it was laid out as a park with avenues of trees and shady walks. The plane-trees were noted over Greece for their enormous size and there was also a sacred olive-grove. Besides the shrine of Academus there were other altars and sanctuaries and of these, one, the altar of Prometheus, was the starting point of a popular Athenian spectacle, the torch-race, in which relays of runners bore a lighted torch to the city. Readers of Plato's " Republic " will recall that the opening conversation speaks of an innovation in this race, when the competitors were mounted on horse-back. By the end of the fifth century the Academy had become a favourite place of resort and a centre of gymnastic exercises.

But the world-wide fame of this pleasant suburban oasis is due to its long association with the philosopher Plato, who lived and taught there from about 360 B.C. until his death in 347; doubtless attracted to it by its popularity with the Athenian youth among whom he chose his disciples. At first he seems to have lectured in the Academy itself, in the intervals of gymnastic exercises; later he bought for 3,000 drachmas a house with a garden close by, and here his school seems to have taken more formal shape, with regular courses of study. Here were written all his later dialogues. So much attached to the place was he that, though it was said to be unhealthy on account of its low, damp situation and the doctors urged him to move, he positively refused to do so. In the Academy he built a shrine to the Muses—the first Museum in the world. When he died he was buried close at hand, and five hundred years later his tomb was still shown to tourists.

His most famous pupil, Aristotle, joined the school at the age of eighteen and remained there as pupil and teacher for at least twenty years. Subsequently Aristotle founded his own school, the Lyceum; but other pupils continued the work at the Academy for nearly a century; it is recorded that lectures were still given in Plato's house and that the scholars built themselves little huts adjoining. In the third century there was a short break in the succession, but the " New Academy " revived the old traditions and continued to teach until the philosophic schools were closed by the Christian Emperor Justinian in A.D. 529. For nearly nine hundred years the Academy had been a centre of learning and research.

The place was thus held in respect throughout antiquity, and there was then every probability

A ROMANCE OF SYSTEMATIC EXCAVATION: THE AVENUE THAT LED TO PLATO'S ACADEMY
It has always been known that the Academy where the world's greatest philosopher lived and taught in the 4th century B.C. was placed in a shady park, a green oasis connected with Athens by a road about three-quarters of a mile long. The very route was lost until the 20th century and it was only after three years of laborious excavation along the Academic road, a late stage of which is seen in the photograph, that the actual site of the ancient Academy was uncovered after fourteen centuries.
Photo by " The Times."

that some of the actual buildings of Plato's time might be recovered by excavation. This has proved to be the case as the result of three years of researches conducted by the Greek Academy at the expense of M. Aristophron.

The Dipylon Gate, whence a visitor left the city to visit the Academy, was located many years ago. From it several ancient roads branched off, bordered by tombs, for this area was the West-

WALLS WHICH ONCE HEARD GOLDEN WORDS
These stones form part of the outer wall of Plato's Academy, only discovered in 1933 although a scene of pilgrimage for nine hundred years after the philosopher's death. Near-by were found golden wreaths once worn by officials of the athletic games.

minster Abbey of Athens. Cicero has told us that the Academy lay six furlongs from the Dipylon Gate ; and the problem before the excavators was to follow up the road leading in the general direction of the Academy for the required distance. The task was laborious but many discoveries of interest rewarded the explorers ; in particular, a fine marble tomb sculptured with battle scenes. In the spring of 1933 it was reported that the actual site of the Academy had been reached and its ruins exposed. What was found formed part of a large gymnasium, with rows of dressing-cubicles for the athletes and a bathing pool. A little further on were laid bare parts of the outer walls of the enclosure, in an early style of masonry, doubtless the very walls that Plato saw. Between the walls and the road were nine stone sarcophagi containing wreaths of gold, presumed to be the graves of presidents of the athletic games.

Further excavation will probably recover for us much more, perhaps even the actual house in which Plato lived. But it is unlikely that the site will ever yield remains of architectural magnificence or of intrinsic value. Athens in the fourth century B.C. lived simply. No splendours of ancient art can be expected here ; but the rather commonplace walls and foundations which have been laid bare will ever have their interest as one of the world's great shrines of thought :

' The olive grove of Academe,
Plato's retirement, where the Attic bird
Trills her thick-warbl'd notes the summer long.'

## The Master Builders.  III.

# The Maya Marvels of Central America

### By L. E. Elliott

#### Traveller and writer on Central and South American Archæology

With illustrations from various sources, and by courtesy of Mr. A. P. Maudslay, the explorer of the Maya sites

BESIDE a sparkling river, curtained with the perpetual green of tropic forest, and backed by tumbled hills, stand the ruins of Copan. Temples and courts, set proudly aloft upon stepped pyramids and terraces, monoliths carved with such depth that they can almost be called statues, stairways with each step elaborately sculptured—here is an extraordinary wealth of eloquent remains, typically Maya in its varied richness, and typically Maya in its strange abandonment.

The ruins of Copan fall within the northern confines of the Central American Republic of Honduras, with the border of Guatemala but a few miles distant. Here the narrow gorge of the Copan River suddenly opens out to form a sunny and fertile valley, varying in width from a quarter of a mile to a mile and a half, until, some nine miles farther along, the hills again close in upon the stream.

All this valley enclosure of, roughly, fourteen square miles, is an archæological treasure-house. Elevated about two thousand feet above sea-level, its climate is

**MONOLITHIC TIME-MARKER AT COPAN**

In the early Maya epoch, stelae, deeply-sculptured stones, such as this, were erected to mark the passage of a five-year period. This particular monument belongs to a comparatively late date in the history of Copan ; it was raised early in the third century of our era.

pleasant all the year round, the heat of the day balanced by chilly nights. But with the exception of a few little haciendas in the folds of the sierra foothills, and a shabby and shiftless little village that crouches near the stately ruins, the whole area of this once important and populous centre is deserted.

The Maya built houses for their gods in stone, however perishable were the dwellings of perishable man, and, despite the fact that all the records of Copan came to an abrupt end nearly sixteen hundred years ago, and despite the centuries of desultory pillaging that succeeded its desertion, enough monuments still stand to prove that here flourished one of the great religious centres of the world.

Not in the valley alone, but upon the adjacent hilltops, up the tributary ravines, extending ten or more miles away, is the handicraft of the Maya builder and sculptor, terraces and ruined temples crowning innumerable summits, glyphs and the fragments of figures of deities half-buried in tropic undergrowth. He

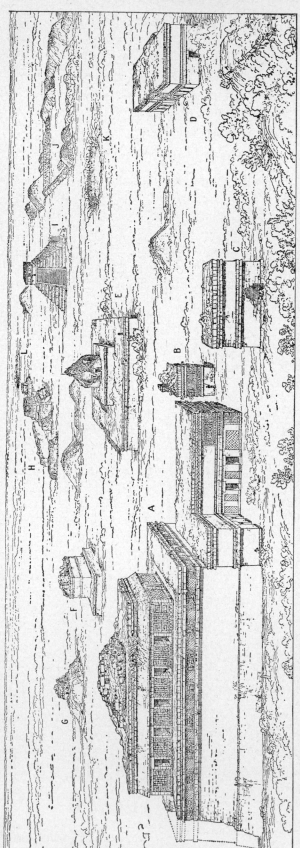

**AN OUTLINE SKETCH OF THE IMPRESSIVE PANORAMA OF CHICHEN ITZA, THE GREAT MAYA CENTRE IN YUCATAN**

All the buildings of this magnificent Maya site, erected after the arrival of the wanderers from the forests of the south, are of the white limestone of the Yucatan Peninsula. The effect is dazzling; richly-adorned edifices of bold design shining snow-white under the pure blue of a burning sky upon the level country, where there are no visible rivers. All the water of the heavy rainfall soaks through the porous limestone forming subterranean streams, and here and there are the natural wells, due to the breaking down of the surface rock, the "cenotes" which made possible the settlement here of a great community. A.—House of the Nuns (Casa de Monjas). B.—(Small annex) the Church (La Iglesia). C.—Larger annex of the "Nunnery." D.—The Akat-Cib (the Writing in the Dark). E.—House of the Snail (El Caracol). F.—The Chichanchob (the Red House). G.—Small Temple. H.—The Ball Court, with Temple of the Tigers and Shields at side. I.—The Great Pyramid (El Castillo). J.—The Court of the Columns. K.—The Cenote Grande. L.—The Cenote of Sacrifice. These names do not denote the ancient use or nomenclature of the buildings, and are merely the inventions of the native workmen employed by explorers.

Reproduced from the "Anthropological Series" by courtesy of the authorities of the Field Columbian Museum, Chicago, U.S.A.

who sees this enchanted valley as the writer once saw it, with the light of a brilliant moon upon the courts and stelae, will also, perhaps, in his imagination, behold it throbbing again with life, see priestly figures in bright and strange garments and feathered head-dresses ascending the stairways, while sacrificial fires flicker before the altars of the gods and the sound of voices rises from a thousand frail houses under the lee of the majestic temples.

Mount the broken steps, stand before one and another of the richly-carved monoliths of Copan, and you are convinced that this confident, boldly-conceived and definitely conventionalised art cannot have sprung full-fledged from a primitive community. Behind it must lie long generations of concept and experiment in art and in the astronomical lore which informed the majority of the records engraved with tireless skill upon scores of stones.

It is too soon to say that all the inscriptions of the great Maya area are concerned with calendrical calculations. A number of these stone writings still baffle the archæologist. But, so far as they have been read, their evidence proves that the deep preoccupation of the learned men of the Maya was with the calendar, and the correlation of religious ceremonial with the calendar.

Long periods of acute observation brought Maya knowledge of astronomy to a pitch of exactitude that would not shame a modern nation, although the latter has the advantage of the telescope. No doubt exists that, in addition to careful observation of the movements of the sun and moon, the Maya astronomers were able to calculate the motions of many planetary bodies, and that they checked their solar and lunar counts by the heliacal risings of the planet Venus.

Copan, however splendid, is but one of the great Maya sites. It is

Ernest Peterffy

## MASSIVE SHRINES AND ENIGMATIC SYMBOLS OF THE LATE MAYA EMPIRE

During the fourth century A.D. the Maya deserted their ancient sites and migrated northwards to Yucatan. Chichén Itzá was one of the chief sites of this Late Maya empire, and among its finest ruins is this stepped pyramid, 85 feet high, with outside staircase leading to the temple on the summit. The upper photograph shows the façade of the Temple of Warriors at Chichén Itzá. The columns at the entrance represent the god Kukulkan, 'the feathered snake which moves in the water,' symbolising the ripple of life.

the most southerly, although below it, on the road to Panamá, strong evidences of Maya ideas abound. Some years ago I picked up near Cuscutlan, in Salvador, a small and exquisite pottery head of pure Maya technique, perhaps carried south by a trader or emigrant. But below Copan there are no temples, no inscriptions—no centres, that is, of learned men. The other points of the triangle of early Maya culture lie north and north-east.

Follow from Copan the northward flow of the river and, after traversing the hills of Merendon, you will reach its junction with the Motagua, a capricious stream scurrying to the Caribbean. Turn east with this water path and, some sixty miles north of Copan, there stand upon the left margin, in deep jungle, the ruins of Quirigua.

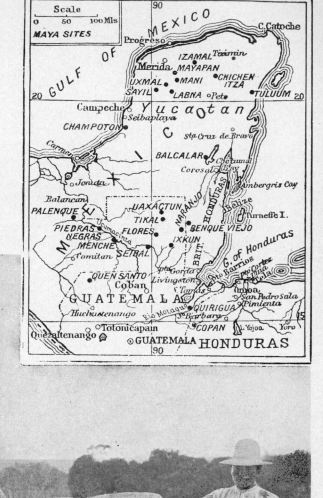

BEAUTIFULLY FASHIONED SERPENT COLUMN FROM A MAYA TEMPLE IN YUCATAN

One of the serpent columns supporting the façade of the temple which crowns the great pyramid at Chichén Itzá, Yucatan. Unlike the architects of the Old World, those of the New did not, in designing columns, derive their inspiration mainly from the vegetable world. Tree motives do not exist. Columns are rare, and, where they exist, are mere broken sections of a wall, or assume the caryatid or snake form (as in this instance). Where they occur they may be taken as evidence of Toltec influence emanating, in comparatively late times, from the Mexican Valley. The sketch map at the top of page, shows the Maya sites of Central America.

**MAYA PRIEST MAKING AN OFFERING OF BLOOD BEFORE A DEITY**

Human sacrifice, though in vogue among the Maya of Yucatan at the time of the Spanish Conquest, was not practised by the early Maya who, contenting themselves with what is called the " penitential rite," pierced their ears and tongues and so offered blood from their own persons. Reproduced here is a remarkable sculpture from Menché, which shows the figure of a god standing with ceremonial staff in hand while a priest kneels in front of the Deity in the act of drawing across the tongue a rope spiked with thorns. A cast of this sculpture is in the British Museum.

221

GRIMLY REALISTIC HANDIWORK OF A SCULPTOR WHO LIVED 1,700 YEARS AGO

This wonderful representation of the head of the death-god of the Maya, carved on a rectangular block of stone measuring 3 ft. 4 in. by 2 ft. 8 in., was found at Copan, and is now preserved among the Maya sculptures in the British Museum. The monument is the work of a man who lived early in the third century of our era.

These twenty-foot-high stelae, magnificently carved in a style distinct from that of their shorter predecessors in Copan, and the huge monolithic animals, render the Quiriguá remains extraordinarily impressive in all this land of ancient wonders.

Copan lies in its sunny upland valley, open to sky and sun ; the noble carvings of Quiriguá stand under a canopy of eternal forest, and the tops of the palms close some forty feet above them like giant feathers of translucent jade. Heavy blue butterflies, as big as birds, tremble above the ferns ; tillandsias and orchids drip fire and honey from a thousand branches ; the still, heat-charged air hangs in the twilight of the forest, and suddenly between the huge buttressed trunks there rise the pale columns of Quiriguá, serene, imbued with tremendous dignity.

All about the main series of tall stelae, or upright stone slabs, carved back and front with richly ornamented

BUST OF THE MAIZE-GOD OF THE MAYA
Originally part of the exterior decoration of a temple at Copan, this is perhaps the most perfect known specimen of Maya sculpture in the round.

figures, plumed in stone with the slender flowing feathers of the sacred Quetzal bird, and inscribed with glyphs, or picture-writings, upon the sides, are other great stones— the enormous "earth monster," and a number of altars carved in the likeness of animals. Hidden in the forest are stepped terraces and the ruined sites of pyramids.

There is no mystery concerning the source of stone for these carvings. As in the case of Copan, the quarries lie fairly close by, while all about are found numbers of hard stone knives and axes, the only tools which the Maya craftsmen employed in the carving of stone. The internal evidence of the date glyphs appears to prove that this was an offshoot of Copan ; the two form the southerly point of the Maya triangle.

To find the other two points one must look almost due north and slightly west for Uaxactun, some three hundred miles away through a maze of mountain and forest, and thence

Early Maya ritual was of a mild character, and tribute to the gods consisted of agricultural produce, birds and small animals offered up on altars like this richly carved specimen at Copan. The nearest approach to human sacrifice before the Late Maya period seems to have been voluntary blood-letting by worshippers by piercing their own ears or tongues, as illustrated in page 221.

## IMPRESSIVE MONUMENTS OF EARLY MAYA RELIGION IN GUATEMALA

Maya date-marking stelae reached their greatest dimensions at Quiriguá, just inside the present border of Guatemala. This city was an offshoot of Copan farther to the south, one of the oldest Early Maya sites, and at one period it replaced the normal columnar stelae by huge sculptured monoliths known as earth monsters, also bearing dates. Their form seems to have been suggested by the alligator; they had a head at each end, and probably symbolised the earth disgorging the sun at dawn and swallowing it at night.

**GORGEOUS DRESS OF MAYA CEREMONIAL**

The figure on this slab is the companion to the priest offering incense shown on the opposite page. He wears an elaborate headdress, crowned with the figure of a heron holding a fish, and in his hand he carries a mask of the rain-god. A jewelled cape, wristlets, and belt, and leg-bandages of jaguar-hide complete his costume.

westward for a lesser space to Palenque. Uaxactun was the most ancient and apparently the longest occupied of all great Maya sites; Palenque, although occupied for a comparatively brief period, has yielded the incomparable treasures of the famous Tablet of the Foliated Cross and the perhaps more beautiful Tablet of the Sun.

An offshoot of Piedras Negras, Palenque seems to have been the artistic parent of Menché. Both display specimens of the finest art of the Maya. The careful studies of Maudslay, made between 1881 and 1894, brought to light series after series of raised buildings with striking characteristics. The Maya architect had no knowledge of the principle of the true arch, and he closed walls by gradually overlapping the construction blocks until they were sufficiently near to be bridged by stone slabs; as a result the interior width of the buildings was comparatively small, with rooms like narrow corridors.

These temples and dwellings are often surmounted by great roof-combs, and the great exterior surfaces from the steps of the foundation-pyramid to the high crest of the building offered scope for the play of Maya skill and artistic imagination.

Of this scope full advantage was taken, and the carved stone slabs, the coloured stucco reliefs and frescoes of the Golden Age of the Maya are without parallel. Seven of the stone lintels of Menché are preserved in the British Museum.

From Uaxactun, a site displaying a sequence of dates that are accepted as running from 212 B.C. to A.D. 340, the later settlement of Tikal appears to have been directed. Also within the triangular enclosure of Copan, Uaxactun, and Palenque are a number of other daughter sites of the same flourishing period—Seibal, Flores, Ocosingo, and Naranjo among them. All have been abandoned to the forest for more than fifteen centuries.

Only a few people have seen the majority of these ruins. Exploration is difficult, the climate not always healthy, and in such regions as that of Petén, where the " Lacandones " live, foreign visitors are regarded with hostility. It is here that persistent reports credit the natives with practising the ancient faith and of making sacrifices of copal and flowers to the old Maya gods. With the exception of Maudslay's excavations at Copan, towards the close of the nineteenth century, practically no scientific digging work has been done, and almost all that we know of this great period of the rise of a true indigenous culture is derived from the monuments.

The daily life of this organized, settled, and peaceful people is exemplified by a few handfuls of stone beads, some weapons and tools of flint and obsidian, a few figurines and fine stone masks, and a dozen or so of pieces of pottery. Not a single scrap of textile is known to exist ; yet we are aware from the vivid portrayals of the stone pictures that the great men of the Maya wore splendid and elaborate garments, intricate head-dresses of mosaic and feathers, finely-made sandals, wristlets, anklets and girdles, and handsome cloaks ; we see that basket-work and rope-making were among their industries.

We know, too, with fair certainty, how long their period of contented occupation of the great centres endured. The efforts of modern scholars have resulted in the fixation of a dating system which is brought into definite relation with our own ; thus, whatever space of time lies behind the creation of Copan as a magnificent ceremonial centre, it is agreed that the first date discovered in this valley is equal to 55 B.C. That is to say, the Maya artists were carving the first stone glyphs of Copan at just about the time that Julius Caesar was preparing the invasion of Britain.

Uaxactun shows dates starting more than a century earlier ; those of Tikal also precede the dating of Copan ; but when the system had been crystallised by the Maya experts it was adopted throughout the great triangle of the Maya area with its inner ring of younger centres, and for over three hundred years every one of the settlements set up, at the end of each fifth year, a dated record in stone. This was the Golden Age of the Maya, a brilliant efflorescence finding its great expression in splendid and beautiful temples. It flourished

MAYA PRIEST OFFERING INCENSE

Stone slab, from the Temple of the Cross at Palenque, showing a figure with the face of the thunder-god blowing an offering of incense through a tube. His head is crowned with a mask of the mythological Moan-bird, associated with clouds and lightning. This energetic example of relief carving belongs probably to the second century A.D.

A MAYA MASTERPIECE OF ARCHITECTURAL MOSAIC

**Example** of Maya architecture from Chichen Itza in Yucatan, affording, as does that in page 228, a good illustration of the skill **of the Maya builder** before he came into contact with the Toltec. The high façade of the building is a mosaic of limestone blocks **so assembled** as to portray a series of masks of the rain-god, whose snout-like nose was borrowed from the tapir, an animal identified **in mythology with the lightning.** The building, La Iglesia, is shown at B in plan on page 218.

until about A.D. 340, soon after the end of the Tenth Cycle of the Maya calendar. Then the whole of this great artistic and scientific effort came suddenly to an end, as if a magic hand had wiped it out.

Not a single glyph was carved within the great triangle after this time, and it is reasonable to suppose that the desertion of the sites by the inhabitants then occurred. Neither spoken tradition nor the historical legends of certain of the emigrant clans, written down soon after the

Spanish conquest, explain this mystery. No guess, suggesting change of climate, invasions of disease, earthquakes or the fear of enemies, sheds a light upon this strange event sufficiently. Though a mural painting in the Great Ball Court at Chichén Itzá shows a battle, Maya monumental carvings are almost uniformly peaceful. Nor do the ancient Maya sites display any sign of destruction other than that of the slow pressure of nature.

The reason of the Maya dissolution remains mysterious, but we know where the dispersed

RECONSTRUCTED MODEL OF A MAGNIFICENT MAYA TEMPLE PYRAMID AT TIKAL

Whereas the Egyptian pyramid was a tomb, the so-called pyramid of the Maya was primarily a substructure of an altar or temple, and as such was invariably flat-topped, a steep outside staircase giving access to the platform. The temple pyramid at Tikal, here shown reconstructed, exemplifies the most imposing stage of Maya architecture. It is the stepped variety of pyramid, built of large blocks of stone closely fitted and freely coated with stucco. Originally much of the ornamental work was coloured

people went. A few probably wandered south without their learned men, and some west, influencing the Quiché and Kakchiquel tribes. But the big mass of the people, led by their priests armed with calendrical lore, went north to Yucatan.

Thanks to painstaking archæological research, their passage may be traced to-day.

The pilgrimage lasted for centuries, and upon the way to the hot and fertile limestone plains of Yucatan they founded a number of sites, such as Santa Rita Corozal in the north of what is now British Honduras, and in more northerly Balcalar. In both of these cases they stopped where they found water, for behind the coral reefs of sun-stricken Corozal are a little lake and a river; the Balcalar site, blazing in the Yucatan heat, is upon the edge of a lake of considerable size, and it was to this lake and the little islet in the middle that the last of the learned Maya made their way after the overthrow of their race by the Spaniards under Hernando Cortés in the early part of the sixteenth century.

DECORATIVE MOSAIC USED BY THE WONDER-WORKING ARCHITECTS OF OLD-WORLD YUCATAN
Uxmal, in Yucatan, an offshoot of Chichén Itzá, is remarkable for the elaborate mosaic decoration of its buildings. One of the finest is the so-called House of the Governor, shown in the lower photograph on this page. This building has many doorways provided with wooden lintels, and the decay of the latter, though responsible for a certain amount of damage, has not seriously endangered the stability of the building. In the upper photograph is shown the detail of a corner, the mosaic being arranged to show a series of colossal grotesque rain-god faces with characteristic trunk-like noses.

The region through which the Maya passed is one of broken mountains, of deep barrancas, luxuriant vegetation in the valleys, and of turbulent streams. Tree-ferns and pink-flowered frangipani trees shade the paths, and here and there the abrupt precipices and gorges are exchanged for open grassy lands or pine ridges. There are few game animals in the forest country. During the Maya wanderings, deer and turkey, no doubt, formed, as they form to-day, the chief prey of the hunts-man. The clans must have paused now and again to plant maize and yucca, peppers and beans and pineapples.

It was while they halted at an unidentified place, known tradition-ally as Chacnouitan, that they "heard of" Chichén Itzá, the chroniclers say. Perhaps they heard of the curious natural wells formed by deep caverns, the cenotes, in the limestone floor of Yucatan. Here they established themselves, priests and artists and artisans, near the great Cenote of Sacrifice, from which a wealth of beautiful specimens of late Maya art, including jade and gold orna-ments, has been taken.

It is a simple matter to visit Chichén Itzá, entering Yucatan by way of the port of Merida. Here is to be seen a magnificent complex of wide plazas and richly orna-mented temples, fine examples of the revivified art of the trans-planted Maya. The ruins are still stately, their intricate mosaics and carvings standing boldly in the clear atmosphere of Yucatan.

Nearer and more accessible, but a day's journey from Merida, are the beautiful sites of Labna and Uxmal. The latter is one of the most marvellous of the Yucatec remains. These were off-shoots from Chichén, and from that mother settlement were also founded Izamal, Sayil, and Mayapan, all displaying splendid monuments; the three chief cities, Chichén, Uxmal, and Maya-pan, formed a famous "League," whose break-up was the signal for internal dissension, the intro-duction of Toltec mercenaries, and the condition

PLUMED MAYA WARRIOR OF ANCIENT YUCATAN

Pilaster from the Temple of Tigers and Shields at Chichén Itzá, showing a fighting-man of the period (eighth to twelfth century A.D.). The warrior wears a plumed mosaic crown, and is carrying a spear-thrower. His wide breast ornament, probably of gold or copper, calls for particular notice; so does his hip shield with the sun device. The temple, of which a photograph appears on page 230, together with a conjectural restoration, contains a series of these wonderfully carved pilasters.

of internecine warfare in which the Spaniards found Yucatan when they first landed in 1517.

Down to the Spanish entry the great sites were periodically visited on religious festivals, although the erection of monuments and record dates had ceased some time previously. But to the eye of the invader the temples and their deities were things of abomination, and no time was lost in

TOLTEC-MAYA TEMPLE BEFORE ITS WOODEN LINTELS PERISHED; AND AS IT IS TO-DAY.

Below is a photograph of the Temple of Tigers and Shields at Chichén Itzá, in its present condition. Above is a restoration of the same building, illustrating the harmonious proportions and beauty in detail which characterised the period of Toltec-Maya architecture. The "tigers (i.e. jaguars) and shields" appear in the frieze, but the outstanding feature is constituted by the rattlesnake columns which are one of the most striking creations of Toltec genius.

destroying all that was destructible, including quantities of precious Maya manuscripts, burnt in huge bonfires by the Spanish priests.

It is to the credit of the Spaniards that they set down what has proved to be the key to the date inscriptions, for the names and signs which the Yucatec Maya told to Bishop Landa are identified with the glyphs of the great ancient temples in the south, and that, teaching the Spanish language to the quick-witted Maya, they gave to apt pupils a medium in which chroniclers set down for the benefit of posterity the famous " Books of Chilan Balam," relating the bare outline of the story of the northerly wanderings of the Maya.

The ruins of Yucatan, magnificent as they are, present no such problem as that of the great cradle of Maya culture. Their extent and the cause of their decay are known. The mystery lies farther south, in the sweltering forests of Central America, in the sites that await a skilful examination. Perhaps on some future day the scientific explorer may bring to light unrevealed stores of ancient learning, and manuscripts may yet be found to shed illumination upon the great mystery of the Maya, whose colossal handiwork, extending, as we have seen, over hundreds of years, had been abandoned and seemingly forgotten when the land was first made known to Europe in the sixteenth century.

ALL THAT REMAINS OF THE CHICHANCHOB, OR "RED HOUSE," AT CHICHEN ITZA

Owing its present popular name to the fact that it had been painted with red cement, this building is a particularly good example of the earlier Yucatec architecture. The upper parts of the inner walls, also the lintels, which are made of Zapote tree wood, still in a remarkably good state of preservation, are covered with inscriptions in Maya hieroglyphics, which, to date, have defied the efforts of all those who have attempted to decipher them.

EXTRAORDINARY FIND OF MASSED ARCHAIC SCULPTURES IN A MYSTERY TEMPLE OF ANCIENT CYPRUS—
Although excavation work on a systematic scale in Cyprus is a comparatively recent development, already discoveries have been made that suggest that the island may yet rival Crete as an archaeological treasure-house. One of the most remarkable finds was at Ajia Irini, on the northern coast, where the Swedish Archaeological Expedition have been excavating a Bronze Age site under the leadership of Dr. Einar Gjerstad. It consisted of a great collection of archaic statuary—some two thousand statues and statuettes.

This remarkable photograph and that in page 236 are given by courtesy of

—"CONGREGATION" OF TWO THOUSAND STATUES SET BEFORE AN EMPTY SHRINE OF AN UNKNOWN GOD

These dumb worshippers were arranged in concentric rows before an altar dedicated to a deity at present unidentified though it is thought that he was a god of fertility. As will be seen from our photograph, the statues are arranged in order of size, the largest at the back, while intermingled with them are numerous votive offerings of a miscellaneous description. The site had been used as a holy place from the end of the Bronze Age, about 1200 B.C., but the "Congregation" is considerably later—from about 600–450 B.C.

Dr. Einar Gjerstad, Head of the Swedish Archaeological Expedition in Cyprus

# Mystery Gods of Early Cyprus

### By E. Royston Pike

#### Author of "Temple Bells," etc.

SOME years ago the papa, or village priest, of Ajia Irini, a little place on the north coast of Cyprus, was digging in his glebe when he struck his spade against some pottery objects. Carefully removing the soil, he brought to light the upper part of a terracotta statue and several smaller terracotta sculptures, which he took forthwith to the Museum at Nicosia There they were examined by the local archaeologists, who were so impressed that it was decided to invite the Swedish Archaeological Expedition which had been working in Cyprus for some little time, under the leadership of Dr Einar Gjerstad, to undertake a systematic examination of the site at Ajia Irini in the hope of making further discoveries

Fulfilment followed close upon the heels of the hope, for the excavators had hardly scratched the surface of the field shown them by the priest when they found evidences—libation tables and vases, sacrificial axes, statuettes of bulls and fragments of offerings—of the site having been occupied for centuries in the far-back past as a religious shrine, as a centre of the bull cultus that in ancient times was so widely distributed throughout the coasts and islands of the eastern Mediterranean. But though these things were interesting enough, they were as nothing compared with what was to follow—with the extraordinary find of a great and absolutely unique array of archaic statuary, arranged about an altar in such a way as to suggest an assembly of worshippers. Numbering about two thousand in all, the sculptures, nearly all of terracotta, vary in size from statuettes about eight inches high to life-size statues. They were found as they had been placed two thousand five hundred or so years ago—in concentric rows in a wide semicircle about an altar, the statuettes in the front row nearest the altar, and the statues placed according to size in the rows behind so that the life-sized figures stood at the back. The general impression is of a congregation gathered together to worship a deity whose ritual evidently centred about the great altar in pages 232 and 233.

What god, what ritual, is not known as yet. The fact that no statue representing the deity has been found suggests that the worship was imageless or aniconic, but a hint as to its nature is given by a

#### SNAKE-WORSHIP IN PREHISTORIC CYPRUS

This statuary group in miniature was unearthed during the excavations at Vounous, near Kyrenia in Cyprus, conducted under the supervision of M. Dikaios. According to the theory propounded by its discoverer, it represents the ritual of a prehistoric cult, combining the worship of the Snake God, the Divine Bull and the Mother Goddess. The tray is fifteen inches in diameter, and the encircling "wall" is 3¼ inches high. It is believed to date from the Early Bronze Age, or about 3000 to 2100 B.C

FIVE OF THE TWO THOUSAND MEMBERS OF THE TERRA-COTTA "CONGREGATION"

The statues and statuettes discovered in situ by the Swedish Archaeological Expedition at Ajia Irini had been arranged, as will be seen in pages 232 and 233, in rows in a semi-circle before an altar but their origin and meaning are still the subject of speculation. Cypriote art, never of high quality, had been somewhat improved at the time of these examples by Egyptian influences.

large oval stone which stands beside the altar. As is well known, oval stones have from time immemorial played a great part in fertility cults as representative of the receptive power of Nature, and thus there is at least a strong likelihood that Ajia Irini was a centre of a fertility cult. The images of the bull that were discovered earlier lends support to the theory, for the bull often symbolized the male principle of generation.

But even though the nature of the worship be established, we are still left uncertain as to the meaning of the serried rows of statues and statuettes. Perhaps the most reasonable theory of those so far advanced has them to be votive sculptures—offerings made to the deity or deities by grateful recipients of their bounty in much the same way as the devout in Catholic lands today hang about the statues of the

Virgin or their patron saint little waxen arms and legs, and erect in chapels on dangerous headlands tablets giving thanks for a safe return to port after a particularly stormy voyage.

PLOUGHING 5,000 YEARS AGO AS TODAY

The excavations at Vounous have thrown considerable light on the everyday life of the Early Bronze Age. Here, for instance, we see a pottery group representing a ploughing scene. The oxen are drawing ploughs very similar to those used in present-day Cyprus; on the verge of the field two women sit beside what is seemingly a cradle.

**CULT BULL THREE THOUSAND YEARS OLD**
At Dali, in the interior of Cyprus, Dr. Einar Gjerstad dug through successive cultural strata until in the lowermost he found traces of a prehistoric cult-place, dating approximately from the Copper Age, about 1200–1000 B.C. Among the finds were five miniature bulls in terracotta which had once stood in a row in a shrine. One of the bulls is here represented.

Whatever the sculptures' import, there is little doubt that they were regarded with the deepest reverence, for when about 525 B.C. the temenos or sacred enclosure was flooded as a result of exceptionally heavy winter rains and the "congregation" was half buried beneath sand and gravel, the statues were left as they were when the flood receded, buried up to the knees or waist, and the additions to their number that were made later were stood on the raised floor-level. The country folk, it is plain, were too pious or too superstitious to lay their hands on what their fathers had set up in that holy spot—with the result, incidentally, that we are provided with an extraordinarily vivid and valuable demonstration of the development of early Cypriote art.

Years afterwards, about 450 B.C. it is conjectured, more floods came down from the hills; the temenos was swamped and this time completely ruined, so that the statues, old and not so old, were buried beneath a thick covering of silt and shingle. And so they remained until in our own day they were recovered in so fortuitous a fashion.

Another site worked over by the Swedish Archaeological Expedition is Dali—the classical Idalion—situated in the middle of the island; and here again the diggings have added considerably to our knowledge of the cults of prehistoric times. At the top of the acropolis, virgin soil so far as the spade of the archaeologist is concerned, Dr. Gjerstad and his assistants laid bare in the lowest culture stratum a cult-place dating back to about 1200–1000 B.C., and among the objects found were five terracotta bulls which had evidently once stood together on a wooden table.

In addition to the activities of the Swedish Archaeological Expedition, excavation work in Cyprus is being carried on by the Cyprus Museum Committee under the direction of M. P. Dikaios One of the sites that has received attention is an Early Bronze Age settlement near Kyrenia, and it was here in the summer of 1931 that there was brought to light the "round, tray-shaped object made of red polished pottery" which is illustrated in page 234, and which, according to its discoverer, is a representation of a temenos or sacred enclosure in which is being performed the ritual of snake worship Three figures with joined hands from which hang two snakes may be discerned represented in relief on the wall on the opposite side of the enclosure to the entrance; possibly they are engaged in a religious dance. In front of them is a kneeling form, and just behind in the left centre sits a larger figure—the high priest of the cult?—on a kind of throne. Other priests are sitting on benches against the wall; six figures of unknown significance are standing in the centre of the ring; and behind the throne to the left may be seen the figures of a man and a woman carrying a child. Just inside the entrance are several horned animals, evidently bulls; there remain two human figures by the entrance, while another is apparently trying to climb over the wall.

Primarily, says M. Dikaios, the ceremony represented is one of snake-worship, akin to that of Knossos, but two other deities are also present— the Mother-Goddess, in the person of the woman holding a baby, and the bull. The persons holding the snakes, he says, seem to be wearing horned head-dresses or bull-masks, symbolizing the divine bull (it is not without significance, perhaps, that on the same site a pair of miniature bull's horns made of pottery, has been found; was it a model, placed in the tomb of the priest who in life wore real bull's horns and danced in honour of the taurian god?); while as for the Mother-Goddess, the woman carrying a child may be, of course, merely an interested spectator or worshipper, but it is worthy of note that near by a ritual vase has been unearthed, of which the stem is composed of a highly stylised representation of the Mother-Goddess stiffly holding her child to her bosom. Then the personage apparently engaged in climbing over the wall—M. Dikaios reminds us that the fertility cults of ancient times were "mysteries" whose rites might be seen only by initiates. This climber, then, may have been one who, excluded from the sacred precincts, yet was resolved to see what was doing on the other side of the wall. So he clambered up—a "gate-crasher" of pre-history!

## THE ZEUS OF PHEIDIAS, LOFTIEST EMBODIMENT OF DIVINITY IN ART

Constructed by Pheidias, the Athenian, the statue of Olympian Zeus which adorned the temple at Olympia in Elis was universally conceded to be one of the Seven Wonders of the World. And this reconstruction in colour makes real for us the seemingly exaggerated expressions of admiration which it elicited from the ancients. "The sight of the figure would make a man forget all his troubles, however worn out he might be with sleeplessness and sorrow," said Dio Chrysostom, the orator.

*From a painting by Charles M. Sheldon, based on Pausanias, and specially made for "Wonders of the Past"*

## The Seven Wonders. II.

# The Statue of Zeus at Olympia

## By A. H. Smith, M.A., F.S.A.

Late Keeper of Greek and Roman Antiquities, British Museum

THE various lists of the Seven Wonders given in the works of Greek and Latin authors always include the statue of the Olympian Zeus at Olympia, by Pheidias. But in comparison with the Pyramids, or even with the Mausoleum, or the Temple of Artemis at Ephesus, the Statue of Zeus (the Roman Jupiter) was a perishable object, and now it is only the shadow of a name.

Except on the minute scale of coins we have no direct copy to give an idea of its details. The excavations at Olympia produced nothing except the foundation and lower course of its pedestal. In literature it is a subject of frequent reference, but we have only one straightforward description, that of the traveller Pausanias, who visited Greece in the latter half of the second century of our era.

In spite of the growing prestige of the Olympic games, there is no reason to suppose that there was an important sanctuary to Zeus at Olympia until after the great national upheaval of the Persian wars. Then the people of Elis determined to erect a worthy Temple of Zeus with a splendid image of the god. The Temple was built between 480 and 450 B.C., but it had to stand empty for nearly a generation until Pheidias should be set free from the construction of the Athene Parthenos and the general superintendence of the adornment of the Parthenon on the Acropolis of Athens. Our knowledge of the form of the new Temple is derived partly from the description of Pausanias, and partly from the excavations carried out by Germans between 1875-1881.

The Temple was a Doric structure with six columns at its ends, and thirteen along its sides. Its inner chamber measured ninety-five feet by forty-three feet, and was divided by two rows of columns into a nave and two aisles. At one end of the central nave were found stones giving the limits of the pedestal of the Statue of Zeus. Here the god sat enthroned. The sculpture, like the Athene Parthenos at Athens, and the Asklepios of Thrasymedes at Epidaurus, was of the work known as chryselephantine—that is, a combination of gold and ivory. Gold plates were fastened about a wooden core of timbering in the form of the draperies, while a striking contrast was supplied by slices of ivory which were used for flesh. The effects of the gold and ivory were then heightened by all the arts of the jeweller, the engraver, the painter. The building which Pheidias had used as his workshop was still known by that name when Pausanias visited Olympia some six hundred years later. An orator, Himerius, observes that Pheidias used but a small workshop, but Zeus was fashioned in it, and so, too, was the Parthenos.

We will now enter the Temple with Pausanias as a guide book, but will take the liberty of abridging Pausanias's description by the omission of mythological detail.

As we enter the doors of bronze we have on the right, in front of a column, Iphitus, crowned by a woman Ekecheiria (Armistice personified), as the attached inscription tells. Pillars stand inside the Temple with upper galleries, and a way of access through them to the statue. There is also a winding way to the roof.

The god, who is made of gold and ivory, is seated on a throne. On his head is a wreath imitating sprays of olive. On his right hand he carries a Victory. She, too, is made of ivory and gold; she carries a fillet, and has a wreath on her head. In the left hand of Zeus is a sceptre, curiously adorned with all the metals. The bird perched on the sceptre is the eagle. The god's sandals are made of gold, and so, too, is his garment. Wrought in the garment are figures of beasts and lilies. The throne is adorned with gold and jewels, ebony and ivory. Upon it, too, beasts are painted and images are wrought.

Between the legs of the throne are four bars, each reaching from leg to leg. These legs are not the only support of the throne. There are also as many columns which stand between them. We cannot go in under the throne as we pass under the throne (of Apollo) at Amyclae. At Olympia barriers like walls fence us out. Of these barriers the one that faces the doors (of the Temple) is coloured dark blue only. The others have paintings of Panaenus, a brother of Pheidias. His Battle of Marathon is painted in the Stoa Poikile at Athens.

On the base which supports the throne and all the rest of the splendour of Zeus are golden figures. I know, Pausanias continues, the measurements which have been recorded for the height and breadth of the Zeus at Olympia, but I cannot commend the measurers, for the dimensions which they give fall far short of the impression on the spectator, and herein it is said that the god himself bore witness to the art of Pheidias. When the statue had just been completed, Pheidias prayed the god to give a sign if the work was to his mind, and straightway a thunderbolt struck that part of the floor where, even to my time, stood the bronze pitcher. That part of the floor which lies before the image is paved with black stones, not white— a kerb of Parian marble runs round the black and retains the olive oil that is poured out.

Pausanias goes on to say that olive oil suited the gold and ivory figure at Olympia because the site was damp, while water was used for the Athene Parthenos at Athens because the air was too dry. At Epidaurus neither oil nor water was required because the figure stood above a well.

The above description of Pausanias was the sole basis for a brilliant restoration made, a hundred years ago, by Quatremère de Quincy, on which is largely based the illustration given in the colour plate. What further progress can now be made ? The excavations have given us the black flooring before the statue with its marble kerb, and also the foundations of the pedestal, which measures 22 feet by 33 feet. Stones of the pedestal have also been found and put together, making the base a mass of masonry some four feet high, but no trace remains of the reliefs which Pausanias saw attached to them. The same excavations showed traces of the footing of the barrier walls, painted by Panaenus. These are thought by many authorities to have joined column to column of the interior colonnades of the temple. On this basis sat the enthroned figure, which is calculated by authoritative writers to have been seven or eight times life size.

The best evidence that we can find for the general appearance of the statue is a bronze coin of Elis, of the time of Hadrian. We see a stately and formal figure of the god, on whose outstretched palm the Victory has alighted with a fillet between her spread hands. No eagle is shown on the sceptre. The throne has a high back, and arms supported, like the arms of the chair of Zeus on the frieze of the Parthenon, by figures of Sphinxes, as described by Pausanias. Beneath the god's feet is an ornate footstool. The bars described by Pausanias join leg to leg, but we see no trace of the pillars between the legs, which were probably set back from the front. The enclosing barrier walls are not indicated.

Pausanias does not attempt to describe the head of the god. It was a common tradition that Pheidias was asked by Panaenus of what type he intended to represent the Zeus, and he replied that he wished to convey in sculpture what Homer had expressed in words : " The son of Kronos spake, and nodded assent with swarthy brows, the king's ambrosial locks flowed downwards from his immortal head, and he shook great Olympus."

If we try to get a more precise idea of the character of the head, we must make use of another unique coin of Elis. The head has long hair, falling straight down the neck, a full beard and a moustache, which, after the manner of early fifth-century sculpture, has long ends falling over the beard. The wreath of olive is carefully and delicately shown. From the indications of the coin, and from our knowledge of the sculpture of the time, it is now clear that we must not look, as our grandfathers were in the habit of doing, among the sophisticated and elaborate statues in the Roman galleries, for an embodiment of the type. If we search our collections for a head of Zeus which, without being a direct copy, yet illustrates the qualities described, we cannot do better than quote a head in the Museum of Boston, to which the late Adolf Furtwängler drew attention, as having just the characteristics of which we are in search.

Apart from the grandeur of the figure itself, the work was noted for the rich variety of its subsidiary sculptures, which formed a mythological text book. The Hours and the Graces stood in groups, three in each, at the top of the throne, above the head of the figure. Sphinxes with Theban youths supported the arms. Below the Sphinxes were reliefs of Apollo and Artemis slaying the children of Niobe. The crossbars had reliefs of Olympic sports, and of Heracles and Theseus at war with the Amazons. Victories supported the legs of the throne. On the base, Aphrodite came up from the sea, in the presence of the gods. The rising sun and setting moon marked the limits of the scene, as on the east pediment of the Parthenon. Finally, the barrier walls at the sides and back of the throne were painted by Panaenus with a group of Greece and Salamis personified, and with eight pairs of mythological figures.

The later history of the statue is lost in uncertainty. The Emperor Caligula, we are told, had a madman's scheme of transporting the Zeus to the Capitol at Rome, and of substituting his own head for that of the god. But his workmen were driven away by terrifying peals of supernatural laughter which broke out when they laid hands on the throne, and the vessel sent to transport it was **struck with** thunderbolts and shipwrecked. The end is unknown. Probably the figure perished at Olympia in one of the earthquakes or barbarian sacks which afflicted fifth-century Greece.

# Peerless Gems of Greek Sculpture

## By Frank Rutter

*WHILE the other sections of WONDERS OF THE PAST are chiefly concerned with the massive works of man in the ages of antiquity, this section is designed to illustrate the beauty of ancient art and craftsmanship in the smaller things, for the element of wonder may inhere in the little not less than in the large. Mr. Rutter, who writes the following chapter of our work, is well known as a writer on modern and classical art.*—EDITOR.

OF all the wonders of the past, what is more wonderful than this—that well over two thousand years ago groups of artisans living in small city-states should have created types of physical beauty which ever since artists of all countries and of all times have endeavoured to excel, but have never surpassed, and only very rarely have equalled?

The beauty of Greek sculpture is not a matter about which debate is possible. To take but one example, which is very well known, the Venus of Milo, so-called because this famous Greek statue, now in the Louvre, was discovered in 1820 near the ancient city of Melos (Milo). The beauty of the Venus of Milo is universally acknowledged, and anybody who pretends that he does not like it is merely adopting a would-be superior pose in order to be different from anybody else.

How did it come about that the sculptors of ancient Greece were able to evolve types of human beauty which have been for a score of centuries the noblest models conceivable by man? There is a reason for everything, and it cannot be doubted that the representation of men and women in Greek art rested upon a solid natural base, namely, the real beauty of the men and women of ancient Greece. The beauty of the originals

before them is, then, the first but not the only cause of the exceeding beauty of the work of the Greek sculptors. Why this race should have been so dowered with good looks is a matter into which we cannot enter deeply, but it was the result of a variety of favourable conditions—the climate, good social habits, free healthy lives spent largely in athletic exercises in the open air, and a pre-natal disposition to beauty brought about by the deep-seated cult of beauty in the parents of the race.

No survey of Greek art, however brief, can afford to ignore the close relation maintained between sculpture and athletics, for this relation lies at the root of the beauty we are endeavouring to analyse. Now, Greek sports differed from modern sports in three ways. In the first place the Greeks paid even more attention to the style of the performance than to the results achieved. With them it was not a question of "winning anyhow," but winning gracefully or not at all. This attitude towards athletics was partly due to the religious character of the Greek games, but since this statement is liable to mislead a modern reader, it must be qualified by an explanation that "it was the intense conviction of the value to man of such strength and beauty as were promoted by the games, which procured them the patronage

**SCULPTURE INSPIRED BY ATHLETES**
This bronze wrestler with every muscle shown taut and alive is one of a pair in the Naples Museum. It is an example of one of the most important aspects of Greek art.
Photo by Alinari

of the gods who represented the state and the race." Modern religion is confined almost exclusively to the spiritual side of man, but Greek religion—if shallower—covered a wider field ; every human power, aptitude, and enjoyment being regarded as something which should be cultivated and perfected for the honour of the gods.

Secondly, in Greece, athletics were more generally practised than in modern times. The Greeks were not spectators of, but participants in, games, and

 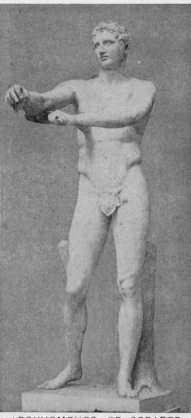

**DORYPHORUS, OR SPEAR-BEARER**
Bronze statue (in Vatican, Rome) of youth with spear. Replica of figure by Polycleitus, a contemporary of Myron. It is known as the " Canon."
Photo by Anderson

**APOXYOMENOS, OR SCRAPER**
Athlete cleaning right arm with scraping-iron, after Lysippus, a contemporary of Alexander the Great. Of Pentelic marble, it was found in 1849 at Rome, and is now in the Vatican.

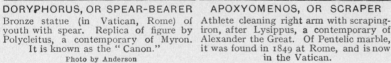

unless he was deformed or enslaved, every young man spent some hours daily in athletic exercises. Thirdly, these young men practised and competed in their games stark naked.

It is impossible to exaggerate the importance of this last characteristic to the sculptor who was thus able to see day after day the bare bodies of the most perfectly made youths strained in every pose of running, wrestling, and disk-throwing. The Greek sculptor began with a knowledge of the human form which a modern artist might spend a lifetime without being able to acquire.

Yet a further cause contributed to the beauty of Greek sculpture. Greek art was not realistic, but ideal. The sculptor was not content to represent faithfully the athlete who might happen to be before him at any moment. He sought an ideal general type through selection from the particular, and after lengthy study by deliberate choice, adaptation, and abstraction, he evolved his ideals. As he differentiated his gods, giving strength to Heracles (Hercules), swiftness to Hermes (Mercury), and grace to Apollo, so he discriminated between his human athletes, giving the runner the ideal build of limb that would suggest his suppleness, and the wrestler the ideal frame that would contain his hardihood and strength.

How greatly the artist was helped by the continual spectacle of athletes in training is proved by the fact that perfection in rendering the male form was attained many years before the ideal rendering of female form became possible. In the earlier periods of Greek art the rendering of men is far superior to the rendering of women, and it was not until about the fourth century B.C. that Greek sculptors generally showed themselves able to portray either sex with equal perfection. The secluded lives led by Athenian women retarded the Attic portraiture of women, while the Spartan maidens who exercised themselves daily like the youths, had no native sculptors to commemorate their forms.

How quick was the eye of the Greek sculptor to seize and record rare perfections of form was shown by Professor Brücke, of Vienna, who, in his great book on " The Human Figure," pointed out that beautiful details in the human body, found but rarely in nature, are common in Greek sculpture. Once the ideal formation of a muscle or a limb was found, it was piously preserved by the continuity of tradition among Greek sculptors, who kept all that was absolutely good in the work of their predecessors, and successively perfected the art by incorporating new beauties amid the old excellences.

Thus Myron (born c. 480 B.C.) was the first to show how to balance the body in strong motion.

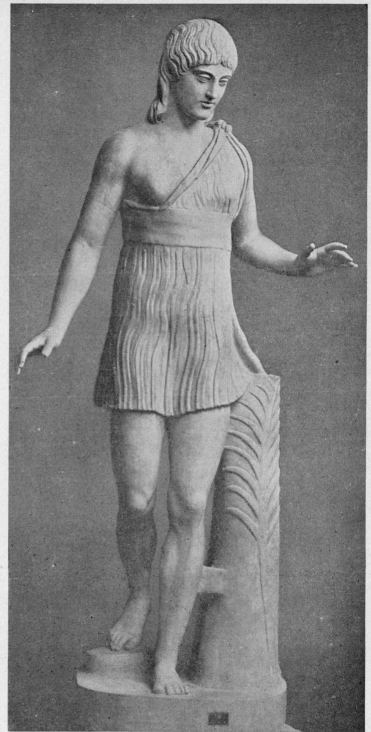

MASTERPIECES IN BRONZE OF FIFTH CENTURY GREEK ARTISTS

These two magnificent statues reflect the attraction which the Greek sculptors found in athletic performances of all kinds when the bodily forms of the contestants were displayed naked or lightly garbed in the palaestra or the stadium. Other examples are reproduced in pages 239, 240 and 244. The Charioteer (left), one of the very few original Greek bronzes now in existence, was found at Delphi. The perfectly natural folds of the drapery that protect the body against the wind, the splendid poise, the calm features and the unemotional concentration of this splendidly virile figure all typify the highest art of Greece in the early fifth century B.C. The Girl Runner (right), a copy in the Vatican Museum of a bronze original, is an example of the Greek girls who were the glory of Sparta in the fifth century. The statue presents the same air of what is sometimes called classic severity, but there is a freedom of attitude and an exquisite appreciation of the lines of the body clearly to be discerned even in this marble copy.

241

THE IDEAL OF WOMANHOOD AS CONCEIVED BY PRAXITELES

As noted in the previous page the Greek sculptor at first concerned himself mainly with male athletes and the naked form of woman was treated comparatively late in Greek art. But Praxiteles excelled in carving bodies half human, half divine in their exquisite proportions, and his Aphrodite of Cnidus was the wonder of the age. As now exhibited in the Vatican Museum, this copy, almost certainly made in Roman times, wears metal drapery.

Vatican Museum, Rome; photo, Mansell

His " Discobolus " or quoit-thrower (see illustration, page 244) is one of the earliest and most precious expressions in sculpture of the beauty of the human figure in action. Balance rhythm and minute perfection of form were the great merits of Polycleitus (c.480 410 B.C.) whom his contemporaries rated as the equal of Pheidias. He perfected the representation of the trunk, and his famous statue, the " Doryphorus," or Spear-bearer (page 240), was known as the " Canon," because it was held to be the perfect type of a male figure. A fair idea of its beauty may be gained from the copy of it, found at Pompeii, and now in the Naples Museum.

Usually the aspect of a Greek statue is that of serene calm, and in the masterpieces of the earlier period, as, for example, the superb " Auriga," or Charioteer, of Delphi (illustrated in page 241), the monumental gravity of the figure is overwhelming in its stateliness; but during the first part of the fourth century B.C., Scopas, who was the foremost sculptor of his time, introduced strong emotion and even passion into the countenances of his figures. No undeniable original of his survives, but his treatment of the eye and brow was considered to be an advance on any previous rendering of these features, and in subsequent works the influence of Scopas is clearly discernible in the treatment of these details.

The expression of mood or feeling was brought to perfection by the Athenian sculptor Praxiteles (c. 400-330 B.C.), whose exquisite modelling of the soft contours of flesh was accompanied by a hitherto unknown power of suggesting intellectuality. The almost complete statue by him of Hermes (see illustration in page 246), discovered at Olympia, illustrates the highest ideal of Greek manhood in its perfect rendering of a noble mind in a body healthy and beautiful.

So far we have confined our attention to the way in which the

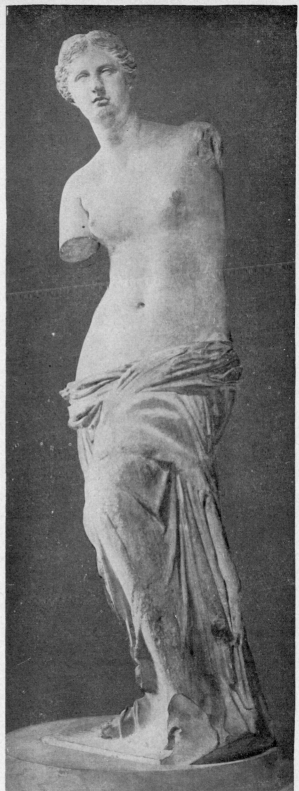

ONE OF THE MOST FAMOUS OF GREEK SCULPTURES: THE VENUS OF MILO

Of Parian marble, and found in 1820 by a peasant near temple ruins in the island of Melos (Milo), in the Greek Archipelago, and now a celebrated treasure of the Louvre, Paris, this glorious masterpiece of an unknown sculptor probably belongs to the second-third century B.C., but was inspired by the canons of an older school. The goddess, known to the Greeks as Aphrodite, and to the Romans as Venus, is supposed to have been holding a shield and gazing at her reflection in the polished surface.

Photo by Alinari

**GRACE OF ATHLETIC ACTION IMMORTALISED IN BRONZE AND STONE: THE DISCOBOLUS OR QUOIT THROWER AND THE WRESTLERS**

Left: this restoration in the Glyptothek at Munich of the bronze original preserves one of the most beautiful studies of the human body ever made, the Discobolus of Myron (fifth century B.C.). To show the perfect proportions of the young man, the result of constant physical training, no artist could have devised a better pose than this, assumed naturally by him when throwing the discus—a sport that brings all the limbs into play, and in which rhythmic movement is essential. The masterly group of wrestlers (also restored in the Uffizi Gallery at Florence), presents an example of the opportunities, fully utilised by Greek sculptors, which were afforded by the magnificent physique of the combatants and the dramatic attitudes into which they were forced by their struggles.

GREEK SCULPTURE AS EXEMPLIFIED IN THE DECORATION OF THE BEAUTIFULLY COLOURED ALEXANDER SARCOPHAGUS

Here is shown part of the great marble Alexander sarcophagus, so called because its beautifully sculptured reliefs commemorate the victorious battles and hunting exploits of the Macedonian king. The tomb is one of several that were discovered at Sidon and are now at Constantinople, and probably once held the remains of a ruler of the Phoenician city. The reliefs, which are the work of a skilled but unknown Greek sculptor, were executed shortly after Alexander's death in 323 B.C. They are remarkable for balance, freedom, and vigour of composition, exquisite beauty of detail, and for their wonderful colouring. The figure seen on the extreme left is probably that of Alexander himself.

Constantinople Museum

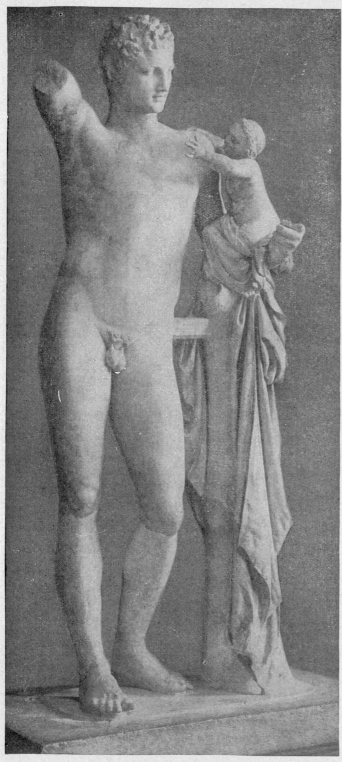

THE HERMES OF PRAXITELES

This, the single undisputed original, in Parian marble, of the work of the
Athenian sculptor, Praxiteles, was discovered at Olympia, Peloponnesus,
in 1877.　The Greek god Hermes, the Roman Mercury, is represented
holding the infant Dionysus in his left arm.　Apart from the mutilation
of right arm and legs, the statue is well preserved.

Photo by Alinari

Greek sculptor obtained his wonderful
knowledge of form and gradually acquired
the power to render all parts of the human
body with ideal perfection. But it would
be totally inaccurate to picture Greek
temples and palaces as places adorned
with cold white statues, attractive only
in form. There is a widespread tendency
to regard Greek art as a " White Art," but
this conception is entirely wrong.

Colour was of the very essence of Greek
architecture, and colour was used not
only for the reliefs and sculpture in the
round which ornamented the exteriors of
these temples, but also for the single
figures or " substantive sculpture " which
we have been considering. Not only were
the figures in decorative reliefs, etc., tinted
throughout, but accessories such as armour
and horse-trappings were added in bronze
or other metal, so that the whole presented
a variegated and vivid effect. That the
Greeks coloured their sculpture is not a
mere conjecture, for careful examination in
recent years of the temple sculpture found
at Olympia, Aegina, and elsewhere has
revealed a number of sculptured fragments still bearing traces of colour.

The charming little statuettes found in
great numbers towards the end of the
nineteenth century at Tanagra, in Boeotia,
give us an excellent idea of the colouring
of Greek statues in the fourth century
B.C. When first recovered from the
ground in which they had been buried
for some 2,300 years, these figurines were
bright with colour as " the flowers that
bloom in the spring," and though some
of the freshness disappeared on exposure
to the air, the examples at the British
Museum give us some notion of what the
original appearance must have been of a
gallery of Greek sculpture.

This use of colour dates from the earliest
times. The limestone sculpture belonging
to the archaic temples of Athens, now
preserved in the Acropolis Museum, show
crude strong colouring. Only a few colours
were used, principally a bright brick-red
and blue, and these were used not
imitatively but arbitrarily to serve a decorative design. Thus men are given blue
hair, oxen are painted green, and no
attempt seems to have been made to
reproduce the colour of nature.

In later times this early crude colouring
gives place to a harmonious tinting more

THE APOLLO OF THE BELVEDERE: SCULPTURED 2,000 YEARS AGO

Statue of Apollo, in Carrara marble, discovered about 1500, in the ruins of Porto d'Anzio, the ancient Antium. Acquired by Pope Julius II., it was placed in the Belvedere Gallery of the Vatican. The left hand and right forearm were restored by Giovanni Angelo Montorsoli (1507-63).   It represents the Greek god, naked save for a cloak secured round the neck and draped from the left arm Apollo is usually represented as a tall, handsome, beardless youth holding bow or lyre, and was the patron of athletes.

in accordance with natural appearances. The most perfect example of Greek colouring extant is the great sarcophagus found at Sidon, now preserved at Constantinople, on which are depicted in coloured relief two scenes from the life of Alexander the Great, one being a lion hunt in which he takes part, and the other a battle scene. In the last-named everything is coloured, the bodies of the horses, the dress and arms of their riders and the footmen, their hair and eyes, even the background. Though the effect aimed at is intentionally decorative, there is no glaring discrepancy with natural appearances, and— greatest marvel of all from a technical standpoint —the semi-transparent colour is laid on in such a way that it mingles with and does not conceal the transparent shine of the natural marble.

Apart from the colour, which constitutes its unique attraction, this relief admirably illustrates the mingling of precision with ideality which is characteristic of Greek sculpture. This is no realistic rendering of any actual incident in the battle, but by selected and carefully composed details it tells the story of the fight. On the extreme left we see Alexander himself overthrowing a Persian horseman who has already turned to fly from him ; next a Macedonian footguard impetuously attacks a Persian infantryman ; in the centre a Greek cavalryman strikes down another Persian ; farther on a light-armed Greek sustains the charge of a Persian horseman, while on the extreme right the veteran Parmenio hurls a Persian general into the arms of an attendant Persian. It should be observed that, though the Greeks are clearly winning, the Persians are more numerous— twelve to six—while the dead bodies on the ground,

ANCIENT GREEK FIGURINES EXCAVATED AT TANAGRA

This delightful little terra-cotta group of two women seated together on a couch conversing was found with a number of others of a similar kind during the modern excavations made in Tanagra, a town of ancient Greece, in Boeotia, near the frontier of Attica. Examples of the artistic handiwork of the Greek potter, they are not only pleasing to the eye ; they have served to throw considerable light on the costumes worn in ancient Greece. There are a number of other examples in the British Museum.
Courtesy of the British Museum

more detailed study, and so great was the reverence for art in those days that the names of these five were handed down in honour to future generations by the historian Dionysius of Halicarnassus.

The Greek gods were idealised human beings. Zeus in sculpture is the ideal Greek father of a family; Apollo is the ideal athlete; and if it can be argued that the Greek sculptors dragged down their gods from heaven to earth, so also it must be universally conceded that they raised the representation of men and women to a divine level which has never been excelled.

four Persian and one Greek, show the proportion of losses on either side.

Thus a perfect synthesis of the progress and result of the battle is clearly narrated, and the story is packed in a design of absolute symmetry. The perfect balance of side with side and group with group is accomplished so tactfully that we hardly notice the science of the composition until we have begun to exhaust the interest of the various duels depicted. Perfect as sculpture, this relief is equally convincing as history. It is a somewhat late product of Greek art, but from every point of view it is a masterpiece.

The idealism of the Greek artist consisted in getting the very best he could from nature and putting it together in the most beautiful way. He always wanted models, and the more models he could get the greater were his resources for creating composite beauty. Thus we are told that when the painter Zeuxis was commissioned to paint a figure of Helen of Troy for the people of Croton, he made it a condition that he should have opportunities of studying the forms of the most beautiful maidens in the city. From the models offered him by the city, he selected five for

**THE WINGED VICTORY OF SAMOTHRACE**

The figure stands in the prow of a trireme, her drapery swept back by the wind. Of Parian marble, found in 1863 at Samothrace, the statue is now in the Louvre, Paris.

Photo by Alinari

## The Study of the Past. VII.

# The Rosetta Stone:
# Master Key to Egypt's Lore

### By H. R. Hall, D.Litt., F.S.A

#### Keeper of Egyptian and Assyrian Antiquities, British Museum

*THE Rosetta Stone is not a wonder of the past. It is a shapeless, broken slab of black basalt inscribed with close-set lines of three different characters. But it is the key that has unlocked for us a treasure house rich with stores of learning and with human interest. Without it the wonder of Karnak and Luxor would be vague and meaningless, the human story of Akhnaton for ever lost beneath the centuries and the tomb of Tutankhamen with all its pomp still buried in the Valley of the Kings; for it revealed to us the meaning of the sacred characters in which the Egyptians had been carving their records for nearly four thousand years. This incalculable value inhering in a thing of little intrinsic wonder surely justifies its inclusion in this section of* WONDERS OF THE PAST; *and here Dr. Hall tells the momentous story of its interpretation. than which no tale of clues and cryptograms could be more thrilling.*—EDITOR.

TO most people the British Museum means, apart from the Library, two things, both ancient Egyptian: mummies and the Rosetta Stone. The block of dark stone tilted on its pedestal at the entrance to the great Egyptian Sculpture Gallery is indeed a monument of transcendent importance, for the inscriptions on its face gave the two first decipherers of the ancient Egyptian writing, Young and Champollion, their first clues. Young did not carry out his researches as far as he might and so lost the glory of being the father of egyptology, but there is no doubt that Champollion owed much to him, probably his inspiration in the first place and then several ideas. Champollion, however, was the first to write an Egyptian grammar, though Young must share with him the glory of having laid the foundation stone of our modern knowledge.

The Rosetta Stone is a block of black basalt, about 3 feet 9 inches by 2 feet 4 inches in dimensions, on which is an inscription cut in two languages, Greek and Egyptian, and in three scripts, Greek and the Egyptian hieroglyphic and demotic. The last is a sort of shorthand first developed about 900 B.C. from the older hieratic, or cursive form of the hieroglyphs, which had gone out of use by the time the Rosetta Stone was made and is not represented on it. The inscription is identical in both languages and is a copy of a decree set forth by the Egyptian priests to commemorate the coronation of King Ptolemy V. Epiphanes, in his ninth year, B.C. 196.

Originally it was set up at Memphis but at an unknown period had been transported to the town of Rosetta on the sea-coast, where it was found by the French troops of Napoleon Buonaparte in 1799. In 1801 it was ceded to the British conqueror of Egypt, together with other antiquities collected by the French savants who accompanied Buonaparte, and brought to England where it was placed in the British Museum as a gift from King George III. From the first it attracted the attention of scholars on account of its bilingual character which gave a hope of possible decipherment, to be brilliantly fulfilled. Two foreign scholars, Silvestre de Sacy and Åkerblad, succeeded in identifying the royal names in the demotic text on account of their correspondence in position to the Greek names. The groups in the hieroglyphic text enclosed within an oval line or "cartouche" were rightly assumed by Zoega on account of this distinction to be royal names. But it was Young who first proved this assumption to be correct and successfully deciphered the name of Ptolemy on the Rosetta Stone, and that of Berenike on another royal decree of the same kind, since he was the first to assume that the signs within the cartouches were alphabetic or quasi-alphabetic and not purely symbolic as had formerly been supposed. On this foundation Champollion in 1822 based his wonderful decipherment of the actual words of the inscription in the hieroglyphs outside the cartouches—which he soon found, by applying Young's and his own results to them, to be in the form of the Coptic language, the tongue in whose modified Greek characters the Egyptian native Christian scriptures had always been written. It was then seen that Coptic was simply a late form of ancient Egyptian.

The royal names were deciphered as follows. It was found that a name within a cartouche corresponding in position to the Greek

ΠΤΟΛΕΜΑΙΟΣ=Ptolemaios (Ptolemy) consisted of the signs ⬭ which were read P-T-O-L-M-I-S, Ptol(e)m(a)i(o)s; the E and A (and in other instances the O) being left out according to the principle, well known to Semitic scholars, of omitting vowels. Then the name ΚΛΕΟΠΑΤΡΑ (Cleopatra) on a bilingual inscription at Philae was found to be the equivalent of ⬭ and in this name it was evident that, arguing from the supposed equivalent of Ptolemy, the letters L, O and P

occurred in approximately their proper positions. The sign ⬭ following ⬭ and the second ⬭ were assumed to be A from the position of the same sign found in the name Berenike or Berenika, so that ⬭ must equal TR and ⬭ equal K, in which case ⬭ would have to equal E. In this case the vowels were obviously given, although in the name of Ptolemy they were not with the exception of O and unless we regard ⬭ (I or Y) as a vowel. Young had noted that the signs ⬭ normally followed a female name so that they could be omitted as simply a feminine termination, which they proved to be.

Now the results from the two names were applied to the word ⬭ which should be the Egyptian equivalent of Alexander. ⬭ was correct for A, ⬭ for L, ⬭ for S, ⬭ for TR, while ⬭ should be E. It was evident that the decipherment was on right lines, for AL. SE. TR was evidently ΑΛΕΞΑΝΔΡΟΣ (Alexander) and the unknown signs ⬭, ⬭, ⬭ must be a second form of K, the sign for N and a second form of S; the whole reading ALKSENTRS. Evidently, as sometimes in the name of Ptolemaios, the O was omitted and the E obviously was also, while the Greek Ξ (X) was quite correctly represented by KS and ⬭ could evidently be either an A or an E and ⬭ a T or a D. The Egyptians spelt the name as best they could in their hieroglyphic script, in which it could have been read Aleksentres or Alkesnotris or any other combination of vowels with the consonantal skeleton of the word; but there is no doubt that they read it Alexandros. The further steps by which the actual language was read in Coptic would take too long to tell. But it was thus from the study of the Rosetta Stone that we derive the knowledge which now enables us to read all Egyptian inscriptions.

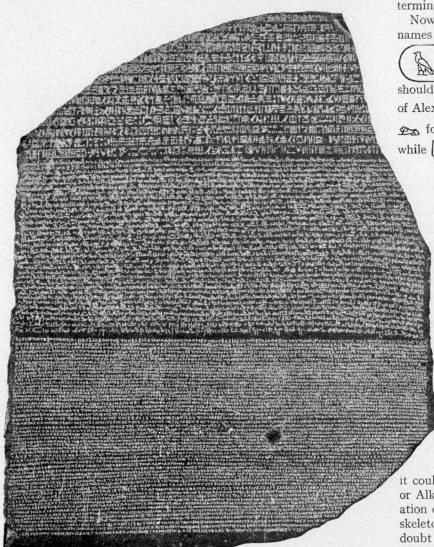

**CLUE TO AN AGE OLD LORE**

One of the greatest triumphs of archæology lay in the discovery in 1799 of the Rosetta Stone from which the meaningless script of ancient Egypt was explained. Its three inscriptions are in hieroglyphic (reading from right to left), demotic and Greek.

*By permission of the Trustees of the British Museum*

## HOW A MARVELLOUS SCULPTURED STAIRCASE WAS DUG OUT

Excavations at the sides of the great platform of the palaces at Persepolis (illustrated in page 54) showed that under 26 feet of brick and rubble débris of the palaces burned by Alexander the Great in 330 B.C., were magnificent sculptured stairways and wall reliefs so large in quantity as to double the known volume of Persian art.  This monumental stairway formed a stately approach to the Apadâna or Hall of a Hundred Columns (see reconstruction in pages 56 and 57).  Sculptured blocks and other fallen fragments, which were found in perfect condition, were replaced by a hoisting tripod.  Details of the sculptures are given in pages 256 and 257.

Courtesy of Chicago Oriental Institute Expedition to Persia under Prof. Ernst Herzfeld. Director Prof. James H. Breasted

## The Royal Palaces. V.

# The Superb Sculptures of the Great Palaces at Persepolis

### By Lewis Spence, F.R.A.I.

*THE ruins of the wonder palaces of Xerxes and Darius have been known since the middle of the 19th century, and much valuable archaeological work upon them has been carried out so that their general construction and even details of their decoration have been revealed as seen in an earlier chapter (see pages 51 to 60). Greater wonders have now come to light. Recent excavations by an expedition of the Oriental Institute of Chicago, under Prof. Ernst Herzfeld, have cleared away vast piles of rubbish and have uncovered reliefs and sculptures of superb qualities and exquisite detail, many of them still as clear cut as on the day on which the ancient Persian artist completed them. The reproductions in these pages are given by courtesy of Dr. James H. Breasted, Director of the Oriental Institute of the University of Chicago.*—EDITOR.

THE manner in which the grandeur of Persepolis was unearthed and restored to modern vision in all its magnificence of sculptured stairway and carven bas-relief is one of the romances of that most "temperamental" of sciences, Archaeology, which, when it reveals new wonders to him, the wayfaring man regards at times as fulfilling his dreams of ancient marvel, while in its more practical mood it seems as dusty as the deserts in which it delves. At Persepolis is nothing but wonder and beauty, the excavation of which must be numbered among the miracles of loveliness of the past restored.

It was in 1887 that Sir Cecil Harcourt Smith visited Persia on behalf of the British Museum Trustees, and advised the dispatch of an expedition to Persepolis, which for more than a generation had been claiming expert attention. In 1892 and the following year moulds were taken from the Palace of Darius, and the resulting casts were housed in the British Museum, the Louvre, and elsewhere. The expedition specialised in the reproduction of the decorated façade of a double stairway built during the reign of Artaxerxes III, and among other activities succeeded in taking a fine mould of the well-known inscription of that monarch.

In 1931 the Persian Expedition of the University of Chicago, under the direction of Dr. Ernst Herzfeld, began operations at Persepolis with the object of examining by excavation the whole area of the terrace described in the former chapter on Persepolis, with the palaces of Darius, Xerxes and Artaxerxes. Part of its intention was the preservation of the buildings and sculptures which cover the terrace and the reconstruction of at least one of the palaces as a specimen of ancient Persian architecture. The excavators were also instructed to reopen the ancient subterranean drainage system and to protect the whole against rain, frost, and the hand of the vandal.

It was found, during the two years' activities of the expedition, that enormous accumulations of brick covered the ruins situated on the platform. These had been caused in the course of five-and twenty centuries by the decay of the walls of the palaces which had been burned by the conquering Alexander the Great in 330 B.C. This débris was twenty-six feet in thickness. The heavy roofs, built of huge beams of cedar, flaming to destruction, had crashed, bearing with them much of the substance of the walls, and time, and perhaps earthquake, had done the rest.

### THE GREAT KING'S HORSE CARVED TO THE LIFE

This detail from the newly discovered Apadana staircase, illustrated in the opposite page, affords an excellent example of the brilliant art and technique of its Persian sculptor some 2,500 years ago. The horse frets at the bit, and eye and nostril and the proud neck breathe actual life.

Courtesy of Chicago Oriental Institute

253

A STAIRWAY OF BEAUTY WHOSE EXISTENCE REMAINED UNSUSPECTED THROUGH A CENTURY OF INVESTIGATION

This beautiful tripylon, or double staircase, enriched with exquisite reliefs was on a higher level than the stairway seen in page 252. It served as a main entrance to the smaller palaces of the Persian kings for their daily use. It is crenelated like the Apadana stairway, and has two groups of sculptures which provide information on the life of ancient Persia that was previously unknown. The symbol of the lion attacking a bull, which is seen constantly in Persian art, figures here in the centre of each outer wall of the staircase. In the background may be seen the ruins of the Palace of Darius, seen also in the photograph in page 54, and by comparing the two illustrations an idea of the relative position of this stairway may be obtained.

Courtesy of Chicago Oriental Institute Expedition to Persia under Prof. Ernst Herzfeld. Director Prof. James H. Breasted

By the new light cast upon the site by the discoveries of the thoroughgoing and nimble-witted American excavators, it came to be recognized that the level of the front part of the terrace is actually lower than had been thought previously. It was found that the great audience Hall of a Hundred Columns, which the Americans called by its Persian name, "the Apadana," stood on a platform nearly ten feet above the level of the terrace, and was reached by a great monumental stairway like an inverted "V," having two sides or approaches from the south and north, the outer walls of which were covered with sculptures of the most splendid description.

It was also found that the smaller palaces which served for the more intimate domestic needs of the Persian monarchs stood on a still higher level, a "tripylon," or double staircase, likewise covered with sculptures, leading up to a platform in front of these. Thus two groups of relief sculptures of the most exquisite character, enriched with figures which greatly extended knowledge of ancient Persian life, were disclosed for the first time by the excavation of these stairways, the irregularities in which the members of the expedition carefully made good by the replacing of the missing parts found among the débris.

The parapets of these fairy staircases are topped by long lines of crenellations, and each of their angles is decorated with the ancient Persian design of a lion attacking a bull, a symbol of astrological significance. The stairway leading to the Apadana consists of two wings, and has a length of about 290 feet. On the main front of this structure is the bas-relief of a great procession of the tributaries of the twenty-eight nations or satrapies of the Persian Empire. The occasion represented is evidently that of the New Year festival, which, among the Persians, was held about the middle of March, and each tribe or nation is separately depicted, its attributes of costume and racial

MAGNIFICENT CARVING OF CROWNED HUMAN-HEADED BULL
Originally one of a pair which formed the capital of a column on the tripylon stairway illustrated in the opposite page, this striking bearded head with its mixed animal and human motives is highly typical of a branch of Persian art inspired by ancient Mesopotamia. Other examples of this art, though less perfect in preservation and less vivid in execution, are seen in pages 51 and 58.
Courtesy of Chicago Oriental Institute

appearance being given the due attention of the observant sculptor.

All these sculptures, when excavated, were found to be practically as fresh as when the last stroke of the chisel completed their contours. That depicting the procession of the tribute-bearers is situated on the southern wing of the Apadana staircase, its northern and opposite wing bearing a representation of the palace guards, Persians, Medians, and Susians, belonging to that famous bodyguard known to history as "The Ten

TRIBUTE SENT BY THE

The tribute bearers from the twen
of ancient Persia, a vast territory
Turkistan to Abyssinia and from t
on the top left, Susians from Bhuzis
with her cubs and Armenians with a
Cilicians, led by a Median, come wit
left). Above, heavily bearded, lo
carry gold vessels and bracelets an
of a chariot dra

## AMONG THE GREATEST WORKS OF ART SURVIVING FROM THE ANCIENT WORLD—

Professor Breasted rightly says of these astonishing sculptures that the best of them " will rank among the greatest works of art that have survived from the ancient world." The reliefs represented here are but nine panels, or portions of panels, selected from a series which total 1,000 feet in length. They show in detail something of the quality of these reliefs which entitles them to be called superb. The tribute bearers in the bottom left panel are Cilicians bringing rams.

Photographs by Chicago Oriental Institute Expedition to Persia under Prof. Ernst Herzfeld.

OF THE PERSIAN WORLD

ons represent the twenty satrapies
om Ferghana, in modern Russian
Sind in India. In the two panels
ith bows, long daggers and a lioness
a stallion. Left centre, a group of
and a pair of rams (enlarged below,
ans with Phoenician caps. They
of horses. Below, a vigorous relief
white stallions.

—SUPERB SCULPTURES NEWLY DISCOVERED ON PALACE STAIRWAYS AT PERSEPOLIS

The frieze on the right is a portion of the central face of the Apadana staircase illustrated in page 252 and represents part of the procession of
tribute bearers of the twenty-eight nations subject to Darius the Great. At the top Arachosians from South Afghanistan lead a camel and
carry vessels of worth; in the centre Sardians from Smyrna in Asia Minor bring a humped bull, shields and lances and, below, are Bactrians
from North Afghanistan with a humped camel and vessels of gold

Reproduced by courtesy of the Director, Prof. James H. Breasted.

Thousand Immortals," the numbers of which were always maintained at full strength.

These carvings, if placed together in a row, would form a panel of relief five or six feet high, and nearly a thousand feet long. They are carved in black stone, capable of a high polish, and this it still retains, although signs are not wanting that the numerous figures chiselled upon it were painted in the most gorgeous colours, as several fragments reveal. By far the most interesting of these are the representations of the tribute-bearers, which afford us a glimpse of actual life in more than a score of Oriental lands at the period of the reign of Darius, between the years 521 and 485 B.C. Here we behold, as though they had posed for the sculptor yesterday, the linea-ments and costumes of the peoples of the old Iranian Empire, including a vast territory which stretched from Ferghana in the north-east to Abyssinia in the south-west, and from the Balkans in the north-west to Sind in the south-east.

Among the races represented we see Arachosians from southern Afghanistan, leading a camel and bearing gifts in pottery bowls, their tight tunics and full trousers somewhat reminiscent of modern Oriental costume. Beneath them stalk Sardians from Lydia, leading humped cattle, and bearing shields and lances, while on a still lower panel are represented tall Bactrians from what is now northern Afghanistan, carrying gold vessels and wearing the antique equivalent of " plus-fours "

Susians from Bhuzistan bear offerings of bows and what might be described as " Kukries," or disembowelling daggers, while others lead a lioness and carry her cubs, at which the dam looks back with maternal solicitude Armenians bring blood horses and costly amphorae, while Cilicians drive large horned rams to the place of tribute.

Solemn looking Scythians from Ferghana in Turkestan, wearing pointed cowls like monks' hoods, bring presents of heavy mantles and spirited horses, and Syrians with elaborately

**THE GREAT APADANA STAIRWAY WITH SCULPTURES UNSURPASSED IN THE ANCIENT WORLD**

This photograph affords a clear view of the northern wing of the monumental staircase that led to the Apadana or Hall of a Hundred Columns, of which a more general view is given in page 252. Thanks to Alexander's mad act of rapid destruction by fire of the main buildings above the stairways these were covered immediately with brick rubbish and undisturbed by man or weather for nearly 2,000 years Hence probably the amazingly clean cut and fresh condition which they and their sculptures present today.

Courtesy of Oriental Institute of the University of Chicago

RUINS OF THE HALL OF A HUNDRED COLUMNS AND TOP OF NEWLY-DISCOVERED STAIRCASE

This photograph, which is complementary to the views reproduced in pages 54 and 252, shows the level at which the new excavations were begun and illustrates the fact that what for centuries had been taken as the great platform of the halls and palaces of the Persian kings is, in the front part at least, an artificial level made up by brick rubbish of the falling palaces and the accumulations of time. Two years' arduous excavation work was required to clear the platform and the stairways. Above all the destruction and decay have soared for two thousand years these lovely ruined pillars. Once they enclosed the magnificence of the " King of kings, the king of lands. the king of this Earth " as Artaxerxes III described himself.

curled beards display gifts of jewelry and pottery, in which their cities excelled. Of equal interest as illustrating the life of the Court, are the sculptures of chariots and mettlesome horses. One such conveyance, drawn by two horses, and driven by a charioteer, was the chariot in which the god Auramazda was thought to ride invisible beside the mortal monarch. It was doubtless believed that his viewless arrows were disposed in the quiver on the left of the vehicle. In another bas-relief the King's horse frets at his bit, restrained by the groom, and a spirited piece shows a couple of servants carrying the monarch's camp-stool

Vivid, and not at all conceived in the prim stiffness of antique art, is another sculpture which represents the Persian and Median guardsmen of " the Immortal " corps in conversation with each other. It might, indeed, be described with justice as the first modern sculpture, and its vitality appears to foreshadow the brilliant movement of the Greek schools. It is an awakening of sculpture, an early sign of stir and passion in the art The inner portion of this splendid stairway was ornamented by sculptures of the Persian Guard, one above each step, as if in the act of mounting the incline.

Similar sculptures adorn the " tripylon " or double staircase which led to the residential palaces Perhaps the most precious thing which emerged from the ruin that covered it is the sculpture of a crowned human-headed bull which formed the capital of one of the columns. The crenellations on this stairway are practically perfect in their preservation. Its sides are carven with other representations of the Guard of Persia, executed in much the same manner, and the motif of the lion and the bull. Above the stairway the remains of a great doorway rear their bulk, the sides bearing sculptures of the monarch accompanied by his parasol-bearers, while over his head spreads the winged symbol of Auramazda

A third and much smaller stairway exhibits tributaries carrying kids, pots filled with provisions and large bundles of weaves or other merchandise, but a strong similarity is to be found between most of the figures in this tributary procession, and they scarcely exhibit the racial individuality of those on the larger stairway. They decorate the inside of this beautiful little incline, the outer walls of which are covered with representations of the " Immortals."

A word must be said about the remains of buildings which were unearthed and, in one instance at least, restored by the American expedition. It became apparent that after the destruction of the roofs, which perished in the incendiary madness of Alexander the Great, the walls, built of sun-dried bricks and decorated by a frieze of enamelled tiles, crashed downward, burying the whole mass deep in brick-dust which hardened in the course of centuries into a thick deposit But the decorative enamelled frieze was carefully pieced together, as was an inscription containing the name of Xerxes.

The Apadana, the traditional scene of Alexander's feast, which ended in a scene of conflagration at the whim of the courtesan Thais, is now desolate and bare, except for the stairway which fronts it and the great pillars, sixty-five feet high, and some seven or eight in number, which remain as the only memorials of its former magnificence But other fluted columns, defaced and broken, litter the surrounding soil.

The Harem of Darius the Great, which was restored by the American Expedition, affords an excellent impression of an edifice of the period. It is a long and rather low building, furnished with many spacious windows, and has a large flat roof with crenellated sides

The superb sculptures of Persepolis seem as though preserved almost miraculously for the amazement of a later age by the rash act of a military despot—not the last instance, indeed, where violence has subserved the strange purposes of Art, embalming her choicest examples until the dawning of a more appreciative age.

BODYGUARD AND TRIBUTE BEARERS ON A PERSEPOLIS STAIRCASE

This finely executed and richly decorated staircase is one of the smaller palace stairways. As on the larger steps of the main stairway the sides are carved with figures, rising step by step, of the royal bodyguard (the "Immortal" corps) and of the bearers of tribute from the nations of the world to the kings of ancient Persia who were thereby confirmed in their brave notions of their own magnificence.

Photo. " The Times "

## HAND-MAIDENS FOR MEHENKWETRE IN THE OTHERWORLD

When the tomb of Mehenkwetre was opened in 1920, these exquisite figures of women attendants, the only large models found among the collection, had stood solemn-eyed and erect for 4,000 years, ever ready to serve their illustrious master, each carrying on her head a basket containing food and drink.  The models were half life-size.

*From a photograph by courtesy of the Metropolitan Museum, New York, specially coloured for "Wonders of the Past"*

# Wonder Models of the Daily Life of Egypt 4,000 Years Ago

## By Donald A. Mackenzie

### Author of "Egyptian Myth and Legend," etc.

*FEW Egyptian finds prior to that of the tomb of Tutankhamen exceeded in direct human appeal the discovery of a complete model representation of the daily life on the estate of a noble of ancient Egypt. The tomb was that of Mehenkwetre, chancellor and steward of the royal palace during the reign of Pharaoh Mentuhotep (about 2,000 years B.C.). The models were found by American excavators in the spring of 1920; some of them are now on view in the museum at Cairo, others in the Metropolitan Museum at New York. The complete series of photographs, with two coloured, is here given by kind permission of the Metropolitan Museum, New York.—EDITOR.*

THE little figures of servants found in ancient Egyptian tombs were called Ushabtis, which means "Respondents" or "Answerers." They were supposed to respond when the soul of the dead master or mistress called upon them to perform whatever service was required. The ancient Egyptians did not believe, of course, that these little wooden figures could, of themselves, do anything. They knew quite well that they would always remain in the tomb in the various attitudes in which they had been carved. What they did believe was that each figure had a spirit, and that the spirit would go to the soul of the mummy in the Otherworld and act as a servant there.

They embalmed the dead, believing that as long as the mummy remained in the tomb so long would the soul exist in Paradise.

Everything placed in the tomb was supposed to be doubled in that Otherworld beyond the sky. That was why the Egyptians took so much trouble to make strong and enduring tombs for their dead and to stuff them with food, clothing, furniture, boats, the figures of servants, and so on. It was supposed that their Paradise was just a glorified Egypt, with richer cornfields, fatter cattle, a more beautiful Nile, finer houses, and a better climate. There the dead would live as they had lived in Egypt. The fields would have to be cultivated and sown and the harvests reaped, and the grain would have to be stored and ground, and loaves would have to be baked. In short, all the work done on earth would have to be done in Paradise, the only difference being that work there would be easier and more pleasant, and that the disasters due to floods or shortage of water experienced on earth would not be repeated in the wonder-land of the new life.

For many centuries the ancient Egyptians were quite content with the idea that everyone who went to Paradise would have to work there. But when we come to study the beliefs that

THE SPIRIT MODEL OF THE RICH MAN'S STEWARD

This model of a trusty steward was placed in the tomb in order that Mehenkwetre should be able to travel in his boat upon the Nile as he might wish in the Otherworld, free from anxiety regarding the safety of his personal luggage, the spirit of the steward being ever present. Note the model trunks beneath the bed, just as they might be on a Nile voyage to-day.

AS SEEN FOR THE FIRST TIME AFTER FOUR THOUSAND YEARS

A remarkable photograph taken actually inside the tomb of Mehenkwetre, and showing—just as they were found—some of the wonderful statuettes and model boats with their crews, with which the Egyptian nobleman had furnished his tomb. His purpose in doing this was that he might not lack for servants in the Otherworld, the making of a material model being supposed to create its spirit equivalent in the spirit world.

existed during the Middle Kingdom period (about 2500 B.C.), we begin to find evidence that those who were not accustomed to manual labour in this world did not like the idea that they would have to sow and reap grain and do other necessary tasks in Paradise—the celestial Egypt. They wanted to live there as they had lived on the earth.

In short, the great lords of ancient Egypt wished to be great lords in Paradise, with their servants about them, ready to respond to orders and to perform whatever task was allotted to them. If the soul of the dead lord wished to sail on the celestial Nile, he must have his boat and his sailors ; if he wanted food, he must have his servants to cook and serve it ; if he wanted his fields tilled and sown and reaped in season, or his cattle herded and counted, or his cows milked,

he must have all these things done for him by his workers. That was why the custom arose in Middle Kingdom times, when Egyptian society was growing complex, of placing these quaint statuettes of workers and domestic animals and models of boats and houses in the tombs.

The earlier figures of servants were shaped like mummies, and on their breasts were inscribed powerful charms, supplied for a price by the priests, to make the soul of the servant obey the soul of the master in Paradise. A characteristic charm of this kind reads as follows :

" O statuette, counted for me, Ra-hotep (the lord), if I am called upon, if I am ordered to do any work which has to be done in the Otherworld, thou shalt act for me at all times, thou shalt cultivate the fields, thou shalt

**HOW CATTLE WERE SLAUGHTERED ON A NOBLEMAN'S ESTATE IN ANCIENT EGYPT**

The Egyptians supposed their Paradise to be just a glorified Egypt, an Egypt with richer cornfields, fatter cattle, a more beautiful river, finer houses, and a better climate, and that there they would live as they had lived in the country of the Nile. That is why they filled their tombs with food, clothing, and so forth. Everything placed in a tomb was believed to be doubled in the happier Otherworld which lay beyond the sky.

draw water, thou shalt remove the sand from water channels. When I am called upon thou shalt respond, ' Here am I.' "

Charms of like character were also written in the " Book of the Dead " under the title, " Chapter for Causing the Ushabti to do the Work of a Man in the Otherworld."

Once the fashion of placing these little figures of servants in tombs was introduced, it became very popular. As time went on the number of Ushabtis increased, and the idea that they were substitutes for their masters gradually died out. The lords no longer feared that they themselves would be called upon to do any work. Their chief concern was to make provision for their own comfort as they had done during life. Some lords had placed in their tombs one figure for each day

of the year, so as to be assured of constant personal service. The later and richer lords, who lived in grander style than did their ancestors, made more and more elaborate provision for their personal comfort in the Otherworld. The tombs were then furnished with numerous statuettes, and, in addition, with wall-pictures, depicting scenes of life, so that these might be repeated in Paradise.

The inscriptions also increased in length and number. Some inscriptions gave orders to employees. Others were really " guide-books," which instructed the lords how to reach the Otherworld.

One cannot help wondering at these ancient Egyptian ideas about making provision for the dead and providing statuettes to solve the servant problem in Paradise. At the same time, one

ENSURING HIS SUPPLY OF SPIRIT BEEF IN THE SPIRIT WORLD

Mehenkwetre gave even more thought to the questions of food and drink than to the matter of clothing. In life, no doubt, he had prided himself, as behoved a great lord of Egypt, on his success as a breeder of fat stock, and he was anxious to maintain this reputation in the Otherworld. Here cattle are seen in their stable, attended by the slaves whose function it was to fatten them.

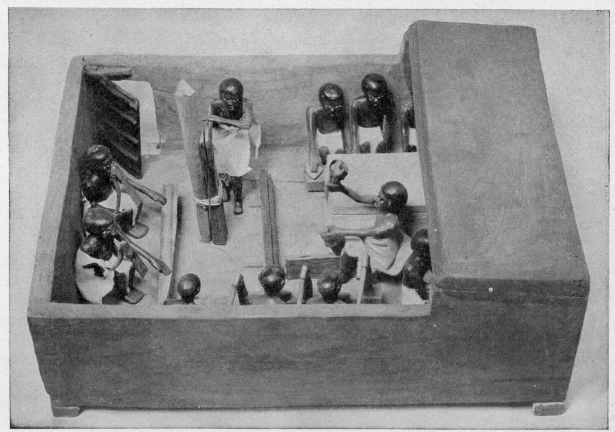

CARPENTERS AT WORK IN THEIR SHOP BY THE WATERS OF THE NILE

When making the arrangements for his future state, Mehenkwetre left nothing to chance. He even provided his tomb with the model of a carpenter's shop, well equipped and surprisingly efficient and up to date. While the central figure is sawing an upright beam into planks, an apprentice on the right is busily engaged mortising with mallet and chisel. This is a better record of a carpenter's shop 2000 B.C. than any photograph of one of our own time could be for future ages.

## CHARMING STUDY OF BUSY LIFE ON THE GREAT WATERWAY OF ANCIENT EGYPT

The kitchen tender is brought alongside, and Mehenkwetre dines comfortably in his cabin while travelling on the waters of the celestial Nile, just as he had been wont to do on earth when journeying, for example, between his country house and Thebes. A closer view of the great man in his cabin appears in page 269, and other boats are seen in colour in the plate facing the same page.

## MEHENKWETRE'S SPIRIT MODELS SHOW HOW THE EGYPTIANS WENT FISHING

Typical of the fishing craft used by the old Egyptians. These canoes, survivals of the earliest type of vessel used upon the Nile, were made by binding together bundles of reeds coated with pitch—the ark of bulrushes daubed with slime and with pitch in which his mother laid the infant Moses. The seine-net between the two canoes holds a goodly haul of little painted fishes.

THAT HE MIGHT STILL HAVE THE SATISFACTION OF COUNTING HIS CATTLE IN THE OTHERWORLD

In this very lively model, herds of cattle are being driven past Mehenkwetre by muscular and active herdsmen, carrying staves. The lord, attended by his son and heir, sits in a sort of grand-stand, surveying his live stock critically. while scribes take note of the number and condition of the beasts. The figures of the men are each about eight inches high. Some of the cattle are seen in their stall in the model illustrated in page 264

cannot but be impressed by the high degree of affection which the burial customs reveal. The living devoted much wealth to ensuring the happiness of those who had departed to another world. No sacrifice was too great; nothing was grudged to the dead. The mourners would rather suffer loss of all they had than deny anything to a dead relative. In that sense, therefore, the custom of constructing expensive tombs and enbalming the dead and purchasing offerings for them was a very beautiful one.

To us the custom makes another appeal. It has a very decided historical value. The groups of statuettes found in the tombs reveal, in a most graphic way, the manners and customs of a great and wonderful people who lived over 4,000 years ago. We are afforded glimpses of daily scenes of life.

Among the Ushabtis are those of house servants and outdoor workers of every class. They are depicted in the actual costumes that were fashionable in the far off days. They reveal by expression and pose their charming manners, their alertness in performing their duties, and their heartfelt sense of duty. Some are solitary personal servants, waiting to attend to a lady, to bind up her hair and furnish flowers and perfumes. They seem so nimble and light-footed that one is assured their movements were not only rapid but almost noiseless.

Other figures are arranged in groups. Here we see herds of cattle driven past a great lord by muscular and active herdsmen who carry staves. The lord sits in a sort of "grand stand," surveying his live stock critically, while his scribes take note of their numbers and condition.

Another little model shows us the cows in their byres and the farm servants feeding or milking them, while a third depicts a slaughter-house, and shows how the Egyptians killed and cut up the animals used for food. Note, too, how the granary scene is depicted. The various workers are lifting the grain and filling it in measures so as to estimate the exact quantity, while records are made by a scribe. Evidently the scribes' "books" are kept in a very exact way. The lord who owns

**THAT HE MIGHT ENJOY THE SHADE OF TREES**

In front of the portico of Mehenkwetre's model house was laid out a model garden such as an Egyptian nobleman, belonging to a race of men who dearly loved flowers and colour, would certainly require in his future state. Egyptians did not think of the Otherworld as a place where gardens grew of their own accord; fields had there to be sown, harvests reaped, and grain stored and ground just as on this earth of toil.

the land can be informed at any moment what quantity of grain has been reaped and how much is contained in the granary. He can be told, too, how much must be reserved for daily use and how much can be sold.

Other models show us the cooks preparing food, the bakers busy baking loaves and cakes, the carpenters at their benches, the boat-builders, the goldsmiths and others plying their trades.

Of very special interest are the models of ships and boats. The River Nile was the great highway of Egypt. It had constantly to be crossed because some estates lay on both banks. When a great lord wished to pass from one city to another,

PORTICO OF MEHENKWETRE'S HOME FOR REPRODUCTION IN PARADISE

This model of the stately portico of his Egyptian home was one of the treasures found in the tomb. It is a nearer view of that which is shown on page 267. Mehenkwetre believed that he would need a house in the Otherworld no less than in this. In fact, he thought that life in the Hereafter would be very much like life in the present, save that it would be easier, perhaps, and more pleasant, and immune from such disasters as are caused, for example, by floods and droughts, purely worldly misfortunes.

or to "go to town" from his country-house, he called for a boat just as a modern lord may call for his motor-car. The Egyptians were the oldest seamen in the world; they were also the finest boat-builders. They made great progress in solving the problems of navigation, and discovered how to steer and adjust the sails so as to tack and come up very close to the wind.

The various models show that they had excellent discipline in their vessels. Every man knew his place and his duty. At the bow stood the "look-out," who took soundings with a long pole; at the stern was the steersman who attended to the steering-paddle. The skipper stood amidships and issued orders, which were repeated by his officers, who were always standing stiffly at attention. In the rowing-boats the men kept stroke, but they sat looking forward and not backward as in modern boats; in the sailing-boat the crew collected round the mast ready to haul the halyards and hoist or lower the sail. The small canoes are of very special interest, because they show us the earliest types of vessels. They were made by binding together bundles of reeds and coating them with pitch so as to make them watertight. Sometimes

the great lords and even the Pharaohs went out in these small boats to amuse themselves by catching fish, or bringing down birds with the aid of throw-sticks or bows and arrows.

In some tombs have been found boats which are without crews. These were used by the souls of the dead to cross the Lily Lake which separated them from the strange and beautiful wonder-land of Paradise. On that lake was a boat which was supposed to be alive, like the swan-boat of Lohengrin. When it was called for it came ashore. The oars were alive, and when the soul said, "Row," they moved of their own accord. A model of this boat might be provided for the dead.

Another idea about the Lily Lake boat was that it was under the direction of a sour and ill-tempered ferryman, who was called "Face Backwards," because he always looked the other way when a soul called to him. It was believed to be necessary to bribe this sinister ferryman.

One bribe was a magic jar of wine which was placed in the tomb. If he could not be bribed the ferryman might be amused, and thus moved to serve the waiting soul as a special favour. A favourite way of providing amusement was to cause a misshapen dwarf to dance a grotesque dance on the shore. A figure of a dwarf was sometimes provided in the tomb for that purpose. Another way to obtain the service of the ferryman was to repeat charms.

One old text puts into the mouth of the waiting soul the words, " Oh, thou (the paddle) in the hand of the ferryman, hear me and bring the boat hither ! " The paddle would then set itself in motion so that the boat might be brought to the beach. Some of the texts threaten the ferryman with dire punishment if he will not serve the waiting soul promptly and willingly.

When the fashion came in of providing model boats with crews in the tombs less was said in the inscriptions about the ill-natured ferryman " Face Backwards." The great lord had a boat of his own and many willing servants, so that he might be enabled to cross the Lily Lake and sail on the celestial Nile. When he reached the Otherworld he found there a mansion and garden provided for him, because models of these had been placed in his tomb. In Paradise he could then enjoy every luxury he had been accustomed to on earth. Even his musicians accompanied him, for statuettes of harpers and pipers had been thoughtfully provided by his relatives. In addition, songs and stories were written on rolls of papyrus so that he might never feel time hanging heavily on his hands.

What a wonderful story of ancient beliefs regarding the Otherworld of the Egyptians these little tomb figures provide ! But they do more than that. They reveal the very high degree of civilization which existed in ancient Egypt forty centuries ago. In some of its aspects that civilization was similar to our own at the present time. Society was well organized. The people of all classes had regularised habits of life. Houses were comfortable and well furnished. Meals were served at stated hours. There was a time for duty and a time for recreation. The ancient Egyptians knew what it was to work hard, and they knew how to enjoy life.

The various workers were carefully trained. As the tomb models show, the men and women were highly efficient, and we know, from the specimens

of their craftsmanship which have been brought to light, that they performed their tasks with thoroughness and exactness. Ancient Egypt was a hive of industry. Its civilization had a setting of Oriental splendour, but it was also veined by great ideals, for a cultivated moral sense permeated every rank of society.

The laws were of a humane character, and were administered without fear or favour. In a papyrus roll (an ancient manuscript) an old sage who gave advice and instruction to men

MEHENKWETRE IN THE CABIN OF HIS SHIP

A large number of portrait models were included among the treasures of the tomb. This shows the Egyptian nobleman cruising leisurely on the waters of the celestial Nile, with minstrels in attendance, one of them fingering the harp.

in positions of responsibility wrote these significant words :

" Forget not to judge justly. It is an abomination to the god to show partiality. This is my teaching."

The great lords who had the Ushabti statuettes placed in their tombs believed that, as worshippers of Osiris, they would be punished for wrongdoing on earth when they reached the Judgement Hall in the Otherworld. In their tomb inscriptions they recorded that they had done their duty, that they had not oppressed the poor, nor ill-treated their workers, and that they had done their utmost to judge justly.

One great lord, named Ameni, who lived about 2000 B.C., had carved on the door of his tomb an inscription which reveals him as an exemplary employer and administrator. It is to the following effect :

" I never afflicted a widow. I never evicted a peasant, nor did I ever ill-use a herdsman. I never took away people (as slaves) for unpaid taxes. No one was miserable in my community ; no one ever hungered in my time. When the years of famine came I ploughed all the fields of my estate and kept the people alive, providing food for all. I gave to the widow. I did not, when I gave out food, favour an influential man above a poor man. Then, in time, came the great inundations of the Nile and all had plenty, but I did not collect the arrears of the field."

This wonderful record gives us an idea of the high sense of duty which existed in the hearts of the best types of landowners and officials in ancient Egypt. The workers, whose statuettes are found in the tombs, were evidently not disciplined by fear alone. They knew something of " the milk of human kindness," and what it was to serve a good master. The theory that they were mere slaves is not supported by the evidence of the texts or by the ancient stories in rolls of papyri.

One story tells that a worker who was bullied and robbed by a man occupying a better position than himself had justice done by making personal appeal to a great lord who championed his cause with success in a court of justice. Another side-light which should not be overlooked is thrown on ancient Egyptian civilization by these statuettes. They were supplied by the priests, who employed large numbers of artisans in the temple workshops. It was a profitable business for them to encourage the wealthy Egyptians to equip their tombs with many models of workers, and to have magical charms and religious texts inscribed on doors and walls, and on papyri rolls.

The priests were all-powerful in Egypt, and, as that country grew more and more wealthy, their demands on the Pharaoh and his lords increased accordingly. It was chiefly owing to their influence that the burial customs became so elaborate, and wealthy men were prompted to expend vast sums so as to ensure their happiness in the Otherworld.

IN THE BUSY GRANARY ON MEHENKWETRE'S WELL-ORDERED ESTATE

In some respects this model (photographed from above), with its wealth of detail, is the gem of the collection, and it throws a flood of light upon the efficiency of the methods which controlled the well-ordered lives of the people of old Egypt. In the chamber on the left scribes, or clerks, may be seen recording transactions and keeping accounts on tablets and papyrus rolls. In the centre and on the right is the granary proper. The men at the top of the flight of stairs are pouring into large bins grain brought up to them in sacks from the lower chamber.

# The Seven Wonders. III.

# The Mausoleum at Halicarnassus

## By F. Norman Pryce, M.A.

Of the Greek and Roman Department, British Museum

BUDRUM is a small Turkish port, with a ruined castle of the Knights of St. John of Jerusalem, beautifully situated on the coast of the Gulf of Kos at the south-west angle of Asia Minor. The district was known in ancient times as Caria, and though nominally a province, or satrapy, of the great empire of Persia, its situation, shut off between the mountains and the sea at the extreme limits of the empire, secured for it a measure of independence.

In the first half of the fourth century B.C. the country was ruled by an active and warlike prince, Mausolus, who fixed his capital on the site of Budrum, anciently called Halicarnassus.

On his death, in the year 353 B.C., his devoted widow, Artemisia, resolved to perpetuate his memory and appease her own sorrow by erecting for him the most splendid tomb ever known, and sent to Greece to secure the services of the most renowned artists of the age. The names of the architects were Satyros and Pythios. The sculptors who were to adorn the structure were Scopas, the greatest Greek sculptor of the century—famed above all for his power to express in stone the most passionate emotions and the most vivid movement—Timotheos, Bryaxis, and Leochares, of whom less is now known, but who in their own age were considered second only to Scopas.

Queen Artemisia reigned for only two years, and then died, consumed by wasting grief for the loss of her husband. The tomb was then still unfinished, but the artists resolved to complete it as a labour of love "for their own fame and a record of their skill." The result was a work of such magnificence and splendour that it ranked as one of the Seven Wonders of the World, and its name, the Mausoleum, has come generally to be employed to denote any elaborate sepulchre.

Descriptions of the building have been handed down to us by more than one ancient writer, but, unfortunately, these are ambiguous and permit of interpretation in various ways, and the dimensions as recorded are suspected by some authorities.

There is thus considerable difference of opinion with regard to many details of the Mausoleum,

ONE OF THE DECORATIVE LIONS OF THE MAUSOLEUM
Several of these splendidly sculptured beasts, all uniform and conventional in design, have been brought to light by the labours of excavators. In 1856, at the instigation of Sir Charles Newton, they were removed for safety to the British Museum. There were probably six such lions, three on each side of a wide stairway leading up to the platform upon which the tomb stood.

and a large number of widely differing reconstructions have been produced.  Generally speaking, however, the building was rectangular, with the short sides on the north and south ; the lower storey, in which was the tomb-chamber, was solid ; bands of sculpture ran round all four sides.  Above

FIGURE OF GRACE FROM THE FRIEZE OF THE MAUSOLEUM

Much of the beauty of the great tomb of Mausolus survived until the 15th century when the Knights of St. John used it to build their castle.  Among the few fragments that still remain is this extremely graceful charioteer from the frieze surrounding the building seen beneath the pillars in the reconstruction in the opposite page.

this was a colonnade of thirty-six columns of the Ionic order of rich golden-white marble, which was surmounted by a pyramid of twenty-four steps, and on the top of the pyramid was a chariot with four horses.  The total height was one hundred and forty feet.  What appeared to ancient sight-seers the most remarkable feature of the building

was the impression of lightness ; the massive pyramid, poised on top of the slender colonnade, appeared to float in air.

There is reason to believe that down to the twelfth century, or even later, the building survived practically undamaged.  But in 1402 the Knights of St. John took possession of Halicarnassus and began to build on the site their castle of St. Peter.

To obtain the necessary building materials they pulled down the remains of the ancient city, and probably about this time the super-structures of the Mausoleum were destroyed.  In 1472 the building was in ruins, and the last of these ruins was destroyed in 1522, when Sultan Suleiman was preparing his great expedition to drive the Knights out of Asia Minor and Rhodes.  The Grand Master of the Order of St. John, realizing the military importance of the castle at Budrum, ordered it to be put in repair.  For this purpose the Knights broke up the base of the Mausoleum and burnt the marble blocks for lime.

While doing this they broke into a large square chamber elaborately adorned with slabs and bands of marbles of different colours, with battle scenes sculptured in relief.  The story goes that the finders at first admired these, and then broke them up.  They then penetrated into an inner chamber containing a sarcophagus.  As night was coming on they returned to the castle, and in the morning when they returned they found that this tomb had been robbed during the night by unknown pirates or brigands.  Thus the grave of Mausolus, after remaining inviolate for over eighteen centuries, was finally destroyed   Shortly afterwards the Knights of St. John were driven from Budrum by the Turks, and all recollection even of the site was lost.

Although this wholesale destruction is recorded of the Knights, yet at times a desire seems to have prevailed to preserve and save some fragments of the priceless sculptures which otherwise would have been fed to their lime-kilns.  At some unknown date a slab of carved frieze was sent to

## THE GLORIOUS SYMBOL OF A CONSUMING GRIEF

This striking reconstruction of the famous tomb of Mausolus at Halicarnassus, now Budrum, Asia Minor, is based on a model in the British Museum constructed after recent investigations into the details of the building. King Mausolus, whose name lives in our language in the word "mausoleum," ruled Caria, from 387–353 B.C. as a satrap, or provincial governor, under the Great King of Persia. The stately monument raised to his memory was inspired by the grief of Artemisia, his widowed queen. Accounted as one of the Seven Wonders of the World, it stood 140 feet high.

## SPIRITED FRIEZE THAT RECORDS DEADLY STRIFE 'TWIXT AMAZONS AND GREEKS

Fragment of the once delicately-coloured frieze of the Mausoleum, rescued in 1846 from the Castle of St. Peter, and now preserved in the British Museum. On the left, the Amazon is drawing back from the attack of her bearded Greek assailant, but has both hands raised, waiting for a chance to hit back with her axe. On the right, she is seen thrown to the ground, the Greek bending over her, ready to deal the fatal blow.

## THE CROWNING GLORY OF THE MAUSOLEUM

A special reconstruction of the four-horse chariot. Some authorities think the king's companion to be a goddess driving his chariot, as Athene is shown on black figure vases driving the chariot of Heracles. But since the figures are in the normal proportions of a man and woman, she probably represents the woman who loved and shared the fortunes of the tomb's dead occupant.

Specially drawn for this work by C. M. Sheldon, from material at the British Museum

Genoa; other slabs were built into the walls of the castle into which a number of marble lions were also inserted. In the seventeenth and eighteenth centuries Western travellers and merchants passing through Budrum observed these fragments, and it was rightly concluded that they must have been taken from the Mausoleum. In 1846 Lord Stratford de Redcliffe, then British Ambassador at Constantinople, obtained permission of the Sultan to remove to the British Museum twelve slabs forming part of the large frieze showing the combat of Greeks and Amazons. In 1856 Sir Charles Newton was allowed to remove the lions and also to excavate on the actual site.

The excavation revealed little more than the foundations and ground plan, and it was evident that the Knights had destroyed everything above ground. Scattered about in the vicinity of the site, however, were discovered a large quantity of fragments of architecture and sculpture, which with great labour were brought

QUEEN ARTEMISIA AND MAUSOLUS HER LORD: STATUES FROM THE GREAT CHARIOT

Mausolus died in the year 353 B.C. and his broken-hearted widow, Artemisia, only survived him two years, dying before the tomb she built for him was finished. These draped statues of the royal pair which crowned the whole building, as seen in the reconstructions in pages 273 and 274, are said to be the work of Pythios, one of the two architects the queen employed. The portrait of Mausolus can be identified from his coins; owing to the mutilation of the head the identification of the female figure is not so absolutely certain. In dignity, grace and treatment of the draperies the sculpture is superb.

Britiah Museum

275

to England and put together in the Mausoleum Room of the British Museum.

The most striking of the sculptures thus recovered are the fragments of the chariot group which surmounted the pyramid. The top step of

**WITH BIT AND BRIDLE STILL ATTACHED**

One of the colossal horses of the chariot group, wonderfully suggestive of physical energy. The original harness, made of gilded bronze, is interesting. In place of a collar, there is a band round the horse's chest; this unites at the crest with another band which passes round the body. When excavated, the chariot group was found in a confused heap. The supposition is that it fell from the summit of the building.

the pyramid has been preserved, showing a horse's hoof in position. Large portions of the colossal bodies of the marble horses, decked out with harness of gilded bronze, still remain, and it is conjectured that the two portrait statues of Mausolus and Queen Artemisia stood originally in the chariot, thus crowning the whole edifice.

The portrait of Mausolus can be identified from his coins. It shows a bearded man, in the prime of life, richly robed, and with an expression of quiet dignity. The head of the companion statue is injured, so the identification as Artemisia, though extremely probable, is not certain; nor is it universally accepted that the statues did originally stand in the chariot. Some authorities have preferred to suppose that they formed part of the groups of statuary scattered about and within the building, of which numerous fragments have been found.

The other decorations of the Mausoleum take the form of three long bands of sculptured frieze which ran round the building, though the level at which they were applied cannot be determined. It has, however, been observed that the least important of the three—a frieze representing Greeks and Centaurs, of which very little remains—is less carefully finished than the others. Probably, therefore, it was placed high up, at some distance from the spectator's eye.

Of the other two friezes one is narrow and of very fine workmanship, but it survives only in small fragments. The subject is a chariot race. The third is the best preserved of all. Twelve complete slabs were taken out of the walls of the castle in 1846; four additional slabs, the finest of all, and hundreds of fragments were discovered during the excavations; and yet one other slab was obtained from a palace in Genoa in 1865. Thus pieced together, the frieze occupies the whole length of the room in the British Museum.

As was the invariable custom with Greek architectural ornaments, the whole frieze was originally bright with colour: blue background, red flesh, white, green, and gold drapery. The weapons of the combatants and harness of the horses were of bronze, and the holes for this metal embellishment may be observed along the whole length. The figures are slenderly proportioned and broadly spaced out against the background, which thereby gives due effect to a certain fondness for oblique lines which is visible in the pose of the figures, nearly all of which are either lunging forward or drawing back with one leg straightened out down to the ground-line. The result is a wonderful spring and movement beating rhythmically along the whole length of the frieze. Never has the rush of battle been rendered with more vigour.

# Olympia and its Sacred Games

## By The Editor

RAIN-MAKING is a great business among primitive peoples in arid lands. It is a large element in their religions, and it is astonishing how nicely the wily old medicine men will organize a sacred rain-making dance which will not have finished ere the first drops begin to fall! An easy step in the practice of magic takes one from rain making to making the fields increase their crops and the useful beasts to bring forth young. To-day, just as in the dimmest past, the highly skilled magicians who can do these things become the chiefs as well as the priests of their peoples. Oddly enough, the most remarkable of the rain-makers in European history ended as victors in a short sprinting race in the Greek games that were held at Olympia.

The story ran that ancient Greek rain-making kings had to stand to battle, every summer, against any young challengers, and prove that their productive strength was as good as ever by killing each upstart and adorning the palace with his head! There was a similar ordeal in the days of early Rome, when the priest-king who served the temple of Diana in the grove of Nemi amid the Alban hills had to defend himself in arms against anyone who tore a bough—" the Golden Bough "—from a sacred tree ; if he fell, the victor took over his post as priest and king of Nemi until, in his turn, he went down before a stronger.

In Rome the problem of maintaining the traditional struggle was eventually solved in a vulgar, practical way by giving fugitive criminals the chance of fighting for the Nemorian kingship. But in Greece the invading Greeks showed finer feeling and reduced the struggle for kingship to a short foot race. Bringing their power of imagination to bear on the difficulty, they produced a romantic legend concerning the fight of one of their early kings and the last of the native monarchs of Mediterranean race, who was killed by his own spear during a murderous pursuit of the young invader of Southern Greece. The pursuit was then mimicked by the short foot race for which any ambitious young Greek could enter. So the real king freed himself from the robes and troubles of the ancient magicians and the gallant winner of the race was honoured as the visible incarnation of a spirit of fertility, at once divine and regal. For some centuries these Olympic games were a local affair, but after the Dorian conquest of Southern Greece Lycurgus (Lykourgos) of Sparta and Iphitos of Elis, in the ninth century B.C., elevated the festival into an affair of general importance. What the scattered British peoples are now doing by cricket and football matches between the motherland and the dominions, under something like direct inspiration from the tradition of the Olympic games, Iphitos and Lycurgus developed into a means of keeping the jarring Hellenic nations consolidated in spirit.

The priesthood of Delphi, the centre of Hellenic religion, helped. An arrangement was made for a truce of god to hold between all Greeks for the festival month, and instead of an annual performance which would have been too great a strain upon the clans, the games were fixed to take place every fifth year at the first full moon after the summer solstice. Underlying superstitions were also altered; the primitive rain-maker almost disappeared ; the victor became Herakles in his most sacred aspect. As such he was greeted, crowned with the divine olive, and led to a feast on a holy bullock of Zeus. Returning to his native city, the winner was clothed in purple and drawn by white horses through a breach made in the ramparts of his town ; in many cases he was worshipped even after death. This was not because he had been a successful athlete, for the Greek love of beauty in strength never went so far as that ; the Olympian hero was adored as an incarnate god.

To him in his successive incarnations was built the glorious festival city of Olympia amid the mountains of the north-western region of the southern Greek peninsula, the Peloponnesos. The beautiful site lay immediately beneath the conical height of Kronos and occupied the angle between the Alpheios river running south and its tributary stream, the Kladeos, forming the western boundary of the sacred precinct. From the hillside there extended the holy grove or " Altis," measuring 218 by 153 yards, enclosed by a wall with three gates, a triumphal arch and a secret entrance. The actual grove had vanished save for one most holy tree, represented by a decayed wooden pillar held together with metal bands and protected from the weather by a small roof on four columns.

This, with a neighbouring altar to the thunder god, was probably the original shrine in the days of contending rain-making kings. About it had grown a forest of works of art. The first was the Heraion, the most ancient temple in Greece, that retained one of its original wooden columns and part of its primitive clay wall with a timber entablature, clearly showing how the Dorian style of architecture had developed out of clay and wood construction. It contained the largest known collection of gold and ivory statues, none later than the sixth century B.C., and a gold and ivory table on which the olive wreaths granted to the victors were laid.

South of this antique work was the more modern glory of Hellas in the age of her splendour—the temple of Zeus, centre of the Greek religion. It was a limestone building in Doric style, 70 yards long, 30 yards broad and 22 yards 5 inches high, erected about 472 B.C., just before art reached its supreme perfection. The western pediment was adorned with sculptures of Lapiths and Centaurs by Alkamenes, and the eastern pediment contained groups by Paionios representing the victory of Pelops over the native rain-making king. By their

great figure compositions these sculptors showed the way to Pheidias who later surpassed them in his designs for the Parthenon at Athens. But in return for what he had learned Pheidias made the Olympian temple more awesome than the Parthenon by modelling in gold and ivory its colossal statue of Zeus. The image, 40 feet high and made of materials costing perhaps two hundred thousand pounds sterling, was enclosed by screens in the nave of the shrine and covered with a purple fabric only removed on solemn festivals. The god was then seen sitting on a throne, holding the figure of Victory in his right hand and an eagle-crowned sceptre in his left. An extraordinary variety of secondary designs in relief and colours covered the throne, footstool, pedestal, barriers and garment of the deity, every scene and figure showing forth the just and merciful ways of the divine father of gods and men.

Yet all the ornament was subdued to the main effect. Upon the mind of every thoughtful Greek of the age of Perikles the unveiled face of the Pheidian Zeus struck with the force of a new

**A TENSE MOMENT IN THE OLYMPIC STADIUM**

In pages 280 and 281 will be found a panoramic reconstruction of the precincts of Olympia; but it must be remembered that all the buildings there shown were not standing in the days of Olympia's greatest renown. The Stoa Poikile (Painted Porch), or Echoing Porch as it was also called, was Macedonian for instance; while the Exedra of Herodes Atticus was not built until A.D. 157. Here we have a reconstruction of the Great Stadium at the culminating moment of the famous foot race; judging the contest on the right are the Hellanodikai, the umpires or "Judges of the Hellenes."

After a reconstruction by Bühlmann

ZEUS AND HERAKLES ENSHRINED IN THE ALTIS AT OLYMPIA

Looming majestic through the cella door is the colossal gold and ivory statue of Zeus, by Pheidias, seen in imagination from the portico of his temple at Olympia. Over the pronaos and opisthodomos, corresponding in position to the end frieze of the Parthenon, were metopes showing the twelve labours of Herakles—almost all of them have been recovered by the Germans and the third from the right here is the well-known one of Herakles relieving Atlas of his task. The statue of the hero on the right is reconstructed by reference to the work of Glykon after Lysippus—the " Farnese Hercules " in the Naples Museum.
After a reconstruction by Bühlmann

religious revelation. Instead of the commonplace strong features of the fierce, omnipotent spirit of the thunderbolt, like a Greek Jehovah, here was revealed a mild and fatherly face with calm eyes and broad brow, inspiring love and awe. Not only was Pheidias the greatest of all men of art ; he was something of a philosophic prophet, working out a gospel in stone and ivory. A reconstruction in colour of his masterpiece faces page 236.

Almost as great in importance as the Temple of Zeus was the multitude of statues of victorious athletes that peopled the open space. It was from the labour of modelling the perfect bodies of young men as Olympian offerings that Greek sculptural art grew in glory. At first each winner had been hailed as " King Herakles." Then, as poetry became the leading art, men of high genius like Pindar acclaimed and spread the fame of the victors by magnificent odes. Finally, when the sculptors completely developed their high craft, their finest achievements in single male figures were used as perpetual memorials of the winners. Something sacred attached to the images, for these represented incarnations of divinity often worshipped, as we have seen, after death. Those who won one game were shown in ideal form ; those

who won three games had their individual features portrayed. There may have been at least five hundred portraits and athletic types of the highest varieties of art before Roman consuls and emperors robbed the holy enclosure of many of its marvellous masterpieces. Even when these barbaric spoilers had seized every athletic figure they thought worth taking, there remained in the second century A.D. some two hundred votive statues for the traveller Pausanias to select for admiring comment from the rest of the marble multitude. None now exists. The only victors that preserve their fame among men are those commemorated in choral lyrics instead of being visibly portrayed in bronze and stone. The verbal music of Pindar has proved more lasting than the marble that Pheidias shaped into the figure of the victor of his day.

East of the sacred enclosure, and divided from it by a fine colonnade decorated by masterpieces of painting, was the famous stadium or foot race course, the 600th part of which was the standard measurement of an Olympic foot equal to 1·05 English feet. The race was a straight sprint from a low starting wall to a low goal wall of 630·818 English feet. On artificial embankments around there was room for 45,000 spectators. Beyond the

Gymnasium        Philippeion        Heraion

Pelopeion

*FAIR TEMPLES AND SACRED PRECINCTS OF OLYMPIA—*

After a reconstruction—

Enclosed Grove of Altis  Agora  Stoa Poikile
Temple of Zeus  Gate of Processions

*—WHERE GREEK MANHOOD COMPETED FOR A LAUREL CROWN*

—by Bühlmann

southern embankment was a great Hippodrome, built for the later game of chariot racing that attracted the gorgeous tyrants of Sicily and aristocrats of Aegina. The chariot race seems to have been founded in 680 B.C. ; the horse race in 648 B.C., together with the horrible game known as the " pankration " ; and the race of soldiers in heavy armour in 520 B.C. The main general event, however, was the old five-fold contest or " pentathlon " —jumping, quoit-throwing, running, wrestling and boxing—that had been organized in 708 B.C. The ancient foot race for godhead was distinct from these events and was rewarded by a separate crown of olive leaves.

Each competitor had to swear he was of pure Hellenic breed, that he contended without any unfair advantage and that he had spent ten months in strict training. Some of the keenest candidates indeed came to Olympia to train. Twelve cities, including Syracuse, Cyrene, Sybaris and Gela, possessed temple treasuries by the enclosure in which were stored offerings and weapons and instruments for their competing young citizens. Ten months before the festival umpires of the games were chosen, numbering first one for each clan but finally fixed at ten. They likewise had to go into training for all details of their work, assisted by heralds, trumpeters and stewards. Under title of Judges of the Hellenes, they occupied a mansion in the enclosure and prepared to feast the victors on a dedicated bull, in a kind of sacrament.

When Olympia came fully to life in the grand festival, the city was one of the supreme spectacles on earth. Republican states sent embassies ; monarchs came in person with lordly retinues ; far-flung colonies from Marseilles to Trebizond, from Cyrene to Cyprus, despatched their best boys and young men with parties of older friends. Gorgeously attired barbarians were attracted by the sight of the most intellectual and enterprising of nations strangely putting off war and business for the chance of winning a handful of olive leaves. " What is the use of trying to subdue men like these ? " said a great Persian commander. " They are eager to struggle without necessity or hope of real reward." Not only was this so, but monarchs, like Hiero of Syracuse, would risk their reputation in the contests. Few were the victors and many the vanquished, and for beaten men there was nothing but shame. Upon them fell the anger of the spectators. Assailed by gibe and ridicule, the best they could do was to creep away over the mountains. According to primitive custom they should have been killed ; instead, as a matter of ritual, they were subject to public dishonour.

In the " pankration " game there was indeed an approach to the original slaying. It was a revival of the lust for blood. The game was a combination of boxing and wrestling in which every form of violence except biting was permitted. A fall did not end the struggle, which continued on the ground until usually the weaker man was strangled or stretched helpless with fingers and toes broken. To the credit of Sparta, she would not allow any of her sons to enter this murderous game. Boxing was also forbidden to Spartans, because a heavy metal instrument was used in the hand with ridges of thick, hard hide.

The maiming and killing brought Olympia into disrepute. Not only the Spartans but other Greeks of the best sort withdrew from the games. Professional strong men entered as candidates, and wagering on the events grew apparently so widespread as to make it worth while for a Thessalian prizefighter in 388 B.C. to bribe three opposing boxers to lose their matches. As one of the boxers who arranged to accept defeat had been champion at the previous festival, there was apparently a good deal of money staked on him. Vainly the later Macedonians and Romans, including Nero, tried by lavish patronage to raise the games again to the old high level.

The sacred festival became a vast fair, with myriads of booths filled with idlers, pleasure-mongers and the scum of society. As Professor Mahaffy remarks : " tumbling, thimble-rigging and fortune-telling, along with love-making and trading, made Olympia a scene not unlike the Derby." In the end, however, there was even less honest competition in the sports than that which still keeps the Derby popular. By ancient custom no woman was permitted to see the games. Even if one crossed the river during the festival, she was killed by being hurled from the steep of Typaion by the southern bank.

But such things were forgotten long before A.D. 394 when by edict of the Emperor Theodosius I. the games were suppressed. The mighty master-piece of the gold and ivory Zeus was destroyed in Constantinople. Then in the sixth century of the modern era a series of earthquakes destroyed most of the temples and a landslip from Mount Kronion buried the buildings at its southern foot. About a century later only the wrecked top of the temple of Zeus was visible. Inundations had buried the city in fifteen to twenty feet of silt, from which a few fine statues including a Hermes by Praxiteles have recently been discovered by German excavators, who uncovered the ruins at a cost of some £40,000 in the vain hope of winning from the ancient site a magnificent harvest of classic statuary.

# The Rock-Hewn Temples of Ellora

## By F. Deaville Walker

### Author of "India and Her Peoples," etc.

#### With Fourteen Exclusive Photographs specially taken by the Author

AMONG the rugged cliffs of Ellora, far away among the desolate mountains of Hyderabad, in Southern India, stands what is probably the finest monolith in the world—a vast temple hewn out of the living rock. It is called the Kailasa, after the celestial palace of the great Hindu god, Siva. The venerable rock temples of ancient Egypt and the red city of Petra, are, strictly speaking, cave temples, for their splendid façades are their only exterior features, and their chambers cave-like excavations in the hillside. The Kailasa at Ellora is totally different from these. Though entirely rock hewn, it is in no sense a "cave" temple.

In the centre of the huge pit-like court in the mountain side from which it has been quarried, this amazing sanctuary stands separate and entire, a perfect Hindu temple, complete in every part, with the whole of its exterior exposed to view—a bewildering mass of magnificently carved pavilions, with elegant pagodas, sunlit terraces, and shady porticoes. It is not architecture; it is sculpture on a vast scale. On three sides rise the perpendicular faces of the rock from which this great temple has been cut away. Undoubtedly, the Kailasa is one of the greatest architectural achievements of India, and it deserves to be numbered among the wonders of the world.

Though the Kailasa cannot claim the hoary antiquity of the great shrines of Egypt, Greece, or even of Rome, it is unquestionably ancient, dating from the eighth century of our era. About the year A.D. 757, Krishna I., of the Rashtrakuta

dynasty, completed the overthrow of the once powerful Chalukyan monarchs of South India, and made himself master of the great upland plains of the Deccan. To commemorate his victory, and as a thank-offering to his patron deity, the conqueror thereupon resolved to excavate a unique sanctuary.

The ancient Brahmans had conceived their great god Siva as dwelling in a heavenly palace far away among the inaccessible snowy peaks and glaciers of the Himalayas, and to this mythical mountain, which

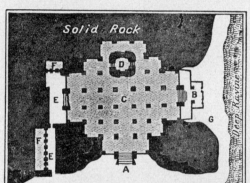

A. Main entrance to Dhumar Lena Temple. B. Side entrance from deep ravine. C. Great hall with pillars. D. Chief shrine surrounded with huge figures (see page 289). E. Side courts cut in rock. F. Small side shrines. G. Waterfall.

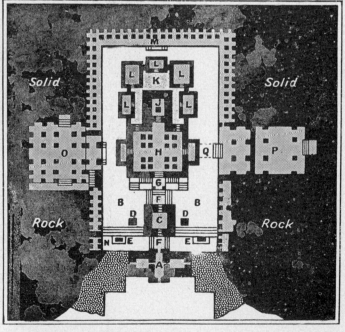

PLANS OF THE DHUMAR LENA AND KAILASA TEMPLES

These two temples are the most imposing of the Hindu remains at Ellora. Top, the Dhuma Lena; below, the Kailasa. There are also magnificent examples of Jain architecture. A. Entrance tower, Kailasa Temple. B. Open court. C. Shrine of Sacred Bull. D. Monolithic pillars. E Monolithic elephants. F. Bridges. G. Main terrace, steps, and entrance to temple proper. H. Main hall. J. Chief shrine. K. Terrace round shrine. L. Small shrines. M. Colonnade round court. N. Shrine of River Goddesses. O. Lankesvara Chapel above colonnade. P. South Chapel. Q. Remains of bridge from South Chapel to main temple.

they called the Kailasa, the abode of their gods, the people turned with the same awe and devotion as the ancient Greeks to Mount Olympus. The victorious Krishna I. resolved to have a Kailasa on earth that should represent and symbolise in every detail the ethereal palace of the snow-capped heights where man's foot had never trod. It was as though Constantine or Charlemagne had resolved to build a cathedral to represent and symbolise the great vision of the New Jerusalem in the Book of Revelation.

As a site for his temple, Krishna I. chose a place among the mountains of the Deccan where the basaltic rocks form a high wall above a verdant valley, and rushing streams fall in beautiful cascades from the cliffs into deep ravines below. For several hundred years Ellora had been accounted sacred, and holy men had made it their abode. Yellow-robed monks of Buddha had found refuge from the rains in small caves in its rocks; as the years passed they enlarged the caves, and with ever-increasing skill excavated wonderful monasteries and chapels in the hillside. Then, as Buddhism waned, the Brahmans began to hew out temples for their own gods near to those their Buddhist rivals were deserting. For Krishna I. the valley had an additional attraction; the rocky wall took the general form of a crescent, like the moon-crest of the god Siva, and here he resolved to create his reproduction of Siva's celestial paradise.

IN THE SILENT COURT OF THE KAILASA TEMPLE, ELLORA

Here is seen the bridge connecting the Shrine of the Sacred Bull with the portico of the main temple. The court beyond is visible through the archway. Through the doorway to the left rock-cut steps lead up to the open terrace above. Of the two large elephants that once stood sentinel beside this doorway, only fragments remain. Remains of a small elephant frieze are on the terrace above. The wall to the left is decorated with scenes from the sacred epic poem, the " Ramayana," in low relief.

MASSIVE COLONNADE AND PILLARED AISLE OF THE LANKESVARA CHAPEL

After the Kailasa itself was finished, a colonnade was cut in the surrounding rock. The top photograph shows (below) a small section of this colonnade. A great chapel, the Lankesvara (108 feet by 60 feet), was excavated above it. The roof is supported by twenty-seven carved pillars of exquisite workmanship. The chapel consists of a shrine-chamber, a nave, and four aisles. one of which is seen in the lower photograph. Notice the dignified simplicity and the great variety in the form of the massive pillars.

ELEPHANT FRIEZE OF THE ROCK-HEWN TEMPLE OF THE KAILASA AT ELLORA STILL SUPERB IN ITS RUIN

This is a larger view of the great rock plinth, 27 feet high, upon which the Temple of the Kailasa stands. It is surrounded with a remarkable frieze of elephants, standing shoulder to shoulder and appearing to carry the temple upon their backs. Although most of their trunks have been broken off and all the elephants have suffered severely from the zeal of Mahomedan invaders, this superb frieze is magnificent even in its ruin, and is one of the greatest achievements of rock sculpture the world can show. The Kailasa is off the beaten track, and probably not one tourist in ten thousand visits this silent, long-deserted sanctuary, which, graceful as well as majestic, is unique; no photograph can do justice to it, no words adequately describe it.

In excavating rock temples, the usual method is to begin with the face of a cliff and dig into it. The method pursued by Krishna's masons was to begin on the top and dig down, as did the masons of Petra (see page 85). On the grassy uplands above the cliffs they marked out an oblong measuring 280 feet by 160 feet. Along the surrounding lines of this oblong they dug long trenches into the rock to a depth of from about 150 feet, thus detaching an enormous central mass from the hillside, and from this central mass they cut the Kailasa.

Imagine the difficulty of planning such a temple from above, and the skill required to carry out the plan with unfailing accuracy and exquisite detail. We do not know how many years were spent on excavating first its exterior form, then its wonderful interior halls and galleries and staircases, and then covering the whole temple, without and within, with magnificent sculpture and bas-reliefs. Nor have we means of knowing if Krishna lived to see any portions of it finished; probably he did not, for he died in A.D. 783. We should like to know how many workmen laboured at the task, how many elephants were required to cart away the rock as it was quarried from around the shrine, how many skilled sculptors worked with hammers and chisels on the decorations of its rock walls, and how many years elapsed ere they laid down their tools and their masterpiece stood complete in all its loveliness.

Then there was a pause, the length of which we do not know. When the work began again, fresh armies of masons attacked the great perpendicular cliffs that encircled three sides of the Kailasa and its surrounding court. In the face of these cliffs, a few feet above the level of the court, they cut pillared colonnades—sculptured cloisters—by which pilgrims might process round the sanctuary. At a still later date two new excavations were undertaken; in the centre of the north cliff, above the colonnade, a large chapel was hewn out—the Lankesvara—measuring 108 feet by 60 feet, the rock roof of which is supported by twenty-seven carved pillars of exquisite design (see page 285).

UNFINISHED SHRINE OF THE RIVER GODDESSES, ELLORA

In this corner of the Kailasa two stone elephants (one shown) represent the rain clouds. In the cliff is the small and unfinished Shrine of the River Goddesses. Within the lower portico are large bas-reliefs of the three great rivers that flow from Siva's throne : Sarasvati, Ganga (the Ganges), and Jumna.

In the cliff to the south, a still more remarkable chapel was cut in three storeys, and connected with the Kailasa itself by a rock-hewn bridge that spanned the court. This South Chapel was never finished, and the bridge has collapsed.

To-day, after more than eleven centuries of exposure to the fierce rays of the Indian sun and the torrential rains of tropical monsoons, the Kailasa is singularly well preserved; it has suffered much more from vandals than from the destructive forces of nature. It stands lonely and majestic,

SIVA'S CELESTIAL PALACE AS SYMBOLISED BY LOVING AND DEVOUT HANDS AMID THE GREAT CLIFFS OF ELLORA

Begun about A.D. 760 by Krishna I. as a thank-offering for his victories, the Temple of the Kailasa, at Ellora, Hyderabad, is a bewildering mass of carved pavilions, with elegant pagodas, sunlit terraces, and shady porticoes  Cut from the living rock, it is wholly symbolical of the heavenly paradise of Siva.  To the right of the photograph is a corner of the main temple. In the centre (connected with the temple by a rock-hewn bridge) is the Shrine of  the Sacred Bull, symbol of  Siva's strength.  Notice the splendid monolith pillar with its elegant carvings There is a similar one on the other side of the Shrine of the Bull (see page 290).  To the extreme left is a corner of the rock from which the whole temple was hewn

## GUARDIANS OF THE SHRINE

This shrine in the Temple of the Milkmaids is a separate chamber with a wide passage cut entirely round, so that worshippers could perform the required perambulations. The idol, or its symbol, originally stood in the dark mysterious chamber with lamps burning before it. The great figures on either side are the guardians of the shrine.

a long-deserted sanctuary. Save for a tiny village in the ravine, the whole place is uninhabited. With the exception of a Government custodian, the visitor usually finds himself alone in the silent courts, and the sound of his footsteps echoes through the long-empty chambers of the shrine. Ellora is off the beaten track, and probably not one tourist in ten thousand visits this amazing temple. Yet no shrine in the whole of India is more worthy of the expenditure of time and money required to explore it.

After the long, dusty tonga ride over the mountains from Aurangabad or Daulatabad, the tourist descends, by a road cut in the side of the ghats, into the vale of Ellora, and after a short, hot walk stands before the

## SHRINE OF THE GREAT DHUMAR LENA CAVE

Next to the Kailasa, the Dhumar Lena is the finest of Hindu caves at Ellora. Its floor measures 149 feet, its roof rests upon twenty-six pillars, and its shrine is an independent square chamber, having a large doorway on each side, the whole being surrounded with the huge carved figures shown above.

HOW HINDU MASTER CRAFTSMEN OF LONG AGO SCULPTURED THE KAILASA FROM A DECCAN MOUNTAIN TOP

The architects of this wonderful temple marked out a big, oblong space, 280 feet by 160 feet, or the top of the cliffs, and then dug deep trenches into the rock to a depth of about 150 feet, leaving an enormous central mass, from which they carved the Kailasa. The photograph shows (right) the Shrine of the Sacred Bull, with a portion of the main temple beyond. In the foreground, at the top of the rock-hewn steps, stands the second pillar, near to which is the broken fragment of a life-sized elephant. There is a corresponding one on the other side. The cliffs around the court are deeply undercut with a colonnade along which the pilgrims marched in procession For centuries this splendid temple has been entirely deserted

entrance to the Kailasa. The entrance tower, which forms a screen to conceal the whole temple from the outer world, is cut like every other part of the temple from the solid rock ; it contains a vestibule and a passage, flanked on either side by chambers on two floors. Passing through and entering the spacious court, we get our first complete view of the Kailasa, and gaze with silent awe. It is unique ; nothing approaching it has ever been conceived by man. Yet it is in no sense a freak or the fantastic design of a disordered imagination. Graceful and imposing, beautiful yet vast, the Kailasa is impressive beyond words. No photographs can do justice to it ; no language can adequately describe it. As we wandered through its porticoes and along its terraces, entranced by its massive strength and elegant design, we expressed amazement.

"Sahib," said our guide in solemn tones, "man did not make this unaided—the gods helped."

"You think so ? " we asked.

"Sahib," answered the guide, "look around you. Could man have made a temple like this without the help of the gods ? "

And as we gazed around, we realized that there was at least this much truth in our guide's contention—that a desire to please the gods was the motive that constrained men to this supreme effort ; it was what Ruskin, in his " Seven Lamps of Architecture " calls " the Lamp of Sacrifice," the spirit that offers to God the best workmanship of which it is capable and the most precious things at its command simply because they are precious and because the labour entailed is great.

The first pavilion that meets the eye is one of exquisitely simple design, two storeys high and covered with carving. It is the Shrine of the Nandi, or Sacred Bull, the symbol of the strength of Siva. Rock-hewn bridges connect it with the gate-tower on one side and the main temple on the other. On either side of the hall stands a stately monolith pillar, both exactly alike, 49 feet high, of remarkable design, and surmounted by another of Siva's symbols—a trident. Near to the base of each pillar is a stone elephant, life-sized, to symbolise the rain clouds that so often gather around the snowcapped heights of the Himalayas. To the left, cut in the face of the cliff, is a small

RICHLY CARVED COLONNADE IN ONE OF THE HINDU CAVE TEMPLES AT ELLORA

The thirty-four rock-hewn temples at Ellora were carved from the mountains of the Deccan, where the basaltic cliffs form a high wall above a verdant valley, and rushing streams fall in beautiful cascades into deep ravines below. The temples stretch along the cliffs for more than a mile and a half, and exhibit remarkable variety in both plan and design. No two are alike in size or shape, and the pillars and bas-reliefs are equally varied. Compare the pillars in this colonnade with those in the other photographs.

SCULPTURED CLOISTERS MIRACULOUSLY UNCRUSHED BY THE MOUNTAIN MASS

On the right stands the great Temple of the Kailasa. To the left is a portion of the colonnade that surrounds the whole court. The rock walls behind the pillars are carved in a wonderful series of great bas-reliefs. They represent the ancient mythological stories about the gods and goddesses—the attempts of peoples of bygone ages to express their conceptions of the Most High. How great must have been the devotion and the architectural daring that cut such a sanctuary from the living rock!

and unfinished Shrine of the River Goddesses, in the lower portico of which are large bas-reliefs of the goddesses of the three great rivers that flow from Siva's throne in the Himalayan Kailasa—Sarasvati, Ganga (the Ganges), and Jumna—and around its balcony are carved vessels of the sacred water.

Above all else towers the chief shrine of the temple, a mighty rock-hewn sanctuary, its highest pagoda rising to a height of 96 feet. It rests upon a solid plinth 27 feet high, around which is a very remarkable frieze of elephants, standing shoulder to shoulder, heads out, and giving the effect of carrying the whole temple upon their backs. Though many of their trunks have been broken off, and all the elephants have suffered severely from the zeal of Mahomedan invaders, this superb frieze is magnificent even in its ruins, and is without doubt the greatest achievement of rock sculpture the world can show.

The interior of the main temple is a hall about 53 feet square, with sixteen pillars supporting the roof. From this, a beautifully sculptured doorway, approached by half a dozen steps, leads into the holy of holies, where a great lingam symbolises the presence and essential attributes of Siva himself. The sacred chamber is small and dark, as is usual in Hindu temples, the darkness symbolising the mystery in which the god dwells. Its walls of solid rock support the lofty central pagoda that surmounts the whole. A raised open-air terrace surrounds the holy place, and on this are five small side shrines, one of which is dedicated to the worship of Siva's son, Ganesha, the god of wisdom, and another (situated immediately behind the principal shrine, in the exact position of the Lady Chapel in a Christian cathedral) is dedicated to Siva's wife, Parvati. There is not a blank wall or undecorated ceiling in the whole of the Kailasa. Huge bas-reliefs of the gods, with figures often eight feet high, confront one everywhere. Colonnades and inner chambers alike are lined with them—these strange mythological figures that symbolise the deeds and the attributes of the god.

SHRINE PILLARS OF A JAIN TEMPLE AT ELLORA
The five Jain temples, richest in design of all the Ellora temples, date from 800 to 1100 A.D. These massive pillars stand before the shrine in the large hall in one of the temples. Notice the fine carving of the fluted pillars and the effective simplicity of base and capital. The entrance is seen to the left.

As we stand upon the high cliff above and gaze down upon this enduring monument of piety, we picture the long string of silent, barefooted worshippers that once filled its courts, processed devoutly around its colonnades, and offered their gifts before its shrine. All have gone. The courts are desolate; offerings are no longer brought; sacred lamps no longer flicker around the sacred, symbolic lingam; the inner shrine is empty. But the Kailasa itself remains—an abiding monument to the devotion of bygone ages.

Even the Kailasa does not exhaust the wonders of Ellora. It is surrounded on either side with cave temples of extraordinary beauty and interest. There are, in all, thirty-four of them, running in a row along the wall of rock for over a mile and a half. To the south end of the line are a dozen of the Buddhist period; then come seventeen Brahman temples, and beyond, five exceptionally fine ones of Jain workmanship. A week is all too short fully to explore their numerous chambers, porticoes, and mysterious recesses. In them it is possible to trace the development of rock architecture from its beginnings in the primitive Buddhist caves to the intricate planning and rich detail that distinguish the Jain period.

Of the Buddhist caves, some were monasteries, with well-cut cells for the monks and halls for common use; others were chapels for the worship of their master "the Lord Buddha." The Hindu and Jain caves are larger, more intricate, and of finer workmanship. The architect and masons had grown bolder and more skilful as the centuries passed, and they successfully carried through schemes their predecessors would not have attempted. Many of the temples have fine forecourts, and some are approached by splendid flights of rock-hewn steps and sculptured porticoes. The general plans, the arrangement of halls and colonnades, and the form of the pillars, exhibit a variety of design that is truly amazing. In these great cool chambers, with their rows of splendid pillars, one pauses to meditate and wonder, and to admire the entrancing vistas of valley and waterfall through the open porticoes. As one passes from shrine to shrine, one's amazement increases and the first adjectives of excitement give place to speechless awe. But their glory has departed. The impetuous rush of Mahomedan invasion drove priests, ascetics, and worshippers from Ellora. With their traditional zeal, the invaders knocked off the heads of the gods, and smashed much of the beautiful stone carving of the temples.

Then a long period of silence settled upon this secluded spot. To-day, one treads reverently through deserted chambers, once sacred; and even those who (in the words of Queen Victoria's famous proclamation) "firmly rely on the truth of Christianity" cannot but be impressed by these marvellous temples in which the ancient peoples of India strove to express their thoughts of the Most High.

**INDRA SABHA: A GEM OF JAIN ROCK CARVING**

The finest of the Jain temples at Ellora is that of Indra Sabha. On a small scale, it reproduces the distinctive feature of the great Kailasa in that it has a central shrine standing independently in a square court—small, but of very fine workmanship. This photograph, taken from a dangerous position on a slippery ledge of rock, shows a corner of the little court and the graceful central shrine, a small square monolith with a doorway on each side and a fine pyramidal roof. It is in every way a gem of architecture, but owing to its situation, it is extremely difficult to take an inclusive photograph of its admirable proportions.

**BEAUTIFUL COURT OF THE INDRA SABHA TEMPLE, SECOND ONLY TO THE KAILASA**

This photograph, taken at the back of the central shrine, shows the fine carvings in the court of the exquisite temple of Indra Sabha, of which another photograph appears in the opposite page. Of the Brahman temples, the Dhumar Lena cave holds pride of second place, but the Indra Sabha is a Jain temple, and were it not for the surpassing grandeur of the Kailasa, would be the jewel of Ellora. Of the two halls at the back of the court, one above the other, the lower one is incomplete.

## The Wonder Cities. V.

# London's Roman Remains

### By R. E. M. Wheeler, D.Lit., F.S.A.

Keeper of the London Museum

FROM the end of the Stone Age the size and position of the Thames estuary made it, with rare interludes, the principal haven for the traffic of the northern seas, and, as witness of this, the river below Kingston has yielded great quantities of prehistoric remains. It might thus be expected that the origins of the city at the head of this estuary would be found embedded in that remote past to which the medieval romancers were fond of ascribing them. From the site of London itself, however, in spite of its accessibility from the sea, scarcely a dozen relics dating from the last 2,000 years B.C. have been recorded. Modern writers have, indeed, sought to reconstruct a " Celtic " London, a city of dwellings built upon piles, and rising above the shores of a marsh or lake. Unfortunately, the piles in question are now known to have been substructures of buildings no older than the Roman period, and the etymology which twisted " London " into " Llyn Din," the " lake city," is equally at fault. The prevalent view (that of Bradley) derives " London " from a hypothetical personal name " Londinos," formed from the Celtic " londos," meaning " fierce." Incidentally, it may be remembered that the Romans, like ourselves, often gave native names to towns or fortresses of their own foundation. The earliest tangible remains of a permanent settlement on the site of London are the potsherds and coins of the Roman city.

The seeming paradox is readily explained. Under natural conditions, the site of London was closely hemmed in by dense woodland, which was formerly co-extensive with the London clay and is now represented by the surviving fragment of Epping Forest. Under primitive conditions, therefore, when the population of the countryside was comparatively small and ill-organized, overland routes through the forest zones were difficult to clear and maintain ; whilst river traffic, which formed the alternative, found easier landing-stages in the higher and narrower reaches. Thus it is that for evidence of a prehistoric " London " we have to look up-stream towards

Mortlake, where the abundance of prehistoric relics indicates a long and intensive occupation before the present era. Only with the appearance of a strong centralised régime, able to organize regular cross-country traffic and to engineer permanent roads, did the site of London itself come into prominence. This it did as the lowest point at which the Thames could be conveniently bridged. For here, and nowhere else between London and the sea, both banks of the river are alike of hard, dry gravel, suitable for bridge-heads. London Bridge was thus destined by geography and geology to become the natural focus of the English road system, and London may be described as the parasite of London Bridge.

It follows that the date of the building of London Bridge is of primary importance. At first sight our historical records seem to preserve a clue. The Graeco-Roman historian Dio, describing the Roman invasion of Britain in A.D. 43, states that the invaders pursued the Britons to difficult fords across the Thames at the point where it " empties into the ocean and at flood-tide makes a lake "—presumably, though not explicitly, in the London district. There the foe eluded their pursuers until some of the Roman troops swam the river, whilst others were able to cross " by means of a bridge a little way up-stream." Whether the bridge was already in existence, or whether it was thrown up during the attack, is not clear, and, since the historian was writing nearly two centuries after the event, he may not have known clearly himself. We must therefore look elsewhere for evidence for or against the existence of London prior to the year 43.

Now, it was not unusual for Roman prospectors and craftsmen to penetrate into " barbarian " lands, and even to form small settlements there, in advance of the Roman legions. Caesar, Cicero and Tacitus all give examples of trade thus preceding the flag in Gaul and elsewhere. Is it possible, therefore, that at London also some of the earliest Roman pottery was, as has been suggested more

Arnold

**LONDON STONE**

Believed to have been, perhaps, a milliarium, or milestone, from which road distances were measured, the stone in the wall of S. Swithin's, Cannon Street, was moved here in 1798 from the other side of the street.

ROMAN SCULPTURE FOUND IN THE WALBROOK

Found in the bed of the Walbrook, which, in Roman days, flowed across the city from near Moorgate to the Thames, this tablet was made by a Roman soldier of the Second Legion stationed at Caerleon in memory of his discharge. The sculpture shows Mithras, the Persian sun god, slaying the bull. In the upper corners, beyond the circle, are the chariots of the sun and moon

House on the east to the southwestern slopes of Ludgate Hill on the west. Within these limits has been found a considerable mass of the earliest red-glazed pottery (the so-called "Samian") which the Gauls had begun to make in imitation of the Italic or "Arretine" ware referred to above. Beyond, from the neighbourhood of the General Post Office to that of the Old Bailey, and across the river Fleet into Fleet Street and Shoe Lane, lay the great cemetery of the earliest Roman Londoners, buried in the vessels of earthenware, porphyry and lead, which can still be seen in the British, London and Guildhall museums. Between the living and the dead, on the site of St. Paul's, those potters whose kilns were found by Sir Christopher Wren when he laid the foundations of his cathedral may already have been working the brickearth of the hilltop. Within less than fifteen years of the annexation of the province, London

than once, brought by adventurous Roman traders who had set up a trading station at a bridge-head on the site some years before the military annexation? There is one small group of evidence which may support this view. In various parts of the City and Southwark have been found a few pieces of red glazed "Arretine" ware—some fifteen or sixteen sherds in all—of a type which was made in Italy in considerable quantities before A.D. 20, and in diminishing quantities after that date. It is possible, therefore, that these sherds *may* represent a short epoch in the history of London prior to the formal Roman conquest. But in the absence of supporting evidence it must be confessed that this handful of sherds is a poor foundation for London, and it is best to be content at present with the one certain fact that, if London existed at all before the year 43, it was then a place of little or no importance.

IN the year of the conquest the Roman armies may, as we have seen, have passed near the site of London. Thereafter, save in an occasional crisis, that site saw little of the legions. Its unrivalled advantages as a distributing centre for commerce now became the dominant factor, and the contemporary historian Tacitus was able to write that in A.D. 60 the town was already "teeming with traders and crowded with merchandise." Modern archaeology is able to amplify this statement by showing us that at this date London already extended from the Custom

MONUMENT TO A GLADIATOR

This tablet, with Greek lettering, was found at Islington—in Roman days, and indeed until the eighteenth century, some way outside London—and seems to commemorate a gladiator, perhaps some favourite of the arena who met an untimely end.

had grown into a township of nearly 200 acres with something of the suddenness with which in modern times the great mushroom cities of America grew under the not dissimilar circumstances attendant upon the opening up of the " Golden West."

Then, in the year 60, fell the blow. The Roman governor and his principal colleagues were away in the north and west, hammering out a frontier for the new province. Colchester, which, as the headquarters of the famous Cunobeline or Cymbeline, had been in effect the capital of south-eastern Britain on the eve of the conquest, had been taken over by the Romans as the working centre of their own civil and religious administration, and a colony of Roman ex-soldiers had been added, in the Roman manner, as a safeguard. Both in its civil and its military capacities, however, the newly organized capital failed in its trust. The incompetence and self-interest of its petty-officialdom spurred the native inhabitants to revolt and, under their queen Boudicca (Boadicea) the rebels swept down upon Colchester, London and Verulam (St. Albans) and " massacred, hanged, burned and crucified " the wretched, defenceless inhabitants to the number of 70,000.

Thereafter the revolt was suppressed ; but deep down beneath the modern street-level to the north and north-west of London Bridge, immediately above the natural surface of the gravel or brick-earth, lie

McLeish

**REMINDER OF ROME ON TOWER HILL**

A piece of the old medieval City wall survives in Trinity Place on Tower Hill, and in the lower part of it is some Roman work, reminding us that the line of London's great wall was first determined by our conquerors from Italy

wide areas of burnt timber, wall-plaster, pottery and coins (including several of Claudius) which still, it seems, bear vivid witness to the words of Tacitus. And when, shortly after the destruction, the quays were rebuilt near by along the river front, they were levelled up with many tons of the débris of the first city. In all these layers the pottery and coins are found to be not later than the year of the revolt ; and the masses of charred timber tell us that much at least of the first London was built of that material, and must have burned in the year 60 as readily as did its successor sixteen centuries later.

FROM the ashes rose a new London, the main outlines of which were destined to remain fixed until after the Middle Ages and are still traceable in the modern plan. In order to understand the nature of its outlines it is necessary to bear in mind the original aspect of the site which moulded them.

The City of London occupies two low hills which rise fairly steeply from the river bank to the height of about forty feet above sea level. The summit of the eastern hill, or Cornhill, is marked approximately by Leadenhall Market ; that of the western, Ludgate Hill, lies close to St. Paul's. Between the two hills, beneath the site of the Bank of England and the Mansion House, the stream known as the Walbrook flowed towards the Thames beside the site of Cannon

Gorse

**WATLING STREET BY ST. PAUL'S**

A Roman road with a flint surface was discovered some twenty feet below the street which runs from Cannon Street to St. Paul's Churchyard. It may have got its name because it originally joined London Bridge to the Watling Street, the Dover–Chester road.

**BATH OF A ROMAN VILLA IN THE STRAND**

On the south side of the Strand, near the church of S. Mary-le-Strand, is a narrow entry called Strand Lane. This site would have been well outside Roman London, which ended at the Hole-bourne river. There seems to have been a country villa here on the hill overlooking the Thames. Its tiled bath, fed by a natural spring, has survived and is open to the public.

and probably twenty feet or more in height, were constructed of Kentish rag and sandstone with intermittent courses of brick and were founded upon the natural gravel of the site. In front of them lay one or more ditches from ten to fifteen feet wide and behind them may have been an earthen bank. At a later date, perhaps when, at the end of the third century and later, the Saxon invaders began to harass our coasts, strong projecting bastions of semicircular plan were added to the wall—probably at two separate moments, for there are minor but definite differences between those to the east and those to the west of the Walbrook. Fragments of these bastions can still be seen at the Tower of London and beneath the courtyard of the General Post Office, whilst the medieval superstructure of another stands in Cripplegate churchyard.

The new walls were some three miles in length and enclosed an area of about 330 acres—an area exceeded by that of only four Roman cities north of the Alps.

Of the buildings within the walls, almost innumerable fragments have been found and destroyed during modern building operations. Few of these fragments have been recorded and, in the absence of systematic observation, valuable evidence of this kind is still being lost almost every day. In one case, however—and that perhaps the most important—certain inferences are possible. At various times on and adjoining the site of Leadenhall Market, at the summit of the hill above London Bridge, have been unearthed the remains of a great building over 420 feet in length, with walls in some places six feet thick and with an apse at the eastern end. The plan seems to have included a nave flanked on the north and south by aisles, and corresponds therefore with the normal design of a Roman "basilica." The plan and size of the building, taken in conjunction with its dominant site, enable us to infer that it formed the principal basilica or town hall of Roman London. Here were the headquarters of the city administration; here prisoners were tried, and here, or close by, was transacted much of the commercial business of the city. The basilica and its adjacent structures combined, in fact, something of the Guildhall, the Law Courts and the Stock Exchange. The walls beneath Leadenhall and Gracechurch Streets

Street railway station, and divided the old city into two equal halves. Farther west, at the present site of Blackfriars bridge, the mouth of the river Fleet, which sprang in the Hampstead and Highgate hills, provided a small but useful harbourage. At the eastern end of the city a less formidable valley flanking Tower Hill formed a convenient limit in that direction. This shallow valley continued northwards and north-westwards and was used by the Roman town-builders as their boundary.

ALONG these natural contours from the Fleet valley to Tower Hill the engineers who laid out the city in the years following the Boudiccan revolt marked, as it appears, the line of the town walls, of which time-worn fragments can still be seen. True, the date of these walls has been much disputed, but the balance of the evidence collected recently by the Royal Commission on Historical Monuments (England) is in favour of the view that, at any rate on the landward side, the defences were built towards the close of the first century A.D. Apart from the direct and indirect archaeological evidence, which need not here be recounted, it is on general grounds reasonable to suppose that the Londoners, who had suffered from the recorded absence of fortifications in the year 60, had learnt from their bitter experience. The new walls, some eight feet thick at their base

Southwark    Fleet River at    Ludgate    Newgate    Aldersgate    Cripplega
              Blackfriars

THE BRIDGE AND RAMPARTS OF ROMAN LONDON FROM THE SOUTHWARK BANK

The first and most important part of London was the bridge to which a junction road ran from the Watling Street to Dover. The above pl. drawn by a French artist, M. Forestier, from material supplied by the Royal Commission, shows the principal gates and the Fleet or Holebou river flowing into the Thames, just beyond the wall at Blackfriars. Trade between Britain and the Continent demanded a distributing centre the Thames estuary, and the lowest point at which the river could be conveniently bridged determined the site of the city.

may, therefore, be regarded as relics of one of the most important buildings in the provinces of Rome, and they represent appropriately by far the largest Roman building yet identified in Britain.

Whether to the south of the basilica stood the open market-place or forum which would be expected in this position is at present uncertain. Various walls have been found in this area, but, in the absence of any precise record in regard to most of them, conjecture is unprofitable.

Other buildings in Roman London are represented for the most part merely by scattered fragments of walling or by remains of floors, which were in a number of cases covered with elaborately patterned mosaics ; for example, the well-known mosaic representing Bacchus riding on a leopard, found long ago in Leadenhall Street and now in the British Museum. These pavements, together with the innumerable fragments of brightly painted wall-plaster

which are unearthed in excavations throughout the city, show that the buildings of Roman London were more brightly coloured than are their modern successors. The remains suggest that most of this decorative work was carried out by craftsmen imported from Gaul or the Mediterranean lands. Only in the fragments of sculpture and of architectural decoration is it possible sometimes to detect the work of the native craftsman.

Apart from the basilica, Roman London must have included many public buildings devoted to secular or religious purposes, and it is possible that one of these should be recognized in the remains of a Roman bathing establishment which is still partly visible beneath the Coal Exchange in Lower Thames Street. Public baths formed a notable feature of Roman town life, and the Thames Street example is large enough to suggest that it was more than the mere adjunct of a private house. Of religious buildings, no structural

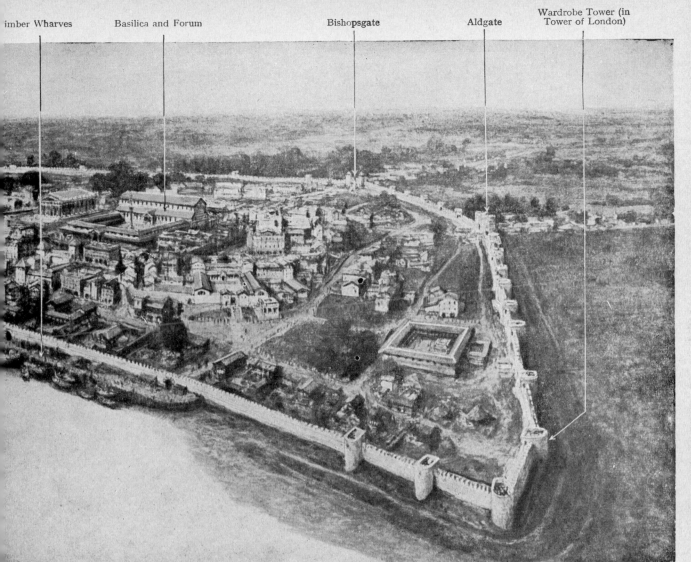

London Museum

**AUGUSTA RECONSTRUCTED FROM THE FINDINGS OF A ROYAL COMMISSION**

There have been many theories regarding the origin of London. The Royal Commission on Historical Monuments concluded that Augusta, the Roman city, was the first London. The beginnings of that city may have anticipated the actual Roman invasion, for it often happened, as in the case of the British Empire, that the arrival of merchant adventurers preceded the official annexation of new territory. Notice the great basilica and forum, marked on the plan, which stood near the site of the present Leadenhall Market.

remains have been recognized, but altars or other dedications to Diana, the Mother Goddesses, Mithras, Cybele and Isis and a few small relics bearing Christian symbols are witness to the former existence of many varied shrines, temples and churches. For the last, the best evidence is the literary record, which has preserved the name of two Roman bishops of London, one of whom, named Restitutus, attended the famous Council of Arles with two other British bishops in the year 314.

Singularly little evidence as to the street plan of the Roman city has been recovered. This plan must be considered in relation with two dominant factors —the position of the city gates and that of the Roman bridge. Of the Roman gates definite remains have been found at Newgate and less certain remains at one or two of the others, but the Roman road system demands that Aldgate, Bishopsgate, Cripplegate, Aldersgate and Ludgate should all be regarded

as of Roman origin; whilst the line of Roman relics found across the river immediately east of the medieval London Bridge suggests that the Roman bridge stood close to its successor.

The other determining feature within the boundaries of the city was the Walbrook, which may be suspected to have divided the Roman town-plan into two distinct parts. Now there is evidence to suggest that this brook was bridged at two points; the first, opposite the east end of Bucklersbury, near the Mansion House, and the other on the south side of Cannon Street. From the northern of these crossings a long drain which may well have flanked a road proceeds north-westwards in the direction of Newgate, and the same line passes beneath the tower of Bow Church, which is recorded to have been built by Sir Christopher Wren on a Roman causeway. It is probable, therefore, that Newgate Street marks a part of the line of one of the principal Roman streets.

Dr. Philip Norman

**UNIQUE PHOTOGRAPH OF THE DESTRUCTION OF LONDON'S ROMAN WALL**

About the year 1880, when the railway to Southend was being constructed, it was unfortunately necessary for the building of the line that this fine piece of the actual Roman wall as we see it here, the least altered by medieval and subsequent repair, should be demolished. Luckily a photograph was secured at the time, so that we can see very clearly what the wall looked like. It was about eight feet thick at the base and some fifteen feet high. A triple course of Roman brick tiles appears amid the mass of ragstone.

To the east of the Walbrook, a line joining the more southerly crossing with a fragment of Roman street found long ago in Eastcheap aligns with the old position of London Stone and cuts through no known Roman building. A parallel line eastwards from the northern crossing of the Walbrook also cuts no Roman building and coincides with a line of arcading—possibly a Roman shop-front—found a few years ago close to Gracechurch Street. Streets drawn in the Roman manner at right angles to these in such a way as to pass the ends of the basilica described above produce a large " insula " or island about 480 feet square, which is, singularly enough, an exact multiple of a land measurement commonly used by the Romans in laying out their towns. The conjecture, therefore, that we may recognize here some of the elements of the Roman plan of London is not unlikely, but further evidence is admittedly required.

OUTSIDE the walls of the city lay the cemeteries, which in a properly regulated Roman town were forbidden inside the walls. Urns, coffins and inscriptions from these cemeteries may be found in several of the museums of London, and not merely are they in many cases of considerable historic interest, but their abundance immediately outside the walls shows that the Roman, like the medieval city, lay almost exclusively within its defences.

A final point demands brief notice. What was the political position of Roman London within the province ? We have seen that at the time of the Roman conquest Colchester, already the native head-quarters, was taken over by the invaders as the new provincial capital. There is no evidence, however, that Colchester maintained the premier position after its failure in the year 60. On the other hand, an inscription found in London and recording a dedication by the Province of Britain to the Divinity of the Emperor suggests that the main centre of Emperor worship, which was normally situated in the capital of a province, was at some period transferred from Colchester to London. Moreover the literary record mentions London as the seat of financial control, and consistent with this is the intermittent issue of coinage from London between 286 and 388, although this privilege may have been shared, perhaps, by other Romano-British cities.

Lastly, the high-sounding title, Augusta, and the use of London, in the fourth century, as a head-quarters by officers such as Theodosius, all suggest that the great centre of the Romano-British road-system was something more than a mere gateway into Britain. Without, therefore pressing the term " capital " too closely, we may say that in a general sense Roman London became at least the main centre of the Roman civil administration.

## The Master Builders. IV.

# The Great Wall of China

## By F. Hadland Davis

Author of "Myths and Legends of Japan," "Japan : From the Age of the Gods to the Fall of Tsingtau," etc.

LESS than fifty years ago reports appeared in English newspapers to the effect that the Great Wall of China was a myth. So far from being a myth, it is the most stupendous example of human achievement. The Hanging Gardens of Babylon, the walls of the Romans, and even the Great Pyramid, are not to be compared with what the Chinese have called the Wan-lich'ang Ch'ên, or Wall of Ten Thousand Miles. It forms the northern boundary of the Chinese Empire, and stretches from Shan-hai-kuan, on the Gulf of Liau-tung, to the Kiayu Pass, near the Tibetan mountains.

Measured in a straight line its length is 1,255 miles, but when we take into account its many sinuosities, we must add to that figure another 250 miles. Its height varies from 15 feet to 30 feet. The breadth at the base is about 25 feet, and at the top 15 feet, but the western section of the Wall is on a less impressive scale, and where the Barrier passes through long stretches of loess formation, the loamy deposit is hewn down in the shape of a wall and faced with brick or stone. Hundreds of years ago, when the Great Wall was a military defence, it was strengthened with over 25,000 towers and 15,000 watch-towers, and to-day, when much of the glory of China's wonder has departed, it is estimated that 20,000 towers and 10,000 watch-towers remain.

The most vivid imagination can scarcely conceive a wall more than 1,500 miles long ; but China is a country of walls. There are so many that if we add their length to that of the Great Barrier they would exceed the diameter of the earth ! It has always seemed remarkable to me that Marco Polo, who wrote so much of what he saw in China during the reign of Kublai Khan, should have left the Great Wall unrecorded. It is almost as extraordinary as the pathetic story of a Chinese peasant who lived close to the Great Barrier, but had not seen it because much labour had bent his back and he had never looked up, though he would take with smiling approval a pill composed of crushed stone from the Great Wall, well mixed with a pulverised mouse ! The amazing Chinese pharmacopœia has a medical use for almost everything.

In 221 B.C. a remarkable man came to the Chinese throne. He assumed the title of Shih Hwang Ti, the First Emperor, and in so doing set aside the long and illustrious line of his predecessors. He abolished the feudal system, and divided the country into provinces ; but our chief interest in his career is to be found in the fact that, like so many of the Pharaohs, he centred his ambition in various building enterprises. He built a great palace in his capital and a hall capable of seating 10,000 people. He caused to be erected in the Imperial Forest Park his wives' palaces, planned in such a way that they resembled a map of the starry heavens. In 214 B.C., having accomplished these and other wonders, he turned

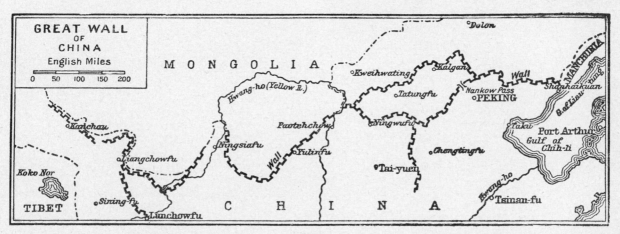

*FIFTEEN HUNDRED MILES OF WALL WIT*

The wild country shown in this section of the Wall would seem to have resulted from some extraordinary convulsion of the earth that t
these mighty mounds, the Wall pursues its course, sometimes at such an angle that even steps are impracticable, and the traveller has to
danger threatened from Mongol or Hun invader, contained its small garrison. At important points these towers were built at intervals o
barrier that this picture suggests. In the western area wide breaches have been made and never repaired, reducing the line to a k

## IN AND OUT AND OVER MOUNTAINS

d into more fantastic mountain tumuli than are to be found in any pictured landscape. Winding in and out and up and down
g its path on all fours. Its serpentine line is occasionally interrupted by square battlemented towers, every one of which, when
a hundred yards. Roughly speaking, **the total length of the Wall is fifteen hundred miles** but it is not entirely the continuous
nd or a flattened track of stubble. **Even so, it is surely the most stupendous of extant engineering monuments of the past.**

**SUMMIT OF THE GREAT WALL OF CHINA WHERE IT CROSSES THE NANKOW PASS**

Winding up hill and down dale, over valley, mountain, desert, and river, the Great Wall of China runs its one and a half thousand mile course from Shan-hai-kuan on the Liau-tung Gulf to Kiayu-Kuan on the borders of the great Gobi Desert, near Su-chow. It was begun in the third century B.C. by Shih Hwang Ti, but not completed until many years afterwards under his successors; indeed, the final touches were only given it during the great restorations under the Ming Emperors in the fifteenth and sixteenth centuries.

*Photo by Underwood Press Service*

his attention to building a wall " one-twentieth of the circumference of the earth." Was his colossal enterprise prompted by personal vanity? Did he wish to leave his name in stone for ever? It is more than probable that in this achievement he aimed at lasting fame; but there is an old Chinese saying, and a true one: " Have no fear of the tiger from the South; beware the rooster from the North." The First Emperor had been warned in a dream that disaster would come from the North. As a Taoist he was extremely superstitious, and gave heed to all manner of signs and portents. However, it needed no prophetic dream to reveal the fact that China's danger lay in the North, for from that quarter the people of the Celestial Kingdom had constantly suffered.

It is said that Hwang Ti pressed into the service of the building of the Great Wall every third able-bodied man in the kingdom. He had previously burnt the Chinese classics, including the revered works of Confucius, and spared only books dealing with agriculture, medicine, and necromancy. It is important to emphasise the burning of the books, or rather writing carved upon bamboo tablets. Wisdom expressed in masterly language has always been China's most precious possession, scholars being regarded as of more account than kings or wealthy merchants. The First Emperor's wanton act was never forgotten or forgiven, notwithstanding that his attempt to suppress the work of great Chinese teachers proved abortive. He is remembered to-day by the learned classes in China, not as the builder of the Great Wall, but as he who burnt the books. If historians have been busy calling him all manner of bad names, Hwang Ti did not hesitate to punish refractory scholars, or judges, who had given offence, by forcing them to work upon the Great Wall. If rich or poor, learned or simple, gave trouble, they were promptly dispatched to add their quota to the vast fabric of stone and brick. We can picture a scholar, familiar with the ethics of Confucius,

306

**WITHSTANDING THE ONSET OF TIME: A WATCHTOWER FORTRESS IN THE WALL**

A particularly well preserved tower is seen in this photograph. More than eighteen thousand of these small fortresses are included within the length of the Great Wall; they vary from forty to fifty feet in height. Nearly all are in ruins. A few are even older than the wall itself, dating back to the fourth century B.C., when they constituted places of refuge and resistance for local settlements. At most of these high points a signal beacon was erected to summon reinforcements when needed.

fumbling with heavy stones. He would only fumble once. Were he seen by an overseer to be inefficient, he would be killed, his body thrown into the Wall and crushed into its foundation. How many perished in this way is not recorded, but such a name for the Great Wall as " The Longest Cemetery on Earth " conveys the impression that China's mighty Barrier contained much that once quickened with human life.

The Great Wall was not completed during the life of the First Emperor, and we do not know how much was accomplished during his despotic rule. It was Liu Pang, first of the Hans, who laboured to put the finishing touches to the tremendous Barrier, and to some of the Ming Emperors is due elaborate reconstruction in regard to the Wall and towers. They faithfully followed the tortuous line planned by Hwang Ti, and it is their work, with more modern additions, that remains to be seen by the traveller to-day.

An undertaking on so vast a scale was inevitably associated with numerous highly-coloured legends. The First Emperor was regarded by the credulous as a great magician who rode a celestial horse whose rapid flight marked out the line of the Great Wall. We are told that Hwang Ti made use of a whip that removed mountains and controlled the waters of the Yellow River. We hear of giants of superhuman strength who performed many marvels in the use of stone, of divinely revealed treasure in the Great Wall, and tales of love and high adventure. With such an accumulation of fanciful stories it is not surprising to find that there are those living to-day who do not regard the Great Wall as a barrier against human foes, but go so far as to suggest that it was a huge stone dragon intended to counteract the effect of evil spirits. Notwithstanding the use made of geomancy in the First Emperor's day and images of deities that still protect certain passes, we are on safer ground if we assume a less fantastic conception and regard the Wall bounding

PORTION OF THE GREAT WALL BY SHAN-HAI-KUAN, ON THE EASTERN OCEAN

This photograph shows the Great Wall crossing the plain between mountain and sea and winding upwards over the barrier, close to its point of commencement at Shan-hai-kuan in the east. It originally abutted right on the shore, but the seaward portion no longer exists. Other parts of it have been destroyed, and in places it is represented by little more than an embankment, but for the greater part of its length it stretches an unbroken line of masonry and brick, marvellously undamaged, for mile upon mile.

Photo by Underwood Press Service

the north and north-west of China as a means of defence against the barbarians. The expense and human suffering entailed in its construction were such that a facetious writer observed: "The Chinese never got over it. But the Tartars did." It must be admitted that the Great Wall, as a military defence, was far from being a success, and was not half so useful as the Grand Canal. The Great Barrier did not prevent the coming of Jenghiz Khan, the first foreigner to rule China, and it was impotent to stay the assault of the Manchus. The amusing account of battle scenes, described in "The Wallet of Kai Lung," is by no

means a travesty of the truth. The Chinese have never been a warlike people, and a far-flung barrier and numerous towers were of little use without efficient soldiers to defend them.

How was the Great Wall made, and what form did it take? We are told by one authority, Dr. W. E. Geil, that the towers were probably built first and the Wall linked up with them. As a rule, the Great Barrier "followed the line of greatest natural resistance," a scheme that necessitated negotiating mountain chains. That such a task was successfully accomplished is one of the most striking examples of human effort

It conveys little idea of the labour entailed when we say that furrows were cut on the crest of mountains, and that between these furrows, about 25 feet apart, were placed huge granite blocks, and upon them clay bricks, in header formation, with a final surface of well-rammed earth. According to local legend goats were used to carry stone to the high ridges, but it is more probable that the blocks and bricks were borne by long-suffering men, who may well have thought of the Chinese saying : " Without tasting of bitterness we never reach the highest " when they were struggling up a pass, between Liang-chow-fu and Lan-chow-fu, where the Great Wall is over 4,000 feet above sea level. Work in the desert regions was naturally of a different kind, and to prevent the encroachment of wind-blown sand it was sometimes necessary to build three outer walls capable of protecting the main line of the Barrier.

It is difficult to define the shape of the Great Wall. It twists and turns like a mighty serpent of stone. It scales mountains, plunges into ravines, bears the heat and dust of the desert, crosses streams, a great grey monster that knows no obstacle, however formidable, unless we except the White Meteor, which deflected its natural course. Seen beneath a blazing sun, the silver glitter of stars, or when it is touched by the white hand of snow, it remains the Wall of Walls, a wonder of beauty and strength and human endurance. It has three immense festoons ; one in the mountains, another in the loess, and a third in the desert. Time has played in a freakish way with the Wall in places, for at one spot it resembles a huge bird with swelling neck and far-stretched tail, but in contrast to this stone oddity is the Great Barrier at Ch'achien-kow, erected by the Emperor Wan Li. Here wall and square towers are still in excellent preservation.

Bearing in mind what the Great Wall must have been in the past, rather than what it is now, with trains rushing through one of its gates, we can conceive its once undiminished glory. Having overcome so many difficulties, having wound its way into depths, stood strong upon the mountain-tops, battled against wind and rain and sand-storm, unmoved by the waters of the Hwang-ho, or by the noise of vast armies, indifferent to the murmur of innumerable caravans, there seems no reason why the Great Wall should come to an

TWO THOUSAND YEARS OF LIFE AND STILL SOUND AND STRONG

Built 2,000 years ago, the tower shown in the photograph remains in wonderful condition. In the carefully built up wall one can see the methodical construction of the ancient Chinese builders. There was once a drawbridge to the entrance, where now the connexion is made by carelessly flung logs.

Sport and General Press Agency

OUTSIDE THE ARCHWAY OF A BRICK TOWER CROWNING THE WONDROUS WALL

The construction of the Great Wall does not appear to have been pursued in an uninterrupted line from beginning to end; rather, it was begun at several points—those crossing the most important routes—and the gaps were filled up later. Moreover, it was only at these points that brick and masonry were employed, the remainder being of undressed boulders and earth, although many of these sections were subsequently strengthened and faced with masonry by the Ming Emperors of a later age.

Photo by Underwood Press Service

end, why the stone mammoth should cease its wanderings so long as it could find foothold in the world. It guarded Peking, the Forbidden City, and ended near the confines of Tibet, the Land of the Living Buddha, passing from mystery to mystery with sublime unconcern, every inch of its winding course rich with human memories. It started within sound of the Yellow Sea, and ended on a precipice, 200 hundred feet high, bounding one side of the Big White North River. The Great Wall was strong and glorious to the last. The stone mammoth stopped, but with raised head on the heights, as if conscious of its tremendous victory.

Two tablets mark the east and west end of the Great Wall. On one is inscribed: "Heaven made the Sea and the Mountains," and on the other: "The Martial Barrier of All under Heaven." There is something reverential about the one, something that shouts of a great work accomplished about the other. What an undulating, curving line of wall between these two tablets! Cities and tombs and monuments have been sheltered behind the Great Wall for hundreds of years, and China's teeming millions have poured in and out of its many gates. We may write of the towns through which the Great Wall passes, of the famous Ming Mausolea, of temples and pagodas, of the "Language Arch" at the Nankow Pass, and of a thousand other sights that are to be seen in the vicinity of the Great Wall, but many will turn with most interest to the Mound of Chin, about a mile from the Black Horse Mountain, where the First Emperor was buried with his wives and concubines and those who built his last resting-place, with its alleged river of quick-silver and grim stories of a coffin that moved at the approach of man. At the top of the Mound is a hole, and to this day the idle throw stones into it. *Stones!* Could anything be more ridiculous? For he who was buried beneath had achieved a triumph in stone, had fashioned across his kingdom the greatest and most wonderful Wall in the world.

## A GATEWAY THAT BARRED THE BARBARIAN PASSAGE FROM THE NORTH

Shown here is one of the vital spots of the Great Wall—the Pa-La-Ling Gate leading to the famous Nankow Pass. Down this pass swept many a horde of would-be invaders of the realm, to be checked and thrown back by the solid barrier they encountered. Because the need of a garrison here was recognized long after wall and towers to the far west had ceased to serve any practical purpose and had fallen into dilapidation. this Nankow section was frequently repaired, and the defensive wall was strengthened by a special system of fortifications.

THE TEMPLE OF ANANDA AT PAGAN : A GORGEOUS PALACE OF A THOUSAND CLOUD-CAPP'D TOWERS

Built of solid brick, strong and massive, yet inexpressibly light in appearance is this amazing temple. The central square measures 200 feet on each side, and has four projecting porches on each face. The crowning pinnacle is 183 feet high, soaring above the top (seventh) storey built in the shape of a Hindu or Jain temple ; the lower storeys are square in shape. Of very solid structure internally, the building is intersected by only two corridors, which are concentric. In the back of each of the four transepts is a statue of Buddha over 30 feet high, representing the great teacher in the four incarnations in which he appeared in this present world. The temple was built in the eleventh century in the reign of Kyansittha

## "THE WALL OF TEN THOUSAND MILES": CHINA'S MIGHTY TRIUMPH IN STONE

At no part of its immense course is the Great Wall of China better built or more complete than at the Nankow Pass. Here it is nearly 30 feet high and 20 feet broad at the base : the lower courses are blocks of masonry, with a brick parapet to crown them, and the towers and watch-towers are in the main unharmed. How the Emperor thought to defend such a mighty line is a mystery. Was it merely a tour-de-force, a boast of power? Among those who were forced to labour on it were all convicted of being in possession of books, and there is a tradition that the bodies of those who died or were killed in its construction—and they were many—were cast into the grim foundations.

*Photo by Underwood Press Service, specially coloured for "Wonders of the Past."*

# The Wonder Cities. VI.

# Pagan : City of Ten Thousand Temples

## By Richard Curle

Author of " Into the East : Notes on Burma and Malaya "

Illustrated with photographs taken by Herbert G. Ponting, F.R.G.S.

OF the dead cities of the world, once the hub of great empires and vast activities and now lying ruined and still, none is more impressive than Pagan. Situated ninety-two miles south-west of Mandalay in Burma, it extends for twenty miles along the banks of the Irrawaddy, and its average depth is five miles. The remains of its pagodas and temples, of which many hundreds can be counted out of a rumoured total of 9,999, thus cover an immense area.

There is no more splendid, solemn and mournful vista than that of Pagan stretching infinitely about one in the deep silence of the wilderness. It has been deserted for over 700 years, and the undergrowth riots about its streets, creeps over its buildings and gives to its huge grandeur an air of irretrievable desolation. And yet on the whole the dry atmosphere of Upper Burma has marvellously preserved Pagan from the decay of time. Much has crumbled, it is true, much has been swallowed by the jungle, but much remains. Pagan viewed from a distance might still be the centre of a mighty kingdom.

A white, sandy track runs through the city, and an occasional bullock cart lumbers along where once gorgeous processions were accustomed to wend their way. In all directions can be seen, as one writer puts it, " countless pagodas in every stage of dissolution, down to mere swelling grass-covered tumuli. Hedges of thorny cactus, fields of millet, acres of purple croton fill up all the intervening spaces."

Perhaps the finest view is to be had from the rest-house on the hill—the town fading on the plain and the broad river flowing into the distance, with the Tangyi hills in the foreground and beyond them the mountains of Arakan. On a peaceful evening this is, indeed, one of the most glorious sights in the whole of Burma.

The little of Pagan that can be seen from the river presents a strange and melancholy appearance. The old pagodas crowning the cliff give one an extraordinary suggestion of loneliness and abandonment, and the thought that behind them, invisible to your sight, lies an immense dead city, powerfully affects the imagination. The peace that surrounds Pagan is weighted with past history. It seems so incredible that man should have raised these innumerable shrines and then have vanished utterly from the scene. The modern village of Pagan, with its 6,000 inhabitants, only serves to heighten the contrast between what was and what is. The visitor to Pagan must assuredly feel the hand of time heavy upon him.

The city was founded in the year 847 by Pyimbya, thirty-third king of the dynasty of Thamok-darit, and it reached its zenith between the years 1010-1204 under kings Anawrata, Kyansittha, Alaung-sithu, and Marapati-sithu. It was under Anawrata that many of the great temples were built. He it was who conquered Thaton in 1050 and transported most of its population to Pagan to help him in his grandiose building schemes. He introduced Sinhalese Buddhism into Upper Burma, though it is probable that there already existed there a form of Indian Buddhism. Indeed, the old Kyauk ku Temple which, unlike nearly all the buildings at Pagan, that are composed of brick, is partly built of stone probably dates from before 1010, and may be held to prove that Buddhism, of a kind, had already taken hold of Upper Burma before the time of Anawrata's religious revival.

The wife of Anawrata was an Indian, and their son, Kyansittha, was consequently half Indian. Alaung-sithu, said to have reigned for seventy-five years, was finally murdered by his son and successor Marathu, who was succeeded by his son, Marapati-sithu. Under this king, who reigned for thirty-seven years, Pagan reached the climax of its greatness and was the most celebrated centre of Buddhism in Indo-China. He was succeeded by Zeya-theinka, who died in 1227.

Twenty-one years later, under Nara-thi-ha-pati— " he who fled from the Chinese "—came the end of the city and the empire of Pagan. The Emperor of China had sent ten nobles to Pagan on a mission, and the king, against advice, had them put to death. To revenge this insult, vast armies from Southern China overran the country and captured the city. The king, it is said, caused many pagodas to be pulled down in order to yield material for defensive works, but all was in vain. The fifty-third king of his dynasty, whose real name was Kyaw-swa, was the last king of Pagan. And since that far off time, which some put about 1250 and others about 1300, Pagan has been little more than a name and a ruin.

Apart from some fragments, there are no remains at Pagan other than religious. But that does not imply that it was essentially a religious city, for it was not. It was the capital of a remarkable state that extended from the gulf of Martaban to the borders of Southern China, and from the bay of Bengal to Cambodia. The inhabitants probably dwelt in mat houses, which have long since powdered into dust while the religious edifices remain. All early Burmese history is steeped in myth and legend, but from out these folk-lore tales we can reconstruct the busy life of Pagan under its kings. In the medieval world of Asia it played an important part. Its wealth and industry, still evident to our senses after 700 years of abandonment, were famed within the East. In the annals of old times the kingdom of Pagan appears illustrious and great, and the whisper of that greatness yet hangs over its incomparable ruins.

As long ago as 1242, Queen Pwazaw wrote: " Pagan is called so because it is the most pleasant and beautiful of all kingdoms. It is also called Arimaddana because it is inhabited by people who are warlike and brave and are able to vanquish their foes, who dread even the sound of its name. Its people always enjoy immunity from danger and are free from pain. They are well versed in every art and possess various industrial appliances. The country is full of useful things, the people are wealthy, and the revenue enormous. It is a glorious kingdom and its subjects are. . . known to be glorious and powerful."

But little of the city, as has been explained, can be seen from the Irrawaddy whose high banks shut out its enormous spaces. One must land and look for oneself, one must spend days there and let the details and the vistas sink into one's consciousness. Nothing can properly convey the marvellous sight that meets the eye. In all

AWE-INSPIRING GUARDIANS OF THE PORTALS OF ANANDA AT PAGAN

Once the busy, beautiful city of King Anawrata, Pagan is now but a miserable little village, and its countless great temples, save for 136 in the care of the Government, are deserted and desecrated. One of the most complete and most beautiful of these literally countless pagodas is the one known as Ananda (Sanskrit: " The Endless "), and these giant leogryphs guard one of its entrances. An excellent illustration of this incredibly wonderful temple appears in page 312.

MAJESTIC EVEN IN ITS DESOLATION: THE PAGODA OF THATBYINNYU

Towering seven storeys high to its graceful pinnacle, and adorned at each corner with a tower on every storey, the Thatbyinnyu pagoda is a most impressive spectacle. The date of its erection is uncertain, but it is supposed to have been built about 1100 A.D. by the grandson of the King Kyansittha mentioned in page 313. Its central tower is 201 feet high, and it differs from the magnificent Ananda temple in that it has only one main entrance instead of four, and consequently only one great Buddha in its inmost shrine.

directions spreads the enormous panorama of the dead city. Its situation is strangely isolated. Beyond the sheer cliffs of the river which winds away glinting and placid into the distance, a low plateau cut by ravines opens before one, with the hungry jungle pressing upon the city and pouring like a stream wherever it can get a foothold. The cliffs themselves are topped by pagodas, many of which lie two-thirds buried in ploughed fields, and one of the most beautiful near the river is the Chauk-pa-hla, which was built in the twelfth century. In the dry weather the whole scene has something of the aridity of a brown desert, but when the rains fall the acacias bloom and the ground is covered with yellow flowers.

The pagodas of Pagan are of every kind. In its heyday it sheltered Buddhist fraternities from Ceylon, Siam, Nepal, the Shan States, Pegu and China, each fraternity living and plotting against the others in their separate quarters, and these have left their mark upon the architecture. There are bell-shaped pyramids, pumpkin-shaped

pagodas, Ceylon dagobas with their knob-like domes, square pagodas, cruciform pagodas. These last, with their vaulted roofs, are the predominant type among the chief buildings and resemble Western ideas of churches rather than Eastern ideas of pagodas. The Government have 136 of the principal pagodas in their charge, and the care now taken of them will do much to prolong the life and keep green the memory of Pagan.

The three principal temples in Pagan are the Ananda, built by Kyansittha, the Thatbyinnyu, and the Gawdawplin, built by Marapati-sithu. The Ananda is the most magnificent of the three. It is a square of nearly 200 feet on each side, with projecting wings that make it 280 feet across each way. It consists of seven storeys, six being square, diminishing in size, and the seventh being shaped like a Hindu temple. It is about 183 feet high. Within, two narrow corridors wind about, and in the rear of each of the four transepts there stands a 30-foot image of Buddha. They represent the four Buddhas of this present world cycle, Kaukkathan,

Kathapa, Gawnagong and Gautama. There is beautiful tile work in the Ananda, and in the niches of its walls there are several thousand carved groups and images depicting scenes in the life of Buddha. The Ananda was built in the eleventh century. Thatbyinnyu, which is 201 feet high, was built about 1100, and Gawdawplin, which is 180 feet high, in 1200.

These three temples lie close together in the heart of the city, but scattered elsewhere, sometimes far distant, are other pagodas of superb appearance and, to this very time, deeply venerated by devout Burmese. The Shwe-Zigon, for instance, one of Anawrata's erections, is said to contain a frontal bone and tooth of Buddha. The golden " hti " upon the summit of its dome is hung with bells. Another venerated pagoda, though not architecturally lovely, is the Nanpaya, which Manuha, the captive king of Thaton, built beyond the Myinkaba stream. It holds four figures of Buddha : three are seated, the tallest being 50 feet in height, and the fourth, which measures 90 feet, is recumbent. The ruins of the king's palace, made of greenstone, are near by.

The largest of all the pagodas in Pagan is the Dhammayangyi, which was begun by Narathu but never completed. It is now in a dilapidated condition. One of the most interesting and perhaps the oldest is the already mentioned Kyauk-ku, inside of whose square tower, now half smothered in jungle, there rests a gigantic figure of Buddha. This temple was inhabited long after the city ceased to live, and it remained a refuge for priests and great nobles down to the year 1637.

It is impossible to give even an approximate list of the memorable pagodas of Pagan. There is the Nagayon whose carving shows the influence of serpent worship, the Mingalazedi with its glazed tiles, the Tangyi-sway-daw with its golden dome above the shining white of its brick, the Maha Bodi covered with niches full of seated Buddhas, the Sulamani, and many other less well known shrines.

Words do not convey much, and here even photographs may fail. Pagan must be seen in its grandeur, its solitude, and its vastness to be entirely comprehended. For 700 and more years it has been drowsing in the wilderness by the river's bank, and one feels that 700 years from now it will be drowsing still.

MOONLIGHT VIEW OF A PORCH OF THATBYINNYU

Truly a wonder temple, Thatbyinnyu must have been an object of universal admiration and an inspiring shrine at which to worship for the followers of Anawrata's new religion brought into Burma from Ceylon. It is in some respects comparable with the wonderful temple of Shwe Dagon, described in later pages. The human figure seems dwarfed by the porch alone : judge then the vastness of the whole building.

Its overthrow by time is slow, but it is sure. At long last Pagan will be a mere hummock in the jungle ; it will disappear into the forest as once, long ago, it rose like a miracle out of the same forest.

# Temples of the Gods. XII.

# Delphi of the Oracle

## By Edward Wright

ON the south-western flank of the huge mass of Parnassus that dominates a mountainous, earthquaking region north of the Gulf of Corinth there was a small rift in the rock from which intoxicating fumes rose. Long before any Greek entered the country the native goatherds had made the spot famous and prophetic rites were carried on under the protection of a snake deity. Out of this extraordinary natural gas well the invading Greeks gradually constructed an oracle, known in the age of Homer by its old snake name of Pytho and changed to Delphi by Dorian conquerors. They set up as presiding deity their favourite god Apollo, fabling that he had killed the snake, formed themselves into a sacred caste from which alone high priests could be chosen, and arranged a league with neighbouring clans for the protection of the wonderful shrine.

Masters of craft were these Dorians; old Egyptian mystery-mongers had nothing to teach them. They did not breathe the deadly volcanic gas of Parnassus themselves, but appointed native mountaineering maids as assistant priestesses. In a hut of laurel boughs the unhappy girls sat on a tripod over the chasm and breathed the fumes until they became half demented. Sometimes they died, but usually they were removed in a raving condition; and their ravings were the oracle of the god. There was no sense in what they said, but the priests interpreted each message —that is, they devised as vague answers as possible to the questions of pilgrims; their real practical work was that of politicians working in the Dorian interests. When their southern kinsfolk, the Spartans, began to rise to power, the influence of Delphi increased. In a higher, disinterested way the priests used religion in an effort to weld the Greeks together into some kind of federated nation. By the seventh century B.C. Delphi was so strong that Solon of Athens, the incarnation of political wisdom, attached his state to the league that centred in the shrine. Foreign potentates, such as the line of Lydian kings ending in Croesus and Amasis (Aahmes II.) of Egypt, sought for Delphian oracles. In the sixth century an exiled group of Athenian nobles built the first historic temple at Delphi, and with the development of the sacred games and the increase in great pilgrim embassies the religious centre became a glorious holy city.

The situation was incomparable in its union of natural grandeur and artistic loveliness. Above, at a height of 8,070 feet, were the five peaks of massive Parnassus where wolf and wild boar roamed the snowfields. About midway down, the mountain slope ceased and an immense wall of cliff a thousand feet high stood above the Delphic hollow, ramparting it from the northern to the eastern sides. A cascading winter torrent had split the cliff into two parts and at the mouth of the chasm a spring welled into a great square basin of rock. This was the holy Castalian spring with whose lustral water ministrants washed their hair

FROM DELPHI, HOME OF ART

In the museum at Delphi is to be seen this exquisite caryatid and acanthus leaf pedestal, fruit of the excavators' toil. Formed of dancing girls from Karyai, it was designed to support a tripod or votive offering.

ALL OF APOLLO'S DELPHIC FANE THAT SURVIVES THE BLOWS OF MAN AND TIME

Heart of the Delphic precinct and scene of the prophetic ravings of the Pythian priestess, the great temple of Apollo is now represented by no more than its foundations, while the Adyton or inmost shrine of the oracle with its vaporous chasm has been so thoroughly destroyed that deep excavation fails to reveal its exact arrangements. At the height of Delphi's prestige the temple was a hexastyle structure, with its outer colonnade in the Doric style and its inner pillars Ionic, built or completed by an exiled Athenian family, the Alkmaionids, in about 415 B.C. What remains to us now, however, appears to be the result of a later restoration that followed the old plan, in spite of the contrary belief of Pausanias.

and pilgrims sprinkled themselves. From the base of the two cliffs and the sacramental fountain a steep slope went down in a series of terraces to the glen of the river Pleistos, on the farther side of which the land again rose sharply to Mount Kirphis.

The general appearance of Delphi was that of a vast rocky amphitheatre ringed with mountains with the city and the oracle set at the top. In the high north-western corner was the stadium for the sacred games; below this was the limestone theatre and then the great walled close of Apollo, with a sacred way twisting upward from the southern gate by the exquisite treasure houses of the principal Greek city states to the most famous of temples. The fane, measuring 197 feet by 72 feet, rested on a large terrace supported by walls of the most perfect masonry. As rebuilt in the fourth century B.C. after an earthquake, and as practically extant in the fourth century A.D., it consisted of an outer Doric colonnade and an inner row of Ionic columns enclosing the great central shrine. Here was preserved beside a perpetual fire a large, conical, carved piece of marble connected with the ancient snake worship but supposed to mark the centre of the earth and therefore called the navel-stone or "Omphalos." By it were a golden Apollo and golden images of the two eagles of Zeus. Below was a dim subterranean chamber enclosing the volcanic rift from which the maddening gas rose.

Upon a column formed of three twining snakes, later removed by Constantine to Constantinople where it is still to be seen in the Atmeidan, there stood a golden trivet. On the trivet was a golden cauldron and in this sat the pale, wild Pythian priestess inhaling the fumes and writhing, while the masters of the oracle took down her broken expressions and interpreted their meaning in remarkably bad verse. In the later period, after one of the virgins had been dishonoured, a single aging woman was employed to inhale the gas and rave. Details of this kind did not matter. The important thing was the practical wisdom shown by the subtle interpreters. For some centuries, between the Dorian settlement and the Persian invasion, they avoided blunders and achieved many successes. They reconciled warring states and directed the colonising ventures of the cities in such a way as to prevent rivalries and wasting conflicts. Streams of pilgrims brought them news of political events in Hellas, of the course of trade and of the last discoveries in the lands of barbarians.

Their special information regarding the gigantic forces of the Persian invader, Xerxes, proved their undoing. Knowing with fair exactness the strength of the Persians, they reckoned that resistance was hopeless. Using the complete machinery of the oracle they counselled absolute submission or flight. After the marvellous Athenian and Spartan

ATHENE'S EMBASSY IN APOLLO'S CAPITAL
Most of the important Greek states had " treasuries " at Delphi—receptacles for votive offerings, consulates, as it were, in the city of the god. The treasury of the Athenians, an exquisite little Doric temple in shape erected with the spoils taken at Marathon, has been rebuilt by the excavators with loving care, since at least four-fifths of its original materials were recoverable.

victories the priests of Delphi were regarded as traitors in Persian pay. The Athenians especially lost their awe of the cowardly oracle and developed that sceptic, searching spirit of intellect from which the modern movement of knowledge was born. Gradually Delphi declined into the resort of the superstitious and if enlightened statesmen condescended to approach the oracle it was for the purpose of obtaining a prearranged message that might induce the unthinking class of freemen to follow the course of policy marked out for them.

The great Delphi or Pythian festival remained, however, a national attraction. By one tremendous mistake the priests had lost for ever the opportunity of federating the clans and directing them in peaceful expansion and warlike adventure; they were no longer able to prevent the Hellas-shattering struggle between the Spartan military class whom they favoured and the Athenian imperialist democrats whom they feared. Yet they still could charm the poetry-loving Athenians by their ancient contest in verse and music and attract the sport-loving Spartans by their athletic games. The original festival at Delphi was devoted to the

GLORIES OF ART THAT ONCE ENRICHED THE SAGEST ORACLE OF ANCIENT TIMES

Clasped like a jewel of many facets in a setting of dark metal, this scene of brilliance gleamed amid the sombre beauties of Delphi; glance from this to the opposite page, trying to combine the one with the other, and some of the majesty of the ancient holy city will be reborn. In the centre of the precinct is the temple of Apollo with the theatre above it on the left and the treasuries of the Greek states grouped below; the one immediately beneath its left-hand column is the treasury of the Athenians. Of the countless works of art that gave the site a whole population in bronze and marble, the Sphinx of the Naxians may here be seen on its column below the temple; the "Auriga" or Charioteer (pictured in page 241) to the left of the steps below the theatre; and the Plataean snake column, described in our chapter on Byzantium, to the left of the colossal statue of Apollo.

After a reconstruction by Tournaire from "Fouilles de Delphes"

320

AMID WILD BEAUTY AND THE PORTENTS OF NATURE: DELPHI'S INCOMPARABLE SETTING

Faced with the gloom and grandeur of the Delphic gorge one has no difficulty in understanding the religious awe of the pre-Hellenic worshippers by the volcanic rift or of the first Greeks who founded there the temple of their own prophetic god, Apollo. Two limbs of the great bulk of Parnassus, the Phaidriadai or Shining Cliffs, approach each other and frame a narrow torrent, wooded at its upper end, that foams down in icy cascades in time of spate. At the mouth of the chasm is another spring, the Castalian, that keeps a trickle flowing in the torrent bed during the severest drought ; and on the slope where the village stands once rose the precinct and city of Delphi. The entire village has since been removed by the excavators.

Photo by Autotype Co.

singing of a hymn to Apollo to the accompaniment of a lyre. At first the singing poets competed every eighth year, but from 586 B.C. the contest was held every fourth year in August. The prize was a laurel wreath. In the earliest time, Homer and Hesiod are said to have been disqualified because they could not play the lyre ; in the latest age Nero was among the winners, but offended by an oraculous answer that seemed to reflect upon his treatment of his mother, he tried to destroy the temple and removed 500 pieces of sculpture.

However this may be, Delphi was almost until her end a wonderful scene of the glories of Greek art. Her wealth invited the plunderer. In the fourth century B.C. the neighbouring Phocians stole her works of gold ; in the following century the Gauls under Brennus tried to sack sanctuary and city but were repulsed by a gathering of the Greek armies. What Delphi lost in works of precious metal yet left her supreme in historic splendour. For it was the custom of Greek states, when victorious over other Hellenic cities or over aliens, to hang a tithe of their spoil about the temple, or devote it to an artistic commemoration of their triumph in the national shrine. Victories and defeats of Athenians, successes and disasters of Spartans and the great adventures of other states down to little nests of Greek island pirates were kept in memory by a countless variety of glorious works in metal and marble. Then, outside the close of Apollo, was the increasing multitude of the statues of victors in the games. Victorious poets were likewise honoured.

Eastward across the ravine from Castely rose the city, some sixteen furlongs in circumference, with its temples to Athene and other deities, a noble gymnasium and small dwelling houses. All the unrivalled scene lasted to the end of the Roman Empire, gathering new works of architecture under Emperors sometimes moved by superstitious reverence for the oracle and sometimes by artistic admiration. But Constantine removed the best treasures to his new capital and finally Theodosius abolished the oracle ; earthquakes destroyed the buildings and closed the vent by which the oracle-working gas issued. In 1891 French excavators removed the modern village of Castri and dug up what earthquakes and spoilers had spared.

AS AN EAGLE MIGHT SEE DELPHI FROM THE CRAGS OF PARNASSUS

Here is Delphi as it appears to-day from the cliffs above after the removal of the village of Castri to another site. In the centre may be seen the rectangular foundations of the fane of Apollo with the Greek theatre above it ; the view of the temple in page 318 is taken from between them. In the upper right-hand corner may be seen the stadium where the Pythian games were held ; while surrounding the temple and stretching down towards the road the enclosure walls may be traced.

## The Wonder Cities. VII.

# Troy: The City Sung by Homer

### By A. H. Smith, C.B., F.B.A.

Late Keeper of Greek and Roman Antiquities, British Museum

THE name of Troy suggests two different subjects of inquiry and study to a modern ear. The one is an archæological question: what is the relationship of the prehistoric city excavated by Schliemann to the other sites of prehistoric culture now known to us, such as Cnossus, Mycenae and so on? The other is a literary problem for study with a " Homer " and a map: how far may the incidents sung by Homer be placed in an actual local setting, accurately known and intimately familiar to the mind of the poet? In the first three-quarters of the last century the distinction would have had no meaning, for the archæological evidence was non-existent and only the surface topography was a subject for study. To the present generation the two problems are distinct, for the one is concerned with actual facts revealed by the spade, and the other with the mind and meaning of the poet and the unchanged natural features of the country.

It is important at the outset to distinguish carefully the various senses in which the name Troy has been and may be employed. In the first place it stands for the city, built by Poseidon for Laomedon, which was ruled by Priam, besieged by Agamemnon and taken by the Greek host. The episodes of a few days of the ten years' siege are the subject of Homer's " Iliad." Of Troy, as of Arthur's Camelot, it may be said:

> The city is built
> To music, therefore never built at all,
> And therefore built for ever.

To some of those brought up as dwellers in this visionary city, the prosaic work of the spade is by no means accounted a gain and they are ready to lament, with the late Andrew Lang, that

> The sacred keep of Ilion is rent
> By shaft and pit ; foiled waters wander slow
> Through plains where Simois and Scamander went
> To war with gods and heroes long ago.

In the second place there is a series of early settlements discovered by Henry Schliemann on a mound called Hissarlik. Thirdly, there is the Greek and Roman town of Ilion; and fourthly, there are the various points at which critics ancient and modern with their Homer in their hand have sought to place the town as most nearly fulfilling the conditions laid down in the wonderful epic.

The present paper deals principally with Troy in the second of the above meanings, but before we turn to the story of Schliemann's discoveries something must be said about the third and fourth, and about the processes by which Hissarlik was arrived at as what must now be called the true site of Troy. From an early period in Greek history proper Ilion or New Ilion claimed to be the direct successor of Priam's Troy. The claim was admitted by a series of eminent tourists. The first of whom we hear was the Persian king Xerxes who, on the march to the Hellespont in 480 B.C., crossed the Trojan plain. On the way he went up to the Citadel of Priam, Herodotus tells us. After he had viewed it and had inquired about every detail, he sacrificed a thousand oxen to Athene of Ilion and his Persian Magi poured out libations to the ancient heroes.

A hundred and fifty years later Alexander the Great visited the Troad, sacrificed to Athene and did everything incumbent on one who claimed to be descended from Achilles. He ran naked up the tumulus of his mighty ancestor, as the custom was, anointed the sepulchral stone at the top and crowned it with a wreath, while Hephaistion placed a wreath on the tomb of Patroklos. He also offered a sacrifice to Priam on the altar of Zeus Herkeios, deprecating his wrath with the race of Neoptolemos, son of Achilles. He exchanged his own armour for weapons reputed to date from the Trojan war. While he was being taken round the sights of the town, he expressed his poor opinion of the Lyre of Paris, and said that it was the Lyre to which Achilles had sung the exploits of good men that he most wished to see.

The claims of the city were similarly recognized by Lysimachos, Augustus and Caracalla. The last-named was enabled by the death of his favourite Festus, which was thought by contemporary rumour to be suspiciously opportune, to repeat the funeral rites that Achilles had performed over the body of Patroklos.

It is therefore evident that through the centuries the town of Ilion was officially recognized as the successor of Homer's Troy and that its inhabitants carefully cultivated the legend. But there is also evidence that those who were critically minded

## WHERE WARRIORS DWELT LONG ERE HOMER SANG

The greatest of the prehistoric cities on the site of Troy was the sixth, but the second, as this photograph shows, was by no means negligible; here A, B and C mark the town walls of the city on the south-west side, while at D are house walls of later periods. It was the evident signs of a conflagration in this second layer that influenced Schliemann to identify it with the city sacked by the Achaean host. The three layers between second and sixth were small settlements rather than towns.

From Dörpfeld's "Troja und Ilion"

doubted the truth of the tradition. It was the general belief that Troy was left utterly desolate after its capture, and the geographer Strabo definitely states that Homeric students questioned the truth of the claim which was prompted by the vanity of the inhabitants of the existing city. He thought that the true site was a place some three and a half miles nearer the mountains, a place called in his day the Village of the Trojans, and he states that according to his authorities the town had had several changes of position and had finally reached its then situation about the time of Croesus, 550 B.C.

The site of this Greek Ilion and Roman Ilium has long been known from inscriptions and otherwise as being at or near the Mound of Hissarlik (Turkish: Hissar, a castle; Hissarlik, a castle and its belongings). This is a low-lying hill projecting into the Trojan plain between two and three miles from the seashore and in the middle between the two chief streams which cross the plain, and which must be the Simoeis and Skamander. But Strabo's scepticism seemed to justify the modern uncertainty as to the true site. In

1791 a French traveller, Lechevalier, put forward an alternative theory which held the field for nearly a hundred years. When Homer (Iliad, Bk. xxii.) describes how Achilles pursued Hektor round the walls of Troy, he says that they came to two fair-flowing springs where the two founts of Skamander rush upwards—one hot and covered with steam, the other as cold as ice even in summer. Lechevalier called attention to an attractive group of springs which issue from the ground not far from the rocky citadel-like hill over the village of Bunarbashi (Spring head), and he decided that this must be the Homeric Troy, and for more than two generations the majority of scholars followed him. Unfortunately, the thermometer fails to confirm Lechevalier's belief that one of the springs is hotter than the other. It was however at Bunarbashi that Dr. Henry Schliemann, under the influence of Lechevalier's theory, first tried the test of the spade. It was only when he found no trace of the expected occupation at Bunarbashi that he transferred his operations to the mound of Hissarlik. Here he carried on a series of campaigns between the years 1870 and 1890. After his death (December 26, 1890) further excavations, according to advanced modern methods, were carried out by Schliemann's widow and Dr. William Dörpfeld. The final publication of the excavations is contained in Dörpfeld's " Troja und Ilion," 1902. English readers will find an interesting discussion of the whole problem in Dr. Walter Leaf's " Troy —a Study in Homeric Geography," 1912.

The mound of Hissarlik is of slight elevation ; it rises some 90 feet above the adjacent plain and about 120 feet above the sea level. It measures approximately 200 by 250 yards.

The excavations, as finally interpreted by Dr. Dörpfeld, show a series of nine superimposed layers of settlement (some of them can hardly be called cities) extending over a very long period of time. Three of these are of outstanding importance, namely the second, sixth and ninth. The first settlement is dated conjecturally between 3000 and 2500 B.C. and is only represented by a few foundations of parallel walls resting on the living rock. These consist of rough stones loosely piled in horizontal courses and cemented with mud. After the destruction of the first settlement a longish interval seems to have succeeded which is represented by an earthy layer over the site.

The second settlement is the prehistoric city assigned to the period between 2500 and 2000 B.C. Its surface level is some 16 feet above the living rock, and it is banked up by powerful retaining walls which enclose a limited area of about 100 yards by 150. The second city is that which was regarded by Schliemann as the city of Priam. It is largely built of unburnt clay tiles and timber resting on foundations and substructures of stone. All parts show traces of destructive fire. A mass of material from the upper part of the buildings buried such lower walls as are preserved for us.

It was in a hiding place in the walls of the second city that Schliemann discovered his " Treasure of Priam." The objects composing the

**BRICK PALACE OF A PRE-HOMERIC PRINCE**

Almost in the centre of the mound lie the remains of a great " megaron " or dwelling house, probably a palace, of the second or burnt city ; at C and K on the one side and to a less extent at P on the other may be seen part of its walls of sun-dried bricks —B is the stone plinth that underlies them. At M and N is the door-pierced wall that separated the forecourt or portico from the central hall. Half of the megaron had to be sacrificed in making the excavation R on the left. H is undisturbed deposit.

From Dörpfeld's " Troja und Ilion "

treasure were found in a cubical mass and, in Schliemann's view, had once been contained in a wooden chest of which he also claimed to have found the key, but the object in question has since been shown to be a corroded chisel. The treasure, now in the Ethnographical Museum at Berlin, consisted of large copper or bronze bowls, of bronze tools and weapons, of many silver vessels and of a large hoard of gold jewelry of a characteristic and primitive kind. It included diadems with pendent chains and basket-like earrings with rosettes and twisted wires. Two splendid pins of twisted gold wire and a bracelet, though not found with the treasure, appear to be of the same period.

The third, fourth and fifth settlements all appear to have been unimportant villages, each placed on the ruins of its predecessor and gradually increasing the height and the area of the mound. The period which lies between the years 2000 to 1500 B.C. is assigned to this group of settlements.

The sixth city is that which mainly concerns us. Powerful bastions and walls spring up from the plain enclosing an area of more than twice the size of the second city. The deposits of the previous towns were brought to a level surface within its area. The sixth city is shown by evidence of architecture and pottery to have belonged to the Mycenean age, that is to the period of a brilliant civilization from 1500 to 1200 B.C. on the shores of the Aegean Sea. This it is now believed was the period dimly recalled in a changed world by tradition and poetry and in which if anywhere the siege of Troy by an Achaean host must be placed.

On the north side of the town the walls of this sixth city are quite destroyed. Possibly the date of this destruction is as remote as the days of Archianax (550 B.C.) who is said by Strabo to have built the walls of the adjacent town of Sigaeum with stones from Troy. What remains is the great wall complete for about three-fifths of the

SORTING NINE TROYS WITH PICK AND SHOVEL

The south-western part of the mound affords a good object lesson of how century must be disentangled from century within the space of a few feet by the painstaking labour of the archæologist. Here A is a tower of the second city; B, C and D are house walls of the third, fourth and fifth settlements; the points marked E represent foundations of the sixth and greatest city; while the wall at the top of the cutting behind which a man is standing belongs to the seventh layer.

From Dörpfeld's "Troja und Ilios"

## BATTLEMENTS BEFORE WHICH HEKTOR FOUGHT AND ACHILLES SULKED

Nine distinct layers go to make up the mound of Hissarlik in the Troad where Schliemann delved for Troy, some of them representing mere settlements, others strong cities where a Laomedon or a Priam might have reigned ; these strata are numbered from the bottom upwards.  Schliemann fixed on the second as representing Homer's Ilion ; maturer criticism has accepted the sixth.   The photograph above shows the ruins (marked A) of the great north-east tower of this sixth city ; B, C and D are walls and steps of the eighth layer, a Greek settlement of historic times ;  E is the retaining wall of the precinct of Athene built in the Roman town, the ninth.
From Dörpfeld's "Troja und Ilion"

ROME AND PREHISTORY CHEEK BY JOWL IN TROY

The great tower and gate on the southern side of the sixth city were badly obscured by the buildings of the ninth, or Roman, period. Here, however, the walls of the projecting tower are visible at O and G. A marks the city wall and the original entrance to the tower. Across one corner of the tower runs the wall of a Roman building marked H; while at I is a wall of the so-called Roman Theatre, more likely the Bouleuterion or Senate-house. N and M mark detached stones of the sixth period.

From Dörpfeld's "Troja und Ilion"

circumference of the citadel on its east, south and west sides, and diversified by towers and gateways. The wall itself is for the most part built of massive squared blocks of local limestone, which received their final dressing in position. It consists of a sloping substructure rising to a height of some 20 feet and surmounted by a vertical parapet wall of 6 feet. It would seem that originally the upper part of the wall consisted of unburnt bricks, of a thickness of 14 feet. This appears to have been rebuilt during the Mycenean occupation, and a narrower stone wall replaced the original brick structure. A parapet was thus formed on its outer side for about a third of its original breadth, leaving a flat terrace wall on its upper surface.

A peculiarity of the wall is that its outer face is built in a polygonal form consisting of a series of short sides of some 30 feet in length. The angles are emphasised by the fact that each side in turn is carefully dressed so as to project some six inches from the face of one of its neighbours. We will make a circuit of this sixth wall from its western end where it is seen at its weakest and roughest. At the south-west angle we come to a gateway which was originally set under the cover of a projecting bastion, but was built up in Mycenean days to concentrate the defence. We pass along a stretch of massive wall—in part demolished to make room for a Roman theatre—and come to a gateway at the most southerly point of the town, protected by a powerful projecting tower.

From here the general line runs to the northeast and again the Mycenean wall is interrupted by a Roman theatre; beyond we reach another projecting tower, in the middle of the south-east face, and still farther on we come to the eastern gate which is carefully masked by an arrangement of parallel walls. The one overlaps the other so that an attacking force could only make an oblique approach in small numbers. Again we follow the line of the wall to the north-east and come first to a small gate, with oblique approach like the last, and then we reach the great north-east tower, the wall of which is still 30 feet high. It contained and protected a well sunk 25 feet deep in the live rock. We have described three-fifths of the wall of the citadel, but it must be understood that the whole is on a surprisingly small scale. The walls described above form roughly a part of the circumference of an ellipse with axes of some 210 yards by 155 yards, and the extant length of wall is only some 370 yards.

Such buildings as remain of the Mycenean city were placed not far from the outer circuit of the walls; they had massive foundations analogous to those of the main walls, but little can be made out as to their character. No doubt other buildings occupied the middle of the plateau, but they were levelled away by subsequent settlements.

The seventh and eighth settlements are those of the historical Greek epoch and they are now represented by unimportant remains of buildings near the edge of the Mycenean city. They may be supposed to have been occupied by a population largely dependent on the succession of visitors like Xerxes and Alexander, brought to the site by its literary interest or by their own vanity.

Nothing remains of the Greek settlements in the middle of the area, which was levelled in Roman times to receive (ninthly) a temple of Athene and other buildings which were prompted not only by Roman interest in Homer but also by Roman pride in the home of their fabled ancestor Aeneas.

The materials of the ninth city were gradually scattered during the succeeding ages in neighbouring churches and villages, and rubbish concealed the surface of the Roman city. A generation ago the site was forgotten, its story was transferred elsewhere, and a whole succession of civilizations, long before Homer and long after him, lay indistinguishable beneath the ploughed surface of an inconspicuous mound in the Trojan plain.

**ILION'S CROWN OF TOWERS ON THE EAST**

At another point on the eastern wall (marked A), a little farther south than the great north-east tower in page 327, may be traced the side walls (B and C) of a projecting tower; at D and E are superstructures built to replace earlier ones of brick The house wall at F and the massive foundation at H both belong to later layers, the seventh and the ninth respectively. The gate leading through the parapet on to the terrace in front of it and so to the tower is easily visible.
From Dörpfeld's "Troja und Ilion"

MENKAURA AND HIS GUARDIAN GODDESSES

The mortuary temple at Gizeh of Menkaura, the Mycerinus of Herodotus, was adorned with several groups of a slate-like green stone. In the one shown here the pharaoh wears the crown of Upper Egypt and is protected by Hathor (left) and the tutelary deity of the Cynopolitan nome or province; other nome-goddesses appear in the other triads.

Boston Museum of Fine Arts

330

## ANCIENT EGYPT'S ARTIST-CRAFTSMANSHIP IN CARVING & CERAMICS—

1. Inlaid coffer, combining maximum of strength with minimum of material; frieze of blue glazed faience tiles with hieroglyphs symbolic of life, power, and stability in gilded low relief.   3. Coffer with inlays of blue faience, white and red ivory, dark ebony and gleaming gold.   8. Carved chair, given to her grandfather, Iuaa, by Amenhotep's daughter, Setamen, fixed by mortice and tenon joints, pegged; decoration on back in gesso and gilt, with frieze of lotus flowers and buds; seat of plaited string.   14. Another chair of state; on each side figure of gazelle and triple life-

*Specially coloured for " Wonders of the Past "*

—EXEMPLIFIED BY SPECIMENS FOUND IN THE TOMB OF IUAA & TUAA

blem.  9. Chariot of Iuaa, in carved wood and leather mesh-work.  2. Painted vases on wooden stands, with symbolical heads on lids.
7. Examples of vases in wood and terra-cotta painted to represent alabaster, glass, black and white diorite, and red breccia.  10. Amulet of
e glaze.  11. Scarab of blue glass and green felspar.  12. Ornamental lid of dummy vase.  13. Kohl (cosmetic) tube of faience with
pper of papyrus pith.  All found in the tomb of Iuaa and Tuaa, whose daughter, Tiyi, in romantic circumstances, became queen of Amenhotep III.

## Ancient Arts and Crafts. III.

# The Exquisite Artistry of Ancient Egypt

## By Donald A. Mackenzie

Author of "Egyptian Myth and Legend." etc.

THE abundance of the exquisite furnishings in the Tutankhamen tomb emphasise the luxurious mode of life that obtained in ancient Egypt during its brilliant Empire period. Not only had the Pharaoh and his courtiers great wealth at their disposal, but were able to employ scores of accomplished artists and designers, and hundreds of highly-skilled and painstaking craftsmen whose devotion to their work and their joy in the efficient performance of it are manifested in these wonderful examples that have been preserved for us for over thirty centuries. Even although no other relics of ancient Egyptian civilization had been discovered, these in themselves are sufficient to indicate that its arts and crafts had a long history, stretching back for many centuries, and that the supreme degree of excellency achieved was cultivated after long and gradual efforts had been made to realize those high and exemplary ideals which the industrious and enthusiastic workers had set before themselves.

Another remarkable feature of the finds is the note of modernity which they strike. The beautiful and highly-decorated furniture was used by a people whose habit of life bore many points of resemblance to our own. These ancient Egyptian aristocrats, for instance, sat in chairs just like modern Europeans. At meals they were waited upon by male and female servants, who brought them the various dishes in order and distributed finger-bowls and flowers. In this respect they differed not only from most Orientals, who squatted on carpets, but even the ancient Romans, who during meals reclined on couches. The Egyptian menu, withal, was as long and varied in character as that of any modern banquet. Even during the Pyramid Age, about two thousand years earlier than that of Tutankhamen, there was abundance at the elaborate meals provided in the houses of the great. A tomb inscription, translated by Breasted, gives an example of an Old Kingdom aristocrat's menu, which includes " ten different kinds of meat, five kinds of poultry, sixteen kinds of bread and cakes, six kinds of wine, four kinds of beer, eleven kinds of fruit, besides all sorts of sweets and many other things."

Another interesting reference to Egyptian customs at meals is found in the Biblical story of Joseph. When that distinguished Hebrew, who had evidently been completely Egyptianised, provided entertainment for his brethren, " they sat before him, the firstborn according to his birthright, and the youngest according to his youth ; and the men marvelled one at another." Apparently they were not accustomed to so much formality. Joseph himself sat apart among the Egyptians, " because the Egyptians might not eat bread with the Hebrews, for that is an abomination unto the Egyptians " (Genesis xliii. ; 32, 33).

There was a form of the caste system in ancient Egypt. It had grown up during the long years of its history

**THE KEEN-EYED SCRIBE**

Reproduced from a coloured statuette found by Mariette in a tomb of the Serapium, this fine figure of a scribe dates back to the fifth or sixth dynasty (c. 2700-2550 B.C. and 2550-2350 B.C.) and the face and form are full of character. The sculptor gives us a complete character study of his sitter, whose attention is riveted upon the subject he is about to record upon the papyrus, while he sits in the immemorial pose of the East.

Louvre, Paris

prior to the time of Tutankhamen. The great lords would not eat with foreigners, nor with their own countrymen who were of lower rank than themselves. Withal, in each social circle, respect was shown to age ; the elders were reverenced. At court functions there were positions of honour and " seats of the mighty," the greatest seat, of course, being that of the Pharaoh, a seat which, by its design and ornamentation, emphasised his pre-eminence among his subjects. That this distinctive custom did not always prevail in ancient Egypt is suggested by a recent study by Dr. Alan Gardiner of an archaic sculptured stone belonging to one of the early dynasties. On it an official is shown " seated upon a throne such as is later reserved almost exclusively to the Pharaoh and the gods." Dr. Gardiner notes in this connexion that " the ceremonial instruments of more recent date " were " objects of everyday use in an earlier age."

By Tutankhamen's time society had grown exceedingly complex, and rank was symbolised by the very furniture, as well as by the colours and designs of the clothing worn. The gorgeous throne found in the tomb could not be used by anyone except the Pharaoh ; the beds and couches were similarly reserved for him, and were consequently placed with his body in the tomb for his exclusive use in the Otherworld.

The use of furniture and the habit of sitting in chairs and stools in quite the modern manner was of great antiquity in Egypt, as has been indicated by the archaic example of a sculptured representation of a seated official which has been referred to. Even in pre-dynastic times, some three thousand years before Tutankhamen's age, the high-born lords and ladies had already made demands on the artistic artisans for comely seats, and for spoons of ivory which had beautifully carved handles depicting figures of animals.

During the early dynasties chairs and stools were manufactured from rare and costly materials in charming designs that take the eye at a glance.

**BRONZE VOTIVE BUCKET**
Examples of these are familiar in museums. They were suspended in tombs, and the decoration, as here, was usually concerned with representations of the gods. In this example there is a fine balance of design.
Turin

Some seats had legs of bulls and cows, which were cut in ivory. Even at that early period ebony was procured and worked with wondrous skill ; and, what is more remarkable still, beautifully inlaid with ivory in artistic designs. When we come to the Old Kingdom times, during which the great pyramids near Cairo were erected, the furnishings of the houses of the great are found to have been of a quite elaborate character. The inlaid ebony chests display a high degree of craftsmanship, while the ivory carving, even when minute, is of supreme excellence.

One of the most beautiful and highly-finished examples of work in ivory of this period is the small portrait of Khufu (Cheops)—one of the builders of the three great pyramids of Gizeh—which was found by Professor Flinders Petrie. Stools and chairs and beds of this age display most exquisite workmanship. Tables were not common ; food was placed instead in gold and alabaster vessels. Chairs were used at meals, but to a more limited extent than during the later Tutankhamen period, for in the tomb scenes the high-born ladies are often represented sitting on mats and carpets in the customary Oriental fashion which still obtains to a large extent, especially in Asia, in our own day.

The touch of artistry and the love of display were not, however, absent in these far-off Egyptian times, which were almost as old to Tutankhamen as his times are to us. Rich carpets and mats and luxurious cushions were provided by highly-skilled artisans. Soft leather was greatly favoured, and not only artistically cut into beautiful designs and elaborately ornamented, but also dyed in most brilliant colours. Stools and chairs had comfortable and beautiful leather seats, and leather was likewise used for beds and for highly-decorated canopies. The royal linens were as fine almost as silk, and were embroidered and coloured according to the fashions of the age, and especially to symbolise the rank of the wearer, for there were royal and aristocratic colours and blends of colours then as in later times.

In the luxurious Empire Age of Tutankhamen the possession and use of furniture became much more prevalent than in earlier times. Indeed, it seems that the aristocrats considered it necessary to sit in chairs and recline on couches so as to emphasise their rank in society. As they sat at meals, the musicians squatted on the floor. The poorer classes were generally represented in tomb pictures and sculpturings sitting or kneeling on the ground or on mats; some have their legs drawn up in front, while others favour the fashion usually adopted by modern tailors on their benches, and

HIGHLY-FINISHED WALL SCULPTURE IN THE TEMPLE OF SETI I. AT ABYDOS

This mural carving is indicative of the high standard of workmanship attained by the craftsmen of the Egypt of 1300 B.C. The king is offering to the god Sekhmet incense in a long-arm censer, while he pours a libation into a bowl over which a bunch of beautifully-carved lotus flowers is seen. Note the ripple of the water as it flows. The god is represented with a falcon head, and is understood to be promising bravery and strength to the king in return for his oblations.

Photo from W. M. Flinders Petrie

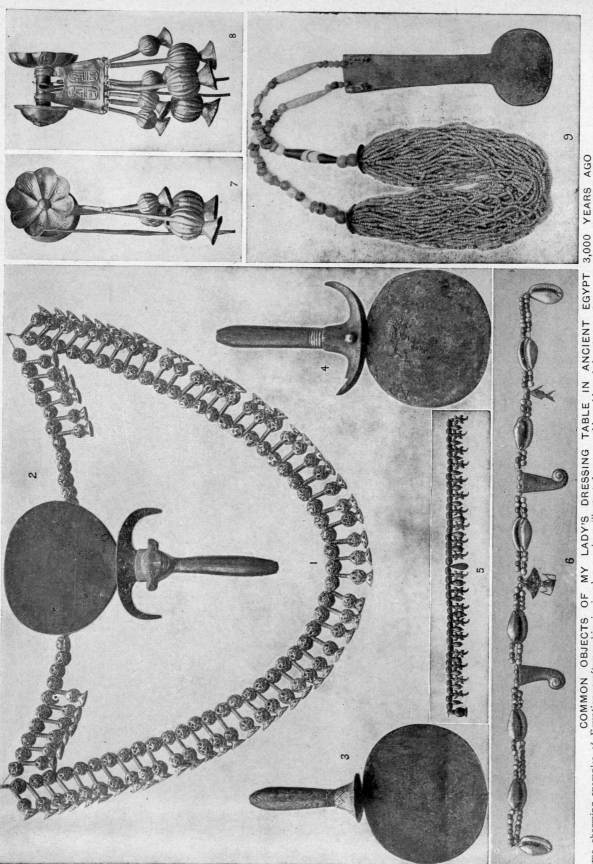

COMMON OBJECTS OF MY LADY'S DRESSING TABLE IN ANCIENT EGYPT 3,000 YEARS AGO

Some charming examples of Egyptian craftsmanship in jewelry are here illustrated. 1. a gold necklace belonging to Queen Tausert, wife of Setnekht; 2. bronze mirror, with handle representing the goddess Hathor; 3. and 4. bronze mirrors with the lotus motif in the handle; 5. necklace of gold and cornelian beads with drops in shape of lizards and flowers and lapis lazuli pendant; 6. necklace of gold, cornelian, lapis lazuli, and felspar beads, some in shape of locks of hair, fish, and cowrie shells, with inlaid pendant; 7. and 8. charmingly shaped jewelry of Queen Tausert found in a small pit in the Valley of the Kings; 9. necklace of glass beads and glazed pottery, with bunch of strings containing numerous small beads and a bronze "menat" or counterpoise. The bunch of small beads went across the chest, while the large beads lay over the shoulders and back, the menat acting as a counter-weight

Photos chiefly from exhibits in the Museum of Egyptian Antiquities. Cairo

by Indian Brahmans when engaged in solitary and silent meditation. Among all classes kneeling was adopted as a position of respect in the presence of a superior or of a deity. The priests kneeled and prostrated themselves in the temples.

The beds and couches of the great, apparently like their chairs, symbolised, as has been stated, their high position in society. Common people slept on their ground mats; the middle classes favoured wicker bedsteads, as did the aristocrats of earlier times, using wooden head-rests of elegant design. Some of the palace couches appear to have been constructed to symbolise by their very loftiness the elevated positions of those for whom they were reserved. In the twentieth-dynasty tomb of Rameses III. (1198-1167 B.C.) an exceedingly high royal couch is depicted, and beside it are steps

coffers used for storing clothing and jewelry were supreme works of art, as may be seen from the illustration in colour of a similar box in page 329.

Amidst the splendour of palace luxury, as in the humblest homes, the children, who have been the same in all ages, amused themselves by imitating their elders. They had their toys and their games; the girls were little mothers and the boys little hunters and soldiers and venders of wares. When the bodies of children were mummified, their parents deposited beside them in the tombs the small vases and bowls and other toys with which they amused themselves during life and were supposed to require in the Otherworld. Little carved and painted dolls have been found associated with the tiny mummies. Some are rudely shaped; others are of quite elaborate

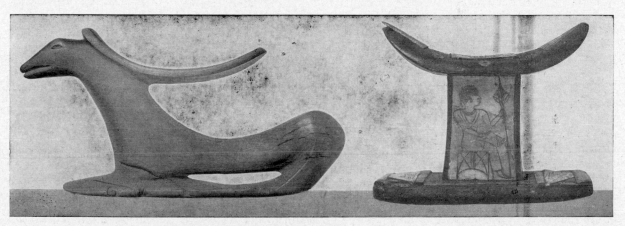

THE HEAD-RESTS USED BY ANCIENT EGYPTIANS GAVE WIDE PLAY FOR FANCY

Although European and American notions of nocturnal comfort may differ from those of the Egyptians, whose pillows were fashioned of wood, as here illustrated, these head-rests were much better adapted for a hot climate than the familiar pillow. The instinct of the Egyptians for decorative ornament is well seen in these examples, the first a happy adaptation of the outline of a hare with ears extended, the second made of light-coloured wood, with ebony inlay and ivory plaques and rosettes. In both, but especially that on the left, is evidence of genuine craftsman's delight. Such head-rests are commonly used among the native races of Africa and are known familiarly by the name of " Kaffirs' pillows."

Courtesy of the British Museum

which were apparently used for climbing into it with appropriate dignity. The cow, lioness, and the so-called " typhonic " (possibly hippopotamus) couches in the Tutankhamen tomb (see the illustration at the foot of page 42) are of this type and resemble the lofty couch of much later date favoured by an Assyrian monarch on a Nineveh marble slab in the British Museum.

Tables were freely used during the Tutankhamen period. Those favoured at banquets, from which food was served, were generally round, and had a single central support, which was sometimes carved in human shape, the figure of a foreign captive being specially favoured. Square and oblong tables had three or else four legs, and were constructed not only of wood but of stone and metal; the surfaces were invariably painted or inlaid with religious symbols and texts. The chests and

character, with hair, strings of diminutive beads, and gaudy attire. Occasionally the dolls have movable arms and legs.

There were, even in these far-off days, mechanical toys, such as workers baking bread or washing clothes; the limbs were attached by pins, and could be set in motion by pulling a cord, just like the modern " jumping jacks." Grotesque monsters with mouths that could be made to gape and close with a snap were also popular. The little balls used in games were likewise placed in the tombs. Evidently there were artisans who employed themselves making toys in ancient Egypt as in modern Europe, and no doubt the custom prevailed of making presents of these in connexion with such occasions as festivals.

But it was not only in toy-making that the ancient artists and craftsmen gave way to flights of fancy and humour. On flakes of limestone (called *ostraca*) and on potsherds, which have been recovered from old rubbish heaps, and are preserved in the museums, the students made trial sketches, while accomplished artists amused themselves by making comic and satirical drawings. One of the latter character shows a fox attired as a priest engaged in performing a temple ceremony, another a mouse driving a chariot and offering a lift to a cat, a third a musician blowing a pipe and inflating himself out of shape, a fourth a little Jew solemnly driving a harnessed monkey, a fifth a Pharaoh and his wife waging war by shooting arrows against one another, as if to suggest that there were occasionally lively domestic conflicts in the royal palace.

In some of these sketches the draughtsmanship is of the highest order. But it was in the solemn tomb paintings, illustrating scenes of life that were to be repeated in the Otherworld, that the energies of the artists were officially directed. These pictures are invariably of a high

**TWO FINE EXAMPLES OF PORTRAIT STATUARY**
Neither name nor circumstance of these two ladies, probably princesses, is recorded, but the exquisite workmanship of their statues confers a sort of immortality on them. The one holding a bunch of flowers is done in limestone, of 18th Dynasty date; the other, 19th Dynasty, is of creamy alabaster.
British and Florence Archæological Museums

order of merit and afford abundant evidence of the exacting training received in the temple schools of art and the wonderful skill with which life-like impressions were conveyed with anatomical exactness, a fine sense of proportion, and an appreciation of the rhythmic flow of free and graceful outline. In the paintings there is a fresh and frank appreciation of pure and vivid colours.

The jeweller's art, like that of the painter's, was of great antiquity. Tomb pictures of the Old Kingdom period show the artisans at work, weighing precious metals, smelting them with the aid of blow-pipes, casting ornaments, and hammering and soldering them. Bracelets, as old as the first dynasty, have been found by Petrie at Abydos on the desiccated arm of a queen, which had been wrenched from the body by tomb-robbers and hidden in a crevice and forgotten. These reveal wonderful workmanship, with ornaments of gold, turquoise, and amethyst artistically blended. Finger rings and flint knives with handles of embossed gold, date back to the

**CASTS FROM AN EGYPTIAN SCULPTOR'S ATELIER**
Among the folk who crowded into Akhnaton's capital city of Akhetaton (Tell-el-Amarna) was a sculptor, one Thothmes, who seems to have filled his studio with plaster casts, taken from both the living and the dead. Perhaps he had in mind the perpetuation of his subjects' features in more permanent form, or possibly he intended the casts to serve as guides for portrait statuary. Whatever the motive that inspired their preparation, these masks are valuable because they show us Egyptians as they really were, whereas most Egyptian sculpture is stylised. Though mainly of Egyptian nobles, some of the casts reveal definitely European features, e.g. the lady, shown full-face and profile in the centre of the illustration above.
British Museum

pre-dynastic age. Beautiful gold chains are as old as the Pyramid period.

By the time of the Middle Kingdom, some five centuries before Tutankhamen's age, the royal ladies of Egypt wore exquisite gold diadems with inlaid gems that have never been surpassed for their arresting delicacy and charm. Two examples of these, found at Dahshur, are preserved in the Cairo Museum. One is of minute and profuse floral design, and is strengthened by shapely Maltese crosses; the other is of more symbolic character, but no less imposing and finely wrought.

NEFERTITI THE LOVELY
The same Thothmes who produced the casts reproduced in the opposite page executed this brilliant essay in feminine portraiture—of Nefertiti, the beautiful queen of the heretic pharaoh Akhnaton.
Berlin Museum

To the same period belong a butterfly of granulated work, suspended to a chain and strong pectorals (breast ornaments), engraved in openwork in gold. Of more elaborate, but rarely of more chaste and graceful character, is the jewelry of the Tutankhamen Age of Empire.

The aesthetic spirit was constantly and successfully cultivated by a religious spirit of devotion to art. In an Old Kingdom tomb scene two craftsmen are employed drilling out very shapely stone vessels with patience and skill. Their feelings

A STUDY IN SOLID DIGNITY
Found in his tomb at Sakkara, the Fifth Dynasty wooden statue of Ka-aper so impressed the native workmen with its lifelike effect of burly authority that they christened it the Sheikh-el-Beled, from a resemblance to a village headman.
The staff and part of the legs have been restored.
Cairo Museum

are rendered articulate by the hieroglyphic texts carved in front of them, for one of them says : " This is a most beautiful vessel " ; and the other answers : " Indeed it is." Evidently the craftsmen found pleasure in their work and aspired to excel.

During the period of transition and change which preceded the reign of Tutankhamen, a distinctive note of naturalism crept into the art products of all varieties. It had already been manifested in the reign of Amenhotep the Magnificent, the father of the " heretic " Akhnaton and the grandfather of Tutankhamen's queen. Two beautiful inlaid coffers found in the tombs of Amenhotep's father-in-law and mother-in-law, and illustrated in colour in page 328 and 329, are notable examples of the new art movement. Both are beautifully shaped, carved, and inlaid. One has a frieze of blue glazed faience tiles, with the signs—" ankh " (life), sceptre (power), and Osirian " dad " (stability) — in gilded low relief. Royal symbols, figures of the king and royal inscriptions, entered into the scheme of the design, which is a perfect unity of symbolism and beauty. The form and workmanship of the coffer is as satisfying to the modern artistic eye as it was to the ancient people to whom it had a religious as well as an aesthetic appeal. In the other coffer the inlays are not only of blue faience, but of white and red ivory, dark ebony, and gleaming gold. The prominence given to the colour blue—that deep rich " Egyptian blue " so greatly admired in our own day—was due to the fact that it was the sacred colour of the god Ammon of Thebes. But its effective use in the scheme of decoration and in association with other colours was wholly due to the promptings of a cultivated aesthetic sense.

Akhnaton appears to have fostered the spirit of naturalism which characterised the art movement

SUPERB EXAMPLE OF PORTRAIT MODELLING
This obsidian head of a Twelfth Dynasty king is one of the sculptor's triumphs for all time. Yet compare its dry, harsh, forceful lines with the gentler intimacy of Old Kingdom work ; the artist who carved it was a genius, but not a lovable genius. Amenemhet III, the pharaoh who reclaimed a large part of Lake Moeris and was among the last of the pyramid-builders, was most probably the original.
Courtesy of Egypt Exploration Society

of his age. In fragments of vividly coloured tiles and in the decoration of furniture the sudden release from immemorial formalism is emphasised to a marked degree. The designers no longer adhered to conventional methods of presenting natural objects, nor did they confine their attention mainly to those which were regarded as religious symbols. They drew with their eyes fixed upon the objects and selected those which appealed to their sense of the beautiful, or those that lent themselves to purely aesthetic use.

The duck-head supports of the folding stool found in the Tutankhamen tomb (illustrated in page 47) are an excellent example of the influence exercised by this new art movement. These ducks have no symbolic significance in themselves. They are purely and simply art objects which attracted the designers and made aesthetic appeal to them. The same spirit is evinced in a fuller and more vivid manner in a fragment of painted pavement found by Petrie amidst the ruins of the palace of Akhnaton at Tell-el-Amarna. Spirited bulls, romping in the marshes, disturb the birds, which take sudden flight into the air, and are depicted with the grace and animation of nature. The colour sense of the artists was richly cultivated, and they revelled in new shades of colour, no longer confining themselves alone to the glaring reds and blues and greens of their predecessors, but introducing those exquisite shades of violet and purple-blues which are seen on the hills of Egypt under certain atmospheric conditions, and the different shades of reds, russet browns, and yellows they seem to have caught from the desert sands and the ridges of limestone and granite in the Nile valley. The sculpture work was profoundly influenced also, as is shown by the examples found at Tell-el-Amarna in 1912 and now in Berlin.

## BEAUTY DESTINED FOR THE DARKNESS OF THE TOMB

This fragment of the statue of a high-born lady illustrates one of the most curious of the funerary practices of the ancient Egyptians. In order to guard against the possible corruption of the mummy and the consequential extinction of the soul, they caused exact likenesses to the deceased to be made, and then by magic ceremonies " brought them to life." In this way the " ka " or double of the dead was furnished with a duplicate body, by residing in which it could enjoy the funerary offerings and also have its existence perpetuated indefinitely in the land of the shades. Dating from the fourth dynasty, the golden age of Egyptian art, the workmanship of this bust is of superlative excellence.

*From a statue in the collection of the late Earl of Carnarvon, specially coloured for " Wonders of the Past "*

The studies of Nefertiti, Akhnaton's queen, one of which is reproduced in page 339 are not surpassed even by the finest products of the Greek age. Indeed, they reveal an elegance and a degree of refinement which contrast sharply with the masculine strength and vigour of Greek sculpturing. The Egyptian lady is more delicately sensitive and feminine than any female depicted by the Greek masters, whose athletic and full-blooded goddesses belonged to an order of women quite different from those gentle aristocrats of the Tutankhamen age.

AN UNKNOWN LADY FROM SAKKARA

As an example of early sculpture in the round, this figure, with its fine free curves, could not well be excelled. Of the same period as the relief of Hesi-ra, also given in this page, she was once known as the wife of the famous Sheikh-el-Beled (illustrated in page 339)

Museum of Egyptian Antiquities, Cairo

HIGH OFFICIAL OF THE PYRAMID AGE

Note the firm modelling of the mouth and jaw in this fourth-dynasty wooden panel of Hesi-ra. Although side-face, the eye is given in full view; but this is an archaic feature running through Egyptian reliefs from the earliest to the latest periods.

Museum of Egyptian Antiquities, Cairo

Here again Egyptian art and religious ideas combine, for it was a religious necessity to the Egyptians to produce "living images" of those they portrayed in stone. The influence of the new art movement, however, was directed towards a more complete realization of nature's own subtle and refined modelling.

The Tutankhamen tomb relics reveal a tendency to revert to immemorial formalism and to overload the designs with religious symbols. But the spirit of exulting freedom remains, and even runs riot in gorgeous and intricate decorative effects,

as shown by a splendid casket on which Tutankhamen is depicted as two human-headed lions in heraldic opposition, wearing the horns and plumes of the god Ammon and trampling his enemies under his royal feet. The stiff and frozen formalism of the symbolism is relieved, however, by

EIGHTEENTH DYNASTY CUTLERY

Chased with hieroglyphics, among which appears the name of Thothmes III., these knives are little different from those in use to-day.

Museum of Egyptian Antiquities, Cairo

products of this character **from** China or Japan. Another **example** of exquisite craftsmanship **is a** **gold** mounted stool **of ebony** and ivory (see page 47). An armless chair of great beauty, with human and other figures cut out on the back which are meant to symbolise the idea of eternal life, is worthy of special mention.

But no piece of furniture from

**GRANDEUR AND VITALITY: EGYPT'S NOBLEST WORK**

Khafra was a fourth-dynasty king, the builder of the second pyramid, and better known by the name given him by Herodotus, Chephren. His diorite statue brings forcibly home to us the unsurpassed freedom and vigour of this period of Egyptian art—in the features, calm ; in the pose, majesty ; and in the body, the beauty of physical health.

**Museum of Egyptian Antiquities, Cairo**

**STATUE OF RANEFER**

One of the first excellences of fourth-dynasty art is the absence of conventionality : but art can lack this and yet be inaccurate. That this fault, too, was avoided, witness the statue of Ranefer.

**Museum of Egyptian Antiquities, Cairo**

the graceful and vigorous modelling of the lion bodies, the generous curves of the tails, and the decorative arrangement of the vultures' wings, while the elaborate scheme of painted decoration forming the borders imparts a dazzling brilliance to the entire scheme. The whole casket is adorned with a minuteness of detail and elaborate finish and variety, which excel the best art

**EGYPTIAN GIRL GYMNAST**
The bold curve of the drawing on this
ostrakon surely gives the lie to those who
speak of the uniform conventionality of
Egyptian art. It dates from about the
nineteenth dynasty.
Museum, Turin

The Egyptians of the Empire period excelled
not only in elaborateness of design, but in the
beauty achieved by simplicity of treatment in
both form and colour. The king's clothes-box is of
beautiful proportion and notable for its black and
white design, with soft brown woodwork in its
supports. Another clothes-box, which contained
clothing for both the king and the queen, has a
curved lid, and is similarly in black and white.
Of delicate shape and finish is a white, fretted
tabouret, while an ebony stool with ivory inlays
of daisy designs is at once gracefully and
exquisitely wrought. Everything the artistic
workmen of Tutankhamen's time touched they
made beautiful. So small and insignificant an

the Tutankhamen tomb is more
wonderful than the throne, which
in itself breathes an air of stead-
fastness, dignity, and aggressive
power. It is shown clearly in
the photograph in page 45. The
arms run from two uraei serpent
symbols of the Pharaoh, each
wearing the "double crown"
of the "Two Lands" (Upper
and Lower Egypt). The legs are
of lion shape, and in front they are
surmounted by lions' heads. On
the chair back, which has a com
fortable slope, are beautiful and
symbolic decorations, while the
arms are exquisitely carved and
otherwise adorned. This is the
first example that has ever come
to light of a throne of an Egyptian
emperor. Its strength and loveliness
reveal not only the splendour of
its age, but the supreme degree
of excellence reached by designers
and craftsmen, who not only
imparted beauty but eloquence
to their work, so that they leave
even a modern admirer in no
doubt as to what they meant,
although they wrought in such
hard material as ebony and ivory.
Among the furniture of all ages
the Tutankhamen throne is of
outstanding merit and charm.

**PORTRAIT STATUARY UNEXCELLED FOR CENTURIES**
In the fourth dynasty art reached a degree of excellence not seen again for many
generations in Egypt. This exquisitely-modelled statue of the Lady Nefert, a
princess of the blood royal, is in a remarkable state of preservation, and beneath
its close-fitting robe, which opens at the neck, the body seems instinct with
warmth and life. The dignified face is surrounded by a ponderous wig which
shows the natural hair on the forehead and is confined by a richly ornamented
bandeau. The statue was found in a ruined mastaba-tomb at Medun, near the
pyramid of king Sneferu
Museum of Egyptian Antiquities, Cairo

object as a buckle for the sandal of the Pharaoh was transformed into a work of arresting and luxurious art, with floral designs in gold, depicted with minute care and instinct with animation and grace. The jewelry and other examples of the goldsmith's art are on a similarly high level.

But no art relics in the tomb are of more surpassing excellence than the symbolic vases cut out of solid alabaster. The wonderful unguent vases especially are of elaborate design, flanked with lotus and papyrus motifs in open work, and in beautiful proportions and wonderfully free and graceful forms. One can only guess at the time employed by the exact and artistic craftsmen who produced these amazing works of art ; their work is flawless, and there are no indications of accidents due to thoughtlessness or carelessness. Not only do they bear eloquent testimony to the taste and inspiration of the designers, but to that loving care and tireless exertion displayed by the ancient craftsmen of unknown names who glorified their age by their exemplary industry and their whole-hearted devotion to the service of art.

The unguent vases symbolise the "Two Lands" (united Upper and Lower Egypt), and are adorned with the Egyptian symbols of longevity, as are so many of the fine products of ancient Chinese craftsmanship of semi-religious character. "A hundred thousand years" is the interpretation of these Egyptian longevity symbols, and apparently that was the period which the priestly supporters of Tut-ankhamen hoped he would enjoy as a result of the pious provision they had made for his welfare in that Otherworld, the wonderland of Paradise, beyond the sky, in association with the gods and goddesses who controlled

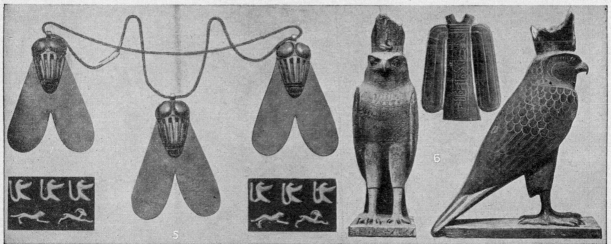

BEAUTIFUL JEWELRY THAT WAS MADE FOR THE USE OF THE DEAD

1 and 3. Two clasps for a necklace in the form of falcons' heads. 2. Inlaid pectoral of the priest Hatiai. 4. Funerary crown of gold threads and flowers with blue petals and carnelian centres, from the treasure of Princess Khnumuit. 5. Golden bees on a chain and collar-pieces, from the treasure of Queen Aah-hotep. 6. Two falcons and a girdle-buckle, specimens of gold and silver inlay-work. Though these jewels were usually made exclusively for the dead, and were consequently of more delicate structure, those of Queen Aah-hotep were worn by her in life. Circa eighteenth dynasty.

Museum of Egyptian Antiquities, Cairo

the destinies of ancient Egypt. The great figures of the cows, lionesses, and "typhonic" wonder-beasts supporting the couches display fine crafts-manship, but are grotesque in design.

These, with other more beautiful objects, breathe the spirit of devotion and loyalty with which the Pharaoh was as consistently regarded after death as he had been during life.

To understand Egyptian art it is necessary to bear in mind that it was, in essence, an expression of religious feeling.

For many centuries it was not only disciplined but hampered by the weight of the religious symbolism imposed upon it. But the very fact that it had its sacred aspect, and therefore its utility, was one outstanding reason why it was

345

sedulously promoted from generation to generation.

The temples were veritable nurseries of Egyptian art, and the skilled craftsmen in their workshops were trained with a degree of thoroughness and care which would not have been possible if it were not believed that they had genuine missions in life. The loving care and the passion for beauty revealed by the art objects of ancient Egypt were undoubtedly fostered by the traditional beliefs associated with the activities of generations of men who believed that they owed the artistic impulse to direct inspiration from the deities whom they worshipped and whom they served.

The reward of the worker was not estimated by money alone ; it was founded chiefly on the conviction that his skill assured for himself that immortality which, by producing religious objects, he helped the Pharaoh, his queen, and his great lords and ladies to obtain.

**FAIENCE SISTRUM     FINE SILVER REPOUSSÉ WORK**

Left: Twenty-sixth dynasty sistrum, a musical instrument connected with Isis-worship.
Right: Silver was known later than gold in Egypt, but the eighteenth and nineteenth
dynasty work in these bowls from Mendes leaves not a trace of the beating or polishing.

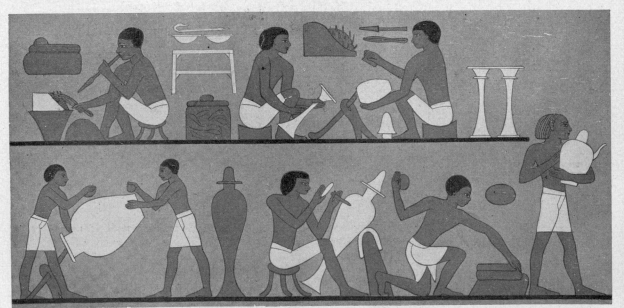

**MAKING GOLDEN VASES THAT RIVALLED THE WARES OF GREECE IN PURITY OF OUTLINE**

The inscription on this wall-painting from the necropolis at Thebes tells us that the goldsmiths are "making vases of gold on
silver." Perhaps the action of the man with a chisel in the lower register points to inlay-work ; although silver-gilt may be what
the artist intends. In any case, the free, accurate curves of the wares reflect no less credit on the painter than on the goldsmiths.

# Temples of the Gods. XIII.

# Sakkara: The World's Oldest Stone Buildings

## By Margaret Murray, D.Lit.

### Assistant Professor of Egyptology at University College, London

*SAKKARA, on the left bank of the Nile, fifteen miles south of Cairo, was the site chosen by the Pharaohs of the Old Kingdom for their necropolis, and its twenty pyramids and still more numerous tombs are of the very greatest importance. For some years the site was excavated by Mr. C. M. Firth on behalf of the Egyptian Department of Antiquities, and on his death the work was continued by M. Jean-Philippe Lauer, assisted by Mr. J. E. Quibell. To M. Lauer I am are indebted not only for information but for the photographs which accompany Dr. Murray's article.*—EDITOR.

THE Step-pyramid at Sakkara is known to be the oldest pyramid in Egypt. It stands in a great enclosure, nearly a mile long, surrounded by a recessed wall of stone, and on one side of the enclosure is a series of remarkable temples and colonnades of the same date as the pyramid. The whole group is the earliest example of stone building in the world. The mud-brick temples of early Babylonia have disintegrated, the wooden structures of early India have perished; only in Egypt the temples of enduring stone have lasted to our time and show what human labour can effect when directed by a master mind.

The remembrance of that master-mind, that great architect, survived for many thousand years, for throughout the long course of centuries his name was preserved till the exotic civilisation imposed by the Romans swept away the native traditions. His name in Egyptian was Imhotep, which the Greeks converted into Imouthes. The magnificent buildings he erected so impressed the minds of the people that he was hailed as a

KING ZOSER, WHO BUILT THE FIRST PYRAMID

The impassive majesty of the more than human Pharaoh is well expressed in this statue of king Zoser, Zeser or Tcheser (circa 2980 B.C.). One of the most ancient specimens of royal portraiture so far discovered, it is made of limestone, and bears traces indicating that it had once been coloured.

demi-god, and after his death his tomb-shrine was a place of pilgrimage. He held the highest positions that any man could hold, short of being the actual Pharaoh; he was a hereditary prince, first under the king, chief architect, and high-priest of Heliopolis. In later times he was said to have been also the chief physician, and was credited with such wonderful powers of healing that the Greeks equated him with their own god of medicine, Asklepios. As the high-priest of Heliopolis he must have been the supreme authority on astrology and astronomy, and would consequently carry great weight in the councils of the Pharaoh. It is possible that he has the credit for medical knowledge which properly belonged to his royal master, for that monarch was also very distinguished as a physician, and it is recorded that he was the first to build a house of hewn stones, and that he greatly patronised literature.

Though it is often said that the pyramids were burial places, this cannot be the case with the Step-pyramid, for king

WESTERN END OF THE STATELY COLONNADE OF THE OLDEST SURVIVING STONE BUILDINGS

The columns at Sakkara are mainly of two types—fasciculated, in imitation of a bundle of reeds, and fluted, which may imitate bundles of long, narrow reeds or thicker reeds cleft down the middle. The second type are seen in the " Little Temple," while above, in the rebuilt entrance to the colonnade, are splendid specimens of the fasciculated columns first erected nearly 5,000 years ago.

Zoser was buried in a great underground tomb at Bêt Khallâf near Abydos. The purpose of the pyramid is therefore a mystery. It was perhaps for the commemoration of the king as a divinity, a place where his godhead could be worshipped while his mortal body was buried elsewhere. For this reason the royal ladies, who were the daughters of the god, were buried in the precincts of the shrine of their divine father.

The Step-pyramid and its surrounding tombs and temples are, as has been mentioned above, the oldest surviving stone buildings in the world. The method of building is, therefore, peculiarly interesting. The want of symmetry shows that they were not constructed according to a plan, nor laid out as a whole, but were the results of circumstances. The enclosure is oblong, the short sides being on the north and south. The pyramid is also oblong, but the short sides are on the east and west. Built against the north side of the pyramid is the funerary temple, which is not in the axis of the pyramid, but lies more to the east. The temple is quite unsymmetrical in plan, and is entered by a series of complicated passages. Just outside the entrance and also built against the north side of the pyramid was the pit in which the splendid statue of the king was found. In the north-west corner of the enclosure was a double row of long, narrow chambers, to which reference will be made later. Near the

north-east corner of the pyramid and parallel with its east side were the great tombs of the two royal daughters.

But the chief glory of the whole group of buildings is the colonnaded entrance into the enclosure with the temple leading out of that colonnade. Ruined though those structures are, their magnificence and beauty are at once apparent. Two great towers flanked the entrance doorway on the outside, then a narrow passage led through the thickness of the wall, and here was carved the representation of an open door. Then the way opened into a wide corridor, where the walls were of white limestone, and twenty pairs of pillars down the centre supported the roof. The corridor terminates in a hall which runs at right angles to the corridor and has four pairs of pillars in the centre. Passing through a doorway in the axis of the corridor the great open space south of the pyramid is reached. The pillars in both the corridor and the hall are among the most surprising works that Egypt has produced, for they exhibit a style which is unknown in any other country till two thousand years later. They are carved to represent bundles of reeds, and are in no case free-standing, but form the ends of solid stone piers.

The temple of the Sed festival leads by a long passage from the corridor ; the direction of both passage and temple is to the north. On each

## THE "LITTLE TEMPLE," A SHRINE OF THE STEP-PYRAMID AT SAKKARA

This photograph shows the "Little Temple" which lies to the south-west of the great open space or court at Sakkara. As will be seen, two of the pillars that supported the temple roof have been repaired and re-erected in their original positions. They are about nineteen feet high, and of a graceful fluted design. The Step-pyramid in the background, built by Zoser, first of the pyramid builders, not as a tomb but as a memorial, is described and pictured in a later chapter on the Pyramids.

side of a central hall are arranged, without regard to symmetry, a number of little chapels or shrines. Between each chapel the wall is carved to imitate a post-and-rail fence of a type well known in early representations of shrines. There is nothing to indicate what gods were worshipped, or whether there was but one divinity, the Pharaoh himself. At the entrance to the temple and at the entrance to every chapel there is carved the representation of a door, either ajar or wide open. This indicated that the deity within was accessible at all times to all comers—his door was never shut against a suppliant. Representations of the ever-open door are found in all the temples within the enclosure-walls of King Zoser; they are the direct opposite of the sculptured doors in the temple of Seti at Abydos, doors which are represented as being shut fast, never to be opened.

This long, narrow temple was for the celebration of the Sed or Tail festival. When the dynastic kings first conquered Egypt their totem was the falcon, and that bird was the personal totem of the Pharaoh till the end of Egyptian history. But in order to be accepted as king by the indigenous people of Egypt, the conqueror had to marry their queen. The conquered people, however, were a cattle folk and their queen's totem was a

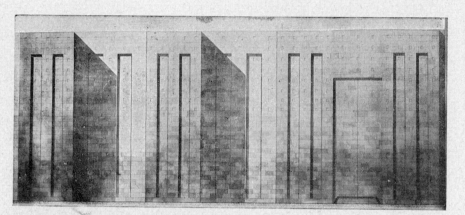

TRIUMPHS IN STONE OF EGYPT'S EARLIEST ARCHITECT THAT GIRDLED SAKKARA'S TEMPLES

Despite the lapse of nearly five thousand years, a considerable portion of the high and massive wall that enclosed the sacred buildings at Sakkara still survives, to tell us of the constructive skill of the ancient builders. Some forty feet in height, the wall was nearly a mile square. The photograph below shows it in its present state; above is a reconstruction drawing.

cow. As a falcon cannot mate with a cow, one or other of the contracting parties had to be transformed, and so the king became a bull. To indicate the change, he was invested with a bull's tail, though originally it was probably the custom to wrap him in the animal's hide. The Tail festival survived till the coming of the Romans, and all Pharaohs were represented in art as wearing a bull's tail. After marrying the queen and being invested with the tail, the Pharaoh was regarded as divine and as the giver of life and fertility to the whole land. The festival was then of the highest importance in the eyes of the king, the priests and the people. More than one Pharaoh erected a special building in which to celebrate it, but none ever equalled Zoser's temple in splendour.

In the north part of the enclosure are a number of galleries hewn out of the rock which underlies the desert where the Step-pyramid stands. In these were baskets of grain and fruit, which must have been placed there in the reign of Zoser, for the seals on the baskets bore the names of Zoser and his predecessor, king Kha-sekhemui. These were clearly store-rooms, but in the south-west part of the

**EXQUISITE DECORATIONS OF THE CHAMBERS OF THE DEAD**
Several of the underground funerary chambers hewn out of the rock were panelled with small glazed tiles, delicate blue in colour and patterned after a reed-mat. Narrow bands of white limestone represent the fastenings holding the reeds together.

enclosure are a series of subterranean galleries containing broken stone vases. Small chambers leading from the galleries were empty. Though no interments were found, it is probable that these chambers are the survival of the burial chambers of the royal attendants, who in early times were slaughtered at the tomb of their master. Other underground chambers were also made in the enclosure, and from one of these a well-built stair leads down into two rooms; the second of these was a long narrow chamber, whose walls were covered with small glazed tiles of an exquisite blue, representing hangings of green matwork. The tiles are inlaid in slabs of limestone, so cut as to represent the binding of the mats. Along one side of the chamber are three

door-like recesses; at the back of each recess was a stone panel sculptured in relief with a scene representing king Zoser performing a sacred dance. Though the relief is surprisingly low the forms are beautifully modelled, the muscles are clearly and delicately rendered, and the figures are instinct with life and vigour; the energy and grace of the dance is well expressed. These panels rank among the masterpieces of Egyptian art. Within the pyramid there are two chambers tiled with similar tiles, though without any sculptured decoration; but it is not known whether there is any connection between them and the underground room just described. One thing, however, is certain; nowhere among the royal pyramids and tombs of Egypt has a more beautiful scheme of decoration been evolved. From the blue-tiled underground room a rock-cut passage leads to a chamber which, though now empty, appears to have been intended for a burial-place. It may have been for the celebration of the mysteries of Osiris with the king as the god

The architecture and the construction of the Step-pyramid and the surrounding buildings are obviously experimental. Some of the experiments were copied by succeeding generations, others do not recur. The reeded columns of the corridor are unknown in that form in later Egypt, though another form of reed-pillar became typical of Egyptian architecture during many centuries. The fluted columns of the princesses' tombs are the earliest example of the type; it recurs in a feebler form in the eighteenth dynasty, but the most vigorous recurrence is in classical Greek architecture, thousands of years later.

In the actual construction, it is clear that the builders were not accustomed to their material, and that their efforts were tentative. They appear to have had little or no knowledge of the weight that stone can carry—hence the solid stone piers in the corridor to support the stone roof. There are no monolithic pillars or enormous blocks of stone, such as we usually associate with Egyptian architecture. The pillars, the walls, and even the pyramid itself, are constructed of small blocks which could be handled and lifted without difficulty by two or three men. The appliances necessary for moving heavy weights—such as rollers, levers, sledges and rafts—were not in existence owing to the scarcity of wood, and it was not until the need arose that large timber was imported from Syria. The style of building shows the technique of brickwork, and the pillars are essentially stone imitations of bundles of reeds. But the genius of Imhotep overcame the technical difficulties. He obtained an immediate and magnificent result, and introduced into the world a new art, the art of building in stone.

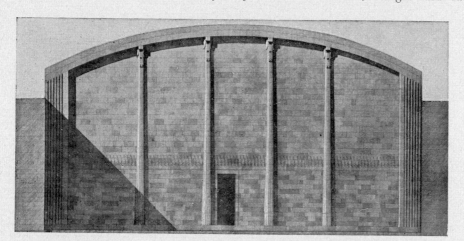

DORIC COLUMNS IN ANCIENT EGYPT THOUSANDS OF YEARS BEFORE THE GREEKS

Below is one of the temples or princesses' tombs which is being partly rebuilt. The columns are fluted and so closely resemble the columns of the Greeks that it is suggested that the Doric architects found in them their inspiration. They are certainly the earliest known examples of this type. Above we see a reconstruction of the temple-front.

## The Wonder Cities. VIII.

# Pompeii : As it Was and as it is To-day

### By George Sampson, M.A.

*T*HE *author of this study, well known as literary critic and editor of the classical writers, has had the advantage of appreciating, during a recent visit to Pompeii, the results of the newer methods of excavation there in progress, whereby the remains of the edifices are skilfully reconstructed on their original lines. We are fortunate in being able to illustrate the subject with a series of contrasting pictures giving photographic views of the existing scenes and conjectural restorations.—*EDITOR.

THE Bay of Naples is justly famed for its beauty. Nature has given the great sweep of coast, the rising verdant shores, the brilliant light, the sea and sky of incredible blue ; and man, placing in the midst the city of Naples mounting in terraces of white among the green up to the height of St. Elmo, has added a touch of civilized beauty to the spectacle. The bay is a deep crescent some twenty miles across, the northern horn being Cape Miseno, and the southern the mountainous peninsula of Sorrento, with Capri lying out to sea. Naples itself stands on an inner crescent that sweeps round from the wooded hill of Posilipo to the shapely mountain called Vesuvius.

This is the most striking object of the bay. To those accustomed to mountain forms it is too much like an imaginary mountain to be real. It is round, even, regular, and isolated, like a child's model of a mountain. It looks made, and, in fact, it was made ; for, in the strict sense, it is not a mountain, but a cinder heap. The whole district is volcanic, but it was the northern, not the southern horn of the bay, that gained notoriety for its subterranean activity. Here are Solfatara, the Phlegraean Fields, the cave of the Cumean Sibyl, and Avernus itself, through which Aeneas descended to the Underworld.

What the ancients noted chiefly about the Bay of Naples, however, was not its volcanic character, but its suitability for pleasure resorts. Baiae, at the Miseno end, was the most **famous of watering-places,**

and luxurious villas were scattered all round the shore. Virgil had a house on Posilipo, and his alleged tomb is shown there to this day. At the southern end, where now stand the suburbs and neighbours of Naples—Portici, Resina, Torre del Greco, Torre Annunziata, and Castellamare— stood Herculaneum, Pompeii, and Stabiae. From the sea's edge up the gradual slope of the slumbering volcano the rich soil produced an abundance of vegetables and grapes, and many small vessels passed in and out of the little harbour at the mouth of the navigable Sarnus, above which there had long been an ordered settlement.

Pompeii itself was built upon a prehistoric lava flow. Like most other places in southern Italy, it had passed under the influence of Greek culture, and Greeks, no doubt, had first established the commercial prosperity of the town. After the Samnite wars (343-290 B.C.) it became a dependence of Rome, and, like the proverbial happy

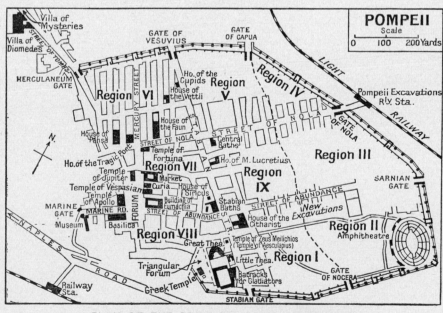

PLAN OF THE PRINCIPAL SITES OF POMPEII

353

THE HOUSE OF PANSA, A POMPEIAN RESIDENCE THAT OCCUPIED A WHOLE ISLAND SITE

Known as the House of Pansa, this building has been restored with great ingenuity in the form of a model, of which the above is a photograph kindly supplied by the Metropolitan Museum of Art, New York, U.S.A. Probably the largest of all the private houses that stood within the city of Pompeii, it occupied a site 319 feet long by 124 feet wide, which the Romans called an insula, and shops and residential apartments faced two of the four streets surrounding it. On the threshold was found a mosaic with the word "Salve" as greeting. The whole outward appearance is curiously modern, and its three-storeyed form a reminder that Roman domestic structures were not confined to houses of one level.

country, had no history. Two centuries of quiet prosperity ended with the struggles of the Social War (91-88 B.C.), in which Stabiae was destroyed, but Pompeii itself suffered little from these disturbances; and we continue to hear of it as a favourite resort of the wealthy Romans.

Cicero himself had a Pompeian villa; the hectic descriptions of Lytton must not delude us into a belief that Pompeii was an exceptionally spacious, luxurious, and perversely wicked city. It was just a normal, prosperous Campanian town, no worse— probably even better—than many a modern commercial city of the same magnitude. At least, Pompeii was not hypocritical; it did not hide away its sins and pretend that they did not exist. Like most Italian towns even of to-day, it was a close-packed, even a huddled, mass of narrow streets and crowded dwellings. The longest line that can be drawn within the walls, from the Herculaneum gate on the west to the Amphitheatre on the east, is less than a mile; the greatest breadth is barely half a mile.

The enclosing walls, pierced by eight portae, measured rather more than two miles. As usual, the population—variously estimated at from 20,000 to 30,000 — had overflowed the walls, and one of the most splendid of the known houses, the Villa of Diomedes, was in a suburb beyond the Herculaneum gate. Pompeii had no special glories of architecture, no vast temples like those at Paestum on the other side of the Sorrentine peninsula, no majestic monuments of Greek genius like those across the water in Sicily. Its exceptional fate naturally tempts us to imagine an exceptional city; but it is the dead and not the living Pompeii that should most amaze us.

The main central street, Stabian Street (anciently the Via Pompeiana) ran south-east to north-west from the direction of Stabiae towards Vesuvius. Two other streets, Nola Street and Abundance Street—the names are modern conveniences—cross this at right angles, dividing the road into three equal portions and the city into six; but east of Stabian Street and parallel with it, a line in the direction of a supposititious street has been drawn from the Capua Gate to the Nocera Gate, cutting the three portions on that side of Stabian Street into six.

The city is thus divided by archæologists into nine "Regions." Of these only three (VI, VII, VIII) have been thoroughly explored; the eastern half of the city has scarcely been touched, a great advantage, as the explorations here are being conducted by the reverent preservative methods of modern scientific archæology.

Pompeii is in some respects an up-to-date city, a model of town planning. The regular occurrence of the peristyled plot of ground within the houses makes it a "garden city," and the straight, geometrically arranged streets anticipate the design of the newest American townships. Almost the only curving street in Pompeii is one of the least respectable. The minor streets are many, and, to modern eyes, very narrow; but no narrower than the streets of old London, as the courts and alleys within the City area testify to-day. Mercury Street in Pompeii is scarcely narrower than the Chiaia in Naples or the Merceria in Venice.

PATHETIC SOUVENIR OF A FAR-OFF TRAGEDY

This is not the actual calcined body of a victim in the destruction of Pompeii, but one of many plaster casts made in the progress of the excavations from impressions left in the debris by bodies overwhelmed by the ashes, the bodies themselves having been resolved into dust. The museums of Naples and Pompeii exhibit a number of these, including several of domestic animals, in the positions where fate overtook them.

The Pompeian streets are all heavily paved (as Naples is) with grey lava slabs, some of them heavily scored by the wheels of vehicles. But vehicular traffic in Pompeii must have been very small—probably nothing but carts for goods. The city fathers of Pompeii did not set up a speed limit, they made speed impossible. Most of the streets could not admit vehicles at all, and those that did, being deep down from the side-walks, like water channels (as they were in wet weather), were "bridged" by large stepping-stones, highly obstructive to traffic.

At intervals by the roadside were fountains, deep square troughs of lava slabs filled by a jet spouting usually from an ornamental head. Not least of the many appealing touches in the dead city are the depressions on the edges of the troughs slowly worn by the resting hands of the passers-by as they bent over the tank, such as that shown in page 362, to drink from the jet.

Pompeii had the usual equipment of public places. Chief of these, of course, was the Forum, a great square bordered on three of its sides by a shaded colonnade, and fronted by handsome buildings for religious or social service. The forum

**WHERE FLOUR WAS GROUND FOR POMPEIAN BAKERIES**
Here is seen a miller's establishment as it exists to-day. The bobbin-like stone, hollowed cone-wise from bottom and top, when placed over the cone seen in the foreground of the photograph, was turned round by wooden levers inserted in receptacles at the waist of the mill, while the grain was poured in at the top and ground to flour in the lower part. Note the ovens in the background.
Photo by Donald McLeish

of a Romanised city, developing from the primitive market-place, became the heart of civic life. Italian life in all ages has naturally been lived more in the open air than ours, and the market-place or forum was the normal scene for any gathering of citizens. The civic rather than the commercial aspect of the place was emphasised, and the markets drew off to some extent, though the business of buying and selling, in the common outdoor Italian way, still went on.

One need only think of St. Mark's Square in the great days of Venice, or of Trafalgar Square, London, supposing it to be enclosed by such edifices as the County Hall, the Abbey, the Cathedral, the Law Courts, and the Exchanges, and to be filled with busy, chattering groups gathered round the bases of statues and garlanded columns, to envisage something like the forum of a Roman city. The Forum of Pompeii was a long rectangle over 500 feet long and more than 100 feet wide. Twenty-two statues, some equestrian, of civic and imperial magnates adorned the square. Steps and stone obstructions prevented the approach of vehicles and, when necessary, the whole space could be closed against pedestrians.

On the northern, uncolonnaded side, the Temple of Jupiter, reached by fifteen steps, projected into the square. At the north-east corner stood the Macellum, a fine provision market, characteristic of an age and people that did not think it necessary to divorce beauty from commerce. Next to this came the so-called Curia, probably a library, and the Temple of Vespasian. The next building, usually called the Building of Eumachia, was probably the wool exchange. At the south-east corner was the small Comitium or voting hall, and along the southern side what we should call the Guildhall, the seat of the municipality. The south-west corner was occupied by the Basilica, devoted to legal and mercantile business. Behind the Basilica stood the Temple of the Pompeian Venus, no goddess of lubricity, but a motherly person who, reverenced with her young son, anticipates a later object of Italian devotion. The Temple of Apollo occupied most of the western side of the square. Here, too, was the table of standard measures.

Away to the south-east, near the Stabian gate, is another " square " which, being an elongated, misshapen quadrilateral, is known as the Triangular Forum. On the south side of this once stood the oldest, and probably the finest, of all the Pompeian buildings, the Doric or Greek Temple,

ONE OF THE MOST CHARMING PIECES OF COLOURED MOSAIC LEFT IN ITS ORIGINAL POSITION

Although probably not the popular place of pleasure that tradition would have it, Pompeii contained many corners that were bright with colour from the effective use of mosaic and gratefully cool in the summer heat from the plash of fountains. The fountain here illustrated was probably the largest and finest of its kind in the city, the chief note of colour in the mosaic being blue, and it must have been an object of admiration and pride to the artistically minded Pompeians.

Photo by Donald McLeish

CORNER OF THE TEMPLE OF JUPITER, LOOKING TOWARDS THE STREET OF MERCURY

In the Forum of Pompeii were grouped the fine Temple of Apollo and the Basilica, or Law Courts, at the south-west corner, with the Temple of Jupiter occupying the north and the buildings of the Market and Eumachia on the east. In the reconstruction the lines of the ruined buildings as they are seen in the lower photograph have been very ingeniously followed, but it will be noticed that the archæologist in this case has not agreed with the one responsible for the complete restoration in the opposite page, in so far as the inscription above the architrave is concerned.

## IN THE FORUM OF POMPEII 1,900 YEARS AGO AND TO-DAY

The lower picture is a photograph of the Temple of Jupiter and its immediate surroundings as these have emerged from excavation, and the upper one is an imaginative reconstruction of the scene 1,900 years ago. A sacrifice is in progress at the altar, which stands in front of the temple portico, and the scene may be regarded as a not unfaithful impression of the public ceremonial at that distant date. The Latin inscription in the entablature over the graceful Corinthian columns of the front may be thus rendered into English : " To Caesar the divine, most excellent emperor, supreme pontiff."

**WHERE GLADIATORS STROVE TO THE DEATH TO MAKE A POMPEIAN HOLIDAY**

Even before Rome, Pompeii was a city given to the fearsome joy of gladiatorial contests, and the local enthusiasm for this brutal form of sport is recorded in many inscriptions still to be seen scratched upon the walls of the houses in the neighbourhood of the Amphitheatre, of which the photograph at foot of the page shows one of the entrances. The reconstruction drawing above animates the scene much as it must have been familiar to those who thronged the Amphitheatre in the days before the city was destroyed.

GENERAL VIEW OF THE AMPHITHEATRE WITH THE MASS OF VESUVIUS IN THE BACKGROUND

Excavation of the Amphitheatre was carried out long before present-day scientific methods of archæological research had been brought to the perfection admirably illustrated in recent work at Pompeii. The old excavators, in digging down from the surface, destroyed almost more than they discovered, and had the Amphitheatre been excavated by gradually clearing the surface of the ground, storing every piece of building material retrieved from the soil, and, when the ancient floor level had been reached, replacing every item in its original position, a still more impressive remnant of the ancient Amphitheatre would have been preserved.

sometimes called the Temple of Minerva, resembling the great temples at Paestum and Segesta, though much smaller than those mighty structures. This was one of the antiquities of Pompeii, for it was already a ruin when disaster fell upon the doomed city. Close at hand are the little Temple of Zeus Meilichios (sometimes called the Temple of Aesculapius), the Temple of Isis (the Egyptian goddess whose worship prepared the way for a mystic and ascetic form of religion that was to triumph over paganism), and the Palaestra where the Doryphoros in the Naples Museum was found.

But the most interesting spot near the Stabian gate is the great open-air theatre, with the smaller covered theatre adjacent. To the tired and dazzled sightseer there is no more delightful place in Pompeii. Here he may sit on one of the upper rows of seats (in his mind's eye he can fill the space with 5,000 spectators) and look across the orchestra and the gladiators' quarters to the great wooded hills beyond. The wise Englishman who has not forgotten to bring a thermos flask of tea can here in comfort review the ancient while he enjoys the modern. Pompeii, especially in summer, is a very thirsty place.

The Amphitheatre, large, but of no special importance, lies far off in the eastern corner of the city. One other set of public buildings deserves brief mention, the baths, of which the chief were the Forum Baths behind the Temple of Jupiter, the Central Baths at the corner of Nola and Stabian Streets, and the Stabian Baths at the corner of Stabian and Abundance Streets. As everyone knows, the bathing process of Roman times was extremely like that which we call a Turkish bath, and hardly needs description. In imperial Rome such late colossal erections as the Baths of Diocletian and the Baths of Caracalla were more like the Royal Automobile Club than the baths in Jermyn Street, London. In Pompeii the baths were just baths, very adequately equipped. Let it be observed that wealthy Pompeian citizens distinguished themselves by spending liberally upon public works; they did not get elected in order to close the baths or the theatres because they did not pay.

FINE BUILDING ERECTED BY A PRIESTESS IN THE STREET OF ABUNDANCE

According to an inscription over the door, this building was erected by Eumachia, a priestess, and may have been used as a wool-sellers' hall. Here we see it in its ruin, and as it may have been in actuality, fronting the Street of Abundance, so called as the headquarters of the jewelry merchants and markets of luxury. A prominent feature of the scene is the public drinking fountain. The visitor can see the stone worn away by those who rested their hands upon the fountain while they drank from its running water. Note the stepping-stone in the side street, so placed to save the pedestrian unnecessary fatigue.

THE HOUSE OF THE BALCONY AND A TYPICAL STREET SCENE OF ANCIENT POMPEII

As illustrating the difference between the old-fashioned method of roughly digging through the accumulated upper soil and chancing the result as the excavations proceeded, in contrast with the present-day system of sifting the mass and literally rebuilding the houses from the material so retrieved, the House of the Balcony here illustrated has been known for many years as the only one of that character, whereas the modern method has proved that most of the houses in Pompeii were so built.   This page gives a most plausible picture of what a Pompeian street was like.

WHERE LAW WAS ADMINISTERED IN THE COMMERCIAL PORT OF POMPEII

Only a few hundred yards from the ancient seaport of the city, which now stands well inland, and built upon the Via Marina at the south-west corner of the Forum, stood the Basilica, of which this photograph shows the state to-day. The restoration in the upper picture makes most effective use of the ruins, and seeks to illustrate chiefly that portion of the building which corresponded to the modern Law Courts, although other parts of it were devoted to commercial uses, the Pompeians, despite their reputation for luxury and voluptuousness, being really an essentially commercial people.

THE STABIAN BATHS, ONE OF THE POPULAR RESORTS OF ANCIENT POMPEII

The art of the archæologist encounters little difficulty in reconstructing the Stabian Baths, as will be seen from the above illustrations, the lower showing the condition of the building as it stands to-day at the corner of the Stabian Road and the Street of Abundance. The interior is extremely interesting, the pipes through which the water was led into them, and those that carried the hot water from room to room, being still in existence. The exterior was gay with coloured paintings, for which Pompeii was famous.

A SPLENDID PRIVATE RESIDENCE AS IT MAY HAVE BEEN BEFORE THE GREAT CATASTROPHE

The dwelling shown in the lower photograph as it stands in ruins to-day is one of the most notable in Pompeii, chiefly on account of the beauty and the interest of its numerous wall paintings. Situated in the north-west quarter of the city, it must have been the residence of one of the notabilities of Pompeii, for the beautiful architectural reconstruction based upon the existing ruins which we print in this page would show that it reached palatial proportions.

Baths, temples, and fora, however, can be found elsewhere. Pompeii is unique, not because of its extraordinary buildings, but because of its ordinary buildings. There are better palaces of Roman times to be found elsewhere, but there are no better houses and shops. It is as if a whole town had been carefully collated, filed, and put away for subsequent reference. Gibbon, who missed little, had no Pompeii to stimulate his marvellous creative imagination. What would he not have given to be able to stand in the House of the Vettii or the Villa of Diomedes! In the fragments of picaresque romance called the "Satyricon" of Petronius, itself contemporary with some of Pompeii's last days, we get interesting glimpses of various "interiors" somewhere in the same neighbourhood. Trimalchio, the freedman, a vulgar profiteer, gives a feast that enables us to envisage not only the kind of food and the manner of service, but the arrangement of the table and the disposition of the guests, who reclined in what seems an uneasy posture, three on a couch, leaning on cushions with the left arm, and feeding themselves with the fingers of the right hand. Three

of these three-seated couches arranged around the table formed the triclinum, a name presently applied to the whole dining-room, of which there were several in a large house.

"By the favour of Mercury," exclaims Trimalchio, maudlin with drink, " I have built me this house. It was a mere cottage, as you know, and now it is a temple. It has four dining-rooms, twenty bed-chambers, two noble porticoes, a store-room on the upper storey, a chamber in which I sleep myself, a sitting-room for this viper (his wife), a capital porter's lodge, and accommodation for a hundred guests." On reaching the house of Trimalchio, Encolpius is greatly alarmed, because the first thing he notices is a huge dog, with the legend "Cave, cave canem!" The dog, however, was merely painted on the walls, which were further adorned with scenes from Homer. On attempting to leave secretly, Encolpius and his companion fall into the water-pool, and have to be dragged out by the hall-keeper.

In reading Petronius we seem to be among the very buildings of Pompeii. Such a house as Trimalchio's would occupy a whole insula, that is,

**A WINE-BIBBERS' CORNER IN ANCIENT POMPEII**

Recent excavation in the Street of Abundance has brought to light this ruin of a wine shop with the earthen bottles in which the wines were stored still intact. These bottles were pointed at the end so that they could be placed into cavities in the earth or into circular holes in the masonry, thus ensuring the coolness of their contents. In this shop flasks and money tills were found.

CHARACTERISTIC EXAMPLE OF THE MANNER IN WHICH THE POMPEIANS DECORATED THE WALLS OF THEIR ROOMS

The particular style of decoration which has come to be known as Pompeian, from its having flourished in that city, and having been preserved in numerous examples among the ruins of the buildings, is admirably illustrated in this photograph of a room in the House of the Vettii. The artists, of Greek origin, who brought this style of mural decoration to perfection, had an extraordinary sense of distance, and were able to make a dull back wall and small room give the illusion of opening out through columned vistas into palatial apartments beyond. Highly coloured, but always with harmonious treatment, the walls of these Pompeian rooms must have been a constant source of pride to the citizens who owned them.

and facing the entrance, there was sometimes an ornamental figure, as in the House of the Faun, where was found the exquisite figure of the Dancing Faun (see page 373), familiar in countless reproductions. From this house came also the magnificent mosaic floor (now in Naples) depicting the Battle of the Issus.

Some houses had a double atrium, a few had none. From the atrium, right and left, opened smaller rooms—triclinia or dining-rooms, and the two alae (or wings) where the aristocratic owner kept the statues or masks of his ancestors and where the others probably kept clothes. Straight across the impluvium from the entrance was the semi-public tablinum, used as a dining or reception room. This completed what we may call the public apartments of a large private

it would be entirely detached, with streets along its four sides; but in the sides of the insula there might be shops, just as there are along the Piccadilly front of the Ritz Hotel, or along the arcade behind the Carlton. An entrance, or vestibule, led to the hall or atrium, with its walls marbled or frescoed, and the floor inlaid with mosaic. At the entrance of one house, the House of the Tragic Poet (Lytton's House of Glaucus), there is just such a dog and legend (though in mosaic) as alarmed Encolpius. The gorgeous atrium was really a development of the smoke-blackened primitive dwelling which had a hole in the roof to let in light and let out fumes. Incidentally it let in water, though this was not in the covenant. In the course of evolution the hole in the roof had become the compluvium, and the pool of water on the floor had become the impluvium, a square, ornamental pool, some eighteen inches or two feet deep, with its handsome marble edges. Before the impluvium.

TWO EXAMPLES OF POMPEIAN WALL PAINTINGS
Dating from the pre-Augustan period, these fine frescoes from the " Villa of Mysteries," near the House of Diomedes, depict the initiation of a woman into the Dionysiac cult. Below, the trembling neophyte is seen being encouraged by the priestess, and (right and above) in a state of exaltation performing a ritual dance.

THE LATEST METHODS OF EXCAVATION TO BE SEEN IN POMPEII

It will be noticed that in this photograph many of the houses are complete in walls and roof, and contrast curiously with the roofless and fragmentary ruins that occupy most of the excavated portion of the city. This is the result of the new method of carefully sifting all the material of each house, marking it, and rebuilding it on the spot. Pictorial "reconstructions," such as illustrate this article, are all very well, but the actual building reconstructed on its original site is an immense advance in archæology.

*Photo by Violet F. Nicholls*

house. Beyond this came the purely family residence. Here the most prominent feature was the peristylium, a garden-court like the small cloister of a monastery, pillared and pent-housed round the sides, and open in the middle. Here flowers grew, and a fountain played, or busts and statues formed a decorative scheme. A house in Region VII gave us the exquisite little Dionysus (wrongly called Narcissus) now at Naples, and a house beyond the Vesuvius Gate yielded the Ephebus.

From the peristylium opened the oecus—drawing-room or dining-room at will—and the exedra, still another saloon. Here, too, came the domestic offices, sometimes a kitchen garden, and a private entrance to the house. Some houses (like Trimalchio's) had a private equipment of baths. The upper storeys were less important, if we may judge from the unobtrusiveness of the stairs. They probably contained slaves' apartments, store-rooms, and so forth. The atrium, with its compluvium opening, of course, was not built over. A Pompeian house, comparatively window-less, was thus dark and cool. Like the modern Italian dwelling, it was built against heat, not against cold. As in other parts of southern Europe, the brazier, not the fireplace, was the means of heating in winter time.

It must not be supposed that there was only one kind of house in Pompeii, but it is a fact that they did tend towards uniformity of style. Architects distinguish several periods of construction. These we need not consider. In general, Pompeii is a "faced" town, its decorative front (of varying kinds) was laid upon a core of brick or rubble, just as marble facings are being laid to-day upon the brick interior of Westminster Cathedral. In most houses the inner walls are covered with fine stucco. The glassy surface of this lent itself to highly elaborate decoration, and here again we have well-marked periods, distinguished by Mau as the Incrustation Period, when the walls were made to imitate the colours of various marbles (example, House of Sallust), the Architectural Period, when the walls were painted with elaborate architectural mouldings to form the frames of painted figures (example, a house in Region V, Casa degli Epigrammi), the Ornate Period, when ornament was freely and fancifully used (example, House of Spurius Mesor, Region VII), and the Intricate Period, when the ornamentation became highly elaborate, and was full of tricks and surprises (example, House of the Vettii, illustrated in page 368).

The pictures painted on the walls vary from simple draped and decorated figures placed in the centre of large panels, to highly elaborate subject pieces ; the complicated Farnese Bull group of statuary at Naples, for instance, appears in the House of the Vettii as a wall painting. There are

370

many landscape pictures, many still-life pictures, and countless Cupids, these being apparently the gnomes and fairies of Pompeii. The House of the Vettii is full of Cupids gaily doing all sorts of things. Sometimes we find the successive incidents of a story all represented in one picture, a device that Titian used centuries later in his Bacchus and Ariadne, a favourite Pompeian subject.

The Pompeians were not afraid of colour. One room in the House of the Vettii has a bold scheme of panels in black and red which the most daring modern colourist might envy. Let it further be said that no more sanitary form of wall covering could be devised. Compared with the Pompeian glaze, modern wallpapers, canvases, and distempers are barbarous.

One of the most remarkable facts about the pictures at Pompeii is that they represent a kind of art that disappeared. Thirteen centuries were to elapse before Italy got back to the freedom of style and truth of representation buried with the walls of Pompeii. In a word, the pictures at Pompeii are modern ; the mosaics at Cefalú and Monreale are ancient.

The outdoor life of Pompeii, like that of modern Italian towns, was vivid and gay. The little open shops (closed at dusk by the same kind of shutters that were put up nightly in London until the roller-blind came in) made a narrow business street like an Eastern bazaar. The taverns had their voluble crowds clamorous for mixed or heated wines. Poorer people cooked at their little charcoal stoves, ate their meals, and performed their toilet operations without embarrassment out of doors, as you may see them do in Naples to-day.

The life of a working street in Pompeii was no doubt almost exactly like that of the Via Lavanaro, in Naples. Heavy stone mills ground the corn. Political sentiments and lampoons were scribbled on the walls, where some of them still remain—mural inscription is a modern as well as an ancient passion. Signs to avert the evil eye appeared over some of the houses, and almost every Neapolitan still wears one. The fountains ran with water, and the projecting balconies or the penthouse roofs of upper loggias gave welcome shade. Those who have tramped the hot basaltic streets of Pompeii under a summer sun think regretfully of the vanished upper storeys and the protection they offered.

So Pompeii ran its busy course, quarrelling with its neighbours, the Nocerines, and shrugging its shoulders at the occasional Campanian earthquake. It was prepared to pay a price for the fertility and beauty that surrounded it. On one side it saw the verdant hills towards Stabiae and the sea ; on the other, it beheld the shapely Vesuvius, not as now, with cloven top, but conical like Fuji,

FOUNTAINS ARE PLAYING AGAIN IN POMPEII AFTER NINETEEN CENTURIES OF DISUSE
Very interesting is this photograph of the fountain in the peristylium of one of the most recently excavated houses in the city, with the holes of the water pipe cleared again from their centuries of dust and ashes, and the water laid on. There is a magic in running water which brings back even to these deserted scenes a touch of life.
Photo by Violet F. Nicholls

and green to the summit. Pompeii could not suppose that there was any difference that need concern them in the eternal hills.

And then the first disaster came. In February, A.D. 63, when Nero was ruling in Rome, a tremendous earthquake broke the city to pieces. So great was the damage that the imperial government doubted whether the place was worth restoration. Restoration, however, went on, and a new Pompeii arose. The dwellings were first rebuilt, naturally with that tendency towards uniformity of style which we have noted, and the greater public buildings were gradually taken in hand. It is insufficiently appreciated that what was finally overwhelmed was not an ancient town, but a new and only partially rebuilt city.

Other, though less violent earthquakes gave evidence of some great subterranean disturbance ; but there was no reason to suspect Vesuvius,

childhood, has a strangely disturbing dream. She was back in the old home, and snow was falling, quietly, steadily, thickly from a black sky. Hours went on, and the snow descended without pause ; but it was not cold snow—it was warm, and suffocating—very suffocating. She began to choke, and woke in a fright to find that the volcano was flooding the city with ashes that silenced all sound, darkened the sky, and filled the air like a palpable fog.

It was in this way that Pompeii perished. First there came a fierce hail of pumice fragments, and after that the volcanic dust, softer than any snow and far more deadly, for it penetrated like water and destroyed those who had sought shelter in closed rooms. In the cellar of the Villa of Diomedes twenty persons perished as they cowered together for safety. All that day and the next the downpour of deadly ash continued. It poured

SOME CURIOUSLY MODERN PORTRAITS FROM THE MURAL DECORATIONS OF ANCIENT POMPEII
In the treatment of the hair and of the dress, these paintings, reproduced from the coloured originals found among the abundant wall decorations of Pompeii, have a curiously modern appearance. Like the other examples we have given, they serve to prove that the artists who found employment in Pompeii had attained to a degree of natural grace and truth which it took the artists of Italy more than a thousand years to reach again.

which, though plainly volcanic in origin (as Strabo had noted half a century before), had never been active in recorded history. Then, on the morning of August 24, A.D. 79, the forces of fire burst through the mountain with appalling fury, and carried high into the air all the accumulated debris of centuries. The top of the cone disappeared, and the present divided summit was formed.

The most immediately destructive of volcanic products is the molten rock or lava that pours from rifts torn in the side of the mound ; but lava had nothing to do with the disasters of 79. The cities of the plain were not burnt with fire from heaven ; Pompeii was drowned in dust, and Herculaneum in dust and water. In a story by Mr. Norman Douglas, the scene of which is laid under the shadow of a Mediterranean volcano, one of the characters, who had lived in America during her

out over Capri on the south, and over Misenum on the north, where Pliny, the Roman admiral and naturalist, was stationed with his galleys. When the news of disaster reached him he gallantly put off to Herculaneum to render aid, but the retreating sea as well as the ash that was filling his ships made landing difficult, and amid the deadly sulphur fumes the old Stoic, fat and asthmatic, quietly died as if he were sleeping.

Two letters of his nephew to Tacitus give us a graphic and authentic account of the disaster.

On August 24, about one in the afternoon, my mother desired my uncle to observe a cloud which appeared of a very unusual size and shape. It was not at this distance discernible from what mountain this cloud issued, but it was found afterwards to proceed from Vesuvius. I cannot give you a more exact description of its figure than by resembling it to that of a pine tree, for it shot up a great height in the form of a tall trunk, which spread at the top into a sort of branches, either because the force of the internal vapour which impelled the cloud upwards decreased in strength as it advanced, or because the cloud being pressed back by its own weight expanded itself in the manner I have mentioned.

It appeared sometimes bright, sometimes dark and spotted, as it was either more or less impregnated with earth and cinders. This uncommon appearance excited my uncle's philosophical curiosity to take a nearer view of it. He accordingly ordered a light vessel to be prepared. As he was going out of the house with his tablets in his hand, he was met by the sailors belonging to the galleys stationed at Retina, from which they had fled in the utmost terror; for that port being situated at the foot of Vesuvius, they had no other way to escape than by sea. They conjured him, therefore, not to proceed and expose his life to imminent and inevitable danger.

In compliance with their advice he changed his original intention, and instead of gratifying his philosophical spirit, he resigned it to the more magnanimous principle of aiding the distressed. With this view he ordered the fleet immediately to put to sea and went himself on board with an intention of assisting not only Retina, but several other towns which stood thick upon that beautiful coast. Hastening to the place, therefore, whence others fled with the utmost terror, he steered his direct course to the point of danger, and with so much calmness and presence of mind as to be able to make and dictate his observations upon the appearance and progress of the dreadful scene.

He was now so near the mountain that the cinders, which grew thick and hotter the more he advanced, fell into the ships, together with pumice-stone and black pieces of burning rock; they were likewise in danger, not only of being aground by the sudden retreat of the sea, but also from the vast fragments which rolled down from the mountains and obstructed all the shore. [Pliny lands, and retires for the night.] In the meanwhile the fire from Vesuvius flamed forth from several parts of the mountain with great violence, which the darkness of the night contributed to render still more dreadful. The court which led to his apartment being now almost filled with stones and ashes, it would have been impossible for him to have made his way out; it was

**THE DANCING FAUN**
Bronze statuette which gave its name to the House of the Faun at Pompeii.

thought proper, therefore, to awaken him. He got up, and joined the rest of the company, who had not been sufficiently unconcerned to think of going to bed.

They consulted together whether it would be most prudent to trust to the houses, which now shook from side to side with frequent and violent concussions, or to flee to the open fields, where the calcined stones and cinders still fell in large showers and threatened them with instant destruction. In this distress they resolved for the fields as the less dangerous situation of the two. They went out, having pillows tied upon their heads with napkins, and this was their whole defence against the storm of stones that fell around them. It was now day everywhere else, but there a deeper darkness prevailed than in the blackest night.

The younger Pliny had remained at Misenum, and tells in a second letter what happened there.

There had been during many days before some shocks of an earthquake, which the less alarmed us as they are frequent in Campania, but they were so particularly violent that night that they seemed

**THE DANCING FAUN**
Another view of the statuette, now in the National Museum at Naples.

to threaten total destruction. My mother flew to my chamber where she found me rising. It was now morning, but the light was exceedingly faint and languid. The buildings all around us tottered, and though we stood upon open ground, there was no remaining without imminent danger; we, therefore, resolved to leave the town. The people followed us in the utmost consternation.

Being advanced at a convenient distance from the houses we stood still in the midst of a most hazardous and tremendous scene. The chariots were so agitated backwards and forwards, though upon the most level ground, that we could not keep them steady, even by supporting them with large stones. The sea seemed to roll back upon itself and to be driven from its banks by the convulsive motion of the earth; it is certain, at least, the shore was considerably enlarged and several sea animals were left upon it. On the other side, a black and dreadful cloud bursting with an igneous serpentine vapour darted out a long train of fire resembling flashes of lightning, but much larger.

Soon afterwards the cloud seemed to descend and cover the whole ocean; it

**SILENUS**
Bronze statuette designed as support for a vase. In the National Museum at Naples.

entirely hid the island of Capri and the promontory of Misenum. The ashes now began to fall upon us, though in no great quantity. I turned my head and observed behind us a thick smoke which came rolling after us like a torrent. I proposed, while we had yet any light, to turn out of the high road, lest we should be pressed to death in the dark by the crowd that followed us. We had scarcely stepped out of the path when darkness overspread us, not like that of a cloudy night, or when there is no moon, but of a room when it is shut up and all the lights extinct.

Nothing was to be heard but the shrieks of women, the screams of children, and the cries of men ; some calling for their children, others for their parents,

GARDEN IN THE HOUSE OF THE CENTENARIO
This spacious stone court with its original marble statues and adornments replaced, and plants growing where doubtless the ancient owners of the garden cultivated them, gives a vivid impression of the peristylium of the Pompeian house.
Photo by Donald McLeish

others for their husbands, and only distinguishing each other by their voices ; one lamenting his own fate, another that of his family, some wishing to die from the very fear of dying, some lifting their hands to the gods, but the greater part imagining that the last and eternal night was come which was to destroy the gods and the world together.

At length a glimmering light appeared, which we imagined to be rather the forerunner of an approaching burst of flames, as in fact it was, than the return of day ; however, the fire fell at a distance from us. Then again we were immersed in thick darkness, and a heavy shower of ashes rained upon us, which we were obliged frequently to shake off lest we should be overwhelmed and buried. I imagined I was perishing with the world itself. At last this terrible darkness was dissipated by degrees like a cloud or smoke ; the real day returned, and even the sun appeared, though very faintly as when an eclipse is coming on. Every object that presented itself to our eyes seemed changed, being covered with white ashes as with deep snow.

Pompeii lay wrapped in this death shroud of ashes. One-tenth of its people had perished. Some died where they had sheltered, some in the act of escaping. The priests of Isis, hastening with their treasures towards the Stabian Gate, were beaten down, and gasped out their last breath

with their impotent gold about them. The fate of Herculaneum was still more dreadful, for upon it fell not merely dust, but torrential rain from the stream thrown up by the mountain ; and when day came, the unhappy city lay stiff in death under a thickening sea of mud which lapse of time has hardened into stone.

When the great convulsion had ceased, the wretched survivors of Pompeii crept back and began groping in the dust for their buried homes. Here the fumes released by their digging claimed still more victims ; but such things as could be reached were removed, and the remains of buildings standing up through the sea of ashes were stripped of everything that could be used. Then the city was left to oblivion, and its very name perished, the site being vaguely known in subsequent centuries as La Civita.

In the sixteenth century, an engineer, cutting a water channel, broke into Pompeii. In 1709, an Austrian count, seeking for antiquities, sank a shaft into the site of Herculaneum. In 1748 more careful digging was begun at La Civita, which was believed to be the site of Stabiae ; but the work of excavation was not systematically pursued until the time of the Napoleonic kingdoms of Joseph Bonaparte and Murat. This early digging, however, was destructive. Everything that was found was removed, and the buildings were stripped of all they contained.

Naples Museum groans with treasures the rightful place of which is the city from which they came, though the problem of protection there would be immensely difficult. Fiorelli (1824-96) was the first humane director of excavation. He it was who adopted the plan of pouring plaster into the hollows where the ash had hardened round dead bodies, and so taking moulds of what had been enclosed. To him we owe the terrible and pathetic figures in the little museum near the Porta Marina, not the least moving being that of the house dog contorted with its last agony.

Modern explorers take moulds of everything, of charred doors and furniture and domestic objects, and are elaborately careful to leave or replace what they find in its appropriate spot. The houses are no longer left bare, but, like the great House of the Vettii, or the House of the Golden Cupids, are allowed to retain whatever is left of their ancient glory. Much of the city has still to be uncovered. Wonderful as the first revelation has been, the later will be more wonderful still. The destruction of Pompeii was a tremendous disaster ; its resurrection has been a miracle.

## The Study of the Past. VIII.

# The Cave of the Cumaean Sibyl

### By F. N. Pryce, M.A.

Assistant Keeper, Department of Greek and Roman Antiquities, British Museum

*ONE of the most fascinating results of present-day archaeology is the light it oftentimes throws on the myths and legends, beliefs and practices, of the ancient world. The story of the discovery of the Cumaean Sibyl's shrine, described in the pages that follow, is an excellent case in point. Thanks to the exploratory skill of Professor Maiuri, Keeper of the Naples Museum and Superintendent of Archaeology in Campania, we are now made acquainted not only with the actual haunt of the Sibyl but also with what may be called the mechanics of the much-venerated oracle. The photographs accompanying the article were taken by Professor Maiuri.—EDITOR.*

THE wise woman gifted with the power of foretelling the future is to be found in the folklore of many lands; the Sibyl of Greece and Rome is but one of her many manifestations What the word Sibyl means no one knows for sure, but we have some reason to suppose that to begin with there was only one Sibyl, perhaps a woman who lived in the flesh and who dwelt near Troy In the course of time, however, men came to believe in the existence of many Sibyls scattered over the ancient world They were pictured as old, old women, savage and morose, who dwelt apart in caves or amid rocks and deserts The howling of the winds through caverns, the uprush of steam from volcanic vents, or the roar of falling waters was the voice of Apollo whose unerring wisdom they in terpreted to Mankind As antiquity imagined them, so Michael Angelo painted them on the ceiling of the Sistine Chapel in the Vatican

Most renowned of all was the Sibyl of Cumae, about whom legend and epic poetry have combined to throw a mantle of romance. Whether there ever was a

historical woman to whom the name was given we do not know, although in the days of the Roman empire her tomb was shown to tourists in the Temple of Apollo near her shrine The story relates that she came from the East, and that Apollo had granted her a year of life for every grain of sand she could hold in her hands She was not immortal, however, and with the lapse

*Continued in page 379*

**ENTRANCES TO THE GROTTO OF THE WISE WOMAN OF CUMAE**

A series of caves discovered in the mountain-side at Cumae, near Naples, by Professor A. Maiuri has been identified as the shrine of the Cumaean Sibyl, the most famous and revered of the Latin oracles. This photograph shows the upper and lower entrances of the grotto.

Long Walls        Mouseion        Statue and Arch of Had

Stadium      Temple of Cronos and Rhea      Temple of Zeus Olympios      Temple and Garden

Bridge over Ilissos

*GENERAL VIEW OF ATHENS FROM THE EAST IN THE—*

*After a restoration—*

Aphrodite      Roman Baths      Hadrian's Wall and Gate      Country House

*—DAYS WHEN HADRIAN HAD ADORNED THE CITY*

—by Bühlmann

377

THE INNERMOST SANCTUARY OF THE SIBYLLINE SHRINE WHENCE THE VOICE OF THE ORACLE ISSUED

Here we see the vault—about 40 feet by 20 feet, and 20 feet high—in which once stood the smoking tripods of the Cumaean oracle. The openings in the roof served as light shafts and also carried the Sibyl's voice to the chamber above. The grotto contains three niches : one, entered by way of a vestibule, where waited those who would consult the oracle, seems to have been the Sibyl's living-room ; the others open to light and air shafts and to a long corridor which played a great part in the proceedings. There can be little doubt that this is the cave inhabited by the Sibyl immortalized in Virgil's majestic lines.

of time she shrank in size until she was shut up in a bottle, crying for death. (To readers of Hans Andersen this little bit of popular mythology will be familiar in another setting). She it was who offered to Tarquin the Proud, last of the Seven Kings of Rome, nine books of prophecies at a high price; when he refused, she flung three books in the fire and vanished. After a time she returned and offered him the remaining six at the same price. The king again refused, whereupon she burnt three more; and then the king paid her the original price for the last three. These were the famous Sibylline books which, consulted in State emergencies, were carefully preserved in Rome until they were accidentally burnt in the civil war of 83 B.C. In the sixth book of the "Aeneid" the poet Virgil tells in stately verse how his hero Aeneas visited the shrine of the Cumaean Sibyl, and learnt from her the fortunes of his wandering band of heroes and the means of passing to the Underworld.

Cumae was an old Greek settlement at the north-west extremity of the Bay of Naples. On the neighbouring Mount Cuma, in a rugged and volcanic region, fit abiding place for a Sibyl, a cave has long been pointed out by tradition as her shrine, and in 1925 the task of exploring this was undertaken by a well-known Italian scholar, Professor Maiuri. The task proved of unexpected magnitude; the cave was of unsuspected depth, with a lining of masonry and a great vestibule before it. Then came a surprise, in the form of a

HOW AN EFFECT OF MYSTERY WAS OBTAINED IN THE GROTTO

The most remarkable feature of the Cumaean cave is this subterranean corridor, 125 yards long and 9 feet wide, lit by means of twelve light-shafts pierced through the side of the hill. It is fully described in the text, page 380. One may imagine the mysterious effect produced by the figure of the priestess as, passing along the corridor, she was now visible, now invisible, to those who had come to consult the oracle.

colossal subterranean gallery two hundred yards long, driven right through the hill from the cave to the opposite side, with light-shafts and huge cisterns for holding water.

All this was highly exciting, but when the exploration was completed Professor Maiuri began to feel doubts. What he had discovered in no way corresponded with descriptions in ancient authors of the Sibyl's shrine. The subterranean passage seemed to be a roadway through the hill, made perhaps for military purposes, and it was not easy to suppose that it would have been cut through a sacred site of such renown. Professor Maiuri, therefore, supposed that tradition was mistaken in identifying this particular cave as the Sibyl's, and resolved to search the vicinity for some other traces. At length, in 1932, fortune gave him his reward

Only a few yards from the first cave a fault in the rock and a growth of bushes concealed a second cave, which was used as a wine cellar Penetrating into this he saw a rock cutting of a form which could be recognized as Greek, and therefore of great antiquity. Then on the upper surface a row of sunken holes was observed, suggestive of the presence of a straight artificial passage along the line of the row. He began to clear the cave, and the result, in his opinion, so exactly corresponds with the ancient descriptions as to leave no doubt that the true cave of the Sibyl has been found.

The innermost sanctuary is a vault measuring 40 by 20 feet and of a height of 20 feet. It contains three niches; one seemed to be the living room of the Sibyl; the visitor entered it through an arched doorway from a vestibule in which were two small stone benches. Originally a door of some kind divided the vestibule from the inner shrine.

THE SIBYL'S SANCTUM BESIDE THE SHRINE

Opening out of the main cave at Cumae is this little niche or chamber in which, it is suggested, the Sibyl actually lived. In the foreground may be seen two stone seats in a kind of vestibule, which probably was separated from the cubicle by a barred gate.

A second niche opened to a light and air shaft; the third niche led to the most remarkable feature, a great subterranean corridor 125 yards long, 9 feet wide, and in places as much as 60 feet in height. This was the entrance to the shrine. Twelve shorter galleries led out from it with openings at the edge of the rock, forming a series of light-shafts. Thus the length of the corridor was divided by bands of light, so that a figure approaching would seem alternately to appear and disappear. Here is a genuine underground temple, of a grandeur and majesty meet for one of the most venerated shrines of the ancient world. Through the rock openings came the hundred voices and echoes of the god's words, which the priestess would interpret and record—on loose palm-leaves, it is said. It would be difficult to imagine anything more awe-inspiring than the twilight of this mighty cave at the end of its mysterious approach.

Of the date of the shrine the only evidence we have at the moment is the shape of the rock-cutting which indicates a very ancient period; perhaps the sixth century before Christ, or even earlier. The cult of the Sibylline oracle died early and Christians then used the cave as a refuge.

# Athens in the Days of her Glory

### By J. L. Myres, M.A., D.Sc., F.B.A.

Wykeham Professor of Ancient History, Oxford; author of "The Dawn of History," etc.

*IN arranging the pictorial diagrams to accompany Professor Myres' brilliant survey of Ancient Athens, no effort has been made to illustrate in any considerable detail the Parthenon or the Theatre of Dionysos, as it has been found desirable to deal with each of these in other sections of our work, the Parthenon coming up under "The Temples of the Gods" for considerably more detailed treatment than would be possible in this chapter dealing with Athens as a whole, while the Theatre of Dionysos forms in its description and illustration an important feature of Professor E. A. Gardner's contribution on the Ancient Theatre in our section on "The Master Builders."*—EDITOR.

FEW ancient cities appeal to the modern world in so many different ways as Athens; and fewer still retain, even in their modern motley of old and new buildings so much of ancient feature and outline.

Rome and Jerusalem have been more continuously inhabited—Jerusalem with smaller alteration of plan and outer aspect, but with almost complete effacement or submergence of older monuments in its disastrous sequence of sieges and captures, Rome, more completely successful architecturally as well as constitutionally in accumulating novelties without sacrifice of the obsolete, but transfigured utterly, more than once, by the shifting of its soul, its seat of will and intelligence, from the Palatine to the Lateran, from Lateran to Vatican across the river, and back from the Vatican to the Quirinal Hill.

Athens, as old as Jerusalem, as richly endowed by its natural situation as Rome, as profoundly significant as either of these cities in human history, more than compensates for the long decadence of its Byzantine history, and for the creeping death which paralysed it under Turkish rule, by the grave aloofness of its monuments from the trivialities of a busy modern capital, and by their coherence—fragmentary as they are—with each other still, and with the site and landscape which they ennoble.

The natural surroundings of Athens are themselves exceptional. The Saronic Gulf of the Aegean Sea, and its counterpart the Corinthian Gulf, which so nearly meets it at the Isthmus, divide the homeland of the Greeks into a northern and a southern half of nearly equal extent, and carry seaboard conditions into the very heart of the peninsula. A little north of this, the narrower channel which separates the island of Euboea from the mainland has always been an avenue of intercourse between the archipelago and central Greece. Both gulfs were the earliest areas to be explored by the nascent civilization of the Cycladic

islands, twin-sister of that of prehistoric Crete, and better situated for such continental enterprises. The mountainous promontory which separates these early water-ways is Attica; and the natural heart of Attica is the Athenian plain, as those earliest explorers were not slow to realise.

Defended from the north by the rugged highlands of Mounts Kithairon and Parnes, which rise to 5,000 feet and reach the coast at either end, and from attack over the Corinthian Isthmus by the steep façade of Mount Geraneia, nearly 4,000 feet high, the whole promontory has enjoyed in all ages a comparative security from attack which made it, in many crises of invasion, a natural citadel and refuge. Like the British Isles, and the net in the parable, Attica has "gathered of every kind," and has bred from chance occupants a peculiar people.

Of the habitable lowlands within the promontory, the westernmost, less well protected against intruders on either hand, has always stood aloof from the rest, and in ancient times formed an independent and usually hostile state. Only for a few brilliant years, at the height of Athenian predominance, was this Megarean section so much as linked with Attica in military and political cooperation. In earlier ages other marginal districts, Eleusis and Marathon, had similar independent existence; and there were even memories of old wars between Athens and the Mesogaia, or "mid-land," which opens south of the Marathon country on to the eastern sea. But in historic times all these had long been incorporated into a single political community, which may fairly be described as the "united states" of Attica.

Of this united Attica, the political centre was Athens; and all free occupants of this promontory-state were alike Athenians politically. It was an achievement of early statesmanship which has no precise parallel; even the beginnings of Rome show no such triumph of political genius over physical obstacles and racial incongruity; and it is this initial marvel which sets Athens always a

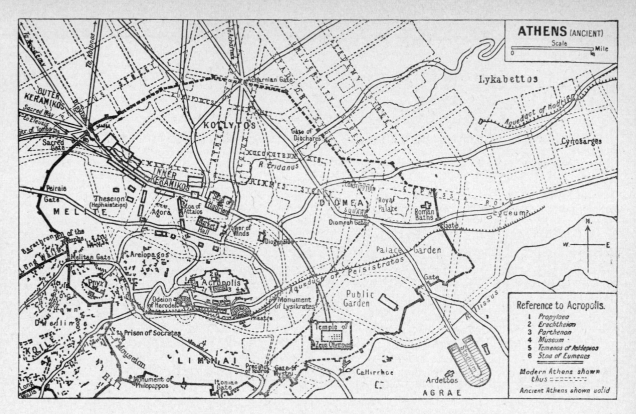

little apart from all other cities of the ancient Greeks, a city-state of the first rank, in an age when the city-state was the highest social structure in existence, and at the same time an anticipation on a smaller scale of the territorial nation-states of the modern world.

The Athenian plain, as has been already noted, was the natural centre of the economic and political life of Attica, its heart and its brain. It is an oblong lowland, sloping from north-east to south-west, and opening on to the Saronic Gulf. The rugged Parnes, already mentioned, bounds it on the north; Pentelikon and Hymettos, almost as lofty and far more impressive, separate it respectively from Marathon and from the mid-land of the promontory; Aigaleos, rather lower, and with two easy passes, divides it from the plain of Eleusis on the west. Somewhat as the rocky island of Salamis screens Eleusis from the open gulf, so the much smaller eminence of Munychia, at the foot of Aigaleos, restricts the shingle foreshore of Phaleron Bay, and provides an almost unparalleled cluster of steep-sided bays and coves, large and small, which were to become the great naval and mercantile harbour-quarter of Peiraeus.

The plain itself is watered by two streams. Kephissos, the larger, rises in the foothills of Parnes and Pentelikon, and has a wide, sunny basin, of which the lower half is alluvial and nearly level. The other, Ilissos, rising between Pentelikon and Hymettos, on the eastern side of the district, has a deeper, narrower valley, with a steep torrent bed and occasional rapids and rocky falls, and then a short open course obliquely through the lowland, to join Kephissos a little above its mouth. Formerly, no doubt, before the shoreline advanced it had its own exit into Phaleron Bay. Neither stream is large enough to form a serious natural barrier, and both are usually dry quite early in the summer; but the Ilissos bed has been a sufficient landmark to keep the seaward foothills of Hymettos always a little aloof from the rest of the plain.

Between these streams a ridge of old marble rock, of like structure with the frontier mountains, runs obliquely out into the plain from its eastern side. Most of it is featureless and inconspicuous, but at its seaward end it first rises into Mount Lykabettos, a steep grey-blue gable of nearly 1,000 feet, and then sinks into a discontinuous plateau sloping rapidly into the lowland, and dissected by the last gorge of the Ilissos, and by smaller torrents off the slopes of Lykabettos.

By these torrents, one flat-topped section of this plateau has been cut away from the rest, and shaped into a roughly oval hill, the world-famous Acropolis, about 512 feet high, precipitous except at its narrow west end, which is connected by an open ridge with the similar but lower cliff-façades of the Hills of the Muses and of the Nymphs, and the broader Pnyx between them, which are the principal divisions of the plateau already mentioned. Close below the west end of the Acropolis, and a little to the north of the connecting ridge, a similar smaller block, of the same rugged formation, presents towards the Acropolis a steep bluff, the Areiopagos, but slopes gently through the district known as Melite, into the claylands bordering the Kephissos, which were to be the " potteries " of the eventual city.

Between the south side of the Acropolis, the steep eastern scarp of the Muses' Hill, and the bed of the Ilissos, which is here almost a gorge, converging and obstructed rainwash makes a patch of wet ground known as Limnai, " the fens " ; and on the north side of the Acropolis the former track of the largest of the torrents from Lykabettos, known as Eridanos, is only marked now by a depression hardly more perceptible to-day than that which gives names to Holborn, Fleet Street, and Ludgate Hill, but was sufficient in early times to set a limit to the Athenian "Agora " or Cheapside, and serve the miscellaneous purposes, defensive and unsavoury, of a drain and a city ditch.

Three thousand years of busy humanity have left little of the soil, and even less of the natural verdure, of this impressive and beautiful site. To refigure " violet crowned " Athens, as Theseus and Kodros loved her, we must clothe the lilac-coloured marble, and its rusty veins and crannies, with soil as red as that of the Mendips, strongly contrasted with the drab and grey alluvium of the plain, the gleaming shingle of Phaleron beach, and the soft cheese-coloured limestones of Munychia and some of the foothills under Parnes. We must afforest Lykabettos and Aigaleos as the government of to-day is doing, with black copses of maritime pine, sprinkle the lower slopes with the bronze-like patina of sturdy oak-woods, and fringe the water-courses with emerald foliage of planes and flickering grey-green poplars.

All arable lands as in the valleys of Judah must " stand so thick with corn that they shall laugh and sing," and in the green shall be splashes of scarlet poppies and anemones, purple bugloss and

ACROPOLIS, PARTHENON, AND PROPYLAEA FROM THE SUMMIT OF THE PNYX
This is the view of Athens that her triumphant sailors caught when returning from the Peiraeus after some successful cruise. From early times Attica was famous—or so its people vaunted—for a clear, pure atmosphere, and for some lambent quality of the sunlight that lent a halo to the gleaming temple-crowned height of the Acropolis when viewed from the sea. Seen distantly, only the flash of the spear-head of Athene Promachos is needed to give the illusion that Ancient Athens still endures.

SOUTH WALL OF THE ERECHTHEION WITH ITS CARYATID-BORNE PORTICO

The foundations in the foreground are probably those of the " Hekatompedon," the ancient temple of Athene, which was partly or wholly destroyed during the Persian invasion, and whose place was taken by the new Parthenon. Beyond it is the south side of the Erechtheion, with the porch of the Caryatides. The part of the building to which this porch, together with the north entrance, gave access was probably built over the old and hallowed tomb of Kekrops, a legendary Athenian king.

PORTICO OF THE SHRINE OF THE CITY'S GUARDIAN GODDESS IN THE ERECHTHEION

This photograph of the delicate Ionic pillars forming its eastern or principal entrance, shows that the Erechtheion is now, alas, but an empty shell. Many have been its vicissitudes: it has been a Christian church and a Turkish harem; it has been scarred by war and half ruined by storms; but such is its intrinsic appeal that attempts have always been made to replace the blocks in position. The part to which this portico gave immediate entrance was the shrine of Athene Polias.

*THE ACROPOLIS, ROCKY HEART OF THE "CITY OF THE VIOLET CROWN"*

The stronghold of the earliest kings of Athens, the Acropolis—a long mass of rock with precipitous slopes—was the fortress-sanctuary of the ancient Athenians, the centre of their cultural life. To-day, as will be seen from this photograph taken from the south-west, it dominates the modern city as it did the old, but only ruined shells, majestic in their decay, remain of the magnificent edifices that in classical times, crowned its summit. In the background are the Propylaea, the Erechtheion and the Parthenon, while in the foreground is the Odeion. *A general view of the city in Greco-Roman times is given in the plate reproduced in pages 276-77.*

Spanish iris, sky-blue borage and forget-me-not, and sheets of marigold and sorrel. This for April weather ; by June, Persephone and her flowers will be in another world, and Demeter will reign in harvest cloth-of-gold. Even then the vines will be green still on the lower slopes, with the velvet texture which is their own ; the fodder-crops and salad-beds in irrigated patches will not have wilted yet, though the gourds and melons will begin to glow among their foliage. The darker green and dense shadows of the fig trees, among the perennial grey lacework of olive groves, will set off the white walls and rose-red tiling of the farmsteads, and the blaze of pink oleander bushes along the torrent banks. Around all, the same unpaintable lilac,

and the names of principal districts of the later city are clearly derived from those of a cluster of early villages nestling in hollows of the craggy plateau. Under the shadow of the citadel in their midst they were at least secure. With the Kephissos plain at their doors they might become wealthy—and the men of the " Plain " were long the predominant partner in the Athenian city-state. With the good will of the " Shore " and the " Highland " to name their two chief rivals in early history—that Athenian state might even become powerful ; for its area was large, as Greek states reckoned territory (being, indeed, about half as big as Yorkshire) ; its position was central, its frontiers unusually strong, and its natural

THESEION AND DISTANT MAJESTY OF THE ATHENIAN ACROPOLIS—
Softened by distance, and with the illusion heightened by the undamaged profile of the " Theseion," the outlines of the Acropolis and its buildings seem to melt into the finished perfection of other years. The " Theseion " on the left, as mentioned in page 399 was probably really a temple of Hephaistos ; beyond it on the right are the towering Acropolis walls, those on the farthest right having been built by Cimon in 468 B.C., and those on the left some thirty years earlier after the Persian invasion, during the ascendancy of Themistokles. In the centre is the bulk of the Parthenon with the Erechtheion on its left, and on a buttress

orange-stained, of the great hills, opalescent among the black clumps of holm-oak, and deep shrubbery tints of myrtle, bay, box-wood, and rosemary ; above all, the pines and the sky, cloudless, saturated with colour like the borage-flowers, and so luminous that every shadow is of a strong purple-blue.

Such was the site of Athens as nature made it. We have now to see what man has done with it. The name itself, in Greek as in English, is plural ;

resources varied and copious. It had the best soil and climate in Greece for the olive, Athene's own gift to her people ; extensive wheatlands, excellent vines on the hillsides, timber enough for early needs of construction and fuel, and beside the fine clays of the " potteries " outside the town, there were in due time the marble of Pentelikon and an inexhaustible silver-mining area in the rugged far end of the promontory, the Cornwall of ancient Attica. Above all—for this mattered most in early times—there was the natural fortress-rock of the Polis; and it was on and around this natural citadel—by good fortune the only one of its kind in the whole region—that the political life of the Athenian people centred, as the political life of Scotland has centred round the castle and "old town" of Edinburgh.

Fragments of early walls, unhewn but massive enough, and traces of a prehistoric palace within their circuit, confirm the first literary reference to the "strong house of Erechtheus," whose ancient kingdom, like the worship of "Our Lady of the Fortress," Athene Polias, goes back in Greek folk-memory at least to the fourteenth century B.C.; the political unification of the people of the

arose which were standing in the fifth century, when Xerxes' Persians occupied and burned the town, and forced the "wooden wall" with which the men of lesser faith had striven on the strength of an oracle to guard the citadel.

That momentary disaster cost us all earlier monuments, but also preserved for us in the fragments of them precious evidence of this older city for which on other sites we look in vain. For it was the foresight of Themistokles (whose larger reading of the oracle of the "wooden walls" had created, only just in time, the first Athenian navy, and whose handling of that naval force had turned the scale against the invaders) that was also the driving force of the hurried reconstruction

—CLEAR CUT AGAINST THE BRIGHT BACKGROUND OF AN ATTIC SKY
of the Propylaea, which may just be seen on the extreme right, the lovely little temple of Athene Nike is silhouetted boldly against the sky. In the foreground are the tops of olive trees, gift of Athene and symbol of the greatness of Athens; for the oil of Attica was esteemed throughout the Greek world, and the need to supply jars was the stimulus which gave pre-eminence to the Athenian potter and distributed the produce of his workshop as far as Greek colonisation penetrated
Photo by the Autotype Co.

promontory by the national hero Theseus, and the liberation of the whole gulf-area from the Minoan sea-kings of Crete, belong probably to the thirteenth; and the heroic choice of King Kodros —who died that Athens might live—averted the worst evils of the Dorian Migration in the early part of the eleventh. These and other memories of older days hallowed the "Rock," the "Council Bluff" at its entrance, and the "Market" in the lower town, long before any of those buildings

"bidding them build, man, woman, and child, sparing neither public nor private edifice that was available," but destroying and utilizing all, "till the walls were high enough to fight from," and Themistokles could reveal to their rivals the success of his manoeuvre. No wonder that from time to time, in Athens, men came upon a forgotten altar, and reconsecrated it "to a god unknown."

Of this hasty barricade short sections remain, largely composed of architectural fragments,

THE ODEION WHERE ATHENIAN PLAYGOERS ASSEMBLED IN THEIR THOUSANDS

As a great centre of art and learning, Athens had many visitors and admirers. Patrons at home and abroad lavished gifts upon her or erected sumptuous buildings within her walls. The interior of the Odeion illustrated above was erected in the Roman round-arched style with three storeys by Herodes Atticus, a rich Athenian, for dramatic performances. At the back of the stage is a massive wall broken by the usual three stage doors and relieved by niches. The tiers of seats coated with Pentelic marble rose in a semicircle on the rocky slope of the Acropolis and sufficed for 5,000 spectators. The whole edifice was once covered with a superb roof of cedar-wood.

tombstones, and other sculptured slabs, such as have lately revealed so surprisingly the hockey and hand-ball teams of Athenian schoolboys of that time. It is through this untidy wall that the famous " Double Gate "—like London's " Temple Bar "—led from the noisy, crowded streets of the " Potteries Within " to the stately calm of the cemeteries which lined the " Sacred Road," by which processions went to Our Lady of the Corn at Eleusis—the Holyrood or the Westminster of the Athenians. Other débris from the devastated town found secure lodgement behind an enlarged curtain wall on the Citadel Hill, similarly patched together, in parts, out of columns and architraves from the ruined temples.

Here they have been recovered in our own time —quaint, grim, gaudily-painted sculpture from temples ; votive statues and terra-cottas, bronzes and painted pottery, chief treasures now of the Acropolis Museum. From them we may judge how rapid, as well as how splendid, was the passage

from primitive and archaic to the mature style and matchless execution of the succeeding century. For it was in the two generations next following the Persian War that Athens, and especially the Acropolis, took on that outward beauty and magnificence which has been her glory ever since.

The Citadel Hill, enlarged and levelled outwards to the new wall, was approached through a palatial Fore-gate, with picture gallery and other buildings annexed. On the right, marking an awkward hummock of rock, once a flanking tower of older defences, rose that exquisite Temple of " Victory-come-to-stay "—surely the happiest alternative to a blasting-charge that ever engineer conceived. Its platform balustrade carries the well-known reliefs of other Victories, winged and hovering still —for victory, too, has its price—before the pathetic Athene mourning her Unknown Warrior.

On the left, as you passed through the five-fold doorway and its inward colonnade, you saw, uncompleted still, the quaint new " House of

Erechtheus," enclosing holy places and still holier relics, with its noble north door, and the stately Porch of the Maidens which was to be the central feature of its unfinished façade. The band of sculpture close below the roof-line struck the eye at once; for on the background of black Eleusinian marble, each figure stood out white as on a Wedgwood vase. On the highest level of the terraced plateau rose the supreme ornament of all, the " Maiden Bower " of the goddess herself, the Parthenon, an oblong building, with a six-pillared portico at each end, within its colonnade of Doric columns, eight to an end and seventeen to a side. Before its eastern end blazed the great altar. Within, the main chamber, 100 feet long like the " Old Temple " which it replaced, guarded inside its internal colonnade the colossal goddess, fully armed, with a Victory on her outstretched hand, wrought all of gold, with the flesh parts in ivory. Around it, in time, were grouped other dedications, and the splendid temple furniture; and the back room, opening to the western portico, served as storehouse for many more.

Another figure of Athene, in gilded bronze, and even larger—for it was 30 feet high—stood in the open between the Temple and the Gate House, a joyous landmark for her ships, for the flash of sunlight from spear and helmet could be seen as soon as you rounded the last cape and set course up-gulf for home. Other sanctuaries, with their altars and worshippers, and monuments innumerable, crowded the pavement of this fortress sanctuary; it was the museum, the record-office, the national monument of a great people, conscious of their achievement, able and willing to be the " School of Greece "; for had they not solved the problem of " culture without luxury " ?

It would have been more in accord with modern taste—and was, in fact, long assumed—that Athenian builders and sculptors should have left the superb marble of the Pentelic quarries unrelieved by colour or gilding. But Athenian marble statues were no more " studies in pure form " than ancient bronzes were studies in " pure verdigris," as the contents of archæological museums might suggest. Bronze, carefully cleaned as modern silver is, and as ancient statues were kept clean by their custodians, is as apt material for rendering the sun-ripened limbs of a southern people, as marble is inadequate to represent humanity

THE OLYMPIEION, OR TEMPLE OF THE OLYMPIAN ZEUS

The fifteen huge marble columns shown above are all that remain of what was one of the largest Greek temples ever built. Foundations were laid for the original temple in the time of Peisistratos c. 530 B.C. Work was resumed c. 174 B.C. by Antiochos IV., Epiphanes, to whose edifice the existing ruins belong, but it was only completed by Hadrian. When the temple was consecrated the Athenians showed their gratitude by erecting a statue of the emperor next to the gold and ivory, or " chryselephantine," statue of Zeus, which was somewhat similar to that reproduced in colour facing page 236 of this work.

THE SHRINE OF "WINGLESS VICTORY": PENTELIC MARBLE TEMPLE OF ATHENE NIKE

This Ionic temple stands on a bastion flanking the Propylaea on the south; the balustrade, adorned with reliefs representing goddesses of victory erecting trophies and presenting offerings in the presence of Athene, has vanished, but the sculptured frieze all that now remains of the temple's superstructure, is still preserved. It represents a council of the gods, among whom is Athene, with her shield, sitting next to Zeus. On the sides are battles of the Greeks with mounted Persians, and at the west a conflict between Greeks and Greeks. The temple, whose date is uncertain, was reconstructed with the ancient stones seen at the sides in 1835.

without careful tinting of the eyes and the flesh parts, and more emphatic colouring of sandals, armour, and drapery; and in Athenian sunlight unrelieved marble surfaces are almost intolerable to the eye, as a stroll down modern Stadium Street will convince you.

Statuary, too, and buildings likewise, had a long history in cruder materials already, before work in marble was achieved; the rough Munychia limestone, like medieval rubble, needed a good coat of whitewash before it was fit to be seen; and over the whitewash colour was habitually applied as it is in the Greek islands to-day, and was in Athens itself within living memory. The fragments of pre-Persian date, both of monuments and of figure-sculpture, are conclusive evidence; and on the Parthenon itself, though the colours have disappeared now, they protected the marble long enough to cause appreciable difference of texture.

No doubt, after Pentelic marble came into common use, its unrivalled whiteness was utilised as it deserved, and later architects, pedantically copying the rain-washed exteriors of old masterpieces were more sparing of colour than their predecessors; but we may safely picture the ancient city, more especially in its early splendour, as aglow with polychrome decoration.

Outside the Acropolis, the fifth century town was an odd mixture of splendour and simplicity —" culture without luxury "—in entire keeping with its motto. Here there were other notable temples, such as the so-called Theseion, which is still almost perfect, of the same simple construction and grave style as the Parthenon; and many smaller shrines of heroes and the " little gods, the gods that bless ". or curse; some of them hardly held a dozen worshippers, and nestled like city churches among the shops and houses.

There were business-like offices for public officials—temples likewise, in many instances, for in ancient life State and Church were one; every servant of the City was a servant of Athene, too, or of some other Power " whom this City observeth." Especially round that immemorial

## "PRISON OF SOCRATES" HEWN IN THE FLANKS OF THE MOUSEION HILL

Among the rock-hewn chambers to the west of the old city is a series which has become known, in the haphazard manner of early archæology, as the "Prison of Socrates." It consists of three excavations cut horizontally into the side of the rock, and one in the "beehive" form of the Mycenean graves; though undoubtedly intended for tombs, they appear to have been later converted into dwellings, perhaps in the stress of the Peloponnesian War, when the countryside flocked for protection to Athens.

## WHENCE ORATORS SWAYED THE ATHENIAN MOB: THE BEMA ON THE PNYX

West of the Acropolis lies another smaller hill, notable, apart from the prehistoric rock-hewn tombs and dwellings by which it is surrounded, for a huge platform on two levels partly cut out of its sloping side and partly retained on the outside by a wall of massive blocks. Here, according to tradition, was the first meeting-place of the Athenian popular assemblies, and here, on the upper terrace, is still to be seen the "bema," or stone rostrum with steps, whence orators addressed the crowd below.

"gathering-ground," the Agora, stood public buildings of special or of general use; long colonnades for covered market and courts of law and business appointments, surrounding irregularly, and with temples and other buildings interspersed, an open space like a fair ground, usually full of stalls and shanties, and mere piles of goods for sale, but easily cleared at a bugle-call, if a meeting was due, by the odd-looking Thracian police, talking heaven-knows-what among themselves, for by custom they were recruited from wild highlanders abroad.

But the greater part of the town, so far as we may reconstruct it from the few streets excavated about thirty years ago by the German Archæological Institute, was very like modern Athens or the older parts of Naples or Rome, only with far less provision for traffic of any kind. The lanes were ill paved and ill drained, the houses small and cramped, the shops open-fronted to the street, like those of Shoe Lane once beloved of tourists. "Who could distinguish from its neighbours the house of Miltiades or of Perikles?" cries an Athenian speaker in the fourth century, lamenting a change of taste which seemed to him significant of a change of morals, too; and we have glimpses, in other chance remarks, of women and children hustled upstairs in a hurry when the master of the house unexpectedly brought home an acquaintance on a matter of business.

Later and more commodious houses had a front passage leading to a little courtyard on to which, on its sunniest side, one of the living-rooms was open for its whole width. The front door opened outwards,

like our stable-doors, to save space within; so you knocked on coming out, or when ejecting slops into the lane, to warn passers-by. And all doors had raised thresholds, as in modern Greek villages, to keep out rain; unlucky to trip up over, but a convenient supplement on a warm day to the scanty chairs and camp-stools.

But the menfolk were not much at home, except

CAPRICIOUSLY PRESERVED: THE "GATE OF THE AGORA"
The "Agora" or market-place proper of classical times lay east of the Acropolis and embraced most of the old "Kerameikos" or potters' quarter; but the portico of Athene Archegetis in the Doric style (erected about the beginning of the Christian era), which is known as the "Gate of the Agora," gave entrance to what was possibly an oil-market to the west of the "Tower of the Winds." Its four well-preserved columns supporting an entablature and pediment show the survival of a fine architectural tradition.

CENTRE OF ATHENIAN LIFE, THE TRADITION-HAUNTED AGORA BELOW THE ACROPOLIS

Dominating the Agora, which lay to the north-west of it, may be seen the Acropolis height with the statue of Athene Promachos, the roof of the Parthenon, and the Propylaea complex. In the foreground is the Agora or market-place, with the Stoa or Portico of Attalos on the left and the Stoa Poikile continuing the line; at the back of it is the Bouleuterion or Senate house and the Tholos, where certain high officials dined at the public expense. In front are the shrine and statue of Eirene and Ploutos, with the Bema or rostrum in the centre of the steps. The small eminence in the right distance is the Areiopagos, and the portico supported by figures is the Stoa of the Eponymoi, with the façade of the Metroon, or Temple of the Mother of the Gods, behind it.

*Specially drawn and coloured for "Wonders of the Past," after the restoration by Bühlmann*

for meals and sleep. The house was the women's domain, and respectable women were not expected to be seen abroad, except for necessary marketing and the laborious journey to the public well or conduit. "The best woman is she whose name is seldomest heard among the men." The leisure time of the men, on the other hand, was spent in the market-place or the drill-ground, in the wine shops or the numerous athletic clubs, where you could get a bath or a chat, as well as a game, or a bout of fencing or wrestling. Work began early, and ended early; festivities ended late sometimes and noisily.

Festivals, religious in origin, and more or less religious in their observances, were as common as saints' days in modern Greece. Some included various kinds of games, especially races between customary points, like the torch-race with elaborate team work from a suburb chapel to the Cave of Pan under the citadel wall, a thank-offering for the issue of the Marathon fight. Many had processions or pageantry, like the hauling of a model ship to the Parthenon, with Athene's new and gorgeous robe for a sail.

And at the Dionysia there were the plays in the theatre, a natural hollow on the south side of the Acropolis, enlarged and improved with marble seats, and at length with a permanent stage instead of the old platform on wheels. Even on a winter day it was seldom too cold to sit thus in the open air muffled up and crowded together, with Ilissos and the purple Hymettos country for a back-scene, and noisy fellows cracking nuts higher up "on the rocks," which served Athenian play-goers for a gallery.

Later, there was a concert hall, too, farther west on the same slope, stone-built to replace the quaint wooden auditorium which the wits called "Perikles' hat," and a long and deep colonnade between this and the theatre, for refuge on wet days, a welcome benefaction from Eumenes, king of Pergamum, whose story is told in later pages.

### CHORAGIC MONUMENT OF LYSIKRATES
A small circular structure of Pentelic marble 21½ feet high, consisting of six engaged Corinthian columns, and erected about 335 B.C., this is the only extant example of a class of monuments that once lined a whole street in Athens, and were designed to support the tripods given as prizes to the successful "choragos" or producer at the theatrical contests of the Dionysiac Festival. The frieze represents Dionysos and the Tyrrhenian pirates.

Few, if any, of the streets showed any engineering skill or architectural pretentions. Probably the most stately was the Street of Tripods, which ran, rather like that which overlooks the Grassmarket at Edinburgh, along the slope above the Agora, with a fine view northward over the plain, to the "black country" of charcoal-burning Acharnai, and the frontier ridges of Parnes. It wound round the citadel's eastern cliffs, as far as the theatre, and was decorated with the monuments of successful performances. One of these only remains, a charming little tower faced with slender columns and carved frieze, with a high plinth below and a lodgment on the roof for the tripod won by Lysikrates, whom it commemorates. Other important thoroughfares led from the market-place

It was in this direction that ancient Athens tended to expand, after it ceased to have military importance ; and the modern palace and fashionable villa quarter are along the same highway. There had been an early suburb, however, on this side, towards the river, as far back as the sixth century B.C., laid out by Peisistratos and his sons around the vast temple of Olympian Zeus, which neither they, nor King Antiochos of Syria, nor the

RESTORATION OF THE STREET IN ATHENS WITH THE TOWER OF THE WINDS

Above is seen a reconstruction of the site where Athenians came 2,000 years ago to learn the latest weather report. Although the porches of the tower no longer exist, this marble-walled structure is not only a beautiful feature but one of the most characteristic buildings in Greece, the date of its erection being probably in the first half of the first century B.C. The bronze Triton which once served as a weather-vane is pointing to Apeliotes, the east wind. Within the tower there can be seen still the round channels which once belonged to a water clock and into which flowed water from a semicircular cistern.
After a reconstruction by Bühlmann

to the Double Gate, and thence dividing, through suburbs, towards Eleusis, to the Academy Gardens, and to Kolonos, another park on a low hill some distance to the north of the city.

The road to Acharnai led through a gate of its own ; there were alternative roads to the port ; and the main road into the midlands of Attica passed eastward up the Ilissos valley along the south slope of Lykabettos. Here, about a mile from the Diomean Gate was the drill-ground, and Lyceum College for scientific and philosophical studies, of which Aristotle was the first director ; and beyond the river bed the racecourse—stadium or stadion—the only public structure of old Athens which has been completely restored, a memorial of the Olympic Games of 1896.

Emperor Augustus in after days lived to see completed, though they all had a hand in its building ; the Emperor Hadrian, a great lover of Athens, finished it in A.D. 129, and installed a great statue of the god, in gold and ivory like the virgin goddess on the Citadel. Of its original equipment of one hundred and four columns, in a double range down each side, with triple rows at the ends, only fifteen are still standing to-day. They are of Corinthian style, 56 feet 7 inches in height. Hadrian also greatly extended this eastern suburb, and his new entrance to it, which still stands, bears on its inner face the words :

" This is Athens, once the city of Theseus,"
and on the outer :

" This is the city of Hadrian, not of Theseus."

The new quarter was known as Novae Athenae or New Athens.

Another great foundation of Hadrian was a public library, of which sumptuous fragments remain north of a Roman extension of the market-place. Other conspicuous Roman buildings are the great music-hall of Herodes Atticus (who also constructed the Stadium already mentioned) and the pretentious monument of Philopappos, which crowns the Hill of the Muses in the south-western quarter of the city.

Mention has already been made of the Areiopagos—the "Mars' Hill" of S. Paul's visit—below the ascent to the Acropolis, and of that middle section of the western plateau opposite, which was known as the Pnyx, perhaps an old nickname, meaning "crowded" or "stifling." As the citadel stands for the military defence of Athens, so round these lesser hills cling the memories of its political development. For it was on the bare crown of the Areiopagos that tradition placed the first session of that Supreme Court which owned no law but the conscience of its members; which, in ages past, had reconciled the claims of justice and mercy in the tragic story of Orestes, and had conducted the grim Avengers, now transformed to be "Gracious Ones," to inhabit thenceforth the rock shelter below this Hill of Dooms. There, after the Persian terror, the guardians of that "law of kindness" held reparation councils till they had set Athens straight, and here, a generation later, were themselves set straight when their work was done.

There, too, long after, "certain philosophers" of Athens which was still if not the "School of Greece" in law and morals, at all events its leading university, drew a wandering scholar, Paul of Tarsus, aside for cool grave discussion of that new theory of his about "Healing and Rising Again," "Jesus and Anastasis," and heard his interpretation of their own "forgotten god." He, too, like themselves, was a "citizen of no mean city," and had freedom of speech among the free.

THE STREET OF TOMBS IN ANCIENT ATHENS

As in the Appian Way at Rome, the Street of Tombs at Athens was also a highway leading into the city. The tombs were usually arranged in rows in order of families, several of which extended down to the Roman period.

After the reconstruction by F. Thiersch

Crowded and stifling, too, the Pnyx Hill must have been on business days, for here, in view of over half the plain, Athenians met, close-ranked, to debate public affairs. The bugle rang out at the appointed hour; the crier went his merry round of the streets, chalking down with his red rope the slacker, the mugwump, and the conscientious objector; the meeting was "made" with a modest quorum of six thousand voters out of about thirteen thousand on the register; the council, a standing committee of five hundred, produced its "orders of the day"; the President offered prayer and signalled to the crier, and at the call, "Who wishes to speak?" the man of the hour—Perikles, or

Alkibiades, or Demosthenes—stepped forward to the platform of the great rock-altar ; and in due course, by open show of hands, it " seemed good to the Council and People of the Athenians " that a Parthenon should be built, or the fleet be mobilised to coerce a revolted " ally," or the " greatest of wars till now " be accepted as a lesser evil than to be bullied by a rival state which had rejected arbitration.

The great semicircle of assembly and its terrace wall are devastated now ; the device of parliamentary representation, which the Athenian Council so nearly anticipated, has made government by referendum a curiosity or a last resource ; but the great altar stands foursquare, and the rock-hewn seats on the terrace above it ; and echoes of those direct appeals which the sea breeze

broadcast through a self-governing people come through to us in Thucydides from the man who " flashed and thundered and confounded Greece."

But Athens, in its great days, was not only a laboratory of fearless political experiment, and of political thinking ; not only, in its own leader's words, " a school of Greece " in the disciplined expression of emotions, and in the constructive criticism of ideals ; it was also, throughout its great days, and for another century, and more, after them, a busy, prosperous centre of traffic and industry, turning the natural resources of Attica —which we have seen were considerable in agricultural and mineral wealth—to the fullest account which the convenient situation of the region permitted, at the very heart of the Greek world. From Solon's wise replacement of corn-growing

THE PROPYLAEA OR CEREMONIAL APPROACH TO THE ACROPOLIS

The Propylaea were a stately system of vestibules and doorways giving access to the Acropolis ; they were the glory of Athens when they were built, and even now that they are in ruins they have in some ways a greater power of fascination than any other building there. And yet misfortune dogged them from their inception ; the original plan of Mnesikles the architect was never fulfilled, partly, perhaps, owing to troublous times that beset the city, and partly owing to religious reluctance to build over ancient sites, which Perikles was no longer able to defy. And in later times storms of ignorance and barbarism have swept across them, the most spectacular disaster being the explosion of a Turkish powder-magazine. The blank wall at the back of this northern wing is that of the ancient Pinakotheka or picture gallery.

Photo by Autotype Co.

by the cultivation of olive and vine, and from the development of silver-mining under the rule of Peisistratos, of the pot-clays of Kerameikos and Kolias under his successors, and of the marble quarries of Pentelikon in the following century, came the raw materials for the service of immigrant craftsmen from older haunts of industry, who were so diligently encouraged throughout the sixth and fifth centuries; though their incorporation into the political fabric of the state met an unexpected and disastrous check just when a more liberal decision might have altered the whole destiny of the Greek people.

And it was the handling of the produce of all these activities, and the distribution of them abroad in exchange for the corn, the timber, the textiles, and the bronze, iron, and other raw materials which Attica could not produce for itself, or could only produce at the expense of more profitable employments, while it could so easily acquire them commercially from elsewhere, that made the livelihood of an ever-growing urban population, and the fortunes of great business families; and what was more important still, created, alongside what had been a city state of agricultural peasant farmers, with accessory home industries, the seafarers and quayside occupants of the great harbour settlement of Peiraeus, the "neighbouring city" of Athens itself, in ancient, as in quite modern times.

The site of this port, nestling among the creeks and coves which encircle the detached eminence of Munychia, at the western horn of Phaleron Bay, has but little early history. Primitive seafaring in those waters, with light, shallow vessels, easily beached at need or when out of use, preferred open roadsteads and a beach of sand or shingle, such as lines Phaleron Bay and many other gulf-heads and delta-fronts in the Mediterranean. Rocky coves, however land-locked, offered too risky navigation to cargo-boats, and were left to fishermen and pirates.

**GATEWAY OF SOLEMN STATE PROCESSIONS**
The Propylaea were composed entirely of Pentelic marble and erected more than 2,300 years ago. Poised beyond them was the 26-foot bronze statue of Athene Promachos that was erected with the booty of Marathon. The goddess was represented in full armour with shield and lance, of which the gilded point gleaming in the sun served as a landmark for sailors rounding Cape Colonna. So fine are the ruins (see the opposite page) that the task of reconstruction is not great.
*After a reconstruction by F. Thiersch*

But when ships of heavier burthen and deeper draught traversed the great gulf of the Levant or the Black Sea, or were "driven up and down in Adria," like the cornship of S. Paul, bringing grain from Odessa or Alexandria or the broad

AS THE ANCIENT ATHENIANS SAW IT: THE EASTERN FACADE OF THE THESEION

The so-called "Theseion" is a temple in the Doric order, as may be seen from its unadorned column-capitals, the most easily recognized feature of this architectural style ; it is also a "peripteros-hexastylos" (see explanation, page 38) with thirteen columns on either side, the length being 104 feet, the breadth 45½ feet, and the height 33 feet. This restoration shows the eastern façade ; the sculptures of the pediment are largely conjectural, but the scenes from the Labours of Hercules in the metopes, or oblong spaces seen beneath the eaves, are extant on this frontage.

*From a reconstruction by André in "Monuments Antiques"*

lowlands of Sicily and Southern Italy, a harbour with a mole and quays, and warehouses thereon, was a convenience, and became a necessity. Still more, when the security of such traffic—involving as it did the food supply of a whole people—became a matter of public concern, the mercantile harbour of a carrying power like Athens, or Samos, or Rhodes, no less than their rivals in Tyre and Carthage, found a naval base and its arsenal an indispensable supplement.

Polykrates, in the sixth century B.C., had made Samos famous as well as prosperous, and a terror to sea-devils, by constructing there the first deep-sea port ; and his tunnelled aqueduct, a full mile long, through the sheltering ridge behind his harbour-fortress, testified to the needs of its crowded population, and had been the model for the far easier achievement of the "Nine-ways Fountain" with which Peisistratos had made industrial Athens habitable about the same time.

In Peiraeus, however, the Athenians enjoyed, by mere bounty of nature, a rock-scarped harbour tenfold more capacious, and securer far against both raids and rough weather than that of Polykrates. Its use came late ; but here it was that, in the nick of time, on the eve of the Persian War, Themistokles persuaded his countrymen to construct that war-fleet which lay secure under the very eyes of its creators, ready against all comers. That fleet it was which made possible the crowning deliverance in Salamis Bay, round the point from Peiraeus itself, and made possible the return of the Athenians and the re-walling of Athens, already mentioned in dealing with the upper town. And it was a task only less urgent, to fortify the naval port, and to surround the whole base of the Munychia prominence with what its massive remnants show to have been the last word in impregnable masonry.

Thucydides, who had lived among eye-witnesses, describes the marvel as it grew: how in the building of it there was no rubble core ; all was of squared stone, from the inner to the outer face ; so wide was it that the wagons passed freely by each other, coming and going upon the wall itself with blocks from the quarries in the hill to the point now reached by the builders. It is the description of a railway viaduct rather than a fortress wall.

The land side thus secured, the harbour mouth was guarded, rather later, by a fortress of similar works ; of its main gateway the flanking towers are visible still. Within, by a triumph of ancient town-planning, by the first master of that rare art in Greece, the broad quay, with its spacious columnar " exchange," or " exhibition building," gave access to broad streets of uniform " gridiron " plan, with squares at the principal intersections, and colonnaded side-walks. Modern Peiraeus does homage to its former self by retracing that old design, as it spreads over the promontory once more. On the sea front were more quays, round fishing coves, and another docking station, with a theatre almost on the promenade, and a larger and more famous one high upon the hillside—their

perennial back-scene just Salamis and the " thousand rippling laughter " of the gulf, and the black peak of Aegina, the " national enemy " for so long ; and on a clear day the castle-rock of Corinth and the snowy gable of the Arcadian mountains.

So planned, and in great part completed, Peiraeus was architecturally the completest contrast imaginable to the crowded dwellings and haphazard thoroughfares and alleys of Athens. Themistokles did not live to see it in its pride ; but a lonely tomb, said to be his, stands far down the promontory, where the traffic hauls close in shore, and the sailor may hail a blessing on the man who built the ships for Salamis.

Again, in due time, less than thirty years later, when the very success of this new business centre and also (we must admit) the not unnatural elation of the Athenians themselves in such prosperity turned neighbours and old rivals into enemies and brought " Dorian war " into Attica, a fresh stroke of constructive imagination and far-sighted strategy linked city and port together by the

BEAUTY OF THE "THESEION" ON THE WEST OF THE OLD ATHENIAN MARKET-PLACE

Like so many of the Greek temples still in part remaining, this, the most perfectly preserved of them all, owes its good fortune to its conversion into a church in the Middle Ages. And yet but little is known of its origin or purpose. As to its date, evidences of style in sculpture and architecture would make it contemporary with the Parthenon, and place it in the fifth century B.C., while with regard to its purpose, it has been universally known as the Theseion from the fact that some of its sculptures portray exploits of Theseus ; but the Theseion is now proved to have stood elsewhere. Perhaps the most likely conjecture, based on statements of Pausanias, is one that would make it the Hephaisteion or Sanctuary of Hephaistos.

RESTORATION OF THE ACROPOLIS, FROM HOAR ANTIQUITY THE—
On a hill dominating the Attic plain there rose the Acropolis, or castle of Athens, where lived the ancient kings, and stood sanctuaries of state. The sole approach was on the west side, which is reconstructed above in all its ancient glory. Theseus, the fifth king, is regarded as the real founder of Athens, and to him Thucydides assigns the synoikismos, or subordination of all the Attic communities to this city as their capital. Originally it consisted of the Acropolis only, but gradually extended in all directions. Persians destroyed the ancient buildings in 480 B.C., but Themistokles and Kimon rebuilt the walls, and Perikles then became the chief founder of those

After the reconstruction by Marcel Lambert

—NUCLEUS OF ALL THE SETTLEMENTS ON THE ATTIC PLAIN

magnificent buildings illustrated here, which even in their present-day ruinous state, still present the finest picture of the unrivalled art of antiquity. Above we see the highly artistic Propylaea, and poised above and behind them the bronze statue of Athene Promachos and the Erechtheion, temple of the tutelary goddess Athene Pollas. On the other side rises the Temple of Nike, built like the Propylaea of Pentelic marble ; while the building that dominates the whole is, according to most authorities, the most perfect monument of ancient art, the Parthenon, far surpassing all other Athenian buildings in the brilliancy of its plastic and polychrome decorations.

famous " Long Walls " from gate to gate, enclosing the crowded, dusty highway between continuous screens of lofty masonry for nearly four miles ; so that the Queen of the Seas, as Athens now was, might deem herself insular, as the hated Aegina had been, and defy the land powers to imperil her. There was an old warning to the effect that " a Dorian war shall come, and dearth therewith," but on the completion of the " Long Walls "

OLYMPIEION AND THE ARCH OF HADRIAN

The Roman Emperor Hadrian was a " Graecophil " and expended much on beautifying Athens. He added a new quarter to the town, to which this arch, 59 feet high, was the entrance, as inscriptions on it record ; it stands close by the Olympieion, whose pillars are visible on the left, and which was also completed by the same monarch. Near by, to commemorate his services to the town, rose Hadrian's colossal statue.

Athenians might well feel that this peril at all events they had forgone.

Yet those " Long Walls " were in a sense the beginning of the end. The sea-road was secure ; but Dorian hatred grew, and croakers, altering one letter, murmured " and death therewith."

And this time the doom fell. The Spartan invasions of 431 B.C. and the following years drove the country population of Attica into false security behind those Walls, camping out, like Smyrna refugees in Athens to-day, " in friends' houses, if they had any, in waste places, temples, shrines, indeed in anything that was not locked up ; in bastions of the walls, and wherever anyone could." This was bad enough, though at least the Walls held. But then came the plague, " and death therewith," as the warning had been ; inexplicable, unavoidable, and usually fatal, though a man might survive disfigured, maimed, or blind for life, or by some special grace recover, as did Thucydides, " who wrote the history."

Other cities suffered, so we hear, but none so irremediably as Athens. It was not so much the loss of life, though the disease cost Athens her supreme leader, Perikles, as well as thousands unknown to fame, save that it is the portrait of such as they that he had drawn in immortal words only a year before, " showing through what kind of training we won our heritage ; in what manner of city and ways of life that heritage has become so glorious ; for the institutions we enjoy preclude envy of our neighbours' ways ; we are rather a pattern for others, than needing to copy them."

What really mattered was the break-up of old ties, old sympathies, old opportunities of intercourse in the stress and horror of such a crisis ; a disease of the soul, clouding the vision as the plague blinded the eye ; sapping the judgement and the will, as the hands and feet of its victims lost their speed and deftness ; corrupting the fine sense of social obligation which alone made possible what Athenians " called democracy, because it is in the hands not of the few but of the many "—for the " many " were Athenians all. And it is their city, of which the fragments are precious to us, because they are the original handiwork of them ; as the work of dramatist and historian was written for them and among them, and has come down to us, preserved through storm and stress because they found it true to the truth which they knew.

Distinguished thinkers, graceful writers and craftsmen, beautiful additions to her series of temples and monuments, Athens continued to produce, or to make her own, in the centuries that followed this turning point of the " Dorian War " and its plague. In the history of Greek achievement they hold high place ; but the torch passed into other hands, and revealed other aspects of the world and of humanity ; and in the history of Athens they are a supplement. When we speak of " ancient Athens," it is to the " pre-war " city that our thoughts, our dreams, and our regrets go back, in which the Erechtheion was rebuilding, and the Parthenon was new.

## The Great Monuments. IV.

# The Wonder of the Obelisk

## By R. Engelbach

Keeper, Egyptian Museum, Cairo

AMONG the wonders of ancient times which have roused the curiosity of mankind for many generations, the obelisk stands almost first. Though the Pyramids make us marvel at the enormous expenditure of labour which they must have entailed, to say nothing of the incredible accuracy of their workmanship, yet the obelisk, as an engineering tour de force, is a greater puzzle than they, and has been the subject of more speculations—some ridiculous in the extreme—than any problem of antiquity. The question is : How did the ancient Egyptians, almost surely ignorant of the capstan, the winch, and the system of pulleys or block-and-tackle, extract these obelisks from the granite quarries at Assuan (Aswan), transport them for hundreds of miles over land and water, and erect them, even in the middle of existing buildings ? We know of obelisks of more than 500 tons which were actually erected, and, if we are to believe the Egyptian and Roman records, some must have weighed over 1,000 tons. We can appreciate the difficulty of such feats the more when we remember that modern removals of obelisks, none of which exceeds 340 tons, always tried the skill of the engineers to the utmost.

As to the *meaning* of the obelisk, strictly speaking I do not think it has a meaning. As we can trace the pyramid back to the funeral-cairn, so I believe we can see in the huge flagstaffs, which always stood before the pylons, the germ-idea of the obelisk. Once a high, thin stone monument is desired, the obelisk is the natural outcome, it being a matter of pride that the monument should be of one block. Let us consider the alternatives : if it were made as thin as a pole, it would not be stiff enough, since granite has no flexibility ; if it had to taper from the width of the base to nothing at the top, its shape would have to be that of a dunce's cap ; if it were of one breadth throughout it would look top-heavy ; if it had not a cap of some sort it would look unfinished, and, finally, if it were of round cross-section it would be almost impossibly difficult to shape or handle, besides being less convenient for inscribing.

No known obelisk dates further back than the twelfth dynasty, that is, to about 1950 B.C.,

when we have one at Mataria of 67 feet high and weighing 120 tons. The 40-foot monolith of the same date at Begîg, in the Fayûm, can hardly be called an obelisk, as it is of unique shape and never stood before a pylon at all ; it is rather a glorified stele. Records of the existence of obelisks extend back to the Old Kingdom, some thousand years earlier, but we know nothing of their size or form.

In ancient times the tops of the obelisks were covered with gold, electrum, or copper caps, to make them shine in the sunlight. According to 'Abd El-Latîf, the Mataria obelisks still retained their copper caps in A.D. 1200. Nearly all the obelisks in Rome, incongruously enough, have been decorated with brazen crosses.

The number of known obelisks is considerable, though there are to-day more obelisks outside Egypt than in it. Though Karnak alone had at least thirteen large obelisks, there are now but three, including one only about 12 feet high, and one which may fall at any time (page 406). These, together with the Luxor and Mataria obelisks, are all that Egypt now possesses, while in Rome there are more than a dozen of various sizes ; Constantinople has two, and England, America, and France have one each. Earthquakes, soil-subsidence, and foreign conquerors have indeed taken a terrible toll. As far back as the time of Ashurbanipal, who took a couple of obelisks to Nineveh (about 690 B.C.), it has been the custom of the foreign controllers of Egypt to take away obelisks as souvenirs, and it is a striking fact that they were able, not only to remove, but to erect them. Though we have no data on the size of those sent to Nineveh, we know that the London and New York obelisks, each of which is claimed as *the* Cleopatra's Needle, had been moved in Roman times from Heliopolis to Alexandria, and one at least had been erected there. These weigh only about 200 tons each, but some obelisks removed to Rome in ancient times weighed as much as 340 tons. With our hydraulic jacks, steel towers, winches, and all the paraphernalia of modern engineering, the removal and erection of an obelisk has been the most difficult task imaginable, and has caused world-wide interest, yet

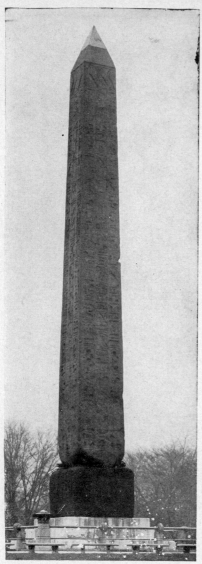

THREE OF THE ANCIENT OBELISKS: IN EGYPT AND IN FOREIGN CAPITALS

Left: One of "Cleopatra's Needles," set up by Thothmes III. (c. 1500 B.C.) at Heliopolis, further inscribed by Rameses II. (c. 1250 B.C.), removed to Alexandria in 23 B.C., and thence to New York, where it now stands. It is 67 feet 2 inches high without the pedestal. Centre: Fellow of that on the left, 68 feet 5 inches high, removed in 1877 to the Thames Embankment; obelisks were usually set up in pairs. Right: Obelisk of Senusret I. of the twelfth dynasty (c. 1980 B.C.), still standing on its original emplacement near Heliopolis—it is the earliest known to us.

Photos by Metropolitan Museum of Art, New York City, and Donald McLeish

among all the literature that has come down to us from Egyptian and Roman sources, there is nothing which throws any real light on how they accomplished such feats.

As an example of what classical authors have to say on this subject, we can turn to Pliny, book xxxvi., chap. 14, where he tells us that the transport of an obelisk under King Ptolemy Philadelphus was done by digging a canal from the Nile to pass under the obelisk, which was lying down, and unballasting two large barges below it, thus letting them take the weight. This may have been true, but it was not the method used by the Egyptians. As to the erection under a king he calls Rhamsesis, he cites a typical dragoman's tale, omitting all

mechanical details, but saying how the king, fearing that the machinery used was not strong enough, had his own son tied to the summit to make the workmen more careful!

At Assuan there is a huge obelisk, 137 feet long, which would have weighed 1,170 tons, lying abandoned, and only partly detached from the surrounding rock. The complete clearance of this monument in 1922 has given us several definite facts about the ancient engineering. It appears that the top layers of rock were removed by pouring water on the granite after it had been strongly heated by papyrus fires. This heating and cooling method is used in the Indian granite quarries at the present day. Having reached

## HOW WERE THE OBELISKS RAISED WITHIN COURTS LESS THAN THEMSELVES IN LENGTH?

Mighty as was the work of hewing an obelisk from its bed, the unfinished block at Assuan teaches us something of the methods employed. More mysterious is the raising of these monuments. One of the most likely theories is illustrated above. A huge brick ramp was constructed, with a rectangular hole near the top whose sides sloped gently towards the waiting pedestal at the bottom; this hole having been filled with sand, the obelisk was dragged up the ramp (1 and 3) until the sand supported its base (2); whereupon, the sand being withdrawn through prepared passages, the base sank on to the pedestal (4, 5 and 6), from which position the block might be pulled upright. A notch in the pedestal in which the base engaged prevented slipping.

a level where the granite appeared to be free from flaws for the desired length, the surface was rendered flat by dressing with large balls of dolerite —a rock akin to diorite—which occur naturally in some desert valleys in Egypt. These balls weigh from 9 to 15 pounds. The outline of the obelisk was next drawn on the flat surface, and a separating trench made around it. A surprising result of the study of the Assuan obelisk is that neither chisels nor wedges were used in detaching it from the quarry; the dolerite balls were the only tools employed. In other words, the obelisk was not cut out but *bashed* out. Whether the balls were attached to rammers and worked by more than one man is a disputable point, but I consider it very probable. Not only the sides, but the

**HEWN FOR HATSHEPSUT AND HER FATHER**
On the left, before the Osiris Court of the Great Temple at Karnak, is the leaning obelisk of Thothmes I., with the pedestal of its companion beyond; like "Cleopatra's Needle" it was employed by Rameses II. for his inscriptions. To the right, behind the pylon, is the obelisk of Queen Hatshepsut, which also formed one of a pair.
*Photo by Gaddis & Seif*

**OBELISK OF RAMESES II. AT LUXOR**
From Roman times obelisks have been prized as souvenirs, and Paris now owns the one corresponding to the subject of this illustration. The pair were erected by Rameses II. before the pylons of Luxor Temple, and the one remaining is about 88 feet high. Note the unimpaired delicacy of its hieroglyphs, each a separate work of art.
*Photo by Gaddis & Seif*

under surface of the obelisk, were detached by bashing. For an obelisk of this size, the detaching would take less than a year. In the quarry we can see how the men were arranged and even how the foremen measured up the work done, but a discussion of all the details of the quarrying is outside the range of this article.

Having detached the obelisk from the quarry, levers and ropes were called into use, and, with the aid of some 5,000 men, it was rolled down from its bed to the spot where a sledge (known from the Deir el-Bahri sculptures) was buried. The sledge was, of course, already on its rollers and track balks. Having dug the sledge and track clear of sand, the obelisk was hauled down

**OBELISKS CARVED UPON THE WALLS OF THE TEMPLE OF LUXOR**

A bas-relief from the Luxor Temple gives a contemporary picture of one of the pylons of that building, and shows the disposition before it of the obelisks, flagstaffs, and colossi. In this instance there are four flagstaffs; the sloping side of the pylon is always recessed to receive the foot, and towards the top may be seen the metal clamps which held them in position. The figure to the right is Amenherkhepeshef, one of the hundred and eleven sons of Rameses II.

Photo by Gaddis & Seif

to the bank of the Nile. Where there was any unevenness in the ground, an embankment was made, and we can see to-day, in the quarries, enormous embankments along which large blocks were transported in ancient times. At the river bank a very large boat was in readiness, covered over by an earth or sand embankment, and the obelisk was pulled over it, and by removing the sand from under the obelisk, it was made to descend gradually into the boat, which was then dug clear and the journey by water begun. The Egyptians were skilful boat-builders, and we have records of boats over 30 yards long. At its destination, probably at high Nile, the boat was packed rigid, the sides removed, and the journey continued on a prepared track to the temple.

As to the erection of obelisks, it is here that speculation has run riot, and perfectly amazing statements have been made on the subject by engineers, architects, archæologists, and by that perpetual thorn in the flesh of the serious student, the reckless exponent of the occult.

(1) that they could introduce obelisks into existing courts whose walls were of less length than that of the obelisk; (2) that many obelisks are so close to the pylons that there would hardly have been room enough for the huge levers which would have been required, and (3) that the pedestal notch—an essential for this method—was never used in the case of the standing obelisk of Queen Hatshepsut (Hatshepsô-wet) at Karnak, as it has come down askew on its pedestal and missed the notch altogether. There are other mechanical objections when dealing with large obelisks.

The other theory is that the obelisk was rolled up a long, high embankment until it nearly overhung the end, and earth was removed from below the obelisk until it was made to settle down slowly on to its pedestal, leaning against the end of the embankment, from whence it could be pulled upright. The great objection to this method is that it is extremely risky; it can well be realized what a delicate process it would be to undercut below a 500-ton obelisk, some 60 feet above the ground, to make it settle down on to a pedestal 15 feet square! The pulling upright would be even more risky, as modern removals have shown that the strongest head-ropes are very unreliable for checking the momentum of such masses. I more than doubt if even the ancient Egyptians would have dared to use this method close to any existing building, knowing that, if the obelisk fell forwards or sideways, it would spread red ruin around it; the use of an embankment is, however, very likely as, in an ancient papyrus, one scribe sets another a problem on calculating the number of

UNFINISHED OBELISK IN THE GRANITE QUARRIES AT ASSUAN

In the quarries at Syene (Assuan), whence came the rose-pink granite of the obelisks, still lies one unfinished shaft which, had it been erected, would have been the largest of all. It measures 137 feet and would have weighed 1,170 tons; but there is a flaw in the granite near its centre which explains its abandonment before completion.

Photo by A. M. MacGillivray

Two theories stand out as being more or less reasonable, though neither is very convincing. One is that the edge of the obelisk was placed so that it engaged in the narrow notch which is found on nearly every obelisk-pedestal, and that it was gradually levered up, the earth being banked behind the levers at each heave, until the obelisk was leaning against an earth bank sufficiently steep to permit it to be pulled into a vertical position. The 35-ton obelisk at Seringapatam was actually raised in this way. The reasons against this method having been used by the ancient Egyptians are

bricks for one nearly a quarter of a mile long and 90 feet high—sufficient for erecting the largest obelisk of which we have any knowledge.

A suggested method, which explains and meets all observed facts, is that the obelisk was not let over the edge of the embankment, but down a pit in the end of it, the pit being of square section, wide at the top and tapering down to the size of the pedestal, with a gentle curve leading from the side from which the obelisk was to enter on to the surface of the embankment. In page 405 is a section through the length of such an embankment, showing the positions of the obelisk at various stages of its descent into the pit or funnel. The gradual lowering of the obelisk down the funnel is done by filling it with sand, which was removed through galleries leading from the bottom of the funnel to the outside of the embankment. From experiments on a scale-model, it was found that there was no tendency for the obelisk to jam against the further wall of the funnel if the sand was removed from the side under the obelisk. A second gallery, on the other side, was, however, necessary in order to clean the surface of the pedestal before the obelisk was pulled upright. The purpose of the pedestal-notch is twofold ; it takes the weight of the obelisk on its inner edge instead of allowing the obelisk to come down on its own edge, thus checking a tendency to twist on the part of the obelisk when being pulled upright. Oscillation after reaching a vertical position could have been avoided by putting a cushion of, say, brushwood between the obelisk and the further wall of the funnel. The sledge is removed in halves before the obelisk descends ; this presents no mechanical difficulty at all.

It will be seen that, in this method, the obelisk must be stiff enough to support its own weight when pivoting about its centre. It has been doubted whether the known obelisks could do so. If one takes the trouble to work out the problem, it is found that in the most extreme case the strain set up would not exceed a safety-factor of $\frac{2}{3}$.

It may not be out of place to give a very brief account of how the removals in modern times of the Vatican, the Paris, the New York, and the London obelisks were performed.

The Vatican obelisk was removed by Domenico Fontana, in 1585, from the Circus of Nero in Rome to the Piazza di San Pietro. The method used was the " heroic " one of bodily lifting it by block-and-tackles actuated by a large number of capstans. A gigantic tower of wood, known as " Fontana's Castle " was erected above the obelisk, the struts being a metre square in section. From the cross-beams of the tower, pairs of block-and-tackles were attached at four points along the

obelisk. It was first raised sufficiently high to enable a cradle, or platform on rollers, to be introduced beneath it, and it was then lowered on to the cradle and pulled to its new site. The re-erection was done in exactly the reverse way to the lowering. The weight of the obelisk was calculated to be 331 tons.

The Paris obelisk was removed by Lebas, in 1839, from its original position before the pylon of Luxor Temple, where it formed, with the existing obelisk, the only pair left in situ. The lowering and raising were performed by means of a huge compound derrick, consisting of five supporting members on each side of the obelisk. Power was supplied by systems of pulleys worked by capstans. It was lowered on to a cradle which ran on a greased way down to the Nile bank, some 200 yards distant. Here it was introduced into a large pontoon-raft from which the prow had been temporarily removed. The raft was towed to France, where the transport and erection were carried out by the same methods. It now stands in the Place de la Concorde, being 75 feet high and weighing 227 tons.

The New York obelisk, which originally formed a pair with the London obelisk at Heliopolis, had already once been removed in Roman times from there to Alexandria and had been erected close to the shore. The lowering was done by fitting it at its centre of gravity with a pair of enormous steel trunnions, supported by a steel tower on each side. The point was lowered (or rather it crashed) on to a tower made of large balks of wood laid criss-cross. A similar wooden tower was then constructed beneath the butt-end, and the tower and trunnions were removed. Each end of the obelisk was raised in turn by hydraulic rams, a course of balks taken away, and the end of the obelisk lowered to the course below, the process being continued until it reached the ground. It was next floated in a wooden caisson to the dock and introduced into a steamship called the Dessouk by opening a port in her bows. At the American end it was placed on a railway and pulled to Central Park, where the trunnions and towers were again used for erecting it. For some of the short moves, the obelisk was rolled on cannon-balls running in channel-irons.

The London obelisk was towed to England in 1877, enclosed in a steel shell, fitted, like a ship, with deck and masts. On its journey it was very nearly lost in a storm in the Bay of Biscay. It was raised on much the same principle as the New York obelisk, but instead of the trunnions, knife-edged steel supports were used bearing on a huge wooden scaffolding. Its last adventure was a wound from a German air-bomb.

SCENE OF THE WORLD'S GREATEST TREASURE HUNT: CHIMU RUINS AT CHAN-CHAN

In spite of the vast hoards of gold which the Spaniards seized and ruthlessly melted down at the time of the Conquest, there is s
little doubt that even greater wealth remains hidden in both Mexico and Peru that treasure hunters have been busy ever sinc
Although more than five million pounds' worth of treasure has been removed from the vast Chimu ruins at Chan-chan, near Truxill
Peru, the 'great treasure' still remains to be found. The high walls of solid hammered clay (bottom) have been breached by gol
seekers, as also have the lower walls which have designs impressed in the clay (top).

# The Lost Treasures of Mexico and Peru

### By Lewis Spence, F.R.A.I.
#### Author of "The Gods of Mexico"

THE tireless hunt for treasure is the keynote to the history of the Spanish American colonies. But those accounts which record rich finds of hidden gold, or the payment of enormous tribute, have failed to rouse the same degree of interest as the greatly more intriguing stories of the presence in secret Mexican and Peruvian fastnesses of hoards of native gold and jewelry still awaiting discovery. There is probably not a village in either of those regions of old romance which has not its legend of buried treasure, and the fact that many of these traditions are vouched for by documentary evidence of a trustworthy character serves to keep them alive. Stories, too, are current in some districts of the existence of hereditary guardians who hand down the secret of the hidden wealth from one generation to another.

Although the native rulers of Mexico and Peru exacted large annual tributes of gold, silver and jewels from the conquered peoples whom they had absorbed into their respective empires, the precious metals do not seem to have aroused in the American races that feverish spirit of covetousness which it astonished them so greatly to find in their European conquerors. But when it became clear to them that the accumulation of gold was the master passion of the Spaniards, they took extraordinary precautions to conceal from the invaders the spots where it was mined or taken from the watercourses, and they began to secrete in inaccessible places such stores of it as in the ordinary way would have been paid as tribute into the royal treasuries of Mexico and Cuzco.

No hidden hoard, perhaps, has aroused so much speculation or has given birth to such a wealth of traditional lore as the treasure of Montezuma, the ill-starred Emperor of Mexico. After his death great efforts were made to discover its whereabouts, in face of what appears to have been a general conspiracy on the part of the natives of all ranks not to divulge the secret. Cortés and his followers had already had an encouraging experience of Aztec treasure trove. Quite by accident they had come upon a built-up doorway in the old palace of Axayacatl, where they had been lodged by order of Montezuma. Breaking down the plaster which covered it, an opening was revealed, and the Conquistadores beheld a large apartment in which were heaped gold and silver bars and ingots, jars of gold-dust, countless cups, vases and platters of gold, ornaments lavishly besprinkled with pearls and quantities of chalchihuitls, or Mexican emeralds, a species of jadeite. This was the treasure of King Axayacatl, the father of Montezuma, the tribute which during his reign had passed into his coffers from the subject provinces, and which he had hoarded against a national emergency. On being weighed, it was found to be worth nearly a million and a half in present currency.

THIS enormous booty inspired the Spaniards to seek for more, and on the death of Montezuma and the subsequent capture of his nephew and successor, Guatemozin, a persistent rumour ran through the army that Guatemozin had given orders that the treasure of his deceased uncle should be carefully placed beyond the reach of the conquerors. Pressure was brought to bear upon Cortés to put Guatemozin to the torture, and thus force him to divulge the whereabouts of the treasure. To this the Spanish leader unwillingly assented; but even in the extremity of his pain the last of the Aztec kings would vouchsafe nothing more definite than that large quantities of gold had been thrown into Lake Texcoco. In an unavailing search expert divers took part. But in a pond in the garden of Guatemozin's palace was found one of those great wheels of gold on which the Aztec symbols of the calendar were engraved.

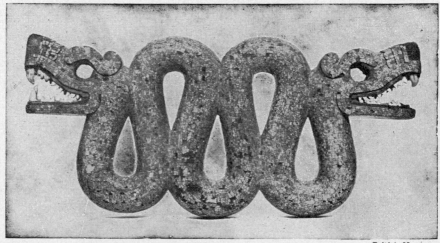

British Muséum

FROM MONTEZUMA'S TREASURE: A TURQUOISE SNAKE

This magnificent piece of mosaic work in turquoise was an item in the great treasure sent by the Aztec King of Mexico, Montezuma, to Cortés for the king of Spain. Large quantities of gold and jewelry were sent to the invading Spaniards as conciliatory gifts, which merely served to whet their appetites for Aztec gold. Extortion produced much more, but it is believed that the bulk of the imperial hoard remained inviolate.

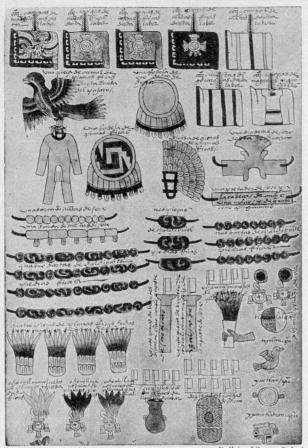

Bodleian Library, Oxford

**EVIDENCE FOR LOST MEXICAN TREASURE**
Cities subject to Montezuma at the time of the Spanish conquest
sent tribute in gold and kind, as seen in these drawings from an
Aztec MS. Here are rich ceremonial costumes, strings of gold
and precious stones and other objects. Aztec signs indicate that
over 40,000 objects are shown in this portion of one tribute.
Nothing of the enormous treasure recorded in this MS. has survived

Generations of treasure hunters have sought un-
availingly for the hoard of Montezuma. On several
occasions documentary evidence has been forthcoming which seemed to point to one or other locality
in the neighbourhood of Mexico City as its place of
concealment, but subsequent examination has invali-
dated an entire series of what seemed to be trustworthy clues. That vast resources other than the
treasure of Axayacatl were at the disposal of Montezuma cannot be questioned. But native subtlety
has proved more than equal to the task of concealing
these in some secret and inaccessible cavern or
retreat in the great mountains which surround the
plain of Mexico, so that after four centuries the story
has come to have an aspect almost fabulous.

In Peru, from the hills to the coast, scarcely a
village is without its legends of the buried treasure
of the Inca. Unlike the fairy gold of the Monte-
zumas, however, this occasionally materialises. On
the execution of Atahualpa, the Inca whom Pizarro
found disputing the throne with his brother Huascar,
the tribute of gold and silver which at his command
was flowing into the Spanish coffers from all parts
of the empire was promptly discontinued, and the
wealth in bars and specie which was on its way to
the Castilian headquarters at Caxamarca was hastily
concealed. The hidden hoard included the great
golden statue of the Luauque, the familiar or guardian
spirit of Atahualpa's father, the Inca Huayna Ccapac,
and with cups, vases, jewels and ritual vessels
amounted in value to many millions sterling. The
secret of its hiding-place was religiously guarded by
the dispossessed royal line of the Inca until the
beginning of last century. Its first official keeper
seems to have been Carlos Inca, who, as head of that
section of the royal family which had submitted to
the Spaniards, dwelt in melancholy state in the
ancient palace of the Colcampata, the ruins of which
still stand on a slope above the city of Cuzco. The
Spaniards do not seem to have been aware that
he knew the place of concealment of the treasure
or he would not long have been left in peace.

TRADITION has it that on one occasion Carlos's wife,
Maria de Esquival, a woman partly of Spanish
race, upbraided him with his poverty and condition.
But the guardian of the Incarial millions, obtaining
from her a promise of secrecy, led her blindfold to
the spot where the treasure was concealed, displaying to her bewildered gaze the heaped bars of
precious metal, the choice vessels and jewels which
had enriched his ancestors in happier days.

Carlos Inca, unable to sustain the constant indig-
nities to which the Spanish authorities subjected him,
eventually went into exile. But he handed down
the secret of the concealed treasure-house to his
heirs in the royal Peruvian succession. Ample proof
of this is to be found in the manuscript of Don
Felipe de Pomares, now in the British Museum. In
1815 the chief Pumacagua, then seventy-one years
of age, resolved to head an insurrection against the
Spaniards. But he lacked the sinews of war. Be-
taking himself to the hereditary guardian of the
treasure, he requested his aid, took the oath of
secrecy, and was conducted to the place of concealment. Blindfold and at night he was led up the
bed of the river Huatanay for a long distance, and
suddenly found himself surrounded by ingots, bars,
and great statues of gold heaped in incredible profusion. He took from the hoard only such a sum
as was necessary to equip his forces, and, returning
to Cuzco, sought the house of a sympathiser, Colonel
Pablo Astete, whose daughter long afterwards
informed Sir Clements Markham that she well
remembered his visit. He was heavily laden with
gold-dust and ingots, and drenched to the skin by
his recent passage through the river. The revolt,
however, was unsuccessful.

Treasure amounting to more than five millions
sterling has already been unearthed from the vast
ruins of Chimu culture at Chan-chan, near Truxillo,
but the ' peje grande,' or great treasure, which a well-
authenticated tradition says is concealed at that spot,
still awaits some lucky excavator. Many expeditions
have closely searched the labyrinthine Chimu ruins, but
so far they have jealously preserved their golden secret.

## The Wonder Cities.  X.

# Kish, the World's Oldest City

### By S. G. Blaxland Stubbs

Joint Author of "Sixty Centuries of Health and Physick," Assistant Editor of "The Universal History of the World"

*IN the popular mind Ur and Babylon have attracted most attention among the immensely important antiquities of ancient Mesopotamia, and separate chapters are devoted to them in this work.   Here some account is given of the tremendous archaeological labours carried out at Kish, within actual sight of Babylon on the opposite side of the Euphrates, by Professor Stephen Langdon, Director of the Oxford-Field Museum Expedition and his colleagues.   The photographs illustrating this chapter have been very kindly lent by Professor Langdon.—*EDITOR.

THE oldest city in the world !  Even though the visible remains of a city proved to justify such a title were but heaps of mud bricks (and they are much more), the mind is thrilled by so definite and tremendous a claim.  We think of the undeniable antiquity of the great cities of Egypt, of Karnak and Thebes, of Memphis and Gizeh, but although Memphis of the First Dynasty takes us back over 5,000 years to 3400 B.C., and perhaps to 4000 B.C. in the predynastic period, they are junior foundations.  At Kish, in Mesopotamia, there had been a city a thousand years earlier.  The first dynasty of Ur, and the even earlier kings from whose days survives the most marvellous craftsmanship in gold known in the ancient world, do but push the life of that great Sumerian city back to about 3500 B.C., while Babylon the great has a total history of little more than 4,000 years.

Professor Stephen Langdon and his colleagues, who have been excavating the vast ruins for many years, have produced evidence of the existence of Kish as a city at least 7,000 years ago.  Although Damascus is sometimes spoken of as the " oldest city," its claim is limited to be the oldest living city.  Full seniority, therefore, remains with Kish.

Civilization as we understand the term has, as yet, no earlier abiding centre.  Human arts and crafts in prehistoric periods, as the French and Spanish cave paintings of the palaeolithic era demonstrate (see pages 143 to 153), had reached an astounding level of achievement at a time perhaps twice as far back as that of the first Sumerian city, but that work was the product of primitive, savage hunters.  At Kish there was a great city, founded in neolithic times, that flourished as the first capital of the mysterious Sumerian race with a continuous history of 2,000 years before the great Sargon of Agade—himself a shadowy, semi-mythical figure in history and archaeology only a few years ago—made the Semites dominant in the land of the great rivers.

The long, unbroken panorama of human life and effort in this Mesopotamian centre, of the struggles and achievements of kingdom after kingdom, of empire following empire, has been reconstructed and established largely by the toil of gangs of Arab labourers under the skilled direction of the scientific archaeologist.  The work of twelve years at Kish, laborious in detail but magnificent in planning and achievement, surely represents one of the outstanding romances of modern archaeology.  The layman may be more readily attracted by the spectacular results of other diggings, of the vast material wealth of a Tutankhamen tomb, or the hoards of gold and silver from graves at Ur, but the mud bricks of Kish enshrine a story of larger appeal to the instructed imagination.

Here, in this waste of ruined cities, on the opposite side of the Euphrates from Babylon, in an inhospitable desert, now without water or plant life and swept by terrifying sandstorms, there still

**QUAINT CARVINGS FROM A PALACE WALL AT KISH**
Vivid and highly decorative, these varied figures of goats, kids and their herd give an indication of the genius of Sumerian artists. They are exquisitely carven and are inlaid in a plaque that once adorned the palace walls at Kish—one of a series in which similar pastoral subjects and martial events were treated.
Courtesy of Professor Langdon

RUINS OF A VAST TEMPLE BUILT BY NEBUCHADREZZAR NOW DUG OUT OF THE MUD AT KISH

This view of one portion of the enormous excavations carried out by the Oxford-Field Expedition at Kish shows the stage which the work had reached in 1930. In the background are the walls of a huge double temple in brick of Neo-Babylonian times, dating from about 600 B.C. This temple, like practically all other ancient buildings of the " land of the two rivers," was made of mud bricks, and the keynote of excavation in modern Mesopotamia is the separation of these baked mud bricks from the dust of the waterless desert that covers them. Although made of such lowly material the buildings themselves were impressive and even grand, as clearly indicated by these temple ruins on their raised platform.

414

FINE BRICK-WORK OF THE TEMPLE OF THE MOTHER GODDESS AT KISH

Kish was a great religious centre throughout ancient times, and its temples were many. Here is seen the upper portion of the great temple of the Mother Goddess. That so much of the building remains indicates not only the great durability of the material used but also the skill and intelligence of the ancient architects. These solid walls show something of the method of laying mud bricks and welding them together with plastic mud. The Mother Goddess was one of the two main deities, and temples in her honour were built and maintained by all the great kings who figured in the long history of Kish.

stood only a thousand years ago, a city which was no mere Troy set on a hill the size of Hanover Square, but an immense concourse of temples, forts, palaces and dwellings spread over an area five miles wide. And this city of Kish had played its proud part not only as capital of the first Sumerian civilisation, but also in the empires of Agade and Babylon with an unbroken rôle, political or religious, down to the end of the Sassanian empire in 650 A.D.

Then, as at Mohenjo-Daro in the sister civilization on the Indus, the great river on which its existence had always depended changed its course and its habits, the canals finally dried up and life died out of the last inhabited districts.

In the beginning the life of this " land between the great rivers " was agricultural, as a vast number of clay sickles of neolithic date prove, and in its main period of prosperity the city was the centre of a great wheat-growing district. It was also a fortified city, for it had almost unlimited political importance and dominated the whole district between the rivers. There were constant wars for the overlordship of this fertile and valuable land.

Two huge mounds seen to-day on the western side of the extensive ruins which stand forty feet high, represent a fortress with a well-buttressed rampart containing spacious rooms, built in Hammurabi's day. These guarded the city on this western side. This fortress is connected by a

massive wall and moat with another fort on the river bank and similar defences, some built by Nebuchadrezzar, exist on other parts of the site.

If it was of obvious political and military importance it was also a great religious centre, for its temple remains are the most extensive yet investigated in western Asia. In the two parts of the city there are three ziggurats (see page 18 for a reconstruction of a ziggurat at Ur), and in both are mounds and towers representing huge temple areas

Kish, as it has been discovered by the Oxford-Field Museum Expedition under the direction of Prof. Stephen Langdon, consists of two parts on either side of the old bed of the Euphrates, now dry. At western Kish in addition to the fortifications already mentioned, there is a huge mound, 90 feet high, of baked red bricks, built about 2080 B.C., which is one of the most prominent objects now seen across the open plain. The city walls, probably those for which Nebuchadrezzar claims the credit, are so extensive and come so close to Babylon (the wall from the Euphrates to Kish was 15 miles long), that even Herodotus appears to have confused them with the walls of Babylon proper.

The earlier site was at eastern Kish, and it is here that the most complete excavations have been made. Professor Langdon and M. Ch L. Watelin have carried their diggings down systematically to virgin soil, to the first evidences of

**ISHTAR AS GODDESS OF BATTLE**
This terra-cotta war chariot is an unusual representation of Ishtar as Goddess of Battle with a weapon in her hand. It is partly restored. A model of an ordinary chariot is illustrated in page 434, and a very early wheel in page 429.

settlement in neolithic times Starting from 5000 B C., that is 7,000 years ago, or somewhat earlier they have revealed a sequence of life and cultures in ten or more stratifications of which at least six are more than 5,000 years old At about 3200 B.C. they came across everywhere in the mounds a layer of fine sand and clay, containing no remains or relics, which was laid down by a great flood—the inundation that for a time blotted out all Sumeria

This is the same great flood as that whose incidence Mr C L. Woolley established at Ur (see page 21), the "Flood" of Babylonian legend, and of Genesis

Examination of the lowest levels of all meant going down nine feet below the modern water level of the plain, so that the work could only be carried on with the aid of hydraulic pumps The sheer mass of excavation work needed to reveal the great buildings was immense as may be gathered from some of our illustrations In 1930. when part of the temple of the Mother goddess had been exposed as it existed in the 20th century B C., it was known that ruins of at least two earlier constructions lay below it. one or more being in the pre-Flood levels The expedition was, therefore, faced with the tremendous task of excavating three or more enormous temples superimposed to a depth of 60 feet

This eastern part of the city is both larger and more impressive than the western Its Sumerian name means "The Mountain of the World" It has more fortifications, a huge cemetery mound 25 feet high and three-quarters of a mile long, a most extensive temple area with two great stage towers—one of which is 75 feet high in its present condition—and two ziggurats, while all around is another large area once covered with temples Here, too, was a great palace of the early Sumerian kings, perhaps built before

4000 B.C All the details of the layout of this side of the city and its vast expanse show clearly that not only was it a busy, densely inhabited city of outstanding political and military value, but even more a revered religious centre for thousands of years. There are great temples to the Earth and Mother goddesses. which were built and rebuilt by the great figures of ancient Mesopotamian history—Sargon, Hammurabi and Nebuchadrezzar among others Ishtar was the principal deity of the older cities, and had shrines there as we know from more than one unusual representation of her as a Babylonian goddess of battle. with a

quiver of arrows on her shoulders and a dagger in her hand, while her left foot rests upon a lion This is a symbol of the war-like goddess who " in the clash of arms and the noise of battle danced on the paved court "

In general, religious practices at Kish were

**PORTRAIT HEAD NEARLY 6,000 YEARS OLD**
This painted Sumerian head, moulded true to life, is ascribed by Professor Langdon to a period of about 4000 B.C., and represents a man who lived nearly 1,000 years before the Flood. It is not only unique but of extreme importance in the story of civilization. A reconstruction drawing by Miss C. L. Legge is given above.

PILLARS, WALLS AND STEPS OF A PALACE BUILT BEFORE "THE FLOOD"

The most ancient of Mesopotamian cities and now known to be the most ancient of the world, Kish was a seat of power in Mesopotamia for 2,000 years before the 30th century B.C. Its very name meant " Universal Dominion." That its kings were cultured and wealthy is proved by the extensive ruins of this palace built over 100 years before the " Flood." The pillars formed part of the colonnade, and its walls were richly decorated, as shown by the plaques illustrated in page 413.

similar to those of later Sumerian and Semitic peoples of Mesopotamia, Ishtar having special prominence as mother goddess and war goddess. Like the Assyrians and Babylonians they buried dogs, for expiatory purposes, beneath the thresholds of houses and preserved clay models of them, several of which Professor Langdon has found. Relics of this religious custom appear to have survived into Roman times, as suggested by the well-known mosaic of a dog in the vestibule floor of the house of the tragic poet at Pompeii.

Sargon the Great of Agade, as he is usually known, was a native of Kish, but he made matricidal war upon his city, captured it and then abandoned it, setting up a Semitic empire at Agade in the 27th century B.C. Mystery has always hung round this great figure whom the Assyrians of a later age regarded as their first national hero. One legend relates that, born in concealment, his mother cast him adrift in a reed basket on the Euphrates, but that he was saved and reared in secrecy—a curiously close parallel with the story of Moses in the bulrushes. He lived to conquer not only Kish but Ur, Lagash and fifty more cities of Sumeria and Elam. His dominions finally stretched, according to his own proclamation, " from the countries of the rising sun to the countries of the setting sun."

But before Sargon's day there were constant wars between the cities of the intra-riverine plain. Umma and Lagash, Kish and Erech fought each other perennially, now one is predominant, now another. The famous " Stele of the Vultures" shows Eannatum of Lagash leading his phalanx of Sumerian spearmen into battle against Umma, and he claims to have " smitten the head of

THE "FLOOD" LINE AT KISH

Visible proof of the Great Deluge which bulks so largely in Sumerian and Babylonian religious literature is afforded by the stratum, 1½ feet thick, of unpierced fine river sand which is marked by the arrow in this photograph. The evidence shows that the city was submerged by a great flood about 3300 B.C.

BUST OF A LATE PERSIAN KING FROM KISH
The great period of time covered by the history of Kish is well exemplified by this bust of a Sassanian king from a Neo-Persian palace of the 4th–5th century A.D. There had been kings at Kish 5,000 years earlier than this unnamed royalty.

tural centre and as a city of residence and trade. When the river changed its course—as the Mesopotamian rivers have done repeatedly before and during recorded history—the city was deprived of essential water supplies and transport and its importance, and its very life waned. Canals were dug to bring the water from the new bed of the river, but they needed constant maintenance and enlargement. In the end the canal system failed and the desert gained the upper hand. So, about the time when Edwin of Mercia was converted to Christianity and Saxon England was in being, the curtain goes down on the last scene in the 6,000-year-long story of this great city, which began its glories while England was a dark land of dense forests and marshes that had but recently emerged from the grip of the last Ice Age

From mud the city rose, out of mud were the bricks of its temples and palaces made and its wheat grown, and to mounds of mud it returned.

Kish " as well. But up to the 30th century B.C., at least, Kish seems to have been the dominant city over a period of about 2,000 years, for its very name came to mean " universal dominion."

Shortly after this time the third dynasty of Kish produced as ruler a figure of romance, a lady with the name of Azag-Bau who raised herself from the poor and unhonoured trade of wine-selling to the throne of Kish. She reigned as queen and queen regent for a long time, at least fifty years. Both the length of her reign and the references to her in surviving tablets make it clear that she was a person of great strength of character.

After Sargon the supremacy passed from Kish to Babylon and although, as we have noted, it long remained a religious centre of great importance and had many periods of prosperity and modified power, it never again obtained " universal dominion." In late Babylonian times it was a prosperous suburb of Babylon, and it revived again under the Sassanians and the Abbasid caliphs, although by the latter period most, if not all, of the ancient site had been abandoned. One immense brick-covered area upon which the early palaces stood had been abandoned as early as 3000 B.C.

From the beginning Kish was dependent upon the Euphrates for its existence, both as an agricul-

ONE OF THE EARLY KINGS
This finely-executed limestone inlay on a slate plaque represents a king of Kish of an early Sumerian dynasty. As an example of early artistic effort it should be compared with the vivid inlays illustrated in page 413. The king is shaven and wears a form of dress unusual on royal figures of the early period. The cone-shaped crown or cap is also unknown in other examples.

# The Splendours of Ancient Pergamum

### By F. N. Pryce, M.A.

Assistant Keeper, Department of Greek and Roman Antiquities, British Museum

FIFTY miles north of Smyrna the river Caïcos, most northerly of the five large streams which flow into the Aegean Sea from the central tableland of Asia Minor, winds through low-lying swamps into the Eleatic Gulf. The coastal plain ceases a dozen miles up-stream, and the river-bed becomes a fertile valley, enclosed by mountains on north and south; and ten miles farther up the valley expands into one of the most extensive and luxuriant basins of all that fertile land. Just where the basin begins to open, two torrents, rushing down from the northern hills to the main channel, isolate a ridge which rises abruptly at its northern extremity to a height of nearly a thousand feet, and slopes gently towards the south-east. At its foot nestles the modern town of Bergama, a flourishing and picturesque place with red-tiled roofs and whitewashed minarets rising out of the foliage. But the eye is held by the rocky crest which towers above, crowned with broken ruins of an older age. It is a princely site, dominating the whole countryside as though marked out by nature to be the seat of empire, and here in ancient time rose the proud city of Pergamum, or Pergamon, for a century and a half a royal capital, and for long afterwards one of the greatest centres of the trade and culture of the ancient world.

The story of Pergamum contrasts curiously with that of the other Greek cities which fringed the western coast of Asia Minor. Their history goes back into the dim beginnings of Greek civilization, but it is mainly a history of subjection, sometimes to a Greek power across the sea, more often to the rulers of the highlands on their east. They never stood long independent in their own strength, nor were they at any time able to impose their will on the interior plateau. Pergamum is a parvenu city, which only appears in history when the others were long past their prime; and its kings derived their prestige and importance from the fact that they subdued the inhabitants of the uplands and extended their rule over the interior from the sea to the Taurus mountains.

In the days of its splendour, court poets invented for Pergamum a history as ancient and distinguished as was possessed by any of its neighbours; but this is manifest fiction, and practically nothing is known of the place until after the death of Alexander the Great, when it was a small hill-town on the top of the crest. The times were troublous. Alexander's generals were dividing up his empire and struggling for supremacy; and one of them, Lysimachos, having made himself king of Macedonia and Western Asia Minor, deposited his state-treasure in this hill-fortress in charge of a trusted officer, Philetairos. But Lysimachos proved a tyrant, and in 283 B.C. all his cities in Asia Minor revolted and transferred their allegiance to his rival, Seleucos of Syria. Two years later Seleucos was assassinated, and Philetairos, seizing the opportunity provided by

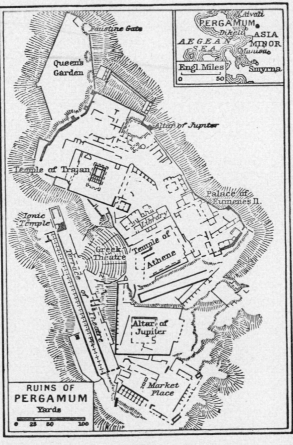

RUINS OF PERGAMUM

the subsequent confusion, declared himself independent ruler of Pergamum, owing fealty to neither Macedonia nor Syria.

An unexpected catastrophe served to divert attention from this insubordination and from the existence of the obscure little state. In 278 B.C. a wandering horde of Gauls, or Galatians, poured out of northern Europe into Greece, spreading destruction and desolation everywhere. Soon afterwards three tribes of them crossed the Dardanelles into Asia Minor, where they became the terror of the local inhabitants, pillaging and sacking the whole land. By the first century of

GRIM REALISM OF THE PERGAMENE SCHOOL OF ART
The vanquished Gaul kills his wife and then himself. The group is spirited and excellent, but so violently emotional a subject would have been abhorrent to sculptors of the best Attic age. The defeat, by Attalos I. of Pergamum, of the terrible Gallic invaders of Asia Minor gave rise to many variations of this motif.
National Museum. Rome. Photo by Brogi

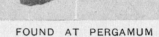

FOUND AT PERGAMUM
This bronze head is in the best artistic tradition, but bears distinguishing marks of the Hellenistic age. Compare the treatment of the hair, for instance, with the more impressionist, even more successful, methods in, say, the Hermes of Praxiteles illustrated in page 246.
By permission of the British Museum

the Christian era, when S. Paul was writing his Epistle to the Galatians, they had settled down into respectable agriculturists, but on their first arrival they seem to have been the wildest of barbarians. In face of this peril and of their own dynastic discords, the Syrian Seleucids could for a long time make no serious effort to reconquer Pergamum, which for forty years under Philetairos and his nephew, Eumenes, continued to grow and prosper. Its authority, however, remained local and circumscribed until the accession in 241 B.C. of Attalos, the cousin of Eumenes, who in the course of a brilliant and warlike reign raised it to the position of a considerable power. Attalos also was the first of the dynasty who assumed the title of king and the insignia of royalty.

His first expedition was against the terrible Galatians, to whom n all probability Pergamum had hitherto been obliged to pay blackmail. In a great battle he defeated them and took much of their territory. The Seleucid kings, alarmed at the growth of the new kingdom, formed an alliance with the Galatians, and the war continued for many years with varying fortune ; in the end, partly by hard fighting, partly by diplomatic address, Attalos emerged victorious, with territory enlarged and prestige enhanced. He next turned his attention to the side of Greece, where the troops of Macedonia were threatening danger, and here came his crowning stroke of statecraft ; he formed an alliance with distant Rome, already beginning

comparatively peaceful, and it was he who largely completed the architectural lay-out of the city, which Attalos seems to have begun and which, when realized, made Pergamum a city unequalled for majesty in the whole ancient world.

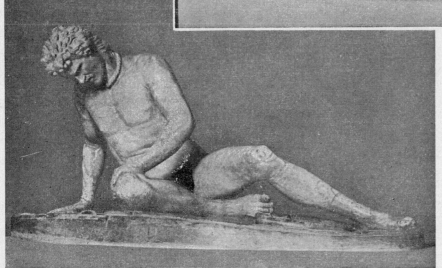

THE FAMOUS "DYING GLADIATOR" FROM TWO ANGLES

Another example of the " Gallic " theme, this statue of a dying Gaul is a copy of a lost original set up by Attalos I. on the terrace at Pergamum ; it was long known as " The Dying Gladiator." For vigour and pathos it is admirable, but it has lost the harmonious curves of earlier figures in a similar attitude, such as the recumbent warriors in the Aegina pediments. Capitoline Museum, Rome. Photos by Anderson

The general idea was that of a semicircle or crescent of great temples and palaces crowning the crest and inner slopes of the ridge on which the old hill-fortress had stood. At the northern and highest end, overlooking the whole, was the royal palace, but this was over-built in Roman times, and its original plan is not now easy to trace. Moving to the south along the gently falling crest, came a row of four large halls opening out of one another. This was the site of the famous library of Pergamum, founded by King Eumenes, and second only in the whole ancient world to the Library of Alexandria. So jealous were the librarians of Alexandria of their rival that they prohibited the export from Egypt to Pergamum of paper (papyrus). But the scribes of Pergamum, though deprived of their usual writing-material, rose to the occasion and produced a substitute which in name still to-day recalls its place of origin (*pergamentum*, parchment). After the library of

its career of world-conquest, and by his fidelity through two trying campaigns won the future mistress of the world for a firm friend. Dying in 197 B.C., Attalos was succeeded by his son, Eumenes II., under whom Pergamum reached the zenith of its prosperity. At first came further wars in which Eumenes fought side by side with the Roman legions, and received broad lands in reward. But the remainder of his reign was

ACROPOLIS OF PERGAMUM, CALLED BY THE ROMANS "PRE-EMINENT ABOVE ALL TOWNS OF ASIA"

Attalos I. had made himself the friend of Rome, thereby establishing the security of his state and widening his dominions; and his son, Eumenes II., by continuing m the same policy, brought such prosperity to the city that he could afford to lavish his wealth on its adornment. This reconstruction shows the Acropolis as it appeared at the height of its glory. The spectator is supposed to be looking northwards: in the foreground is the Altar of Zeus within its enclosure, and behind it the terrace where Attalos erected statues of the Gauls; beyond that again is the old fortress-wall, and within it a square with porticoes on two sides containing the small Temple of Athene  In the distance to the left is the later-built Temple of Trajan.

After the reconstruction by F. Thiersch

RECONSTRUCTION OF THE THEATRE AND SOUTH FACE OF THE ACROPOLIS AT PERGAMUM

The two reconstructions on this and the opposite page should be taken in conjunction, as they embrace roughly the same section of territory, this view being from the west while the other is from the south. Here in the foreground may be seen the theatre : a broad terrace runs behind the stage, with the small temple of Caracalla at its extreme left. On the Acropolis itself, commencing from the left, are the Temple of Trajan, the colonnaded square with the Temple of Athene, the Terrace of the Statues, and on a lower level the Altar of Zeus. Where the Acropolis hill sinks towards the plain below the Altar of Zeus we see the small Temple of Dionysos, and finally, on the extreme right, the beginnings of the Agora, or market-place.

From Thiersch's "Königsberg von Pergamon."

423

GREEK THEATRE AT PERGAMUM WHERE ART FLOURISHED UNDER A LIBERAL KING

Owing to its steepness and its great height the Greek theatre at Pergamum is one of the most imposing to be seen anywhere. During the second century B.C. Pergamum was among the most renowned homes of art and literature in the Graeco-Roman world, and even rivalled Alexandria. Its library shared an equal repute with that of Alexandria, and its scribes have the credit of inventing parchment: Romans indeed thought that the sculpture and the architecture to be found within its walls was the most wonderful in the whole world. This illustration of the theatre shows admirably the way in which Greek architects took advantage of the natural contours of the hillside in building this type of structure; hence no two theatres are ever alike.
after "Altertümer von Pergamon IV."

FALLEN TOWERS THAT GIRT THE ACROPOLIS OF PERGAMUM, MISTRESS OF ASIA MINOR

Though Pergamum owed its wealth of art and literature to an era of peace, won by friendship with Rome, it was essentially a fortress-town, and originally appealed to Lysimachos when he posted Philetairos there by reason of its defensible qualities. The illustration above of Pergamum as it is to-day helps us more easily to realize this; it shows the steep way from the lower city to the Acropolis, which, girdled with frowning bastions on its hilltop, dominates the fertile plain beneath. But it was not only the plains but all Asia Minor which once owned the sway of the enterprising city, tor under the guidance of a series of far-seeing rulers Pergamun attained an eminence which only bowed to the advancing might of Rome, her erstwhile friend.

After "Altertümer von Pergamon IV"

PORTION OF FRIEZE FROM THE ALTAR OF ZEUS
This frieze, representing as it does the Battle of Gods and Giants, was well fitted to typify the struggle of Pergamum with the barbarian Gauls.    A goddess is shown poised to hurl a snake-wreathed jar at a fallen giant, above whose head may be seen the remains of one of the life-like serpents which writhe in restless turmoil through the whole scene.
Kaiser Friedrich Museum. Berlin

reasons which led the kings of Pergamum to leave untouched this venerable monument of earlier days.

Continuing southward and passing beyond the old fortress wall, a broad terrace is reached, commanding a superb view of the valley. Here Attalos had ranged a series of sculptures in commemoration of his victory over the Gauls ; the originals have perished, but copies of some have been identified in various museums, the most famous being the Dying Gaul of the Capitoline Museum at Rome. Long known as " The Dying Gladiator,'' and the inspiration of Byron's " Butchered to make a Roman holiday,'' this statue is now recognized as a representation of one of the terrible barbarians whom Attalos subdued and as a direct copy of one of the figures set up by him on the terrace.

Next to the terrace came the most splendid monument of all, the Great Altar of Zeus, built apparently by Eumenes. It consisted of a huge base over a hundred feet square, on the top of which was the altar of sacrifice surrounded on three sides by colonnades, and open on the fourth side to a broad staircase cut into the base. Around the base ran a continuous frieze of sculpture, of which the surviving fragments have been pieced together in Berlin. Some idea of the scale of the whole may be gained from the fact that the frieze was over a hundred and fifty yards long. It is the most extensive and most ambitious example of Greek art that has remained to us. The subject is the Battle of the Gods and Giants, a theme frequently treated by the Greeks as emblematic of the contest between civilization and barbaric force, and of special significance therefore to the people of Pergamum, constantly mindful of their barbarian neighbours. In the slab illustrated in page 427, Victory floats down to the goddess Athene, who drags a giant backwards by the hair, while the Earth, the mother of the giants, rises from the

Alexandria had been partly destroyed, Cleopatra asked Mark Antony to repair the loss by granting her the books at Pergamum. He consented, and it is said that two hundred thousand volumes were thus transferred to Alexandria.

In the centre of the crescent was a large open square contained on two sides by stately double-storeyed porticoes, on the third by the wall of the old hill-fortress, for this had only extended thus far along the crest ; the fourth side was open to the precipitous side of the ridge. Within this enclosure stood a small and unpretentious temple of the Doric order, dedicated to Athene. This is the oldest building of the series, dating from the time when Pergamum had not achieved greatness and was but an insignificant town on the hilltop. Plain and unadorned, of coarse local stone, it seems out of place in the midst of its surroundings of gleaming marble, but we may easily guess the

ground to plead for the life of her child. In technical brilliance this frieze has never been surpassed, but the general effect is restless and unsympathetic; we miss the quiet pathos which the older sculptors of Attalos were able to give to their representation of a dying foe.

The semicircle was completed on the south by an Agora, or space for the public assemblies of the city; this was surrounded by porticoes, and contained a temple of Dionysos. Lastly, unity was given to the whole composition by a magnificent colonnaded terrace, which ran along the chord of the semicircle at the level of the Agora. Two smaller temples adjoined this terrace, and behind it, in the centre of the whole, was a theatre of the usual Greek form, a semicircle of tiers of seats climbing up the hillside, cut into the living rock.

Such was the group of buildings which crowned the summit of Pergamum, and which the German excavations of 1879-1885 revealed to us. The city proper lay still further to the south, and extended in terrace after terrace down the hill to the valley-level. During the present century the Germans resumed work with the view of investigating this lower city, but the work has of necessity been left uncompleted. Many houses, a market place, and a gymnasium on three terraces have been discovered, and the main road up the hill has been traced; under the paving of this runs a complicated system of water-pipes, conveying water from the distant mountains to the highest point of the city.

With the death of Eumenes in 159 B.C., the greatness of the independent kingdom of Pergamum declined; the two remaining kings, Attalos II. and Attalos III., did little further towards the embellishment of the city. It was as the ally of Rome that Pergamum had prospered, and Rome, now supreme and no longer in need of an ally, regarded its independence with suspicion and its wealth with jealousy. In 133 B.C. the last king of Pergamum, realizing the inevitable, on his deathbed bequeathed the kingdom to Rome, and Pergamum henceforth became the capital of the Roman province of Asia. The change, however, did not affect its material prosperity; in the first century A.D. a Roman official could describe it as " pre-eminent above all other towns of Asia." In Roman times the population seems largely to have transferred from the hill to the valley, where a new quarter sprang up on the site of the modern

**BATTLE OF GODS AND GIANTS FROM THE ALTAR OF ZEUS AT PERGAMUM**
Victory crowns Athene, who is dragging a giant by the hair preparatory to slaying him. He is already in the toils of a mighty snake, and Rhea—Mother Earth—pleads for the life of her son as she rises from the ground. This slab from the altar-frieze gives a vivid idea of the whole, whose keynote is strife and violent motion. It belongs to the second school of Pergamene art, and though in some ways it marks the highest achievement of this age, we miss the restraint of the earlier sculptors of the age of Attalos.
Kaiser Friedrich Museum, Berlin

## RECONSTRUCTION OF THE GREAT ALTAR OF ZEUS AT PERGAMUM

The magnificent Altar of Zeus built by Eumenes II. to the south of the Temple of Athene on the Acropolis was the glory and the crown of Pergamum. Its appearance is here reconstructed, with the exception of the frieze representing the Gigantomachia which surrounded the base of the structure; this is shown in its present damaged condition, but more detailed examples of it are illustrated in pages 426 and 427. The altar was dedicated to Attalos, who had become the city's hero after his defeat of the Gauls.

Kaiser Friedrich Museum, Berlin

town. No excavations have as yet been made in this area, though the ruins of baths and an amphitheatre are to be distinguished. The old palace of the kings, crowning the summit of the hill, was partly pulled down, and on its site was built a large temple dedicated to the Emperor Trajan.

It is disputed whether the allusion made in the Book of Revelations to the church in Pergamum as " dwelling where Satan's seat is " may simply refer to the fact that Pergamum was the headquarters of the official worship of the Roman emperors in Asia, or whether it may not be a direct reference to the Great Altar of Zeus. In any case, there is reason to believe that the destruction of the altar and the other monuments must be ascribed to the early Christians in their desire to efface all vestige of heathen worship. The sculptures when found bore marks of deliberate defacement, and the buildings were largely torn down to provide materials for a Christian church, and for a new wall around the summit; for with the decay of prosperity in the Roman world Pergamum became again the little town on the hill-top. As such for centuries it maintained an obscure existence, then in the fourteenth century came the Turks, after which the rocky crest appears to have been left uninhabited.

## The Study of the Past. X.

# When and Where Did Civilization Begin?

### By M. C. Burkitt, F.S.A.

#### Lecturer in Archaeology and Anthropology at Cambridge University

THE ordinary person is, I fancy, apt to imagine that the growth of civilization has been a continuous process beginning with man's first evolution from the animal state and culminating in the conditions which surround us to-day. More particularly the inhabitant of London, New York, or any other great city may be forgiven for thinking, as he listens to his wireless or drives himself in his car to see the latest ' talkie ' film, that the modern Babylon in which he lives is one of the final products of this process.

But that there has really been such a continuous growth of civilization is very questionable. For there have been many civilizations, not one. They have arisen, flourished for a time, and fallen again, often leaving few traces of their splendour behind them. The reasons for these waxings and wanings have been various ; sometimes an internal loss of vigour, sometimes barbarian invaders, sometimes climatic changes may have been responsible for their disappearance ; the point just now is that the climb to our present high level of civilization has surely not been up a steady gradient to a final summit, but is, rather, proving to be like the ascent of a mountain side when each succeeding peak seems to be the final one, but is in reality cut off from another perhaps higher scarp by a valley of greater or less depth.

What, however, do we mean by a civilization, and what constitutes one ? The great essential is some sort of social organization in which men can live together for their mutual advantage. There must be opportunities for specialisation, without which improvements cannot come. There must be leisure to think, to cultivate the intelligence as well as the practical abilities ; so that together with material progress, which by utilising nature eases the burden of human life, there will develop an enlarged mental outlook engendering in its turn what must be called art and religion. That mankind as a whole has been able to produce these necessary organizations is due to the gregarious habits of human nature. It has been suggested that our earliest forebears hunted in packs, and that had they not done so, had they rather, like the cat, stalked their prey stealthily and singly, we their descendants could never have created a civilization, properly so called. We should never have learned to have good manners, to work together, to pool our resources for our mutual good, in fact to organize ourselves ; we should have remained as untamed as is that delightful if somewhat sinister animal the cat.

But of course the evolution of all these excellent qualities took long ages to accomplish, and we do not find the traces of anything that can be described as civilization until many thousands of years after the first appearance on the globe of man himself. This seems to have happened towards the end of the Tertiary epoch, that is to say, some time after the clay upon which London is largely built had been laid down in a shallow estuary, and some time before the great Ice Age had northern Europe in its arctic grip. The period is so remote that we cannot date it in years, we can only measure it in geological language. The difference between our first ancestor and his predecessors was probably at first purely mental ; one branch of the simian stock concentrated in developing the organ of the brain, and as a result there grew up all that we are rightly proud of to-day.

The story of human development can be divided into three main periods— the Ages of Stone, Bronze and Iron respectively. We are still living in the last

Oxford-Field Museum Expedition

### THE OLDEST KNOWN WHEELED VEHICLE

Wheels—instruments of prime importance in the movement of civilization—seem to have originated among the Aryan-speaking peoples. These two solid wheels of a chariot were disinterred with the skeletons of the animals that drew it at Kish, the Sumerian city of Babylonia, built about 3200 B.C.

**PALAEOLITHIC MAMMOTH-HUNTERS ENGINEERING THEIR KILL**

Before the invention of agriculture, while men still lived by hunting, concentration of population would have entailed starvation. Single-handed, however, a palaeolithic man would have had small success in trapping and killing the huge beasts that then roamed the earth, and so small communities of hunters came into being. Dr. Karl Absolon's discoveries show that in Moravia the mammoth-hunters drove their quarry into pitfalls and killed them by dropping heavy bomb-shaped stones, slung perhaps in straps, upon their skulls

of these. In the middle period the uses of iron were unknown, but copper and its alloy with tin, bronze, was extensively used. In the first period, the Stone Age, man had not learnt to work with metal at all, and all his weapons and tools were made of stone, bone, or wood. Towards the end of this age, however, he had found out how to tame and domesticate animals and how to cultivate crops; previous to this his food supply had depended on his skill and success as a hunter. We know little of the earliest hunters except what we can guess from their stone implements; but the last of the hunting peoples formed in western Europe 10,000 years or more ago what we can only describe as the first true civilization.

The hunters of the Reindeer Age, as this period is called, lived under the shelter of overhanging rocks on the sunny sides of valleys or in the mouths of caves. They made delicate and beautiful implements of flint and bone ; we have found their bone needles with neatly-made eyes that are no longer and not very much coarser than an ordinary darning needle of to-day. With these, no doubt, the women sewed skins together to make garments while their husbands were out hunting. Their bone tools were often elaborately decorated with delicate engravings of animals, and little statuettes have been found. They buried their dead with care, sometimes leaving tools and necklaces of shells with the corpse, and, most wonderful of all, they painted and engraved surprisingly good and faithful pictures of animals, some of them now extinct like the mammoth and woolly rhinoceros, on the walls of deep caves into which they can only have penetrated with the aid of some artificial light. These painted caves were no doubt sacred places where ' sympathetic magic ' rites took place in the belief that the supply of game pictured on the walls would thereby be increased or the hunter's success ensured.

There is some evidence that a caste of artist-medicine-men-priests existed who actually made the paintings and conducted the rites. Life must have been very strenuous. Nevertheless, when we excavate their ' homes ' or stand in their cave temples gazing at their astonishing works of art and remember the degree of thought that these pictures imply, we cannot but recognize that man had here evolved a genuine and remarkable civilization.

THE end of the Reindeer Age coincided with a change of climatic conditions in Europe. The mean annual temperature rose considerably : the great Ice Age had come to an end. A knowledge of agriculture, domestic animals and pottery-making now gradually became general, and a simple village life developed. But though these aids to the growth of a civilization had appeared, and the security of human life must have increased enormously, we have found little that indicates any upward growth in the mental outlook of the people. All the wonderful art of the Reindeer Age had disappeared with the hunters and nothing comparable seems to have taken its place. Thus in our pursuit of civilization we must now leave Europe with its rather unexciting herdsmen-potters and turn our eyes to areas farther south and east, where the uses of copper and bronze have by now been discovered.

### HARVESTING IN EGYPT IN THE LATE STONE AGE

Discoveries made in the Fayum by the British School of Archaeology in 1927 included material evidence of the agricultural methods practised in Egypt in pre-Dynastic times, that is, before about 3400 B.C. The sickles were made of palm leaf stem with a groove in which finely chipped flint blades were fixed with bitumen ; the corn was cut close to the ears, threshed with thick sticks and then carried in baskets to high ground, where it was stored in basket receptacles sunk in the earth (inset) and covered over with mud.

### FERTILISING INUNDATION IN THE VALLEY OF THE NILE, A CRADLE OF CIVILIZATION

Before the Dynastic period in Egypt Kingdoms of the North and of the South were established in the Valley and the Delta of the Nile, and even before that there is evidence of a distinctively Egyptian civilization from end to end of the Valley, and this again was preceded by a definite culture—the Badarian. According to Prof. Childe the latter stage was reached between 6,000 and 5,000 B.C. To the Nile with its two seasons of flood and sparsest flow Egypt owes its fertility, and on its banks settled civilizations arose in very early times.

Most people are aware that a high degree of civilization existed in ancient Egypt, popular attention having been focussed lately on the glorious furnishings of Tutankhamen's tomb in particular, Yet already 2,000 years earlier than this—before 3000 B.C. —the Egyptians had evolved a genuine civilization. In the last few years, mainly as a result of the expedition conducted by Mr. C. Leonard Woolley, Mesopotamia has been found to rival Egypt in respect to the antiquity and glories of its past. His own account of his excavations at Ur, with illustrations of some of his remarkable discoveries, is given in pages 19 to 26. The queen's headdress is probably the most notable thing of its kind that has yet been found, while the lapis and carnelian inlays and the fluted gold vessels show an artistic genius and a craftsmanship which it would be hard to surpass to-day. Nor must we forget the bull-headed musical instruments, the game board and the chariots —the latter showing that the uses of the wheel had been discovered before 3000 B.C. The owners of these beautiful objects lived in large cities; they had two-

storeyed houses and temples and ramparts. When important personages died numbers of retainers and oxen were buried with them, from which we must infer that they had a quite elaborate belief about life in another world. Like the Egyptians, they too had a writing of their own.

The civilization which the spade of the archaeologist has unearthed in the islands of the Aegean is not less wonderful. It had its focus in Crete. Here great palaces full of all kinds of beautiful objects have been excavated. There were even bathrooms and a drainage system. And, once more, not only have we evidence for an advance in ideas of material comfort, but art and a religious system were well developed, as is evidenced by the beautiful frescoes and elaborate tombs which have been found. Except for the fact that these three civilizations were of the Bronze Age— iron was not discovered till much later—and that therefore all tools and weapons were made of bronze, it is probable that an Englishman of the early nineteenth century, just before the coming of steam and electricity, transplanted back to those times, would

GRAVE OF BABYLONIAN CIVILIZATION BESIDE THE EUPHRATES

Obvious explanations suggest themselves for the riverine location of large human settlements—fertility of the well-watered valleys and plains, rich pasturage and facilities for river transport and communication. The delta land of Mesopotamia indeed owes its existence to the Euphrates and the Tigris, and here flourished the Sumerian civilization, the earliest of which there is historical knowledge. Its culture preceding 3000 B.C., including highly skilled metal work which must have begun a thousand years earlier, would compare with that of Athens under Pericles. Not long afterwards Babylon arose higher up on the Euphrates, to dominate awhile and then to disappear.

have been able to adapt himself quite comfortably to the daily life of his hosts. He would certainly not have felt that he had fallen back into savagery.

Our purpose here, however, is not to describe the wonders of these long-past civilizations, but to consider how and why they grew up where they did, and whether they were merely isolated phenomena, or whether our own civilization to-day is not in some way their direct descendant.

The banks of great rivers like the Nile and the Euphrates have ever been likely places for human settlements. Water for crops and herds was there always available, and communication between village and village would be easy. But not all river banks at all periods have produced great civilizations, and we must search farther for an explanation.

It is common nowadays to hear that a depression is approaching our western seaboard from far out on the Atlantic or from Iceland and that soon there will be rain in northern Europe. Some thousands of years ago, however, the highway of these depressions lay farther to the south, and the life-giving rain must have fallen over areas even as far south as the North African desert. As a result many countries which we are accustomed to think of as parched and arid wastes must have then been fertile and capable of cultivation. This perhaps partly explains why we have to look for the civilizations of 5,000 years ago in the areas we have just described rather than in northern Europe.

Some more questions arise from these considerations. Is it not possible that other great areas now desert, such as the Gobi in Asia, were also once fertile fosterers of flourishing civilizations? The answer is 'quite possible.' But owing to the inclement conditions now prevailing, it is not always easy to find traces of these problematical civilizations. Again, is the growth of a civilization purely a question of climate and environment, and is humanity so automatic that, given suitable conditions, a fine progressive civilization will appear? And, similarly, will our own civilization fade away if the climate of northern Europe changes again? The answer to

Howard Carter, Tomb of Tutankhamen

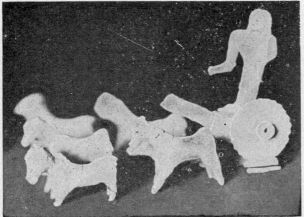

Oxford-Field Museum Expedition

these questions is not easy. There is much of truth in the statement that humanity is the plaything of climate. But climate alone cannot produce a civilization. The people living under the favourable conditions must possess within them a germ of progress—a germ which is largely a mental or spiritual groping for betterment. This germ can remain dormant for a long time ; when the right environment is encountered it grows spontaneously, or, more often, is fertilised by hybridisation, as when a people is partially conquered by vigorous invaders. The civilizations of early Egypt and Mesopotamia are examples of such a cross-fertilisation. Once germinated, the plant springs up with a rapid growth but, equally, dies away when conditions deteriorate.

Thus we see that in ancient times great civilizations grew rapidly and persisted perhaps for long periods, only to fade away in the end. But we ask ourselves : was there not some contribution to human progress passed on from one to the next ? Perhaps yes. But in what does this elusive something consist ? Surely not in mere material betterment. Perhaps then in the realms of art ? Yet are we to-day more worthy than the fresco painters of Crete—or even than the cave artists of the Reindeer Age ?

Courtesy of Sir John Marshall

## AMENITIES OF SOCIAL LIFE TWO THOUSAND YEARS BEFORE THE AGE OF IRON

Sanitary systems are better evidence of civilization than jewelry, and excavations at Mohenjo-Daro show that in this respect ancient Indo-Sumerian social conditions 5,500 years ago were surprisingly advanced. Most of the houses had their own wells and bathrooms connected by covered drains with large conduits of brick in the streets outside. Below these ruins are the layers of nine earlier cities not yet excavated. The toy chariot, above, with its team of asses—horses were not yet known—was found at Kish. Iron was not introduced into Egypt until some 2,000 years later, in the time of Tutankhamen, in whose tomb the earliest known iron-bladed weapon (top) was found.

## Temples of the Gods. XIV.

# Baalbek: Splendid in its Ruin

## By Richard Curle

Author of "Wanderings, a Book of Travels and Reminiscence," etc.

ABOUT midway between Beirut and Damascus, at a dreary station in the plateau called Ryak, the railway for Aleppo branches northward. It is but half a dozen miles along this line that the ruins of Baalbek lie clustered in their mighty fragments. As you wander through them, it is like wandering through a wilderness of stone raised tier upon tier. The perfect and vast proportions of the ruins expand about you, and in their fallen grandeur they are probably more impressive to modern eyes than they must have been in the days of their glory.

What astonishes one at first sight about these ruins is, indeed, their tremendous extent. That is an emotion which no photograph can arouse, and which, in fact, cannot be conveyed adequately in words. Their total length is about 950 feet, and at their widest they are about 650 feet. They are a mixture of Roman work, Byzantine work, and work of a later period. The order of entering is as follows: A flight of steps, the Propylæa, an hexagonal forecourt, the Great Forecourt (with an altar in the middle of it), another flight of steps, the Temple of Jupiter-Baal, sometimes called the Temple of the Sun.

To the left, half-way between the Great Court and the Temple of Jupiter-Baal, lies the Temple of Bacchus, and grouped around this temple are the remains of various other buildings.

The Great Court measures 440 feet by 370 feet. In olden days it was bordered by covered halls, decorated with statues. Some of these halls are still in a

**FRAGMENT OF A ONCE SPLENDID CORNICE**

Fallen section of cornice in the Temple of Bacchus at Baalbek, from which some idea may be gained of the commanding beauty of the decorative art of the ancient builders.

fairly good state of preservation, though weeds grow in the pavement-niches of the court, and your only companions are lizards and grazing animals.

It is this neglect which gives Baalbek so infinite an appeal. The spick and span ruins of the West, where every stone is carefully guarded, have a sort of adventitious vulgarity thrust upon them. But here you may witness the greatness of silent decay. Wild flowers and grass flourish unhindered amid the stones, bushes sprout through the crevices of the walls, everywhere nature is covering up with merciful oblivion the gaunt skeleton of the ruins. Thus there is something extraordinarily natural and soothing about Baalbek. If it gives you an emotion of tragic happenings, it also gives you an emotion of the deepest serenity. You can sit there for hours dreaming uninterruptedly of the past.

In the Temple of Jupiter-Baal but six columns out of fifty-four remain upright. The three last that fell, fell in the earthquake of 1759. This must have been a particularly splendid building, for the columns are sixty feet in height and their Corinthian capitals are twenty-two feet in circumference. In one of the side walls there are three great stones, raised twenty feet above the ground, that measure each sixty-four feet by thirteen feet. One may well wonder at the engineering skill of past ages that succeeded in getting these monsters, weighing twelve hundred tons apiece, into position. They were quarried about half a mile away, and there, lying still in the quarry, is an even larger stone, sixty-eight feet by fourteen feet,

CLOSER VIEW OF THE CORINTHIAN CAPITALS SEEN IN THE OPPOSITE PAGE

This photograph has a particular value in enabling the reader to form some idea of the massiveness of the architecture of the Temple of Bacchus in Baalbek, the figure of the Arab seated on the stone roof of the portico giving an indication of the immense size of the tall and graceful columns which carry the architrave and frieze.

which may simply have proved too titanic to shift into position. Perhaps nothing brings back the past of Baalbek so intimately and vividly as the sight of this stone. It makes one feel somehow as though one had been present personally at the very building of the temples ; it makes one see the human problems that faced the architects. That stone has been lying there, maybe, for nearly two thousand years ; but looking at it, one suddenly realizes that the men who quarried it and then failed to move it were men like ourselves.

But if the shifting of these stones presents a curious problem, the marble pillars of the temples present a still more curious one. It has been shown that these were probably brought from the interior of Egypt, and it has been calculated that three years must have been required for their journey. What a weird and hazardous journey it must have been, and how sacred a place Baalbek must have appeared in the eyes of these early idolaters. The beginnings of its history are lost in the mist of legend ; but though the buildings we see are mainly Roman, dating from the era of Antoninus Pius (A.D. 86-161), it is probable that the site knew former temples sacred to the worship of Baal as the controller of human destiny.

**EAST END OF THE VESTIBULE OF THE TEMPLE OF BACCHUS AT BAALBEK**

From this glimpse of the ruins we can gather some notion of the dignified beauty of the building in the day of its splendour. The leaf work throughout this temple was particularly beautiful, anticipating in the decorative nature of its treatment and the care of the chiselling the lovely Byzantine work of a later day. Huge masses of the ceiling have fallen in, and the Turks have ruined many of the columns by extracting the iron clamps for the sake of the metal.

Photo by F. M. Good

GENERAL VIEW OF THE TEMPLES OF BACCHUS AND JUPITER-BAAL ON THE ACROPOLIS AT BAALBEK

The observer in this photograph is looking towards the north and sees in the right foreground the south side of the Temple of Bacchus, while on the left and beyond uprear the six remaining columns of the great Temple of Jupiter-Baal, which extended to the right a greater distance than is covered by the photograph. The great temple was an immense structure with a massive forecourt on the east, reached by a wide and dignified staircase. The main part of the temple lay behind the smaller Temple of Bacchus, and was known as the Court of the Altar, a Christian basilica at a later date being built amid the ruins. Massive walls enclosed the whole group of buildings, and portions of these still remain.

Photo by F. M. Good

438

**THE TRILITHON AT BAALBEK: SOME OF THE MIGHTIEST STONES EVER MOVED BY BUILDERS**
But for the figure of the Turk in the above photograph, it would be difficult to estimate the immensity of the stones employed in this, the outer wall of the Acropolis at Baalbek. Three great stones are contained within the middle course of the masonry, each measuring 63 feet long by 13 feet high and 10 feet thick. The means whereby they could be lifted and placed in position on the top of a sub-structure, already 23 feet high, must have called for the exercise of immense power, and would puzzle the most expert builders of to-day. It has been thought that the name of the Trilithon, or " three-stone," applied to the great Temple of Jupiter-Baal may have originated from the use of these particular stones.
Photo by Donald McLeish

To the side of the Temple of Jupiter-Baal, as we have seen, lies the smaller but better preserved and more exquisite Temple of Bacchus. Here there are nineteen pillars still erect out of a total of forty-six. These are Corinthian pillars, and they are fifty-two feet in height. The ornamented cella of the portal is finely intact, and its beautiful design is one of the most fascinating things in Baalbek. But, indeed, even in this waste of shattered stone there are many out-of-the-way corners where one may come unexpectedly upon friezes and carved designs in a singular state of preservation. What is moving about Baalbek is its mingled vastness and delicacy. It combines grandeur of immensity with an artistic sense of proportion and with a marvellous felicity of carving.

These vast ruins include terrace upon terrace and fragments of numerous strange erections. The two temples are but the crown of the setting, and in ancient days were hemmed about by a long formality of approach. One may suppose that many priests and servers dwelt within the precincts, and that when the whole building was extant it resembled a small town rather than a temple. As a religious centre of the Roman Empire it probably possessed considerable political significance, and no doubt it was a place of scheming as well as of worship. One may picture governors of provinces arriving in hot haste, emissaries from Rome, legionaries from the distant parts of Asia. The high priest would read the omens, and action would be decided upon. The temples of Baalbek,

439

GREAT PORTAL OF THE TEMPLE OF BACCHUS

A nearer view is given here of the real gem of the Temple of Bacchus at Baalbek, with the middle stone of the lintel sunk from its original position, the photograph having been taken before the stone was replaced as shown in page **441**. Vines and garlands are richly carved, while satyrs and bacchantes gambol in the frieze along the lintel of the great door.

Photo by F. M. Good

NEAR VIEW OF THE FINE STONE CARVING

Fortunately much of the beautiful carving around the main portal of the Temple of Bacchus remains, despite the ravages of barbaric hands, and in this photograph we are able to distinguish more clearly the richness and confident beauty of the work.

Photo by Donald McLeish

in short, never knew the cloistered life of the old Christian monasteries.

If we consider its history, we may be surprised that it has not all long since vanished into dust. Probably no building has been more disturbed by battle, by changing faiths, and by the fury of fanaticism. It was attacked in 635 by Abu Abaida after the conquest of Damascus. It was pillaged in 748. In 1090 it passed into the hands of the Seljuks, and in 1134 into the hands of Jenghiz Khan. In 1175 it was taken by Saladin, and in 1260 it was dismantled by Hulagu. In 1400 it was sacked by Timur, and in 1517 it was seized by the Turks, in whose hands—often only nominally—it remained until the settlement after the European War. Indeed, its final scene of war was when it was occupied by the British in October, 1918. It has been, in turn, in the possession of infidels, Christians—Theodosius (A.D. 346-395) built there a Christian basilica, the ruins of which were cleared away in 1899-1904—and Mahomedans. Each new religion ravaged the memorials of the former, and each new war for its possession took toll upon its mighty architecture. Earthquakes, too, have done their worst. It has survived because it was built on a colossal scale. Baalbek was first known of in Europe in the sixteenth century: now it is certainly one of the most famous ruins in the world.

It is all the more wonderful to look at because of its desolate surroundings and the air of stillness and neglect that hangs over its courts and temples. At its feet an Arab village, squalid and mean as only an Arab village can be, and with a population of about 5,000, serves only to heighten the solemn grandeur of the noble remains. Baalbek faces

THE SPLENDID MAIN PORTAL OF THE SHRINE OF BACCHUS AT BAALBEK

Even in the state of utter ruin into which the temple has fallen, such a picture as this calls up at once a mental vision of the architectural splendours which made the shrine of Bacchus at Baalbek one of the most beautiful of its kind in all the world. Vine leaves, as befits the god to whom the temple was dedicated, are a noticeable motif in the carving, which is rich and luxuriant, but never oversteps the line into the florid and over-decorated.

Photo by Donald McLeish

441

## HOW THE NORTH SIDE OF THE TEMPLE OF BACCHUS LOOKS TO-DAY

Relatively small when compared with the original dimensions of the Temple of Jupiter-Baal, the Temple of Bacchus is to-day one of the best preserved and most beautiful of the antique buildings of Syria. The date of its erection takes us back to the second century of our era, but it was possibly completed as to its decoration and enrichment by the Emperor Caracalla, between A.D. 211 and 217. About two years before his assassination, near Edessa, Caracalla visited both Syria and Egypt.

*Photo by Donald McLeish*

across the plateau—Baalbek is, itself, 3,850 feet above the sea—the long range of the Lebanon, and at night, especially, it has a tragic dignity of reserve. The pregnant silence of history seems to hover over it, and standing there amid the ruins one felt the very whisper of its turbulent past. Delightful orchards surround Baalbek, white with their spring blossom at the season of my visit, and the soft gurgle of the irrigation canals was the only sound that broke the immemorial silence.

Yes, it was easy at such an hour to recreate the past, and to feel its invisible tentacles around one. In those far-off centuries, when all was in pristine order and the Roman gods were worshipped in the temples, together, probably, with a remnant of Baal worship, the sight that met a traveller's eye must have been one of unparalleled

magnificence. In the middle of that huge plain, lying between the Lebanon and the Anti-Lebanon, there arose a great sweep of tiered buildings, that must have stood forth in their shining newness like some splendid monument built to outlast the ages. Who were the people that worshipped there, and why were these temples built so far from the customary haunts of men? Perhaps in those days an enormous town, constructed like the present Arab village of little more than mud, encircled the temples. Those wanderers of the far-flung Roman Empire must surely have found in Baalbek—it is practically certain that they did—a site holy already to the local inhabitants. There, both as an act of worship and of conquest, they raised this tremendous shrine to their own gods, superstitiously not ignoring the spirit of the gods that were.

442

## RUINS OF THE ONCE GLORIOUS TEMPLE OF THE JUPITER OF HELIOPOLIS

Baalbek is referred to in ancient Assyrian and Egyptian inscriptions as Balbiki, indicating it as a centre of Baal worship, and the Greeks, identifying Baal with their sun-god, Helios, named the place Heliopolis. When the Romans came into possession they accepted Helios as Jupiter, and so the great temple, of which the ruins are shown above, was dedicated to Jupiter of Heliopolis, whose worship spread into Italy itself. Antoninus Pius (A.D. 138-161) was the imperial initiator of these temples, whose broken stones can still awaken our wonder.

Photo by F. M. Good

But if we consider Baalbek through the centuries, imagination is appalled at the scenes of violence and devastation that went on around its walls, and that undermined it gradually from age to age. Names famous and terrible in history float across its annals, and are swallowed into darkness. What massacres and sackings Baalbek has witnessed! If only stones could speak, how fantastic and gruesome would be the unfolded tale! I know that, as I strolled about the empty courts, whose ruin and decay were doubly strange in the breath of the green spring, I seemed almost physically conscious of a mourning spirit. Perhaps no place in the world has felt more heavily the hatred of man and the bitterness of religious strife. Now it is incredibly peaceful—peaceful in the grandeur of death. Baalbek is like a warrior whose fight is over and who, fearless and fervent to the end, rests finally and in full content from his labours.

At certain times of the year Baalbek is visited by many European and American tourists, and an hotel has been put up near by for their reception. I will never forget how, in the cold silence of the night, I went out on to an upper balcony and gazed upon the ruins in the moonlight. The pillars above the vast, vague mound rose clear into the sky, and away beyond them the range of the Lebanon, austere and dim, stretched indefinitely on either side. About the whole scene there was an extra-ordinary emotion of classical aloofness. And, indeed, what finally strikes one most about Baalbek is perhaps just this feeling of aloofness. Baalbek is so completely different from everything around it, so infinitely greater, so infinitely more dignified. It is as though from a giant past it had degenerated into a plaything of a race of pygmies; it is like a blind Samson shorn of its strength.

INTERIOR OF THE TEMPLE OF BACCHUS AT BAALBEK AS IT IS TO-DAY

This photograph of what is known as the cella or naos of the temple, meaning the part enclosed within the four walls exclusive of the portico or peristyle, shows how the side walls were divided into fields by fluted semi-columns. In the elaborately decorated niches stood some of the statues which once adorned the shrine of the deity known to the Greeks as Dionysus, god of wine and fruitfulness and promoter of civilization, and to the Romans as Bacchus. The cella is about 87 feet long and 73 feet wide. On each side of the entrance are piers containing spiral staircases.

Photo by F. M. Good

# Cave Tombs and Chair Burials of the Mysterious Etruscans

## By the Editor

*ALTHOUGH the Etruscans are still one of the most mysterious of the ancient races, much light has been thrown on their beliefs and practices by the funerary relics that have been dug up from their graveyards. As will be seen from the photographs—specially taken in the Etruscan Museum, Florence—in the following pages, the Etruscans developed a system of burial that is without parallel in the history of human sepulture.—EDITOR.*

ONE of the most interesting and least known of the ancient races that established themselves and flourished in Europe was the race that dominated that part of Italy once known as Etruria—the modern Tuscany and Umbria. Controversy still continues as to the precise origin of these Etruscans, but some day it may be possible to trace that very remarkable people to their original home on the coast of Asia Minor, or perhaps on one of the eastern islands of the Aegean or Mediterranean

Although the Etruscans developed a splendid civilisation in Italy at least eight centuries before our era, and must have come from their Aegean home with an already high cultural equipment, involving expert knowledge of all sorts of metal work, from weapons of war and the chase to the most delicate pieces of gold jewelry, and with a language quite distinct from any of the Greek dialects, but using an alphabet closely similar to ancient Greek and possibly derived from a common source, and although their many colonies in Italy grew rich and powerful, over-spreading an immense area of Italy while Rome was still an unimportant town on the Tiber, yet they were eventually absorbed into the great Roman Empire without leaving any deliberate historical record of themselves. And this, too, despite the fact that they gave to Rome its first dynasty of kings, the Tarquins, as well as the symbol of the Republic, the historic " fasces", or axe surrounded by a bundle of rods, and that numerous Italian place-names recall them to this day, the Tyrrhenian Sea and even the Adriatic having derived their appellations from Etruscan names

The monuments of their civilisation are numerous and yield a vast amount of information to the scientific enquirer, but the inscriptions which they bear—a rough estimate of the total places these at about nine thousand—are so brief, seldom more than the bare names of persons, that even the greatest experts in the ancient tongues of the

INSIDE ONE OF THE BEEHIVE TOMBS OF THE ETRUSCANS
As a general rule Etruscan tombs were circular and either sunk into the volcanic rock or raised like monster beehives above the ground. The tomb seen in this photograph dates from the 6th century B.C. It is paved with stone flags and walled with tufa blocks, while the vault of overlapping stones is supported by a rectangular pillar consisting of massive slabs of stone.
Photo, Alinari

**HOMES FOR THE DEAD LIKE THOSE OF THE LIVING**

Cinerary urns modelled from dwelling-houses are occasionally met with in the burial-places of the prehistoric Etruscans. The little "soul-house" shown above, though perhaps it is of rather later date than the other ossuaries depicted in this article, may be regarded as fairly typical.

possibility of a Hittite origin, in support of which, but certainly not in proof thereof one could mention quite a number of Etruscan sculptures in flat relief which are as Hittite in character as the great bulk of Etruscan art later than the seventh century, B.C., is Greek in style if not in inspiration—if such a happy discovery could be made, it would add greatly to the interest of their story and enable the history of the most remarkable of all Italy's invaders to be written in all its romance and adventure for it would illumine the great sections of darkness which it still contains

In this brief chapter, however, my intention is not to attempt any description of the development of the Etruscan people in that part of Italy where over a period of two or three hundred years, beginning in the ninth century, B.C., they made many important settlements originating from the immigration of powerful families and clans or tribes who established themselves at various points along the western coast of Italy and a little inland up the river valleys, subduing the local Italians and building fortified camps which eventually

Mediterranean peoples have been unable to reconstruct from them anything of the Etruscan language If some day an ancient script or some lengthy epitaphs in the same alphabet came to light among the ruins still to be explored along the Aegean shores, and the Etruscans could definitely be identified with such ancient peoples as the Lydians, the Lycians, or the Carians—and Mr. Randall MacIver, our best English authority on this strange people, does not exclude the

**MOUND-STUDDED NECROPOLIS OF ETRURIA**

At Cervetri—the ancient Caere—is a wonderful Etruscan necropolis. The great mound-and-circle tombs seen in this photograph are round drums, 45 to 55 yards in diameter, carved out of the soft tufa rock, or built up of courses of oblong blocks of masonry. On the basis of this rock or masonry tambour, earth was heaped up to form a conical mound.

From Randall MacIver 'The Etruscans," Clarendon Press. Photo, Alinari

### SEPULCHRAL CHAMBER OF A BEEHIVE TOMB

Here we see the interior of one of the great mound-and-circle tombs shown in the photograph in the opposite page. The sepulchral chambers are carved in imitation of houses, with beams and rafters and representations of weapons and many domestic implements. The niches formed the " loculi " or funerary couches for the dead.

### RECONSTRUCTED INTERIOR OF A ROCK-HEWN BURIAL PLACE

This is a reconstruction of an elaborate mortuary chamber at San Girolamo, near Volterra, such as was appropriated to a single Etruscan family. The alabaster caskets are original ; some forty in number, each contains the ashes of a member of (probably) the Atia family. They have lids of the " anthropoid " type and their sides are decorated with carvings representing scenes taken for the most part from stories forming part of ancient Greek mythology.

Photo, Alinari

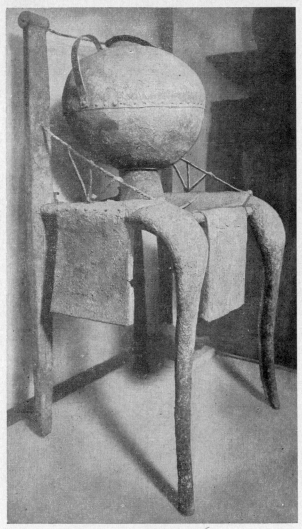

**THRONED IN DEATH AS IN LIFE**

One of the most curious of Etruscan burial customs was the
enclosing of the remains in funerary urns placed on chairs or
thrones of beaten bronze. In the later burials bronze tables
and terracotta domestic utensils were placed before the burial
chair, ready for use in the world beyond.

American museums—we must be content with the
little that has been said about them here, as this
brief chapter is meant only to draw attention to a
peculiar and entirely characteristic form of their
burial rites.

The illustrations which accompany these notes
are, I think, well calculated to attract the attention of the reader. I shall not readily forget the
surprise with which I first looked upon the various
objects here photographed in the Etruscan museum
at Florence—surely the most interesting of all
that city's treasuries of the past. Anything more
grotesque, indeed more childish, than this form of
sepulture could hardly be imagined of a civilised
people To burn the body after death and place
the remains—for we must always remember that
ancient cremation was never so efficient as the

**PORTRAIT-CROWNED CINERARY URN**

The pottery sepulchral urns such as this remarkable specimen
are interesting developments from the bronze ossuaries of the
type shown in the upper illustration. It has been suggested
that perhaps here we have the origin of the portrait bust. This
particular urn dates from the ninth or eighth century B.C

developed into villages and towns. They were
attracted to Italy, and especially to that western
part of it which lies between the Apennines and
Campania, mainly because of the copper mines to
be worked there and the iron which was found in
large quantities, especially in the island of Elba,
due east of which, and at no great distance up the
river Bruna, one of the most important of the
twelve great cities of the Etruscans, Vetulonia,
was situated Fascinating as it would be to
reconstruct from the abundant vestiges of their
civilisation which are still to be found in the great
cemeteries left by this strange people—for it is
paradoxically in their graveyards that they live
for us today, the wonderful contents of which
may be studied in various museums throughout
Italy, and even in certain collections that have
been brought together in Paris, in London and in

PROBABLE ORIGIN OF THE BUST: ETRUSCAN BURIALS IN POTTERY URNS

Of these three further specimens of funerary urns of the "portrait-bust" type, the one on the right dates from the ninth or eighth century B.C. Its two companions are several hundred years later, and it is interesting to observe how the passing of time was accompanied by a considerable measure of artistic degeneration.

modern system whereby the entire body is utterly reduced to ashes—in a large terracotta jar, or perhaps a jar of beaten bronze, the lid of which in the earliest models bore no suggestion of human form, but was gradually given some conventionalised f e a t u r e s of the human head, sometimes merely the outline of a warrior's helmet, was not greatly at variance with burial customs of other peoples in the near east. But out of this the Etruscans developed a pathetic effort at reconstituting for the dead s o m e t h i n g of the surroundings of the life they had surrendered.

Here some Egyptian influence may be t r a c e d, a l t h o u g h the idea of supplying the dead with all the trappings and facilities of every-day life was widespread t h r o u g h o u t the ancient world and endures among barbaric races to this

CRUDE FEATURES IN BRONZE

Another of the bronze chair burials is seen in this photograph. The features crudely drawn on the lid serve to mark an intermediate stage between the quite non-human urn such as the one shown in the upper illustration in page 448 and the "portrait-busts" such as those reproduced above.

day. But in the hands of the Etruscans this form of burial and all that it implies led to a disposition of things in the funerary chambers which approached almost to the comic. We are first to conceive the disposal of the cremated remains within the funerary urn and to observe the lid of that in the course of a generation or two being changed from its original u t i l i t a r i a n purpose into a crude representation of the head of the deceased, and the next step of adding arms thereto was obviously a naïve advance in the direction of helping the dead person in the underworld of the cave. The urn was next placed on a chair, usually made of bronze—and how modern some of these chairs look to our eyes!—and in front of the chair in that chamber of the shades, they came to place bronze tables and on the tables bronze and

ANIMATED FRESCOES IN THE CHAMBERS OF THE DEAD

In their striving to make the last resting-places of their dead resemble as closely as possible the homes of the living, the Etruscans painted the interior walls with representations of convivial scenes, banqueting, dancing, and so on. One of the most celebrated of these painted sepulchres is the " Tomb of the Leopards " at Tarquinii, dating from the 5th century B.C. In the portion of its frescoes shown above, a noticeable feature is the two women (indicated by their white skin and garments) who are sitting at the tables and participating freely in the pleasures of their menfolk.

Photo, Alinari

terracotta specimens of the things used by the dead in their daily lives before they descended into the tomb, so that they should be ready for use in the new and vaguely-conceived life of the spirit to which they had passed.

It was in this way that the Etruscan tombs gradually became filled with innumerable valuable objects of jewelry, weapons of war and the chase, household ornaments and votive offerings, such as the huge bronze cauldrons of the types which were specially wrought and dedicated to the Olympian gods. So that from some of these tombs a procession of objects almost as multifarious, and not less instructive than those that issued from the wonder tomb of Tutankhamen, has been brought forth as the result of the intensive exploration of recent years

The changes of fashion which create so much diversion when we scan them in the old pages of such a publication as *Punch*, and which have furnished within the last few years a whole library of books to amuse us in contemplating the comic aspect we ourselves presented forty or fifty years

ago, and the still more comic appearance of our grandfathers and grandmothers, are scarcely less noteworthy in the study of these Etruscan tombs. There were periods throughout the long centuries of Etruscan evolution when their burial customs underwent complete change. The form of their tombs was at times modified by local geological conditions, although throughout the thousand years of their endurance they remained faithful to the original plan of a circular enclosure, whether that was erected above the ground or hollowed out of the volcanic rock below.

But at one time we find them practising the rite of inhumation, at another placing the whole body in a large and often richly decorated sarcophagus, and again practising cremation and disposing of the calcined remains either in the jar-like urns already mentioned, in little " soul-houses," miniature copies of Etruscan dwellings, or in small-size sarcophagi, sometimes beautifully sculptured from alabaster, but more often moulded in terracotta.

Again, we find the actual tomb assuming the exact proportions and characteristics of the interior of an Etruscan house    Tombs there are to be seen in which every detail of an actual dwelling house are reproduced in stone, the wooden rafters being carefully carved out of the tufa, the window recesses and the doors as faithfully reproduced as though it had been an abode for the living instead of a dwelling of darkness for the dead.

In many of these large house-like interiors we find an anteroom and an inner room.  It was within the inner room that a magnificent bronze bedstead was erected, and the bodies of the husband and wife laid to rest upon it as though they were in readiness to arise from it at the break of a day that never dawned.  Most of their household utensils surrounded them in their nuptial chamber of death, and in niches around the walls of the outer apartment small sarcophagi were stored, containing the remains of their family.

Many wonderful tombs have been explored, and one of the finest is reconstructed in every detail in the Etruscan Museum at Florence.  In this scores of these little sarcophagi, many of them bearing

beautifully carved or moulded figures, no doubt resembling in some respect the person whose remains were interred within, are ranged around the crypt-like vault, in the centre of which stands the large and imposing sarcophagus of the head of the family and his wife, both of whose effigies in semi-recumbent positions are sculptured life-size resting on the lid.

In the tombs of this latter type there was not the same effort to supply the dead with the materials of everyday life, which either implies some temporary change of ideas concerning the future life or merely the absence of suggestion, for once a body had been cremated and placed within a small sarcophagus upon a shelf the impulse to surround it with the familiar objects of its life on earth could not have been so strong as it was in the case of burial in the anthropoid jars, where a crude suggestion of the departed still adhered to the form of the urn.

Where the ground did not permit of digging a shaft down into the volcanic rock and hollowing out below the surface either a large crypt with one

ETRURIA'S MOST PRETENTIOUS FORM OF BURIAL

The final and most sumptuous stage in Etruscan burials was when the casket containing the ashes developed into a sarcophagus showing the dead man reclining at full length on a couch, accompanied in many instances by his wife.  A case in point is the alabaster sarcophagus seen here : the gold necklace about the woman's neck was actually found in the tomb.

Photo, Alinari

TOMB OF THE VOLUMNII AT PERUGIA CARVED IN THE LIVING ROCK

In the vicinity of the great Etruscan settlement on the borders of Umbria, the tomb of the Volumnii is one of the finest examples of the sepulchral burial-chambers. Carved out of the solid rock, it is fashioned after the interior of a rich man's home, and in the niche at the back are still preserved intact the beautiful sepulchral urns belonging to the family by whom the tomb was made. This splendid sepulchral chamber dates from the third or second century B.C.

Photo, Alinari

or two sustaining pillars, or a square imitation of a house interior, sometimes even plastering the whole of the walls and painting them with bright colours —in one particular case representing in plastic relief all the common objects of an Etruscan household including the geese and hens, as well as the scissors and pots and pans and chairs and table—tombs were built above the level of the ground. Even so, they started usually with a circular enclosure of stone, rising in something of a beehive form, so that Etruscan cemeteries as they grew, presented an extraordinary appearance as of scores of great beehives, and to this day these strange homes of the dead form a very distinctive feature of the landscape in certain parts of Tuscany.

Mention of the decorated interiors of the tombs demands a word or two further, as there was a period when, possibly influenced by contemporary Greek design, the interiors were brightly illuminated with the most animated frescoes representing scenes of gaiety, the pastimes of the people, banqueting and so forth. Indeed, from some of the pictures in these tombs a totally wrong impression of the Etruscans was for many centuries

entertained. In most of these frescoes are to be seen women seated alongside of their men, and to the Greek mind this was almost offensive, as the Greek kept his women in the background, never taking his wife to the sports or showing her off in public places. It was Greek writers, therefore, who put it about that the Etruscans were a peculiarly licentious people who took a pride in being seen in the company of women, the only sort of women the Greek mind could imagine being those of their own Hetaira class. It is extraordinary that in Etruscan society, the fact of women having attained to a position unheard of in Greece, being regarded as almost the equals of their husband in all the affairs of life, admitted freely to their husbands' society and to that of their friends, should in the uncomprehending minds of critics have produced the idea of a licentious people, which it must be admitted a few of the mural decorations in some of the tombs might be held to substantiate ; but the probability is that these ribald dances so depicted were associated with some few and not characteristic members of the young Etruscan nobility.

RECONSTRUCTION OF THE THREE PYRAMIDS AT ABUSIR WITH THEIR TEMPLES AND APPROACHES

Of the two outer pyramids at Abusir, other than the central one of Sahu-ra (see model in page 462), one was built by King Userkaf and the other by King User-en-ra, or Neuserre, both of the fifth dynasty; they were known as "Ab-ast" and "Men-ast" respectively. They are not as big as the more noted pyramids of the fourth dynasty, and signs are not wanting that by this time the centralised power of the Pharaohs was waning. Beneath the shadow of these monuments of the remote past our wonder is merged in that strange sadness induced by dead cultures and vanished empires. To a sightseer of Tutankhamen's days they would have appeared scarcely less venerable in their antiquity than they do to-day

*After Herr Borchardt, by permission of Messrs. Henrichs, of Leipzig, from his "Grabdenkmal des Königs Ne-user-ra"*

# The Great Monuments. V.

# The Pyramids of Egypt

## By T. Eric Peet

Professor of Egyptology, Liverpool University

*A N account of the Great Pyramid of Cheops has been written for this work by another contributor, and falls, according to our editorial plan, into the series of articles on the Seven Wonders. Here Professor Peet describes the pyramids of Egypt generally: what they are, who built them, their number, which is larger than is generally supposed, of what material, and by what means they were erected.—*EDITOR.

THERE can be little or no doubt that the fascination exercised by ancient Egypt over the thinking beings of all ages is due first and foremost to two things—her mummies and her pyramids. She claims recognition by the fact that she evolved a means of preserving the bodies of her dead from decay, and the tombs of her greatest rulers from destruction at the hands of man and time. The child who enters a museum directs his first steps to the mummy-room; the tourist's first excursion in Egypt is to the pyramids of Gizeh.

And yet there is nothing in Egyptian civilization with regard to which more foolish and incorrect ideas prevail in the popular mind than these two very subjects—pyramids and mummies. There is an intimate connexion between the two. They illustrate one and the same idea—the pathetic efforts made by the Egyptians to preserve their dead from interference and corruption. The body was mummified because it was believed that even in the after-life it would still be needed, and that if it went to pieces a kind of second and more fatal death would occur. The pyramid was piled over the tomb-chamber partly, at least, in order to conceal the exact whereabouts of the body, and to prevent evilly-disposed persons from destroying it and so bringing about this second death.

The main questions which may be asked about the pyramids, and which we shall endeavour to answer here, are the following: What are the pyramids, and by whom were they built and when; where, and how many are they; and of what material and by what means were they built?

The purpose of the pyramids has aroused the curiosity of all ages. In a book written in the middle of the last century we find solemnly enunciated the opinion that they were the store-houses which Joseph built to store up grain against the seven years' famine. And yet, even before the decipherment of the Egyptian language, there was never any doubt upon the matter, for the Greek historians and travellers state quite unequivocally that the pyramids were the tombs of kings; while the Arab rulers of Egypt in the Middle Ages were wont to ransack them for the wealth supposed to lie within or beneath.

The pyramids then, are tombs, and they are the tombs of kings, and occasionally of queens and other members of the royal families. The proofs of this lie, first, in the fact that the royal coffins, and sometimes even the remains of the bodies, have been found within or beneath them, and secondly, in the fact that the Egyptians' own statements on the subject, both on the walls of these pyramids themselves and elsewhere—quietly ignored by those who prefer their own imaginings to hard facts—leave no doubt on the matter. Such beliefs as that the Great Pyramid of Gizeh served during its construction as an observatory for watching the motions of certain stars are the phantasy of dreamers who can blind themselves to the facts, and are unworthy of serious consideration.

How many, and where are the pyramids? Popular belief for the most part recognizes only three, those of Gizeh, about five miles south-west of Cairo. As a matter of fact, there are very many more than this. They may be divided into two main groups. The first occupies what is known as the Great Pyramid Field, which extends along the west bank of the Nile for a distance of sixty miles from Abu Roash (due west of Cairo) in the north, to Hawara in the south. The other, with which we shall deal but lightly here on account of its minor importance and late date, is in the Sudan around Meroe and Napata, and is the burial-ground of the Ethiopian kings—some of whom also ruled Egypt—of the eighth century B.C. onward, and their Meroitic successors. It is only of late years that these tombs have been scientific-ally investigated by the Harvard-Boston expedition under Reisner; and excavation is still in progress.

In addition to these two great groups of pyramids there were others, notably at Thebes, opposite the modern Luxor. Here, for example, still lie the remains of the pyramid and pyramid-temple of

King Mentuhotep III. of the eleventh dynasty, excavated some years ago by the Egypt Exploration Society, and more recently an American expedition has discovered that King Mentuhotep V. of the same dynasty also began for himself a tomb near the same spot. The Abbot papyrus, which contains an account of the plundering of royal tombs in the twentieth dynasty, records the examination by state inspectors of ten royal pyramids dating from

again, we next reach Sakkara and its pyramids of the fifth and sixth dynasties. These are from one point of view, despite their ruined condition, the most important of all the pyramids, for the walls of their chambers are covered with inscriptions. These, as may be imagined, are of a funerary character. Their value is twofold: in the first place, they provide a mine of information concerning early Egyptian religion, and in particular

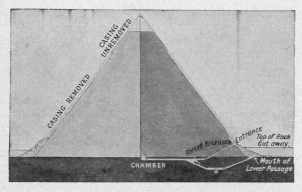 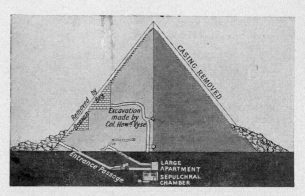

**SECTION THROUGH THE SECOND GIZEH PYRAMID (LEFT) AND THE THIRD PYRAMID (RIGHT)**
The Pyramid of Cheops is unusual, having the burial chamber in its centre. The section through the second pyramid shows the more normal arrangement, and indicates the extant portion of the original stone casing. Large portions of the third pyramid were removed by Osman Bey in a frantic search for treasure, as shown by the right-hand section, but the tomb-chamber, with the mummy and its sarcophagus, were not discovered until 1838. These were then shipped for England, but were lost on the journey.

the thirteenth to the eighteenth dynasties, nine of which were intact and one broken open. These were doubtless comparatively small monuments, and only slight traces of a few of them now remain.

We may, therefore, return to the more important and interesting northern group in the Great Pyramid Field. The most northerly pyramid is to be found at Abu Roash, eight miles due west of Cairo; it is the tomb of King Razedef of the fourth dynasty, about 2900 B.C. Next, four miles to the south, lies the famous Gizeh group, the tombs of the great kings of this same dynasty, Cheops (Khufu), Chephren (Khafra), and Mycerinus (Menkaura). East of the first are three smaller pyramids, doubtless designed for members of the royal family, and three more lie to the south of the pyramid of Mycerinus. Round about this group of royal tombs are the mastaba-tombs of the courtiers and nobles and their families, rectangular structures of stone, with walls slanting slightly inwards, containing chambers often sculptured and painted, and concealing the entrances of the underground burial pits.

Moving southward and passing by the unfinished pyramid of Zawiyet el Aryan, we reach Abusir, where are the slightly less imposing brick pyramids of three great kings of the fifth dynasty, roughly 2750-2625 B.C., together with the temples which they built in honour of the sun-god. Moving on

its beliefs regarding death and the after-life, and in the second they are the earliest surviving specimens of any length of the written Egyptian language.

In addition to this group, Sakkara boasts yet another pyramid, interesting as being the earliest known to us. It is built in steps or stages, and known to the tourist as the Step Pyramid. It stands to-day 197 feet in height, and is peculiar in that its base is not, as usually, a square, but a rectangle, 394 by 351 feet. It is the tomb of King Zeser of the third dynasty, who ruled roughly 2980 B.C., and who also possesses a second tomb —as more than one Egyptian monarch did—at Bet Khallaf, 300 miles farther up the Nile.

Still farther to the south is Dahshur, where lie buried under their ruined pyramids some of the great monarchs, the Amenemhets and Senusrets, of the twelfth dynasty, 2000-1788 B.C. After this there is a gap in the long line of pyramids until we reach Lisht, where there are two more of this same dynasty. Yet farther south, at the entrance of the oasis of the Fayyum, lie three isolated pyramids, that of Amenemhet III. (twelfth dynasty) at Hawara; that of Senusret II., of the same dynasty, at El Lahun; and that of Sneferu, an early king of the fourth dynasty, at Medum. The last is one of the most imposing features of Egyptian landscape. It stands on a mound, partly artificial, 120 feet in height, and rises in three

## GRIM BULK THAT HAS DEFIED THE WEATHERING OF FORTY-EIGHT CENTURIES

No more impressive example can be imagined of the overwhelming dignity that attaches to mere magnitude than that presented by the three great pyramids of Gizeh. In order of antiquity as of dimensions, the Great Pyramid of Khufu (Cheops), seen here on the right, ranks first; it is dealt with in detail in a later chapter. Next in order is the Pyramid of Khafra, or Chephren (centre), part of whose limestone casing remains at the summit. Smallest and youngest of the three, but still more than 4,700 years old, is the Pyramid of Menkaura—Mycerinus.

WARDEN OF THE DESERT MARCHES, THE GREAT PYRAMID OF CHEOPS

To realize the position of the three pyramids at Gizeh in relation to Memphis, modern Cairo, and the rest of Egypt, it would be advisable to consult the colour map in a later page. Above is the Great Pyramid of Khufu, or Cheops, as he is known to Greek writers, seen from the plain; the Egyptians called it "Khut." It will be discussed more fully later, but, in connexion with Prof. Peet's conclusions in page 462, it is worth mentioning that as many as 300,000 men are recorded by the historian Diodorus to have been employed on the work of its construction.

steep steps, or stages, to a height of 114 feet, with a flat, not a pointed, top.

Such is a brief description of the pyramids of the Great Pyramid Field with their dates. Before we can go any further into the details of some of the more interesting of these tombs we must first explain the relation of the pyramid to the important group of buildings which lay about it.

A pyramid, as has been stated above, is a tomb. More exactly it is a tomb-chapel. The Egyptian tomb of any pretensions to size invariably consisted of two essential parts, a tomb-chamber and a tomb-chapel. The former was in most cases an underground chamber containing the body in its coffin of wood or stone; the latter was a building above ground, made of brick or stone, perhaps in some cases of wood, in which the relatives of the dead man or the funerary priests attached to his tomb made the daily offerings of food and drink for his consumption. Thus the typical tomb of the noble of the fourth dynasty was the mastaba described already, a rectangular building of stone, with slightly sloping walls, containing the small rooms in which the offerings were made. Under

this lay the tomb-chamber, cut in the solid rock, and entered either by a pit or a staircase generally concealed by the mastaba.

In the third dynasty the royal tomb had been of a similar type, but much larger, and built, in the cases known to us, of brick. But towards the end of the dynasty Zeser introduced a new type of royal tomb, the pyramid. There are some who believe that the pyramid is simply a developed mastaba with a pointed top. Architecturally there may be a germ of truth in this, for some of the pyramids do seem to have been begun as mastabas and afterwards given successive outer coatings and finished off in a point. Other Egyptologists, however, would see in the pyramid the embodiment of a totally new idea.

At Heliopolis, in the Delta, not far north of Cairo, was the centre of sun-worship in Egypt. Here, in the Sun Temple, was preserved a sacred pyramidal stone called the "benben." Now the summit of a pyramid or an obelisk was known in Egyptian as "benbent," possibly from its resemblance in shape to the sacred stone, and if this idea is correct it would seem that both the obelisk and the pyramid were closely connected with sun-worship. In this case it would be in no way extraordinary that at a period when sun-worship was coming more and more into prominence in Egypt, the king should give to his tomb a form expressive of his adherence to the solar cult, with which, incidentally, current beliefs concerning death and the hereafter were intimately bound up, as is evident from the inscriptions in the Sakkara pyramids.

However this may be, the fact remains that for centuries from the fourth dynasty onward each king aspired to build himself a tomb in the shape of a pyramid. As the type developed the offering-chambers ceased to be placed inside the pyramid itself, and took the form of an imposing pyramid-temple built on to its east side. The burial chamber still lay in the solid rock beneath the pyramid (with a few exceptions) and was entered by a staircase or sloping passage, often approached by a concealed opening in the north face of the pyramid not far above its base. But this was not all. The pyramids were mostly built on the high desert plateau, many feet above the level of the cultivation, and it was a long and rough climb to reach them. To remedy this, a second smaller temple was built for each pyramid down in the cultivation, a kind of introductory or entrance-temple, and from this a covered inclined passage led up into the pyramid-temple proper on the plateau above. Thus in the flood-time visitors to the tomb would be carried in their boats to the landing-stage of the introductory temple, where they would disembark. After a short preliminary ceremony there they would advance up the covered incline to perform in the temple proper the ceremonies for which they had come.

**SECOND PYRAMID OF GIZEH, WITH ITS CAP OF POLISHED STONE**

An obscure king succeeded Khufu, and then came Khafra, or Chephren, the builder of the second pyramid at Gizeh, known to the Egyptians as "Ur," and here viewed from the summit of the Great Pyramid. Figures convey little of its immensity, but, with its height of about 450 feet and its base-line of 700 feet, it is calculated to contain some 60,000,000 cubic feet of rock. The polished stone with which the whole building was once cased has long since vanished, with the exception of the topmost portions.

Photo by Donald McLeish

**MEDUM PYRAMID OF KING SNEFERU, RENOWNED AS A WARRIOR-KING**

Another important site is that of Medum, where stands the pyramid of King Sneferu; he is reckoned either as the last of the third or the first of the fourth dynasty—there appears to have been no real break between the two. In any case, Sneferu is the first king of Egypt who really takes shape as a historical figure, inaugurating as he did a great period of prosperity, raiding the Sudan, conquering the Sinaitic peninsula, and establishing there a settlement of turquoise and copper miners.

Photo from W. M. Flinders Petrie

**CLOSER VIEW OF THE THIRD DYNASTY STONE PYRAMID AT DAHSHUR**

The earlier pyramid at Dahshur here illustrated is one of two built of stone which are almost certainly to be attributed to the successors of King Zeser; of them little is known except that they must have maintained the prosperity of his reign to erect such imposing monuments. In a sense, these are the first pyramids, certainly the first to assume the conventional pyramidal shape, for, in contrast to the Step Pyramid, the courses of masonry were faced so as to give them an unbroken outline.

STRANGE OUTLINE OF SNEFERU'S PYRAMID RISING FROM THE SANDS OF EGYPT

Sneferu built for himself two pyramids, but it was probably in that at Medum that he was buried ; the other one dominates the group at Dahshur. The Medum pyramid, 114 feet high, is of a curious shape, as may be seen, having three steps of 70, 20, and 25 feet respectively ; it was in a tomb close by that the beautiful statue of the Lady Nefert illustrated in page 343 was found. The official entrusted with the care of this pyramid, we know from inscriptions, was Ka-nefer ; it was one of the highest offices of the realm.

Photo from W. M. Flinders Petrie

The relation of these component parts of the pyramid group has only been fully understood through the excavations of the last thirty years, notably those of the second and third pyramids of Gizeh, and the pyramids of Abusir. Every finished pyramid thus consists of four parts, the pyramid proper, the pyramid temple, the covered incline, and the introductory temple in the plain.

We may now apply this scheme to the famous pyramids of Gizeh. Of that of Cheops, the Great Pyramid, we shall say little, for it is described in another part of this work by Dr. Margaret Murray. Suffice it to say that, in addition to the usual burial chamber cut in solid rock beneath its centre, it has—and in this it is almost unique—a series of chambers of unusual form within its core. Its original height was about 481 feet, and the four sides measured 755 feet 8 inches, with a maximum error of no more than an inch. The angle of slope of the faces is 51 degrees. Some of the stones used weigh sixteen tons, and yet so perfect is the masonry that the joints between stone and stone average only one-fiftieth of an inch.

The second pyramid, that of Chephren, has sides 706 feet 3 inches in length, and its original height was 472 feet. It was cased with a fine outer coating, granite below and limestone above, which has now totally disappeared except near the top. It has two entrances, one some distance up the north face, and the other at the ground level.

STEP PYRAMID OF ZESER AT SAKKARA, FORERUNNER OF ALL ITS KIND

The pyramids at Sakkara form a series of great interest extending over a long period, and of these none is more important than the "Step Pyramid," first of all pyramids, built by King Zeser or Tcheser, of the third dynasty (c. 2980 B.C.). With the rise to power of this dynasty in Egypt the archaic period began its era of greatest prosperity, signalized by the change from the "mastaba" to the pyramid as a royal tomb and the increasing use of stone instead of brick as a building material.

Photo from W. M. Flinders Petrie

## PYRAMIDS AT GIZEH SEEN THROUGH THE FEATHERY PALMS THAT FRINGE THE NILE

Seen unforeshortened by perspective, as here, the pyramids tend less to rob each other of their size. About their base, and especially by the small pyramid of Menkaura on the extreme left, may be seen smaller pyramids erected to cover the bones of royal kinsmen and lesser personages of the court; there were also many mastaba-tombs, for in death as in life the perfect courtier wished to be near his king. It must be remembered that these mighty structures are purely and simply tombs, and those who try to find other purposes for them are as likely to be disappointed as the old Khalifas who ransacked them in vain for treasure. Of more practical use has been their casing of polished stone, pillaged ceaselessly by the architects of Cairo.

*From a photograph taken and coloured in Egypt by H. A. Fawcett, M.R.C.S., D.P.H.*

EARLIEST STONE MONUMENT OF GREAT SIZE, THE STEP PYRAMID OF SAKKARA

The pyramid of Zeser is about 200 feet high and is built in six " steps," decreasing upwards from 38 to 29½ feet in height. Its shape and method of construction show clearly that it is in the transition stage from the " mastaba," for it is rectangular instead of square, the base measurements being 351 and 394 feet : indeed, although of stone and not of brick, there is evidence that it was commenced as a mastaba and added to afterwards. The architect was probably the famous deified Imhotep.

Both descend at an angle for 100 feet, where they turn horizontal. Finally they coalesce and lead into a rock-chamber, discovered by Belzoni in 1816, containing a solid red granite sarcophagus.

The pyramid-temple of this pyramid has been completely excavated, but is in a sadly ruined condition. Its entrance-temple is now known to be the so-called Sphinx Temple which lies below the plateau and has been cleared and visited by tourists for many years. The Sphinx itself is

PYRAMIDS OF BRICK AND STONE AT DAHSHUR WITH 1,000 YEARS BETWEEN

The pyramids at Dahshur belong to two widely separated ages in Egyptian history, of which, strangely enough, the earlier produced the finer structures by far. The ruinous brick pyramid in the foreground, for instance, was built by a king of the twelfth dynasty (c. 1900 B.C.), during the Middle Kingdom, when less labour was expended on such unproductive works and stone only used for facing. In the background, however, may be seen an early stone pyramid which is second only to that of Zeser at Sakkara.

MODEL OF THE PYRAMID OF SAHU-RA, SHOWING THE TEMPLES ATTACHED

King Sahu-ra, of the fifth dynasty built himself the pyramid at Abusir known as " Kha-ba," whose model here illustrated is intended to show the four component parts of such structures in their relations to each other. First comes the entrance-temple on the edge of the flood-limit, next the covered way, here divided and foreshortened (see colour plate facing page 461). This leads to the pyramid-temple where the priests officiated ; and finally, the pyramid towers above the tomb. evidence perhaps of sun-worship.

Metropolitan Museum of Art, New York City

part of the arrangements of this pyramid. It is a vast piece of natural rock carved in the form of a lion, with the head of King Chephren, and lies on the right of the covered way as one goes up from the entrance-temple to the pyramid-temple.

The third pyramid, that of Mycerinus, was 215 feet high, and had a side of 346 feet 2 inches. Part of the granite casing which covered the lower part of it still remains. Several attempts to enter it were made in the early nineteenth century, and it was eventually opened by Colonel Howard Vyse. The entrance is in the north side, 13 feet from the base. A sloping passage leads down to a burial chamber where was found part of a wooden coffin, shown by its inscription to be that of Mycerinus, and now in the British Museum. From this chamber another passage leads to a farther chamber, in which was found a magnificent basalt sarcophagus. This was placed on a ship bound for England, but after touching at Leghorn the vessel disappeared and was never heard of again.

One question still remains to be answered. How did the Egyptians contrive to erect these vast piles of immense blocks of stone? On few subjects has so much nonsense been talked, and there are those who actually believe that steam or electricity was used. In reality the answer is perfectly simple—endless labour, endless patience, and almost endless time. So soon as a king of the

fourth dynasty came to the throne practically the whole available labour of the land was conscripted for the construction of his pyramid. In the dry season men were busy cutting the blocks at the quarries. When the floods came rafts were floated up to the mouths of the quarries, and with no more scientific apparatus than ropes, levers, and wooden rollers, the blocks were placed on the rafts. The journey thence to the pyramid site was a simple matter. Here by the same means the blocks were worked off the rafts and up a paved inclined slope or ramp to their position on the pile.

As the height increased a spiral incline was probably left in the masonry of the pyramid itself, up which the blocks were laboriously man-handled by vast gangs of men working day after day, and year after year. Let him who disbelieves this simple explanation spend a week in an excavating camp in Egypt. There he will see stones of the same size being moved by the same old means. When Reisner was working at the third Gizeh pyramid thirty of his Arab workmen moved from off the temple area in a few weeks over 400 granite blocks fallen from the pyramid casing, and weighing from one to seven tons each, with no other tackle than levers, rollers, ropes, and a couple of improvised trucks. " If there is an order," they said, " we will build a pyramid."

## Ancient Arts and Crafts. IV.

# Masterpieces of Roman Sculpture

## By Frank Rutter

*MR. RUTTER, who in a previous article has painted for us a vivid picture of the spirit that produced the Greek masterpieces, now turns to Roman sculpture with the excellences peculiar to it, and discusses an art which, buried as it were beneath the mighty ruins of Rome's more obvious qualities, long remained unrecognized; and has only recently been reinstated in its true aesthetic position—an archæological discovery as genuine as any.*—EDITOR.

NO city is more famous than Rome, no age more celebrated than that of its first emperor, Augustus; yet no art has been more unjustly slighted than that belonging to Imperial Rome's greatest period—namely, the era which stretches from the reign of Augustus to that of Constantine.

"A decadent anti-climax to the art of Greece," that was the old-fashioned view of Roman sculpture, which was commonly considered to be no better than a more or less feeble imitation of the sculpture of Greece. Modern research—among which must be mentioned the valuable work done by the British School of Rome—has altogether revolutionised critical opinion, and to-day it is recognized that many of the innovations which were formerly held to be the peculiar characteristics of Christian art had their origin in the despised sculpture of pagan Rome.

Roman art now stands out as the bridge which links the masterpieces of ancient Greece with those of the Italian Renaissance. It attempted and partially solved problems which the Greeks had avoided, problems which were not again tackled and finally conquered for nearly a thousand years. It created the "continuous style," which became a model of monumental narrative for centuries to come, so that the spiral reliefs of Trajan's Column are the ancestors alike of Giotto's Biblical frescoes and of Hogarth's "Marriage à la Mode" series; and finally it gave a new direction to art, substituting a search for individual character in place of the standardisation of an ideal beauty based on the regularity of proportions.

How did it come about that a race which made contributions so important as these to the progress of art remained so long uncelebrated for its artistic prowess? The old prejudice against the art of Rome was due to several causes. In the first place the Romans themselves set a bad example. While justly proud of their achievements in other fields, they were inclined —like many Englishmen —to believe that in matters of art foreigners had merits superior to that of their own countrymen. No Roman author took the trouble to write the biographies of Roman artists, and consequently the very names of the greatest Roman sculptors are unknown to us. Generous to a fault in their praise of what Greece had achieved in the past, the Romans underrated the value of the work of their own contemporaries. This example of depreciation has been widely followed.

Secondly, owing to the great changes Rome underwent in the first century — for example, the great fire of Nero

**PORTRAIT OF THE EMPEROR VESPASIAN**
This is a notable example of the manner in which the Roman sculptors of the first century anticipated the "impressionism" of the nineteenth century sculptor Rodin. The bust, in the Museo delle Terme at Rome, is altogether a masterpiece in its forceful delineation of character.
Photo by Alinari

and the extensive public works carried out by Trajan in the second century and by the Antonines later—comparatively few examples of Augustan and earlier sculpture are now in existence. Further, of the few great monuments that remain the majority are in pieces, and the fragments belonging to them are scattered in different museums and in various cities.

Thus one of the noblest monuments of Augustan Rome was the Ara Pacis (Altar of Peace), set up by the Senate in 13 B.C. in honour of the emperor's victorious return from a double campaign in Gaul and Spain. The sides of this altar were decorated with allegorical reliefs and with a wonderful frieze of a procession in which the emperor, his attendants, and the Imperial family figure. Fragments of this great altar may be found in the Vatican, the Villa Medici, and the Museo delle

Terme at Rome, in the Uffizi at Florence, and at the Louvre in Paris. With unwearying zeal the Austrian savant, Professor Eugen Petersen, worked for years at the patient identification of the fragments, and was eventually able to reconstruct it photographically and display its beauties in a monograph published in 1902.

To perceive the pristine grandeur of a monument which time has mutilated and dispersed to this extent requires a considerable exercise of the imagination, and it is easier to grasp the peculiar properties of Augustan sculpture by the more intimate study of a detail. The beautiful altar with the plane-leaves (see page 465) in the Museo delle Terme, Rome, is a splendid example of what has been called the "illusionism" of Augustan sculpture. The bull's head, above the crossing branches, has a magnificent simplicity

**BEAUTIFUL SLAB FROM THE SOUTH FRIEZE OF THE ARA PACIS AT ROME**

A fragment of the great altar dedicated to the " Peace of Augustus " by the Roman Senate in 13 B.C. On the extreme left is the beautiful Antonia and her husband, the Elder Drusus, leading their child Germanicus. In the background an old woman puts her fingers to her lips to admonish this couple for talking during a sacred procession. The old man, third from the right, has been identified as the great art patron Maecenas. The slab is now in the Uffizi Gallery at Florence.

Photo by Brogi

**THE EMPEROR COMMODUS AS HERCULES**
This handsome bust, in the Palazzo dei Conservatori at Rome, marks the technical advance of the later Roman sculptors, who were the first to suggest the glance of the eyes in a life-like manner. Note the undercutting in the hair and beard.
Photo by Anderson

in the Flavian age, and particularly during the reign of Domitian (A.D. 81-96), during whose sovereignty the triumphal arch begun by his brother Titus was completed. The Arch of Titus is one of the most imposing monuments still to be seen in the Roman Forum, and the two sculptured panels inside the arch (see page 516) are famous as illustrating one of the most striking events in history, the capture of Jerusalem. Little notice, however, was taken of their artistic qualities until Franz Wickhoff, in 1894, startled the world of art by placing these reliefs on a level with the masterpieces of Velazquez. Commenting on the panel which shows Roman soldiers carrying off the sacred utensils from the Temple at Jerusalem, the table for the shewbread (Exodus xxv. 23), the trumpets which called the people together (Numbers x. 2), and the seven-branched candle-stick (Exodus xxv. 31), Wickhoff wrote:

" We are to believe that the people are moving there before our eyes ; we are no longer to be reminded of pictures ; rather, the plastic art tries to attain by its own methods the same effect as would a highly developed art of painting— the impression of complete illusion. Beauty of line, symmetry of parts, such as a conventional art demands, are no longer sought for. Everything is concentrated on the one aim of producing an impression of continuous motion. Air, light, and shade are all pressed into the service and must help to conjure up reality. The relief has

and realism, while the leaves themselves are modelled with a subtlety that shows not only a close observation of natural form but also an appreciation of the atmosphere that envelops and softens forms. Here is an example of one of the triumphs of the Roman sculptor—namely, his ability to create the " illusion " of reality. This was brought about largely by the suppression of a definite outline, so that, in the work illustrated, the edges of the leaves appear to melt into the air as they would in Nature.

This was the first aesthetic advance made by Rome, its conquest of an effect which the Greeks had not attempted or realized. Further progress was made

**ALTAR DECORATED WITH BOUKRANION AND PLANE-LEAVES**
This altar, with its bull's head and plane-leaves, discovered near the Castello Sant' Angelo and at present in the Museo delle Terme, is a masterpiece of the Augustan " illusionist " manner. Note the simplicity and naturalism of the details and the way in which the edges of the leaves seem to melt into the surrounding air.
Photo by Anderson

' respiration,' like the pictures of Velazquez. But as it is the real and not painted air that filters in between the figures, it follows that all the master's art is brought to bear on such a skilful arrangement of groups as, in spite of the compression, may allow air to pass between, above, and around the figures, thus helping to supplement the modelling, even as the sunlight which, when it breaks in, awakens these figures to magic life. To allow natural illumination to contribute to the perfecting of the artistic effect was one of the boldest innovations." In this relief and in the other, which shows the emperor in his four-horsed chariot, the difficult problem of depth—that is to say, of rendering the third dimension pictorially—has been almost conquered, for, owing to the skill with which the figures have been cut out of the marble block in varying depths, we seem not only to look along the line of the procession but to be able to penetrate its ranks.

While not disputing the remarkable merits of these reliefs on the Arch of Titus, Mrs. Arthur Strong, the greatest English authority on Roman sculpture, has pertinently called attention to their limitations : " That the sculptor does not yet fully command the resources of art is shown by the disproportion between the arch and the human figures, and in the absence of the most elementary laws of perspective, which might enable the sculptor to place the arch in some sort of just relation to the orientation of the procession. This is evidently conceived as passing straight in front of the spectator, yet the arch is placed in a three-quarter view, so that none of the figures are really going through it, but are passing between it and the frame of the relief."

**WONDERFUL RELIEFS ON THE LOWER SPIRALS OF TRAJAN'S COLUMN**

For the position and surroundings of the Column of Trajan see the photograph in page **517.** The portion here illustrated is taken from the base of the column and shows two of the spiral windings. On the lower band the Roman army is seen issuing from the gate of a fortified city (Viminacium) and crossing the Danube by a bridge of boats, while "Father Danube" (left centre) from his cave stretches out his right hand in encouragement. The upper band shows works of fortification in progress.

Photo by Alinari

TWO VIEWS OF THE LOVELY ANTINOUS MONDRAGONE IN THE LOUVRE

This famous head, the last type of ideal beauty created by the antique world, illustrates the temporary reaction in favour of Greek ideals during the reign of Hadrian. The feminine grace of this boy's countenance has nothing in common with the virility that marks the native art of Rome, such as we see in the reliefs of Trajan's Column, or the portrait of the warlike Trajan himself. Antinous was the favourite of the Emperor Hadrian, and was drowned in the Nile in A.D. 122.

Photos by Alinari (left) and Giraudon (right)

Nevertheless, the sculptors of the Arch of Titus gave the truest rendering of space that had yet been known, and their masterpieces remained unrivalled in this respect for thirteen centuries—in fact, till the discovery of the laws of perspective in the fourteenth century began a new epoch in both painting and sculpture.

Possibly it was the failure to discover these laws which caused this "impressionist sculpture" to be only a transient phase of Roman art; on the other hand, there are not wanting critics who maintain that this search after an intensified realism was deliberately abandoned by later sculptors who considered this style ill-suited to the deliberate aims of architectural decoration.

However this may be, the fact is incontestable that the next great movement in Roman sculpture, during the reign of Trajan, shows a complete change of style. Trajan's Column, which still adorns the forum associated with his name, must always rank with the greatest creations of the human genius as shown in sculpture. From a merely material point of view it is a wonderful monument. This column is encircled by a spiral sculptured band some 217 yards long, and about one yard high, though the band increases in height as the spirals approach the top of the

column to allow for the perspectival diminution. On this band, which winds twenty-three times round the column, the story of the emperor's two Dacian campaigns is told in 155 sculptured pictures containing 2,500 figures, yet these renderings of different episodes in the campaigns are so neatly dovetailed into one another that the whole forms one continuous and uninterrupted narrative.

Wickhoff, who was the first to apply the term "continuous" to this style of composition, was also the first to analyse its epoch-making character as a work of art: "Extreme naturalness of movement is here combined with an ideal treatment of time. This makes it possible to crowd victory and battle together into a narrow space. In the midst of the fray, which runs its course at one end of the design, the emperor is thundering against his enemies, while the other end is occupied by a peaceful scene in which Roma welcomes the hero and Victory crowns him. The spectator who has assimilated this work knows that a new sphere has been opened to art, and therefore will not be surprised that a narrative style which could produce such a masterpiece held its own for fifteen centuries, survived the decline of artistic power, and accompanied the revival of art among foreign peoples, because no other kind of narrative

PORTRAITS OF AN OLD MAN (LEFT) AND CARACALLA (RIGHT)

The national characteristics of Roman art are impressively displayed by the bust of an old man in the Vatican Museum, which dates from the Republican period. The bust of Caracalla has been called " the most striking portrait left us by antiquity." It is in the Royal Museum, Berlin.

Photos by Alinari (left) and V. Bruckmann (right)

MEDALLION FROM THE ARCH OF CONSTANTINE

The Arch of Constantine consists in part of materials from an earlier period (see page 519). This vivid impression of an imperial boar-hunt dates from the reign of Domitian and has atmospheric qualities similar to those of the Arch of Titus.

Photo by Anderson

could approach it in force and vitality."

From a purely naturalistic point of view the sculpture on Trajan's Column may appear a retrogression. It will be observed that not only is the relief lower than in the sculpture on the Arch of Titus, but that rows of figures are pressed against each other and arranged in superposed tiers. The attempt to render space is abandoned, but in its stead there is a conscious decorative aim which was afterwards to set an example and a standard to the painters and tapestry-weavers of medieval Europe. Further, the sculptured band of the Trajan Column introduced into Europe a new story-telling art which became of supreme importance to humanity when Biblical subjects took the place of pagan triumphs. Not only did Raphael, Michaelangelo, and other giants of the Renaissance admire the drawings of the figures on Trajan's Column and openly borrow actions and details therefrom for their own works, but every story-teller in paint, from Giotto to Hogarth, owes the origin of his art to the creative genius of these unknown Roman sculptors.

Under Trajan's successor, Hadrian, there was a temporary reaction towards Greek models, which found supreme expression in the one type of ideal beauty evolved by Rome—namely, the Antinous. The obscure Bithynian youth, whose beauty made him the favourite of Hadrian, whose early and mysterious death on the Nile led to his deification, captured the imagination of the Roman world and added a new classic type to art. The exquisite Antinous Mondragone

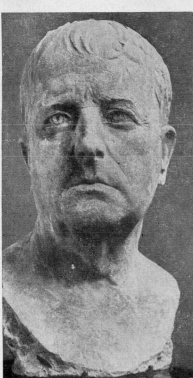

## SOME ROMAN BUSTS

The woman and two men in the top row remain unidentified, but the busts are masterpieces of sculptural realism. The powerful head (left) in the second row is also nameless, but the youth is Augustus and the beautiful girl is Antonia daughter of Mark Antony. Below is an unknown man and Servilia, a great Roman dame who was mistress of Julius Cæsar One and all impress the beholder with a sense of the sculptor's mastery of his medium, and are evidence that the Romans, so renowned for their achievements in law and war, were capable of almost comparable triumphs in the sphere of art

## REGAL DIGNITY OF THE AUGUSTUS OF PRIMA PORTA AT ROME

The most celebrated portrait of Octavianus Augustus, first Emperor of Rome, this statue was found in the Villa of Livia at Prima Porta and is now in the Vatican Museum. It is all Roman in its dignity, but at the same time indicates the classic revival which marked his reign. Greek influence can be traced in its clear outlines and in the details of the cuirass with its allegory of the wearer's victory over the Parthians and (below) the Earth and her children rejoicing in the blessings of peace.

**Photo by Alinari**

(see page 467) at the Louvre shows the perfection of this last classic type, but it is an exotic work, so Greek in its conception and treatment that it can hardly be considered a true representative of Roman art. Roman sculpture excelled in portraiture as well as in decorative and commemorative reliefs, but its forte was not the creation of ideal types, it was the lifelike rendering of particular individuals.

Strong traces of Greek influence can be found in Antonine and Aurelian sculpture, but under Septimius Severus and his son Caracalla the native Roman art revived with a new vigour, and while the "continuous" style once more became the fashion, its effect was heightened by a new technical device. Sculptors now cut deeper and, by working away the background, figures were shown in brilliant relief against a dark niche of shadow. This strong contrasting of light and shade had a fine colouristic quality which may be seen in the portraiture of the

MODEL OF SOUTH FAÇADE OF THE ARCH OF CONSTANTINE
All the grandeur that was Rome is embodied in this noble structure, with its "unsurpassable harmony of proportion." Many portions of it were taken from earlier monuments, because Constantine wished to emphasise the legitimacy of his right to the diadem by portraying himself among those earlier emperors to whom he claimed to be related. For the present condition of the arch, see page 519.
Metropolitan Museum of Art, New York City

TRAJANIC FRIEZE ON THE ARCH OF CONSTANTINE
In this spirited rendering of the tumult of battle the bareheaded Emperor, with flying cloak, is shown galloping over bodies of the dead, while before him are barbarians suing for mercy. Originally designed for the decoration of Trajan's Forum, this panel, with others, was removed to adorn the Arch of Constantine. Together with that on the following page, the photograph was taken with considerable difficulty, the panel being about 30 feet above the road.
Photo by W. M. Flinders Petrie

period, as well as in the sculpture of the Arch of Constantine.

Of all the monuments of ancient Rome the Arch of Constantine is perhaps the grandest in its structure and the most completely preserved. To the student of sculpture it is additionally interesting because it is an epitome of the different stages of Roman art. For this arch is decorated in great measure by sculptures taken from earlier monuments, so that on its face we can trace the progress and development of Roman sculpture. The earliest portions are the eight circular medallions, arranged in two sets of four on each front of the arch, which represent imperial scenes of hunting and sacrifice; these probably date from the reign of Domitian, and are typical of the art of that period in their

**AURELIAN PANELS ON THE COMPOSITE ARCH OF CONSTANTINE**

The panel on the left shows the Emperor Marcus Aurelius with one attendant (Bassaeus) haranguing the attendant soldiery from a raised dais. The panel on the right depicts the Emperor's sacrifice on the Capitol in thanks for his victory. In these and other panels the original head of Marcus Aurelius has been replaced by a head resembling that of Constantine. Although these sculptures show traces of the Greek influences which had marked the reign of Hadrian, they have lost none of the Roman vigour and variety.

Photo by W. M. Flinders Petrie

impressionism and treatment of space. The medallion of the boar-hunt is especially remarkable for its lively naturalism. "The breathless gallop shown as a flight through the air, the panting pursued beast below, the attempt at foreshortening in the group on the left, are all," writes Mrs. Strong, "in the same line of artistic endeavour as the panels of the Arch of Titus."

The two slabs inside the central archway and the two which adorn the shorter sides of the attic or upper storey, though ruthlessly torn apart, form a continuous whole, which dates from the time of Trajan and relates his exploits. The rush and swirl of the whole composition is splendidly exemplified in the panel which shows the emperor, with flying cloak and bare head, charging on horseback over the heaps of dead, while barbarians meet him suing for mercy, and behind him crowd his trumpeters. "A severe design is combined with an animation unknown to previous art," says Mrs. Strong, and it was this series which inspired Wickhoff to write that fine appreciation of Trajanic art which has been quoted.

The eight smaller panels on the two fronts of the attic form part of a series of reliefs belonging to the period of Marcus Aurelius. Three other panels of this series are in the Palazzo dei Conservatori, Rome. The triumph of the emperor forms the subject of these reliefs, and among the barbarian chiefs two distinct types may be recognized—the Sarmatian, with wild and tangled hair, and the German, with round head and short whiskers. Probably these panels were removed by Constantine from the arch erected to Marcus Aurelius in honour of his double victory over the Germans and Sarmatians. While betraying the revival of Greek influence in the sharp clearness of their outlines, these panels show remarkable variety in the composition of similar subjects and are full of drama and dignity. Striking in the simplicity of its arrangement is the " Address to the Army," in which the emperor, with one attendant, is raised high above the crowding soldiery, whose heads form a straight line at right angles to the imperial group, while the decorative effect is enhanced by the perpendicular lines of the ensigns and lances seen against the portico. These soaring upright lines also convey a sense of triumph, and a similar device was employed to the same end by Velazquez in his famous picture known as "The Lances," or "The Surrender of Breda." Finally, we have typical examples of Constantinian sculpture in the "River-gods" of the side arches and in the "Victories" at the base of the columns, all of which have the deep under-cutting and the strong light-and-shade effect which are characteristic of the period.

From the examples already given it is manifest that we can no longer regard Roman sculpture as a mere uninspired imitation of Greek models, and while admitting the great influence of Greece, it should be emphasised that the Romans had wonderful models nearer home in the masterpieces of Etruscan sculpture. These also played their part in the formation of the Roman styles, and it was perhaps Etruscan rather than Greek influence that was predominant in Roman portraiture. In this department of sculpture the outstanding achievement of Rome was its discovery of beauty in character. Here, again, the artists of pagan Rome anticipated a characteristic of Christian art and prepared the way for an art that was to be human rather than divine.

When we look at the "Head of an Old Man" (see page 468), which experts assign to the republican period before Augustus, we learn that a searching realism was native to Roman art. Nothing could be farther from the idealism of Greek art than this early work. Another later but equally superb example of masterly characterisation is "The Shoemaker, Gaius Julius Helius" which rivals a painted portrait by Jan Van Eyck in its scrupulous rendering of the hairy wart on the left cheek.

Though the portraits of the emperors have long been used by historians for illustrative purposes, their intrinsic merit as works of art were till recently unacknowledged. The Austrian scholar, Alois Riegl, was the first to point out the innovation in the treatment of the eye introduced in the portrait busts of the Antonines.

This innovation consisted in "showing the iris as a bean-shaped segment filled with two dots to indicate the points of light." The bust of "Commodus as Hercules" (page 465) admirably illustrates this new departure, which permitted a more profound psychology in portraiture. It also shows the brilliant colour effect produced by the deep under-cutting of the period. A later development, also making for an increased liveliness, was a half turn of the head, as seen in the magnificent "Portrait of Caracalla" at Berlin. It has been described as "the most striking portrait left us by the antique," and for massiveness and vitality its equal cannot be found before the masterpieces of Donatello in the fifteenth century.

EQUESTRIAN STATUE OF MARCUS AURELIUS

The archetype of all subsequent equestrian statues, this splendidly decorative monument, standing in the Piazza del Campidoglio at Rome, holds a unique place in the history of art. The naturalness of the group is in keeping with the characteristics of Roman sculpture—not imagination, but sanity, dignity, and restraint.

Felton

HADRIAN'S WALL ON ITS WAY EASTWARD TO BORCOVICIUM

Just past the clump of trees seen in the photograph is the fort of Borcovicium, and in the nearer distance is one of those castella or mile-castles which were built at regular intervals o; one Roman mile along the 73-mile line of wall from the mouth of the Tyne to Solway Firth. Each of these castella served as a temporary garrison of about 100 men. The Borcovicium camp was about five acres in extent and was the second largest of the Northumbrian stations. Cilurnum further o; having half an acre more to its credit; but the largest in the whole length of wall was Amboglanna (Birdoswald) in Cumberland. These camps were from two to eight miles distant from each other and their accommodation was, roughly, for 500 soldiers.

## The Master Builders. V.

# Hadrian's Wall: Relic of Roman Britain

### By Jessie Mothersole

Author of "Hadrian's Wall"

*THE writer of this contribution is the author-artist of an admirable work describing the whole length of Hadrian's Wall with the pleasantest historical and topographical allusiveness. The book in question, first published in 1922 by Mr. John Lane, of the Bodley Head, London, is illustrated entirely with Miss Mothersole's own drawings in colour and in black and white ; but for the purposes of* WONDERS OF THE PAST, *in which the pictorial documents must be, wherever possible, direct photographic reproductions, a series of admirable photographs has been secured by the author ; these, with the exception of the one in page 485, have been taken by Mr. John Gibson, of Hexham. Those desiring to pursue the subject beyond the bounds of a single chapter can be recommended to Miss Mothersole's book, the title of which is "Hadrian's Wall."*—EDITOR.

"HADRIAN'S WALL," as marked in the atlases of our schooldays, cutting Great Britain into two separate halves, has always suggested, by its position and its attractive name, something romantic and mysterious and stimulating to the imagination. Who has not in childhood wondered what was still left of it, and what it really looked like " when it was new " ?

The reality was far more wonderful than anything we are likely to have pictured to ourselves. Imagine a great wall, 8 feet thick and (including its parapet) nearly 20 feet high, faced with beautifully worked stone ; see this wall stretching on for mile after mile, a distance of 73¼ miles, from the mouth of the Tyne to the Solway Firth ; climbing high hills, descending into valleys, crossing now a broad river, or again, a small stream ; keeping always to the highest possible ridges of the hills ; shirking no difficulties, but simply " carrying on " till its object is attained, and making a complete cleavage between north and south. Such was the wall itself when it was made ; but also in its course it linked together no less than 14 large forts ; and there were built into it, as an integral part of its construction, 80 small forts or milecastles and about 160 wall-turrets or watch-towers.

Thus we see that the wall was no bare monotonous line of masonry, but included 254 distinct fortified posts, large and small. Fourteen of these were forts built to accommodate 500 or 1,000 men, and contained streets, chapels, offices, colonnaded courts, barracks, officers' dwellings, granaries and workshops, each fort being surrounded by a little town containing the soldiers' families and the hangers-on of the garrison, with a well-appointed bath-house as the centre of its social life.

The country through which this barrier runs is partly low-lying and fertile, partly wild and desolate. Lonely enough it is for the most part to-day, though once it was astir with the activities of the Roman legions who built the wall, and afterwards it resounded to the tramp of the auxiliaries who manned it. Soldiers from nearly every part of the then known world met along this narrow line. From the banks of the Rhine, the Danube and the Seine, from the shores of the sunny Adriatic and of the North Sea, and from the Spanish Peninsula, they came at the command of Rome to hold these outposts in the Northumbrian solitudes.

To follow the course of the wall on foot is to give yourself up entirely to its guidance, letting it lead you where it will ; and, if at times all trace

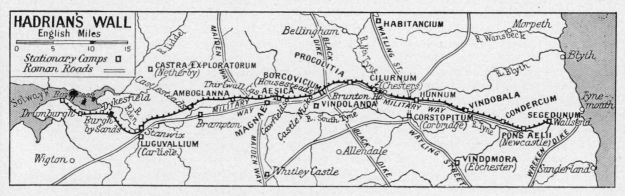

THE GREAT WALL ON PEEL CRAG, 900 FEET ABOVE SEA-LEVEL

Shown here is the southern aspect of the wall where the upper facing-stones have been restored; the northern face has not been touched. Repairs in the wall were necessary to keep sheep from falling down the crag, and it was therefore thought best to rebuild it carefully, as nearly as possible in the Roman manner. The photograph shows clearly the barren " wastes " on the north of the wall; it was taken soon after the rebuilding, when heaps of stones were still lying about. These are now overgrown with grass.

of it has disappeared, seeking the clue until you find it, and following on again. And it has much to reveal to you all along its course.

Not only can it still be traced over the greater part of its 73-mile course, with long stretches of solid masonry bearing witness to its past glory, but there are also splendid ruins of the forts, mile-castles, and watch-towers. And this is in spite of the fact that the whole structure served as a convenient quarry to the neighbourhood for centuries. Indeed, a list of the churches, castles, peel-towers and farmhouses which have been built out of materials stolen from the wall leaves one wondering that any of it still remains to be seen. One writer after another has discussed the question of the wall, its history and its purpose, ever since 1587, when Camden, the antiquary, attacked the subject in his " Britannia "; but it is only within the last generation that through modern methods of digging it has been proved beyond a doubt who was the builder, and what was the true relation between the different parts of it.

Besides the wall itself, with its mile-castles and turrets, and its associated forts, there is an earth-work known as the Vallum, running to the south of the forts, and consisting of a broad ditch between earthen mounds. This has always been the greatest

puzzle of all to the antiquaries, but seems now to have yielded up its secret at last.

Briefly, the history of the wall and Vallum appears to be as follows. Agricola, that most famous figure of first century Britain, had been appointed governor of this turbulent province in the year A.D. 78. In the short space of seven years or less he was successful not only in overcoming rebellion in various parts of the island, and greatly extending the sphere of Roman rule, but also in making peace seem more attractive than war to the southern Britons, and inducing them to build dwellings and temples in the Roman style and to send their sons to Roman schools. They even learnt to take a pride in speaking Latin and wearing the toga. However, the newly conquered north still remained intractable, and in that region Agricola's forts, arranged in a network over the country, were as necessary when he left the island as they were when he first built them. These forts included a series across the Tyne-to-Solway isthmus, along the line of a road he had himself constructed, known since Saxon times as the Stanegate. It probably extended the whole 40 miles from Corbridge in the east to Carlisle in the west.

Some thirty years after Agricola's recall, there appears to have been a great native rising when

Roman garrisons in the north were wiped out, and certain of the Agricolan forts completely overthrown. The frontiers were always more or less disturbed, so when the Emperor Hadrian, who succeeded in A.D. 117, visited the province to put into practice there his policy of consolidating rather than extending the frontiers of the Empire, it is not surprising that he " found many things to put right," as his biographer Spartian tells us.

He began at once on his new frontier scheme. It is even possible that the new line of forts along the frontier was already on the way to completion, in accordance with his instructions, before he actually arrived in the country. These forts were mostly to the north of the Stanegate line ; and in the hilly districts in the centre, where a bold ridge of basalt falls in rocky precipices facing northward, they were perched as high as possible on the ridge, so as to have the widest outlook over the enemy's country. Contemporaneously with the forts, or perhaps later, the Vallum was constructed as a civil boundary line under the protection of the forts, to mark the northern political limit of the Roman province of Britain.

Apparently, this original scheme of forts and Vallum did not prove wholly successful in its purpose of preventing raids and incursions from the north. Anyhow, it was thought necessary to enlarge some of the forts, so that the garrison could be increased. Even this did not solve the problem. The forts were five or six miles apart, and it would be almost impossible to keep such careful guard over these long distances as to prevent armed bands from slipping through in the dark, and making short work of any sentries who might be there to bar their way.

So the great wall came into being, as the last word in the defensive problem, linking up the forts, and including a mile-castle every seven furlongs and two wall-turrets between every pair of mile-castles. A fine military road between the wall and the Vallum, running from fort to fort with branches to the mile-castles and turrets, completed the scheme. The whole elaborate system of works was carried out in a very short space of time, certainly between the years A.D. 119 and A.D. 127, under the direction of Hadrian's propraetor, Aulus Platorius Nepos, whose name appears with that of his imperial master on slabs found at four different mile-castles on the wall.

Between eighty and ninety years later, the wall and its forts and turrets underwent a thorough

ONE OF THE BEST-PRESERVED ROMAN BUILDINGS IN ENGLAND

The bath-house at Chesters lies quite outside the walls of the Fort of Cilurnum, on the edge of the North Tyne. It was completely covered by soil washed down towards the river, which accounts for its excellent preservation ; as the photograph shows, the tops of the walls are at the present level of the ground. The view is taken looking north ; in the foreground are seen the flues that crossed under the floor and served to heat one of the hotter rooms—perhaps the " calidarium."

STREET OF BARRACKS IN THE FORT OF CILURNUM, WHERE SPANISH OUTPOSTS BRAVED A NORTHERN CLIME

Five long, narrow rooms on either side of the street make up this group of barracks; they open on to a portico supported by columns, some of the bases of which remain. It is probable that each room housed ten men of the Asturians who formed the garrison, and that there were six of such groups of ten rooms in this northern part of the fort; the Asturians were horse soldiers from Spain. A deep stone gutter runs down the middle of the street. When these rooms were excavated they were full of pottery, bones, oyster shells, and all kinds of rubbish. The walls were carefully restored in the winter of 1919-20, for, with exposure to the frosts and rains, they run the risk of disintegration if they are not kept in repair.

HOW ROMANS OF RANK KEPT WARM IN THE WINTER DAYS

Careful arrangements were always made by the Romans for heating their principal houses, even in such outlying posts as the forts of the great wall. The commandant's house at Cilurnum was heated by the hypocaustal system in the usual way, that is, by forcing hot air under the floors and along flues in the walls. For this purpose the floors were supported on pillars, as here shown. Those nearest the furnace were of tiles, mortared together; those farther away were stone columns broken short. All bear marks of fire.

reconstruction under the Emperor Septimius Severus. They had suffered much during the disturbances of the previous fifty years. The work of restoration was so extremely well done that the idea seems to have arisen that he was the actual builder of the wall, and certainly several ancient writers appear later to have given him the credit for it. That is why Camden, with many who followed him, calls the great wall " The Wall of Severus," and it was only towards the middle of the nineteenth century, when the Rev. John Hodgson, the historian of Northumberland, started a new theory, based on the study of inscriptions, that Hadrian began to come into his own. Not for another seventy years was his claim fully established; and then modern methods of digging,

and observation of floor-levels, with coin and pottery evidence, proved him to have been responsible for forts, stone wall and Vallum alike. It is impossible in a short article to give details of the evidence, but it is clear and irrefutable.

We have seen that under the term " Hadrian's Wall " are included: 1. A series of frontier forts, built of stone; 2. An earthwork, known as the Vallum; 3. A massive stone wall, with mile-castles and watch-towers. We will now consider these in the order in which they were constructed.

## 1. The Forts

Seventeen forts are now generally included in the list of those along the line of the wall, but of these only fourteen were afterwards linked up into one

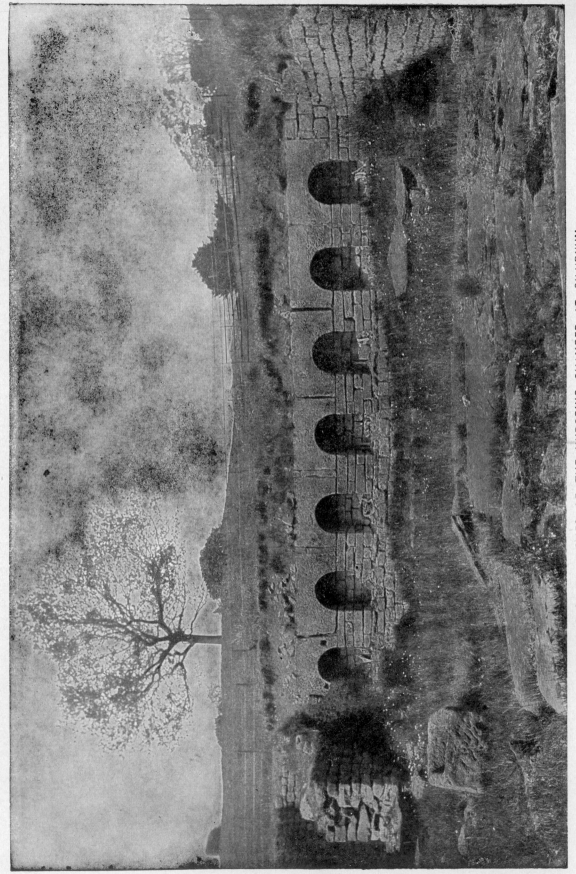

THE SEVEN NICHES OF THE UNROBING CHAMBER AT CILURNUM

The largest room of the bath-house at Chesters (Cilurnum) is one near the entrance, which is thought to be the unrobing and anointing chamber; it has a flagged floor, and along its west wall are seven round-arched stone niches, each round head being cut out of a single stone. Much discussion has arisen as to the use of these niches, and it is suggested that they were cupboards for the bathers to hang up their clothes. Nothing of the sort has been found elsewhere, and they make quite a striking feature seen from the far side of the North Tyne, towards which they face. Each niche is 3 feet high, 2 feet wide, 1½ feet deep, and 8 inches above the level of the floor.

BARRACKS AT CILURNUM AND A ROMAN WINDOW

Another view of the barracks at Cilurnum is presented above ; in the foreground are seen heaps of bones and other rubbish found in the chambers when they were opened. The lower picture shows part of a room in the bath-house at Cilurnum, the walls of which are preserved up to the window-level. This is very unusual ; only one other example is known in England. Pieces of rather opaque glass were found on the ground outside. The room has an apsidal end ; and the structure of the flues for heating it is seen to follow the semicircular plan of the walls, with a cross-flue up the centre.

## ROMAN SENTRY-BOX AND A FAMOUS BRIDGE

The upper picture shows a wall-turret at Brunton, near Chollerford, the best-preserved specimen that has been uncovered. In the lower picture we see the eastern land-abutment of the Roman bridge which carried the Military Way across the North Tyne to Cilurnum. The great wall is seen joining the tower, just below the wooden fence. The massive stones of the abutment are linked by rods of iron, and in their midst lies embedded the pier of an earlier bridge, pointed at one end.

structure with the wall. Of the remaining three, two lie to the south of both wall and Vallum on the Stanegate, and were, no doubt, Agricolan sites, and the third (at Castlesteads in Cumberland) lies between the wall and the Vallum.

The names of the forts, with the Roman equivalents where known, are as follows, from east to west :

1. Wallsend .. .. Segedunum
2. Newcastle .. Pons Aelii
3. Benwell Hill .. Condercum
4. Rudchester .. Vindobala
5. Halton Chesters .. Hunnum
6. Chesters .. .. Cilurnum
7. Carrawburgh .. Procolitia
8. Housesteads .. Borcovicium
9. Chesterholm .. Vindolanda
10. Great Chesters .. Aesica
11. Carvoran .. .. Magnac
12. Birdoswald .. Amboglanna
13. Castlesteads
14. Stanwix
15. Burgh-by-Sands
16. Drumburgh
17. Bowness

Of these, Cilurnum, Borcovicium, Aesica and Amboglanna offer at present the best opportunities for studying on the spot the construction and plan of the forts, but the position of a good many more can be traced, even by the ordinary tourist. The exact site of the fort at Burgh is one of the more recent discoveries along the wall line, made in the spring of 1922.

The area enclosed within the fort walls varies, some being four or five acres in extent, others about half that size. All are parallelograms in plan, with rounded corners, are enclosed by a wall at least five feet thick, surrounded by a ditch, and had gateways north, south, east and west—double-portalled gateways with round arches, closed by two-leaved wooden doors swinging on pivots shod with iron. There was a guard-chamber on either side of each main gateway, and turrets were placed round the walls. In the centre stood the headquarters building, containing the "sacellum" or Chapel of the Standards, and office rooms. The commandant's house at Cilurnum shows beautiful stone mouldings outside, and painted plaster walls inside, and has elaborate private baths.

At Cilurnum and Borcovicium the stone thresholds of gateways are grooved by the constant passage of chariot wheels, the width between the wheels being 4 feet 6½ inches, just the same as between the wheel-ruts in the streets of Pompeii. The best preserved building on the wall line is the bath-house at Chesters (Cilurnum) on the North

PRINCIPIA OR HEADQUARTERS BUILDING AT BORCOVICIUM

In the foreground is the beautiful base of a column, the first of a row of six which supported the portico of an open court. On the right was a row of five rooms, the central one being the "sacellum," or Chapel of the Standards. Another open court stood on the left, surrounded on three sides by a portico ; the entrance to the Principia was in the east wall of this court. This view was taken looking southward, across the valley of the Tyne.

THE GREAT WALL DESCENDING LIMESTONE BANK

At this point the wall is about five feet high, and runs through fields parallel to Wade's Road, the direct route from Newcastle to Carlisle. In early summer this strip of wall is a blaze of gold from the gorse which grows upon it. The photograph shows well the character of the facing-stones, though they have become loosened and irregular. The site of a mile-castle which has never been excavated is located on the top of the hill in the distance, just on the left of Wade's Road.

Tyne. One chamber still stands 9½ feet high, with twenty-three courses of stones. A large flagged chamber, probably the unrobing room, contains seven round-arched stone niches, whose purpose is not known, but it is suggested that they were cup-boards for the bathers' clothes. Another room shows part of a splayed window-opening, and window-glass was found underneath. It is very rarely that Roman buildings are found to reach the window level. This building is one of the best preserved in England, having been covered up and protected by the soil that was washed down towards the river.

## 2. The Vallum

The Vallum is now recognized as a civil boundary, or "limes," consisting of a flat-bottomed ditch, with an earthen mound on either side of the ditch at a distance of 24 feet away. It extends for 66 miles, from Newcastle to Dykesfield, thus missing the full length of the wall by 7¼ miles.

The late Professor Haverfield, assisted by Mr. and Mrs. T. H. Hodgson, spent years of patient work in excavating the Vallum, locating it where it was lost, discovering its true purpose, and ascertaining that it is not earlier in origin than the forts, because it bends round to the south to avoid them.

Mr. F. Gerald Simpson and Dr. R. C. Shaw have recently found causeways crossing the Vallum where gaps have been made in the mounds; and they infer that the ditch was filled up and the mounds were lowered to facilitate the carrying of building materials across the Vallum when the wall was being built. When the wall was finished, some of the causeways were cleared out, and the earth thrown up on the edge of the ditch to form an additional mound, the presence of which had not been convincingly explained by anyone before.

## 3. The Great Wall

The great wall is built of concrete, of immense strength, and faced with stone blocks very regular in size. A V-shaped ditch, 10 to 15 feet deep, and 35 to 40 feet wide, defended it on its northern side, and, where necessary, was hewn out of the hardest stone. A very remarkable instance of this occurs on Limestone Bank, near Chesters, where the ditches of both wall and Vallum are hewn out of basalt, great boulders of which lie scattered about in confusion. The wall forms the north wall of the mile-castles, whose east and west walls are bonded into it. They measure about 60 feet by 50 feet. Very good specimens are to be seen uncovered in the hilly regions at House-steads, Cawfields and Castle Nick.

The wall-turrets are sentry boxes, 12 feet by 10 feet, recessed into the wall. Some were destroyed by Severus when he repaired the wall. Excavation of turrets by the late Mr. J. P. Gibson and Mr. F. G. Simpson has yielded much valuable evidence, and thirty are now awaiting their turn to be opened.

The best examples of wall-turrets which can now be seen are at Brunton, Black Carts near Chesters, and Mucklebank, on the Nine Nicks of Thirlwall.

One of the most remarkable features along the line of the wall is the Roman bridge which continued the barrier over the North Tyne, near Cilurnum. There are traces of two bridges: the later one was twice as wide as the earlier, wide enough to carry the military road of Hadrian. Both bridges rested on stone piers in the bed of the stream, but the later one had very massive land-abutments which encroached on the stream, and made the water-passage much shorter: and it is suggested that this later bridge was built at the same time as the great wall, to carry out the idea of making an impassable barrier against raiders of every sort. Portcullises may have filled the water-openings when the stream was running low.

In a very illuminating article on "The Purpose of the Roman Wall," in the "Vasculum" of October, 1921, Mr. R. G. Collingwood shows that the wall was never designed to be itself a fighting-ground; its object was to provide an elevated sentry-walk which should at the same time be an obstacle to unauthorized persons who wished to cross the boundary of the Roman province. It was, in effect, one continuous watch-tower, 73 miles long. Mr. Collingwood also shows that the Roman auxiliary of the period when the wall was built, and for 200 years later, carried weapons (two throwing-spears and a short sword) wholly unsuitable for warfare from the top of a wall

THE MOST ROMANTICALLY SITUATED MILE-CASTLE ON THE GREAT WALL

Known as Castle Nick mile-castle, this fort lies in a narrow depression, or "nick," in the hills; the nick has been named after it, "Castle Nick," and then the castle in its turn has been named after the nick. Only the north gateway is visible in the picture. The south gateway is exactly opposite, at a distance of 62 feet; the walls still stand 5 feet high. The sheet of water is Crag Lough, with Hot Bank farmhouse on the side of the hill beyond.

NORTH GATEWAY OF THE FORT OF BORCOVICIUM

This was the usual double gateway with twin semicircular arches, inner and outer. The central pier from which the inner arches sprang is clearly seen; also the remains of the guard-chambers, one on either side. The purpose of the great stone tank in the foreground is unknown. The wall is seen running towards the plantation, and then taking its farther course over the hills beyond, to the Sewingshields Crags. An unusual feature is a gateway to be seen in the right centre of the photograph; elsewhere the only means of crossing from one side of the wall to the other was through a fort or mile-castle. A hollow in the ground near the angle of the wall, once taken for an amphitheatre, is now proved to be an ancient quarry.

## BORCOVICIUM WHEN IT RANG WITH THE TRAMP OF ROMAN LEGIONARIES

Borcovicium was one of the seventeen large forts that defended Hadrian's Wall, and upon the remains excavated near Housesteads Mr. Forestier has based this drawing. The military road entered the fort through the west gate (left), the Porta Decumana, under a double arch between two flanking towers, after crossing a double ditch by a wooden bridge. There were similar gates on the north, south and east sides of the fort, with pent-roofed turrets, used as guard-rooms, at intervals between them on the rampart walls. The long buildings aligned from west to east are barracks and granaries : the Commandant's house, including the look-out tower, and officers' quarters are in the centre, about the colonnaded atrium. Hadrian's Wall formed the north wall of the fort, from the north-east corner of which it can be seen resuming its course along the edge of the hills. This reconstruction drawing should be compared with the photograph in the opposite page of Borcovicium to-day.

12 to 15 feet high, and that the width of the rampart walk, 3 or 4 feet, was much too narrow for anything but sentry purposes; also that, for the same reason, catapults and ballistæ could never have been used except at the forts and mile-castles.

Rudyard Kipling's vivid picture of fighting on the wall in "Puck of Pook's Hill," refers to a late period in the Roman occupation, when the bow and arrow had begun to be used; but in considering the purpose of the wall, it is necessary to take into account only the conditions which prevailed at the time when it was built.

Fresh excavations are constantly being carried on along the line of the wall, as opportunity offers, and thus new facts are being gleaned. It may be that in a few more years a whole flood of further light will have been thrown on the subject; but the position now, contrasted with the doubt and uncertainty that existed as to its origin and history only a comparatively short time ago, is like broad daylight following a murky night.

Even the most ardent student of archæology must feel that the beauty and variety of the country through which the wall runs adds much to its attractiveness. A walk from end to end takes us, it is true, through two large cities, Newcastle and Carlisle, but it also leads through peaceful pastoral regions; it brings us along rocky ridges, whence we look southward across the green valley of the Tyne and northward over the vast moorland wastes flecked with floating cloud-shadows and surrounded by a girdle of hills. Here, indeed, is the true wall country, where we feel the spring of the mountain turf under our feet, where the air is filled with the scent of the wild thyme, and in our ears is the musical cry of the curlew circling overhead.

The ruins themselves, on these lonely heights, rival in stateliness and in extent the ancient monuments in Rome herself; and as they stand in their stubborn endurance, having defied for so long the attacks of man and of the elements, they speak to us of the strength of character, the hardihood, the love of law and order, which characterised Rome at her best, and made her the worthy guardian of civilization against all the forces of reaction.

ROMAN MILESTONE THAT HAS WEATHERED THE STORMS OF 1,850 YEARS

On one of the roads made by Agricola, about 80 A.D., stands a milestone, 5 feet high. The road has been known since Saxon times as the Stanegate; it probably ran all the forty miles from Corbridge to Carlisle. Other milestones, found near the road, have been placed in the museums; this is the only one still standing. A portion of the Stanegate can be seen in the middle distance, with the mound of the Fort of Vindolanda rising above it on the left.

GATEWAYS AT BORCOVICIUM AND CILURNUM

Upper picture : West gateway at Borcovicium, looking south-east. The central piers that supported the semicircular arches, the stone thresholds, and the position of the guard-chambers can all be noted. At the foot of the hillside on which the fort stands runs Wade's Road, and Grindon Lough is seen beyond. Lower picture : The east gateway of Cilurnum, with the guard-chambers on either side ; the great wall joins the southern guard-chamber. Beyond the distant trees flows the North Tyne.

489

# What the Dawn-Man was Like

## By Sir Arthur Smith Woodward

Formerly Keeper of the Geological Department, British Museum

THOSE who study the structure of the human body are satisfied that many of the peculiar arrangements in its parts can only be explained by supposing that the immediate ancestors of man lived in trees. It has been well said, indeed, that if there had been no trees on the earth, man would not have been here in his present form. The animals which most resemble man—the monkeys and apes—still live in forests and climb nimbly among the branches, and it is interesting to notice that the few remains of remote prehistoric man hitherto discovered among fossils exhibit more resemblances to the corresponding parts of apes than do the same structures in any race of modern man. Apes and man, therefore, seem to have descended from common ancestors. In the apes, which remained among the trees, the brain scarcely increased in size or showed any improvement, but the jaws and teeth grew more powerful as weapons, the arms became longer for swinging, and the toes acquired greater strength for grasping. In man, on the other hand, who soon adapted himself for living on the ground even away from forests, the brain rapidly increased in both size and complexity, so that he flourished by his wits rather than by bodily prowess. His jaws lost their power as weapons, and his comparatively feeble arms served his purposes in a new way by the dexterity of their hands, which added to his equipment by making useful implements of wood, stone and bone.

It is still unknown where the forerunners of man first abandoned their life in trees, for fossil remains of them are extremely rare. Apes and men, indeed, are so wary that they escape from floods and many other accidents which would kill and bury most ordinary animals. Old and feeble apes are usually caught and eaten by leopards and other beasts of prey. None of the apes bury their dead, and it is likely that the earliest man-like creatures resembled them in that respect. Various geological discoveries, however, suggest that humanity began somewhere in central Asia, and it seems most hopeful at present to search that region for the earliest remains. On the tropical southern fringe of Asia, in a river deposit in Java, we have already found fragments of perhaps the oldest ape-like man or man-like ape, the Pithecanthropus, while a few miles from Peking in China, the skulls and portions of the jaws and teeth of another primeval man and a woman, Sinanthropus with many peculiarities of an ape, have been dug up in the floor of a cave which they seem to have inhabited. None of these remains, however, were associated with any recognizable implements or other indications of the man's mode of life.

The earliest ancestor of modern man, of whom we know a little and can infer more, was found far away from the supposed original abode of the human race. His remains were accidentally buried in a river-gravel which was washed together in a tumultuous heap by a torrential flood round the present situation of Piltdown, a hamlet near Uckfield, in Sussex. Only parts of his skull and lower jaw have been recovered, but they were associated with a few implements and other indications of his home surroundings, so that it is possible to learn something of the circumstances of his life. He must have been in all essential respects a man, but he still retained so many traits of an ape, and lived so completely as a child of nature, that he has been well described as representing the dawn of humanity. His proper name, indeed, is Eoanthropus, or 'dawnman.'

The skull of the Piltdown dawn-man is as large as the average human skull of the present day, but is unusually low in the crown and very broad

**OLDEST KNOWN BONE IMPLEMENT**

Measuring sixteen inches in length by four inches wide and one inch thick, this tool was cut from the thigh-bone of an elephant, and evidently was originally perforated just below the pointed end. The method of its fashioning indicates that its maker knew also how to work in wood.

How the implement was cut from an elephant thigh bone

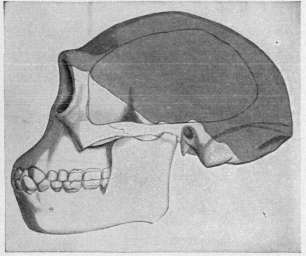

## APE-LIKE MAN AND MAN-LIKE APE

In 1891 Dr. Eugéne Dubois found at Trinil in Java fossilised fragments of an Early Pleistocene human being. From the skull-cap, shown here in dark shading, Mr. Forestier made the reconstruction drawing (top right) of his probable aspect, the resemblance of which to that of the chimpanzee beside it explains the scientific name Pithecanthropus or ape-man.

behind. This peculiar breadth and squatness means that he had a stout and inelegant neck. The brain case is much thicker than usual, and in the fine spongy texture of the bone is quite unlike that of any other human skull hitherto known. It must have been especially well adapted to receive blows without sustaining damage. Possibly disputes were settled by blows, for the face and jaws are not much larger than those of some later races of primitive man. The canines, or corner teeth, which are such powerful weapons in the great apes, and are used by them for fighting,

are still a little prominent in the dawn-man—entirely different from those of modern man—but they are too feeble to have been of much use for attack and defence. The ways of the ape had already been superseded by those of a creature with keener wits, and old weapons were giving place to new.

The brain of the dawn-man, as shown by the impression which is left on the inside of the brain case, is completely human, and is as large as that of some of the lower races of man still living. Those regions of the brain, however, which are instrumental in the higher realms of thought and association of ideas, are imperfectly developed. Although dawn-man could undoubtedly speak, therefore, his powers of conversation must have been less than those of even the lowest modern man. They would suffice only for the most elementary needs.

Of the body and limbs of the dawn-man nothing is known ; but it is reasonable to infer from the skeletons of a somewhat later extinct race of man which have been discovered, that he had comparatively short and stumpy legs, with an ungainly and incompletely upright gait. His implements suggest that his hands were about the same as those of modern man. If he could be seen alive he would be recognized at once as human, but his stooping, stumpy, shuffling form would betray his lowly grade.

The flooding of the old river at Piltdown, which buried at least the skull and lower jaw of the dawnman, also engulfed in its eddy enough of his belongings to show that he was living on its bank. He was still merely a wandering hunter, without either domestic animals or crops, and one may infer from analogy with certain surviving wild tribes of man that his only habitations were temporary shelters made of boughs of trees. We know that he fed on the flesh of game, because near his remains

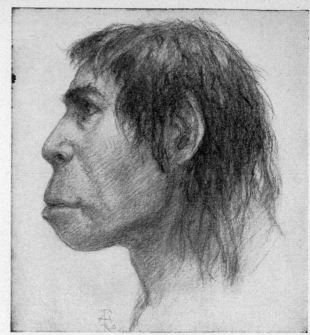

was found a broken leg bone of a deer bearing marks of the tool with which he had split it to extract the marrow. We also suspect that he fed on hard fruits of some kind—perhaps acorns, nuts and seeds—for among his stone implements is a lump of flint which has been well battered by use as a pounder. Burnt flints occur in all directions, and they were once found with pieces of charcoal. These, of course, might be only the relics of a forest fire, but some of the flints are cracked in the same way as others which are definitely known to have been used by later prehistoric men as 'pot-boilers.' Such stones were placed among the glowing embers until they were very hot, and were then dropped suddenly in sufficient numbers into water to raise its temperature even if not actually to boil it. The dawn-man, so far as we know, had not learned to make pots to hold water, but like certain existing savages he may have used skins for the purpose.

The dawn-man of Piltdown was certainly many generations in advance of the time when his early forerunners picked up any convenient stone for use as an implement without any further shaping. He was also fortunate in finding close at hand an unlimited supply of pieces of flint, which could readily be chipped to give sharp edges and points to supply his needs. He never took any further trouble, however, in shaping the stone after his chipping had produced enough sharpness. He was sufficiently keen-witted to know that to attain the desired result he must first split the flint to make one nearly plane face, and then he need only work a little round the sharp edge of the flake thus formed. Each implement evidently served many purposes—in fact, all the purposes of a hunter's simple domestic life. There are no hunting weapons, and game, as usual

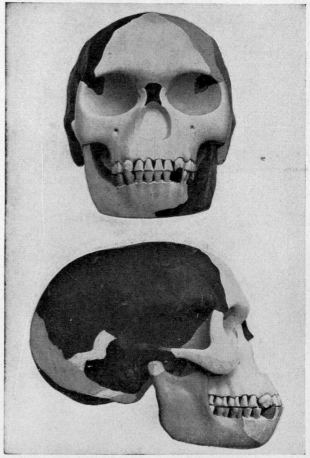

DAWN-MAN AND HIS PEKING CONTEMPORARY

Sir Arthur Smith Woodward prepared this reconstruction of the Piltdown skull, the dark portions being the fragments actually found. Mr. Forestier's drawings above show the probable appearance of this Eoanthropus and the contemporary Sinanthropus (left).

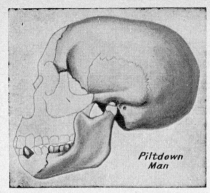

Piltdown Man

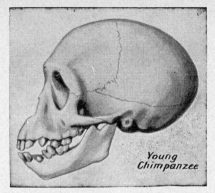

Young Chimpanzee

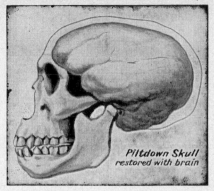

Piltdown Skull restored with brain

In conformation the skull of Eoanthropus (left) bears great resemblance to that of the young chimpanzee (centre), particularly in respect of the lower jaw. In cranial features, however, the Piltdown race approximated to modern man, a cast taken from the interior of the skull showing that the brain contained within the thick brain-case (right) was definitely human in size and character.

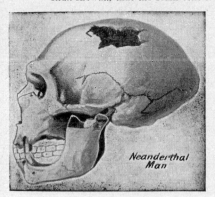

Neanderthal Man

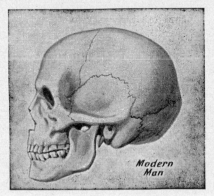

Modern Man

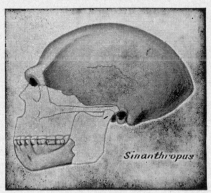

Sinanthropus

STAGES OF SKULL DEVELOPMENT FROM APE TO MODERN MAN

Of the two skulls of Sinanthropus found in 1929 and 1930 the earlier one shown here (right) is that of a female, as is, perhaps, the skull of the Eoanthropus in the upper row. Comparison of these skulls shows that the mental capacity of the latter was superior to that of the Peking man and also that his cranium approximated much more nearly to the modern human cranium (centre) than did the cranium of Neanderthal man (left), who yet came so much later in the evolution of the human race.

with primitive tribes, must have been caught in pits and snares.

With the stone implements, dawn-man must have been able to cut pieces of wood, for among his belongings which have been recovered from the eddy in the Piltdown gravel is a large piece of worked bone which is cut just as if it were a plank of wood. This unique bone implement, which is sixteen inches long, four inches wide, and one inch thick, was split and cut out of the thigh bone of a very large elephant, one of the two gigantic species of elephant which are known to have lived in the British part of Europe at the time (for the British Isles had not then become separated from the rest of the continent). It is cut to the shape of a wedge at one end, evidently the useful end, and to the shape of the blade of a cricket bat at the other end, evidently the handle. On one side, near the pointed end, there must have been originally a perforation, through which a thong of some kind could be threaded; but the outer bar of the perforation has broken away, and there seems to have been an attempt to make a new perforation a little further inwards which was never finished. This perforation might have been made by a flint borer, also found at Piltdown, which shows distinct marks of wear by use. This bone implement is the oldest piece of worked

bone yet found anywhere. Its shape is unlike that of any implement either of wood or bone made by existing wild races of man.

The dawn-man of Piltdown, therefore, notwithstanding his remoteness from our time and the striking traits of ape in his bodily frame which have been eliminated in later races of man, had already made a good start in that domination of nature which is the characteristic feature of humanity. His overgrown brain had given him superior wits, with subtle craft as a substitute for the struggle of tooth and claw. Family and tribal life, and the beginning of definite speech, had led to co-operation, by which he could compete with and capture the more powerful beasts around him. His discovery of fire, and the use of skins as clothing, had enabled him to venture into regions where his life would otherwise have been insupportable. His use of stone and bone, and presumably wood, for implements had exercised his inventive faculties, with no little success. The beautiful symmetry of the carefully cut rounded end of the bone implement suggests the beginning even of some appreciation of art. Dawn-man, indeed, was no longer a mere creature of circumstances. He was well advanced in that inventive and adventurous spirit which has always been the mainspring of human progress.

## The Wonder Cities. XII.

# The Splendours of Imperial Rome

## By Edward Hutton

Author of "Rome," "Italy and the Italians," etc.

BY good fortune, the last of the historians of ancient Rome, Ammianus, has left us a vivid description of the Eternal City on the morrow of the removal of the seat of Empire by Constantine from Rome to Constantinople, while it was still in all its glory, its unapproached magnificence unspoiled, its classic architecture, its treasures of sculpture and every art, its forums and baths and palaces still perfect and intact, in all the splendour of their unsullied beauty.

The occasion of his most graphic record was the visit and triumphal entry of the Emperor Constantius, the son of Constantine, in April, 357. He was received by the magistrates and Senate. The streets were lined with an innumerable multitude, so that the Emperor is said to have affected surprise that the human race should thus suddenly be collected on the same spot. He was lodged in the ancient palace of Augustus, he presided in the Senate, and harangued the people from the tribunal which Cicero had so often ascended. He was present at the games of the circus, and accepted the crown of gold prepared for the ceremony.

His short visit—the Emperor had not been present in Rome for thirty-two years—was employed in viewing the monuments of the Eternal City. In his company was a Persian prince who had taken refuge in his train. Together they visited the Forum, and together were overwhelmed and astonished by the marvellous beauty of the city. They admired "the awful majesty of the Capitol," beheld with wonder the mighty Baths of Caracalla and Diocletian, which in their vast extent resembled provinces, "the massy greatness of the amphitheatre of Titus" (the Colosseum), the Pantheon like the whole quarter of a city, rounded smoothly, and fair with lofty pillars and arches, the columns bearing the figures of former princes, the wonderful Theatre of Pompey, the noble Temple of Peace. Above all they were amazed by the Forum of Trajan with its column, "a work unique under the whole heavens, wonderful, worthy as we consider of the approval of the gods." So much did they admire this incomparable structure that Constantius thought to mark his advent by imitating the equestrian and colossal statue he had seen there, till the subtlety of his Persian guest remarked that he must first command such a stable to be made if he could. And with the malice of his race he added that one thing only had pleased him : to find that men died at Rome as well as elsewhere.

We who visit Rome to-day, and contemplate all that splendour in ruin, can only have an imperfect idea of the sentiments which the Imperial City inspired when in all her glory and majesty. No city of the medieval or of the modern world is comparable with her. The medieval cities were villages filled with hovels grouped about a few fine buildings at best ; our modern cities, triumphant in their energy and their ugliness, are none of them to be thought of for a moment beside Imperial Rome.

It is, in fact, extremely difficult for us to realize what Rome was in the long years of her splendour. She was the capital not of a country, however great, but of the world. Her

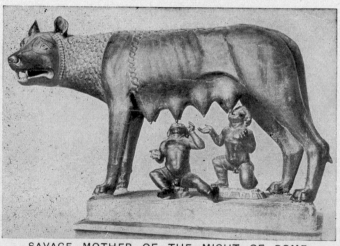

**SAVAGE MOTHER OF THE MIGHT OF ROME**
According to the old legend Romulus, the eponymous hero of Rome, and his brother Remus were suckled by a she-wolf ; and a statue representing this is known to have stood in the neighbourhood of the Temple of Jupiter Capitolinus. While it is doubtful whether this is the statue, with the exception of the twins it dates from the fifth century B.C.
Capitoline Museum. Photo by Anderson

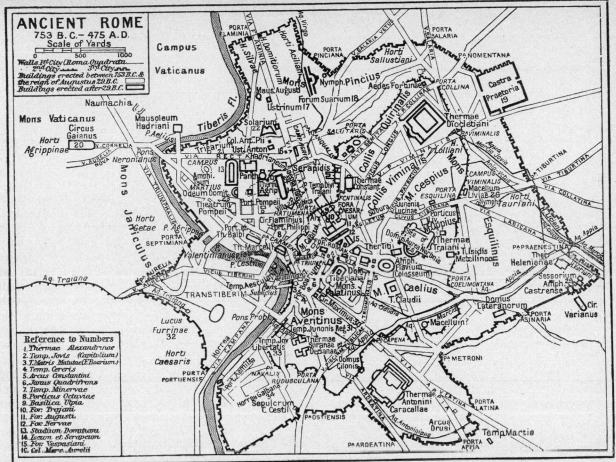

English names of places indicated by numbers. 1. Baths of Nero restored by Alexander Severus. 2. Temple of Jupiter (Capitol). 3. Temple of Mater Matuta (Cattle market). 4. Temple of Ceres. 5. Arch of Constantine. 6. Arch of Janus with Four Faces. 7. Temple of Minerva. 8. Colonnade of Octavia. 9. Basilica of Trajan. 10. Forum of Trajan. 11. Forum of Augustus. 12. Forum of Nerva. 13. Stadium of Domitian. 14. Temple of Isis and Serapis. 15. Forum of Vespasian. 16. Column of Marcus Aurelius. 17. Crematorium. 18. Swine Market. 19. Camp of Praetorian Guards. 20. Circus of Caligula. 21. Training Stables. 22. Sundial. 23. Concert Hall of Domitian. 24. Voting Enclosures of Julius Caesar. 25. Public Villa. 26. Provision Market of Livia. 27. Cattle Market. 28. Golden House of Nero. 29. Court of Law. 30. Great Circus (Circus Maximus). 31. Temple of Juno. 32. Grove of Furrina. 33. Temple of Jupiter and Liberty. 34. Granaries of Galba.
Latin terms and their equivalents in English : *Aqua*, water, aqueduct ; *collis*, hill ; *horti*, gardens ; *mons*, mount ; *pons*, bridge ; *porta*, gate ; *thermae*, baths ; *vicus*, street.

Empire, in the sonorous words with which Gibbon opens his History, " comprehended the fairest part of the earth and the most civilized portion of mankind." But so beneficent was her work, the unity which she founded and maintained, that the same writer goes on to say that " if a man were called to fix the period in the history of the world during which the condition of the human race was most happy and prosperous he would, without hesitation, name that which elapsed from the death of Domitian to the accession of Commodus (A.D. 96-180)."

No one, no man of European tradition and education that is, can visit Rome for the first or for the hundredth time except as a pilgrim. The reason for this is not exclusively Christian at all ; it is that Rome was the creator, and that twice over, of all that we mean by Europe, of all that we mean by civilization. No other city in the world has half her claim upon our allegiance. She

is the mother of us all. When she created Europe, the British, too, in their far island, became a part of that which she had made ; and that unity which was the Roman Empire was not only unquestioned but so unquestionable that every province of that great administration thought Roman thoughts and moved in a single polity which, for years after its material dissolution, men could not bring themselves to believe had passed away. Finally, to crown all, in the moment of her maturity, she accepted the Christian religion and philosophy.

To obtain some vision of Rome on the eve of that great decision which determined the future of mankind, let us imagine two men coming up the Via Appia from Brindisi to Rome. One of them would in all probability have been a Christian, though perhaps not openly. On the fifth day of their journey in their light travelling carriage they would first come in sight of the city and the marvellous panorama we still see to-day over the tragic majesty of the Campagna, across which stretched the mighty aqueducts—the Aqua Marcia and the Aqua Claudia—the bases of the Alban Hills and the blue Sabine Mountains, with lonely Soracte in the distance—surely the most noble landscape in the world—being clustered round with villas and gardens. Presently the ancient road would begin to be enclosed with tombs, as indeed was every road leading to a Roman city; at the sixth milestone the Casale Rotundo or Cotta's tomb, probably raised by Messala Corvinus, the poet and friend of Horace, to his son; then the old villa which we know as Roma Vecchia; and then the vast mausoleum of Caecilia Metella, whose circular structure, sixty-five feet in diameter, still fills us with astonishment.

Perhaps as they approached the city thus in the earliest dawn they would hear the song which Pliny heard, caught and struck, in spite of himself, by its freshness and blitheness, the sound of children's voices, as the Mass was sung in the sanctuary of some great neighbouring villa, about which, in the catacombs underground, the dead lay, thousand upon thousand, no longer without hope.

The way would be noisy now with business, and there would be a great throng about the gate—the Porta Appia, where they would alight, for one seldom drove within the walls. Just outside the gate, still in all its splendour, stood a temple and grove of Mars, on high ground and approached by an avenue. Within the gate, where the aqueduct crossed the paved way, they would pass under the Arch of Trajan which still stands there, though then it was splendid with marble, with presently the tomb of the Scipios on their right, and so, the way now thronged with people on foot or in litters, they would come, where the Arch of Drusus crossed the way, to the vast Baths of Caracalla on their left, as large as a town, and capable of accommodating more than 1,600 persons at a time.

Perhaps they would turn into these baths for refreshment after the dust and weariness of the journey. They would be welcomed at their entrance by the " ostiarius," or porter, then as now chosen for his size, and by the " capsarius," or wardrobe-keeper, who would take charge of their wraps. There they would find and greet their friends and acquaintances, hear the news,

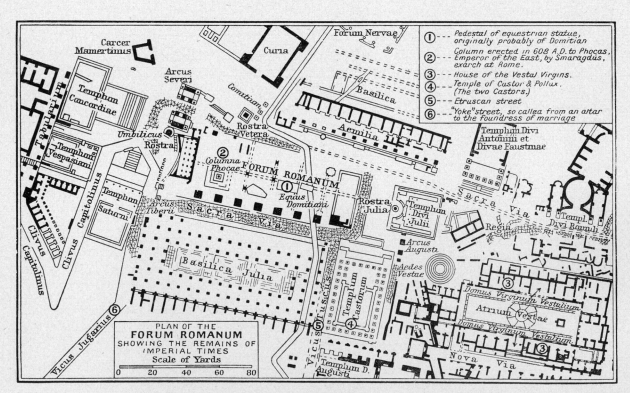

The old Forum at Rome was originally a marsh lying between the Palatine and Capitoline hills. After being drained by the Cloaca Maxima it was long used as a market-place and centre of barter, with a smaller space to the north, the Comitium, reserved for popular assemblies (comitia). With the expansion of the population, however, it was found necessary to transfer the comitia to the Forum and use subsidiary fora for purposes of trade; the Forum also being employed for spectacular events and the transaction of legal and commercial business. Nevertheless, further enlargements were always required, and these were supplied by the erection of adjoining Basilicas, and the great Fora of the Emperors Latin terms employed in the above map with equivalents in English: *Aedes*, temple; *arcus*, arch; *atrium*, court; *basilica*, hall for legal and civic proceedings; *carcer*, prison; *clivus*, slope of a hill; *comitium*, space for public assemblies, etc.; *curia*, senate-house; *D.*, *Divus*, deified (i.e. dead); *Regia*, official house of the Pontifex Maximus (high-priest); *Rostra*, public tribunal; *Tabularium*, Record-office; *Umbilicus*, "navel," centre of Rome; *via*, road; *vicus*, street.

RUINS OF THE BATHS OF CARACALLA, FROM WITHIN AND FROM WITHOUT

A Roman bath was something moderns do not possess—gymnasium, turkish-bath, restaurant, and club in one—and all carried out in a spirit of sumptuous lavishness beyond the dreams of latter day luxury. The baths mainly built by Caracalla, though begun by Septimius Severus in A.D. 206, were the most beautiful, though not the largest, in Rome. In the lower photograph may be seen portions of their tesselated pavement and fragments of mosaics fallen from the upper storeys. They had room for 1,600 bathers.

Photos by Ewing Galloway and Donald McLeish

RECONSTRUCTION OF THE SOUTHERN PORTION OF ROME AS IT APPEARED IN THE DAYS OF ITS GRANDEUR

1. **Capitoline Hill,** with its temples and **many** public buildings. 2. Basilica Ulpia. 3. **Forum of Trajan,** erected A.D. 111-114, and in ruins in the tenth century. 4. Forum of Augustus, **built** after the battle of Philippi, 42 B.C., **and excavated in 1888-89.** 5. Forum of Nerva or Transitrium and Temple of Minerva. 6. Forum of Vespasian and Temple of Peace. 7. Temple **of** Venus. 8. Basilica Aemilia, built by Aemilius Lepidus, 179 B.C. 9. Temple of Faustina and Antoninus, dedicated A.D. 141, in the interior of which was built the Church of S. Lorenzo in Miranda. 10. Portico of Livia. 11. Baths of Titus and Trajan. 12. Colosseum. 13. Colossal statue of Nero as god of the sun, 118 feet high. 14. Temple of Venus and Roma. 15. Basilica of Constantine, originally built by Maxentius, A.D. 306-312. 16. House of the Vestals. 17. Temple of Vesta, where the sacred fire was kept alight by the Vestal Virgins. 18. Triumphal Arch of Augustus. 19. Temple of Castor and Pollux, first founded in 484 B.C. after the battle of Lake Regillus. 20. Basilica Julia, founded by Julius Caesar, 46 B.C. 21. Rostra, or platform from which public orators made their speeches, erected by Augustus. Nos. 14-21 were included in the old Forum. 22. Arch of Septimius Severus, erected A.D. 203 **to** commemorate the victories of the emperor and his sons in the East. 23-25. Imperial palaces on the Palatine Hill. 26. Circus Maximus, which held over 200,000 spectators. 27. The Velabrum quarter. 28. Theatre of Marcellus, completed 13 B.C., accommodating about 14,000 spectators.

From the reconstruction in plaster by Professor Marcellani

COLUMN OF MARCUS AURELIUS AND THE CIRCULAR TEMPLE OF VESTA

Left: Erected in honour of Marcus Aurelius by the people of Rome, this marble column is modelled on that of Trajan (see page 517), but is of inferior workmanship. It is 97¼ feet high, excluding the base and the later additions of the pedestal and statue of S. Paul, and the shaft, 11½ feet in diameter, is composed of 28 drums. The spiral reliefs portray battles in the Marcomannic war. Right: This beautiful little temple has received more admiration, perhaps, than any other of the remains in Rome. It consists of a circular cella 26 feet across, surrounded by twenty Corinthian columns of Parian marble 32 feet high, the total circumference being 156 feet. Widely known as the Temple of Vesta, it was more probably dedicated to Matuta, and took its present form in the reign of Augustus. only the original roof and entablature having been replaced since his time.

Photos by Donald McLeish

and read the newspapers or " Acta Diurna." They would select the kind of bath they desired, cold, tepid, warm, shower, or perspiration bath. The bath over, they would then take a walk up and down the beautiful grounds, while others, less weary, would indulge in athletic sports, or gymnastics, to prepare for the delights of the table. After the luxurious meal, these gigantic thermae could supply every kind of entertainment. There were libraries, concerts, literary entertainments, readings of the latest poems or novels, popular shows, or just conversation with one's friends, and not least with one's women friends.

These baths, vast and magnificent though they were, were by no means the only thermae in the city, or even the largest. The Baths of Agrippa, of Nero, of Vespasian, and Titus were already in existence when they were built, and the Baths of Diocletian were even larger. The thermae were, in fact, more than baths, they were vast, but not exclusive, institutes. We have nothing to compare with them in any city of the world to-day. They bear witness to a social civilization far beyond our own. These Baths of Caracalla, for instance, were a mile in circumference, and were open at certain times for the free use of every citizen. The vast domes were covered with magnificent mosaics, and the walls lined with precious marbles from Egypt and Numidia. Even the pipes and taps and fittings generally were of silver and bronze, while in the various halls and porticoes stood many famous statues—the Farnese Bull, the Venus of the Capitol, the Venus Callipyge, the Hercules and the Flora of Naples, the Dionysus of the British

ROME'S MOST IMPRESSIVE RUIN: THE COLOSSEUM FROM AN UNUSUAL ANGLE

To the visitor of to-day the might and grandeur of the old Imperial City is summed up in the vast ruins of what is known as the Colosseum. This, however, was not its original name; it was called the Flavian Amphitheatre, after the family during whose reigns it was built. It was begun by Vespasian in A.D. 72, dedicated by Titus, and finally completed by Domitian. The last recorded entertainment took place in the eleventh century, and from then onwards its uses have been many, in particular as a convenient quarry for Roman architects, to which is due the disappearance of at least two-thirds of the original structure.

Photo by Florence Farmborough

Museum. It was not uncommon for a rich man to bequeath a sum of money to throw open the baths to all for a day, or a week, or even for ever.

From the Baths of Caracalla, following the Via Appia past the Temple of Virtue and Honour, and under the Caelian Hill, one would presently come to the Porta Capena. In front rose the Palatine Hill, covered with the glorious Imperial Palaces, gleaming in the sun, tier after tier of white marble, touched here with gold, there with the colours of infinitely various and precious marbles and loveliest gardens; and facing the Porta Capena the Septizonium, the seven-zoned structure of Septimius Severus, which formed the façade on this side for this hill of palaces. Beneath lay the great Circus Maximus, in the narrow valley between the Palatine and the Aventine, even then dark with groves of ilex.

Turning here to the right, still following the Triumphal Way, between the Palatine and the Caelian Hills, at the end of the vista might be seen the great Triumphal Arch of Constantine, and

beyond, towering into the sky, what Gibbon calls the "awful majesty of the Flavian Amphitheatre," the Colosseum, with which, so mighty was it, our own half barbarous ancestors were wont to confound the very city itself, the destiny of Rome.

While stands the Colosseum,
Rome shall stand;
When falls the Colosseum
Rome shall fall;
And when Rome falls—
The world.

As one passed up that way towards the arch and the vast structure which dwarfed it, one might note on the right, on the summit of the Caelian Hill, the Temple of Claudius, surrounded by a beautiful shining colonnade of marble. On the left of this Way of Triumph, at the foot of the palaced Palatine, lay the vast Hippodrome, and beyond, the lovely porticoed Temple of Apollo.

Beyond the arch what a spectacle met the sight! Nothing in our world is comparable with it, and be sure it outshone all our imagination can build of what it was in the days when it stood complete.

501

THE FORUM ROMANUM AS IT WAS, SEEN FROM THE COURT OF THE HOUSE OF THE VESTALS
Compare this reconstruction with the photograph in the opposite page, as the two embrace exactly the same view. The spectator must for the moment become a Vestal Virgin, and look down the Sacred Way towards the Capitol from within the Atrium Vestae. On the left will be the Temple of Vesta (not the Temple of Matuta, see page 499), with the Temple of Castor and Pollux behind it ; on the right a portion of the Regia, repository of the priestly archives, and of the Temple of Julius Caesar ; and in the far background the Tabularium, or " Record Office " ; the remaining features being as described in pages 506 and 511.
Restoration by J. Hoffbauer

502

ALL THAT TIME HAS SPARED FROM THE GLORIOUS YESTERDAY OF THE FORUM ROMANUM

Alas for the Eagles! The very centre of the centre of the world—for the Umbilicus Romae was in the Forum, and Rome was the hub of the nations—had become a rubbish-heap when in 1870 men began to excavate these poor vestiges. The stumps of the circular peristyle of the Temple of Vesta are in the foreground; two of the only three remaining pillars of the Temple of Castor and Pollux are seen to the left; of the Temple of Saturn but eight Ionic columns remain, and three Corinthian columns of the Temple of Vespasian. To the right is the still solid Arch of Septimius Severus, and to the left of that the column of Phocas.

## THE PANTHEON AS IT WAS WHEN ROME WAS MISTRESS OF THE WORLD

Mystery shrouds the original construction of the Pantheon. Though persistently attributed to Marcus Agrippa (27 B.C.), it is now supposed that the present structure is of much later date, only the portico dating from his time, as the inscription states. In any case it is the most wonderfully preserved of all Rome's monuments, a fact which it owes to its dedication as a church in A.D. 608. The building, as this reconstruction shows, is circular and crowned with a dome; its only light is admitted through a hole in the top

## ONCE A TEMPLE, NOW A CHURCH: THE PANTHEON AS IT IS TO-DAY

Eight granite columns support the pediment of the portico, with eight more in two rows behind, giving a frontage of 37 yards and a depth of 15. Through continual raising of the surrounding soil the base of the structure is now below the level of the ground. It was originally dedicated to those gods who were connected by legend with the ancestry of the powerful Julian family.

Beyond the flashing, uptossed waters of the Meta Sudans, a great fountain, of which only the brick core now remains, towered up the vast Flavian Amphi-theatre, encased in marble and bronze. It seems to have been the most as-tounding, though not certainly the most beautiful, thing in the city, and it is still the most amazing ruin in the world. It had been begun by Vespasian in the gardens of the Golden House of Nero. Without, it consisted of four arcades, the first Doric, the second Ionic, the third Corinthian, the fourth a wall upheld by Corin-thian pilasters and pierced with windows. Within, the walls were lined with seats, tier above tier.

Around the arena stood a high, massive wall, and above this was the pavilion where the seats of honour were placed for the Emperor and his family, for the Vestal Virgins, and the great officers of state. Above, again, were the seats for the senators, the magistrates, the military knights, and then for the male citizens. The women sat in the highest part of the building under a colonnade. The whole, capable of holding 50,000 persons, was sheltered from sun and rain by an awning supported on masts, and the arena could be flooded with water for naval fights. It became the monstrous stage upon which Christianity faced Paganism and all that the Colosseum stood for, its cruelty and indifference, and overthrew it for all time.

A little to the west of the Colosseum stood that Colossus, thirty-one metres high, which Nero had raised in his own likeness in bronze, and which Vespasian changed into a statue of the sun, for it was all covered with gold and stood upon a huge pedestal. Turning away from the vast theatre where agony and death were staged as a spectacle to amuse the populace, one gazed down the Sacred Way, to the Triumphal Arch of Titus, past the noble portico of the Temple of Venus and Rome.

This great temple, which stood on the low hill at the bottom of the Forum facing the Capitol, was a double temple, the largest and most magnificent in Rome. It stood on an enormous platform, 145 metres long and 190 wide, on the north side of the Sacra Via.

**INTERIOR OF THE PANTHEON IN PAGAN TIMES**

The interior of the Pantheon is of majestic and harmonious proportions, being roofed by a dome whose spring starts from a point half the total height from the ground; this height—142 feet—is, moreover, the same as the span of the dome. In the 20-foot walls are three apses, the place of the fourth being taken by the door, and four recesses, symmetrically placed; and in the eight resulting spaces are small shrines. Above this run two cornices between which is now a row of fourteen empty niches not shown in this reconstruction, and from the upper springs the dome.

On the platform was a great colonnade consisting of a single row of enormous columns of grey Egyptian granite at the sides, and a double row of columns at the ends. At the west end was a single wide flight of steps; at the east end were two smaller flights, facing the Colosseum. It was so large that it seemed to be not merely a temple, but one of the tremendous imperial Forums.

At the south-west corner of this vast building stood across the Sacra Via the Triumphal Arch of Titus, ennobled with great sculptures in relief telling of the fall of Jerusalem. The Sacra Via, or Sacred Way, was the oldest and most famous street in Rome. It ran from the shrine called the Sacellum Streniae in the Colosseum valley, beside the Temple of Venus and Rome, close under the southern colonnade, and passed under the Arch of Titus through the Forum. It was about five metres wide, and beside it stood the most ancient and sacred shrines of the Roman people. It led to the

## TWO RECONSTRUCTIONS OF THE WESTERN BUILDINGS IN THE FORUM ROMANUM

To the left of the lower reconstruction is the façade of the Temple of Castor and Pollux, and beyond it the Basilica Julia; beyond that again the Arch of Tiberius and Germanicus (visible in the upper picture), and the Temples of Saturn, Vespasian and Concord in that order; below the temples, the Rostra, and in the background, the Arx. Two scenes of contemporary life are also here depicted: above, the historic remission by Trajan of debts to the State; and below, a religious procession before the Temple of Castor and Pollux.

Top illustration from the painting by G. Lessi, after restorations by G. Gatteschi

## SOUTHERN CORNER OF THE FORUM ROMANUM AND PALACE OF TIBERIUS

The centre of Roman civic life was the Forum Romanum; though Emperors might give their names to later and more magnificent enclosures, the older Forum could never lose the sanctity of established custom. In this reconstruction, from the left, are the Temple of Venus and Rome, the Temple of Julius Caesar with the Rostra Julia below, the Temple of Vesta, the Temple of Castor and Pollux, and the end of the Basilica Julia; while the palatial building in the background is the Domus Tiberiana on the Palatine.

*From a reconstruction by R. Lanciani*

## EASTERN END OF THE FORUM ROMANUM, WITH ARCH OF TITUS IN THE DISTANCE

In the foreground are the original blocks of the " Via Sacra," or Sacred Way; not far beyond where they cease was the limit of the Forum Romanum. Originally the road curved to the left and led round in a semicircle to the Arch of Titus, seen in the background. On the left of the photograph are pillars of the Temple of Antoninus and Faustina (see page 512) and next come two broken dedicatory columns. To the left of the Arch of Titus part of the Colosseum is just visible, and in the right foreground are the three lonely columns of the once magnificent Temple of Castor and Pollux.

*Photo by Donald McLeish*

## THE FORUM ROMANUM AS IT WAS IN THE DAYS OF THE CAESARS

In pages 502 and 506 have been given restorations of the western end of the Forum Romanum ; this is a view of the same Forum looking east, with only the Basilica Julia left unrestored in the foreground to give an uninterrupted view. The plain-fronted building on the left is the Curia, or Senate-house, with part of the Arch of Severus on its left and the Basilica Aemilia on its right. Between the Basilica and the Temple of Julius Caesar at the end is the Temple of Antoninus, with the Basilica of Constantine behind.

## CENTRE OF THE FORUM ROMANUM AS IT APPEARS TO-DAY

On comparing this illustration with the one above the reader will note the good preservation of the Curia. This is only apparent, as after it had been dedicated as a church it was rebuilt several times in much the same form. In the centre is the Column of Phocas, which does not appear in the reconstruction as it belongs to a later date (A.D. 608). On the extreme right of the reconstruction may be seen the façade of the Temple of Castor and Pollux, but the only three columns remaining are not included here (see page 507).

Photos by Boyer d'Agen

## TEMPLE OF VENUS AND ROMA, ARCH OF TITUS AND TEMPLE OF JUPITER STATOR

A reconstruction of the Temple of Venus and Roma appears in page 510. In this reconstruction also it may be seen in the background rising above its surrounding colonnade. Below it is the Arch of Titus (see page 516), and to the right the Temple of Jupiter Stator, built or rebuilt by Atilius Regulus in 294 B.C., but fabled to have been originally founded by Romulus. To the right of the picture the Clivus Palatinus commences the ascent of the Palatine Hill (see page 514).

*After a reconstruction by G. Gatteschi*

Capitol and the Temple of Jupiter Capitolinus, and was the ceremonial way followed by every dictator and every emperor who had been accorded a triumph. It was about as full of sharp turns as the way through the Mall and the Horse Guards Arch to Westminster Abbey from Buckingham Palace—to compare great things with small—and it fell more sharply beyond the Arch of Titus than that road does anywhere in its course. The climb up to the Capitol must always have been far more formidable than the climb up Ludgate Hill to S. Paul's Cathedral.

The view from the Arch of Titus towards the Capitol must have been one of the most noble in Rome. The palaced height of the Palatine, covered with the most splendid buildings in the world, stood to the south. To the north appeared the immense arches and enormous bulk of the Basilica of Constantine. Before one lay all that was greatest and most ancient in Rome, the Capitol, crowned by the mighty temple of Jupiter ; and in the valley before one the vast atrium of the Vestal Virgins, their ancient circuar fane, the Regia, the Temples of Romulus and Antoninus and Faustina ; and beyond, the Forum itself with the Rostra, the Basilica Aemilia to the north, the Basilica Julia to the south ; and beyond, again,

the Temples of Saturn, of Vespasian, and of Concord under the Capitol, with the Triumphal Arch of Septimius Severus beyond the Temple of Janus on the north side. Terrace upon terrace, portico upon portico, temple heaped on temple, forum passing into forum, innumerable columns beyond innumerable columns, till the eye, amid the ordered medley of glorious stone, found the Column of Trajan in the beautiful Forum of the Emperor, towering on high over another series of temples, which would seem to have been as numerous as churches are in the modern city.

It would be impossible, in the space of a single article, to consider all these buildings, even in the most superficial manner. We must be content here to name them. But in the space between the Arch of Titus and the Forum, which the Sacra Via entered at the Fornix Fabianus, two or three great buildings cannot be passed over. The enormous Basilica of Constantine, called the Basilica Nova, was rather the work of Maxentius than of Constantine. The Basilica, which stood on a vast platform, was of peculiar form, consisting of a central nave 80 metres long, 25 wide, and 35 high —higher, that is, than the nave of Westminster Abbey, the highest Gothic nave in England. The two side aisles were each 16 metres wide. The

## CAPITOL AND TEMPLE OF JOVE AS THEY APPEARED FROM THE PALATINE HILL

The Capitoline Hill lies immediately behind the western end of the Forum Romanum, and is divided into two eminences, of which the southern was called the Capitolium and the northern the Arx, or citadel. It was on the Capitolium that the Temple of Jupiter Capitolinus (seen above) once stood; it was of an unusual shape, having three distinct cellae dedicated respectively to Jupiter, Juno, and Minerva. Founded in 509 B.C., it was three times rebuilt, in the days of Sulla, by Vespasian, and by Domitian.

Photo by Boyer d'Agen

## COLUMNED GRANDEUR OF HADRIAN'S VAST TEMPLE TO VENUS AND ROMA

At the opposite end of the Forum to the Capitol, on the north of the Sacred Way beyond the Arch of Titus, stood the double Temple of Venus and Roma, with its two cellae back to back, and facing towards the Colosseum and the Forum. A mighty structure, it was designed by the Emperor Hadrian himself, begun in A.D. 121 and finished in A.D. 138; at either end were porticoes of ten columns each, and the whole stood upon an artificial platform surrounded by a colonnade of 180 columns.

From a reconstruction by G. Gatteschi

TRIUMPHAL ARCH OF THE EMPEROR SEPTIMIUS SEVERUS IN THE FORUM

Most of the features in this reconstruction have been illustrated and described in the other reconstructions of the western end of the Forum (which actually runs north-west and south-east, but the term is used for convenience). The Tabularium at the back, however, is better shown here than elsewhere; its exact use is not certain, but archives of some sort were deposited in it; also the arch on the right, erected in honour of Septimius Severus, the Emperor who died and was buried at York (Eboracum).

From a reconstruction by R. Lanciani

façade was towards the east, but Constantine erected a second entrance in the middle of the south consisting of a porch with porphyry columns approached by a long flight of steps. Opposite this new entrance he built a second semicircular apse in the north wall, the original apse being in the west wall. The walls of brick, six metres thick, the huge porphyry columns, the enormous height and space, made it one of the most remarkable buildings in in the whole of Rome.

On the west, beside this great Basilica, Maxentius built a temple in honour of his son Romulus. In the rear of this stood the Templum Sacrae Urbis, the two temples being converted in the sixth century into the Church of

ARCH OF SEVERUS AND PILLARS OF THE TEMPLE OF SATURN

Erected in A.D. 203 to commemorate the victories in the East of Septimius Severus (146-211) it is 75 feet high and 82 feet broad. Its marble columns, statues, and bas-reliefs have been much mutilated, while the six-horse chariot in which the Emperor was shown had disappeared before the arch was excavated in 1803. The road is the old Clivus Capitolinus

Photo by Donald McLeish

PORTICO OF THE TEMPLE OF FAUSTINA AND ANTONINUS

After the death of his wife Faustina in A.D. 141 the Emperor Antoninus erected a temple to her; and after his own death in the year 161 his name was added to hers in the inscription. Of this temple, which stood at the eastern end of the Forum and to the north of it, only a portico of ten lovely columns of Euboean marble is visible, the interior of the temple being now occupied by the Church of San Lorenzo in Miranda.

Photo by Donald McLeish

this therefore, southward, and like it within the extended Forum, stood one of the most famous buildings in Rome, the Atrium of Vesta and the Temple of Vesta. Though not a consecrated temple, it was the most sacred spot in Rome, round in form, and contained the sacred fire, the Palladium, and other sacred things. It was built of white marble with twenty fluted columns connected by bronze gratings. The roof was dome-shaped, with an opening in the centre for the exit of the smoke of the Sacred Fire. Near the temple were statues of an ox and a ram.

Beside the temple stood the Atrium Vestae, the House of the Vestals. It consisted of an open peristyle surrounded on all sides by rooms on two and three storeys, the central court, 69 metres long and 24 wide, being surrounded by a colonnade of forty-eight Corinthian columns of cipollino. Beyond the temple, from north to south, stood the Temple of Julius, behind the Rostra Julia, where the body of Caesar was burned, the Arch of Augustus, the Temple of Castor, and the Temple of Augustus right under the Palatine Hill.

SS. Cosma and Damiano. A much earlier building, dating from the best years of the Empire, stood beside the Temple of Romulus—the Temple of Antoninus and Faustina. It had lovely cipollino (or granular limestone-mica) columns 17 metres high, with Corinthian capitals of white marble supporting an entablature also of white marble surrounding the whole building.

In front of this temple, on the other side of the Sacred Way, stood the Regia, said to date from Numa, and to have been the house of the Pontifex Maximus. It remained his headquarters. He was in some sort the governor of the Vestals. Beyond

All three temples were surrounded and upheld by columns of marble.

We now come into the Forum proper, the centre of the life of the city. One can imagine it thronged with noisy crowds, as now it is overrun by the groups of cosmopolitan sightseers shepherded by their guides. Here all the famous men of the great Roman story have passed by and paused and debated. Here Horace met his bore. The noble and sacred space, sacred to human liberty, was framed by the columned Basilica Aemilia and the Curia Julii on the north, the great columned Basilica Julia and the temple of Saturn—the latter the most holy

GREAT HALL IN THE PALACE OF DOMITIAN AS IT WAS
Above the pillared walls is a highly ornate cornice, surmounted again by a band of frescoes and a roof of panelled vaulting.
From a painting by E. P. Wüscher-Becchi after designs by G. Trabacchi

place in Rome after the Temple of Vesta—on the south. Between them stood the Arch of Tiberius.

Then, under the Capitol itself, stood from south to north the columned Porticus Deorum Consentium, the columned Temple of Vespasian and the Temple of Concord with its great columned portico. In front stood the great Rostra facing the Forum, and above, on the Capitol, the great columned Tabularium. To the north, on the height above, stood the Temple of Juno, where now Ara Cœli stands. To the south, on the similar height, stood the Temple of Jove, where Palazzo Caffarelli stands to-day.

Standing there and gazing out over what may be called the greatest of all human achievements—the

PALACE OF DOMITIAN ON THE PALATINE HILL
The Palatine Hill has achieved etymological immortality by passing into the common language under the form of "palace." The Palace of Domitian here shown restored and in its present state was one of the magnificent structures by which it gained this repute. But where now are the costly marbles from Paros, Euboea, Numidia, Pentele, the statues in their niches, the mosaics, frescoes, and tessellated pavements, and the gilded bronze?

SHOPS AND SHOPPERS IN A BUSY ROMAN STREET ON THE PALATINE HILL

At the point where the Sacred Way passed under the Arch of Titus, coming from the Forum, a road known as the Clivus Palatinus branched off to the right and led up a narrow valley in the Palatine Hill to the vast complex of imperial buildings at the top. The photograph shows the site of this street to-day as seen from the Arch of Titus, which is described in page 516; while the reconstruction has peopled the same spot again with all the bustle of Roman street life. Note especially the wayside fountain on the right: the article on Pompeii has made familiar the excellent water-supply of Roman towns.

Photos by Boyer d'Agen

514

City of Rome, the soul of the Empire, the creator of Europe—the whole of the heart of that unequalled and incomparable thing lay at one's feet : the Forum and the Sacred Way filled and encompassed with columned temples and basilicas of marble shining in the sun, away to the vast Colosseum. To the south stood up all the beauty of the Palatine, with its infinite palaces of marble, and its gardens and laurels and ilexes and fountains, its gold and precious stone. To the north lay the exquisite and perfect Forum of Trajan, with its sky-kissing column, itself surrounded by other Fora scarcely less lovely, the Forum of Augustus to the west, the Forum of Vespasian beyond it, the Forum of Julius to the south, and across them lay the vast columned Basilica Ulpia, close by the Temple of Trajan, the Temple of Mars, and the Temple of Peace. Thousands of men have gazed upon that sight which we shall never see, and loved it above everything, yet none guessed perhaps that he was looking upon something that would fall and decay and disappear as utterly as the leaves fall and are dust. Nothing that man has made since is comparable with it ; beside it Paris is a mere hut village, London nothing more than a mole's labyrinth.

Did a man never muse there, as the sun set and the shadows passed from column to sun-kissed column over the beloved city ; did a man never dream that as the sunlight passes, as the shadows pass, this too would pass away ? No man would have dared to dream just that. For Rome, Eternal Rome, lay there under his eyes with the whole world in her embrace —yes, her embrace, for we were all her children and to her owe everything. No, she cannot pass away—she is the Eternal City. As the shadows fall we too may see lying across the city that darkest shade which has the form of a dome and is still upreared in the name of a universal government, heir of the Imperial, enthroned in the hearts of men.

And when one has seen all this from the Capitol as in a dream, and when one has seen the ruin of it with these mortal eyes—the Forum a brickfield, covered with wild flowers, the Palatine an incredible ruin among which is a wilderness of roses —one has seen but a part of that incomparable whole which was the Rome of the Emperors.

Far away to the south, on the top of the Esquiline Hill, rose the vast baths of Diocletian, vaster even than those of Caracalla of which I have spoken. To the south of them and not far from the Colosseum rose the Baths of Trajan. Nor were these all. Under the Quirinal stood the Baths of

PYRAMIDAL TOMB OF GAIUS CESTIUS

This pyramid, a noble structure 116 feet high faced with marble slabs on a square base, is the tomb of Gaius Cestius, a contemporary of Cicero. The sides at the base measure 33 yards each way. It stands just within the medieval Porta San Paolo, seen in the background, originally built on the site of the Porta Ostiensis by the great Belisarius.
Photo by Ewing Galloway

Constantine, and about the Pantheon to the west of the Via Lata, the medieval and modern Corso, stood the Baths of Nero and the Baths of Agrippa.

The Pantheon, which in its main part stands and remains the chief, if not the only, Roman building still more or less intact and in use, was begun by Agrippa in 27 B.C. and, with the Baths, the stagnum and Euripus, formed the great group of public buildings he founded in this part of the Campus Martius. The Pantheon was a temple containing four statues and probably especially dedicated to the ancestral deities of the Julian family : Mars, Venus, and the deified Julius. The great dome is still one of the wonders of the world.

Vast mausoleums, too, rose in various parts of the city : the Mausoleum of Hadrian, the Mausoleum of Augustus. The former is still used as a castle—the Castello Sant Angelo—and in its huge strength and height and bulk no modern building, not even S. Peter's, is so impressive.

ARCH OF TITUS WITH PANEL SHOWING GOLDEN SPOILS FROM THE TEMPLE AT JERUSALEM

The position of the Arch of Titus has been indicated in many of the restorations of the Forum Romanum, and will also be found in the plan in page 490. The nature of the carvings on it (see the right-hand photograph) leave no doubt that it was erected to commemorate the fall of Jerusalem in A.D. 70, but the application of the title "divus" to the Emperor Titus in the inscription indicates that the building was dedicated after his death in A.D. 81. The arch was constructed of Pentelic marble and has two Corinthian columns on either side, above which runs a frieze of soldiers; in the space between gateway and frieze are Victories and figures of Rome and Fortune; and under the arch are the spoils of Jerusalem, including the seven-branched candlestick, while in the corresponding panel, not illustrated here, the Emperor himself is shown in his chariot.

Photo by Donald McLeish

516

THE COLUMN TO-DAY, WITH TRAJAN REPLACED BY S. PAUL

Trajan's column has suffered but little in the course of centuries, and the fine spiral reliefs of the Dacian wars which adorn it are still the best study for the military institutions of their day. The total height of the column including the base is 127½ feet; the shaft itself being of the same height as that of Marcus Aurelius (see page 499): and 34 blocks of marble went to its construction (18 to the shaft).

FORUM TRAJANUM AND TRAJAN'S COLUMN RESTORED

After the successful issue of the Dacian war Trajan began the construction of the Forum known by his name between the Quirinal and the Capitol. It was completed in A.D. 114. Magnificent colonnades enclosed it on three sides and the Basilica Ulpia completed the fourth, beyond which could be seen the summit of Trajan's memorial column, which he never lived to see, as he died abroad before its completion.

**ACKNOWLEDGMENT IN ENDURING MARBLE OF A ROMAN EMPEROR'S BOUNTY**

Two incidents in the reign of the Emperor Trajan seem to have moved the gratitude of the Romans so much that they engaged the art of the sculptor—unless we may trace the finger of the Emperor himself in these representations! Marble balustrades from the Forum give the two scenes: the formal remission of debts from individuals to the State, and the investing of an endowment for the education of poor children (shown here). The reconstruction in page 506 also portrays the former eventful ceremony.

Photo by Donald McLeish

**SACRED CISTERN AND STATUES IN THE COURT OF THE HOUSE OF THE VESTALS**

Beyond the eastern limit of the old Forum, and on the southern side of its later extension, was the House of the Vestal Virgins, with its courtyard. The duty of these maidens, six in number and chosen from the highest patrician families, was to keep burning the Sacred Fire in the Temple of Vesta (see page 502); marriage was permitted them after thirty years of service, but for unchastity before that time they were buried alive. In this photograph may be seen the Sacred Cistern in the courtyard and statues of Head Virgins of the second and third centuries; on the left arches of the Basilica of Constantine.

Photo by Donald McLeish

## IN HONOUR OF CONSTANTINE: BEST PRESERVED OF ROME'S TRIUMPHAL ARCHES

The sculptured arch spans the Via Triumphalis a short distance from the Colosseum, thereby corresponding roughly to the Arch of Titus on the Via Sacra, and was erected to commemorate the victory of Constantine over Maxentius in A.D. 312. Such of the sculptures as date from that period show an obvious decline in art; but some earlier buildings were partly employed for its construction, so that many of the features are of excellent workmanship. The arch itself has three openings.

## SOME OF THE THREE HUNDRED TOWERS ON THE WALLS OF AURELIAN

The walls of Rome have been several times extended, from the old fortifications of the Arx and the Palatine, and the wall of Servius Tullius enclosing the Seven Hills on the left bank of the Tiber, to the inclusion of the Janiculum and the Vatican Hill on the right bank, and the Walls of Aurelian begun in A.D. 271 and completed in 276. This photograph shows a section of the Aurelian Walls; much of the work is original, but subsequent Emperors and Popes have restored or destroyed extensively.

*Photos by Anderson*

## VIVID RECONSTRUCTION OF THE MAGNIFICENT BATHS OF DIOCLETIAN—

In the great public baths which ministered to the needs and the pleasures of the entire population, Imperial Rome developed an institution which has no parallel in modern life. Caracalla's baths covered an area as large as that occupied by the Houses of Parliament in London. Diocletian's baths were even larger. In this reconstruction drawing the Frigidarium or great swim-

## —ONE OF THE GREATEST ARCHITECTURAL GLORIES OF IMPERIAL ROME

ming bath is on the left; the Tepidarium, which was the main hall in which the bathers undressed and where they rested after taking the hot baths, was marble-paved and superbly decorated; on the right were the Calidaria, or chambers where hot baths were taken. Besides serving their purpose as baths the Thermae provided every facility for public exercise and amusement.

## HOW TIME HAS DEALT WITH THE TOMBS OF THE APPIAN WAY

In ancient cities it was not usual to have burials within the walls, and many of those found in Rome itself **were** due to later extensions of the city area. Most thickly populated by the dead were the borders of the old Appian Way without the walls, laid down by Appius Claudius in 312 B.C.; among the tombs being that of Caecilia Metella, illustrated in page 524, and shown in the reconstruction in the distance, on the right of the road. Trees now grow among the shattered tombs.

Photo by Donald McLeish

## A WAR-SCARRED TOMB, THE CASTELLO SANT' ANGELO BY THE TIBER

A history of the vicissitudes through which this building passed since it was converted into a castle would be a history of the Middle Ages. But in the days of Imperial Rome it was a tomb, built by Hadrian about the year A.D. 130 to contain the bones of himself and his descendants. The reconstruction (top) shows that it consisted of two diminishing circular structures surrounded by pillars, on a square base, the whole being surmounted by a conical roof. In some ways it reminds one, therefore, of the traditional shape of the Lighthouse of Pharos.

**FORTIFIED TOMB ON THE APPIAN WAY**
Standing by the great Appian Way is the mighty tomb
of Caecilia Metella, daughter of Quintus Caecilius Metellus
Creticus and wife of Crassus, son of the Triumvir. Like the
Sant' Angelo castle it is circular, resting on a square base, and
was similarly used as a fort in the Middle Ages. The tower
is 70 feet in diameter, and there is evidence that the roof
was conical before it was replaced by battlements.
Photo by Donald McLeish

tells us that the nine great parks
of London, with a total of 2,000
acres, represent a thirty-ninth
portion of the city's area, while those
of Imperial Rome, lying over the
chain of hills for two miles at
least on either side the Tiber,
represented an eighth. Rome was
like a great white rose in the
midst of these green leaves.

And so we must think of her in
the confusion of our world to-day
as the incomparable and visionary
city, of which we hear in our
earliest years, always as of something to be desired and sacred,
whose history we learn as well as,
if not before, our own, and whose
title is Eternal. Men loved her then
and have loved her since, even in
her ruin, as no other city, not even
Athens, was ever loved. She was
the head and front of our world.
She was the Capital.

But when I have named all these—as though an
ancient traveller from Barbary had recapitulated
to his friends in a country far from Rome what
had struck him most in the Mother City—what
have I done to bring before the reader the greatness, the splendour, the majesty, the beauty, the
living wonder and glory of Rome ? Nothing. One
must fill the streets and Fora of the Eternal City
with Romans and Provincials, with slaves and
Barbarians, with people from the whole world—
for Rome was ever Cosmopolis. One must hear the
noise of the great town, the confused voice of a
vast multitude ; one must stand in the Forum
Romanum and see Caesar go by in triumph, one
must enter and see the senators in their curule
chairs deliberating the destiny of mankind, a
sight so august that, as we know, it appalled the
barbarian ; one must see sunrise and noontide
and evening come in the ways of the city.

And I have said nothing of the gardens. Yet
no modern capital of Europe or America can be
compared with Imperial Rome for the number and
extent of its public parks and gardens. Lanciani

**ALTAR TO AN "UNKNOWN GOD"**
On the west of the Palatine Hill stands a strange little altar
with an antique inscription dating from about 100 B.C. "Sei
Deo sei deivae sac[rum]"—sacred to an unknown god or
goddess. The Sextius Calvinus who restored it was probably
the praetor who founded the town of Aquae Sextiae.
Photo by Donald McLeish

# Arts and Crafts of Ancient Britain

## By Sir Bertram Windle

### Author of "Life in Early Britain"

THE Celtic races seem to be first known in that portion of western Europe where the Danube, Rhine, Rhone and Elbe have their origin. In the eighth century B.C. we find them, or at least a tribe of them, established at Hallstadt in the Salzkammergut, probably attracted there by the salt mines, which still exist in that spot. This was in the Early Iron period, and there is a definite form of culture to which is given the name Hallstadt.

Two centuries later a much more important culture was in existence at La Tène, a Gallic town at the northern end of Lake Neuchâtel in Switzerland, a culture which spread far and wide and is recognizable in its artistic products by a "motif" known as the flowing spiral, of which more shortly will be said.

The Celtic peoples linguistically consisted of two groups, P and K (or Q) Kelts. The former used P where the latter used K (or Q), e.g. pen, a head—as in Pen-maen-mawr, "the great stone head," or Ken (more properly ceann), a head—as in Kenmare, "the sea head." The former are the linguistic ancestors of the Brythonic speakers of Wales and Brittany; the latter of the Goidelic or Gaelic speakers of Scotland, Ireland and the Isle of Man. The general belief to-day is that the K-Celts first appeared in England circa 1150 B.C., arriving, armed with leaf-shaped bronze swords, at the Thames and the Wash as well as the Wessex ports. Moving westward, they passed by the upper Severn and the Bala gap into Wales and then they moved across the channel to Ireland.

Later invasions which brought the La Tène culture may perhaps have been around 450 B.C.

These later invasions brought into Britain one very important implement, namely the potter's wheel. Plenty of rough pottery had been made in Britain during the Neolithic Period and up to the arrival of these immigrants, but it was what is known as hand-made, that is, it was roughly moulded, as to-day is moulded the pottery of people like the Akikuyu and other primitive races, and as all the pottery in the American continent was moulded before the coming of the Spaniards. It is remarkable what symmetrical vessels can be produced by skilled workers without the wheel, but without that implement only a few can attain to the skill which the multitude can acquire with this mechanical aid. Such wheel-made pottery we find, for example, in the famous cemetery at Aylesford, and it is easy even for an untrained eye to discern the great difference that there is between it and even the best funerary pottery of the earlier time.

Another art which the Celts introduced, one of great beauty and interest, was that of enamelling. Their knowledge of this art is alluded to by an early writer, and in its essentials it resembles that in use to-day. Enamels are a kind of glass coloured with various pigments (like stained glass) and deposited in a molten condition on a metal background. It is obvious that if they are to be arranged in patterns and not to be mere smudges of colour, these fluid glasses must be confined within limits, at least until they cool and solidify. There are two methods of doing this. The first, called "cloisonné" and largely used by the Japanese for many years and by them and others to-day, consists in soldering down wire barricades shaped to correspond with the desired patterns within which the molten glass can lie without mixing with its neighbours. But the other method, also employed to-day, the method used by the Celts, is known as "champlevé" and consists in excavating recesses in the metal background into which the molten glass may be poured. The Celts used enamels of various colours; these included red, blue, yellow and green.

It is now time to speak of their artistic motifs, and specially of the flowing spiral already alluded to. In the later parts of the Palaeolithic age, in those cultures known, from their classical sites, as Magdalenian and Aurigniacian, there was a wonderful

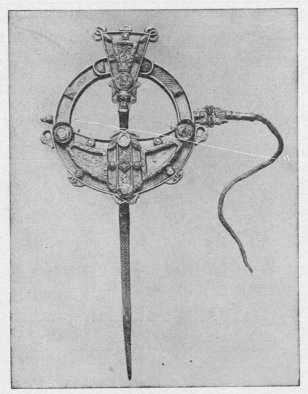

**THE TARA BROOCH**

The Tara Brooch, now in the Dublin Museum, represents the high-water mark of the Celtic jeweller's art. Fifteen hundred years ago Irish noblemen and their ladies wore such brooches but few were as richly ornamented as this superb example.

**THE EIGHTH CENTURY BOOK OF KELLS**

The Book of Kells (see p. 528) dates from the eighth century, and its beautiful illustrations include scenes from the Life of Christ and portraits of three Evangelists. The finest of the Irish illuminated MSS., it is to-day one of the most treasured possessions of Trinity College, Dublin.

outburst, especially in Spain and in France, of a naturalistic art which delineated animals of various kinds, also fishes, with wonderful fidelity. With the coming of the Epipalaeolithic period that wonderful chapter in artistic history was closed, nor did anything at all resembling it reappear until many centuries later. Not in that which followed nor in that with which this chapter deals. There is very little attempt to represent animals or birds, still less man, and what attempts there are of the Celtic period are lamentably bad : and very unimportant if we omit the zoomorphic figures on the funerary buckets found at Marlborough and at Aylesford. These, it seems tolerably certain, were imported from Gaul and cannot be described as British, and in any case were a very debased following of Etruscan originals.

But in another direction the Celtic artists and, more especially at a later date, their goldsmiths and scribes reached a pitch of excellence which has never been excelled, even if ever attained, and that was in the region of geometrical decoration. We may think of this kind of decoration as consisting of two classes— straight lines and curves. The former was constantly used in the Neolithic period for the ornamentation of pottery and other things with criss-cross lines, chevrons and the like, and these and other simple forms were very naturally also employed by the Celtic designers. But their forte lay in curved geometrical figures. Did they originate this idea ? That we cannot say. Mr. Romilly Allen, who is an authority on this subject, says that the Celts never invented any new ideas, but that once they had picked up an idea from someone else—a thing for which they

had a great aptitude—they gave it such a strong Celtic tinge as to make it unrecognizable even by those from whom it was borrowed.

" Wait till you hear me tell that story to-morrow night ! " said a great Irish raconteur to a friend of his and mine after listening to a good tale ill-told at a Cambridge High-Table. My friend's account was that when it was so told the original narrator laughed as loudly as anyone else and was equally delighted with the perfect novelty of the story.

Where the spiral came from no one quite knows ; perhaps it may have had an Aegean origin. But it made its way across Europe, as George Coffey showed, and is met with, for example, in great display on the huge stone at the entrance to the marvellous sepulchral chamber at New Grange in Co. Louth, Ireland. It is found on the curious stone balls which are almost a speciality of Aberdeenshire ; it is found in goldsmiths' work, and at times so closely resembles what we know to have been examples of Mycenaean art that we shall probably not go far wrong in agreeing with Coffey that there was its origin, and that it made its way into Scotland and Ireland via Scandinavia.

The flowing spiral is not close and compact, but like the long trailer of some climbing plant, and once the eye has grasped what it is there never can be any difficulty in recognizing it wherever it is encountered. Go right across to the west of Europe, and in County Galway is a great natural stone, about four feet in height, at Turoe, perhaps a stone of great sanctity, where this decoration can be seen. Go down to the south of the same island and in the Museum of University College, Cork, there are three curious long cones of thin bronze, most beautifully made and with their edges united by the tiniest of bronze rivets—a marvel of workmanship. They were almost certainly the ornaments of some kind of head-dress ; were found in slob-lands along the river Lee below Cork, and show the same flowing spiral. Very commonly the spiral was adorned with leaf forms, and one of the most beautiful examples of this is to be met with in the scabbard which formed part of the finds at the Crannoge of Lisnacroghera in Ireland. The same curve was used by wood-workers, for it is to be found on the wooden bowl discovered at the lake village near Glastonbury in Somerset, a copy of which is in the British Museum. And this form of curvilinear geometrical art is to be met with on many of the ornaments and articles of daily use of that period. As an example let us consider the backs of the bronze mirrors found in various places, of which those discovered at Birdlip, Gloucestershire, are beautiful instances.

As much as space will admit has now been said respecting the type of art employed, and we must now turn to some account of the kind of objects to which it was applied. To continue with warlike objects, of course there were swords and daggers, and there is at Colchester Museum the bronze, undecorated helmet of a Celtic warrior from St. Albans, a Celtic town before it became the Roman Verulamium. It is shaped like what is known as a hunting cap, but it is probable that the peak was worn at the back to protect the neck from missiles and blows. Perhaps here may be mentioned the horse-trappings, bits and appendages which have been found in various places, and sometimes, as in the fine examples discovered in the Polden Hills, Somerset, adorned with beautiful designs in enamel.

From these we may turn to articles for personal use or adornment. Besides their mirrors, the ladies had metal combs and also chatelains. But the fibulae or brooches form a group of great magnitude and much interest. The true fibulae are just more or less glorified safety-pins ; the simplest kind of fastening which can be imagined. Large numbers may be seen in all museums, and without delaying over them we must direct attention to the far more elaborate pennannular brooches.

This kind of brooch, which belongs rather to Christian than pagan Celtic art, is in use to-day among the Ouled Nail of North Africa, who close their garments with it just as the Irish nobles and their wives did fifteen hundred years or so ago. The ornamentation of these brooches reaches the high-water mark of the jewellers' art, and the best example is what is known as the Tara brooch, which is in the National Museum in Dublin.

THE decoration on both faces of this large and richly adorned example is unsurpassed of its kind. The torque was a twisted metal collar made of bronze or gold, and worn by men. They, as well as the women, wore armlets and wristlets of the same metals, twisted or otherwise ornamented and at times enamelled. In connexion with these must be mentioned the curious gold lunulae which,

Lawrenc-

THE ANCIENT TOWER OF S. COLUMB'S CHURCH AT KELLS IN COUNTY MEATH

From Kells in County Meath came what is acknowledged to be the most perfect illuminated manuscript in Irish Christendom—the Book of Kells. But Kells as the headquarters of the famous missionary S. Columb retains several architectural traces of the Christian brotherhood who settled here, and among them is the old church tower of which the base is shown in the photograph. This part was rebuilt in the last quarter of the sixteenth century, but the rude sculptures seen on the left must date from nearly a thousand years before.

when first discovered, were claimed to be the golden sickles with which the Druids detached the mistletoe, but which are now recognized as head or neck ornaments. Most of them are of Irish provenance and are decorated with the straight line, not the curvilinear geometrical ornamentation—chevrons and the like.

It may here be mentioned that there is little doubt that in the times with which we are concerned Ireland was the El Dorado of the Western world, and that most of her gold, stream and not vein, was then collected by the people of the day, a fact which accounts for the extraordinary richness in gold ornaments of the Dublin Museum, in spite of the untold quantities of objects which have been found and surreptitiously melted down for bullion.

Jet necklets have been found occasionally in England, as at Middleton Moor in Derbyshire, but the finer and more numerous examples come from Scotland. Necklaces of glass beads of divers colours are also amongst the ornaments of the period.

Something must now be said concerning the marvellous examples of Celtic art in early Christian times. When the Celt, especially in Ireland, took to Christianity, he took to it with all his heart, and the great monasteries of the Celtic type—quite different in discipline from the Benedictine abbeys of later introduction—were of great size and existed in considerable numbers. In the abbeys lived, no doubt, the men who cultivated the wonderful art of script and illumination which we find in the few gospels and other works of a religious kind which have come down to us, for large numbers must no doubt have been lost or destroyed in the destruction of the religious houses at the time of the change of religion in these islands. There is admittedly no more beautiful example of an illuminated manuscript than the Book of Kells, now in the library of the University of Dublin, a work which was seen and commented on by Giraldus Cambrensis in his Irish journey. It dates back to the eighth century, and its ornamentation includes the circles, knots and triskeles which we have met with in other cases and in that of the last named, especially on the backs of mirrors.

The Book of Lindisfarne, or Durham Book, is an English example, but none the less of Irish inspiration, for S. Aidan was brought from Iona to Lindisfarne, where the book was made, and Iona had its origin from S. Columba. A point to be noted in these books is the poor drawing of the human frame where introduced, quite in accord with what was previously said as to the characteristics of Celtic art. In the Gospel Book of MacDurnan, dating from the ninth century, there is, as title page to the Gospel of S. Matthew, a figure of that saint which is purely Byzantine, and clearly was copied by the illuminator from some such source. It is quite out of harmony with the rest of the decoration. The Book of Deir, of the same century, shows this art in its degradation; poor spirals, many contractions in the Latin (there is a curious Gaelic gloss in the margins) and execrable figure drawing. These books, being of great value, were supplied with metal cases, and a fine example is that known as the Soisgeal Molaise.

A GALWAY MONOLITH AND CELTIC METAL WORK FROM LINCOLNSHIRE AND AYLESFORD

Sculptors of the La Tène period, like the smiths, worked from a geometrical basis which they overlaid with a floral pattern. In the monolith (left) at Turoe House, County Galway, the spiral scrolls are evidently an imitation of embossed metal work. The bronze shield (centre) found in Lincolnshire and now in the British Museum, dates from the beginning of the Christian era, and was originally backed with wood or leather. It is a splendid example of La Tène metal and red enamel work. The bucket (right) comes from Aylesford.

## THE SCULPTURED WEST FRONT OF ARDMORE CATHEDRAL, AND AN ALTAR ON HOLY ISLAND

In the seaside village of Ardmore, in County Waterford, Ireland, are the rough stone remains of the Cathedral and Oratory of S. Decian, who, legend says, was a predecessor of S. Patrick in the conversion of Ireland. The two tiers of sculptured niches on the Cathedral's **west** wall (bottom) are probably of the seventh century. Of the same period were the ruins of S. Caimin's Church and the wonderful **panelled** altar (top) on Holy Island, which is set in the waters of Lough Derg, County Clare. S. Caimin died in 653.

A PIT GRAVE AT AYLESFORD, AND AN INSCRIBED MONOLITH AT CRAG

The ancient Celts cremated their dead and buried the ashes. The most important of the Aylesford discoveries in 1886 was that of a pit grave (left) containing bronze utensils mingled with fragments of cinerary earthenware. The bucket shown in the photograph held brooches and calcined bones. These relics are ascribed to the third La Tène period. The monolith (right) is at Crag in County Derry, and bears on its surface the line and dot characters of the Ogham alphabet, devised in Ireland. Two names of the dead are represented by these signs.

The Domnach Airgid or Silver Lord's (book) is more probably a reliquary, and marks the end of the real Celtic work, for the ornamentation is obviously affected by Gothic influences. But, then, it belongs to the fourteenth century. It was the work of one, John O'Barrdan. The Ardagh Chalice in the Dublin Museum is the high-water mark of the Celtic (or any other) jewellers' art as applied to religious objects, and is profusely decorated even to the under surface of the foot. Here again we meet with triskeles and curvilinear ornament. The Cross of Cong; the pastoral staff of Clonmacnoise, showing the shape of that episcopal appurtenance as it was at that day, and very different from the later Gothic, with the arm-shrine of S. Lachthin, must not be omitted from mention; nor the bells, often ornamented, which were carried about by wandering prelates and priests, nor the cases made for their protection, the most elaborate of which is the so-called bell-shrine of S. Patrick.

A FEW words must be said about the high crosses like those at Clonmacnoise and elsewhere, which were such a glory of the art of the Celts in the Christian period. These are wheel crosses, that is to say the arms of the cross are embraced by a stone circle from which the ends project. The figure of the Redeemer is small and within the ambit of the circle. On the top of the cross is a small representation of a roofed building of the type used for reliquaries. The cross and circle are at the top of a tall pillar with a pedestal, and the sides, face and back of this shaft are covered with that knot-work which is so marked a characteristic of this art. The crosses of Cornwall, like that, for example, at Sancreed, are smaller examples, marked by the same characteristic of the figure being unduly small in comparison with the shaft.

A BRITISH BRIDLE-BIT

This Early British bridle-bit was discovered at Risa, near Hull, and is now in the British Museum. Its red and blue enamel decoration has more than a merely artistic significance, for the red enamel was used as a substitute for the red coral of earlier days, which was credited with magico-religious properties

# Palmyra, Queen City of the Desert

## By Edward Wright

*SITUATED midway between the Syrian coast and the upper course of the Euphrates river, Palmyra was probably an old desert trading centre long before King Solomon, according to tradition, extended his power there. When the Romans and Parthians were contending for the dominion of the Middle East, the Palmyrenes increased in power and riches. By A.D. 260, when the finest works in the city were being built, the desert city was in a position to challenge both the Persian and Roman Empires. The Grand Colonnade, of 1,500 splendid columns, with arcaded streets branching from either side, the triple-gated Triumphal Arch, the Palace and Judgement Hall of Zenobia, and the finer parts of the immense fortress Temple, were probably erected during the reign of Zenobia. The city fell to the Romans under Aurelian in A.D. 273.—EDITOR.*

FOUR days' hard travelling from Damascus, over the flowering valley and outlying limestone ridges of the Lebanon mass, brought a rider by the portal pass to the Syrian wilderness of sand and salt lakes. Leftward of the pass, a long range of yellow heights, stretching from the Euphrates river, ended in a wall-girt, castle-crowned mountain. On the right, another tower-dotted crest linked with a second line of peaks and scarps, which, like a rampart of civilization, blocked out the desert and curved back towards Damascus The desert, in the latter part of the third century of the Christian era, had not been able to invade the cultivated field. It was then the tide of civilized life that ran outward through the gap between the two mountain ranges, and spread in power and beauty into the wilderness.

As the rider climbed the pass, a marvellous spectacle was unfolded. There was an ancient oasis of palm trees at the foot of the mountains, and the high, green fronds peeped at the traveller as he rose, and then became mingled with the stone foliage of a forest of Corinthian columns, and the carven work of immense ranges of arcades. As the top of the pass was reached, the oasis city of Palmyra shone like a fairy mirage of the desert, on a background of sun-scorched sand, seamed and patched with bitter salt, Within a thirteen-mile circuit of ramparts, connecting with the walled and castled mountain, was an immense array of pillars. Little houses had tiers of little columns; mansions had ranges of larger columns; scores of temples had lofty columns, and giant fluted drums rose into leafy capitals by a great palace and greater Sun Temple. Small streets and large squares had each their pillared arcades, and the many private gardens were, like cloisters, framed in columned coolness. Intersecting the maze, in a line running from the foot of the castled heights to the principal temple, was a Grand Colonnade, with pillars fifty-seven feet high, supporting a massive, ornate entablature. It began with a magnificent triple Triumphal Arch, from which stretched four rows of columns, forming a wide, central, arcaded highway, with two footways on each side. Midway on this road of triumph two splendid palaces, with colossal statue-work, soared into the blazing sky, and lesser colonnades branched continually from the main thoroughfare. In the vast shadowed bazaars, crowded with Syrians, Saracens, Jews, and Greeks, shone the silks, carpets, jewels, and fine fabrics of India and Persia.

Century after century, from the days when Alexander the Great overran Babylonia, the Palmyrenes had built themselves shade from the sun and shelter from the sandstorm by means of arcades of Corinthian pillars. In their Temple of the Sun, the architectural style they adopted from the later Greeks was developed with an overwhelming effect of splendour. Being the fortress treasure-house of the city, the temple was surrounded with a wall, some seventy feet high, the massive strength of which was lightened in

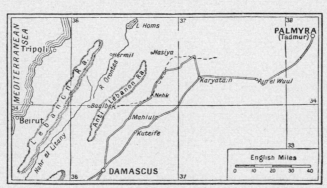

MAP INDICATING THE POSITION OF PALMYRA

appearance by pilasters supporting an overhanging, solid work of carven stone that was both beautiful and useful in defence. Between the pilasters were windows that further broke the vast surface of the wall in an ornamental way, and provided openings for archers, if needed. The doorway

WHERE EASTERN ART AND WESTERN SPLENDOUR MET
Local tradition may be right in calling a mass of ruins near the Triumphal Arch Zenobia's Palace and Judgement Hall at Palmyra. The elaborate carving on doorpost and lintel seem to mark it as a royal residence, built, one would like to think, by Odenathus for his lovely queen, Septimia Bath-Zabbai.
Photo by F. M. Good

was an example of resisting power and grace. Thirty-two feet high and sixteen feet wide, it was made out of monoliths for jambs and lintels, but the single blocks of stone were exquisitely sculptured. Within was a court, set with rows of columns seventy feet high, from the middle drum of each of which projected a bracket on which rose statues of citizens who had deserved well of the city. These statues overflowed the temple court, and adorned the pillars of the Grand Colonnade.

In the middle of the spacious square, ascended by a flight of stairs and encircled by a single row

of Ionic columns with finely wrought bronze capitals, was the temple. It was forty paces long and sixteen paces broad, with the entrance at the western side, and the sanctuary at the eastern end. Here, on the ceiling of lovely designs with zodiacal emblems, was the most perfect carving in Palmyra, and here the ancient Syrian cult of the sun, in the latter part of the third century of the Christian era, was still strongly held. Such was the costly, artistic labour spent upon the temple that the great polished columns, if measured end to end, were some six miles long. Near by was a smaller temple dedicated in A.D. 130 to an imperial visitor, the Emperor Hadrian.

In addition to the enormous range of classic architecture in Palmyra, there were remarkable examples of a kind of native building scattered in profusion round the base of the neighbouring mountains. They were great tower tombs, most of them over one hundred feet high, with vaulted caves beneath, each containing nearly five hundred embalmed bodies of Palmyrenes. Many of the lower interiors were finely painted and carved, and small statue groups of scenes from family life were placed by the mummies. Here could be traced, in little personal ornaments left with the dead, the history of Palmyra for some thirteen hundred years, since the days when Solomon is said to have held the mountain gate to Mesopotamia. Assyrian, Hittite, Egyptian-Nubian, Persian, Macedonian, and Roman cultures had left their mark on the life of the outposts of the great desert, until the city grew strong enough to win independence, and aim at empire herself.

It was the peculiarity of Palmyra that she flourished most in adversity. When the Parthian or the Persian was at war with Rome, the desert city balanced freely between the two mighty contending forces, and enriched itself by acting as trade broker between them. When the northern trade routes from Antioch and Aleppo to the Orient were closed by warfare with the Parthians, Palmyra began greatly to prosper. And when the southern trade route through Petra (described in pages 83 to 90) was ruined by the greed of the Romans, every Roman campaign in upper Mesopotamia increased the far-ranging power of the Palmyrenes.

By the middle of the third century of our era, practically all the commerce between India, Persia, Southern Arabia and the Far East on the one hand, and all the Mediterranean world on the other hand, poured through the gorgeous city that held the mountain pass in the Syrian desert. Rome alone took yearly at least one million sestertii of Indian merchandise, and depended upon Palmyra not only for luxuries, but likewise for aid in eastern wars. In every campaign in Mesopotamia, Rome anxiously waited to learn what was the Palmyrene policy.

As soon as the power of the Parthian weakened, the Romans encircled Palmyra with their legions.

Their Emperor Severus, after breaking the Parthians, reduced Palmyra to the status of a Roman colony, and procured the assassination of the chief man of the city, Odenathus, who had plotted a revolt. The Romans had always despised the caravan traders as an unwarlike race, while envying their enormous wealth and fearing the political power which the merchants skilfully exercised in their desert buffer state between two rival empires. Severus seemed to have put an end to all danger from Palmyra, and prepared the way for extracting its riches.

The Palmyrenes, however, were not at the end of their resources. In spite of their luxurious, silken, scented ways of life, they had a hard core of Semite character. In them, the smooth shrewdness of the Syrian was blended with the vehement strength of the Saracen, as the desert Arab was

**DESERT-GIRT FORTRESS: PALMYRA'S CASTLE FROM THE GRAND COLONNADE**

On each pillar of the Grand Colonnade was a projecting bracket bearing a statue of some illustrious Tadmorene. These numerous pillars, so beloved by the old architects of Palmyra, make the city look to-day like a magic city of stone conjured from the sands. From the castle in the background a magnificent view may be had over the ruins and the circling desert, but the present structure is Moslem work, built of stone from an older fort once within the circuit of the walls.

Photo by F. M. Good

ALL THAT REMAINS OF THE FOUR ROWS OF PILLARS WHICH FORMED THE HIGH STREET OF THE WONDER CITY OF PALMYRA

What varied pageantry must have passed between the colonnades of Palmyra's triumphal way! Victorious legions bearing the spoils of far campaigns—lithe and keen-eyed desert men like the Beduin of to-day, or Roman veterans of staider mien, the flotsam of Rome's eastern defeats; Zenobia, armed like Athene, speeding in her chariot among her statesmen on some martial errand; sad bands of foreign captives; and endless caravans laden with precious merchandise which enriched the high-born traders and made their city the mistress of the East. For her wealth did not rest on the produce of her workshops or the soil, but on a complete control of the trade-routes connecting the Mediterranean with legendary lands beyond the sunrise.

Photo by F. M. Good

534

FLUTED SHAFTS WHICH STAND IN SOLITUDE ON THE WESTERN CONFINES OF THE DESERT CITY OF PALMYRA

Turn where one will, and still the pillars rise, until one wonders that the architects had time to build anything else! Smooth and fluted, with Ionic or Corinthian capitals and elaborate entablatures, their style is ornate and without the classic restraint of an earlier period; but their finished effect must have been more than impressive, and it would be presumption to find fault with craftsmen who could work in such exquisite detail as is shown in the ceiling of the Temple of the Sun God, and of which examples can be found littered everywhere among the ruins. Seldom have the artistic impulses of East and West blended in such harmony as in this strip of northern Syria.

Photo by F. M. Good

535

TENDRILLED VINES THAT ATTEST THE SKILL OF PALMYRA'S STONE-CUTTERS

Wonderfully preserved in the dry Syrian atmosphere, gems of craftsmanship adorn huge blocks which lie piled in hopeless confusion round the lonely pillars which once supported them. Tradition, supported by the Bible, asserts that Solomon founded "Tadmor in the Wilderness," but this may be the error of a scribe who misread his text or wished to magnify that monarch's dominions. At least it must have been of some account then, but it does not enter history until Mark Antony thought it rich enough to plunder.

Photo by F. M. Good

already called. Partly by marriage and business connexion with Beduin chiefs along the caravan roads, and partly by successful, quiet desert campaigns and enlistments of Saracen fighting-men, they were the practical, secret masters of the larger part of Arabia. By way of preparing for battle, the elder son of the assassinated chief of the city took over the leadership of the urban militia and the conduct of affairs. The younger son, named Odenathus, after his father, went into the desert, and trained the Beduin cavalry and spearmen. But his supreme stroke of military policy was his love marriage with a wonderfully beautiful Saracen girl, Bath-Zabbai, daughter of Zabbai, a sheikh of the Beni-Samayda tribe, who had a Greek wife, claiming direct descent from Cleopatra of Egypt. Zabbai quickly rose, with the influence of his son-in-law, to the rank of an army commander at Palmyra, and with another Arab as commander-in-chief, drew the horsemen of the northern wastes into tents round the city.

Meanwhile, the extraordinary power of the city, as a balance between two hostile empires, was suddenly restored in A.D. 241 by the resurrection of Persia, under a fanatic line of Sassanian monarchs, whose armies swept through Mesopotamia and advanced on Antioch. When Syria was overrun, Palmyra was in extreme peril, but, as in similar circumstances in Parthian invasions, the city, confident in the strength of fortifications extending to the Euphrates, and in the natural defences of the desert, drew profit out of danger. She prolonged her influence along the border of Palestine, reaching past the wheat granary of the Hauran, and taking control of the middle trade route running from the desert towards Nazareth and Akka. Complete mistress of the commerce between the Eastern and Western civilizations, and with Arabia in her service, she produced in her Beduin Queen, Bath-Zabbai, now better known by her Romanised name, Zenobia, the herald of Mahomet and his world-conquering Caliphs.

The husband of this extraordinary woman of genius opened the diplomatic game with Rome and Persia. When the Emperor Valerian, recognizing that the work of Severus was undone, visited Palmyra in order to win its free and friendly cooperation in his campaign against the Persians, Odenathus the younger played the part of a grateful client. Apparently forgetting what the Romans had done to his father, he accepted the dignity of a consulship, and Valerian with his legions crossed the Euphrates, and in A.D. 260 met the host of Sapor of Persia. Then ensued a disaster under which the Mediterranean world rocked to its foundations. The Emperor of Rome was taken prisoner, and his skin, stuffed with straw, was preserved as a trophy in the Zoroastrian temple. Antioch was stormed and sacked, and city after city opened their gates to the barbaric victor.

Odenathus sent Sapor rich gifts and a letter of congratulation, in the hope of saving Palmyra. But his city was the key position on the old Persian line of march to Palestine and Egypt, and Sapor wanted more than gifts from him. "Who is this Odenathus that thus presumes insolently to write to his master?" said the Persian. "Let him, with hands bound behind him, prostrate himself before our throne! Otherwise swift destruction shall be poured upon him, his people, and his land."

Checked in Cilicia, Sapor angrily turned to make good his threat and lay waste Palmyra. Then it was that Zenobia flamed out over a world of men at war, and, as the greatest warrior woman in history, made her menaced city the home of an immortal romance. As wife of the Palmyrene chief and daughter of his Saracen commander, Zenobia, by her beauty and prestige, exercised an inspiring influence over the wild Beduin army encamped by the city walls. Sweeping out on horseback from the palace by the Grand Colonnade, she began to conduct reviews and, with the aid of her father and kinsmen, learnt to manage manoeuvres. The Arab horsemen had not then met a great disciplined army, and they had to be taught how to act flexibly and steadily together in mass. In training them Zenobia trained herself into a commanding genius for war.

This is no mere romantic view of the Lady of Palmyra, but the contemporary, considered judgement of the best soldier of her age—Aurelian, the saviour of Rome, who had good reason for studying the career of Zenobia, and wrote out his admiring view of her for the enlightenment of the Roman Senate. Odenathus, with his subtle talent for political strategy, was the best partner for the genius of Zenobia. Still playing the part of a Roman consul, he collected remnants of the legions that Sapor had shattered, reorganized them, and brought them into the Palmyrene service. Then under the personal direction of Zenobia, the Arab cavalry, the Palmyrene heavy horse and armour-clad infantry, with the Roman forces, made

PALMYRENE STONEWORK BUILT INTO THE WALL OF A MOSQUE

After its capture by Aurelian, robbed of its queen and its trade routes, the glory of Palmyra was gone. First the seat of a Roman garrison, refortified under Diocletian, almost deserted at times, and later repaired by Justinian, it enjoyed a brief rebirth of prosperity before finally succumbing to the forces of Islam, when its stones were hurled asunder and its temples used as forts. Here we see some beautiful specimens of carved stonework built wholesale into the wall of a mosque.

Photo by F. M. Good

GRAND TRIUMPHAL ARCH AND TEMPLE OF MALAK-BEL, THE SUN GOD, PALMYRA

Looking at its still impressive pile through the ruins of the Triumphal Arch, one cannot wonder that Aurelian, Emperor of Rome, spent three hundred pounds' weight of gold and eighteen hundred pounds' weight of silver to repair the Temple of the Sun, after the damage done by his soldiers at the sack of Palmyra. Covering over fourteen acres, with its circuit of more than a mile, its court of 374 columns 70 feet high, its statues and pavements, and the beautiful carving of its central shrine, it must have formed a fitting frame for Zenobia when, bare-armed and helmeted, she went forth to review her troops after due sacrifice to Malak-Bel, or held her court upon the temple steps.

Photo by F. M. Good

538

**TRUNCATED STUMPS OF PALMYRA'S PECULIAR TOWER TOMBS**

All round the city of Palmyra, at the foot of the forbidding hills, stand these grim towers of mystery—some squat, some rising to a hundred feet or more, but all built roughly to the same plan. Here, in niches or " loculi " arranged about the walls of their storeyed chambers, and in some instances in extensive vaults beneath, the Palmyrenes deposited the embalmed remains of their dead. The two figures at the base will show the size.

Photo by F. M. Good

a rapid, secret march through the desert, and surprised the Persian army west of the Euphrates river. The Beduins were the spearhead of the attack. They broke clean through the enemy, in that characteristic Saracen charge that the world was to know well later. The Palmyrenes and Roman legionaries completed the rout. Sapor escaped with the loss of his treasures and spoils— and accompanied by his wives!

Zenobia did not pursue the defeated Persians over the river. Whether or not she had some of the blood of Cleopatra in her veins, the effect was the same. She had learned to speak both the Egyptian and the Greek languages. Greater in intellect than Cleopatra, and probably not less beautiful, she did not drift with events and look out for passing chances, but strongly swayed things to serve her power. The reason why she left Sapor in peace was that there was another Roman army she designed to break to her will. A Roman general in northern Syria had thrown off his allegiance to Rome, and set up as Emperor of the Middle East. As such he threatened Zenobia's supremacy. Playing still, under the skilful direction of Odenathus, the role of a faithful agent of Rome, Zenobia marched against the usurper, and took and executed the rebel leaders.

In recognition of these achievements, Odenathus was proclaimed Augustus by the Roman Senate, with the approbation of the Roman world. Then, as Emperor of the East, alongside Valerian's degenerate son, who was Emperor of the West, the husband of Zenobia raised Palmyra to a practical equality of power with Rome. The man, by his political talent, constructed an empire on the woman's soldierly genius. Zenobia's forces, under her father Zabbai and his friend Zabdas, drove the Goths from Asia Minor, defeated the Persians under the walls of Ctesiphon, and held the field from Armenia to Arabia. Unhappily, Odenathus was murdered by a nephew, whom he had punished for insubordination, and on his death, about the year 267, Zenobia ruled alone as Regent of the East, in the name of her elder son.

On one side of her was the Persia she had crippled ; on the other side Rome was apparently foundering, and her provinces dropping away, under rebel army leaders. Zenobia, an absolute monarch, had everything required for lasting success, save moderation. The appearance of a pretender in Egypt gave her the opportunity for which she had been waiting. Her colonial army of seventy thousand troops routed the Egyptian forces, and gave her the long-desired throne of her reputed ancestor—Cleopatra, with half the civilized world for her empire.

There have been women who inherited great dominions, but the Beduin's daughter who personally carved out for herself an absolute power, stretching from the Caucasus mountains to the Libyan desert, is without a peer in history. She far surpassed in actual achievement the myths of Semiramis. In the days of her supreme glory, life in Palmyra was the most romantic of pageants.

Helmeted, bare-armed, in a robe clasped by a diamond buckle, she would walk to the assemblies of her people, or march on foot for long distances with her troops, messing with her officers, who included many Persians she had won over.

She had the brown skin of the Saracen, with black eyes of glancing fire, full lips, pretty white teeth, and an expressive face. Her person was graceful in repose and winsome in movement, her voice clear and strong, and in stately addresses and familiar talk her brilliant mind could stoop to enchant a common soldier or enrapture a philosopher. In fact, Longinus, the neo-platonic thinker, was drawn by her grace and strength of intellect from Athens to Palmyra, and became her chief counsellor. And if Longinus wrote the treatise "On the Sublime," the best piece of ancient literary criticism extant may be said to reflect

WHERE THE DEAD PALMYRENES SLEPT IN TOMBS RESEMBLING THE HOUSES OF THE LIVING

A more distant view of some of the towers of Palmyra; the lofty tomb on the right was built for one Iamlichos and is dated A.D. 82. It was hoped that these remote burial-chambers would yield treasures of artistic or archæological interest, but in every case the hand of the despoiler had been before, and beyond a few broken statuettes and votive tablets, torn cerements, desecrated bodies, and piles of scattered bones, there is little to reward the explorer who would risk the ascent.

Photo by F. M. Good

## THE STONES ARE STANDING, BUT THE GREATNESS THEY COMMEMORATE HAS PASSED AWAY

Facing the Temple of the Sun at Palmyra was this Triumphal Arch, and from it there ran that colonnaded street of shady sidewalks and numerous statues which bisected the city and was its principal feature. Standing at the western end and looking down its fourfold ranks of columns, thronged with busy life, to the noble arch which bounded the vista, the old Palmyrene master of caravans must have been inspired with the same dreams of empire that urged his queen to disaster and her counsellor to death.

Photo by F. M. Good

the fine taste and generous range of appreciation of Zenobia's court.

Of her taste in architecture, the Grand Colonnade, the triple Arch of Triumph, and other majestic ruins in Palmyra still eloquently speak. To complete her portrait we must add that, amid all the dazzling magnificence in which she lived, she had the good housewife's passion for thrift. She usually walked or rode on horseback rather than go to the expense of a chariot. There were few damsels in her palace, the work of the royal household being done by aged men.

She saved money, no doubt, because she looked to the final struggle for complete dominion. She had to reckon with Rome. For, unrestrained in ambition after the death of her husband, she stood forth as successor to the Persian in hostility to the Roman power. For some years, everything favoured her. She met the Roman Emperor Gallienus in battle and scattered his army, and took, as usual, some of its remnants into her service. Rome, however, was not so decisively enfeebled as to submit to a masterful alien woman; the army officers killed Gallienus, and started a strong movement of reform, and raised to supreme power a foreign farm labourer—Aurelian—who was to prove a match in strategy for the daughter of the Beduin sheikh. After settling affairs in Europe, Aurelian marched through Asia Minor, and arrayed his forces for battle by Antioch in the early part of A.D. 272.

For more than twenty years Zenobia had been accustomed to break Roman legions by shock cavalry tactics. At the head of her troops, she launched her Saracen horse. As usual they scattered the Roman horse, but, unexpectedly, found no infantry immediately behind them. Aurelian had placed his foot soldiers behind the Orontes, and he did not bring them forward until the Arab cavalry was worn out by chasing the light Roman horse. So Zenobia, through over-confidence, met her first defeat. Collecting her forces, she stood again to battle higher up the Orontes. Again her Arab horsemen were irresistible, but her medley of foot could not sustain the attack of the re-organized Roman legionaries. With

fragments of her beaten army, the Empress retreated to Palmyra, and there stood a long siege, meanwhile doing her best to negotiate a fighting alliance with Persia.

Here let Aurelian himself speak, in his letters to the Senate of Rome :

The Romans tell me that I am waging war against a woman, as though Zenobia were contending against me by her own strength alone, and not with that of a host of foes. I cannot describe to you how many engines of war she has. There is no part of her ramparts which is not furnished with two or three ballistas. Tormenting fire is poured down upon us. . . . My accusers would not know how to praise me enough, if they knew this woman—if they knew her prudence in council, her firmness of purpose, the dignity with which she directs her army, her munificence when need requires it, her severity when it is just to be severe. I must remark that the victory of Odenathus over the Persians, the flight of Sapor, the march to Ctesiphon, were her work. I can assert that such was the dread of this woman among Orientals and Egyptians, that she held in check Arabians, Saracens, and Armenians.

Daring to the last, the Empress arranged all the details of the defence of her capital and, leaving Zabdas in command, rode out at night on a she-camel. With a few companions, she passed the Roman lines, and in five days reached the Euphrates. Her design was to bring a relieving army from Persia. But as she entered a boat to cross the river, some Roman cavalry galloped up and seized her. In consternation the Palmyrenes at once surrendered, Aurelian returned to Rome, and Zenobia, bound in golden chains, graced his triumph ; but hearing that Palmyra had been utterly destroyed by her conqueror, she refused all food and is said to have died of starvation.

Her two sons, however, seem to have married into the Roman aristocracy, and a century after Palmyra had been laid in ruin, like another Carthage, and her children, women, and men slaughtered, some of Zenobia's offspring were senators of decadent Rome. Her own race still remembers her, and amid the stately ruins of her city they relate traditional details of her life that no historian has yet fully gathered. In due time the Saracens avenged her, and the chasm they succeeded in making in the civilization of the Mediterranean is still unbridged.

A COIN OF ZENOBIA
(Enlarged)

# The Great Pyramid

## By Margaret A. Murray, D.Lit.

Asst. Professor of Egyptology at University College, London

*IN pages 453-462 Professor Peet has told, with much instructive detail in a little space, the story of the pyramids of Egypt without special reference to the Great Pyramid, the chapter here given having been reserved to form one of our series on The Seven Wonders. Among the illustrations accompanying Professor Peet's contribution are several that show the Great Pyramid in various aspects. The two chapters should be studied in conjunction.—*EDITOR.

OF all the Seven Wonders that astonished the ancient world the Great Pyramid not only survives to modern times but still retains its hold upon the popular imagination. It is one of the few structures from the distant past that have defied the ravages of time and the still more destructive ravages of man. The chief damage that it has sustained is the stripping off of the outer casing, which was intact only five hundred years ago ; it was torn off by the rulers of medieval Egypt, partly in a wild hunt for concealed treasure, partly as a convenient quarry from which to obtain worked stones. Yet the amount of stone removed was comparatively small, and the Great Pyramid still stands firm and solid as the rock on which it is founded, vying with the everlasting hills in grandeur and immutability. Seen by moonlght or in the clear air of the dawn, in the rosy glow of the sunset, in the fierce glare of a summer noontide, or rising like a lofty mountain above the morning mists of the valley, the Great Pyramid dominates the landscape and fires the imagination.

The master mind that conceived the idea of this huge structure

**KHUFU, BUILDER OF THE GREAT PYRAMID**

King Khufu, or Cheops, the fourth-dynasty monarch who made his name famous for all time as the builder of the Great Pyramid at Gizeh, is also perpetuated by this inimitable ivory carving.

*Photo, Egypt Exploration Society*

reigned over Egypt for more than sixty years, and was known to his people as Khufu, to the Greeks in later days as Cheops. Herodotus tells us that he was " a most flagitious tyrant, he shut up all the temples and forbade the sacrifices." Herodotus had obviously received his information from the priests, to whom Khufu's action would, of course, have appeared iniquitous, but read in the light of the later history of Egypt it is evident that we have here one of the many episodes in that long struggle for power between the king and the priesthood which continued throughout the whole historic period until the Persian conquest put an end to it. The idea that the Great Pyramid was built by slave labour is probably false. During the three months of the inundation the whole land was under water and no agricultural work could be done ; the Pharaoh then set the labourers to large public works, and during that period they were fed and housed. The Great Pyramid may therefore be regarded as the monument, not of a tyrant, but of a wise and beneficent ruler who saved his people in the dread days of scarcity.

NORTH FACE AND ENTRANCE OF THE MOST ROYAL TOMB EVER PLANNED BY HUMAN ARCHITECT

Has ever man conceived such a tomb for himself as the mightiest of Egypt's early dynasts ? Kings and dynasties there had been in Egypt before, but Khufu was the first to give imperial prestige to the land whose divided wealth and resources had been welded by his predecessors into a conquering power ; pyramids there had been before, but never before or since the days of King Khufu has a pyramid been planned or constructed so immense as this, the Great Pyramid at Gizeh that after ages were to hail as one of the world's Seven Wonders. Long since rifled of the poor body it housed, it stands on a rocky platform west of the Nile, not far from Memphis, ancient seat of the king who built it

Photo by Donald McLeish

544

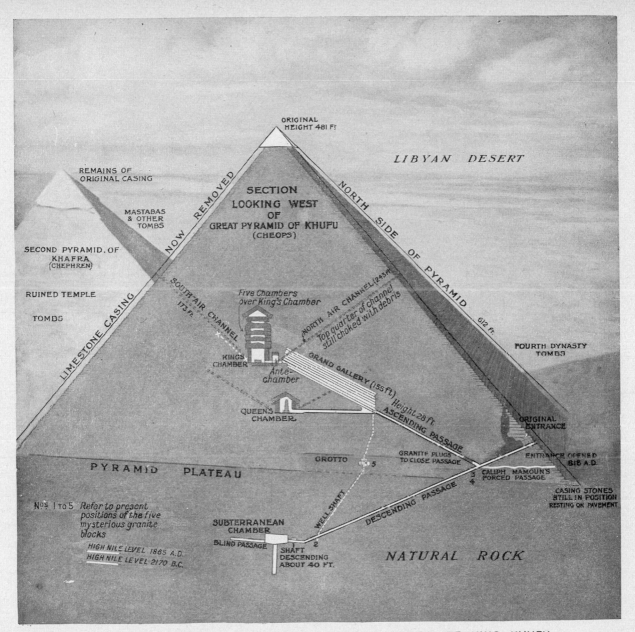

ORIGINAL
HEIGHT 481 Ft

*LIBYAN DESERT*

SECTION
LOOKING WEST
OF
GREAT PYRAMID OF KHUFU
(CHEOPS)

REMAINS OF
ORIGINAL CASING

MASTABAS
& OTHER
TOMBS

SECOND PYRAMID. OF
KHAFRA
(CHEPHREN)

RUINED TEMPLE

TOMBS

NOW REMOVED

NORTH SIDE OF PYRAMID

612 Ft.

LIMESTONE CASING

SOUTH AIR CHANNEL
175 ft.

NORTH AIR CHANNEL (245 ft)
Top quarter of channel
still choked with debris

*Five Chambers
over King's Chamber*

KINGS
CHAMBER

*Ante-
chamber*

GRAND GALLERY (155 ft)
Height 28 ft

ASCENDING PASSAGE

QUEEN'S
CHAMBER

FOURTH DYNASTY
TOMBS

ORIGINAL
ENTRANCE

PYRAMID PLATEAU

GROTTO

5

GRANITE PLUGS
TO CLOSE PASSAGE

WELL SHAFT

DESCENDING PASSAGE

3
4

CALIPH MAMOUN'S
FORCED PASSAGE

ENTRANCE OPENED
818 A.D.

CASING STONES
STILL IN POSITION
RESTING ON PAVEMENT

Nos 1 to 5 *Refer to present
positions of the five
mysterious granite
blocks*

HIGH NILE LEVEL 1865 A.D.
HIGH NILE LEVEL 2170 B.C.

SUBTERRANEAN
CHAMBER

BLIND PASSAGE

2

SHAFT
DESCENDING
ABOUT 40 FT.

*NATURAL ROCK*

UNIQUE CHAMBERS AND GALLERIES OF THE PYRAMID OF KING KHUFU

The pyramid that King Khufu built to be his sepulchre 5,000 years ago is notable not only for exceeding all its kind in size, but by reason also of its internal structure. It is calculated to contain at present 85,000,000 cubic feet of masonry as against the 60,000,000 of the Second Pyramid; but, apart from this, it differs in having two chambers built in its very heart as well as the normal subterranean one. Compare this section with those of the Second and Third Pyramids in page 454. The numbers here refer to the position of five strange isolated blocks, unique in being completely pierced with drill-holes; their purpose or original location is unknown.

**The** ancient Egyptian name of the Great Pyramid is Yakhet-Khufu, "Horizon (i.e., burial-place) of Khufu." The name shows that this gigantic bulk of masonry was actually erected as a tomb, the only other evidence being the sarcophagus in the so-called "King's Chamber."

The entrance to the pyramid is on the north face, from which a sloping passage descends, partly through the masonry and partly through the rock, to an underground chamber. This passage offers a clear and uninterrupted view of the northern sky, a fact which has given rise to the belief that the Great Pyramid was built for astronomical observations. The underground chamber was probably intended to be the burial vault, but it was never finished, and the resting place of the mightiest of Pharaohs is unknown.

About 63 feet from the entrance another passage leads upwards in the mass of the pyramid, and at the junction of the ascending and descending passages is the end of a plunderer's tunnel. The plunderer in this case was no less a person than

RUGGED STEEPS OF THE GREAT PYRAMID AS IT IS TO-DAY

In its pristine finished state the Great Pyramid was encased in an outer skin of polished limestone, the whole of which has been stripped off within the last 500 years with the exception of a few stones still in position on the pavement at the north-east angle. As shown in the drawing on the opposite page, this outer casing was adjusted upon a surface of partly dressed stones, forming a giant stairway up which travellers can ascend to the summit with the assistance of stalwart Arabs.

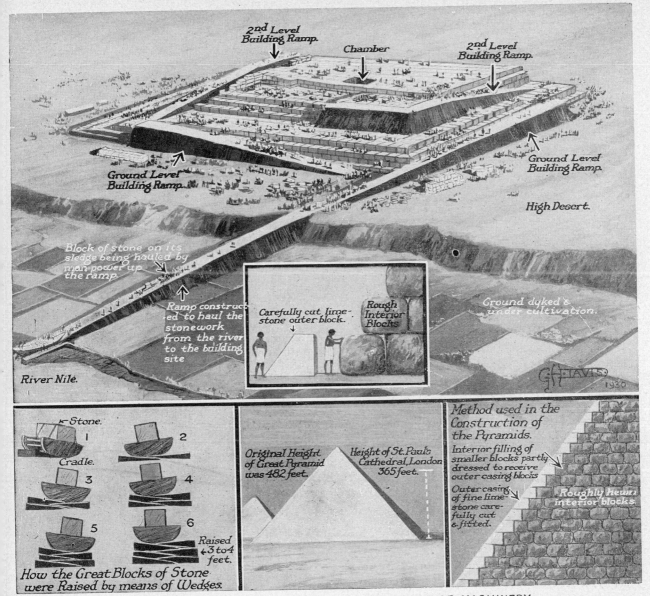

Labels on the illustration:

2nd Level Building Ramp.

Chamber

2nd Level Building Ramp.

Ground Level Building Ramp.

Ground Level Building Ramp.

High Desert.

Block of stone on its sledge being hauled by man power up the ramp

Ramp constructed to haul the stonework from the river to the building site

Carefully cut limestone outer block.

Rough Interior Blocks

Ground dyked & under cultivation.

River Nile.

Stone.

Cradle.

1 2 3 4 5 6

Raised 3 to 4 feet.

How the Great Blocks of Stone were Raised by means of Wedges.

Original Height of Great Pyramid was 482 feet.

Height of St. Paul's Cathedral, London 365 feet.

Method used in the Construction of the Pyramids.

Interior filling of smaller blocks partly dressed to receive outer casing blocks

Outer casing of fine limestone carefully cut & fitted.

Roughly Hewn Interior blocks.

## HOW THE PYRAMID WAS BUILT WITHOUT THE AID OF MACHINERY

How stupendous was the task of building the Great Pyramid may be dimly realized when it is remembered that nothing of the nature of cranes, pulleys or mechanical tackle was invented in that remote period. Every stone used in its construction—and they are computed to number 2,300,000, averaging in weight 2½ tons each—had to be hauled by man-power over prepared ramps to its destined level and lifted into position by wedges. After the site was prepared the actual building is credibly said to have occupied 100,000 men for twenty years.

the Khalif Mamoun, a medieval ruler of Egypt, who had heard the tradition that the pyramid was a storehouse of hidden treasure. Stories of life-sized cocks made of gold and precious stones, of ewers cut from a single emerald, of coined gold lying in heaps, so inflamed his desires that he spent an enormous fortune in breaking into the solid structure, to find nothing more than an empty sarcophagus without even a lid.

To prevent access into the upper chambers the ascending passage was plugged up with blocks of granite, which formed an impenetrable barrier. But it is evident that the builders did not intend the structure to be entirely closed, for the true

entrance to the pyramid was by a turning stone which Strabo says gave at once on to the descending passage. It is probable that the door fitted so closely that it was indistinguishable on the outside from the other stones, and it is also probable that the secret of it was known only to the priests of the pyramid.

The ascending passage increases suddenly in width and height, and becomes the Grand Gallery. The stone floor has a ramp on each side; and the centre portion, up which the breathless visitor painfully climbs, is scored across with deep horizontal grooves; these were probably made to facilitate the moving of the granite sarcophagus.

**WITHIN THE GREAT PYRAMID**

This is a view looking up the Grand Gallery. On either side are visible the raised ramps that border the passage, while the deep grooves in the floor were probably intended to help the haulage of the huge granite sarcophagus found in the " King's Chamber."

Photo, Underwood Press Service

the King's Chamber, which would otherwise have been crushed by the superincumbent mass. In the two uppermost of the five chambers the two names of Khufu are written in red paint on the blocks ; this was done by the quarrymen of long ago when they hewed the stone out of the quarries of Turrah, marking each block with the king's name and the place where it should be set. These are the only inscriptions found in or on the pyramid, though Herodotus says that there was an inscription on one of the outer faces ; and 'Abd El-Latîf, who was more than a thousand years later than Herodotus, also mentions inscriptions on the outer casing.

Where the ascending passage enters the Grand Gallery a horizontal passage leads southward to the " Queen's Chamber." This is also an unfinished part, for though the roof and walls are of the finest ashlar masonry the floor is quite untouched and rough. The names of the two principal rooms in the pyramid, the King's Chamber and the Queen's Chamber, were given by the Arabs in modern times, probably because of their likeness to the burial niches of the Moslems, the ceiling of a man's being flat, of a woman's pointed. From both chambers two airshafts lead out to the surface of the pyramid ; they were to bring in air to the workmen ; when the work was finished and the airshafts no longer required, the outer casing of the pyramid effectively blocked the apertures.

At the junction of the ascending and horizontal passages a well-shaft was sunk through the masonry and the rock down to the descending passage near the underground chamber.

The ascent of the pyramid is an event to be remembered, but to most a visit to the interior is even more impressive. The black impenetrable darkness ; the utter stillness ; the feeling that above and around and below are solid masses of stone reared by hands long dead ; the knowledge that one of the mightiest of the mighty trod those floors and hoped to rest for ever within the structure ; all combine to make the Great Pyramid one of the most mysterious and solemn of all the ancient buildings in the valley of the Nile.

The Grand Gallery ends as suddenly as it began in a short, horizontal passage which leads through an ante-chamber into the so-called King's Chamber. The reason for making this chamber is still a problem ; it contains a sarcophagus, but the actual burial place was below the ground. It does not stand in the middle of the pyramid ; it is not in line with the diagonals, and it is not vertically under the apex ; the reason of the asymmetry is not known. The sarcophagus, carved from a solid block of granite, is 7 feet 6 inches long, 3 feet 3 inches wide, and 3 feet 4 inches high. It has been cut to hold a lid, but it is possible that the lid was never brought into the pyramid. When struck the sarcophagus gives out a note sounding like the tolling of a knell.

Vertically in line above the King's Chamber are five little chambers ; they are thought to be placed there to relieve the weight of stone over

# The Wonder of the Mummy

By G. Elliot Smith, M.A., M.D., Litt.D., F.R.S.

Professor of Anatomy, University of London

THE ancient Egyptian practice of preserving the bodies of the dead has excited the wonder of mankind for many ages. It has aroused the curiosity of those who have visited or read about Egypt ever since the time of Herodotus, the first tourist to put on record his impressions of Egypt and its strange customs almost twenty-four centuries ago. For nothing excited his amazement more than the information he gathered with reference to mummies and the methods of the embalmer's art.

It is, however, with feelings other than those of mere curiosity that we must contemplate the practice of an art which has made it possible for us to gaze upon the actual faces of the men and women who dominated the civilized world thirty centuries and more ago. But the study of this strange practice reveals much more wonderful results than the sentimental interest of seeing these mighty rulers of antiquity and experiencing the feeling of the reality of ancient history. For the invention of embalming was very intimately connected with the development of the essential arts and crafts of civilization and of many of man's deepest beliefs. It was also responsible for creating the literary symbols that give expression to such aspirations as " this corruptible shall put on incorruption and this mortal shall put on immortality." Among the ancient Egyptians the first glimmering of the idea of immortality was suggested by the possibility of rendering the corpse incorruptible ; and in their case the logical sequence suggested in the Christian burial service of to-day was something more than a mere verbal analogy.

The carpenter's craft was originally devised for the purpose of making coffins for the dead, and it was intimately related to the invention of mummification in Egypt. The art of working stone, not merely making rock-cut chambers, but also shaping stone for building, was also prompted by the same desire ; and it is no exaggeration to say that the craft of the stonemason and the art of architecture are both due to the attempt to preserve and protect the bodies of the dead more effectually. So also portrait statuary developed from the need to preserve an image of the dead when it was realized that the mummy itself lost its semblance to the deceased as he was during life.

The wonder of mummification thus depends not only on its sentimental appeal, but on the part it played in originating several of the most essential elements of civilization and shaping the nascent beliefs of mankind for all time. But apart from all these admittedly serious claims upon

SARCOPHAGUS OF IUAA, FATHER OF QUEEN TIYI

Made of a coarse-grained wood, covered with pitch, and ornamented with figures and hieroglyphs in stucco-gilt, the sarcophagus contained three separate nested coffins. The inscriptions record Iuaa's various titles and include prayers to the gods of the West on behalf of the deceased, who was husband of Tuaa and father of Tiyi, the queen of Amenhotep III.

Museum of Egyptian Antiquities, Cairo

RICHLY DECORATED COFFINS CONTAINED IN THE SARCOPHAGUS OF IUAA

All the coffins are mummiform in shape. 1. Outer coffin, covered with pitch and ornamented in stucco-gilt; face and hands gilt; hair represented by black and gold stripes; eyebrows and lashes of dark blue glass, iris of black obsidian, and whites of white marble; broad necklace of gold. 2. Second coffin, coated with stucco and gold and silver foil and richly inlaid with glass of various colours; face of gilt; hands of gold foil; below the vulture, with outstretched wings, the goddess Nut is represented standing. 3. Inner coffin, specially notable for the exquisite modelling of the face; here also, below the vulture with outstretched wings, is a standing figure of Nut in low relief.

Museum of Egyptian Antiquities, Cairo

the attention of the historians of art and belief, the practice of embalming is such a bizarre and gruesome business that it is a question of psychological interest and wonder to discover how mankind was impelled to resort to such a repellent custom. Great as is the dislike which the modern European experiences at the mere thought of cutting, or in any way mutilating a dead body, although long centuries of practice of the anatomist's art should have familiarised him with the idea and reconciled him to its usefulness and necessity, it is difficult for us to realize the intensity of the feelings with which a people like the ancient Egyptians must have regarded such desecration. For they did not attempt to preserve the bodies of their dead by artificial means until they had acquired the most profound respect for, almost approaching to worship of, the corpse, and the most intense loathing of any such mutilations as

are unavoidable in the practice of embalming. Yet, paradoxical though it may seem, it was precisely these ideas of the importance and sanctity of the dead that impelled the Egyptians to try to preserve the body and to persist in their attempts to attain this aim in spite of all the gruesome and disgusting results incidental to the experimental stages of the invention of so strange a custom.

Insistence has been made upon these aspects of the practice of embalming to impress upon the reader's mind the fact that mummification is a very strange and fantastic procedure, and that the attainment of any success in the practice involved many years of gruesome experimentation. It took the Egyptians two millennia to attain any measure of real success in the art, even though in Egypt conditions are perhaps more favourable than in any other land. Hence when we find scattered throughout the world arbitrary methods of preserving the dead which reproduce the procedures devised by the Egyptians only after centuries of persistent effort it is altogether unreasonable to pretend that the people in outlying parts of the world who practise these distinctively Egyptian devices did not acquire them either directly or indirectly from Egypt.

Thus another wonder of the study of mummies is the irrefutable demonstration they afford of the diffusion of elements of ancient civilization from Egypt to various localities in Africa and Europe, Asia and Oceania, until early in the Christian era they reached Peru and Central America, as well as the North-West Coast.

But before considering this world-wide spread of the custom of embalming let us consider how this wonderful procedure came to be invented in Egypt, and how it underwent an unbroken series of changes in technique during the thirty-five (or perhaps forty) centuries of its practice there.

In discussing problems relating to ancient Egypt it is not an easy matter for most people to form any precise conception of the remoteness of the period in time with which we have to deal. The mere enumeration of thousands of years fails to convey any definite idea to those who are accustomed to reckon things in the past by events rather than by the use of arithmetical figures.

MUMMIFORM COFFIN FOUND AT ABYDOS

In Abydos, an ancient centre of Osiris worship, it was the dearest wish of every pious Egyptian to be buried, or even to have his mummy placed temporarily. The necropolis vaults and their contents have suffered much from robber hands, but the mummy shown above, apparently of the Ptolemaic period, was found intact in its mummiform coffin.

From "The Cemeteries of Abydos II.," by T. Eric Peet

Most of us have been taught to look upon the time of the Norman Conquest as a very remote period, and to regard the Roman invasion of Britain as having occurred almost at the dawn of history. Yet at the time of Julius Caesar the practices which we are about to study had reached in Egypt almost the last stage of their decadence after having enjoyed—to our certain knowledge—a vogue for a span of time considerably longer than, perhaps nearly twice as long as, that which separates Caesar's time from ours. This carries us back to a period compared with which that of Homer seems quite recent. It was many centuries earlier than the time when the Pentateuch was put into writing or before "Joseph commanded his servants the physicians to embalm his father Jacob." But to get any clear idea of the factors that brought about the invention of embalming we have to add to this long span yet another series of years as great as that which separates the date of William the Conqueror's landing at Hastings from our time!

Even at that remote

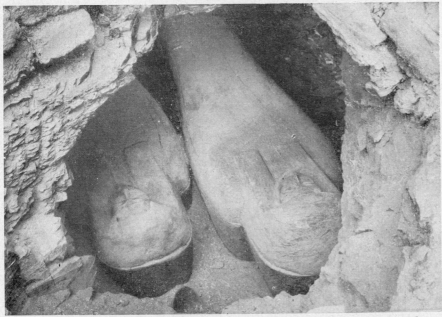

MUMMIFORM COFFINS HIDDEN FOR MORE THAN 2,000 YEARS

Two "anthropoid," or mummiform coffins containing mummies of the twenty-fifth dynasty (712-663 B.C.), discovered near Deir el-Bahri, in a rock-cut tomb where they had been hidden so successfully that they were only revealed by the modern excavator seeking all things likely to throw light on the life and customs of the distant past.

By courtesy of the Metropolitan Museum of Art, New York

period, roughly sixty centuries ago, the Egyptians were building up the earliest real civilization. They had devised the practice of agriculture and the methods of irrigation. They had domesticated cattle and used milk as food with the barley they cultivated. They had learned to fashion pottery of a simple grace and elegance of form that has never been surpassed, and they had attained a remarkable degree of skill in working flint and the hardest stoneware in a manner that bears ample testimony to their technical skill and to their possession of the moral qualities of patience and restraint. They were already acquainted with gold, and had conferred upon the relatively useless yellow metal the arbitrary value that has made it so potent an instrument of good and evil ever since. They knew, also, how to weave linen.

Custom had already imposed on this population a regular and orderly mode of burying their dead in

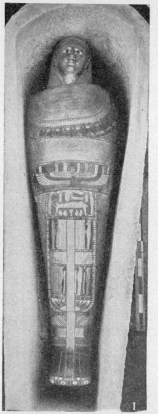

definite cemeteries, in a position and with a geographical orientation strictly defined by convention, along with a set of objects which the deceased had treasured in this life or his relations believed he might need in the next.

It was this custom of burying valuables with their dead which led indirectly to the acquisition of the knowledge which suggested the idea and demonstrated the possibility of the artificial preservation which we call mummification. The earliest Egyptians at present known to us had already commenced those nefarious practices which have been continued by their successors ever since then—I refer to the plundering of the graves of their contemporaries, and, in later times, of their predecessors also. When powerful Pharaohs like Rameses the Great, whose acts were accomplished in the glare of the publicity that illumines a throne, dared to mutilate his own father's monuments, merely to

EXAMPLES OF AN ART THAT WAS PRACTISED IN EGYPT FOR AT LEAST 4,000 YEARS

1. Cartonnage case of an unknown Egyptian priestess of the Ptolemaic period.   2. Coffin and mummy of an unnamed princess ; the mummy is not now in the coffin.   3. Mummies of Greek children from the Fayyum, A.D. 200. That on the left is prepared with bitumen, and head and shoulders are covered with a gilded cartonnage, and the child is holding a bunch of red flowers in the left hand.

their history, from the most remote times until the present day, the inhabitants of Egypt and Nubia freely indulged in such easy methods of enriching themselves, in defiance of their belief in the sanctity of the remains of their dead.

Thus it happens that a considerable proportion of graves, even of the earliest known predynastic period, are found to have been desecrated and their contents damaged to a greater or less extent ; and in many of these there is unmistakable evidence to show that the robberies were committed by contemporaries of the deceased—that is, by people who knew whether the graves contained the bodies of rich or poor, men or women.

This practice of rifling graves had very important consequences. For it made even the earliest

**MUMMY-WRAPPINGS OF THE ROMAN AGE**
The wrapping of mummies was carried out with the minutest care, and was an art in itself, especially when we realize that all these interwoven bandagings were kept in place without the aid of fastenings or adhesive material of any kind whatsoever.
From "Roman Portraits and Memphis (IV.)," by W. M. Flinders Petrie

attain a greater fame or notoriety, and others, like Akhnaton, who desecrated even his royal father's tomb out of spite against his religious professions, or, rather, the better to emphasise his devotion to a new religion, is it to be wondered at that the common people should have satisfied their more insistent desires and obtained useful and valuable objects from the graves of their contemporaries, when they could do so in secrecy and without running any of the risks that attended the royal vandalism ?

However strong a restraining influence their religious beliefs may have exercised against the committal of such acts of desecration, we have the most positive and conclusive evidence that the temptation of the immediate gains that might accrue from grave-plundering often proved too strong for these people ; and at every period in

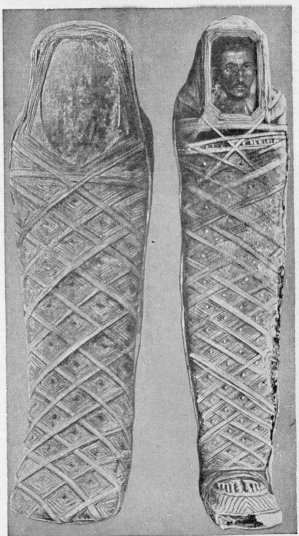

**STILL MORE ELABORATE WRAPPINGS**
Two other styles of wrapping are here shown ; in both examples the bandages form rhombus patterns, but in the one on the left each cavity has a square of gold-foil at the bottom, while in the other case these squares are replaced by gilded stucco buttons.
From "Roman Portraits and Memphis (IV.)," by W. M. Flinders Petrie

Egyptians aware of the fact that the bodies of their dead did not always suffer corruption when placed in the ground, but were often preserved in an imperishable form. The hot, dry sands desiccated the bodies in many cases so that the skin and flesh, the hair, and even the eyes, were completely preserved. The discovery of this phenomenon, no doubt, set these people wondering whether the survival of the bodies of the dead did not also mean a prolongation of their existence. Perhaps it prompted them to provide them with food and raiment and all the other things needed in their daily " life " and enjoyment.

As the belief in the reality of this prolongation of existence developed, and ampler supplies of food and equipment were made, the tomb had to be made larger until eventually it became a suite of large rooms in one of which the corpse was lodged in a coffin of wood, stone, or pottery. But it soon came to be realized that these ampler provisions for the welfare of the dead defeated the very object which had prompted them. For in the large tombs the body was no longer preserved as it often was when placed in contact with the hot, dry sand in the simple grave. But the importance of such preservation had become so insistent that (somewhere about the time of the first dynasty, 3400 B.C.) attempts were made artificially to preserve the body, using common salt, perhaps also crude natron, and various resins for the purpose. The trees that provided these resins which could preserve the body, and so, as the Egyptians believed, prolong existence, were regarded as life-giving, i.e., divine, and identified with the god Osiris, the prolonger of existence.

The fundamental aim of mummification in Egypt throughout more than thirty centuries of its practice was to secure for the dead the same fate as tradition had accorded Osiris, and to enable them to be identified with the god who had attained the boon of immortality. This conception shaped the whole ritual of embalment and the funerary ceremonies.

The earliest actual mummy known to exist at the present time is in the Museum of the Royal College of Surgeons, in Lincoln's Inn Fields. It was found in 1892 near the Pyramid of Medum, by Professor Flinders Petrie, who assigns it to the time of Sneferu (third or fourth dynasty). Although the identity of the tomb from which it came is not quite certain, and there is some doubt as to the time in which it was embalmed, it can be referred with certainty to the Pyramid Age. The only question concerning its age that is still in dispute is whether it should be assigned to the period of the fourth dynasty (2900 to 2750 B.C.), when the Great Pyramids were built, or to the

fifth (2750 to 2625 B.C.). Judging from the technical procedures adopted in wrapping and treating the body (in comparison with the data collected by Professors George A. Reisner and Junker at the necropolis of the Gizeh Pyramids), it is more probable that it belongs to the time of the fifth dynasty.

But although the Medum specimen is the earliest actual mummy, definite indications of attempts at mummification have been found (the specimen brought to light by Mr. J. E. Quibell, at Sakkara, in December, 1911, is now in the Museum of the Royal College of Surgeons, London) as early as the second dynasty (c. 3,000 B.C.), and on theoretical grounds it is probable that experiments in embalming were made at the time of the first dynasty (3400 B.C.), or even earlier.

In the Sakkara specimen the body was swathed in a large series of bandages, which were so moulded as to retain the shape, particular attention being devoted to the restoration of the face and head. Although it would be erroneous to call this mass of linen and the skeleton enclosed within it a mummy, the corrosion of the innermost bandages (those originally in contact with the skin) indicates that some attempt had probably been made to embalm the body. But in the Medum specimen, which is actually a mummy, the superficial bandages are impregnated with a resinous paste, and the surface is skilfully modelled to reproduce the form of the corpse, special attention being given to the face, the details of the eyes and moustache being brought out by the use of green and brown paint. Inside this resinous carapace the body itself is well preserved. Although this specimen is unique Professor Junker found a series of bodies of the same age that had been subjected to somewhat analogous processes, stucco plaster being used instead of resinous paste. Sometimes the whole body was encased in this material, in other cases the head only was so enclosed.

The chief interest of these processes is the evidence they afford of the two aims of embalming : (a) to preserve the body, and (b) to make a lasting portrait of the deceased. At first the attempt was made to convert the wrapped mummy itself into a portrait statue, but when this was found to be impracticable a statue was made of stone, wood, or plaster (apart from the body), and painted to reproduce the lifelike appearance of the deceased. The ideas that inspired this new art are revealed by the words used by the Egyptians themselves to define their achievement. The sculptor was called " the vivifier," and the word for " to carve " was " to give birth," " to create," " to give life." The artist was, in fact, believed to have made " a living image," a reproduction

**FUNERARY CHAMBER WHERE EGYPTIAN MUMMIES AWAITED RESURRECTION**

No people have ever taken such elaborate means to preserve inviolate the bodies and personalities of their dead as did the Egyptians. The embalmed corpse was enclosed in several coffins sealed in an outer sarcophagus of stone, and this was walled up in a chamber excavated deep in some cliff and reached through a long tunnel. One of the latest of such vaults to be discovered, dating from Rameses the Great, is depicted here. It was excavated near Luxor, and the funerary chamber, richly sculptured by one Nefir-Rempit, contains several fine sarcophagi.

**FOOT-CASE OF AN EGYPTIAN MUMMY**
The feet of the Egyptian mummy, like the head, were frequently provided with a case on which they were modelled as though exposed. The modelling of the feet here illustrated (from a cemetery of the Graeco-Roman age at Hawara) is of peculiar accuracy and delicacy and shows the Egyptian method of tying sandals.
From "Roman Portraits and Memphis (IV.)," by W. M. Flinders Petrie

**MUMMY OF SETI I.**
The head of Seti I. second Pharaoh of the nineteenth dynasty, is wonderfully preserved, but the rest of the body has suffered grievously from the depredations of ancient tomb-robbers who tore the wrappings in search of loot.
Museum of Egyptian Antiquities, Cairo

New York). These are the earliest royal mummies so far recovered, having been embalmed about 2050 B.C.

In addition to this interesting fact two other circumstances render this series of mummies unique. The method of embalming revealed in the bodies of these queens differs from that of all other Egyptian mummies, although it was described more than sixteen centuries later by the Greek traveller Herodotus, and again later still by Diodorus, the Sicilian. Another interesting feature of these mummies is the fact that two were tattooed, and afford not only the earliest examples of this strange practice, but also the only ones that have come down from ancient Egypt.

Egyptian embalming attained its greatest success in the period represented by the eighteenth, nineteenth, twentieth, and twenty-first dynasties,

of the deceased that was so lifelike as to ensure the continuation of his existence. It gave him a fresh lease of life, a new birth ; it was, in very truth, a recreation of his existence.

The thousand years that followed the embalming of Ranefer have left us singularly little evidence of the practice of mummification. Several mummies of the Middle Kingdom (c. 2000 B.C.) have been found by Messrs. Garstang (at Benihasan), Quibell (at Sakkara), Lythgoe, Mace, and Winlock (at Lisht and Thebes). Most of these were in such a fragile condition that they could not be moved.

In the ruined pyramid of King Mentuhotep II., at Deir el-Bahri (Thebes), the mummies of six of the wives or concubines of this Pharaoh of the eleventh dynasty and a child have been found by officials of the Cairo Museum and by Professor Naville, Dr. H. R. Hall, and Mr. Herbert Winlock (working respectively under the auspices of the Egypt Exploration Fund, the British Museum, and the Metropolitan Museum of

**CLOSER VIEWS OF SETI IN THE AUSTERITY OF DEATH**
Death cannot blur the masterful delineations of character in the features of Seti I., and we can well understand how under such kings the power of Egypt reached its zenith in the nineteenth dynasty. He made a magnificent tomb in the Valley of the Tombs of the Kings at Thebes ; but his body was found in the cache at Deir er-Bahri, where it had been hidden for security.
Museum of Egyptian Antiquities. Cairo

mummies of the four Thothmes, Amenhotep II., Iuaa, and Tuaa, the parents of Queen Tiyi, are so well preserved that looking upon them we can form a very clear picture of these famous rulers as they were when alive. But in the nineteenth dynasty (1350–1205 B.C.) the famous Pharaohs Seti I., Rameses II., and Merenptah were even more successfully embalmed, for their mummies now reveal them to us in all their strength and dignity, as the weakness of many of their successors in the later part of the nineteenth and the twentieth dynasties is equally demonstrated.

Amid the disorganization of the closing years of the twentieth dynasty the weakness of the government left the royal necropolis in the

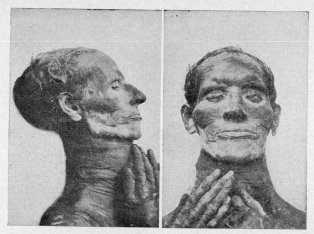

**MUMMY OF IUAA: PROFILE AND FULL FACE**

It was found in the tomb of Iuaa and Tuaa, in the Valley of the Tombs of the Kings, in 1905, enclosed in the sarcophagus and coffins illustrated in pages 549 and 550. The linen mummy straps were covered lavishly with stucco and gilt ornamentation.

Museum of Egyptian Antiquities, Cairo

from 1580 B.C. to 945 B.C. The expulsion of the Hyksos rulers was followed by the conquest of Palestine and Syria. From these countries, as well as from the Sudan, East Africa, and the incense country in Southern Arabia, to which the Egyptian sovereigns of the eighteenth and the succeeding dynasties sent expeditions, abundant supplies of resins, balsams, and wood were obtained which enabled the embalmers to carry the practice of their art to a higher pitch of success than was ever achieved in Egypt before or after this period. During the eighteenth dynasty especially the technique of mummification revealed rapid progress, and the

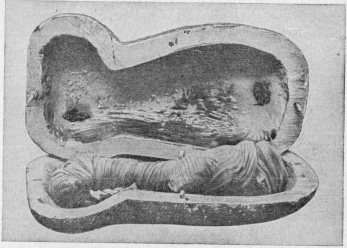

**MUMMIFIED JOINT IN A WOODEN CASE**

Joints mummified and in wooden cases were found by Mr. Theodore M. Davis when in 1905 he discovered the tomb of Iuaa and Tuaa on the west side of the Nile at Thebes. On this occasion Mr. Davis was accompanied by Mr. Arthur Weigall and Sir Gaston Maspero.

Museum of Egyptian Antiquities, Cairo

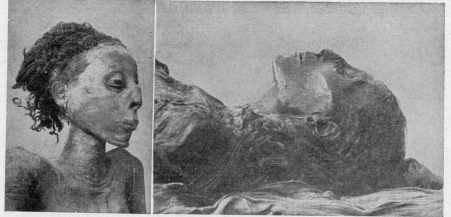

**THOTHMES IV. AND A GRUESOMELY LIFELIKE QUEEN**

Left, mummy of a queen of the twenty-second dynasty; right, mummy of Thothmes IV., a Pharaoh of the eighteenth dynasty. The mummy of the queen (c. 900 B.C.) shows how practices altered with time, as artificial eyes have been inserted and the contours of the face filled out by packing with mud beneath the skin.

Bibân-el-Mulûk at the mercy of grave-robbers. Hidden away in the recesses of the desolate Valley of the Tombs of the Kings was the vastest collection of gold and precious jewelry and furniture that was ever, perhaps, accumulated in one place until the United States of America acquired the world's gold. The discovery of the remarkable tomb of Tutankhamen has given us some idea of the lavishness with which royal tombs were equipped; and **if this youthful nonentity** could command such vast wealth at a time when the State was impoverished, our imagination fails to picture what must have been put into the tombs of such powerful emperors as Thothmes III., Amenhotep III., Seti I., and Rameses the Great, who could command the resources of the whole civilized world of their time.

The temptation of this vast accumulation of wealth hidden away in a deserted ravine led to the inevitable result when the civil power of Egypt became weakened in the twentieth dynasty, and robbery on a vast scale took place. Practically every royal tomb in the valley, with the single remarkable exception of Tutankhamen's, was not merely rifled but despoiled of all its gold and valuables. But before this wholesale plundering took place stealing on a smaller scale had been taking place. The men whose business it was to construct and furnish these rock-cut tombs had opportunities for rifling other tombs in the neighbourhood. Many records have been preserved from ancient times relating to the trials of men suspected of tomb-robbing in the Bibân-el-Mulúk, and in some cases giving the confessions of the

guilty men. But insufficient food and unhealthy working conditions often produced strikes among the necropolis workers, and no doubt such industrial disturbances were an important factor in impelling the strikers to plunder tombs. We have records of such strikes in the twenty-ninth year of Rameses III. (1164 B.C.) and in the reign of Rameses IX. (about 1130 B.C.). In the "Asiatic Review" of April, 1923 Mr. Warren R. Dawson collected all the available data with reference to these strikes and robberies in the Valley of the Tombs of the Kings—and a very interesting story it is.

When order was once more restored in Egypt attempts were made to repair the damaged mummies of the famous Pharaohs, and after many vicissitudes and, in some cases, a couple of centuries of repeated moving from one hiding-place to another, more than thirty of the kings' and queens' mummies found a resting-place for twenty-eight centuries in the famous cache at Deir-el-Bahri (where they were found in 1881), nine others in the tomb of Amenhotep II. (where they were found in 1898), and others elsewhere. The records of these events and the inspectors' reports are

MUMMY OF AMENHOTEP II., WHO DIED ABOUT 1420 B.C.

When the tomb of Amenhotep II. was discovered in 1898 by M. Loret in the Valley of the Kings, eleven royal mummies were found. Ten of these were removed to the museum at Cairo, but that of Amenhotep II. was left in its stone sarcophagus, where it still lies in state beneath the glow of an electric lamp. In 1901, despite precautions, the tomb was forced by modern representatives of the ancient tomb-robbers, who cut through the wrappings of the mummy in quest of royal treasure.

found inscribed upon the rough coffins into which some of these rifled mummies of dead royalty were placed for greater protection.

One of the immediate effects of the labours of the priests of the twentieth and twenty-first dynasties in restoring these mummies was a profound modification of the technical processes of embalming. Realizing how imperfectly many of these mummies retained any semblance to a living man or woman, the embalmer of the twenty-first dynasty set to work to devise new methods to make the mummies more lifelike. Materials, such as linen or mud, were introduced under the skin, and the whole body modelled so as to correct the shrunken and distorted form so often seen in the earlier mummies. Artificial eyes were inserted, and special measures (the use of wax plates) were taken to protect the nose, mouth, ears, and eyes from distortion. Finally, the skin was painted. But having done this the embalmer imagined that he had at last accomplished the aim after which his predecessors had been persistently striving for more than twenty centuries. He had made a mummy which was both the actual body of the deceased as well as his portrait statue. Hence they attempted to make it as complete a restoration of the whole man or woman as it was possible to do.

From the earliest times it was the custom to remove from the body most of its organs, so as to facilitate its successful preservation. But the heart and kidneys were so important that the embalmer aimed at leaving them in situ in the body. Of the organs that were removed four were regarded as specially important, and after being carefully embalmed they were placed in four jars (usually called canopic), which were put in the tomb with the mummy, sometimes in a special case. These four sets of organs—liver, lungs, stomach, and intestines, respectively—were placed under the protection of the four sons of the god Horus, and after the eighteenth dynasty the four jars were distinguished by differently-modelled lids—human-headed (liver), baboon-headed (lungs), jackal-headed (stomach), and hawk-headed (intestines). But in the twenty-first dynasty, when the effort was made to render the mummy complete, it became the custom to restore these preserved organs to the body. A model of the appropriate son of Horus was made of wax (or mud or pottery) and wrapped up with the organ committed to its

care so as to make a neat parcel swathed in linen bandages, which was then replaced inside the body along with the other parcels packed in sawdust.

The technique of the elaborate process of restoring the mummy's form became so complex and difficult that disastrous failures often occurred. This led to a rapid degradation of the art of embalming. But as interest in the preservation of the body itself diminished, more and more attention was devoted to the decoration of the surface of the wrapped mummy. Hence in the later phases, and especially during the Greek and Roman periods, gaudily-decorated mummies and mummy-cases became common.

Even when Christianity was introduced into Egypt, and the early bishops of the Church forbade the practice of mummifying the dead, people refused to abandon a practice to which their ancestors had been habituated for more than thirty centuries. But if the exhortations of such devout bishops as St. Anthony the Great failed to put a stop to embalming, the more vigorous methods of the followers of Islam did succeed after the Arab conquest of Egypt in destroying the most distinctive invention of Egyptian civilization.

Though the practice of mummification was thus brought to an end in Egypt, it has survived elsewhere. In early times the Egyptian custom was adopted in Palestine and Syria, and at least as early as the sixth century B.C. along the whole north coast of Africa. But it also was adopted in Nubia and the Sudan, in Uganda, and the basins of the Niger and the Congo. Later on it spread farther afield in Africa, for example to the Zimbabwe region of Rhodesia, and also the Canary Islands and Madagascar.

But with the wider diffusion of culture in later centuries it spread to Europe and India. From the latter and Ceylon it spread to Burma, the Malay Archipelago and Indo-China, to New Guinea, Australia, and Melanesia, and then in the early centuries of the Christian era it reached the islands of Polynesia and Peru and Central America. At the same time it was being diffused around the eastern littoral of Asia along the Aleutian islands to the north-west coast of America.

Thus the practice of embalming affords one of the most unmistakable tokens of the influence of Egypt in devising elements of civilization which in time were diffused throughout the world.

THUPARAMA, IN WHICH IS ENSHRINED THE COLLAR BONE OF THE BUDDHA

Though small in size, Thuparama, at Anuradhapura, is one of the most sacred among the dagobas because it enshrines the collar bone of the Buddha which it was built to cover in the reign of King Tissa (247-207 B.C.). The present shell is nineteenth century work, but the ancient core and the circle of graceful shafts that stand on the platform invest it with peculiar attraction. No one has yet probed the meaning of these slender granite columns capped by exquisite carvings of dwarfs and sacred geese in life-like action.

Photo by F. Deaville Walker

# The Great Dagobas of Ceylon

## By G. E. Mitton

### Author of "The Lost Cities of Ceylon"

*THE Island of Ceylon is rich in relics of a past civilization, but here only the Great Dagobas are dealt with. This article is included under the sectional heading of "Temples of the Gods" for the convenience of editorial arrangement, for while dagobas are certainly sacred edifices, they are relic shrines like the Indian stupas or commemorative monuments, and not in the strict sense of the word temples. The other relics of the ancient civilization of Ceylon are dealt with in a later chapter —that on the "Lost Cities of Ceylon."*

ONLY after the diffusion of Buddhism did the custom of burying supposedly sacred relics under vast mounds of bricks become popular. The pagodas of Burma, which are, perhaps, the best-known examples of this sort of relic shrine, are usually bell-shaped, rising into a spire and capped by a "hti" (tee) or umbrella, hung with bells which tinkle in every wind. The Siamese pagodas are very much fined out, and have no umbrella, and in a general way suggest the architecture of the Angkor Vat in Cambodia. The Chinese pagodas are more towers than anything else, and keep practically the same breadth to the summit, like a square and highly decorative factory chimney.

Far less known than these are the rounded masses of millions of bricks found in Ceylon, and called "dagobas." There are indeed piles, somewhat similar, in India, where they are called "topes," such as the great tope at Sanchi, and the evolution of these has probably been by way of the tumulus.

The word pagoda came to us from the early European adventurers in the East, and is not Indian like dagoba, stupa and tope. Dagoba means relic receptacle, but it is not by any means certain that all of these gigantic piles were relic receptacles ; in fact, evidence suggests that some were merely commemorative monuments.

The best known, though not the largest of them, at the ancient city of Anuradhapura is most certainly a relic shrine. That exceedingly valuable national chronicle, the "Mahawansa," gives us an obviously authentic, if somewhat highly embroidered, account of the way in which this splendid monument came into existence. It appears that the form was not in any way copied from already existing examples in Southern India, but was evolved independently on the spot.

King Dutugemunu (101 B.C.), having obtained a collection of relics of great sacredness, asked the bricklayer what form the proposed shrine should take, and he, dashing his hand into a golden pot full of water, pointed to the bubbles that arose and floated on the surface. Whether this is true or not, a floating bubble gives a curiously exact outline of what these piles must have been like when first built. Though the bricks have settled and sunk, and in some cases there have been disastrous landslides, yet we have still existing some huge bubble-shaped domes rising to startle us by their dimensions and unusual shape.

During the ages when the cities of Ceylon lay desolate in the jungle, these rounded elevations were rapidly clothed with bush and scrub, like the rest of the ruins of temples, tanks, pavilions and other remains. Huge roots as thick as a man's thigh worked themselves insidiously in between the bricks and clamped themselves to the interior work ; the ever grasping ficus sent down its octopus-like branch-roots and clutched the masonry in its tentacles, so that when the cities were rediscovered and restoration set to work about the end of the nineteenth century, it was found impossible to eradicate them altogether. Much was cut away, but to wrench out such roots would have been to cause a landslide.

Such a catastrophe has occurred, indeed, in the case of Ruanweli, the most sacred of the larger dagobas. This is certainly a true relic shrine for it had a secret chamber in the interior into which none but monks were permitted to penetrate. The dagoba is now angular or triangular in outline, and capped by a modern copper spire. It is one of the Eight Sacred Places of the Buddhist community in Anuradhapura, and is therefore not under the control of the Archæological Commissioners. It was originally 120 cubits, or 270 feet, high—a Ceylon cubit being reckoned as 2 feet 3 inches—and is now about 178 feet, rising from terraces laid with limestone blocks.

At the foundation the king placed eight golden and eight silver vessels and eight bricks made of gold and many bricks of silver. Thus, its name of

KIRI, THE MILK-WHITE DAGOBA, STILL IN THE JUNGLE'S GRIP

Here is one of the only two large dagobas remaining at Polonnaruwa. The ficus trees had grown over it and thrust down their roots, sometimes as thick as a man's thigh, into the cracks in the pure white coating of chunam which once covered the dome. It was from this marble-like exterior that the name arose. To-day, with infinite patience, the growths which were slowly tearing it apart have been removed, and the dagoba stands cleared, a rather melancholy object, it is true, but saved from destruction.

Ruanweli (gold dust) was well earned. On the top of these was laid a heap of perfumed flowers blessed by the chief abbot. Among the deposited relics was placed a golden figure of the Buddha decorated with precious stones. Upon a solid foundation, beaten down by the feet of elephants enclosed in leathern pads, was reared this mighty " drum," made, so far as we can judge now, of equal diameter and height. It originally stood like its fellows on three plinths or procession terraces, together 15 feet high, the paved platform being about 470 feet across. The retaining wall was set with elephants' heads facing outwards ; these were covered with the white lime called chunam which shone like marble, and each had a pair of real ivory tusks. Only a few of the brick cores remain.

Altars, or thrones, for the Four Buddhas of this world cycle stood against the drum on the terrace, facing outwards at the four cardinal points. These were richly carved in string courses and had three wings. Something of the same kind may be observed elsewhere; in the famous Pagan temples the Ananda has four shrines at the cardinal points with presentments of the four Buddhas. There were guard houses at the approaches, one of which (restored) remains. The grandeur of Ruanweli still makes an appeal in its decay, though marred by hideous flimsy erections of modern Sinhalese taste on the platform. But at its perfection, when covered, as we are told was the case, by one king with red clay into which were stuck fragrant flowers until it resembled a gigantic nosegay, or crowned with a jewelled tee—another king throwing over it a " net covered with diamonds "—it must have been a resplendent object.

It was not quite completed when Dutugemunu, after a reign of twenty-four years, lay dying, and was carried out to a granite slab to rest his eyes on this and the Brazen Palace, his proudest works. His devoted brother had had a framework made to cover the uncompleted dome, and over this was thrown a great cloth to resemble a finished whole.

**AMBUSTALE DAGOBA ON THE SACRED MIHINTALE HILL**

Eight miles from Anuradhapura, high up on the sacred hill of Mihintale, the Ambustale Dagoba stands on the very spot where King Tissa, two centuries B.C., met the apostle of Buddhism and became converted to that faith. Flights of well worn stone steps, fringed by maidenhair fern, lead up beneath the steep hillside to Ambustale surrounded by dark groves of palms. The monks who tend the sacred spot shelter in the caves of the rocks, over the entrances of which droops the gorgeous hibiscus.

Greater even than Ruanweli are the two giants of the jungle, Abhayagiri and Jetawanarama. By a curious accident, at some date in their past history the names of these two got transposed, as is now fairly substantiated ; thus Jetawanarama, which is now the highest (249 feet, counting the steeple), was that magnificent pile of 180 cubits (405 feet) built about 88 B.C. by a set of monks in rivalry with those of the Sacred Bo-tree. This great dagoba was handed over to the Buddhist committee in 1909 on certain conditions, one of which was that no trees were to be felled, as expert opinion considered this would endanger the structure. However, the conditions were not observed, and in the following year the Archæological Commissioners had to step in to prevent further destruction.

Sir Emerson Tennent, writing of this dagoba, made the following computation : " The materials are sufficient to raise 8,000 houses, each with a 20 foot frontage ; they would construct a town the size of Ipswich or Coventry."

This presumably refers only to the bricks, but the enormous stone blocks on the surrounding processional platforms must also be reckoned in the material and labour. The steeple and tee are very grand, and wrought with bold mouldings. Tradition says that a large disk on each side was once covered with sparkling gems, after the manner of the " htis " of the Burmese pagodas. The diameter of this drum is now 360 feet, not so far below what it was originally in height.

The steeple of Abhayagiri (so-called) was ruinous, and rebuilt by prison labour in 1890. It is possible to ascend to the summit by the winding path left by the workmen, and from an elevation of about 230 feet (from the platform) survey the surrounding country. The most striking objects are the domes of the two sister dagobas rising from a sea of dark green foliage like rocks in a bay. Elsewhere there are stretches of green cleared land, and glimpses of the enormous lakes, or tanks as they are called, for the storage of water.

It has been reckoned that if the dome of Abhayagiri was carried down to ground level it would be exactly hemispherical. The total area enclosed by the outer boundary wall is 11 acres. The oldest topes seem to have been always dome-shaped, usually something less than a hemisphere, thus approximating closely to the floating bubble, with base circular, quadrangular or polygonal.

By an interesting calculation it has been shown that the apex of the third pyramid at Gizeh would fall within the steeple of Abhayagiri, and its angles at the base coincide with the angles of the drum. The stone-paved platform is decorated with altars, now ruinous, and some very finely carved many-headed cobras on stelae or panels. The carving on the uprights is unusually good, one showing a female figure. The great flights of steps at the entrances are 27 feet wide, thus making an open approach which enables the platform to be seen.

The only thing in Burma comparable with these massive piles is the Myinmu pagoda on the banks of the Irrawaddy River, and this, though a huge pile of bricks, is shapeless, and not hemispherical. It has round the base an elaborately carved stone railing, like that of the famous Sanchi tope in Central India.

The only other dagoba at Anuradhapura which is large, though not comparable in size with these, is Miriswetiya, a name explained by the story that the king (Dutugemunu) who built it did so as an atonement because, in his greed to devour a chilli-curry (Miriswetiya) of which he was particularly fond, he forgot to make his usual offering of a part of it to the monks. Miriswetiya is a mere shell, and its dome has completely gone. The two enclosing walls afford a home to an innumerable company of bats, who, to the delight of visitors, fly out about dusk every evening like twisting clouds of spray or smoke. The walls are 101 feet in diameter, but only 82 feet in height now. The altars or thrones are unusually well preserved.

At the later city Polonnaruwa, the capital from the ninth to the thirteenth century, the dagobas have lost their attractiveness of outline. We are told that Parakrama, the great hero-king of the twelfth century, built no less than 101 dagobas at this place, but the only two that survive with any completeness are the Rankot dagoba and the Kiri or milk-white dagoba. The former is said to have been due to Parakrama's second queen. It is about 200 feet in height and 180 feet in diameter. It was once crowned by a golden umbrella, thus recalling the " htis " of the Burmese pagodas. Its present tee or crown is in good condition, and has figures outlined upon it. A great deal of cutting and tearing out of giant roots had to be done here in 1905-6.

The Rankot dagoba has shrines at the cardinal points and eight smaller ones in pairs between, a special feature. Both it and the Kiri dagoba, which is about half the height, are stilted drums, higher than their base diameters, and thus they lose impressiveness. The latter gained its name from being covered with chunam, which gleamed like marble from afar.

The dagobas already mentioned all belong to one type, though varying in size. There is another sort, much smaller and more bell-shaped, which has as a distinguishing feature many pillars on the platform. The principal one of this kind is Thuparama, only second to Ruanweli in its sanctity, for it was built to enshrine the right collar

**ABHAYAGIRI, SECOND OF THE MIGHTY MONUMENTS AT ANURADHAPURA**

This dagoba has retained the evenness of its outline better than any of its fellows. It is second in size of the three great stupas. A new brick erection built by the monks on the summit now replaces the truncated steeple, and it is possible to climb to this by a steep path. From the summit the other two dagobas rivalling Abhayagiri can be seen rearing themselves above a sea of jungle. On the stelae found on the platform are unusually perfect carvings.

**JETAWANARAMA DAGOBA, THE LARGEST OF ITS KIND NOW EXISTING**

Jetawanarama, a gigantic hill of bricks at Anuradhapura now covered with jungle growth, rises to a height of 240 feet and was originally much higher. It rests on a platform 100 feet wide, and was built about the end of the first century B.C. It is the largest of all the dagobas known to exist. The pillars of the ruined entrances to the processional platform can be seen in the photograph, also the dwarf guard-stones and the stone vases surmounting the pedestals on each side.

bone of the Buddha in the reign of King Tissa (247 B.C.). It was originally only 33 feet in height, and of an inverted basin shape, but surmounted by a conical steeple of such large dimensions in proportion to the drum that it carried on the lines. It was rebuilt by devotees in the nineteenth century and now rises to 63 feet and is much more bell-like than at first.

Seen from a good distance it suggests, indeed, a pagoda rather than anything else. It stands on a high platform reached by flights of wide steps, with door guardians in attendance. Its charm lies in the collection of beautiful granite columns which surround it. These are in four rows at varying distances from each other, and the columns in each row vary in height from 24 feet to 14 feet 6 inches. The shafts are monolithic, and the capitals beautifully carved with designs of capering dwarfs, sacred geese and, in the case of some, carved fringes 14 inches deep embracing the shafts. They are arranged in quadrants to allow of entrance, and many are surmounted by a boss or pad. It seems impossible they could at any time have carried a roof. To begin with, they are too slender and not high enough. They have provoked much conjecture, and it is imagined they may have been used to hang festoons of flowers from, or to support the paintings of the Buddha's incarnations carried about on festival days. Another dagoba very similar in dimensions to Thuparama, and with similar columns, is Lankarama.

About eight miles from Anuradhapura the hill of Mihintale rises to a height of about 1,000 feet. Up the sides of this hill are long flights of stone steps set by pious kings of bygone ages to aid pilgrims in their ascent. Fringed by maidenhair fern, and grand in their straight simplicity, these outdoor staircases are very impressive. It was on this hill that King Tissa was hunting the elk

when he met the apostle Mahinda and was converted to Buddhism with all his followers. The spot on which this historic meeting took place is now occupied by the Ambustale dagoba, which rests on a platform about three-quarters of the way up the hill. It is a kind of hollow amid

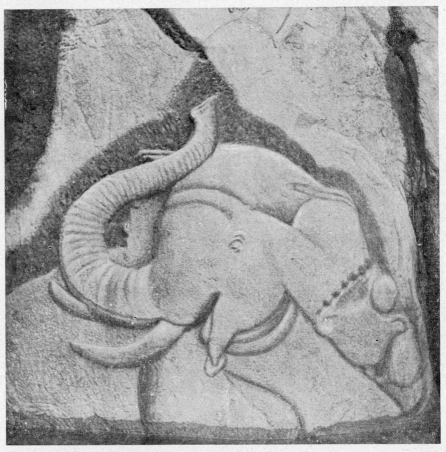

CARVING OF UNUSUAL VITALITY AT ISURUMUNIYA

In depicting elephants the ancient Sinhalese have no rivals. This splendid head is cut in relief on a sheer rock face arising from a deep pool at the rock temple of Isurumuniya. The work must have been carried out under exceptional difficulties owing to the position. The temple lies about a mile outside the great ruined city of Anuradhapura.

Photo by Mrs. Maynard

steeply rising rocky eminences. This dagoba is also of small size, and is surrounded by columns, but they lack the grace and finish of the Thupurama or Lankarama columns. The monks in attendance live in gloomy rock-hewn dwellings amid the limestone boulders close by.

High above it, and above the palm groves on the steep hillside, set like a wen on the topmost eminence, is the Et Vehera dagoba, built over a hair which grew over the left eyebrow of the Buddha. This is a mere tumulus. It is about 90 feet in height, and is approached by flights of steps. On the southern side the granite cliff falls sharply to the plain.

## The Wonder Cities.   XIV.

# Jerusalem under Herod the Great

### By J. Garstang, M.A., D.Litt., D.Sc. (Oxon)

Professor of Archaeology in the University of Liverpool, and formerly Director of the British School of Archaeology at Jerusalem and of the Department of Antiquities for Palestine

AMONG the numerous transformations that Jerusalem has undergone from its foundation in the far off days of the Jebusites until to-day, none was more radical than that accomplished by Herod the Great. At this epoch, it may be said, the old order changed and a new Jerusalem came into being. The general arrangement of the city still reflected the ancient civilization and conformed with customs and institutions established by the Israelites, but already the seeds of Hellenism were taking root and the new order was becoming visible above the soil—indications of a more vigorous civilization, destined soon to overrun the old. Even the temple itself, at the culmination of its splendour, took now an entirely new aesthetic appearance under the dominating influence of Hellenistic art in that stage of development which is familiarly called "Graeco-Roman."

It is this Hellenised Jerusalem of Herod the Great that interests Christendom most profoundly, for it was the Jerusalem of Christ. Many would like to visualise the city as it then was, or at least to know, if not to see, what remains in fact of that period.

Yet the inquiry is not easy and most of the fanciful reconstructions of the Holy City, however well intentioned, are not to be trusted. The historian Josephus has indeed left us very precious descriptions of various features—palaces, monuments, ramparts, canals, water systems, tombs and so on—but the literary sources still require more critical examination or await a final collation with the archæological remains upon the site. And the recognition of these material remains is no easy task, involving the presence of a trained archæologist and a life devoted patiently to investigation. For years little or no excavation has been possible, and the results already obtained by the learned Dominican Fathers of the Ecole Biblique (now the official Archæological School of France in Palestine) have only been gleaned as and when public works or other enterprises within the city have afforded the opportunity.

The casual visitor, familiar with contemporary monuments of antiquity elsewhere, splendid alike in their preservation and character, such as those in Thebes, Athens, Pompeii, and Timgad, might look in vain for any material trace of

**"TOMB OF ABSALOM," A LINK WITH HEROD'S DAYS**
Looking across the Kidron valley towards Ophel are three rock-hewn funeral monuments that undoubtedly date from Herod's time. Of these the so-called "Tomb of Absalom," square in shape and surmounted by a concave cone, is only carved in the solid rock as far as the cornice, above which it is built up of beautifully worked stone.
Photo by the British School of Archæology at Jerusalem.

CITY OF JOSHUA, DAVID, SOLOMON, HEROD—

In this reconstruction of Jerusalem as it was under Herod the Great, we are supposed to take up much the same point of view as that in page 574, to stand on the Mount of Olives and gaze over the Kidron valley in the foreground, over the great Sanctuary and the Upper City beyond, out to where the horizon hides Joppa (Jaffa) and the distant sea. Occupying the centre of the panorama is the Temple of Herod with its courts and buildings spread out on the summit of Mount Moriah, and the grim fortress of Antonia which Herod built to guard it and to serve as a secondary citadel—so soon to stand the ghastly siege of A.D. 70. In the nearer wall of the enclosure is the Shushan Gate facing a causeway over

## —IN THE DAYS OF ITS ULTIMATE SPLENDOUR

the Kidron. Below the south wall of the temple on the left lies Ophel, the Zion of David and the Jebusites, and behind it the Tyropoeon valley spanned by " Robinson's Arch " at the south-west corner, and " Wilson's Arch " farther north. On the opposite or northern side beyond Antonia lies the quarter known as Bezetha. Lying round the Tyropoeon valley is the Lower City with the Upper City, or Jerusalem proper, on the height beyond ; it is crowned in the left distance by the towers of Herod's Palace and drops steeply away to the valley of Hinnom or Gehenna.

*After the painting by H. C. Selous, by courtesy of the London Society for Promoting Christianity Among the Jews*

FOUNDED BY HEROD BUT CALLED THE "TOWER OF DAVID"

Probably few ancient cities have so suffered from haphazard nomenclature as Jerusalem ; at every turn there are names that seem to take us back to the days of the kings and earlier, whereas in fact the remains of even the Jerusalem of Herod's time are not numerous. Such is the " Tower of David " in the citadel, claiming by its title a specious glamour of antiquity—though the lower courses prove their Herodian character by massive size and drafted joins, so that by ordinary standards they are old enough.

Photo from Prof Garstang

Jerusalem in its glory. He will see, quaintly picturesque but not reflecting in any sense the period of his search, a medley of constructions without character, or of modern buildings leaning against others of Arab or medieval origin, themselves perhaps superimposed upon Byzantine foundations or covering the remains of the Roman "colonia" of the second century. It will appear to him as though the Jerusalem of Herod was not only destroyed but utterly effaced by the legions of Titus in 70 A.D. Of the temple itself not one stone is visible upon another ; the magnificent

## WHERE JEWS MOURN THE RUIN OF THEIR ONCE GLORIOUS TEMPLE

On the western wall of the Temple enclosure, now the girdling wall of the Haram el Sherif, is a spot where devout Jews gather once a week to bewail the destruction of the Sanctuary. There, they believe, are stones from the original Temple of Solomon, and indeed it may be that some such are buried beneath later masonry; but as they stand, the magnificent blocks visible in this photograph are undoubtedly part of the structure built by Herod the Great, father of that Herod before whom Christ was tried.

Photo by Underwood Press Service

**RELICS OF AN HERODIAN VIADUCT**

Just south of the Wailing Place of the Jews, and not far from the south-west corner of the Haram enclosure, are remains of a bridge that once spanned the Tyropoeon valley. On the outer side of the present wall these remains are known, after their excavator, as "Robinson's Arch"; and on the inner side, shown here, a pier and the spring of a span may still be seen.

Photo by the British School of Archæology at Jerusalem

very few, and they may be rapidly indicated. First, we have the great ashlar walling founded on rock, and some column bases in position, preserved in the basement of the Russian institution near the Holy Sepulchre; secondly, there is the similar massive masonry of drafted stones forming the lower visible courses of the corner of the temple enclosure (the Haram of to-day), stretching from the spot known as the Wailing Place of the Jews, past "Robinson's Arch," around the south-west corner and along the south wall as far as the south-east corner of the enclosure; thirdly, similar masonry is also to be seen in the citadel enclosure, particularly the foundations of the "Tower of David"; fourthly, there are certain walls and buildings already excavated on Mount Ophel, the ridge that leads upwards from the Pools of Siloam to the temple area; and finally, traces of a Jewish quarter may be found on the eastern slopes of Mount Zion overlooking Ophel.

In this short list of Herodian remains we have not included the well-known "Ecce Homo Arch" in the "Via Dolorosa,"

monument that now rises in the sacred enclosure was the later creation of Christian architects working for the first Mussulman Khaliphs, decorated according to the taste and tendencies of Islam. Even the few remains of the period that the visitor will see will probably be so obscured and out of setting that he is likely to be more impressed by such foolish modern names as the "Tower of David" or "Herod's Palace," and to preserve the image of the structures so named, however involuntarily, in any mental picture he may have formed of the Holy City.

The remains of the period on which correctly to base the outline of such a picture are indeed

a striking monument of the Roman age, but to be fitted only doubtfully and with difficulty into the picture of Herod's Jerusalem that we are striving to create. These authentic remains are few indeed; they may be counted on the fingers of one hand. In the mind's eye they must be enclosed not by the medieval walls of the modern city, but by a circuit reaching farther to the south enclosing the ridge of Ophel and the hill of Zion. In this circuit the foundations of the citadel and the portions of wall adjoining, together with the line of the opposite eastern wall east of the Haram el Sherif, are the only present landmarks. The northern wall is more doubtful.

It has often been argued that the present north wall preserves the general line ; but it is to be pointed out that the remains visible in the basement of the Russian Hospice, the origins of which are traceable to the period of Herod, were adapted to all subsequent transformations of the city, in particular to the Forum of Aelia Capitolina and the Temenos of Constantine. Their presence and character may be taken to indicate the limit of the city to the north-west in the time of Herod. With the city wall so uniting and enclosing the visible remains of the period which have been mentioned and the rest of the area still blank in the mental picture we are striving to create, we may now proceed to fill in the plan with general indications and certain details culled from ancient writers or from the results of topographical research.

To the north of the hill of Zion, that is to say in the vicinity of the present citadel and the Tower of David, rose the Palace of Herod, a vast series of luxurious buildings adorned with colonnades and peristyles, courts and gardens. The general scheme of arrangement was apparently Oriental, but the style and decoration probably differed little from an Alexandrian palace of the later

Lagides. This inference is based on the character of architectural fragments accidentally discovered. Excavations have still to uncover this, one of the most famous and most imposing buildings of the period. On the same height, but towards the east, arose the palace of the Hasmonean princes ; it would seem to have preserved its local Jewish aspect, but little or nothing material is known about its fabric. Farther south (beyond the present wall) on the easterly slope of the same hill of Zion, clearances have brought to light (under the Byzantine levels and the Roman remains of the period of Aelia) traces of an interesting Jewish quarter of the age of Herod, including streets, dwellings, store-rooms, a mill and other features.

Farther east, beyond the depression that still marks the exit of the Tyropoeon valley, rises the gentle slope of Ophel, which leads up from the Pools of Siloam by the side of the Brook Kidron, as far as the present southern wall of the city. This historic site is now to be excavated under the auspices of the present administration of Palestine, which has invited the collaboration of all archæological societies within the League of Nations. All the educated world, Christian, Jew and Moslem

VAULTED "STABLES OF SOLOMON" BENEATH THE TEMPLE COURT

From time immemorial, in order to provide a large and level site for the temple, the summit of Mount Moriah must have been extended by substructures ; but the existing vaulted chambers known as "Solomon's Stables," just inside the wall by "Robinson's Arch," appear to be even post-Herodian. For in the foreground a Roman capital may be seen built into a square column, and the arch itself (visible here in the left background but better shown in page **572**) is incorporated in the structure of the wall.
Photo by the British School of Archæology at Jerusalem

JERUSALEM, THE CITY IN THE ABUNDANCE OF WHOSE GLORY ISRAEL TOOK DELIGHT

Apart from its religious significance, and even leaving out of account its claim to unsurpassed literary style, the Bible is a most fascinating historical document; and in it no more enthralling tale is unfolded than that of the chequered story of Jerusalem. Her beginnings are shrouded in a mist of interesting conjecture; she was early peopled by the Jebusites, a tribe thought to be of Semitic origin from the name of one of their kings, Adoni-zedek. We know from Joshua xv. 63 that, in spite of being surrounded by the people of Israel, the Jebusites could not be expelled from the city, and indeed there is no record of their expulsion, it being accepted that they were later merged in the Israelites. This view is from the Mount of Olives, east of the city; in the left foreground is the Tomb of Absalom (see page 567), and the Mosque of Omar is seen rising above the Harem el Sherif

Photo by F M Good

574

EVIDENCE FROM SAMARIA OF THE CHANGES WROUGHT BY HEROD ON JERUSALEM

The old capital of the northern kingdom of Israel, founded by King Omri, carries in its name an epitome of the history of Palestine and Jerusalem. The word Samaria is a Hellenised form of the Aramaic Shameravin; but the name of the modern village, Sebastiyeh, is a corruption of Sebaste, which in its turn is Greek for Augusta. Augustus, Emperor of Rome, had given Samaria to Herod the Great who lavishly fortified and adorned it, and renamed it after his Imperial patron; it underwent a transformation similar to that at Jerusalem, but more of the ruins remain to tell the tale. Here is the terrace of the temple erected by Herod in honour of Augustus; to-day the inhabitants use it as a threshing-floor.

Photo by Donald McLeish

575

alike, will follow the progress of discovery with living interest. We are told that the crest of the hill was levelled in the Roman age to facilitate the development of the city plan ; but it would appear that the statement refers to the upper part, possibly indeed that which now lies between the Haram and the city wall, where the Stadium of Aelia was constructed. It may be hoped, and no one can realize this without some emotion, that it still remains for the excavator to uncover the traces of the ancient fortress of the Jebusites, of the first City of David, and maybe the tombs of the Kings of Judah. Of Herod's work there is little trace as yet, but from the indications still visible it may be believed that Herod had already arranged and decorated the approaches to the Pools of Siloam in the style of the Roman Nymphaeum of Jerash or of Amman, beyond the River Jordan.

Overlooking Ophel from the opposite slope of the Kidron valley, above the modern village of Silwan, there are to be seen three splendid funerary monuments which may be attributed with some certainty to the period of Herod the Great. These are known familiarly by the names : the Tomb of Absalom, the Grotto of S. James and the Pyramid of Zacharias. Though forming a group, and contemporary in date, these tomb structures present an interesting variety of design and treatment. The first is square in plan, carved in the living rock as far as the cornice from which point it is built up of good ashlar blocks. Above the architrave the square plan gives way to a circular structure which is bound together as it were by a rope moulding and is crowned by an incurving monolithic peak. The four sides of the solid base are decorated with an Ionic façade, two

WHAT AN HERODIAN BASILICA MUST HAVE LOOKED LIKE

Herod Hellenised Jerusalem, but beyond scanty remains in the Russian Hospice there is little wherewith to reconstruct the secular part of the city in his time ; and in order to obtain an idea of its appearance one must go to other towns of Palestine Hellenised, or Romanised, at about the same date. In the Church of the Nativity at Bethlehem, for instance, Roman columns and capitals are admirably preserved ; indeed the whole building even to-day must look strangely like a Basilica of Herod's period, with its fine vista of unfluted Corinthian columns receding to the background on either side.

**ECCE HOMO ARCH IN THE VIA DOLOROSA**

One of the "stations" on the Via Dolorosa, or Christ's path to the Cross, is known as the "Ecce Homo Arch"; here it was, according to tradition, that Pilate exclaimed: "Behold the man!" It is, however, extremely doubtful whether the masonry dates from Herodian times; more likely the arch was an entrance in Aelia Capitolina—but see page 579. The central span bridges the street, but the side arch on the north, as shown here, has been used for the choir of the Church of the Sisters of Zion.

Photo from Prof. Garstang

COLUMNS LIKE THOSE THAT MUST HAVE ADORNED JERUSALEM

Before the advent of Herod the Great Jerusalem must have looked far more like the modern town than it did after his embel-lishments—and still more so after its conversion into the Roman colonia of Aelia Capitolina. Colonnades and porticoes were the main features of Herod's improvements, and other towns besides Bethlehem may be enlisted in forming a mental picture of their appearance; this photograph shows the portico of a Roman temple of Herodian date standing in lonely ruin at Jerash.

Photo by the British School of Archæology at Jerusalem

columns between the corner pilasters, while a frieze of design familiar in other tombs of Roman character that may be seen in the district round Jerusalem completes the somewhat severe and dignified scheme of decoration.

The Pyramid of Zacharias is similar in general design but it is entirely carved in the living rock. The cornice curves outwards in Egyptian fashion and the whole is surmounted by a plain pyramid giving a further Egyptian suggestion. The Grotto of S. James, which lies between these two monuments, is altogether different in character, being hewn in the cliff face with even a rock-carved portico, this time of Doric character, recalling the rock tombs of Beni Hasan in Egypt and similar structures of Lycia in Asia Minor. Each tomb thus has its special character, and the three form a group of unique interest among the numerous varieties of tombs around Jerusalem. Further, it is to be gathered from a passage in Josephus that these tombs, the two former at any rate, are to be attributed to Queen Helen of Adiabene, the devout lady who sent corn from her modest kingdom near the Euphrates, in northern Mesopotamia, to the relief of Jesusalem in the time of famine mentioned in the Acts of the Apostles; for after her son's accession her body and that of her brother were sent to Jerusalem to be interred in the " pyramids " which she had constructed; these, we are told, were three in number, and they were three furlongs outside the city. No other funerary monuments or tombs around Jerusalem answer nearly so well to this description, and though only one can properly be called a pyramid and their distance from the nearest point of the city wall as it was then can only have been one or two rather than three fur-longs, yet the description and indications are relatively so detailed and suggestive that the accuracy of the identification can hardly be doubted. These monuments may accordingly be attributed to the period under review with as much certainty as any other antiquities of the site.

## ROMAN STYLES IN ARCH AND FOUNTAIN AT JERASH

Jerash was the old Gerasa, a town on the farther side of Jordan not far from Ramoth-Gilead. In the upper photograph we see the ruins of its triumphal arch built in Herod's age; those who wish to find a place for the Ecce Homo Arch in the Herodian Jerusalem think that it must have been of this type. Below is a drinking-fountain of the same era at Jerash, showing how the façades of public buildings in the most distant regions were adorned at this time in the Roman manner.

Photos by the British School of Archæology at Jerusalem

GROTTO OF S. JAMES AND PYRAMID OF ZACHARIAS

A little to the south of the "Tomb of Absalom," illustrated in page 567, are two other funeral monuments; one is hollowed out in the rock, and known as the "Grotto of S. James" from a legend that the Apostle hid himself there after the arrest of Christ, while the other is called the Pyramid of Zacharias. Completely rock-hewn like the first, it yet stands isolated as though built up, and with its plain surface is more Egyptian in appearance than the Tomb of Absalom. All three are Herodian in date.

Photo by the British School of Archæology at Jerusalem

When we approach the city wall again at the Golden Gate, a doubt must arise as to the origin of this entrance which, notwithstanding the visible traces of reconstruction and remodelling, remains one of the most beautiful vestiges of antiquity in Jerusalem. The structure in general may be recognized as Byzantine work of the seventh century A.D., but doubtless it stands upon the foundations of the Shushan Gate of the time of Herod, and has embodied a number of features of that period of the temple. Two massive monoliths, originally door jambs, are now used as pillars, rising actually above the level of the top of the wall. Their proportions recall again the pillar which still lies prone in the enclosure of the Russian cathedral to the north-west of the city.

Passing within the sacred enclosure no traces of Imperial work greet the eye. The platform itself is much higher than aforetime, so that even the embers of the awful fire kindled by the soldiers of Titus lie buried deeply below an artificial accumulation of subsequent ages. Recent trenching done for purely practical purposes by the Moslem

authorities failed to disclose more than a few detached and meaningless worked stones, though the cuttings penetrated the bed of chips and débris in places to a depth of 3 metres. Even at the lower level found in the stables of Solomon (surely, by the way, a misnomer for Suliman), though the wonderful system of vaults which carries the southern extension of the platform is traditionally very ancient, it is none the less impossible to assign the work as a whole to the period of Herod's temple. For there may be seen buried in the structure, and no longer serving any purpose in the new scheme, the inner continuation of that Imperial viaduct that united the temple area to the western hill, over the Tyropoeon valley; this viaduct is well indicated and well known from the remains familiarly called "Robinson's Arch," visible in the external masonry of the enclosure. The masonry of this arch, the Imperial character and date of which are not disputed, and its relation to the main wall of the temenos, indicate that the lower courses in this sector of the enclosing wall of the temple area are an original structure of Herod the

## ARAB SPLENDOUR AND CLASSIC GRACE ON THE HARAM EL SHERIF

A special chapter in this work is devoted to the Temples at Jerusalem, to-day all that remains of that majestic succession of buildings is the level wall-girt platform on the summit of Mount Moriah, the Haram el Sherif. The Mosque of Omar, or more correctly the Kubbet el Sakhra (Dome of the Rock), which stands in the centre, is Moslem work of the seventh century but a glimpse of an epoch closer to that with which we are here concerned is afforded by the arcades round the mosque platform, with their ornate Corinthian column-capitals—obvious elements from architecture of an earlier date

*Photo by Donald McLeish, specially coloured for " Wonders of the Past "*

Great. In it perhaps there lie embedded the enclosure and some features of the age of Solomon, but even this is doubtful. The masonry conforms essentially in character and setting with other temenos walls of undoubtedly Herodian character, particularly that of the Mosque of Hebron that encloses the cave of Machpelah and the traditional cenotaphs of the patriarchs.

But the focus of our interest is the temple, the site of which is certainly the Haram el Sherif, enclosed by the walls we have described. The Sacred Rock that outlasts all human endeavour to embellish or enclose it is covered at present by The Dome, a splendid example of medieval art that now marks by another turn of the wheel the second shrine of Islam. The enclosure itself has been altered and remodelled; nevertheless, contemporary archæology—thanks particularly to the researches of the Palestine Exploration Fund (1864-9)—is able to discriminate the phases of its evolution. Careful and detailed comparison with masonry unquestionably of the period of Herod

(particularly the Haram of Hebron mentioned above) enables us to regard with some certainty as portions of the Herodian enclosure the lower part of that magnificent stretch of the present wall from and including the Wailing Place of the Jews (itself perhaps indeed of earlier origins but now reconstructed), past Robinson's Arch, round the south-western corner of the enclosure, and all along the southern wall as far as the return of the south-eastern corner. This and the Rock itself are the most tangible remains. Several columns and decorated fragments to be seen in " Solomon's Stables," and certain other indications, such as the column that still rests in its quarry bed (like that greater one of Baalbek) in the compound of the Russian hospital and cathedral, provide the architect with elements from which to reconstruct in theory, but with a degree of certainty that warrants the attempt, the great southern portico, called historically the Royal Basilica, the most monumental of all the porticoes with which the esplanade was embellished at this period.

FINE STONEWORK OF THE RUINED SYNAGOGUE OF ESTHER

In consequence of the lavish embellishments whereby Herod the Great Hellenised Jerusalem, followed after about a hundred years by its destruction in A.D. 70, its subsequent transformation into a Roman colonia under the name of Aelia Capitolina, its reinstatement in Byzantine times as the centre of Christianity, its capture by the Mahomedans under Omar in 637, and all the later flux and reflux of the Crusades that have left it a Moslem city since 1244, there are but few ruins that suggest the original home of the Jewish faith. The fine stone moulding, however, of this ruined synagogue at Kefr Birim on the Sea of Galilee, fabled to be the burial place of Queen Esther, shows the blend of East and West that was evolved.

Photo by F. M. Good

### THE ROUGH AND NARROW WAY THAT WOUND FROM JUDGEMENT HALL TO CALVARY

From the north-east of the city the Via Dolorosa, most sacred of Jerusalem's streets, runs tortuously upwards to the Church of the Holy Sepulchre. Every Friday the Franciscan Fathers pass this way on a pilgrimage that commemorates Christ's bearing of the Cross from the Hall of Judgement to Calvary. Still narrow and often difficult to climb, it was, according to tradition, in this street that Simon the Cyrenian took the Cross from Our Lord, and the route is marked by chapels, each indicating one of the fourteen Stations of the Cross.

**ARAB TOMBS GUARDING THE GOLDEN GATE**

The Golden Gate is Byzantine work in the main, but it embodies some masonry of Roman workmanship. It owes its name to a Latin mistranslation of " the Gate which is called Beautiful "; but this was almost certainly within the Temple Court, while the Golden Gate is in the eastern wall of the Haram, probably on the site of the Shushan Gate of Herod. It was in 810 that the Arabs closed it up; but there is still a tradition current that some Friday a Christian conquerer will enter by it.
*Photo by F. M. Good*

In an attempt to realize the style and decoration of the Sanctuary itself in the age of Herod, which the tests enable us to restore in considerable detail, we must be guided by the architectural decoration of numerous contemporary buildings: the temples of Si'ah and of 'Araq-El Emir in Trans-Jordania, the Haram of Hebron already mentioned, as well as numerous examples or ruins typical of the Syrian Basilica, Agora, Stadium, Baths and so on in other Herodian towns of Palestine, such as Samaria. Above all must be borne in mind the series of funerary monuments in the vicinity of Jerusalem : the Pyramid of Zacharias and the Tomb of Absalom in the valley of the Kidron, described above ; the well known but misnamed Tombs of the Kings ; the tomb of Herod's own family at Nikephurich, as well as many other buildings and ruins less known but not less expressive of the architectural and decorative tendency of the age. The magnificent Corinthian peristyle with which Herod adorned the approach to the Senate House in his native city of Ascalon gives a just idea of what must have been the appearance of the colonnades and porticoes

that surrounded the temple, and, with even greater certainty, of the monuments outside the temple area devoted to games and contests.

Another monument realized by the munificence and pride of Herod was the fortress on the crest of Bezetha that protected the approach to the Sanctuary from the north-west. Ever since the origins of the temple some form of artificial defence existed in this zone, though gradually pushed southwards by the extension and development of the sacred area. Herod himself finally moved it and surrounded it by a formidable fosse, constructing a monument which was at once fortress and palace. This he named after his Imperial master—a fact that would alone suggest the taste and style in which the work was carried out, even if there were no material indications such as the remarkable remains that may still be seen.

Returning thus from this rapid survey of the area to our starting place in the crypt of the Russian hospice, eastward of the Holy Sepulchre, there remains in conclusion the question of the significance of the several Corinthian columns first mentioned in our summary. The answer is not difficult, for a number of similar features are to be found in and about the small shops of the adjoining bazaar, fronting therefore on a permanent thoroughfare. These betoken the existence, whether in Herod's period or in the remodelled plan of the city in the second century, of a "Via Principalis," flanked, as was the Roman custom of those days, by an avenue of columns, and running generally in the line of the present street of shops. Such avenues are distinctive features of the cities of this age at Samaria and Jerash, where rows of columns may be seen to-day still standing in position. The origin of this feature may be traced on Palestinian soil to an earlier Hellenistic age, for excavations at Ascalon have shown that before Herod built his sumptuous forecourt to the Senate House of the city there ran through the same area a causeway flanked by rows of columns connected by a screen wall on either side. This avenue, though less ambitious in conception and smaller in execution, was nevertheless the prototype of the more sumptuous approaches through the Herodian, or as it might be said, the "Augustan" city. More generally also it may be inferred from the analogies presented by these other cities that so far as was feasible in the existing state of the city the efforts of Herod were directed to initiating a definite town plan, somewhat like that carried out with deliberation but "ab initio" at Jerash. There the town was laid out on virgin ground, with its central principal street and cross streets at regular intervals, all decorated with colonnades and the junctions with appropriate features; the quarters or areas thus enclosed were allocated to special groups of buildings, the "zones" of the modern town plan. Doubtless this could not be realized by Herod in Jerusalem, a city that had already developed through centuries of Oriental and distinctively non-classical traditions. It was not until after the total destruction of the city by Titus that it became possible to lay out a new city upon a classical plan. This work was carried out by order of the Emperor Hadrian in the second century: but it was not Jerusalem that arose from its ashes, it was no longer the holy city of the Jews, the annexe of their thousand-year-old temple that was reconstructed; but a new Roman city by the name

of Aelia Capitolina that was built out of the historic ruins of centuries.

Notwithstanding the complete change which the city underwent, and the consequent interment of nearly all the vestiges of the Herodian city, we have seen that some elements for the reconstruction of the picture of Jerusalem in the time of Christ do exist, and that a temperate imagination may visualise with confidence the general outline and appearance of the city at this age. Doubtless the facilities which are now offered to research in accordance with the mandate of the League of Nations will soon enable much fresh detail to be added to the picture.

By one standing on the Mount of Olives, in the east, which still, as of old, gives the best point of view, there would be seen in the foreground, where The Dome now stands above the Rock in the sacred enclosure, the Temple at the culmination of its development, the legitimate pride and glory of the Jewish nation, with its imposing circuit of sumptuous colonnades and porticoes, and its courts rising, as it were, in échelon, right up to the inner Sanctuary, where the majestic pylon gleamed with its covering of marble and its gilded surfaces. To the north (dismissing from our mental view all the modern walls and buildings) there arose the powerful mass of Antonia, the fortress that dominated and at the same time protected the sacred area on that side. To the south, the uninterrupted sequence of dwellings and palaces fell gradually away right to the foot of the hill of Ophel, as far as the Pools of Siloam. The main eastern wall followed the same course on the brink of Kidron, turning westward at the extreme points indicated to enclose the city. On the slopes of the western hill (Mount Zion) were grouped and ranged other quarters relatively more recent but not less populous than the old, crowned on the western horizon by the imposing silhouette of Herod's Palace. At no period of its history could the Sanctuary and City have presented a more inspiring aspect. The rhythm and harmony of Graeco-Roman art, so beautifully rendered against the Oriental sky, restrained the louder tendencies of Herod himself, while infusing order and taste into the traditional chaos of the city.

## The Master Builders. VI.

# South America's Marvels in Masonry

### By T. Athol Joyce, M.A.

#### Author of "South American Archæology," etc.

*DESPITE all the mystery and romance that have gathered around the name of the Incas, that curious empire of the Andes is a mere affair of last night when contrasted with the dim yesterdays of the ancient civilizations of the East. But much that is usually looked upon as Inca work, standing in the countries where the Conquistadores implanted the more vigorous civilization of Spain, is in no measure Inca, but pre-dates by ages the period during which that strange people flourished. In the following chapter Mr. Athol Joyce, a leading authority on South American archæology, lightly sketches the work of both Incas and pre-Incas, considered as the master builders of South America.*— EDITOR.

THE region of South America which holds the remains of more than one great culture-period consists of the highlands and narrow Pacific slope between the River Ancasmayu in Ecuador and the River Maule in Chile.

It thus comprises a large part of the modern Republic of Ecuador, practically the whole of Peru, the Bolivian uplands, and the northern extremity of Chile. This was the extent of the great Inca Empire as found by Pizarro in 1533. So remarkable was this state in its detailed organization, so wonderful the products of its craftsmen, potters, weavers, gold-workers and stonemasons, that all masterpieces of ancient art and architecture found throughout this vast region are to-day popularly attributed to the Inca people.

Yet the Inca only had their beginnings about the year A.D. 1100, when, coming from the south, they settled in the city of Cuzco ; and it was not until about A.D. 1400 that they completed the conquest of the coast. Even Cuzco itself, the capital city of the Inca empire, and now the oldest living city of the South American continent, shows abundant traces of occupation by an earlier race of architects who played with vast masses of stone as though they were pebbles and left behind them structures which seem as enduring as the living rock itself.

Cuzco is a tragic wonder. As you stand upon the Sacsahuaman hill, dominating the city, a strange and moving scene lies spread beneath the mellow Peruvian sky. Clouds hang in the soft blue, and a gentle breeze stirs the barley upon the terraced slopes of the hills. Deep in the hollow formed by enclosing mountains, green-veiled and purple-shadowed, lies the ancient capital, from which you have climbed by narrow cobble-stoned pathways. Every step has deepened the feeling that it is inadequate to say that there are Inca ruins to be found in Cuzco : it *is* Inca, or pre-Inca. Nearly every building is imposed upon the wreck of dignified

Inca walls, and in many cases these Inca walls rest in their turn upon the massive blocks of polygonal masonry erected by their predecessors. The fine stone-work of the ancient civilization mocks the rickety stucco of the intrusive European. Admirably cut stones have been pitched into every cottage wall, and a glance inside any humble courtyard shows the brown-skinned housewife cooking the family meal over a fire sheltered by carved blocks, fashioned in centuries now long dead. Tawdry chapels of Spanish colonial days have been built upon noble Inca foundation-walls composed of squared stones, and, throughout one narrow, dirty lane, the early stone-work rises on either hand from foot-level, to tower high above head-level in simple and majestic lines.

As you climb, you rub shoulders with the "Indians," the veritable descendants of the Inca and their subject tribes. Their dark, heavy, patient faces are set in perpetual sullenness, their eyes subdued ; it seems as though these native folk had been oppressed by eternal grief ever since that day when they saw their last divine ruler executed upon a scaffold in Cuzco's main plaza by the omnipotent Spaniard. This quietude emphasises the sense of age, for Cuzco is a hushed city ; the Indian voices are low-pitched ; there are no street-cars and very little traffic. The passing of mules and llamas—the latter a relic of the dead culture—through the deep and stony ways strikes no modern or incongruous note.

Perhaps the spirit which broods over Cuzco is the spirit of stone ; stone in its austerity, muteness, and endurance, because the peculiar genius of the South American architect, who, from the technical point of view, was a better builder than even the Maya of Central America or the Mexicans, led him to achieve his effects by the mass and perfect fitting of his blocks and to dispense with decoration in the form of carved or stucco ornament.

MARVELS OF THE BUILDERS' ART SET AMIDST THE MARVELS OF NATURE

Like so many of the Greek temples, Inca ruins, impressive enough in themselves, owe no little of their imposing effect to the majesty and austerity of their surroundings. Here the circular edifice of Intihuatana may be seen in the background; behind it, overshadowing and brooding upon it, are mighty mountains, some of the lesser giants of the Andes range which helped to keep the Incas from the conquest of the coast for about three hundred years. The ruins are at Pisac at the head of the Yucay Valley, or Urubamba Ravine, in which is also situated the wonder city of Machu Picchu; it is a ravine of the Andine chain, and contains the most glorious natural scenery and most impressive remains in the whole district.

In any consideration of aboriginal American architecture two points must be kept in mind. The first is that iron was unknown throughout the two continents, and therefore all masonry must have been worked with stone tools. It is true that the Peruvians possessed tools of copper, which, owing to accidental admixtures of tin, were, in some cases, bronze. But even bronze is unsuitable for the working of stone, and the blocks used in building must have been shaped with tools of stone. The second point is that these primitive architects were ignorant of the principle of the arch. Their only method of roofing was by using beams, or by building inwards with overlapping courses until the space between the walls could be bridged with stone slabs. As a matter of fact we know, from the reports of the early chroniclers, that usually the roofs of the principal buildings were constructed of thatch, often elaborately worked, and of great density and thickness.

The Inca, especially during the later empire, worked with stone blocks of moderate dimensions, cut approximately to size, and squared. They built without mortar, and the stability of their walls, and their beauty, is the result of perfect adjustment and accurate bonding. Beyond this

THE IDOL OF THE INCA'S PALACE AT KALASASAYA

This man-shaped idol stands near the palace of Kalasasaya, at Tiahuanaco, and legend says he answered all questions put to him. Both the idol and the valley were therefore called Ramac, which signifies "He who speaks." The idol holds a sceptre with a condor-like head in his right hand, and in the left an object which, many writers believe, represents a number of slate tablets inscribed with the hieroglyphics or pictographic writing of the country.

is the sense of form and proportion which characterises all their edifices, or at least those which survive. Rectangular buildings are the easiest of achievement for the primitive architect, if the principle of the bonding of corners is known, as it was to the Peruvian builder. But the Inca achieved circular and even apsoidal buildings of perfect symmetry. The finest of these, as a work of masonry, is the apse of the great Temple of the Sun, the lower portion of which is now incorporated in the church of Santo Domingo. Here enshrined was the great golden disk which represented the sacred luminary, hidden from Spanish eyes by the Inca at the conquest and not yet discovered. Here, too, were preserved the desiccated bodies of the earlier rulers, sitting enthroned and bedecked in the precious ornaments to which their divine rank entitled them in life.

Another remarkable instance of circular building is seen at Pisac, close to Cuzco, where the remains of a temple and observatory still bear witness to the skill of the Inca mason. The main structure, circular in form, and beautifully built, is known as the Intihuatana. Here were set up the pillars, the shadows of which, measured at noon, enabled the Peruvians to calculate the solstitial periods, and thus to rectify their calendar.

But though the Inca architect aimed at an austere effect, achieved through the massiveness of his material and the perfection of its jointing, unobscured by any form of carved ornamentation, he was apt to relieve the monotony of a long plane surface by a series of blind niches, broader at the bottom than at the top. Such niches are peculiarly characteristic of the Inca period, and Inca doorways are made in the same almost Egyptian form.

But the pre-Inca masonry is the more marvellous, and it is true to say that no people have played with stone in so facile a fashion as the Peruvians and Bolivians of the earliest cultural periods. The masons of that epoch, beginning, as we believe, in the first or second century before our era, used blocks of any size or shape, keying the one into the other by means of re-entrant angles. Such a process involved enormous labour, because each block was carved to fit one position only. And yet in Cuzco alone there are miles of such work,

THE SEMICIRCULAR TOWER, MACHU PICCHU

Some of the most perfect masonry in all the stupendous work of Machu Picchu is in this little flattened semicircle of a tower. Within the tower may just be seen a sacred rock that has at some time been cracked by fire ; below it is a cave, part natural, part artificial. The walls are adorned with niches and windows.

each joint, after centuries, and despite the action of earthquakes, lying as true as when the stones were first laid, with no mortar to hold them.

Ignorance of the principle of the arch is a serious handicap in the construction of buildings of more than one floor, yet the South American architect achieved the feat, usually by building a lower storey of great solidity, which could support a smaller structure above. The upper structure occupied only a small proportion of the roof-space of the lower, and was therefore fronted by a broad promenade. Buildings of this nature have been found on some of the islands in the Bolivian

Lake Titicaca, which were sacred to the Sun, where temples and " nunneries," the bourne of countless pilgrims, were constructed under the Inca regime. But one building amongst the Inca ruins stands alone. This is the Temple of the great god Viracocha, erected to celebrate the first great Inca victory over the surrounding tribes, a victory which proved the foundation of a great empire. Rectangular in form, with a length of 330 feet and a breadth of 87 feet, it is divided by a central wall which even now stands 40 feet high. It is built of clay bricks, on walls of stone, and the central wall is pierced by numerous doorways with lintels some 14 feet above the ground. Above the doorways was fitted an upper floor, supported by pillars, the stone slabs or wooden joists of which fitted into holes still apparent in the structure of the outer walls. This building is, from the technical point of view, one of the most remarkable in South America. The combination of stone and "adobe" is in itself unusual, while the height, carried up in a perpendicular line, renders it unique.

The growth of Inca power, and the ever-widening extent of Inca domination, were marked by the

NICHES IN THE ORNAMENTAL WALL AT MACHU PICCHU

A wall which abuts on the semicircular tower at Machu Picchu is notable for the beautiful symmetry of the niches in it, those hall marks of the Inca builders ; between each niche is a projecting squared knob of stone. The wall itself is built of specially selected white granite of such fine grain that it gleams like marble.

## THE MARVELLOUS STONE OF TWELVE ANGLES IN A STREET OF CUZCO

With the ancient history of Peru the Incas are indissolubly associated in our minds; but the Incas cannot have ruled for more than about 300 years before Pizarro and his Conquistadores arrived, and some of the most wonderful remains in Peru are indubitably pre-Inca. Such is the inimitable polygonal masonry, which still abounds to-day in the streets of Cuzco—whence comes this crowning example of its class, the famous block of twelve angles and re-entrants, jointed snugly and without mortar to its almost equally amazing neighbours. In the upper photograph is seen another portion of the same wall.

erection of settlements built in the typical Inca style. Such settlements were, in fact, fortresses, erected at strategical situations which dominated important passes in the mountainous country to which the Inca were bred. Many of these settlements were recreated upon the foundations laid by that earlier generation of stone builders who achieved the early polygonal masonry of Cuzco. Apart from the ruins on the islands of Lake Titicaca in Bolivia, the most important Inca sites lie to the north of Cuzco. The wonderful site of Ollantaitambo, the fortress guarding the Vilcomayo valley, though so closely connected with the last pages of Inca history, belongs really to the pre-Inca period. Machu Picchu is more representative, and is truly one of the world's wonders, as much by reason of its geographical setting as its perfect masonry. Even here are traces of pre-Inca work, but the major portion of this wonderful

complex, astride a saddle between two abrupt river-canyons, is Inca. Further north still, the hand of the Inca builder is evident at the terraced site of Huanuco Viejo, and even beyond, at many isolated sites as far as Ecuador.

The pre-Inca builders wrought on a larger and bolder scale, employing stones of all sizes, from blocks weighing a few pounds, to huge masses of many hundredweight. But each individual block was wrought to fit its neighbours, keyed in to them by means of re-entrant angles, and so perfectly adjusted that the Spanish conquerors credited the Peruvians with the knowledge of a process whereby stone could be softened, so that it could be cut like chalk. Much of this polygonal masonry survives, eternal, in Cuzco: one celebrated block, with no less than twelve angles, is shown to the visitor in the wall of a narrow street. But the most stupendous example of this class of

DOOR AND WINDOW IN A STONE-BUILT INCA PALACE AT COLCANCHA

Inca palaces or "country houses" of the ruling class are to be observed in many parts of the country, although most of the buildings have been so laid under contribution to supply material for modern dwellings that the ruins are extremely scanty. A palace at Colcancha, however, of which this is a photograph, is in a fairly good state of preservation; a door (with a man standing in it) and a window may be seen, the latter being a feature uncommon in Inca architecture except at Machu Picchu.

STAIRCASE LEADING TO THE KALASASAYA IN THE RUINS OF TIAHUANACO

In the uplands of Bolivia, between La Paz and the great lake of Titicaca, the very home of the megalithic culture of the region, are ruins of what must have been a considerable city—would be now, indeed, were not the railway track and the neighbouring village of Tiahuanaco built almost entirely of its stones. And in the midst of the site is the Kalasasaya, a temple or a palace to judge by its size. Leading up to its pillar-surrounded platform between two standing monoliths is this staircase of monolithic steps.

architecture stands proudly upon the Sacsahuaman hill just outside the city. Here is a triple rampart, raised of colossal stones, each wall built in a series of salient angles, from which an attacking force could be taken in flank. Every stone that could be dragged from its place has been taken to serve the uses of the modern population. Yet so much remains, so much has defied the looter, simply because it is too massive, too big, for the strength of modern man to handle; though it was not too big or massive for the early master builders to erect. So it stands, stark and threatening, grey and old, triumphant over time, the work of giants, but little disturbed by the pilfering of modern pygmies.

Other marvels in stone lie all about. As you ride your horse upon the slopes of this sunny, grassy hill, you discover that every

AN ARCHITECTURAL MEDLEY AT TIAHUANACO

Above is a typical illustration of the use made nowadays of the building material left by Inca and pre-Inca alike. In the photograph we see a Spanish church built upon prehistoric foundations, and two idols guarding the church door.

STUPENDOUS PRE-INCA MASONRY AT SACSAHUAMAN NEAR CUZCO AND THE—

In the upper photograph are to be seen the triple lines and mighty polygonal masonry of the fortress of Sacsahuaman, near Cuzco. For a third of a mile these cyclopean lines stretch one behind the other across the top of a neck of land, complete with a defensive system of salients and re-entrants which must have made them almost impregnable ; some of the blocks weigh more than 20 tons and stand 20 feet high.   Below, a comprehensive view of the incredible town and fort of Machu Picchu and the country, beautiful and terrible,

—EYRIE-LIKE TOWN OF MACHU PICCHU OVERHANGING THE URUBAMBA CANON

in which it is perched. Wonderful works are to be found in spots seemingly inaccessible to man, beautifully hewn monolithic stairways climb dizzily about the precipices, and above all stands sentinel the peak of Huayna Picchu. On the left are the laboriously cut and very fertile terraces which served the inhabitants for fields, descending the sheer side of the hill. There is a theory that this was the original home and stronghold of the Incas from which they descended to conquer Cuzco and eventually the whole country.

ANCIENT INCA DWELLING FOR THE LIVING AND THE DEAD
Strange towers, in which the Incas interred the remains of their families, dot the high plateau of Bolivia—part of the ancient Peruvian Empire. The Incas refused to be parted even after death, and in these Chullpas, or Houses of the Dead, the relations of those buried in the lower chamber continued to live despite the gloom and darkness of their windowless abode.

Ollantaitambo, to the north of Cuzco, a site intimately connected with the history of the late Incas, but prehistoric in origin. The geographical situation is remarkable, and no better description has ever been written of it than that of the gifted traveller Squier, which runs as follows :

"Their principal works were built at a point where a low ridge extends nearly across the valley. This ridge had been terraced up with high vertical walls, rising from the very bed of the stream on every side to the height of nearly 100 feet. Held by any considerable body of men, it commanded completely the passage of the valley. The river pours with arrow-like rapidity between these terraces and the rocky escarpment opposite, along the face of which runs the narrow and dizzy pathway over which all travellers to Ollantaitambo are obliged to pass. From this point forward for a league the valley is narrowed to a mere cleft between mountains rising in rugged masses, but with almost vertical fronts, to enormous elevations. The brain reels in straining to discern their splintered summits. Dark and chill, this is one of the grand portadas, or mountain passes, of the Andes, leading to the plains of the Amazon, of which the early chroniclers write with undissembled awe. The river looks black and sinister in the subdued light, and its murmur subsides into a hollow roar. The shrubs of broom become scant and small, and their flowers are few and mean. In front rises for ever the white, ghastly Chicon."

In so stupendous a setting it was only a master builder who could construct an imposing architectural complex. But the primitive Peruvian rose to the occasion, and his terraced citadel is worthy of the setting. It rises tier upon tier to the topmost stronghold, the upmost terraces being constructed of enormous slabs, some of which have measurements of 13 by 7 by 5 feet.

The centre-point of megalithic craftsmanship, however, appears to lie outside Peru. In Bolivia, on the high plateau, some 13,000 feet above sealevel, is the dead and destroyed city of Tiahuanaco. This desolate site, its ruins spread over a vast

outcropping rock has been carved in "seats," steps, and terraces ; or channelled with zigzag runnels, terminating in deep basins. Beneath such rocks many burials have been found, and a credible theory holds that the "seats" were the platforms on which were ranged the ancestral mummies at the periodical festivals to the dead ; and that the channels served to convey to the august dead the libations of "chicha" (maize-beer) poured out above their last resting-places.

Masonry of the pre-Inca type is found at many sites throughout Peru, suggesting that the Incas, in their course of conquest, followed the footsteps of a previous race of conquerors. Thus, at certain strategic points, guarding mountain passes, the sites of important fortresses in the Inca period, there are stupendous remains of this earlier age. One of the most impressive of these sites is

plain ringed by peaks of unexplored mountains, on the borders of the mighty upland sea of Titicaca, is one of the most remarkable megalithic sites in the world. One of the principal features is a kind of rectangular Stonehenge, a vast " plaza," enclosed by series of mighty monoliths and approached by a stairway composed of giant monolithic steps. Within the enclosure still stand a gateway, door-posts, and lintel, cut from a single block and covered with carving, probably representing a ceremonial dance in honour of the god of rain and thunder, whose image is the central feature.

In the neighbourhood the plain is strewn with mighty blocks, accurately carved, tenoned, and recessed, which must be the elements of some great architectural complex. But it can never be reconstructed unless the neighbouring town of La Paz is destroyed and the railway torn up. The builders of the town and the engineers used the early site as a stone-quarry. La Paz was built from Tiahuanaco, and the railway runs on the finely-carved stone-work, now converted to road-metal, of architects of a greater genius.

Archæological evidence shows that the builders of Tiahuanaco established a great empire through-out the highlands, and even effected the conquest of part of the coast, but the coast-dwellers, even at this early period, about the commence-ment of our era, were no mean builders in spite of certain limitations. Stone they had not, but they erected wonderful cities of clay bricks. These cities were extraordinary agglomerations, veritable human ant-heaps. The ruins of Chanchan, near Truxillo, are a case in point. The whole settlement is a complex of continuous building, recalling the " cities " of the Pueblo Indians of North America. Roughly square, it is divided into four " quarters " each surrounded by its own containing-wall. Within each quarter, the chambers adhere one to the other as the cells of a bee-comb, and it is evident that many of the " by-streets " must have run along the tops of the walls. At the great site of Pachacamac, near Lima, the centre of the worship of the great creator-god of that name, was another important city, which maintained its sanctity even in Inca times. The Inca, indeed, insisted on

MONOLITHIC GATE AT TIAHUANACO, ONE OF THE MOST ANCIENT OF AMERICAN MONUMENTS

Surmounting the age-old doorway is an image of the rain god surrounded by little carved figures believed to be performing a ceremonial dance in his honour. It will be observed that a number of these figures have been left uncompleted, and archæologists consider that some tragedy—earthquake or war—overwhelmed the sculptors in the midst of their work. The monolith, one of the oldest in the Western hemisphere, was probably split and overthrown during an earthquake, but it has since been erected on its old site, as the above photograph shows, amid the ruins of Tiahuanaco, where, possibly, it once graced a pre-Inca palace or temple.

IMPRESSIVE TEMPLE RUINS WHERE "THE CHILDREN OF THE SUN" WORSHIPPED THE GOD VIRACOCHA

The Incas, who considered themselves a sacred race and the progeny of the sun and moon, worshipped their "parents," the evening star, the spirit of thunder and the rainbow, together with other gods, of whom Viracocha was the presiding power. This great temple, ascribed to him, is at Racche in the Titicaca district. Here were sacrificed objects most prized by the people—grain, fruits, a few animals, and products of their own industry. It is worthy of note that the Inca temples were never polluted, like those in Mexico, with the blood of human victims.

building there a temple to the Sun, their own tribal deity, but the mighty clay-built pyramid, crowned with the shrine of Pachacamac the god, still remained the bourne of countless more conservative pilgrims up to the Spanish conquest.

Apart, then, from the question of material, the early coastal cities are distinguished by their complexity, and by the practice of erecting their shrines on lofty pyramidal foundations. Such pyramidal erections, undoubtedly of very early date, have been found as far north as Truxillo. But they are also distinguished by their ornamentation. The severe style of the highlands relied for its effect upon form and mass. The coastal architect embellished his buildings with moulded ornament in relief, and some of the ornamented walls of ruined Chanchan provide remarkable examples of clay-work. The distinction prevailed even after the Inca conquest. Stone being unobtainable on the coast the Inca turned to clay. But he preserved his formal tradition. The Inca buildings in the coastal region reproduce the stone buildings of the highlands in all their severity of form and lack of ornament. The only concession is shown in the breaking of a blank space of wall by means of niches, of the same pattern as the stone-built niches permitted by inherited tradition.

Yet the great buildings, of which so many portions survive, the forlorn monoliths, carved with an accuracy of detail which few civilizations can parallel, represent only a small proportion of the labour of the early Peruvian stone-worker. The aqueducts and the cultivation-terraces, the so-called "andenes," though far less spectacular, were only created at the expense of incredible human labour. The Peruvians were an agricultural people (for the herdsmen of the uplands were, on the communistic system, rationed from the plantations), but the crops of inland Peru were grown, for the most part, on mountain-sides so steep

RAIN AND THUNDER GOD ON THE GREAT GATE AT TIAHUANACO

Above is a near view of the god of rain and thunder carved on the lintel of the monolithic gateway illustrated in page 595. The dead and desolate city at Tiahuanaco in Bolivia where this gateway stands is of special interest, as it affords proof not only of pre-Inca art and culture but of pre-Inca empires as well. Though situated in the uplands round Lake Titicaca, there is evidence that its sway extended as far as the dwellers by the coast. And as for the conquest of things material, no more startling proof than the gateway could be desired of the masses its inhabitants hewed and handled with their implements of stone. Yet the extent of their conquests was as nothing compared with the subsequent Inca Empire.

LIKE A RIVER-WORN CANYON IN LIVING ROCK: MASONRY OF THREE CULTURES IN CUZCO

Cuzco has a claim to be one of the oldest cities in the world, as almost as much of its still standing architecture is ancient Peruvian as modern; the ancient portions, however, seldom extending above the lower courses. But in one narrow street at least, the Callejon de Loreto, the prehistoric masonry towers up to a height of 20 feet or more throughout the whole of its length and on both sides, a wonderful vision of strength and durability. In parts of the town three separate strata may be seen; first a few courses of polygonal masonry, next a layer of Inca architecture consisting of smaller and squared but still beautifully laid blocks, and finally, to crown the whole, some haphazard and flimsy dwelling-houses of to-day.

that the necessary soil could only withstand the pressure of rain by the support of containing-walls. Hence a system of terrace-cultivation, involving the construction of thousands of miles of masonry, which prevented the precious humus from being washed down the mountain-sides.

The Peruvians of the interior built their country, line upon line of masonry up every precipitous slope, with stairways leading from terrace to terrace. The imagination stands almost paralysed when it attempts to contemplate the extent of human labour by which such a feat was accomplished, but the contemplation of the result furnishes some idea of the astounding perfection of Peruvian social organization in the early days.

Then the aqueducts: the coast is a rainless area, and even in the highlands an organized system of irrigation was of supreme importance. Water was brought over amazing distances from far sources in the mountains, and many cities are still supplied by means of stone conduits, the origins of which have been lost and never traced again.

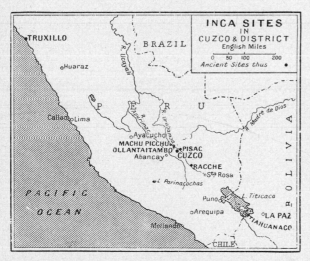

Engineering feats of this description are sufficiently surprising in the interior, but when the coast is taken into consideration they become amazing. On the aqueducts the prosperity of the coast depended. The Inca conquered the highly-civilized coastal population by intercepting the water-supply in the mountains, and the fact that the Spanish conquerors neglected to keep the aboriginal aqueducts in repair provides the reason why many once populous settlements stand deserted in coastal deserts, once green and fertile. Few peoples have handled stone, whether in mass or in detail, with such facility as the South American of the Pacific slope, in spite of the fact that his tools were of the same material. But no people has made so extensive a use of stone, and no people has a greater claim to the title of master builder.

AN AYMARA GOD WHICH THE INCAS OVERTHREW

There is a trace of the Celestial in the slanting eyes of this little stone god which predates the rise of the Incas; but there is, nevertheless, a strong resemblance between it and the features of this native of La Paz, a servant in the museum of that town, where the idol is housed. In spite of Inca and Spanish conquests, the aboriginal inhabitants have altered but little.

Keystone

SHEER HULK OF AN IMPERIAL GALLEY: A MASTERPIECE OF ROMAN SHIPBUILDING

Although the recovery of the imperial galley from the depths of Lake Nemi has disappointed the expectations of people whose imaginations had been fed on legends of the orgies for which it once provided the stage, it has yielded much of immense value and interest to the archaeologist. The hull measures 197¼ feet by 60 feet over all. Pine and larch, spruce and oak, were all used in its construction, and the hull was completely cased in lead outside with a layer of wool packed between the wood and the metal, these three components of the structure being fastened together with long, flat-headed copper nails. The finds included a quantity of bronze tablets, coins, handles, hinges, joints, keys, nails, lead tiles, cement paving slabs, and some bronzes.

## The Study of the Past.  XII.

# The Wonder Ships of Lake Nemi

## by the Editor

SOME twenty miles to the south-east of Rome, among the lovely Alban hills, which seem to have been shaped for the landscape of romance, lies the storied land of the Castelli. In the days of Imperial Rome it was starred with pleasure palaces of the emperors, such as Domitian's, from whose remains the town of Albano was originally built, and superb villas of the great patricians, like that of Cicero, which covered a princely parcel of land between Tusculum and Frascati. In the Middle Ages it became a land of castles built by great barons the Conti, the Orsini and a score of others whose names are still familiar to every Roman. Hence the term 'Castelli.' A lovely and historic land.

The hills are of volcanic origin, and among them lie two famous lakes that are the craters of long extinct volcanoes : the Alban Lake and Lake Nemi. Both are beautiful, but Nemi, the smaller, is the more picturesque. The surrounding country in ancient times was more wooded than we see it to-day. It was famed for its groves when the grove was as essential to religious rites as the columned chapel of a later day. Most famous of all these sacred groves was that of Diana at Aricia, on the banks of Nemi, whence the lake was known as the Mirror of Diana. Here the goddess had her principal sanctuary, whose oldest priest was himself supposed to be a god of the forest and the chase and, as Virbius, was worshipped with Diana.

Among all the shrines of ancient Italy this has always been regarded with peculiar interest from the barbarous custom which secured the succession to its priesthood. The priest was known as King of the Woods or Groves (Rex Nemorensis), and he was always a runaway slave. To obtain the coveted office the runaway slave had to break a bough from a particular tree in the grove and with this engage the reigning priest in single combat. Any combatant who succeeded in snatching a bough from this tree had the right of challenge, and if he killed the priest he took his post as lord of the temple and the grove by

The still glassy lake that sleeps
　　Beneath Aricia's trees,
Those trees in whose grim shadow
　　The ghastly priest doth reign,
The priest who is the slayer,
　　And shall himself be slain.

So much for the legendary interest of Lake Nemi, in which we are less concerned for the moment than in its association with the Roman emperors as a haunt of pleasure. Tiberius is known to have resorted there at times to enjoy the delicious mountain air and the lovely scenery, while being rowed about in a barge that was large enough to afford him luxurious accommodation at nightfall. But Caligula, who succeeded him in the year 37, and is credited with squandering in one year the six millions of money left by Tiberius, is believed to have built the two or three 'wonder ships of Nemi' which have given to the lake its latter day fame.

Lake Nemi is only three and a half miles in circumference, its total area covering no more than seventy acres. Facts to remember in considering the story of its pleasure ships. When I first saw it, many years ago, I was keenly disappointed in the scene which imagination had invested with gloomy grandeurs and romantic surroundings. On a day of pouring rain these defied all efforts to reconstruct. It was Rex Nemorensis that attracted me thither, for I had scarcely hoped to be able to see through the waters of Nemi, had I found them as crystalline as I found them opaque, the decaying timbers of those almost fabulous galleys of Caligula in which tradition, aided by certain ancient writers, had made that imperial debauchee and his immediate successors enjoy for a few brief years their voluptuous pleasures in a setting of natural beauty.

One knew that various efforts had been made from

Alinari

**LION HEAD THAT CAPPED A BOLLARD**

In an attempt in 1895 to salve the submerged vessels some fine bronzes were recovered which are now in the Museo Nazionale in Rome. They included three lion heads, each with a ring in the mouth, probably used for mooring small boats.

What the galleys may have looked like when they served the extravagant and scandalous pleasures of the emperor Caligula just nineteen hundred years ago—he reigned from A.D. 37 to 41—is suggested by this imaginative reconstruction drawing by Professor Mancini, a leading Italian archaeologist. The drawing, it should be mentioned, was made before the pathetic hulk shown below was exposed to view in 1930.

## CALIGULA'S PALATIAL HOUSEBOAT 1900 YEARS AGO AND NOW

Before the drainage operations were begun in 1928 Lake Nemi was 112 feet deep. This photograph shows it as it appeared in February, 1930, with one of the two imperial galleys uncovered; the other vessel was so deeply embedded in the mud that attempts to recover it were abandoned. The narrowness of the lake, which only covers an area of seventy acres in all, renders it almost certain that the galleys were never intended to be rowed about its surface, but were palatial houseboats moored beside the bank.

P. & A.

**HOW LAKE NEMI'S WATERS WERE DRAINED AWAY**

Previous attempts to raise the submerged vessels from the water having failed, it was suggested that the water might be drained away from under the vessels. Signor Mussolini sanctioned the grandiose scheme, and a firm of Milanese hydraulic engineers secured the contract and began work in 1928. These are some of the powerful electric pumps by which the immense undertaking was accomplished.

appear to have been with the pleasure ships of Lake Nemi, which for close upon two thousand years have been sources of speculative discussion. What were they in reality? How came they to be sunk? Both questions are now capable of a reasonable answer, which differs radically from most of the ideas entertained about them in the past.

Various explanations of their sinking have been given. That there was anything catastrophic in the event is highly improbable, and, from the position of the hulks, it is improbable that they sank beneath the water as the result of top-heaviness in some extraordinary storm. More likely it is that after having provided Caligula for three, or at most four, years with the pleasures he had sought, and Claudius and Nero who followed him in turn finding lessening delight in their use, or having more exciting pursuits to occupy themselves with elsewhere, the ships were allowed to lie neglected at their moorings. Their most valuable treasures would be removed to the safer housing of the Palatine palaces, while the destructive forces of nature, rotting their timbers, slowly dragged the vessels down to the oozy places at the bottom of the lake, where for eighteen hundred years or more they have been lying.

These two (or is it three?) most famous of the 'galleys' of Rome were never ships at all. They have been rather aptly described by one Italian antiquary as 'floating kiosks.' Numerous fantastic reconstructions of them have been drawn by imaginative artists. Some of these show the larger of the two vessels as a great trireme with its three banks of oars, requiring hundreds of slaves to ply them, and with the most florid decorations along the hull; pavilions, temples and a multitude of luxurious detail on the superstructure which, given an unexpected gale such as blows up at times even in the mild climate of Alban Hills, would have served admirably to heel over the whole gorgeous equipment.

All such notions of these pleasure boats or barges may be dismissed now that we can look upon the skeleton of the actual thing. In any case, it is improbable that there would have been such elaborate provision made for the mobility of a craft so large in an area so restricted. A few sweeps would have taken it from shore to shore. We shall, I think

time to time to recover from these sunken pleasure galleys some of the splendid treasure of bronze and sculpture they originally contained; and, indeed, in the museum at Rome, and elsewhere, such objects of decorative utility as bronze animal heads with mooring rings for attendant craft, which had been taken from the wrecks, were to be seen. But no one at that time had proposed so bold a scheme for the recovery of the galleys themselves as that which the quick mind of Mussolini, with dictatorial power behind the mind, accepted from Prof. Arduino Colasanti, and was able to put into action in October, 1928. The chief fruits of this have now been gathered. A lean and disappointing harvest, let it be said at once!

While ancient tradition is nearly always a reliable guide to the locality of some time-marking event—and few indeed are the ancient traditions which were entirely compact of imagination—it is a safe rule for the student to bear in mind that the ancient chroniclers of these traditions esteemed it a virtue that their tale should lose nothing in the telling, and in time immense areas of embroidery are woven around a tiny patch of original fabric. So it would

Alinari

ROMULUS'S LEGENDARY FOSTER-MOTHER
This ringed wolf head is one of two found with the lions' heads recovered in 1895 and is preserved with them in the Museo Nazionale, Rome. The head projects from a bronze box fitted to the head of a beam and could not have resisted any great pull

form a much better notion of what these pleasure ships were like if we think of them as immense house boats, their hulls built like great barges, possibly following somewhat the lines of the pleasure vessels on the Nile to which the Ptolemies were partial.

They were designed essentially to enable the emperor in the torrid days of summer to enjoy the coolness and refreshment of living and sleeping upon the waters of this hill-surrounded lake. They might indeed be described as the first of the floating palaces, if one may use a phrase that has become so identified with the development of modern liners on the Atlantic route. And they were doubtless furnished to a degree of fantastic luxury which no houseboat of any modern millionaire who might desire to rival Caligula in voluptuous tastes could attain.

For some thirteen centuries they had lain rotting in their watery graves, with never a soul to take a passing interest in their story, until with that wonderful reawakening of curiosity in all forms of classical culture which came with the Renaissance, imaginative men dreamed of refloating them and enriching the world with further examples of Roman arts and crafts. Leon Battista Alberti, a great architect of the middle fifteenth century, was the first of these. He had the active patronage of Cardinal Prospero Colonna, but his efforts produced the most disappointing results. About a century later, in 1535 to be

precise, a sort of diving bell invented by one Lorena, would have enabled a systematic exploration of the hulks to be made, but De Marchi, who had charge of the enterprise, failed to do anything by attempting to do too much. He tried to raise the larger of the galleys by means of a cable, which broke. In 1855 some valuable objects were recovered, and since then various partial explorations of the wrecks have yielded some valuable bronzes.

Then came the grandiose scheme of draining away vast quantities of the water to expose the galleys by lowering the level of the lake. No 'treasures,' alas, are reported as having been recovered from the muddy bottom. All that the remains establish is that Roman ship-builders were astonishingly modern in their methods. For the rest, the imaginative reconstructions of the artists find little justification in the barge-like structure now revealed, and they at least will not thank Mussolini for laying bare the gaunt and unpicturesque ribs of the greatest of Caligula's 'wonder-ships.'

DRUSILLA, DEIFIED SISTER OF CALIGULA
Support is lent to the theory that the Lake Nemi barges were Caligula's by this graceful bronze statuette recovered some years before the 1928–1930 operations. It stands three feet high, and on good grounds is believed to represent Caligula's sister Drusilla.

## BEAUTIFUL RECONSTRUCTION OF THE HANGING GARDENS OF BABYLON

Of all the Seven Wonders of the Ancient World, the Hanging Gardens of Babylon have left us least, in stone or story, wherewith to build a picture of their beauty, but from what evidence there is this lovely reconstruction has been produced. The gardens have borrowed their shape from the Babylonian temple-tower : trees and flowers mass every terrace, and a circling canal gives coolness to the air. Inspired like so many mighty works by love, they were built by King Nebuchadrezzar to delight the eyes of his Median bride. Comparison with the reconstruction drawing in page 607 will reveal the essential similarity of the drawing and painting

*Specially painted for " Wonders of the Past '*

A TURNERESQUE CONCEPTION OF WHAT THE GREAT CITY OF BABYLON WAS LIKE IN THE DAY OF ITS GLORY

One reconstruction of the Hanging Gardens of Babylon has been given in the colour plate facing page 605; above is another striking piece of creative imagination by the architect, Mr. William Walcot, not indeed of the Hanging Gardens in particular, but rather intended to give an epitome of the life of that gorgeous city. The idea is that of a great central building used for all civic purposes, and covered with wicker dwellings which the notables of the town were permitted to erect there; and the whole effect may suggest the general appearance of the famous gardens. But it must be emphasised again that the work is frankly imaginative, designed to create a mental picture of Babylon as it once appeared rather than to give an archaeologically accurate reconstruction.

Reproduced by permission from an etching by Mr. William Walcot; copyright reserved by the publisher, Mr. H. O. Dickins, 9, Great Pulteney Street, London

CRUMBLED RELICS OF THE GARDENS THAT WERE THE GLORY OF BABYLON

To Nebuchadrezzar II, who reigned from 604 to 561 B.C., is chiefly due the credit for the rebuilding that made Babylon the greatest city of the world of that time.   The royal palace occupied the greater part of the Kasr, or Southern Citadel, and excavations as shown in the lower photograph justify the reconstruction drawing above.   It was here that the Hanging Gardens were situated, these being actually terraces overlaid with earth to a depth sufficient to support trees as well as flowers and flowering shrubs, and irrigated by water pumped into cisterns at the summit.

where—in the words of Professor Myers—" a stone door-socket was a rich gift of a king to his god, and was rescued from one ruin after another, to be re-used and proudly re-dedicated," it is still harder for us to imagine whence, and at what cost, all the stone that must have been required for the gardens was obtained.

In point of grandeur and immensity, the Hanging Gardens cannot be compared with Nebuchadrezzar's colossal palace, or with the Temple of the God Bel Marduk, Babylon's protecting deity—a towering eight-storeyed structure, crowned with two vast gold-laden shrines. But for beauty, grace, and charm they were unmatched. They occupied a square, with a circuit of rather more than a quarter of a mile, immediately to the north-east of the principal court of the royal palace.

The use of the term " hanging " in connexion with these gardens is, though generally accepted, in many ways unfortunate. The word gives a false impression, and it is not a fair translation either of the Greek " kremastos " or of the Latin " pensilis." To the Romans " pensilia " conveyed the idea of balconies.

Balconies—balconies raised one above another ; that is exactly what the Hanging Gardens were. They comprised, in fact, a series of wide, stone terraces, supported by arches, and rose, like a giant stairway, to a height of 350 feet, the whole structure being strengthened by a surrounding wall 20 feet thick. On each of the terraces was a layer of mould so deep as to make it possible not only for plants and flowering shrubs to be grown, but fruit-bearing trees as well.

The gardens were irrigated by means of hydraulic pumps which raised water to a reservoir on the highest terrace. On top of the numerous arches the builders laid reeds and bitumen, and, above these, thick sheets of lead. This served to prevent moisture from the soil leaking through and so damaging the spacious and superbly decorated apartments constructed in the vaulted spaces between the arches below.

A wide flight of steps ascended from each terrace to the one above. Picture these lofty terraces, their many arches festooned with flowering creepers, and all the platforms ablaze with the most gorgeously scented and coloured flowers which Asia—indeed, the then known world—could produce, shaded from the too hot sun by trees laden in their seasons with rich and luscious fruits : picture, in this paradise of sybaritic and Oriental luxury, in the heart of great Babylon, the Median queen holding her splendid Court, then you will be able to appreciate something of the glamour and glory of the Hanging Gardens.

Now, in imagination, mount the wide staircase up from the relentless glare and cruel heat of the long Mesopotamian summer into the shade of one of those arched chambers, furnished with exquisite treasures of Eastern art : sink on a soft divan, and feel the dry, hot air blowing deliciously cool upon you through the continuously watered vegetation without, while minstrels make soft music, while slaves anticipate your slightest wants, while the life of the great city throbs below—then, surely, you will call the Hanging Gardens a wonder, a conception worthy of the king who was feared and respected as the greatest monarch upon earth.

What remains of the Hanging Gardens ?

More than is commonly supposed. Excavations carried out in 1903 brought to light, in a square immediately to the north-east of the ruins of Nebuchadrezzar's great palace, a vaulted crypt or cellar, the foundation of a building wholly unlike any other traced on the site of ancient Babylon.

And evidence survives that stone was used extensively in its construction. Inscriptions on tablets found on the stairway leading to the crypt suggest that these cellars once served as refrigerators, as places for preserving perishable foods.

On either side of a central passage are the remains of seven vaulted chambers, closely resembling in design the arched apartments of the Hanging Gardens of legend. This quadrangle is surrounded by a thick wall and, outside this, on the north and east, separated from it by a narrow corridor, is another series of chambers.

There is little doubt that this masonry once served to support the fairy palace built, as a symbol of love, by the king who led the Hebrews into captivity, and who is the best known to us of all the historic characters of the long, long ago. The position of the ruins, their construction, and size all point to this one conclusion. And the surmise is supported by evidence which appears to be still more convincing.

In one of the outer chambers there is, to quote from that authoritative work, " The Excavations at Babylon," by Robert Koldewey, " a well which differs from all other wells known in Babylon or elsewhere in the ancient world. It has three shafts placed close to each other, a square one in the centre, and oblong ones on each side, an arrangement for which I can see no other explanation than that a mechanical hydraulic machine stood here, which worked on the same principle as our chain pump . . . This contrivance . . . would provide a continuous flow of water." How strange that this utilitarian detail should be the only surviving proof that the Hanging Gardens once existed in all the glory with which legend has invested them !

# Chosroes' Palace at Ctesiphon

## By the Rev. W. Ewing, M.C., D.D.

Formerly of the Palestine Exploration Fund, Author of "Arab and Druze at Home"

IN the far-spreading plains of Irak little that is picturesque or beautiful arrests the eye. Itself the gift of the mighty rivers, but for Euphrates and Tigris the country would be unrelieved desert. The greenery of spring swiftly withers, and the land is baked hard and brown by the suns of summer. The surface is broken by canals, fragments of earthworks, remains of old irrigation systems, and great marshes. Many are the mounds that cover ruined cities of the ancient world—archæological treasuries.

About twenty-five miles down stream from Bagdad, on the eastern bank of the winding Tigris, stands the famous Arch of Ctesiphon, the surviving residence of the renowned White Palace of Chosroes I. The vaulted roof of the great hall of audience looks in the distance like a gigantic arch. I first saw it on an evening in March, 1917, during the thrilling pursuit of the Turks to Bagdad. A mirage caused an optical illusion, lifting high the solid block of masonry so that it dominated the landscape. It is by far the most striking remnant of antiquity in all that region.

The Parthians founded Ctesiphon. In early years it shares the obscurity that shrouds so much of Parthian history. That people's home lay in the uplands south-east of the Caspian Sea. They acquiesced in the conquests of Cyrus and Alexander. About 250 B.C. they rose against the Seleucid Empire and, led by one Arsaces, who challenged and slew the Greek satrap, established their independence. Their dominion gradually widened until, under Mithridates I., distinguished alike as soldier and statesman, a great empire was built up which lasted 400 years, and proved a formidable rival to Rome in Asia. In luxury, extravagance, and display the Parthian court resembled that of the Achaemenians. In other respects it fell far short. Little worthy the name of art or letters has survived. Our knowledge of the Parthians is drawn mainly from the records of their foes.

The court spent the summer in the north. With the approach of winter the splendid household of the kings, with their glittering hosts attendant, moved to the sunny south. Their pavilions were spread in the plain of Ctesiphon, east of the Tigris, over against Seleucia, a city built by Seleucus on the western bank, which had succeeded to the honours of Babylon. Gradually the village of Ctesiphon swelled into a great city, which became the capital of the Parthian Empire.

In A.D. 16 Artabanus became king. The Roman Vitellius, by intrigue and treachery, compassed his flight, and set up Tiridates in his stead. The new king was acclaimed by a vast multitude ; but of him, with his youth and soft Roman breeding, his subjects soon grew weary, and the grim Artabanus, wearing the wretched garb of his exile, was welcomed back to his royal city.

The Emperor Trajan brought ships on rollers across country from the Euphrates, and in them crossed the Tigris against Ctesiphon. Osroes, the successor of Pacorus fled. Trajan easily took the city. His spoil included the king's golden throne. He constituted Lower Mesopotamia a province, and on the plain of Ctesiphon, amid great pomp, set over it a creature of his own, with the style of " King of Parthia," the imperial hand placing the diadem upon his brow. But the emperor's plans miscarried. In the spring of A.D. 117 Osroes returned, expelled the puppet king, and re-established his own authority.

Not till A.D. 165 was the prestige of Roman arms restored. Seleucia received the Roman generals as friends. Ctesiphon they attacked as enemies. Yet both were overwhelmed by the same fate. Cassius wrought havoc with the splendid buildings of Ctesiphon, plundered the temples, sought out the treasures, and departed with a rich booty. From this blow, fatal to Seleucia, Ctesiphon soon recovered. In A.D. 198 Severus, in spite of stout resistance, captured the city. The males were slaughtered, 100,000 women and children were taken captive. Much precious metal, and the chief ornaments of the palace, were carried away. By an act of blackest treachery Caracalla inflicted the last spasm of anguish endured by Parthian Ctesiphon. The soldiers, betrayed and unarmed, were, with the rest, slaughtered like sheep and the city was given over to pandemonium. Mani, founder of the Manichaean sect, is said to have been born at Ecbatana (A.D. 215), and educated at Ctesiphon, where also he was crucified.

In A.D. 226 a new chapter in history begins ;

the Persian Ardashir overthrew the Parthians, made Ctesiphon his residence, and founded the powerful Sassanid dynasty. He rebuilt Seleucia and erected other suburbs, the group forming al-Madain, "the cities" of the Arabs.

Odenathus, prince of Palmyra, besieged but did not take Ctesiphon in A.D. 261. It was taken and sacked by the Emperor Carus (A.D. 283), who forthwith died mysteriously in his tent during a thunderstorm. Strongly fortified as it was by river, walls, and morasses, Julian attacked the city in A.D. 363. Diverting the course of a canal, he brought boats from the Euphrates and crossed the Tigris. The Persians, defeated in the plain, fled to the shelter of their walls, leaving to the victor a great spoil, including precious metals, splendid arms and trappings, beds and tables of massive silver. Judging the city impregnable, Julian passed on, and soon died of wounds. In A.D. 420 a council met in Ctesiphon under the Archbishop of Seleucia, which received the Nicene faith and the canons approved by the churches in the West. And in A.D. 531 there came to the throne the greatest, perhaps, of all the Sassanian princes, Chosroes I., who built the White Palace. His grandson Chosroes II. is said to have taken the true cross from Jerusalem to Ctesiphon. His son returned it to Heraclius, who restored it to Jerusalem.

The rise and progress of Islam brought a new and ruthless enemy to the gates of Ctesiphon. In A.D. 637, the year after his victory at Kadisiyeh, Saad moved against the city. Panic-stricken at the Moslems' sudden crossing of the river, the defenders fled. An almost incredible booty fell to the conqueror. The great hall of the White Palace was consecrated as a place of prayer. Here Saad gave thanks, ascribing his victory to the Lord of Hosts. Here the Friday service of Islam was first celebrated in the land of Persia.

Finding Ctesiphon unhealthy, the Arabs migrated to the new cities of Kufa, Bagdad, and Basra. From the deserted towns materials were taken for the building of Bagdad. Scattered heaps of rubbish alone mark the sites of Seleucia and the other suburbs. But the solid brickwork of Chosroes I., hard as iron, withstood the pickaxes of al-Mansûr, and the noble arch remains. Within sight of it Townshend fought the battle of November, 1915, securing his retreat against overwhelming odds.

Of the beauty and splendour of Ctesiphon in its regal days there is ample evidence. Girt by a loop of the great river, it stood like an emerald in a chain of sapphires. Rich soil and plentiful water made easy the creation of "paradises," shady gardens with fountains and flowers, and fruitful orchards. Not far off were royal hunting-seats embowered in greenery, and parks where lions,

wild boars, "bears of remarkable fierceness," and other animals were kept for princely sport.

The palace, temples, and mansions of the nobility were of great magnificence. Wealth was lavished upon their adornment and furnishing. Here was the very home of luxury and display. Here also was the centre of imperial treasuries. Conqueror after conqueror had been enriched by her spoils; yet all were insignificant compared with the prodigious booty taken by Saad. It included vast stores of silver and gold, costly robes, precious stones, and jewelled arms; musk, camphor, amber, and delicious perfumes; a horse of gold with emerald teeth, neck set with rubies, saddle of silver, and trappings of gold; also a camel of silver with foal of gold. Chosroes' armoury contained helmet, breastplate, greaves, and arm-pieces, all of solid gold adorned with pearls, six "cuirasses of Solomon," and ten costly scimitars. But the chief prize was surely the royal banqueting carpet, seventy cubits long and sixty broad, representing a garden, with ground wrought in gold, walks in silver, meadows of emerald, rivulets of pearls, trees, fruit and flowers of sparkling diamonds and other precious stones. When the works of art and the fifth part of the entire booty had been set apart for the Caliph, so enormous was the remainder that the share falling to each of Saad's 60,000 soldiers was about £312.

The White Palace of Chosroes I. was the central glory of Ctesiphon, and the most splendid example of Sassanian architecture. A noble structure, with portico of twelve lofty pillars of marble, its height was 150 feet, its breadth 180 feet, and its length 450 feet. The spacious central hall, open in front, was 115 feet long and 85 feet high. Stars of gold gleamed on the blue vaulted roof, figuring the motions of the planets among the signs of the zodiac. A foiling of semicircles adorned the front of the great arch. Here the king, sitting on a throne of gold, heard causes and dispensed justice. Vaulted chambers that stood on either side and behind have disappeared. Part of the main façade remains, facing eastward, with its striking ornamentation of doorways, double-arched recesses, pilasters, and string courses.

Recall for a moment the beauties of the past, Parthian and Persian pomp and pageantry, the luxury and wealth that roused the cupidity of kings and emperors, the mighty ramparts, the changing scenes of victory and defeat; then look upon this grey ruin, rising wearily over an empty wilderness, and a sense of the transiency of human splendour overwhelms the spirit. The old river sweeping past in all its pristine strength, the wind sighing among the reeds, seem to murmur a dirge over the long-vanished glories of Ctesiphon.

**WHERE PERSIAN PRINCES FEASTED AND GAVE AUDIENCE: THE ARCH OF CTESIPHON**

As recently as 1864, when this photograph was taken, the whole of the right-hand façade of the Arch of Ctesiphon was still standing. To-day it has disappeared, and with it large portions of the vault, as may be seen by consulting the other photograph in this page. The mighty building was erected by Chosroes, a Sassanid monarch who came to the throne in A.D. 531, towards the end of the great dynasty which was founded by Ardashir in the third century A.D., and revived the glories of the Persian Empire.

**VAULT OF THE WHITE PALACE AT CTESIPHON, SCENE OF MANY BITTER FIGHTS**

The "Arch of Ctesiphon" is actually all that remains of the vast vaulted audience chamber of the White Palace, the triumph of Chosroes the Great. The whole building was once 150 feet high; the great hall is 85, and though a marble portico has disappeared, the front was always open to the sky—indeed, with its blue-painted, star-spangled roof it must have seemed like the vault of heaven itself. In the foreground here are troops of the Mesopotamian Expeditionary Force, heroes of the last of all the battles it has seen.

Photo from the Rev. Dr. Ewing

**STREETS AND BUILDINGS OF A ROMAN TOWN REVEALED BY AIR PHOTOGRAPHY**

Although the existence of a Roman 'camp,' or more properly town, at Caistor near Norwich has long been known, it had never been properly excavated until 1929, largely because of the lack of detailed knowledge. The city area consists of two fields under cultivation, surrounded by a ditch with lengths of Roman wall. When this surprising aerial photograph was taken in a dry summer the streets of the city and the plan of the foundations of some of the buildings were revealed by pole streaks in the barley which was then growing. The barley growing upon the streets and wall-foundations was paler than its better-rooted neighbours. A plan based solely on this air photograph is given in the opposite page.

## The Study of the Past. XIII.

# Aerial Discovery of the Hidden Past

### By Dr. E. Cecil Curwen, F.S.A.

Author of " Prehistoric Sussex "

EVERY race, every generation that has come and gone, has left its mark upon our land in more senses than one. Let us see how true this is in the most literal sense. Just as a deal table that has seen much service is covered with the scratches and stains that result from the uses to which it has been put, so the face of the habitable parts of the earth is scarred and worn with the results of human activity dating from the earliest times down to the present day. As we go about the country we are so familiar with the sight of roads, hedges, ponds, walls and buildings, that it does not occur to us to regard them as mere scratches on the world's surface, nor are we always able in the medley of such marks to distinguish order or reason in any but the most obviously recent ones.

Viewed from a few thousand feet up in the sky all is different. Man himself appears neither bigger nor more important than a germ seen through a microscope, and his works appear proportionately small. It is possible to take a comprehensive view of them, to see them in relation to large areas of country, and in many places to distinguish order and system in a number of marks which, if seen on the ground at all, are unintelligible, and to realize that these are scratches that have been made by past generations or earlier races.

The idea of studying archaeology by means of photography from the air was begotten by a balloonist in the latter part of last century, and developed by aviators in Mesopotamia during the Great War, but the man who has been most responsible for bringing it forward as an indispensable adjunct to the study of archaeology in Great Britain is Mr. O. G. S. Crawford, Archaeology Officer to the Ordnance Survey and Editor of 'Antiquity.' Public attention was first drawn to this new weapon of research by his brilliant rediscovery of the line of the Stonehenge Avenue, which appears to have been a broad processional way, bounded by ditches on either side and leading to the temple. In 1923 he was looking through some old photographs that had been taken by the R.A.F. on Salisbury Plain two years before, and he was able to discern on them quite distinctly the faint parallel lines of the avenue curving away through the modern fields right down to the river Avon at West Amesbury. The line of this avenue has been so thoroughly obliterated by modern cultivation (except for a short length close to Stonehenge itself) that it is not discernible on the ground at all, and there has been much speculation as to its original course. As early as 1723 the antiquary Stukeley had been able to trace out about half of it, but the rest had already been lost. But to-day, 200 years after Stukeley, the whole course can be traced clearly from the air, leading from Stonehenge by the easiest gradients right down to the river Avon. In order to confirm this discovery, Mr. Crawford carried out excavations at three points on its course, and at every one he found the buried ditches exactly at the places indicated in the photographs.

SOME of the stones of Stonehenge have been identified as having been brought from Pembrokeshire. It has therefore been suggested that this avenue may have been the route by which they were conveyed from the nearest point of the river, after having been brought by sea round Land's End and up Southampton Water.

Perhaps one of the most spectacular revelations on the part of air photography is afforded by the remarkable picture of the Roman town at Caistor-by-Norwich. The site of the town was already known, but the new revelation was the plan of the streets and of some of the actual buildings. These streets and foundations appear as light streaks on the grey background of the picture, and herein lies the greatest wonder of this new weapon of discovery, for the observer looking at these light streaks is not looking

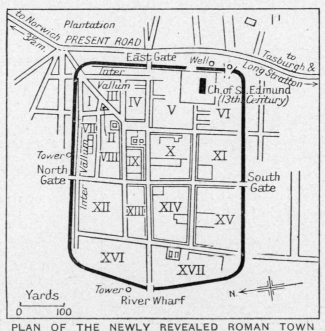

PLAN OF THE NEWLY REVEALED ROMAN TOWN

Charted from the astonishing air photograph in the opposite page, this plan gives a detailed lay-out of the city identified with Venta Icenorum and dated about A.D. 320. The vallum, or ditch, was apparently constructed after the town was built, since the streets in places appear to be continued outside the town walls.

From Crawford and Keiller, ' Wessex from the Air,' Oxford Press

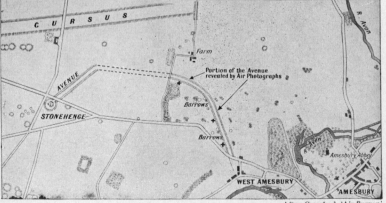

After Crawford, 'Air Survey'

**NEW LIGHT FROM THE AIR ON STONEHENGE**

What is assumed to have been a processional way which led to the famous temple at Stonehenge is seen in this photograph and diagram. Most of the avenue has been destroyed by ploughing; while that shown in the upper part of the photograph has not been destroyed the lower portion is ordinarily invisible on the ground, and is only revealed from the air by the altered colour of the corn. The crosses in the diagram mark the points where the air photographs have been verified by excavation

at actual Roman roads, nor even at parched ground covering them, for he sees nothing but barley growing ! The plan of the Roman town is etched out in growing barley. The explanation is that the barley which is growing on the thin soil overlying roads and foundations of walls is paler in colour than its more robust neighbours which are growing on deeper soil, and this pale barley collectively shows up as light streaks which reproduce the plan of the streets. The value of a photograph like this is immense when excavation is in prospect, for it shows the excavators exactly where they may most usefully open up the ground.

MORE frequently, however, ancient earthworks are revealed by the deeper colour of crops growing over disturbed ground. This is especially the case in country where there is but little mould overlying a chalk subsoil. If an ancient earthwork has been levelled by ploughing, the ditches and pits which had originally been dug in the solid chalk are now filled up with a mixture of more or less loose chalk rubble and mould, which provides much better rootage for crops than can be found over the undisturbed chalk. Hence corn growing over such hidden ditches or pits is more luxuriant and of a darker colour than its neighbours, and shows up in air-photographs as dark bands or spots which betray the positions of the ditches or pits. This effect is best observed in dry summers and may not be obtained in a wet year. In this way many prehistoric settlements and burial mounds have been discovered, especially in Wessex.

A very remarkable discovery of this kind was that of the site of what may be described as a wooden edition of Stonehenge in the parish of Durrington, Wilts. An Air Force officer was flying over the site in June, 1926, and noticed in a field of growing wheat a large, dark circle within which were a number of dark dots. He photographed it, and showed his results to archaeologists. As a result, Mr. and Mrs. B. H. Cunnington have carried out extensive excavations, from which they conclude that there once stood here a circle, or rather six concentric circles, of timber uprights, from one to three feet in diameter, and all surrounded by a wide ditch. It appears that this was a structure similar to Stonehenge, but

The dark circle near the hayricks in the distance marks the ditch that once surrounded a temple similar to Stonehenge, but made of wood. Within the ring can be seen dark dots that represent the pits in which the wooden pillars stood. In the centre of the picture the smaller circles mark the ditches that surrounded burial mounds. All these are revealed by a deeper colour of the corn.

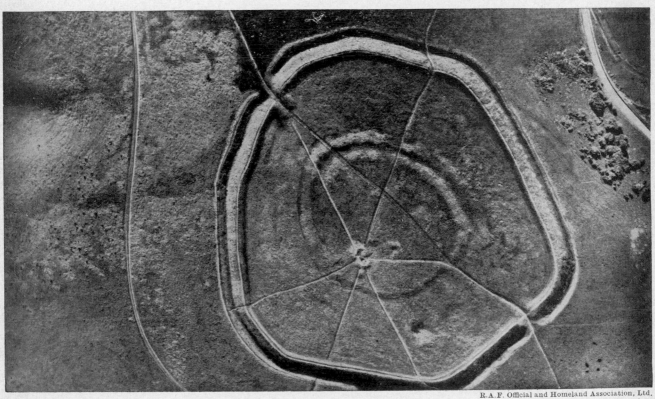

The well-marked outer ring in this photograph of the Trundle hill above Goodwood racecourse is the earthen wall of a Celtic hill-city that flourished from about 500–100 B.C. This photograph, from Dr. Curwen's 'Prehistoric Sussex,' first drew attention to the fainter inner ring which represents a neolithic settlement of rare type, dating from not later than 2000 B.C. Here Dr. Curwen excavated and found, among other objects, neolithic pottery and the skeleton of a young woman buried about 3,700 years ago.

THE AEROPLANE UNCOVERS SITES HIDDEN FOR THOUSANDS OF YEARS

Ordnance Survey and 'Prehistoric Sussex'

Less spectacular than the foregoing, but just as important from the point of view of the science of archaeology, was the discovery of the nearly obliterated banks of an older hill-fort within the area of the well-known ramparts of the Trundle at Goodwood (Sussex). Though visible on the ground, this had not been noticed until it was revealed by an air-photograph taken in 1925. This led the writer to carry out excavations in 1928 which proved that, while the great ramparts must be assigned to some period in the last five centuries before Christ, when they formed the defences of what was then the capital city of the district—the lineal ancestor of the modern Chichester—the half-obliterated banks revealed by the air-photograph belong to one of those rare and exceptionally interesting hill-forts which are characteristic of the later stone age and cannot well be less than about 4,000 years old.

This type of fort has only been recognized within the last few years, more particularly since Mr. Alexander Keiller

constructed of wood instead of stone, and it has therefore been given the very appropriate name of 'Woodhenge.' The question of its date is not finally settled, but there is no doubt that it cannot be less than 3,000 years old. Another very similar example has recently been discovered near Norwich.

If the darker colour of the corn had not revealed the ditch and the holes in which the wooden uprights had stood, this remarkable monument of antiquity would still be lying unrecognized under the ground. It has been truly said that the very processes of agriculture which were responsible for the obliteration of such sites are now, thanks to air-photography, instrumental in their discovery.

R.A.F. Official

**CELTIC CULTIVATION SEEN AGAIN AFTER CENTURIES**

In the lower photograph of part of a large ploughed field near Ann's Farm, Cholderton, Wiltshire, can be seen a criss-cross pattern of faint lines. These are the outlines of prehistoric Celtic fields, destroyed by modern agriculture, but still visible from the air, though scarcely distinguishable on the ground. The upper photograph shows prehistoric Celtic fields on Windover Hill, near Eastbourne. These fields are easily distinguished from the Saxon and medieval English kind, which were longer and narrower.

began in 1925 his systematic excavation of the best-known of such sites, on Windmill Hill near Avebury in Wiltshire. The chief characteristic of these forts, of which perhaps a dozen examples are known in Britain, is that they are defended by one or more rings of ditches which are interrupted by numerous causeways of undisturbed ground, the purpose of which is not fully understood. When excavated, the ditches yield quantities of pottery of a hitherto uncommon type—fragments of vessels that had round bottoms and little lugs for handles, sometimes perforated for suspension with cords. The study of this type of hill-fort is very much occupying the minds of archaeologists at the present time, and every new site discovered throws fresh light upon a little-known period of our prehistory.

ROMAN FIELD-WORKS USED IN TITUS' CAMPAIGN AFTER JERUSALEM FELL

This Roman camp, near the Dead Sea, formed part of the siege-works thrown up by the Romans under the Emperor Titus when they besieged the last remnant of the resisting Jews in the fortress of Masada in A.D. 71, which completed the conquest of Judaea begun by Vespasian in A.D. 67. Even the emplacements of the legionaries' tents can be distinguished

But it is not on prehistory alone that air-photography is able to throw light. History also has its dark periods, and of these none needs illuminating more than that of the coming of the English after the collapse of the Roman Empire—let us say the fifth and sixth centuries of our era. The written records of the period are disappointingly inadequate, and are not free from suspicions of doubtful authenticity and political or racial partiality. The problem is not unlike that which confronts the police after the commission of a crime : which of the two is likely to give the more reliable reconstruction—the statements of the accused or the investigations of finger-prints and footprints carried out by a skilled detective ? The former, of course, need to be checked by the latter, and so it is with the case in point.

Two conflicting views of the period of the Anglo-Saxon conquest are held, and these, presented in their most extreme forms, are as follows : either the English came in and stole Britain from the Romanised Britons, whom they murdered and exterminated, or the English settled down alongside the Britons, ruled them, and ultimately amalgamated with them without any loss of continuity of the life of the people as a whole. The problem is a very complex one, for it is probable that each of these views is more or less true of different districts. Where, however, air-photography has examined the footprints and finger-prints, as it were, the evidence is all in favour of the virtual extermination of the earlier race, with a complete break in the continuity of rural life.

This conclusion is based upon a study of the agricultural systems of the two peoples as revealed in the case of the Britons by air-photography and excavation, and in the case of the English principally by documentary evidence. The two chief differences lie in the characteristic situations of the villages and in the shape of the fields. British villages were almost always situated on hilltops, while the Saxons chose valleys and plains and cleared the forests. The sites of the Saxon manors are substantially the same as the villages of the present day, and these are very rarely found to stand on the sites of pre-existing British settlements. Both Britons and Saxons tilled little fields which each contained about one acre of land, but while the Saxon acre was a long, narrow strip, the British (or ' Celtic ') field was relatively short and broad. The outlines of these old fields have been perpetuated because the process of ploughing, even on a slight slope, tends to form terraces, which are especially noticeable on the chalk hills. Even where modern ploughing has destroyed the old terraces, or ' lynchets,' as they are called, their outlines may appear on air-photographs as blurred white lines revealing whole systems of prehistoric fields, the outlay of which differs fundamentally from that of the Saxon system, which is known from reliable documentary evidence. The reason why air-photography rarely, if ever, reveals the Saxon fields is that the latter occupied the same ground and were delimited by substantially the same boundaries as those still cultivated at the present day in the neighbourhood of villages which date back to before Domesday.

It is evident, therefore, that with fundamental changes in the outlay of the fields and the sites of the settlements there must have been a complete and absolute break in the continuity of rural life on the arrival of the English, and this can only be explained by supposing that the older race was

**THE GREAT PALACE OF A CALIPH WITH ITS COURTS AND GARDENS FULLY DISPLAYED**

Even when considerable ruins of buildings remain above ground aerial photographs can provide views which could not be equalled by months of ground survey work. This aerial plan of the great palace of Mutawakkil, a ninth century caliph, at Samarra, whither the capital had been transferred from Bagdad, shows clearly that the aeroplane provides an extraordinarily powerful new instrument for archaeology.

R.A.F. Official

**THE ARCH OF CTESIPHON FROM THE AIR**

Even so well known a ruin as this is illuminated by aerial photography, for ground photographs fail to show that it was not merely an arch but a huge open palace hall, the audience chamber of Chosroes' White Palace. Other photographs of the arch appear in page 611.

enslaved or exterminated, allowing the newcomers to make a completely fresh start on their own lines. This period, therefore, presents an absolute contrast with that of the Norman Conquest, in which rural life went on with new masters but otherwise very little change. But in regard to this question every district must be studied on its own merits, for the principles which governed the English settlement of Sussex and Hampshire are not necessarily the same as those which obtained in Devon or Shropshire.

What has been said above will illustrate the possibilities of air-photography in elucidating the problems of our own past history. Opportunities abroad are just as great, and in Mesopotamia and Palestine an unlimited field of discovery is opened up. The desert is being found to be full of the ruins of ancient cities, one of them near the Tigris being twenty miles long and three miles wide, spaciously laid out with houses, gardens, roads and canals. These ruins represent the city of the Caliph Mutawakkil, who flourished about A.D. 850. In the Judaean wilderness the siege-works constructed by the Romans at the siege of the fortress of Masada—the last stand made by the Jews in A.D. 71—are still to be seen in their entirety, even the emplacements of the rows of tents occupied by the legionaries being clearly visible in the air-photographs.

Enough has been said to illustrate the possibilities of this new weapon. It remains for us to go on using it in making fresh discoveries.

## Temples of the Gods.   XVI.

# The Gods of Ancient Greece

### By W. R. Halliday, M.A., B.Litt., Hon. LL.D.

#### Principal of King's College, London

*IN the Greek pantheon were many gods, major and minor.   Here we give representations of the more important, taken from authenticated statuary now preserved in the great museums.   The Aphrodite (or Venus) of Milo was given in the chapter entitled " Peerless Gems of Greek Sculpture," as were the Apollo of the Belvedere and the Hermes of Praxiteles.   As regards the names it is only since about the middle of the nineteenth century that these have been commonly given in Greek form, earlier English writers, the poets in particular, deriving their inspiration from the French and consequently using the Latinised forms—Venus for Aphrodite ; Mercury for Hermes, etc.*—EDITOR.

GREEK civilization came into being as the result of a mixture of races.  During the latter part of the second millennium B.C. a series of invasions of fair-haired Northern peoples, who were armed with iron weapons, over-whelmed the civilization which had been built up in the Aegean area during the Bronze Age. Although it has hitherto proved impossible to decipher the writing of the people of the Bronze Age, the general cha-racter of their religious beliefs and practices is revealed by their art.

Their religion, it would seem, presented two main features.  The first is the worship of a goddess of nature, who dwelt upon the mountain tops and is often represented in art between attendant lions or wild animals.  Asso-ciated with her, but apparently subordinate to her, is an armed male figure representing, probably, a divine con-sort or lover.  This goddess reminds us of a type of divinity charac-teristic of Anatolia in historical times, the great mother-goddess of Asia Minor, with her constant but variously

**THE FAMOUS MOURNING ATHENE**
Zeus is fabled to have had a headache : as a drastic remedy Hephaistos cleft his head with an axe, whereat Athene sprang forth armed with a battle-cry, to be the goddess of war and wisdom.  Her Roman name was Minerva, and the owl was sacred to her.  This relief shows her with spear and helmet.
Acropolis Museum, Athens.  **Photo by Alinari**

named lover, Adonis, Attis, or Thammuz.  There can be little doubt that this diety of the Bronze Age affected the Greek conception of certain goddesses. In particular, Our Lady of the Wild Beasts, the Huntress Artemis, Aphrodite, and even, in certain of her aspects, Athene, are closely connected with this pre-Hellenic god-dess.  The place of her worship was in natural sanctuaries, caves on the mountain side, or in small shrines, which were either placed in the open air or situ-ated within the palace of the king.  In cult the divinity was repre-sented, not by a statue, but by a sacred tree or by a pillar, which was sometimes surmounted by the sacred double axe.  To this " fetish " the god-dess was summoned at the moment of worship by music or by hymns of invocation, and her advent is often pic-torially represented by the device of a dove settling upon the pillar.

The second prominent feature of the religion of the Bronze Age was the worship of dead chieftains.  Thus, not

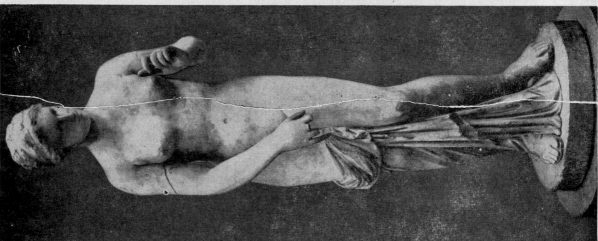

## ALEXANDER IN THE GUISE OF A GOD

The final stage in the development of the ancient Greek religion was the deification of men of superlative fame and achievement. One of the first, and perhaps the greatest, of these "men-gods" was Alexander the Great, and the statue pictured above shows him apparently in the guise of Zeus.

Glyptothek, Munich; photo, Bruckmann

Anderson

Anderson and Mansell

## RELIGIOUS DECAY AND ARTISTIC DECLINE

With the passing of time the statues of the Grecian deities betrayed a definite declension from the early idealised types: diminishing reverence was revealed in the emphasizing of the weak and sensual. This tendency is seen in the statue of Jupiter-Serapis (a combination of the Greek Zeus and the Egyptian Sun God) reproduced above, but more obviously in the Venus (right) found at Ostia.

are the best known. The ritual of these seems to have consisted primarily of a magical dramatic representation of the annual death of nature in winter and its rebirth in spring. But this drama of death and rebirth held promise of a similar rebirth of the mortal worshipper, and those who were privileged to become initiated into these magical secrets appear to have found in their contemplation hope of eternal bliss.

Orphism and the mystery cults represent, it will be noticed, quite a different religious attitude to

SILENOS AND HIS YOUNG PUPIL

Dionysos, already illustrated in page 622, is here shown in even more effeminate guise, and attended by his mentor Silenos, son of Pan. The followers of Dionysos were satyrs, or Thracian horse-divinities, whereas Pan was an Arcadian goat-divinity; but the latter was soon attracted into the Dionysiac circle.

The Louvre, Paris

that implied by the worship of the gods of the city-state. In the first place their appeal is universal, not civic or tribal. Before the end of the seventh century B.C. the " Homeric Hymn to Demeter " extends an invitation to all Greek-speaking persons, irrespective of their narrower nationality, to become initiated in the Mysteries of Eleusis. The Orphic brotherhoods and the initiates of the Mysteries thus formed religious societies, member-ship of which did not coincide with the membership of any political or social group. The worshipper

is here regarded as an individual personality, rather than as a member of the body politic.

Again, the centre of religious interest has shifted from this world to the next. The new gospel is one of salvation addressed to the individual soul ; the Orphic preachers were in consequence the first proselytizers in the ancient world.

Another important religious development in post-Homeric times was the revival of the worship of the mighty dead. There are already traces in the " Odyssey " of the existence of hero-cults, and the author of the eleventh book betrays a knowledge of the ritual peculiar to the worship of the powers of the Underworld. For, whereas the head of the victim sacrificed to Olympian gods was held back to look upwards at the moment of sacrifice, and its flesh was subsequently eaten by the worshippers at a banquet, in sacrifice to the nether powers, the throat of the victim, with its head depressed to look downwards, was cut over a trench dug in the ground and the offering was consumed by fire, none of its flesh being eaten.

Hero-worship spread all over Greece. Many of the heroes were no doubt legendary figures, and some may even have been " faded gods " of ancient local cults, but all were thought of by their worshippers as historical persons who had once lived and died and had afterwards received apotheosis. The majority of these cults possessed a strong local character ; they present in most respects a close analogy to the phenomena of saint worship in Christianity and Islam. Divination and healing were almost invariable features of the hero's activities, and the method normally employed was that of incubation, i.e., the inquirer or patient slept at the tomb or shrine and was visited during the night by the hero.

By the fifth century the apotheosis of legendary figures had developed into the practice of canonising distinguished persons immediately after their death. Thus, for example, the Spartan general, Brasidas, was worshipped as a hero by the people of Amphipolis immediately after his death in 422 B.C. Throughout the fourth century B.C. individualism became increasingly dominant in every department of life and art ; at the same time the city-state was disintegrating. The creation of Alexander's empire at the close of the century marked the passing of its day. Together with the city-state there declined inevitably that part of Greek religion which was intimately bound up with it. Further, philosophic rationalism had discredited mythology, and, by demonstrating the causes of natural phenomena, had undermined the belief in the constant interposition of heaven in terrestrial affairs. The gods of Olympus survived, it is true,

**A NEREID, ONE OF POSEIDON'S TRAIN**

The Nereids were nymphs of the Mediterranean; Thetis, mother of Achilles, was one, and Amphitrite, illustrated in page **625**. They symbolised all the phenomena of ocean—the white-capped waves, the pellucid depths, the phosphorescence. Are the mermaids of modern fairy-story their half-forgotten echoes?

The Museum, Naples    Photo by Brogi

far as men could judge from their bitter experience, alone decided, without regard for merit or desert, the fortunes of themselves and their contemporaries.

On the other hand, the arbitrary power, which kings possessed, of dispensing happiness or misery, led to the frequent deification of living monarchs. For this the later developments of hero-worship had prepared the way, and the more than mortal claims and achievements of Alexander the Great had rendered easy the last step. From this Graeco-Oriental deification of the man-god developed later the worship of Augustus and Roma, which bound together the provinces of the Roman Empire in the common cult of the reigning emperor and the imperial majesty of the Eternal City.

**DEMETER, GODDESS OF HARVESTS**

Demeter, known to the Romans as Ceres, was the goddess of corn, and more broadly of the growth and death of vegetation. It was the legend of the annual return of her daughter, Persephone, from Hades, which gave the Greeks their first hopes of a future life.

Courtesy of the British Museum

but mainly as quasi-allegorical expressions of the theological tenets of philosophy.

At the same time the emotional needs of individualism maintained the popularity of the Otherworldly elements in Greek religion, and, as times became more and more difficult upon earth, men grasped with yet greater eagerness at hopes of happiness beyond the grave. The mystery religions were reinforced by foreign allies. Thus, at the close of the great period of Greek civilization, the great mother-goddess with her divine lover, whom we have already met in Crete, returned in her Asiatic forms to exercise a dominating influence.

In conclusion, two characteristic developments of the Hellenistic age, which were to become of some importance in the religious history of Rome, deserve attention. They are both products of the incalculable insecurity and misery of the time. On the one hand, the apparent injustice of the regulation of terrestrial affairs led to the negation of a beneficent Providence, and to the consequent deification of capricious Chance, which, so